SOCIAL
PSYCHOLOGY

THIRD EDITION

SOCIAL PSYCHOLOGY

David G. Myers

Hope College
Holland, Michigan

McGRAW-HILL PUBLISHING COMPANY

New York   St. Louis   San Francisco   Auckland   Bogotá   Caracas
Hamburg   Lisbon   London   Madrid   Mexico   Milan   Montreal
New Delhi   Oklahoma City   Paris   San Juan   São Paulo
Singapore   Sydney   Tokyo   Toronto

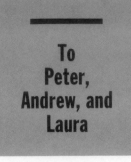

**To
Peter,
Andrew, and
Laura**

SOCIAL PSYCHOLOGY

2 3 4 5 6 7 8 9 0   VNH   VNH   9 4 3 2 1 0

ISBN 0-07-044283-5

This book was set in Century Expanded by Waldman Graphics, Inc.
The editors were Alison Husting, Scott Spoolman, James D. Anker, and James R. Belser;
the designer was Jo Jones;
the production supervisor was Friederich W. Schulte.
New drawings were done by Fine Line Illustrations, Inc.
Von Hoffmann Press, Inc., was printer and binder.

See Acknowledgments on pages 577–579.
Copyrights included on this page by reference.

Library of Congress Cataloging-in-Publication Data

Myers, David G.
    Social psychology / David G. Myers.—3rd ed.
        p.   cm.
    Bibliography: p.
    Includes indexes.
    ISBN 0-07-044283-5
    1. Social psychology.   I. Title.
    [DNLM: 1. Psychology, Social.   HM 251 M9957s]
HM251.M897   1990
302—dc20
DNLM/DLC
for Library of Congress   89-12275

ABOUT THE AUTHOR

David G. Myers is the John Dirk Werkman Professor of Psychology at Hope College, where he has taught for 22 years and has been voted "Outstanding Professor" by students. Dr. Myers' love of teaching psychology is evident in his writing for the lay public. He has authored or co-authored eight books and written for many magazines, including *Saturday Review*, *Psychology Today*, and *Today's Education*.

Also an award-winning researcher, Dr. Myers received the Gordon Allport Prize from Division 9 of the American Psychological Association for his work on group polarization. Dr. Myers' scientific articles have appeared in more than two dozen journals, including *Science*, *American Scientist*, and *Psychological Bulletin*. He has served his discipline as consulting editor to the *Journal of Experimental Social Psychology* and the *Journal of Personality and Social Psychology*.

In his spare time he has chaired his city's Human Relations Commission, helped found a Community Action center which assists poverty-level families, and spoken to numerous collegiate and religious groups. David and Carol Myers are parents of sons ages 23 and 19 and a 12-year-old daughter.

CONTENTS
in brief

CONTENTS

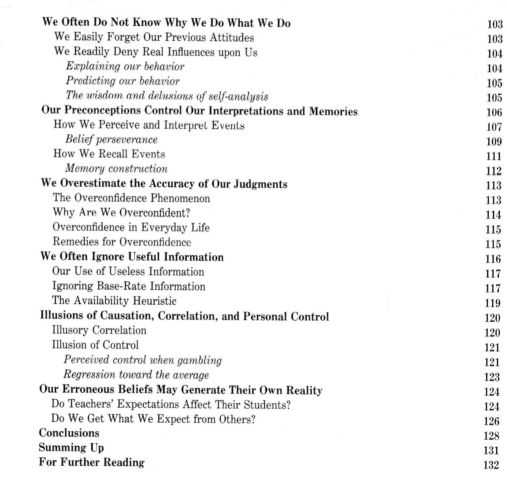

**CHAPTER
4**

**CHAPTER
5**

PART TWO

SOCIAL INFLUENCE

CHAPTER 6

**CHAPTER
7**

CONFORMITY   201

**CHAPTER
8**

PERSUASION   235

**CHAPTER
9**

GROUP INFLUENCE   269

**CHAPTER
10**

**CHAPTER
11**

**CHAPTER
15**

PREFACE

I n all of recorded history, human social behavior has been scientifically studied in but one century—our century. Considering that we have barely begun, the results are gratifying. Such psychologists have gleaned significant insights into belief and illusion, love and hate, conformity and independence. Much mystery remains, yet we can now offer partial answers to many intriguing questions: Will people act differently if we can first persuade them to adopt new attitudes? If so, how best to persuade? What leads people sometimes to hurt and sometimes to help another? What kindles social conflict, and how might we transform closed fists into open arms? Answering such questions expands our self-understanding and sensitizes us to social forces at work upon us.

When invited to write this book I envisioned a text that would be at once solidly scientific and warmly human, factually rigorous and intellectually provocative. It would reveal social psychology as an investigative reporter might, providing an up-to-date summary of important phenomena of social thinking and social behavior, and of how such phenomena have been uncovered and how they are being explained. It would be reasonably comprehensive in its coverage of the discipline, yet would also stimulate students' *thinking*—their propensities to inquire, to analyze, to relate principles to everyday happenings.

Presenting concepts concretely enough to enable students to gain some proficiency in working with the ideas prohibits an exhaustive catalog of theory and research. How, then, does one select material for inclusion in a "reasonably comprehensive" introduction to the discipline? I sought to present theories and findings that are neither too esoteric for the typical undergraduate nor better suited to other courses, such as developmental and personality psychology. I chose instead to emphasize material that casts social psychology in the intellectual tradition of the liberal arts. By the teaching of great literature, philosophy, and science, liberal education seeks to expand our thinking and awareness and to liberate us from the confines of our current environment.

Social psychology can contribute to these goals of liberal education. Many undergraduate social psychology students are not psychology majors; virtually all will enter professions other than social psychology. By focusing on humanly significant issues, one can present the fundamental content that preprofessional psychology students need in ways that are stimulating and useful to all students.

The book opens with a single chapter that introduces our methods of inquiry. The chapter also forewarns students of how findings can seem obvious—once you know them—and of how social psychologists' values penetrate the discipline. The intent is to give students just enough to prepare them for what follows.

The remainder of this third edition is organized around its definition of social psychology: the scientific study of how people *think about* (Part One), *influence* (Part Two), and *relate* (Part Three) to one another.

Part One on social thinking examines how we view ourselves and others. For example, Chapter 3 introduces attribution theory and then looks in greater depth at three intellectually provocative concepts: the fundamental attribution error, the self-serving bias, and the benefits of self-efficacy.

Part Two explores social influence. By appreciating the cultural sources of our attitudes, and by learning the nature of conformity, persuasion, and group influence, we can better recognize subtle social forces at work upon us.

Part Three considers the attitudinal and behavioral manifestions of both negative and positive social relations. Thus this reorganized section flows from prejudice to aggression, and from attraction to altruism, and concludes by exploring the dynamics of conflict and peacemaking.

Applications of social psychology are both interwoven throughout every chapter and highlighted with the applied chapter that concludes each section. The applications chapter, "Social Thinking in the Clinic," now includes material on social psychology's contributions to the study of health.

This new edition also features an increased multicultural emphasis. This can be seen not only in visible additions, such as the color photo essay on "Social Behavior around the World," but also throughout the book in the integration of research from various cultural settings. The book's focus remains on the fundamental principles of social thinking, social influence, and social relations as revealed by careful empirical research. But these principles are more and more illustrated transnationally, thereby broadening students' awareness of the whole human family.

In addition to the reorganization of Part Three and the enhanced multicultural emphasis, the book is thoroughly updated. More than 600 citations are new to this edition.

Finally, readers will find new pedagogical aids—added subheadings to organize the material, end-of-chapter suggestions for further reading, and a glossary to supplement the conceptual definitions appearing in the text margins. There are additional—and abbreviated—"Behind the Scenes" personal reflections by selected investigators. And there have been countless abbreviations of old material to accommodate these new features without lengthening the book.

Social Psychology, third edition, is accompanied by a comprehensive teaching-learning package. Martin Bolt's acclaimed *Teacher's Resource Manual* contains a wealth of classroom ideas, including dozens of ready-to-use demonstrations. For many students, the most helpful supplement to this text will be Bolt's *Study Guide*, which provides chapter objectives, chapter reviews, practice tests, and ideas and resources for papers. Finally, Ann Weber has again provided a carefully developed test-item file—over 1500 basic knowledge and application items.

IN APPRECIATION

Although only one person's name appears on this book's cover, the truth is that a whole community of scholars have invested themselves in it. Although none of these people should be held responsible for what I have written—nor do any of them fully agree with everything said—their suggestions made this a better book than it could otherwise have been.

This new edition still retains many of the improvements contributed by consultants and reviewers on the first two editions. To the following esteemed colleagues I therefore remain indebted: Robert Arkin, University of Missouri; Martin Bolt, Calvin College; Anthony Doob, University of Toronto; William Froming, University of Florida; Ranald Hansen, Oakland University; Elaine Hatfield, University of Hawaii; Bert Hodges, Gordon College; William Ickes, University of Missouri at St. Louis; Chester Insko, University of North Carolina; Edward Jones, Princeton University; Billy Van Jones, Abilene Christian College; Martin Kaplan, Northern Illinois University; Douglas Kenrick, Arizona State University; Norbert Kerr, Michigan State University; Charles Kiesler, Vanderbilt University; David McMillen, Mississippi State University; Arthur Miller, Miami University; Teru Morton, Vanderbilt University; Darren Newtson, University of Virginia; Paul Paulus, University of Texas at Arlington; Royce Singleton, Jr., College of the Holy Cross; Mark Snyder, University of Minnesota; Garold Stasser, Miami University; Homer Stavely, Keene State College; Elizabeth Tanke, University of Santa Clara; William Titus, Briarcliff College; Tom Tyler, Northwestern University; Rhoda Unger, Montclair State College; Mary Stewart Van Leeuwen, Calvin College; Ann Weber, University of North Carolina at Asheville; Gary Wells, Iowa State University; and Kipling Williams, Purdue University.

This third edition gained from new cover-to-cover reviews before, during, and after its drafting. For countless constructive criticisms and for saving me from many errors, I am grateful to: Robert Arkin, University of Missouri; Susan Beers, Sweet Briar College; George Bishop, University of Texas at San Antonio; Martin Bolt, Calvin College; Dorothea Braginsky, Fairfield University; Russell Clark, Florida State University; Jack Croxton, State University of New York at Fredonia; Philip Finney, Southeast Missouri State University; Stephen Fugita, University of Illinois at Chicago; Marita Inglehart, University of Michigan; Judi Jones, Georgia Southern College; Janice Kelly, Purdue University; Arthur Miller, Miami University; Chris O'Sullivan, University of Kentucky; Nicholas Reuterman, Southern Illinois University at Edwardsville; Linda Silka, University of Lowell; Stephen Slane, Cleveland State University; Ann Weber, University of North Carolina at Asheville; Bernard Whitley, Ball State University; and Midge Wilson, DePaul University.

Hope College, Michigan, and the University of St. Andrews, Scotland, have been wonderfully supportive of these successive editions. Both the people and the environment provided by these two institutions have helped make the gestation of *Social Psychology* a pleasure. At Hope College, poet-essayist Jack Ridl helped shape the voice you will hear in these pages, and Kathy Adamski has again contributed her good cheer along with her secretarial excellence.

Were it not for the inspiration of Nelson Black of McGraw-Hill, it never would have occurred to me to write a textbook. Alison Meersschaert, McGraw-Hill's director of Basic Book Development, guided and encouraged the formative first edition. Editor Alison Husting nurtured this new edition, suggesting numerous creative touches along the way. James Anker has again coordinated the teaching package. And James Belser has patiently guided the process of converting each of the editions from rough manuscript into finished book.

To all in this supporting cast, I am indebted. Working with these four dozen people has made the creation of this book a stimulating, gratifying experience.

David G. Myers

CHAPTER

1

INTRODUCING
SOCIAL
PSYCHOLOGY

———

hat is social psychology? Let's consider some down-to-earth examples of the questions that intrigue social psychologists.

The Amazing Cyranoids. Do our preconceptions bias our impressions of others' behavior? To find out, Stanley Milgram (1984) created what he called "cyranoids"—people who, like a character under the influence of Cyrano de Bergerac in a play of the same name, echo someone else's thoughts. Unwitting people would meet and talk with a child. The child, however, merely echoed remarks that Milgram, eavesdropping from the next room, transmitted through a wireless receiver into the child's ear. In one study, high school teachers interviewed an 11- and a 12-year-old boy, each of whom provided a mouth through which Milgram, a brilliant scholar, could speak. The teachers were asked to probe the limits of the child's knowledge "so that you would be able to recommend a grade level for each subject."

The teachers were impressed with the two children. But were they able to discern the brilliance of the person they were actually talking with? Milgram noted that

> The opinions teachers formed of our child cyranoids depended as much on the teacher as on the child, and the questions asked and avoided. Teachers varied in how they approached their questions, the best of them allowing the cyranoids' responses to guide their interview, the worst never seeing beyond the possibilities of an average 11-year-old.

> Moreover, we see how general preconceptions did not allow the teachers to get anywhere near the appropriate grade level of the cyranoid in some subjects. After all, to assign a Ph.D. to a 10th-grade class of social studies does no great honor to his Harvard degree. . . . As the source, I was hoping they would ask the cyranoid about Freud, Jung, Adler, or at least Darwin and Wittgenstein, but some teachers stuck to fractions and parts of speech.

These misimpressions make one wonder: How vulnerable are we to others' misjudgments? More generally, what determines the impressions we form, of both ourselves and others?

Are Ten Heads Dumber Than One? President John F. Kennedy, like most other U.S. presidents, enjoyed the support of a bright and loyal group of advisers who collaborated in his decision making. One of their first major decisions was to approve a Central Intelligence Agency plan to invade Cuba. The high morale of the group fostered a sense that the plan couldn't fail. Since no one sharply disagreed with the idea, there appeared to be consensus support for the plan. After the resulting fiasco in Cuba's Bay of Pigs (the small band of U.S.-trained and U.S.-supplied Cuban refugee invaders was easily captured and soon linked to the American government), Kennedy was heard wondering aloud, "How could we have been so stupid?" Reflecting on the group's decision making, Arthur Schlesinger, a member of the Kennedy inner circle, later reproached himself in his book *A Thousand Days* "for having kept so silent in the cabinet room. I can only explain my failure to do more than raise a few timid questions by reporting that one's impulse to blow the whistle on this nonsense was simply undone by the circumstances of the discussion" (1965, p. 255). So, how are we affected by our participation in groups? Or, to broaden the question, to what extent and in what ways do other people influence our attitudes and actions? And how might we as individuals resist unwanted social pressure or get a group to consider our point of view?

To Help or to Help Oneself? As bags of cash tumbled from an armored truck on a fall day in 1987, $2 million scattered along a Columbus, Ohio, street. Some motorists stopped to help, returning $100,000. Judging from what disappeared, many more stopped to help themselves. When similar incidents occurred several months later in San Francisco and Toronto the results were the same: Passersby grabbed most of the money (Bowen, 1988).

What situations trigger people to be helpful or greedy? For that matter, what stimulates us to like or dislike, and to be friendly or antagonistic toward one another?

What are the common threads running through these questions? As diverse as they are, they all deal with how people view and affect one another. And that is what social psychology is all about. As we will see, social psychologists attempt to answer such questions by using the scientific method. They aim to study attitudes and beliefs, conformity and independence, love and hate. To put it formally, we might say that ***social psychology*** is *the scientific study of how people think about, influence, and relate to one another.*

> **Social psychology:**
> The scientific study of how people think about, influence, and relate to one another.

Social psychology is still a young science. We keep reminding people of this, partly as an excuse for our incomplete answers to some of the questions raised above. But it is true. The first social psychology experiments were not reported until the very late 1800s and no book on social psychology was published before this century. Not until the 1930s did social psychology assume its current form. And it was not until World War II, when psychologists contributed imaginative studies of persuasion and soldier morale, that it began to emerge as the vibrant field it is today (Smith, 1982). In just the last two decades the number of social psychology periodicals has more than doubled. More and more, social psychologists are applying their concepts and methods to social concerns such as emotional well-being, health, courtroom decision making, and the quest for peace.

But what are social psychology's concepts and methods? How does the field differ from sociology and from other areas of psychology? What are the social psychologist's research tactics and how might we apply these in everyday critical thinking? And are social psychologists' concerns and methods influenced by their personal and cultural values? In this chapter, these are our questions.

SOCIAL PSYCHOLOGY AND THE OTHER DISCIPLINES

We social psychologists are keenly interested in how people think about, influence, and relate to one another. But sociologists, personality psychologists, and even novelists and philosophers are also curious about these matters. Let us briefly consider the similarities and differences between social psychology and some of these related fields.

SOCIAL PSYCHOLOGY AND SOCIOLOGY

Social psychology is often confused with sociology. Sociologists and social psychologists do share a common interest in studying how people behave in groups. Nevertheless, social psychology's subject matter and methods differ from those of sociology. Most *sociologists* study the structure and functioning of *groups*, from small groups to very large groups (societies). The *social psychologist* is usually interested in the *individual*—how a person thinks about other people, is influenced by them, relates to them. Thus while social psychologists are interested in groups, they generally want to ascertain how groups affect individual people, or how an individual can affect a group.

For example, while a sociologist might be interested in how the racial attitudes of middle-class people as a group differ from those of lower socioeconomic classes, the

The social psychologist is interested in the individual within the group.

social psychologist would be more interested in how racial attitudes develop within the typical individual. For instance, does merely labeling people as members of some group—as football players, Blacks, sorority women, the aged—lead one to overestimate both the similarity of people within the groups and the differences between the groups? (The answer, by the way, turns out to be yes.)

Although sociologists and social psychologists use some of the same research methods, social psychologists rely much more heavily upon experiments in which they *manipulate* a factor such as the presence or absence of peer pressure to see what effect it has. The factors that sociologists study are typically hard to manipulate. So they often use surveys to study, say, the relationship between people's socioeconomic class and their racial attitudes. Obviously, ethical considerations also preclude sociologists' experimenting with such factors as people's economic levels. One just doesn't manipulate someone's long-term economic well-being to see its effect on racial attitudes. A social psychologist, however, might very briefly induce some people to feel frustrated to see how this experience affects their attitudes toward other people.

Social psychology also differs from social work. Social psychologists are eager to see their principles applied to widespread problems such as crime and marital breakdown, but the problems themselves are not the primary focus of social psychology.

SOCIAL PSYCHOLOGY AND PERSONALITY PSYCHOLOGY

Social psychology and personality psychology both focus upon the individual person, so they, too, are closely related. Indeed, the American Psychological Association includes them in the same journals (the *Journal of Personality and Social Psychology* and the *Personality and Social Psychology Bulletin*). Their difference lies in the *social* character of social psychology. Personality psychologists give greater attention to our private internal functioning and they have a special concern for *differences* between individuals—for example, why are some individuals more aggressive than others? Social psychologists focus more on our common humanity, on how people, in general, view and affect one another—for example, how social situations can lead *most* people to act kind or cruel, to conform or be independent, to feel liking or prejudice. As we will see, our attention is typically so focused on other individuals that we often attribute their behavior to their inner dispositions, failing to notice social forces at work. If we see a stranger talking angrily, we may ignore or discount the anger-provoking situation and assume the stranger is a hostile *person*.

There are other differences. Social psychology has a shorter history. Many of the heroes of personality psychology—people like Sigmund Freud, Carl Jung, Alfred Adler, Abraham Maslow and Carl Rogers—are deceased. Because of its more recent history, all but a few of social psychology's leading contributors are alive and active. Also, social psychology has fewer famous "heroes"—people who have invented grand theories—and many more unsung heroes—creative researchers who are contributing smaller-scale theories. We will meet some of these people in the autobiographical "Behind the Scenes" inserts sprinkled throughout this book.

LEVELS OF EXPLANATION

The perspectives from which we can study human beings are organized into academic disciplines ranging from basic sciences such as physics and chemistry up to integrative disciplines such as philosophy and theology. Which perspective is most relevant depends on what it is you want to talk about. Take love, for example. A physiologist

"You can never foretell what any man will do, but you can say with precision what an average number will be up to. Individuals may vary, but percentages remain constant."
Sherlock Holmes, in Sir Arthur Conan Doyle's
A Study in Scarlet, *1887*

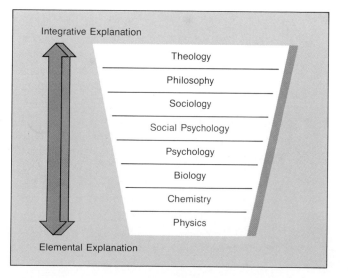

FIGURE 1-1
Partial hierarchy of disciplines. The disciplines range from basic sciences that study nature's building blocks up to more integrative disciplines that study whole complex systems. A successful explanation of human functioning at one level need not contradict an explanation at other levels.

might describe love as a state of arousal. A social psychologist would examine how various characteristics and conditions—good looks, similarity of the partners, sheer repeated exposure to one another—enhance the emotion of love. A poet would extol the sublime experience that love can sometimes be. A theologian might describe love as the God-given goal of human relationships. Because an event, like love, can often be described simultaneously at various levels, we need not assume that one level is *causing* the other—by supposing, for example, that a brain state is causing the emotion of love or that the emotion is causing the brain state. The emotional and physiological perspectives are simply two ways of looking at the same event.

It is also important to remember that one type of explanation need not compete with others. Successful scientific explanation, for example, need not discredit or preempt the perspectives of literature and philosophy. Thus an evolutionary explanation of the universality of incest taboos (in terms of the genetic penalty one's offspring pay for inbreeding) need not preempt a sociological explanation (which might see their function as preserving the family unit), or a theological explanation (in terms of moral truth). These various explanations of the incest taboo can complement rather than contradict one another.

If "all truth is one," then different levels of explanation should in fact fit together to form the whole picture, just as different two-dimensional perspectives of an object may be assembled into a more complete three-dimensional picture. Once we recognize the complementary relationship of various explanatory levels, we are liberated from all the useless argument over whether human nature should be viewed scientifically

"Knowledge is one. Its division into subjects is a concession to human weakness."
Sir Halford John MacKinder, 1887

Different sciences promote different perspectives that often seek to answer the same questions.

or more subjectively. It is not an either/or matter. The scientific and subjective perspectives are both valuable for their own purposes. Although this book pays particular attention to the fruits of scientific research, we need not demean the rich insights of other approaches. Sociologist Andrew Greeley (1976) explains: "Try as it might, psychology cannot explain the purpose of human existence, the meaning of human life, the ultimate destiny of the human person." Social psychologists ask some very important questions, but these are not among them.

In short, humans can be viewed from multiple perspectives, each incapable of answering questions raised by other perspectives. Social psychology is *one* important perspective from which we can view and understand ourselves.

HOW WE DO SOCIAL PSYCHOLOGY

Unlike other scientific disciplines, social psychology has 5 billion amateur practitioners. While few of us have firsthand experience in nuclear physics, we are the very subject matter of social psychology. From daily observations of people, each of us forms many ideas concerning how people think about, influence, and relate to one another. Professional social psychologists have an edge on the amateurs because they observe human behavior more painstakingly, often with experiments that create miniature social dramas in which cause and effect can be pinned down more precisely. Most of what you will learn about social-psychological research methods will simply be absorbed as you read the remaining chapters. But let us go backstage now and take a brief look at how social psychology is done. This glimpse behind the scenes will be just enough, I trust, for you to appreciate the evidence discussed throughout this book.

Most social-psychological research is conducted either in the **laboratory** (a controlled situation) or in the **field** (everyday situations outside the laboratory), and the research is either **correlational** (asking whether two factors are naturally associated) or **experimental** (manipulating some factor to see its effect on another). Understanding the difference between correlational and experimental research is crucial if you are to be a critical reader of psychological research, especially as reported in newspapers and magazines.

Field research:
Research done in natural, real-life settings outside the laboratory.

To illustrate the advantages and disadvantages of correlational and experimental procedures, consider a practical question: Is college a good financial investment? Surely you have heard claims made about the economic benefits of going to college. But these claims are sometimes nothing more than the optimistic speculations of college recruiters and administrators. So let's consider the claims. How might we separate fact from falsehood in assessing the impact of college upon students' later earnings?

CORRELATIONAL RESEARCH: DETECTING NATURAL ASSOCIATIONS

First, we might ascertain whether any relation—or *correlation*, as we say—exists between people's educational levels and their earnings. For example, if college is a good financial investment then college graduates should, on average, earn more than those who don't attend. And, sure enough, Figure 1-2 shows that college graduates have a whopping income advantage. So, can we now agree with college recruiters that higher education is your gateway to economic success?

"College degrees boost lifetime earnings."
American Council on Education (1983) newsletter headline

Before we answer yes, let us take a closer look. We know for a fact that formal education has been associated with earnings. That is indisputable. But does this nec-

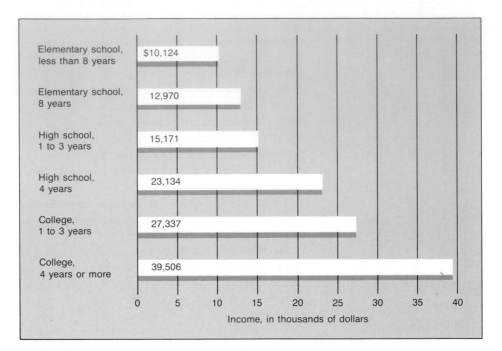

FIGURE 1-2
Income of families, by education of head of household. *In thousands of dollars*

essarily mean that education *causes* higher incomes? Perhaps you can identify factors other than education that might explain the education-earnings correlation. (We call these factors *variables* because people will vary on them.) What about family social status? What about a person's intellectual ability and achievement drive? Might these not already be higher in those who go to college? Perhaps the higher earnings come from some combination of these variables, and not the attaining of a college degree. Or perhaps education and earnings are correlated because those who have money in the first place can most easily afford college.

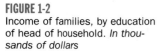

Correlational research:
The study of the naturally occurring relationships among variables.

Correlation Need Not Imply Causation

The education-earnings question illustrates the most irresistible thinking error made by both amateur and professional social psychologists. When two factors like education and earnings go together, it is terribly tempting to conclude that one is causing the other, *if* we are predisposed to believe such a conclusion. During the 1980s, football commentators were fond of noting a correlation between yardage gained by Dallas Cowboys running back Tony Dorsett and the game outcome: When Dorsett gained over 100 yards, the Cowboys nearly always won, but they were in grave danger of losing when Dorsett gained fewer than 100 yards. The implication was nearly always that Dorsett *caused* the Cowboys' outcome. To some extent this was surely true. But so was the reverse. A Cowboy victory *caused* Dorsett to go over 100 yards—because when the Cowboys were winning they would give the ball to Dorsett to run out the clock on the ground (Gilovich, 1989).

Consider two examples of the correlation-causation issue from the realm of psychology. If a particular style of child-rearing is associated with the personality traits of children exposed to it, what does this tell us? If as Freud believed, children who receive harsh, demanding toilet training become uptight and compulsive, does this validate what has been called Freud's "Scott Tissue theory of personality"? With every correlation, there are at least three possible explanations (see Figure 1-2). The effect of the parents on the child ($x \rightarrow y$) is one. You might, however, be surprised at the strength of evidence for how children affect their parents ($x \leftarrow y$) (Bell & Chapman, 1986). Or maybe, as explanation 3 in Figure 1-3 suggests, there is a common source (z) to both the child-rearing style and the child's traits. Perhaps the characteristics of both parent and child are rooted in their shared genes. Or maybe the toilet-training technique and the child's personality are both the result of the whole parent-child relationship.

As a second example, consider the very real correlation between self-esteem and academic achievement. Children with high self-esteem tend also to have high academic achievement. (As with any correlation, we can also state this the other way around: High achievers tend to have high self-esteem.) Why do you suppose this is? Some believe that a "healthy self-concept" contributes to achievement. Thus, boosting a child's self-image may also boost the child's school achievement. Others argue that high achievement produces a favorable self-image. A string of gold stars by one's name on the spelling chart and constant praise from an admiring teacher may boost a child's self-esteem. But careful studies of a nationwide sample of 1600 young men, by Jerald Bachman and Patrick O'Malley (1977), and of 715 Minnesota youngsters, by Geoffrey Maruyama and others (1981), revealed a surprising result: Self-esteem and achievement were *not* causally related. Rather, they were correlated merely because they were both linked to intelligence and family social status. When they extracted the effect of intelligence and family status, the correlation between self-esteem and achievement evaporated. Similarly, John McCarthy and Dean Hoge (1984) dispute the idea that the

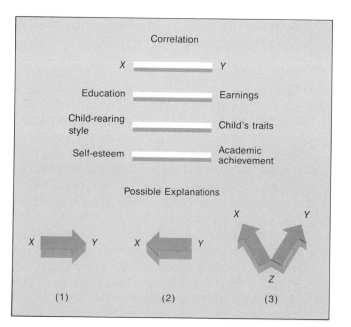

FIGURE 1-3
When two variables are correlated, any combination of at least three explanations is possible.

Researchers have found a modest but positive correlation between adolescents' preference for heavy metal music and their having attitudes favorable to premarital sex, pornography, satanism, and drug and alcohol use (Landers, 1988). What are the possible explanations for this correlation?

correlation between low self-esteem and delinquency means that low self-esteem causes delinquency; rather, their study of 1658 teenagers suggests, delinquent acts lead to a lowered self-esteem.

In short, the great strength of correlational research is that it tends to occur in real-world settings where it can examine important factors like race, sex, and education that cannot be manipulated in the laboratory. Its great disadvantage lies in the ambiguity of its results. Knowing that two variables, such as education and income, go up and down together enables us to predict one, knowing the other. But this does not establish cause and effect.

Fortunately, statistical techniques have now been developed that *suggest* cause-effect relations in correlational research. They do so by pulling apart obviously related factors (like education, family status, and aptitude) to isolate the predictive power of each. They can also take into account the sequence of events (for example, by ascertaining whether changes in achievement tend more to precede or follow changes in self-esteem). Yet the moral of the story remains: Correlational research enables prediction but cannot tell us whether changing one variable (such as education) will *cause* change in another (such as income).

Survey Research

Random sample:
Survey procedure in which every person in the population being studied has an equal chance of being selected.

How, then, do we measure variables such as education and income? One way is by surveying representative samples of people. Survey researchers obtain a representative group by taking a **random sample**—one in which every person in the total group has an equal chance of being chosen to participate. With this procedure any subgroup of people—red-haired people, for example—will tend to be represented in the survey to the extent they are represented in the total population.

One amazing fact is that whether the survey researcher is studying the characteristics of people in a city or in the whole country, surveying about 1200 randomly selected participants will enable the researcher to be 95 percent confident of describing the entire population with an error margin of 3 percent or less. To visualize this, imagine a huge jar filled with beans—50 percent red and 50 percent white. Someone who randomly samples 1200 of these will be 95 percent certain to draw out between 47 percent and 53 percent red beans regardless of whether the jar contains 10,000 beans or 100 million beans. If we think of the red beans as supporters of one presidential candidate and white beans as the other candidate's supporters, we can understand why, since 1950, the Gallup polls taken just before U.S. national election days have, on the average, diverged from election results by only 1.4 percent.

Bear in mind that such polls do not actually predict voting; they only *describe* public opinion as of the moment they are taken. Public opinion can shift, as it did toward candidate George Bush during the 1988 U.S. presidential race. To critically evaluate surveys we must also bear in mind four potentially biasing influences: unrepresentative samples, the order in which questions are asked, the response options, and the wording of questions.

Unrepresentative samples Not only does a survey sample's size matter but also how closely the sample represents the population being studied. In 1984, columnist Ann Landers accepted a letter writer's challenge to poll her readers on the question of whether women find affection more important than sex. Her question: "Would you be content to be held close and treated tenderly and forget about 'the act'?" Of the more than 100,000 women who replied, 72 percent said yes. An avalanche of worldwide publicity followed. In response to critics, Landers (1985, p. 45) granted that "the sampling may not be representative of all American women. But it does provide honest—and valuable—insights from a cross section of the public. This is because my column is read by people from every walk of life, approximately 70 million of them." Still, one wonders, are the 70 million readers representative of the entire population? And are the 1 in 70 readers who participated representative of the 69 in 70 who did not?

The importance of the representativeness of the survey sample was effectively demonstrated in 1936, when a weekly news magazine, *Literary Digest*, mailed a postcard presidential poll to 10 million Americans. Among their more than 2 million returns, Alf Landon won by a landslide over Franklin D. Roosevelt. But when the actual votes were counted a few days later, Landon carried only two states. Why the polling error? Because the magazine had sent the poll only to people whose names had been obtained from telephone books and automobile registrations—thus omitting those who could not afford either (Cleghorn, 1980).

Sampling bias can plague even the best of contemporary surveys. Simultaneous political opinion polls, each supposedly having a 3 percent error margin, commonly vary from one another by more than 3 percent. Philip Converse and Michael Traugott (1986) attribute such discrepancies partly to the some 30 percent of those sampled who either refuse to cooperate or are unavailable, making the obtained sample not a perfect random sample. For example, when voters were surveyed by phone during the 1984 presidential race, those answering when their home was first called favored President Reagan by a slim 3 percent margin. After the interviewers persisted in calling back those not home until reaching them, President Reagan's margin increased to 13 percentage points (indicating, incidentally, that conservative voters spend less time at home).

Order of questions   Given a representative sample, the survey researcher must also contend with other sources of bias, such as the order in which questions are posed. Asked whether "the Japanese government should be allowed to set limits on how much American industry can sell in Japan," most Americans answered no (Schuman & Ludwig, 1983). Simultaneously, two-thirds of an equivalent sample were answering yes to this same question—because they were first asked whether "the American government should be allowed to set limits on how much Japanese industry can sell in the United States." Most of these people had said that the United States has the right to limit imports; to appear consistent and even-handed, they then said that Japan should have the same right.

Response options   Consider, too, the dramatic effects of the number of response options. When Joop van der Plight and his coworkers (1987) asked English voters what percentage of Britain's nuclear energy they wished came from nuclear power, the average preference was 41 percent. Others were asked what percentage they wished came from (1) nuclear, (2) coal, and (3) other sources. Their average preference for nuclear power was but 21 percent. A similar effect of response option occurred when Howard Schuman and Jacqueline Scott (1987) asked Americans "What do you think is the most important problem facing this country today—the energy shortage, the quality of public schools, legalized abortion, or pollution—or if you prefer, you may name a different problem as most important." Given these choices, 32 percent felt that the

DOONESBURY   by Garry Trudeau

Survey researchers must be sensitive to subtle—and not so subtle—biases.

quality of public schools was the biggest problem. Among others simply asked, "What do you think is the most important problem facing this country today?," only 1 percent named the schools. Remember: The form of the question may guide the answer.

Wording   The precise wording of alternatives may also influence answers. One poll found that only 7 percent of Americans thought government programs should be cut back if they cut out "aid to the needy." Yet 39 percent would kill funds if the "needy" item was called "public welfare" (Marty, 1982). Even very subtle changes in the tone of a question can have large effects (Schuman & Kelton, 1985). "Forbidding" something may be the same as "not allowing" it. But in 1940 when two comparable samples of Americans were asked either "Do you think the U.S. should forbid public speeches against democracy?" or "Do you think the U.S. should allow public speeches against democracy?" 54 percent said the U.S. should "forbid" such speeches while 75 percent said the U.S. should "not allow" them. And while 81 percent of Americans agree that "Women with young children should be able to work outside the home," 71 percent also agree that "Women should stay home if they have young preschool children" (*Public Opinion*, 1984, 1985). Survey questioning is a very delicate matter. Even when people say they feel strongly about an issue, the form and wording of a question may affect their answer (Krosnick & Schuman, 1988).

EXPERIMENTAL RESEARCH: SEARCHING FOR CAUSE AND EFFECT

The near impossibility of discerning cause and effect among naturally correlated events prompts most social psychologists to create laboratory simulations of everyday processes whenever such are feasible and ethical. We might liken these simulations of life to what aeronautical engineers do. Do they begin by observing how flying objects perform in a wide variety of natural environments? The variations in both atmospheric conditions and flying objects are so complex that they would surely find themselves perplexed about how to use such data to design better aircraft. So, instead, they construct a simulated reality, one that is under their control—a wind tunnel. Now they can manipulate the wind conditions and ascertain the precise effect of particular wind conditions on particular wing structures.

YOU GET WHAT YOU ASK FOR

Not only answers to survey questions, but also important everyday decisions are influenced by how an issue is posed. Amos Tversky and Daniel Kahneman (1981) posed the following problem to their students at Stanford University and at the University of British Columbia:

> Imagine that the U.S. is preparing for the outbreak of an unusual Asian disease, which is expected to kill 600 people. Two alternative programs to combat the disease have been proposed. Assume that the exact scientific estimate of the consequences of the programs are as follows:

Those given the following two choices favored Program A by about 3 to 1:

> If Program A is adopted, 200 people will be saved.
>
> If Program B is adopted, there is ⅓ probability that 600 people will be saved, and ⅔ probability that no people will be saved.

But when the same two choices were stated differently, Program B was favored by 3 to 1:

> If Program A is adopted, 400 people will die.
>
> If Program B is adopted, there is ⅓ probability that nobody will die, and ⅔ probability that 600 people will die.

How might you respond to the way something is framed—perhaps like those who respond more positively to ground beef described as "75 percent lean" rather than "25 percent fat"? Or like those who prefer a new medical treatment described as having a "50 percent success rate" over one that has a "50 percent failure rate" (Levin et al., 1987, 1988)?

The moral: the way everyday decisions are framed can make a big difference.

Control: Manipulating One Variable While Holding Others Constant

Like aeronautical engineers, social psychologists experiment by constructing social situations that simulate important features of our daily lives. By varying just one or two factors at a time—while holding all other things constant—the experimenter pinpoints how changes in these one or two things affect us. Just as the wind tunnel helps the aeronautical engineer discover basic principles of aerodynamics, so does the experiment enable the social psychologist to discover basic principles of social thinking, social influence, and social relations. And just as the ultimate aim of wind tunnel simulations is to understand and predict the flying characteristics of complex aircraft, so also social psychologists do experiments in order to understand and predict.

The experimental method is used in about three-fourths of social-psychological research studies (Higbee et al., 1982), and in two out of three studies the setting is a research laboratory (Adair et al., 1985). To illustrate, consider effects of television on children's attitudes and behavior (to be discussed more fully in Chapter 12, "Aggression"). Children who watch lots of violent television programs tend to be more aggressive than those who watch few. This suggests that children might be learning some of their behavior from what they see on the screen. But, as I hope you now recognize, this is a correlational finding. Figure 1-3 reminds us that there are at least two other cause-effect interpretations that do not implicate television as the cause of the children's aggression. (What are they?) Social psychologists have therefore brought television programs into the laboratory where they control violence viewing by exposing children to violent or nonviolent programs and observing how it affects their behavior.

For example, Robert Liebert and Robert Baron (1972) showed young Ohio boys and girls either a violent excerpt from a gangster television show or an excerpt from an exciting track race. The children who viewed the violence were subsequently most likely to choose to press vigorously a special red button which supposedly would transmit a burning pain to another child. (Actually, there was no other child, so no one was really harmed.) Such experiments indicate that television *can* be one cause of children's aggressive behavior.

Research and application   As this experiment illustrates, social psychology is fascinating partly because it mixes everyday experience and laboratory analysis. Throughout this book we will be keeping one foot in each by drawing our data mostly from the laboratory and our illustrations mostly from life. In fact, there is in social psychology a healthy interplay between laboratory research and everyday life. Hunches gained from everyday experience have inspired much laboratory research, and such research has illuminated important facets of human nature, deepening our awareness of what is before us. This interplay is evident in the research on children's television. What people saw in everyday life suggested some experiments. Network and government policy makers are now well aware of the results of these experiments. So, what we see in life can often be scrutinized in carefully managed experiments, the results of which may then be applied to social problems.

However, generalizing from laboratory to life should be done cautiously. The laboratory, for all it may aid us in uncovering some basic secrets of human existence, is still a simplified reality. It tells us what effect to expect of variable X, all other things being equal—which in the complexity of life they never are. Moreover, as you will see, the participants in many social-psychological experiments are college students. While this may help you identify with them, college students are hardly a random sample of all humanity. Would the same results be obtained with people of different ages, educational levels, and cultures? This is always an open question, though experience has taught us to distinguish between the *content* of people's thinking and acting—their attitudes and norms, for example—and the *process* by which they think and act—how their attitudes affect their actions and vice versa, for example. The content probably varies more from culture to culture than does the process. People of different cultures may hold different opinions, for instance, yet form them in similar ways.

So far we have seen that the logic of experimentation is very simple: By constructing and controlling a miniature reality we can vary one factor and then another and discover how these factors, separately or in combination, affect people. The laboratory experiment allows us to test ideas gleaned from life experience, and with due caution we can relate our findings to the real world. Now let us go just a little deeper and see how an experiment is done.

Every social-psychological experiment has two essential ingredients. One we have just considered—*control*. We manipulate one or two factors, while attempting to hold constant all other factors. The other ingredient is *random assignment*.

Experimental research: Studies which seek clues to cause-effect relationships by manipulating one or more factors, while controlling others (holding them constant).

Random Assignment: The Great Equalizer

Recall that we were reluctant to credit college with the higher incomes of college graduates because graduates may benefit not only from their education but also from their social backgrounds, aptitudes, and so forth. A survey researcher might measure each of these likely other factors and then note the income advantage enjoyed by college graduates above and beyond what would be expected from these other factors. Such statistical gymnastics are all well and good, but the researcher can never adjust for all the possible factors that might, in addition to attending college, differentiate graduates from nonattenders. The alternative explanations for the income difference are

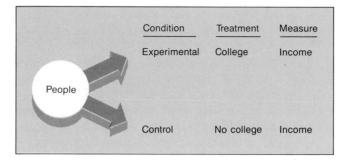

FIGURE 1-4
Randomly assigning people either to a condition which receives the experimental treatment or to a control condition which does not can give the researcher confidence that any later difference is somehow caused by the treatment.

limitless—perhaps ethnic heritage, or sociability, or good looks, or any of hundreds of other factors that the researcher has never thought of.

So, let us for the moment give free reign to our imagination and see how all these complicating factors might be equalized in one fell swoop. Suppose someone gave us the power to take a group of high school graduates and ***randomly assign*** some to college and some to other endeavors. Each person would have an equal chance of being assigned to either the college or noncollege condition of our pretend experiment. So the people in both groups would, in every conceivable way—family status, looks, aptitude, and whatever—average about the same. Random assignment would roughly equalize all these previously complicating factors. Any later income difference between these two groups could therefore not be attributed to any of these factors. Rather, it would almost surely have *something* to do with the variable we manipulated. Similarly, if an experiment on malaria in Central America revealed that only people assigned to sleeping rooms with unscreened windows catch it, this would not mean that unscreened windows by themselves *cause* malaria; but it would indicate that the cause has something to do with lack of screens.

Random assignment:
Assigning participants to the conditions of an experiment such that all persons have the same chance of being in a given condition. This equalizes the conditions at the beginning of the experiment. Thus if participants in the different conditions later behave differently, it will rarely be due to pre-existing differences among them. (Note the distinction between random *assignment* in experiments and random *sampling* in surveys.)

The Ethics of Experimentation

Our college example also illustrates why some experiments are neither feasible nor ethical. Social psychologists would never manipulate people's lives in this way. In such cases we rely upon the correlational method and squeeze all the information we can out of it.

In other cases, such as the issue of how children are affected by watching television, we briefly alter people's social experience and note the effects. Sometimes the experimental treatment is a harmless, perhaps even enjoyable experience to which people give their knowing consent. Sometimes, however, researchers find themselves operating in that gray area between the harmless and the risky.

Social psychologists often venture into that ethical gray area when they design experiments which really engage people's thoughts and emotions. Experiments need not have what Elliot Aronson, Marilyn Brewer, and Merrill Carlsmith (1985) call ***mundane realism.*** That is, laboratory behavior (for example, delivering electric shocks as part of an experiment on aggression) need not be literally the same as everyday behavior. For many researchers, that sort of realism is, indeed, a not-too-important, mundane matter. But the experiment *should* have ***experimental realism***—it should absorb and involve people. Experimenters do not want their people consciously playacting or ho-humming it; they want to engage real psychological processes. Forcing

Mundane realism:
Degree to which an experiment is superficially similar to everyday situations.

Experimental realism:
Degree to which an experiment absorbs and involves its participants.

people to choose whether to give intense or mild electric shock to someone else can, in this sense, be a realistic measure of aggression.

Achieving experimental realism often requires deceiving the participants. If the person in the next room is actually not receiving the shocks, the experimenter does not want the participants to know this. If they knew it, the experimental realism would be destroyed. Thus, about one-third of social-psychological studies (although the number has decreased over the last 15 years) necessarily involve deception (Vitelli, 1988).

Experimenters also seek to hide their predictions lest the participants, in their eagerness to be "good subjects," merely do what's expected. In subtle ways, the experimenter's words, tone of voice, and gestures may inadvertently "demand" desired responses. To minimize such ***demand characteristics,*** experimenters typically standardize their instructions or even write or tape-record them.

Researchers often walk a difficult tightrope in designing experiments that will be involving, yet ethical. To believe that you are hurting someone, or to be subjected to strong social pressure to see if it will change your opinion or behavior, may be temporarily uncomfortable. Such experiments raise the age-old question of whether ends justify means—whether the insights gained can justify deceiving and sometimes distressing people. Thus social-psychological research is now reviewed beforehand by an ethics committee to ensure that people are treated humanely. Ethical principles developed by the American Psychological Association (1981) urge investigators to:

- Tell potential participants enough about the experiment to enable them to give their ***informed consent.***
- Be truthful. Deception should be used only if justified and if there is no alternative.
- Protect people from harm and significant discomfort.
- Treat information about the individual participants confidentially.
- Fully explain the experiment afterwards, including any deception. The only exception to this rule is when the feedback would be brutal, making people realize they have been stupid or cruel. The experimenter should be sufficiently informative *and* considerate that people leave feeling at least as good about themselves as when they came in. Better yet, the participants should be repaid by having learned something about the nature of psychological inquiry. When treated in such ways, few participants mind being deceived (Christensen, 1988).

EXPLAINING AND PREDICTING: USING THEORIES

Although basic research often produces practical benefits, such applications are not our only reason for doing social psychology. Many of us are in the profession because we have a hard time thinking of anything more intrinsically fascinating than our own human existence. If, as Socrates counseled, "The unexamined life is not worth living," then simply "knowing thyself" better is a worthy enough goal.

As we wrestle with human nature to make it give up its secrets we usually organize our ideas and findings into theories. A ***theory*** is an integrated set of principles that explain and predict observed phenomena. Some people wonder why social psychologists are so preoccupied with their theories: Why don't they just gather facts? In response, our aeronautical engineering analogy is again useful. The engineers soon would be overwhelmed if, without any guiding principles, they tried to develop, merely by trial and error, an exhaustive catalog of the ways in which different wind conditions affect different wing structures. So, instead, they formulate broad concepts or theories, about how air movements interact with wing structures, and use the wind tunnel to test

Demand characteristics:
Cues in an experiment that tell the participant what behavior is expected.

Informed consent:
An ethical principle requiring that research participants be told enough to enable them to choose whether they wish to participate.

"Nothing has such power to broaden the mind as the ability to investigate systematically and truly all that comes under thy observation in life."
Marcus Aurelius, Meditations

Theory:
An integrated set of principles that explain and predict observed events.

Hypothesis:
A testable proposition that describes a relationship that may exist between events.

predictions derived from these concepts. Whether in aeronautical engineering or in social psychology, theories are a scientific shorthand.

In everyday conversation, "theory" often means "less than fact"—a middle rung on a confidence ladder going down from fact to theory to guess. But to any kind of scientist, facts and theories are different things, not different points on a continuum. Facts are agreed-upon statements about what we observe. ***Theories*** are *ideas* that summarize and explain facts. "Science is built up with facts, as a house is with stones," said Jules Henri Poincaré, "but a collection of facts is no more a science than a heap of stones is a house."

Theories not only summarize, they also imply testable predictions, called ***hypotheses.*** Hypotheses serve several purposes. First, they allow us to *test* the theories on which they are based. By making specific predictions, a theory puts its money where its mouth is. Second, predictions give *direction* to research. Any scientific field will mature much more rapidly if its researchers have a sense of direction, rather than haphazardly collecting isolated facts. Theoretical predictions suggest new areas for research; they send investigators looking for things they might never have thought of. Finally, the predictive feature of good theories can also make them very *practical* as well. In a world torn by strife and conflict, what would be of greater practical value than a complete theory of aggression, one that would predict the conditions under which to expect it and how to control it? As Kurt Lewin, one of the founders of modern social psychology, declared, "There is nothing so practical as a good theory."

Say we observe that crowds of people sometimes explode violently. We might therefore theorize that the presence of other people makes individuals feel anonymous, thus decreasing their inhibitions against doing harm. Let's let our minds play with this anonymity theory for a moment. Perhaps we could test it by constructing a laboratory experiment similar to execution by electric chair. What if individuals in groups were asked to simultaneously administer punishing shocks to a hapless victim, without knowing which of them were actually shocking the victim? Would these individuals administer stronger shock than individuals acting alone, as our theory predicts? Or we might manipulate anonymity: Would people hiding behind Halloween masks deliver stronger shock than people who were identifiable? If the results confirm our hypothesis, this might suggest some practical applications. Perhaps, for instance, incidents of police brutality could be reduced by having officers wear large name tags and drive cars identified with large numbers.

But how do we conclude that one theory is better than another? A good theory does all its functions well: (1) It effectively summarizes a wide range of observations, and (2) it makes clear predictions that can be used (a) to confirm or modify the theory, (b) to generate new exploration, and (c) to suggest practical application. When theories are discarded, usually it is not because they have been falsified, but because, like an old-model car, they have been replaced by newer, better models.

But do social psychology's theories provide *new* insight into the human condition? Or do they only describe the obvious?

IS SOCIAL PSYCHOLOGY SIMPLY SOPHISTICATED COMMON SENSE?

Many of the conclusions presented in this book will probably have already occurred to you, for the subject matter of social psychology is all around you. Every human being daily observes people thinking about, influencing, and relating to one another, so there is bound to be some accumulated social wisdom. For centuries, philosophers, novelists, and poets have observed and commented upon social behavior, often with keen insight. Might it therefore be said that social psychology is only common sense dressed in new jargon? Social psychology has been the object of two contradictory criticisms. One is that it is trivial because it documents the obvious; the other is that it is dangerous because its findings might be used to manipulate people. Is the first objection valid— does social psychology simply formalize what any good amateur social psychologist already intuitively knows?

THE I-KNEW-IT-ALL-ALONG PHENOMENON

One problem with commonsense explanations is that we tend to invoke them *after* we know the facts. Events are far more "obvious" and predictable in hindsight than beforehand. Baruch Fischhoff and others (Slovic & Fischhoff, 1977) have demonstrated many times that when people are told the outcome of an experiment, the outcome suddenly seems unsurprising—certainly less surprising than it is to people who are simply told about the experimental procedure and its possible outcomes. People overestimate their ability to have foreseen the result.

Likewise, in everyday life we often do not expect something to happen until it does. We then suddenly see clearly the forces that brought it to be and so do not feel surprised. After President Reagan's victory over Jimmy Carter in 1980, commentators—forgetting that the election had been "too close to call" until the final few days of the campaign—found the Reagan landslide unsurprising and easily understandable. When, the day before the election, Mark Leary (1982) asked people what percentage of votes they thought each candidate would receive, the average person, too, foresaw a slim Reagan victory. When, the day after the election, Leary asked other people

In hindsight, events seem far more obvious and predictable than before they occur.

what result they *would have predicted* the day before the election, most indicated a Reagan vote that was closer to the final result. Jack Powell (1988) found a similar knew-it-all-along effect after the 1984 Reagan triumph over Walter Mondale. Finding out that something had happened made it seem more inevitable. As the Danish philosopher-theologian Sören Kierkegaard surmised, "Life is lived forwards, but understood backwards."

If the I-knew-it-all-along phenomenon is pervasive, you may now be feeling that you already knew about it. Indeed, almost any conceivable result of a psychological experiment can seem like common sense—*after* you know the result. The phenomenon can be crudely demonstrated by giving half of a group some purported psychological finding and the other half the opposite result. For example, tell half that:

> Social psychologists have found that, whether choosing friends or falling in love, we are most attracted to people whose traits are different from our own. There seems to be wisdom in the old saying, "Opposites attract."

Tell the other half that:

> Social psychologists have found that, whether choosing friends or falling in love, we are most attracted to people whose traits are similar to our own. There seems to be wisdom in the old saying, "Birds of a feather flock together."

When asked to "explain" the result and then indicate whether it is "surprising" or "not surprising," virtually all will find whichever result they were given "not surprising."

As these examples indicate, we can draw up on the stockpile of ancient proverbs to make almost any result seem commonsensical. Nearly every possible outcome is conceivable, so there are proverbs for almost all occasions. Shall we say with John Donne, "No man is an island," or with Thomas Wolfe, "Every man is an island"? Does "haste make waste," or is "he who hesitates lost"? If a social psychologist reports that separation intensifies romantic attraction, someone is sure to reply, "Of course, 'Absence makes the heart grow fonder'." Should it turn out the reverse, the same person may remind us, "Out of sight, out of mind." No matter what happens, there will be someone who knew it would.

"A first-rate theory predicts; a second-rate theory forbids; and a third-rate theory explains after the event."
Aleksander Isaakovich
Kitaigorodskii

Karl Teigen (1986) must have had a few chuckles when asking University of Leicester (England) students to evaluate actual proverbs and their opposites. When given the actual proverb "Fear is stronger than love," most rated it as generally true; but so also did students who were given its reversed form, "Love is stronger than fear." Likewise, the genuine proverb "He that is fallen cannot help him who is down," was rated highly; but so too was "He that is fallen can help him who is down." My favorites, however, were the two highly rated proverbs "Wise men make proverbs and fools repeat them" (authentic) and its made-up counterpart, "Fools make proverbs and wise men repeat them."

The **hindsight bias** creates a problem for many psychology students. When you read the results of experiments in your textbooks, the material often seems easy, even commonsensical. When you subsequently take a multiple-choice test on which you must choose among several plausible outcomes to an experiment, the task may become surprisingly difficult. "I don't know what happened," the befuddled student later bemoans. "I thought I knew the material." (A word to the wise: Beware of the phenomenon when studying for exams, lest you fool yourself into thinking that you know the material better than you do.)

Hindsight bias:
The tendency to exaggerate one's ability to have foreseen how something turned out, *after* learning the outcome. Also known as the I-knew-it-all-along phenomenon.

The I-knew-it-all-along phenomenon not only can make social science findings seem like common sense, it also can have pernicious consequences. It is conducive to arrogance—an overestimation of our own intellectual powers. After the invention and acceptance of the typewriter, people, in hindsight, said it was a machine that demanded invention and that, once invented, had to be a success. But to Christopher Latham Sholes, creator of the Remington, its success was not so obvious beforehand. In an 1872 letter he confided that "my apprehension is [that] it will have its brief day and be thrown aside."

Moreover, because outcomes seem as if they should have been foreseeable, we are more likely to blame decision makers for what are, in retrospect, their "obvious" bad choices than to praise them for their good choices, since these, too, seem "obvious." Thus *after* the Japanese attack on Pearl Harbor, Monday-morning historians could read the signs and see the "inevitability" of what had happened. Likewise, we sometimes chastise ourselves for our "stupid mistakes"—perhaps for not having better handled a situation or a person. Looking back now, we see how we obviously should have handled it. (Recall Arthur Schlesinger's regret "for having kept so silent" during discussions of the CIA plan to invade Cuba's Bay of Pigs.) But sometimes we are too hard on ourselves. We forget that what is now obvious to us was not nearly so obvious at the time.

The conclusion to be drawn is *not* that common sense is usually wrong. Conventional wisdom often does apply—under certain conditions. The point is that our common sense is often *after the fact*—it describes events more easily than it predicts them. We therefore easily deceive ourselves into thinking that we know and knew more than we do and did.

We have seen what social psychology is, how its research is done, and how it differs from common sense. There is but one other matter to which we should be sensitized before embarking on our journey into the discipline.

Of course, sometimes common sense is wrong. For centuries, our daily experience told us that the universe revolved around the earth. But then science contradicted what our eyes told us and, eventually, dethroned the commonsense view.

SOCIAL PSYCHOLOGY AND HUMAN VALUES

Social psychology has no scientific answer to questions of human values: What ends are ultimately desirable? What ought we to do? What vision of the good life is worthy of our aspirations? Although social psychologists have no privileged answer to these questions, their personal values nevertheless penetrate their work in several subtle and not-so-subtle ways.

OBVIOUS WAYS IN WHICH VALUES ENTER THE PICTURE

We have seen already how values influence our ethical standards in doing research. But even before we reach this stage of a research project, our values have already entered the picture—beginning with our choice of the topic. It was not merely by accident that the study of prejudice flourished during the 1940s as fascism raged in Europe, that the 1960s saw increased interest in aggression as riots and a rising crime rate plagued America, that the 1970s provided a new wave of research on sex-role socialization and sex-role stereotypes, and that during the 1980s there was a resurgence of essays and studies concerning psychological aspects of the arms race. Such trends are products of the decades in which they occur.

Value considerations may also influence the type of people attracted to various disciplines. At your college are the students attracted to the humanities, the natural sciences, and the social sciences noticeably different? Some have suggested that psychology and the other social sciences attract people who are eager to challenge tradition, people who would rather shape the future than preserve the past (Campbell, 1975; Moynihan, 1979).

Finally, values obviously enter the picture in a very different sense—as the *object* of social-psychological analysis. Social psychologists have investigated how values are formed, how they can be changed, and how they influence our attitudes and actions. None of this, however, tells us which values are "right."

NOT-SO-OBVIOUS WAYS IN WHICH VALUES ENTER THE PICTURE

Less often recognized are the subtle ways in which value commitments masquerade as objective truth. The social sciences seem especially vulnerable to the expounding of values disguised as facts. Unlike workers in the physical sciences, whose analyses are more value free, and in the humanities, where values are more openly discussed, psychologists and sociologists are more often blind to their implicit values. Here are three not-so-obvious ways in which values enter social psychology and related areas.

1. Science Has Subjective Aspects

There is a growing awareness among both scientists and philosophers that science is not so purely objective as commonly thought. Contrary to popular opinion, scientists do not merely read what's out there in the book of nature. Rather, they interpret nature, using their own mental categories. In our daily lives, too, we view the world through the spectacles of our preconceptions.

The point is easily demonstrated. What do you see in Figure 1-5? Can you see a dalmatian dog on the right sniffing the ground at the center of the picture? Until they are given this expectation, most people are blind to what those who have the preconception are able to see. But once your mind has the preconception, it controls your interpretation of the picture—so much so that it becomes difficult *not* to see the dog. This is the way our minds work. While reading these words you have probably been unaware, until this moment, that you have been looking at your nose. Our minds block from our awareness something that is there, if only we were predisposed to perceive it. This tendency to prejudge reality on the basis of our expectations is one of the most important facts about the human mind.

A classic demonstration of how our presuppositions control our interpretations was provided by a Princeton-Dartmouth football game some years ago (Hastorf & Cantril, 1954; see also Loy & Andrews, 1981). The game lived up to its billing as a grudge match; it turned out to be one of the roughest and dirtiest games in the history of either school. A Princeton All-American was gang-tackled, piled on, and finally forced out of the game with a broken nose. Fistfights erupted, and further injuries occurred on both sides.

"Science does not simply describe and explain nature; it is part of the interplay between nature and ourselves; it describes nature as exposed to our method of questioning."
Werner Heisenberg,
Physics and Philosophy

Not long after the game, two psychologists, one from each school, showed films of the game to students on each campus as part of a social-psychology experiment. The students played the role of "objective" scientists, noting each infraction as they watched and who was responsible for it. As you might suppose, the Princeton students were much more likely than the Dartmouth students to see their Princeton players as the victims rather than the agents of illegal aggression. The Princeton students, for

FIGURE 1-5
What do you see?

Social representations:
Socially shared beliefs. Widely held ideas and values, including our assumptions and cultural ideologies. Our social representations help us make sense of our world.

example, saw twice as many Dartmouth violations as the Dartmouth students saw. There is an objective reality out there, but—in science as in everyday life—we are always viewing it through the spectacles of our preconceived beliefs and values.

Because the community of scholars at work in any given area often share a common viewpoint, their assumptions may go unchallenged. What we take for granted—the shared beliefs that European social psychologists call our ***social representations*** (Billig, 1988; Moscovici, 1988)—are our most important but least debated convictions. Sometimes, however, someone from outside the camp will call attention to what is being taken for granted. Some of social psychology's previously unexamined assumptions are now being illuminated by feminists and by Marxists, both of whom stand somewhat outside the camp of traditional social psychology. Feminist critics are calling attention to subtle biases (for example, to the political conservatism of many scientists who favor a biological interpretation of gender differences in social behavior—Unger, 1985). Marxist critics are calling attention to competitive, individualistic biases (for example, assuming that conformity is bad and that individual rewards are good). Such biases can affect what we "see" as we design and interpret our experiments. (Of course, any such group has its biases, too.)

So what do we conclude: That because science has its subjective side we should dismiss it? Quite the contrary: The realization that human thinking always involves interpretation is precisely why we need scientific analysis. Observation and experimentation help us clean the spectacles through which we view reality. By constantly checking our beliefs against the facts, as best as we can discern them, we restrain our biases.

2. Psychological Concepts Have Hidden Values

Values also influence psychology's specific concepts. This is apparent in psychologists' attempts to specify the good life. We refer to people as mature or immature, as well-adjusted or poorly adjusted, as mentally healthy or mentally ill, as if these were statements of fact, when they are really disguised value judgments. The personality psychologist Abraham Maslow, for example, was well known for his sensitive descriptions of the characteristics of "self-actualized" people—people who, with their needs for survival, safety, "belongingness," and self-esteem satisfied, go on to fulfill their full human potential. Few readers notice that the initial selection of the self-actualized persons to be analyzed was done subjectively, by Maslow himself. Thus the resulting description of their self-actualized personalities—spontaneous, autonomous, mystical, and so forth—is a statement of Maslow's personal values. Had Maslow begun with someone else's collection of heroic personalities—people such as Napoleon, Alexander the Great, and John D. Rockefeller Sr.—the resulting description of self-actualization would have been quite different (Smith, 1978).

Psychological advice likewise reflects the advice giver's personal values. When mental health professionals advise us how to live our lives, when child-rearing experts tell us how to handle our children, and when some psychologists encourage us to live free of concern for others' expectations, they are usually propounding their personal values, not just sharing their technical expertise. Many people, failing to realize this, are quite willing to abdicate their own judgment to the "professional" judgment. Because value decisions should concern us all, we had best not abdicate them to the scientist and professionals. Science can help us discern how better to achieve our goals, once we have settled on them. But questions of ultimate moral obligation, of purpose and direction, and of the meaning of life are not directly addressed by a science of behavior.

The pervasiveness of hidden values can also be illustrated in the research-based concepts of personality and social psychologists. Our labels reflect our judgments of what we have observed. Pretend you took a personality test and the psychologist, after scoring your answers, announced "You scored high in self-esteem. You are low in anxiety. And you have exceptional ego-strength." Ah, you think, I suspected as much, but it feels good to know that. Now another psychologist gives you a similar test. For some peculiar reason this test even asks some of the same questions. Afterward, the psychologist informs you that you are apparently quite defensive, for you scored high in "repressiveness." How could this be, you wonder. The other psychologist said such nice things about me. It could be because all these labels describe the same set of responses (a tendency to say nice things about oneself and not to acknowledge problems). Shall we call it high self-esteem or defensiveness? The label reflects the researcher's value judgment about the trait.

That value judgments are often hidden within our social-psychological language is no reason to malign social psychology. It's true of all human language. Whether some-

Psychological advice reflects the
advice-giver's personal values.

one engaged in guerilla warfare is labeled a "terrorist" or a "freedom fighter" depends
on our sympathy with the cause. Whether someone involved in an extramarital affair
is practicing "open marriage" or "adultery" depends on one's personal values. "Brainwashing" is social influence we do not approve of. "Perversions" are sex acts we do
not practice. Remarks about "ambitious" men and "aggressive" women, or about "cautious" boys and "timid" girls, convey a hidden message, do they not?

   To repeat, values lie hidden within our definitions of mental health and self-esteem,
our psychological advice for living, and our psychological labels. Throughout this book
I will call your attention to additional examples of hidden values. The point of these
examples will, I trust, never be that the implicit values are necessarily bad. It is simply
that scientific interpretation, even at the level of our labeling of phenomena, is a very
human activity. It is therefore quite natural and inevitable that social psychologists'
prior beliefs and values will influence what they think and write. For example, when
I picked postcollege income as a way to measure the effect of college, did this convey
a subtle message (which in this case I don't really believe) that the primary purpose
of a college education is to maximize your potential earnings?

SOCIAL PSYCHOLOGY IN THREE WORLDS

Psychology's roots are international as well as interdisciplinary. The pioneering experimenter, Ivan Pavlov, was a Russian physiologist. Child watcher Jean Piaget was a Swiss biologist. Sigmund Freud was an Austrian physician. But it was in the United States that these and other transplanted roots flourished, thanks to abundant laboratories, sophisticated equipment, and a wealth of trained personnel. Surveying the world scene, McGill University social psychologist Fathali Moghaddam (1987) describes the U.S. as the psychological first world—the superpower of academic psychology, especially of social psychology. Social psychology's "professional center of gravity" is in the United States, observes Michael Bond (1988) from the Chinese University of Hong Kong. Because Canadian and U.S. social psychology are intermeshed—even, Moghaddam believes, "indistinguishable"—we could as well speak of one "North American" social psychology.

The other industrialized nations form social psychology's second world. Great Britain, for example, shares with North America a strong tradition of scientific psychology. But because of its much smaller university system, Britain has only one-twenty-fifth as many academic psychologists as does the United States. Some social psychologists in Britain, West Germany, France, and the other European countries are contributing new approaches. Their methodology supplements laboratory experiments with natural observation of social discourse and behavior. European and North American social psychologists share interests in the intrapersonal and interpersonal levels of explaining social behavior, but Euro-

pean scholars tend to give more attention to the intergroup and societal levels as well (Doise, 1986; Hewstone, 1988). Thus their views may question U.S. individualism; conflict, they say, arises not so much from the misperceptions of individuals as from a power struggle between groups. The European political agenda stimulates their interests in social issues such as unemployment, political ideology, and relations between different linguistic and ethnic groups.

The developing nations, such as Bangladesh, Cuba, and Nigeria, form social psychology's third world. Hampered by their limited resources—Nigeria, a relatively powerful third-world country, has but 58 academic psychologists—such countries have had to import their psychology from the first and second world nations. Yet their problems are distinctive; pressing issues related to poverty, tribal conflict, and traditional agricultural life-style demand attention. In third-world societies, social psychologists seldom have the luxury of exploring the basics of human nature, nor can illiterate people answer questionnaires.

A complete social psychology would draw upon the insights of psychologists in all three worlds in describing processes of social thinking, social influence, and social relations common to all humans. Such a social psychology is thinkable if the three worlds of social psychology will be mutually sensitive and supportive, will work cooperatively rather than in isolation, and will exchange knowledge and experience.

3. There Is No Bridge from "Is" to "Ought"

Naturalistic fallacy:
Defining what is good in terms of what is observable. For example: What's typical is normal; what's normal is good.

One of the most seductive errors tempting those in the social sciences is converting one's description of what *is* into a prescription of what *ought* to be. Philosophers have called this the **naturalistic fallacy.** The gulf between "is" and "ought," between scientific description and ethical prescription, remains as wide today as when philosopher David Hume pointed it out 200 years ago. Thus no survey of human behavior—say, of sexual practices—logically dictates what is "right" behavior. If most people don't do something, that does not make it wrong; if most people do it, that does not make it right. As we contemplate what ought to be, you and I may welcome information about what is. But ethical decisions must in the end be made on their own merits.

The well-known research on moral development by developmental psychologist Lawrence Kohlberg (1981, 1984) is a case in point. Kohlberg observed that moral thinking unfolds through a consistent series of stages, just as physical development occurs in a predictable sequence. Few people, however, ever reach the "highest" stage

BEHIND THE SCENES

After being born in Iran and educated in England, I joined hundreds of thousands of Iranians returning home after the revolution of 1978. I soon found that my new Ph.D. ill-equipped me for work in a culture that was suspicious of Western psychology and demanding that my teaching and research reflect Iranian concerns and values. Through my experiences there, and subsequently with the United Nations Development Programme, I became aware of the urgent need for a psychology that is appropriate to the poor and illiterate masses of Third World people. Believing that internationalizing psychology will benefit psychologists in all three worlds, I am now working to bridge the gap between social psychology in North America and other parts of the world and to educate psychologists for work in the Third World.

Fathali M. Moghaddam,
McGill University

of moral development, the "postconventional" level of self-chosen moral principles. Experiments have therefore been undertaken to ascertain how people may be stimulated to achieve higher levels of "maturity" in their moral thinking. Notice here a subtle shift from objective *des*cription of stages of moral thinking to *pre*scription of the postconventional stage. Kohlberg's scheme seems to provide a scientific basis for our own moral thinking [which Norma Haan (1978) and Carol Gilligan (1982) believe is especially characteristic of individualistic and rationalistic males], thereby providing a handy rationale by which we social scientists can judge opposing moral philosophies as immature.

My purpose here is not to quarrel with the value judgments implicit in Kohlberg's very influential description of moral development. The point is simply that there is no way we can move from objective statements of fact to prescriptive statements of what ought to be without injecting our values.

In such ways, both obvious and subtle, social psychologists' personal values may influence their work. We do well to remember this, and also to remember that what is true of them is true of each one of us: Our values and assumptions color our view of the world. Those who have known only their own culture assume its view of the world. To discover how our values and social representations shape what we take for granted, we can encounter a different cultural world—as from time to time we will do throughout this book.

SUMMING UP

SOCIAL PSYCHOLOGY AND THE OTHER DISCIPLINES

Social psychology is the scientific study of how people think about, influence, and relate to one another. Sociology and psychology are social psychology's parent disciplines. Social psychology tends to be more individualistic in its content and more experimental in its method than other areas of sociology. Compared to personality psychology, social psychology focuses less attention on differences among individuals and more attention on how people, in general, view and affect one another. There are many additional perspectives on human nature, each of which asks its own set of questions. Successful explanation of human functioning by one perspective does not contradict other perspectives.

HOW WE DO SOCIAL PSYCHOLOGY

Most social psychological research is either correlational or experimental. Correlational studies, sometimes conducted with systematic survey methods, ascertain the relationship between variables, such as between amount of education and amount of income. Knowing two things are naturally related is valuable information, but it usually does not indicate what is causing what. When possible, social psychologists therefore prefer to conduct experiments in which cause and effect can be pinned down more precisely. By constructing a miniature reality that is under their control, experimenters can vary one thing and then another and discover how these things, separately or in combination, affect people. Participants are randomly assigned to an experimental condition, which receives the experimental treatment, or a control condition, which does not. Any resulting difference between the two conditions can then be attributed to the experimental treatment. Ethical problems often encountered in conducting experiments have necessitated the development of ethical standards for research.

Social psychologists organize their ideas and findings into theories. A good theory will distill a bewildering array of facts into a much shorter list of predictive principles. These predictions can be used to confirm or modify the theory, to generate new exploration, and to suggest practical application.

IS SOCIAL PSYCHOLOGY SIMPLY SOPHISTICATED COMMON SENSE?

Social psychology's findings may sometimes seem obvious. However, experiments indicate that outcomes are generally far more "obvious" after the facts are known than they are beforehand. This hindsight bias tends to make people overconfident about the validity of their intuition.

SOCIAL PSYCHOLOGY AND HUMAN VALUES

Social psychologists' values penetrate their work in obvious ways, such as their choice of research topics. Less easily recognized are subtle ways in which values permeate social psychology. There is a growing awareness of the subjectivity of scientific interpretation, of values hidden in the concepts and labels of social psychology, and of the gulf between scientific description of what is and ethical prescription of what ought to be. This penetration of values into science is not unique to social psychology, nor is it anything to be embarrassed about. That human thinking is seldom dispassionate is precisely why we need systematic observation and experimentation if we are to check our cherished conjectures against reality, and why social psychologists in different cultures are eager to exchange their ideas and findings.

FOR FURTHER READING

To see social psychology firsthand in its primary sources, skim, for North American social psychology, the *Journal of Personality and Social Psychology* or *Personality and Social Psychology Bulletin*, both published by the American Psychological Association.

To sample European research in social psychology, see the *European Journal of Social Psychology* (published by the European Association of Experimental Social Psychology) or the *British Journal of Social Psychology* (published by the British Psychological Society).

For a carefully selected sample of influential articles from the literature of social psychology, see Amy Halberstadt and Steve Ellyson's *Readings from the First Century of Social Psychology* (McGraw-Hill, 1990).

Three paperback books nicely introduce social psychology's methods:

Aron, A., & Aron, E. (1990). *The heart of social psychology*, 2nd edition. Lexington, MA: D. C. Heath. Provides a personal glimpse of what motivates social psychologists, based on extensive interviews with leading researchers.

Dane, F. C. (1988). *The common and uncommon sense of social behavior*. Belmont, CA: Brooks/Cole. An informal account of social psychology's purposes and methods, based on close analyses of a well-chosen sample of recent experiments.

Hunt, M. (1985). *Profiles of social research: The scientific study of human interactions*. New York: Russell Sage. A gifted science writer provides a behind-the-scenes tour through the wonder and excitement of social research. Depicts the human drama—the joys, struggles, and dilemmas—of doing such research.

PART ONE

SOCIAL THINKING

PART ONE

SOCIAL THINKING

*Change the way people think and
things will never be the same.*

Steven Biko

This book is organized around its definition of social psychology: the scientific study of how we *think about* (Part One), *influence* (Part Two), and *relate* (Part Three) to one another.

These chapters on social thinking examine how we view ourselves and others. In varying ways, each chapter confronts an overriding question: How reasonable are our social attitudes, explanations, and beliefs? Are our impressions of ourselves and of one another generally accurate? In what ways is our social thinking prone to bias and error, and how might we bring it closer to reality?

Chapter 2 explores the links between our attitudes and behaviors: Do our attitudes determine our behaviors? Do our behaviors determine our attitudes? Or does it work both ways?

Chapter 3 analyzes how we explain other people's actions and our own. For example, when do we attribute people's actions to their circumstances ("She was angered by the insult") and when to their own dispositions ("He is an angry, hostile person")? Do we explain our own actions similarly?

Chapter 4 looks at the amazing and sometimes rather amusing ways in which we form beliefs about our social worlds and reveals a half-dozen ways in which we are prone to err.

Chapter 5 examines the implications of this research on attitudes, explanations, and beliefs for the mental health professions. For example, how do people explain their emotional and health problems? And how might psychologists and physicians diagnose people more accurately and treat them more effectively?

CHAPTER
2

BEHAVIOR
AND ATTITUDES

D uring the 1988 presidential campaign, candidate George Bush appealed to undecided voters by standing on the New Jersey shoreline and declaring his commitment to clean water and air. But some people wondered, as people wonder about any politician: *Was this the real George Bush?* Did Bush's campaign statements reflect his genuine attitudes? Or, as his opponent alleged, was Bush a "born-again environmentalist," whose attitudes were better reflected in his prior support of Reagan administration environmental policies? After Michael Dukakis was nominated as the Democratic Party's presidential candidate, similar questions emerged: Did Dukakis' professed support of a strong national defense, emphasized with TV images of him riding around in an M-1 tank, reflect his heartfelt attitude toward the military? Or was he, as Republicans alleged, "Mr. Weak on Defense."

Attitude:
A favorable or unfavorable evaluative reaction toward something or someone, exhibited in one's beliefs, feelings, or intended behavior.

When we question Bush's ***attitude*** toward, say, environmental funding, we refer to his beliefs and feelings related to such spending and his resulting inclinations to support or oppose it. Taken together, such favorable or unfavorable *evaluative reactions*—whether exhibited in beliefs, feelings, or inclinations to act—define a person's attitude toward something (Breckler, 1984; Jamieson & Zanna, 1989; Zanna & Rempel, 1988). Attitudes provide an efficient way to size up the world: When we have to respond quickly to something, how we *feel* about something can guide how we react.

Generally, we assume that the different ways an attitude can be exhibited are related—that, for example, a person who *believes* that a particular ethnic group is lazy and aggressive may *feel* dislike for such people and therefore *intend to act* in a discriminatory manner. Any of these three dimensions can be tapped when assessing people's attitudes. (You can remember them as the ABCs of attitudes: *a*ffect (feelings), *b*ehavior (intention), and *c*ognition (thoughts).)

The study of attitudes is close to the heart of social psychology and historically was one of its first concerns. It is therefore fitting that we begin our journey into social psychology with a close look at the impact of social thinking: how do your attitudes affect your actions?

DO OUR ATTITUDES DETERMINE OUR BEHAVIOR?

To ask whether our attitudes determine our behavior is to ask a fundamental question about human nature: What is the relationship between what we *are* (on the inside) and what we *do* (on the outside)? Philosophers, theologians, and educators have long speculated about the connection between thought and action, character and conduct, private word and public deed. The prevailing assumption, which underlies most teaching, counseling, and child rearing, has been that our beliefs and feelings determine our public behavior. So, if we want to alter the way people act, we had best change their hearts and minds.

"The ancestor of every action is a thought."
Ralph Waldo Emerson,
Essays, First Series

"Thought is the child of Action."
Benjamin Disraeli, Vivian Grey

ARE WE ALL HYPOCRITES?

"In the beginning," social psychologists wholeheartedly shared the assumption that to know a person's attitudes is to predict that person's actions. But in 1964, Leon Festinger concluded that research had in fact not found that changing people's attitudes will change their behavior. Festinger also advanced the radical notion that the attitude-behavior relation actually works the other way around, with our behavior as the horse and our attitudes as the cart. As Robert Abelson (1972) put it, we are, apparently, "very well trained and very good at finding reasons for what we do, but not very good at doing what we find reasons for."

An even more damaging blow to the supposed potency of our attitudes came in 1969, when social psychologist Allan Wicker reviewed several dozen research studies covering a wide variety of people, attitudes, and behaviors. Wicker offered the shocking conclusion that the expressed attitudes of a group of people usually predicted little of the variation in their behaviors. For instance, students' attitudes toward cheating bore little relation to the likelihood of their cheating. People's expressed convictions regarding the church had but a modest relationship to church attendance on any given Sunday. Self-described racial attitudes predicted little of the variation in behavior that occurred when people confronted an actual interracial situation.

*"Between the idea
And the reality
Between the motion
And the act
Falls the Shadow"*
T. S. Eliot, The Hollow Men

If people don't play the same game that they talk, it's little wonder that attempts to change behavior by changing attitudes often fail. Warnings about the dangers of smoking only minimally affect smoking among those who already smoke. Increasing the public's awareness of the desensitizing and brutalizing effects of a prolonged diet of television violence has stimulated many Americans to voice a desire for less violent programming—but ironically, they still watch media murder as much as ever. Appeals for safe driving habits have had far less effect on accident rates than have lower speed limits and divided highways (Etzioni, 1972).

At about the time that Wicker and others were offering their assessment of the potency of attitudes, some personality psychologists began to suggest that personality traits—at least those measured by our best-known personality tests—also fail to predict our behavior (Mischel, 1968). If we want to know how helpful people are going to be, for example, we usually won't learn much by giving them tests of self-esteem, anxiety, or defensiveness. If the situation makes clear-cut demands, we are better off knowing how most people act, or so many studies seemed to suggest. Likewise, many psychotherapists began to argue that talking therapies such as psychoanalysis seldom "cure" people's problems, and that therapists should instead work directly on modifying the problem behavior and forget about analyzing personality defects that hypothetically underlie the problem.

All in all, the developing picture of what controls our behavior seemed to focus on factors outside us—external social influences, for example—and to play down internal factors such as attitudes and personality traits. The emerging human image was that of little billiard balls that have different stripes and colors to be sure, but that are all similarly buffeted by the forces upon them.

"It may be desirable to abandon the attitude concept."
Alan Wicker (1971)

In short, the original thesis that our attitudes determine our actions was countered during the 1960s by the antithesis that our attitudes determine virtually nothing. "Aha!" you may be thinking. "Thesis. Antithesis. Now for the synthesis." And so it happened. The surprising finding that what people say often differs from what they do sent social psychologists scurrying to find out why. Surely, we reasoned, our convictions and feelings make a difference sometimes.

The luxury of hindsight enables us to impose order on the findings. In fact, what I am about to explain seems so obvious now that I find it hard to imagine why most social psychologists (myself included) were not thinking this way before the early 1970s. I must remind myself that the truth is obvious only once it is known, and that today's "obvious" synthesis sometimes becomes tomorrow's controversial thesis.

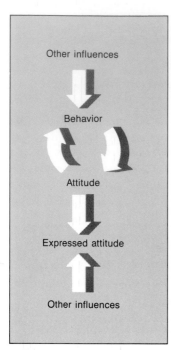

FIGURE 2-1
Our expressed attitudes may imperfectly predict our behavior, because both are subject to social influences.

Note the deception here, and recall from Chapter 1 that professional ethics approve such deception only when necessary and justified.

Bogus pipeline:
A procedure for detecting people's attitudes. Participants are first convinced that a new machine can use their psychological responses to measure their private attitudes. Then they are asked to predict the machine's reading, thus revealing their attitudes.

WHEN DO ATTITUDES PREDICT BEHAVIOR?

The reason we so often act contrary to our expressed attitudes is that, as Figure 2-1 suggests, our behavior and our expressed attitudes are both subject to social influences. One social psychologist counted forty separate factors that complicate the relationship between attitudes and behavior (Triandis, 1982). If we could just neutralize the social influences—making all other things equal—might our attitudes accurately predict our behaviors? Let's see.

Minimizing Social Influences on Expressed Attitudes

Unlike a physician measuring heart rate, we social psychologists never get a direct reading on people's attitudes. Rather, we measure their *expressed* attitudes. And expressions are behaviors, which, like other behaviors, are subject to outside influences. In Chapter 1 we saw that the way we pose a survey question can affect the answer given. So also can the conditions under which the person responds. This was vividly demonstrated when the United States House of Representatives once overwhelmingly passed a salary increase for itself in an off-the-record vote, then moments later overwhelmingly defeated the same bill on a roll-call vote. Fear of criticism had distorted the true congressional sentiment on the roll-call vote. We often tend to express what we think others want to hear.

Since people often don't wear their hearts on their sleeves, social psychologists have longed for a "pipeline to the heart" that would enable them to know people's concealed attitudes. Edward Jones and Harold Sigall (1971) therefore devised a **bogus pipeline** method for measuring people's attitudes. It's not a real pipeline, but it is the closest thing we have to one. In one experiment, conducted with Richard Page, Sigall (1971) had University of Rochester students hold a locked wheel, which if unlocked could turn a pointer to the left, indicating disagreement, or to the right, indicating agreement. When electrodes were attached to their arms, the fake machine supposedly measured miniature muscular responses that were said to gauge their supposed tendency to turn the wheel left (disagree) or right (agree). To demonstrate this amazing new machine, the researchers asked the students a few questions, on which the experimenter had already secretly ascertained their attitudes. After a few moments of impressive flashing lights and whirring sounds, a meter on the machine announced the student's attitude—which was nothing more than the attitude position the student had earlier indicated. The procedure convinced everyone.

Once the students were convinced, the attitude meter was then hidden and they were asked questions concerning their attitudes toward Blacks and requested to guess what the meter revealed. How do you suppose these White collegians responded? Compared to other students who responded through a typical questionnaire, those responding by the bogus pipeline admitted more negative belief. It was as if they were thinking, "I'd better reveal my opinions lest the experimenter think I'm out of touch with myself." For example, those responding to the paper-and-pencil scale rated Blacks as being more sensitive than other Americans; those responding through the bogus pipeline reversed these judgments. Displays of racial prejudice are generally considered gauche among today's sophisticated collegians, but the bogus pipeline was able to cut through the feigned attitudes.

Experiments with the bogus pipeline have produced additional interesting results. For example, Joseph Faranda, Joseph Kaminski, and Barbara Giza (1979) found that men and women students at the University of Delaware expressed similar attitudes about women's rights and roles when questions were asked with a paper-and-pencil test. But when using the bogus pipeline, men expressed much less sympathy toward women's rights than did women. (I suspect some of us are now thinking we knew-it-all-along: "Most college men are closet chauvinists.") Even a simpler variation of the bogus pipeline—telling people their attitude reports will later be double-checked with a lie detector—triggers more honest attitude reports (Jamieson & Zanna, 1983). All these studies suggest one reason that expressions of attitude may not predict other behaviors: People's real attitudes are sometimes distorted when expressed.

Minimizing Other Influences on Behavior

If people's expressions of attitude are affected by outside influences, their other behaviors are probably even more so. As Chapters 6 to 9 will illustrate again and again, social influences can be enormous—enormous enough sometimes to induce people to violate their deepest convictions. Thus, before Jesus's crucifixion his disciple Peter denies knowing him; presidential aides may go along with actions they know are wrong; politicians may say what they believe voters want to hear.

"Do I contradict myself? Very well then I contradict myself. (I am large, I contain multitudes.)"
Walt Whitman, Song of Myself

Given that on any occasion we are affected not only by our inner attitudes but also by the situation we face, would *averaging* many occasions enable us to detect more clearly the impact of our attitudes? Predicting people's behavior is like predicting a baseball player's hitting. The outcome of any particular time at bat is nearly impossible to predict, because it is affected not only by the batter, but also by what the pitcher throws and by unmeasurable chance factors. By considering many times at bat we neutralize these complicating factors. Thus, knowing the players, we can predict their approximate batting *averages*. Or to use an example from research, people's general attitude toward religion poorly predicts whether they will go to church next Sunday (because church attendance is also influenced by the weather, the preacher, how one is feeling, and so forth). But people's religious attitudes predict quite well the total quantity of their religious behaviors over a period of time (Fishbein & Ajzen, 1974; Kahle & Berman, 1979). The moral: The effects of an attitude on behavior become more apparent when we look at a person's typical or average behavior rather than at isolated acts.

Measuring Attitudes Specific to the Behavior

Other conditions further improve the predictive potency of attitudes. As Icek Ajzen and Martin Fishbein (1977; Ajzen, 1982) point out, when the measured attitude is general—say, an attitude toward ethnic minorities—and the behavior is very specific—say, a decision whether to help a particular Hispanic person in a particular situation—we should not expect a close correspondence between our words and our actions. Indeed, report Fishbein and Ajzen, in twenty-six out of twenty-seven such research studies, attitudes did not predict behavior. But attitudes *did* predict behavior in all twenty-six studies they could find in which the measured attitude corresponded closely to the situation being considered. For example, we can expect that attitudes toward the general concept of "health fitness" will poorly predict specific exercise and dietary practices. The likelihood of people's jogging is more likely to depend on their opinions about the costs and benefits of *jogging*. Thus, to change people's health habits through persuasion, we should alter their attitudes toward *specific* health-related practices (Olson & Zanna, 1981; Ajzen & Timko, 1986).

So far we have seen two conditions under which our attitudes will predict our behavior: (1) when the other influences upon our attitude statements and our behavior are minimized and (2) when the measured attitude is specifically relevant to the observed behavior. One other condition is suggested by Figure 2-1: An attitude should better predict behavior when it is made potent.

Maximizing Attitude Potency

Our attitudes lie dormant when we act automatically, without pausing to consider them. Often we act our well-learned "scripts," not stopping to reflect on what we're doing. In the hallway, we may respond similarly to friends and to strangers with an automatic "Hi." We answer the restaurant cashier's question, "How was your meal?" by saying "Fine," even if we found it tasteless. Such mindless action is often adaptive. Since we normally concentrate on only one thing at a time, acting without premeditation frees our minds to work on new problems. As the philosopher Alfred North Whitehead argued, "Civilization advances by extending the number of operations which we can perform without thinking about them."

Bringing Attitudes to Mind

"Thinking is easy, acting difficult, and to put one's thoughts into action, the most difficult thing in the world."
Goethe

In novel situations our behavior is less automatic; when there is no well-learned script we usually think before we act. If people were prompted to think about their attitudes before acting, might they then be truer to themselves? Mark Snyder and William Swann (1976) wanted to find out. So two weeks after 120 of their University of Minnesota men students indicated their attitudes toward affirmative-action employment policies, Snyder and Swann invited them to act as jurors in a sex-discrimination court case. Only if the men were first induced to remember their attitudes—by being given "a few minutes to organize your thoughts and views on the affirmative action issue"—did their attitudes predict their verdicts. Similarly, people who take a few moments to review their past behavior tend to express attitudes that better predict their future behavior (Zanna et al. 1981). The conclusion from this and other experiments is that our attitudes will guide our behavior only if they come to mind. Attitudes that don't come readily to mind often lay dormant when opportunities to act on them arise (Fazio, 1987; Kallgren & Wood, 1986).

"Only individuals who know what they believe and who know the implications of what they believe for what they do are in a position to put their beliefs into practice."
Mark Snyder (1982)

Self-conscious people are more in tune with their own attitudes (Miller & Grush, 1986). Thus another way experimenters have induced people to focus on their inner convictions is to *make* them self-conscious: for example, to have them act in front of a mirror (Carver & Scheier, 1981). Perhaps you can recall suddenly being acutely aware of yourself upon entering a room having a large mirror. Making people self-aware in this way promotes consistency between words and deeds (Gibbons, 1978; Froming et al., 1982). For example, Edward Diener and Mark Wallbom (1976) noted that nearly all college students *say* that cheating is morally wrong. But will they follow the advice of Shakespeare's Polonius, "To thine own self be true"? Diener and Wallbom set University of Washington students to work on an anagram-solving task (said to predict IQ) and told them to stop when a bell in the room sounded. Left alone, 71 percent cheated by working past the bell. Other students, made self-aware by working in front of a mirror while hearing their tape-recorded voices, were truer to themselves—only 7 percent cheated. It makes one wonder: Would eye-level mirrors in stores decrease shoplifting by making people more conscious of their attitudes against stealing?

"Without doubt it is a delightful harmony when doing and saying go together."
Montaigne, Essays

The Potency of Attitudes Forged through Experience

Finally, we acquire our attitudes in a manner that sometimes makes them potent and sometimes not. An extensive series of experiments by Russell Fazio and Mark Zanna (1981) indicates that when our attitudes are rooted in our experience—not just in hearsay—they are far more likely to endure and to predict our subsequent actions. One of their studies was conducted with the unwitting assistance of Cornell University. A housing shortage forced the university to assign some first-year students to several weeks on cots in dormitory lounges while others basked in the relative luxury of their permanent rooms. When questioned by Dennis Regan and Fazio (1977), students in both groups espoused equivalently negative attitudes regarding the housing situation and how the administration was dealing with it. But when given opportunities to act upon their attitudes—to sign a petition and solicit other signatures, to join a committee being formed to investigate the situation, to write a letter on the matter—only those whose attitudes were rooted in direct experience with the temporary housing acted upon their attitudes. [As this experiment also hints, people are especially likely to act in accord with their attitudes when it is in their self-interest (Borgida & Campbell, 1982; Sivacek & Crano, 1982).] Other research by Fazio and Zanna, William Watts (1967), and Steven Sherman and colleagues (1983) indicates that, compared to attitudes formed passively, those which are forged in the hot fire of actual experience are more clearly defined, more certain, more stable over time, more resistant to attack, and more readily remembered.

Experience-based attitudes are also thought through more (Wu & Shaffer, 1988). And thoughtful attitudes—especially attitudes that have been pondered by analytic people—are less subject to whims of the moment. When, say, it comes time to vote,

People who have thought a great deal about issues are more likely to vote according to their attitudes.

people who have thought a good deal about an issue are more likely to go vote their attitudes (Cacioppo et al., 1986). Thus, compared to 20-year-old college students, adults with a longer history of life experiences have more potent attitudes (Sears, 1986).

To summarize, our attitudes predict our actions (1) if other influences are minimized, (2) if the attitude is specific to the action, and (3) if, as we act, we are conscious of our attitudes, either because something reminds us of them or because we acquired them in a manner that makes them strong. When these conditions are not met, our attitudes seem disconnected from our actions.

Do these three conditions seem obvious? In hindsight, it may be tempting to think we knew them all along. But remember: They were not obvious to researchers in 1970. Nor were they obvious to the West German university students who were unable to guess the outcomes of published studies on attitude-behavior consistency (Six & Krahe, 1984). As we saw in Chapter 1, the outcomes of research studies generally are not obvious—until they are obtained and explained.

"The view that attitudes have essentially no effect on behavior can be rejected with a high degree of confidence."
Peter Bentler & George Speckart (1981)

So it is now plain that, depending on the conditions, the relationship between our attitude statements and our behavior can range from no relationship to a substantial one. La Rochefoucauld, the seventeenth-century French writer, was correct: "It is easier to preach virtue than to practice it." Yet we can breathe a sigh of relief that our attitudes are, after all, *one* determinant of our actions. This conclusion is reinforced by findings that people's attitudes can indeed predict their actions two weeks, two months, or even two years later (Kahle, 1983; Kahle & Berman, 1979). To return to the philosophical question with which we began, there *is* a connection between what we are and what we do, even if that connection is often looser than most of us would like to believe.

Now we turn our attention to the less commonsensical idea that our behavior determines our attitudes. It is true that we sometimes stand up for what we believe, but it is also true that we come to believe in what we stand up for. If social psychology has taught us anything during the last twenty-five years, it is that *we are likely not only to think ourselves into a way of acting but also to act ourselves into a way of thinking.*

Much of the research that documents this conclusion has been inspired by social-psychological theories. However, instead of beginning with these theories, I think it more interesting to reverse the order and first present the wide-ranging evidence that behavior affects attitudes. I invite you to play theorist as you read this evidence. Speculate *why* actions affect attitudes, and then compare your ideas with three explanations proposed by social psychologists.

DOES OUR BEHAVIOR DETERMINE OUR ATTITUDES?

"In doing we learn."
George Herbert, Jacula Prudentum

How do we learn to bicycle, type, play a musical instrument, or swim? As with much we learn, we must *do* it to know it. We can read books on bicycling, but we cannot *know* bicycling until we have done it. But is this effect of action limited to knowing physical skills? Consider the following incidents, each based on actual happenings:

Sarah is hypnotized and told to take off her shoes when a book drops on the floor. Fifteen minutes later a book drops and Sarah quietly slips out of her loafers. "Hey, Sarah," asks the hypnotist, "why did you take off your shoes?" "Well . . . my feet are hot and tired," Sarah replies. "It has been a long day." The act produces the idea.

George has electrodes temporarily implanted in the region of his brain that controls his head movements. When the electrode is stimulated by remote control, George always turns his head. Unaware of the remote stimulation, he thinks this activity is spontaneous and when questioned always offers a reasonable explanation for it: "I'm looking for my slipper," "I heard a noise," "I'm restless," or "I was looking under the bed" (Delgado, 1973).

Carol's severe seizures were relieved by surgically separating her two brain hemispheres. Now, in an experiment, a picture of a nude woman is flashed to the left half of Carol's field of vision and thus to the nonverbal right side of her brain. A sheepish smile spreads over her face and she begins chuckling. Asked why, she invents—and apparently believes—a plausible explanation: "Oh—that funny machine" (Gazzaniga, 1985). Frank, another split-brain patient, has the word *smile* flashed to his nonverbal right hemisphere. He obliges and forces a smile. Asked why, he explains that "this experiment is very funny."

Such illustrations hint at a wide-ranging effect of what we do on what we "know." Indeed, the mental aftereffects of our behavior are evident in so rich a variety of experimental and social situations that we can but sample from the smorgasbord. The following examples will, nonetheless, indicate the power of self-persuasion—that our attitudes can follow behavior.

ROLE PLAYING

The word *role* is borrowed from the theater and, as in the theater, refers to prescribed actions—actions expected of those who occupy a particular social position. When stepping into a new social role we must perform its actions, even if we feel somewhat inauthentic. But generally our sense of phoniness does not last long.

Recall a time when you stepped into some new role—perhaps your first days on a job, or in a sorority or fraternity, or at college. That first week on campus, for example, you may have been supersensitive to the new social prescriptions and tried valiantly to meet them, to root out your high school behavior. At such times we often feel artificial; self-consciously we observe our new talk and actions, because they aren't naturally ours. Then one day an amazing thing happens: We notice that our insincere sorority enthusiasm or our pseudointellectual college talk no longer feels forced. We have begun to absorb the role. Granted, we chose the role. Yet now it has begun to fit as comfortably as our old jeans and T-shirt.

"No man, for any considerable period, can wear one face to himself and another to the multitude without finally getting bewildered as to which may be true."
Nathaniel Hawthorne

Consider experiments on the effects of acting out a role. In one study, young women smokers who played the emotional role of lung cancer victims subsequently reduced their smoking more than those merely given factual information about the dangers of smoking (Janis & Mann, 1965; Mann & Janis, 1968). Another experiment engaged some students in a game that simulated conflict with the Soviet Union. As a result of playing the simulation—which was intended to make students more understanding of the Soviets—those students who played the role of U.S. advisors developed attitudes toward Russia that were more hostile (Trost et al., 1989).

In a real life situation, researchers observed industrial workers who were promoted to foreman (a company position) or shop steward (a union position). The new roles demanded new behavior. And, sure enough, the men soon developed new attitudes (Figure 2-2). The foremen became more sympathetic to the management's positions, the stewards to the union's (Lieberman, 1956).

This latter study hints at the tremendous importance of our vocational role. The career you choose will affect not only what you do on the job, but also the attitudes and values you are likely to develop. New teachers, police officers, soldiers, and managers usually internalize their roles with significant effects on their attitudes and per-

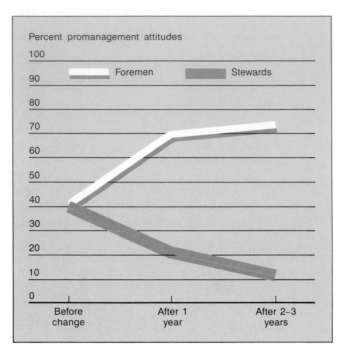

FIGURE 2-2
Workers promoted to the role of union steward or that of company supervisor developed attitudes compatible with their new role. (Data from Lieberman, 1956.)

"My whole personality changed during the time I was doing the part."
Ian Charleson on his role as serene and devout Olympic hero Eric Liddell in Chariots of Fire (quoted by Magnusson, 1981, p. 188)

sonalities. The marines "make a man out of you"—not just by indoctrination, but by having you act out the new role requirements.

The effect of behavior on attitude is evident even in the theatre. Self-conscious playacting may diminish as the actor becomes absorbed into the role and experiences genuine emotion. In William Golding's novel *Lord of the Flies*, a group of shipwrecked English boys descend to uncivilized, brutal behavior. When a movie version of the book was made, the youngsters who acted it out became the creatures prescribed by their roles. The movie's director, Peter Brook (1964), reported that "Many of their off-screen relationships completely paralleled the story, and one of our main problems was to encourage them to be uninhibited within the shots but disciplined in between them" (p. 163). Jonathan Winters has remarked that a hazard for stand-up comics like himself is that "you get to believing your own stuff." Indeed, after several years of constructing fantastic characters, Winters underwent therapy to treat a confused personal identity (Elliott, 1986).

SAYING BECOMES BELIEVING

There is abundant evidence that most of us—not just George Bush and Michael Dukakis—adapt what we say to please our listeners. Social psychologist Philip Tetlock (1981b) has found that the policy statements of American presidents tend to be quite simplistic during the political campaign (for example, "To bring down the deficit we need major cuts in government spending"). Immediately after the election their statements become more complex—until the next election year. Similarly, we are readier to tell people good news than bad, and we adjust our message toward our listener's position (Manis et al., 1974; Tesser et al., 1972; Tetlock, 1983). In one experiment, even faculty members writing supposedly candid letters of recommendation to graduate

"Good God! He's giving the white-collar voters' speech to the blue collars."

Impression management: In expressing our thoughts to others, we sometimes tailor our words to what we think the others will want to hear.

schools were more glowing in their comments when the students reserved their right to inspect the letters (Ceci & Peters, 1984). These aren't really lies, mind you; we just shade our views this way or that, depending on whom we're addressing.

Thomas Jefferson recognized this effect in 1785:

> He who permits himself to tell a lie once finds it much easier to do it a second and third time, till at length it becomes habitual; he tells lies without attending to it, and truths without the world's believing him. This falsehood of the tongue leads to that of the heart, and in time depraves all its good dispositions.

"I had thought I was humoring [my captors] by parroting their cliches and buzz words without personally believing in them. . . . In trying to convince them I convinced myself."
Kidnap victim Patricia Campbell Hearst, Every Secret Thing

Experiments bear out this point. People induced to give spoken or written witness to something about which they have real doubts will often feel bad about their deceit. Nevertheless, they begin to believe what they are saying, *provided* they were not excessively bribed or coerced into doing so. Especially when there is no compelling external explanation for one's words, saying becomes believing (Klaas, 1978).

Once we have uttered our modified message, we tend to believe it. Tory Higgins and his colleagues (Higgins & Rholes, 1978; Higgins & McCann, 1984) confirmed that "saying becomes believing" by having university students read a personality description of someone and then summarize it for someone else who was known to either like or dislike this person. The students not only gave a more positive description when the recipient liked the person, but also then liked the person more themselves. And

ACTING ONESELF INTO BELIEF: SAYING IS BELIEVING

University of Oregon psychologist Ray Hyman (1981) describes how by acting the role of a psychic he convinced himself of his own psychic powers.

> I started reading palms when I was in my teens as a way to supplement my income from doing magic and mental shows. When I started I did not believe in palmistry. But I knew that to "sell" it I had to act as if I did. After a few years I became a firm believer in palmistry. One day the late Stanley Jaks, who was a professional mentalist and a man I respected, tactfully suggested that it would make an interesting experiment if I deliberately gave readings opposite to what the lines indicated. I tried this out with a few clients. To my surprise and horror my readings were just as successful as ever. Ever since then I have been interested in the powerful forces that convince us, [palm] reader and client alike, that something is so when it really isn't. (p. 86)

when asked to recall what they had read, they remembered the description as being more positive than it was. In short, it seems that we are prone to adjust our messages to our listeners, and, having done so, to believe the altered message. So it may indeed have been, or become, the real Bush and Dukakis speaking.

THE FOOT-IN-THE-DOOR PHENOMENON

Can we not all recall times when, after agreeing to help out with a project or to join an organization, we eventually ended up far more involved than we ever intended, vowing that in the future we would say no to such requests? How does this happen? Experiments suggest that if you want people to do a big favor for you, one technique is to get them to do a small favor first. In the best-known demonstration of this *foot-in-the-door* principle, California housewives readily agreed to a small request to sign a safe-driving petition (Freedman & Fraser, 1966). Compared to other women who were not approached for the small favor, these women were three times more likely to comply later with a bigger request to place an ugly "Drive Carefully" sign in their front yards.

Foot-in-the-door phenomenon: The tendency for people who have first agreed to a small request to comply later with a larger request.

Although the effects are not usually so dramatic, many other researchers have confirmed Freedman and Fraser's finding (Beaman et al., 1983; Dillard et al., 1984). Several of these studies have tried to elicit altruistic acts, such as contributing to a charity. For example, Patricia Pliner and her collaborators (1974) found 46 percent of Toronto suburbanites willing to contribute to the Cancer Society when approached directly. Others, asked a day ahead to wear a lapel pin publicizing the drive (which all agreed to do), were nearly twice as likely to donate when the Cancer Society came calling. Likewise, 53 percent of the residents of one middle-class Israeli city contributed to a collection for the mentally handicapped when approached by canvassers working for Joseph Schwarzwald and his colleagues (1983). Two weeks earlier, other residents had been approached to sign a petition supporting a recreation center for the handicapped; among these 92 percent contributed. The effect has even occurred with young children, who by second grade seem to have the necessary concept that "it's good to be consistent" (Eisenberg et al., 1987).

"You will easily find folk to do favors if you cultivate those who have done them."
Publilius Syrus, 42 B.C.

Note that in these experiments the initial compliance—signing a petition, wearing a lapel pin—was voluntary, never coerced by threat or bribe. We will see again and again that when people bind themselves to public behaviors *and* perceive these acts to be their own doing, they come to believe more strongly in what they have done. Why does this happen? What, for instance, produces the foot-in-the-door effect? One possibility is that the initial act affects the person's *attitude* toward such action. If this occurs, then shouldn't we expect the greatest compliance when the small request corresponds closely to the large request? Anthony Greenwald and his coresearchers (1987) offer a practical example. They approached a sample of registered voters the day before the 1984 U.S. presidential election and asked them a small question: "Do you expect that you will vote or not?" All said yes. Compared to other voters who were not asked their intentions, they were 41 percent more likely to vote.

Robert Cialdini and his collaborators (1978) further demonstrated the effects of commitment by experimenting with the ***low-ball technique,*** a tactic reportedly used by some new-car dealers. After the customer agrees to buy a new car because of its extremely good price and begins completing the sales forms, the salesperson removes the price advantage by charging for options the customer thought were included, or by checking with the boss who disallows the deal because "we'd be losing money." Folklore has it that more customers will stick with their purchase, even at the higher price, than would have agreed if the full price had been revealed at the outset. Cialdini and his collaborators found that this technique does indeed work. For example, when introductory psychology students were invited to participate in an experiment at 7:00 A.M., only 24 percent showed up. But if they first agreed to participate without knowing the time and only then were asked if they would participate at 7:00 A.M., 53 percent came. Experiments with University of Missouri-Columbia students by Jerry Burger and Richard Petty (1981) indicate that the low-ball technique is effective partly because once a commitment has been made, one feels obligated to the requester.

The foot-in-the-door phenomenon is well worth being aware of so that we won't be naively vulnerable to it. Someone trying to seduce us, financially, politically, or sexually, usually will try to create a momentum of compliance. Before agreeing to the small request, think about what will follow.

Marketing researchers and salespeople have found that the principle works even when we are aware of a profit motive (Cialdini, 1988). Our harmless initial commitment—returning a card for more information and a gift, agreeing to listen to an investment possibility—often starts us toward a larger commitment. The day after I wrote the last sentence, a life insurance salesperson came to my office and offered a thorough analysis of our family's financial situation. After finishing his presentation, he did not ask whether I wished to buy his life insurance, or even whether I wished to engage his free service. His question was instead a small foot-in-the-door, one carefully calculated to elicit my agreement: Did I think people should have such information about their financial situation? I could only answer "yes," and before I realized what was happening had agreed to such an analysis.

Salespeople sometimes also exploit the power of small commitments when trying to bind people to their purchase agreements. In many states there are now laws that allow customers of door-to-door salespeople a few days to cancel their purchases. To combat the effect of these laws, many companies use what the sales-training program of one encyclopedia company calls "a very important psychological aid in preventing customers from backing out of their contracts" (Cialdini, 1988, p. 78). They simply have the customer, rather than the salesperson, fill out the sales agreement. Having done so themselves, people are likely to live up to their commitment.

The foot-in-the-door can be corrupting. As we will see in Chapter 7, "Conformity," evil sometimes results from gradually escalating commitments. A trifling evil act can

Low-ball technique:
A technique for getting people to agree to do something. People who have agreed to (but have not yet performed) an initial request are more likely to comply when the requester makes the request more costly than are people who are approached only with the costly request.

All my life I've been a patsy. For as long as I can recall, I've been an easy mark for the pitches of peddlers, fund raisers, and operators of one sort or another. Being a sucker contributes to my interest in the study of compliance: Just what are the factors that cause one person to say yes to another person? To help answer this question I conduct laboratory experiments. I also spent three years infiltrating the world of compliance professionals. By becoming a trainee in various sales, fund-raising, and advertising organizations I discovered how they exploit the weapons of influence, and how we can spot these weapons at work.

Robert B. Cialdini,
Arizona State University

make the next evil act easier. To paraphrase another of La Rochefoucauld's *Maxims* (1665), it is not as difficult to find one who has never succumbed to a given temptation as to find one who has succumbed only once.

This process of step-by-step commitment, of spiraling action and attitude, contributed to the escalation of the ill-fated U.S. involvement in the Vietnam war. After making and defending difficult decisions, political and military leaders seemed blind to information incompatible with their acts. They noticed and remembered comments that harmonized with their actions but ignored or dismissed information that undermined their assumptions. As Ralph White (1971) put it, "There was a tendency, when actions were out of line with ideas, for decision-makers to align their ideas with their actions."

ACTIONS AND MORALITY

The action→attitude sequence occurs not just with shading the truth but with more immoral acts as well. Cruel acts corrode the consciences of those who perform them. Harming an innocent victim—by uttering hurtful comments or delivering electric shocks—typically leads aggressors to disparage their victims, thus helping to justify the hurtful behavior (Berscheid et al., 1968; Davis & Jones, 1960; Glass, 1964). In all the studies that have established this, people were most likely to justify their action if they were coaxed, not coerced into it. When we agree to do a deed, we own more responsibility for it.

"Our self-definitions are not constructed in our heads; they are forged by our deeds."
Robert McAfee Brown, Creative Dislocation—The Movement of Grace

In everyday life, oppressors similarly disparage their victims. We tend not only to hurt those we dislike, but to dislike those we have hurt. In times of war, soldiers generally denigrate their victims, as in American soldiers' dehumanizing references to Vietnamese people as "gooks." This is yet another instance of the spiraling effects of action and attitude: The more one commits atrocities, the easier it becomes. The same holds for prejudice. If a group holds others in slavery, it is likely to perceive the slaves as having traits that justify continuing the oppression. Our actions and attitudes feed one another, sometimes to the point of moral numbness.

These observations suggest that evil acts not only reflect the self; they shape the self. Situations which elicit evil acts therefore gnaw at the moral sensitivity of the actor. The following depicts what happened to one man who testified that he was but a small cog in the Nazi machine.

Cruel acts often beget cruel attitudes.

Q: Did you kill people in the camp?

A: Yes.

Q: Did you poison them with gas?

A: Yes.

Q: Did you bury them alive?

A: It sometimes happened. . . .

Q: Did you personally help kill people?

A: Absolutely not, I was only paymaster in the camp.

Q: What did you think of what was going on?

A: It was bad at first but we got used to it.

Q: Do you know the Russians will hang you?

A: (Bursting into tears) Why should they? *What have I done?* (Arendt, 1971, p. 262)

Fortunately, the principle works in the other direction as well. Moral action has positive effects on the actor. Experiments demonstrate that when children resist temptation, they tend to internalize their conscientious behavior if the deterrent is strong enough to elicit the desired behavior, but mild enough to leave them with a sense of choice. In a dramatic experiment, Jonathan Freedman (1965) introduced elementary school children to an enticing battery-controlled robot, but instructed them not to play with it while he was out of the room. Freedman used a severe threat with half the children and a mild threat with the others. Both were sufficient to deter the children. Several weeks later, a different researcher, with no apparent relation to the earlier events, left each child to play in the same room with the same toys. Fourteen of the eighteen children who had been given the severe threat now freely played with the robot; but two-thirds of those who had been given the mild deterrent still resisted playing with it. Having made the conscious choice not to play with the toy, they apparently internalized their decision, and this newly acquired attitude controlled their subsequent action.

Other experiments confirm the effect of moral action on moral thinking. For example, those who teach or enforce a rule generally internalize and follow it better after doing so (Parke, 1974). In Alcoholics Anonymous, a "pigeon"—a new member—is said to be "someone who came along just in time to keep his sponsor [mentor] sober." By actively encouraging new members, sponsors sustain their own commitment to sobriety.

INTERRACIAL BEHAVIOR AND RACIAL ATTITUDES

If moral action helps create moral attitudes, might not more positive interracial behavior lead to the reduction of racial prejudice? Such was part of social scientists' testimony prior to the Supreme Court's 1954 decision to desegregate schools. The argument ran like this: If we wait for the heart to change—through preaching and teaching—we will wait a long time for racial justice. But if we legislate moral action, we can, under the appropriate conditions, indirectly affect heartfelt attitudes. Although this idea runs counter to the popular notion that "you can't legislate morality," the evidence (see Chapter 15) suggests that substantial cognitive change has, in fact, followed on the heels of desegregation. For example:

> Since the Supreme Court decision the percentage of White Americans favoring integrated schools has more than doubled.

> In the ten years after the Civil Rights Act of 1964 the percentage of White Americans who described their neighborhoods, friends, co-workers, or fellow students as all-White declined by about 20 percent for each of these measures—a significant increase in interracial behavior. During the same period, the percentage of White Americans who said that Blacks should be allowed to live in any neighborhood increased from 65 percent to 87 percent (ISR Newsletter, 1975).

> More uniform national standards against discrimination were followed by decreasing differences in racial attitudes among people of differing religion, class, and geographic region. As Americans came to act more alike, they came to think more alike (Greeley & Sheatsley, 1971; Taylor et al., 1978).

This evidence does not prove the point, for there are other ways to account for these altered attitudes. But it is consistent with the contention that our attitudes follow our behavior.

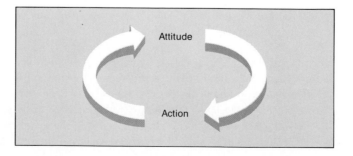

FIGURE 2-3
Attitudes and actions generate one another, like chickens and eggs.

"We do not love people so much for the good they have done us, as for the good we have done them."
Leo Tolstoy, War and Peace

Experiments support the contention that positive behavior toward someone fosters one's liking for that person. Doing a favor for an experimenter or another subject, or tutoring a student, generally increases one's attraction to the person helped (Blanchard & Cook, 1976). (Note that these experiments complement those which demonstrate that *harming* another leads people to denigrate their victims.)

In 1793, Benjamin Franklin tested this idea that doing a favor engenders liking. As clerk of the Pennsylvania General Assembly, he was disturbed by opposition from another important legislator. So Franklin set out to win him over:

> I did not . . . aim at gaining his favour by paying any servile respect to him but, after some time, took this other method. Having heard that he had in his library a certain very scarce and curious book I wrote a note to him expressing my desire of perusing that book and requesting he would do me the favour of lending it to me for a few days. He sent it immediately and I return'd it in about a week, expressing strongly my sense of the favour. When we next met in the House he spoke to me (which he had never done before), and with great civility; and he ever after manifested a readiness to serve me on all occasions, so that we became great friends and our friendship continued to his death. This is another instance of the truth of an old maxim I had learned, which says, "He that has once done you a kindness will be more ready to do you another than he whom you yourself have obliged." (Rosenzweig, 1972, p. 769)

SOCIAL MOVEMENTS

The effect of a society's racial behavior on its racial attitudes suggests the possibility, and the danger, of employing the same idea for political socialization on a mass scale. Such was clearly evident in Nazi Germany, where participation in mass meetings, wearing uniforms, demonstrating, and especially the public greeting "Heil Hitler" es-

Our political rituals—the daily flag salute by schoolchildren, singing the national anthem—use public conformity to build private conformity to patriotism.

tablished for many a profound inconsistency between behavior and belief. Historian Richard Grunberger (1971) reports that

> The "German greeting" was a powerful conditioning device. Having once decided to intone it as an outward token of conformity, many experienced schizophrenic discomfort at the contradiction between their words and their feelings. Prevented from saying what they believed, they tried to establish their psychic equilibrium by consciously making themselves believe what they said. (p. 27)

The practice is not limited to totalitarian regimes. Our own political rituals—the daily flag salute by schoolchildren, singing the national anthem—use public conformity to build a private conformity to patriotism. I recall participating in air-raid drills in my elementary school not far from the Boeing Company in Seattle. After we repeatedly acted as if we were the objects of Soviet attack, many of us came to fear the Russians. Observers noted that the civil rights marches of the 1960s were as important for their strengthening the demonstrators' commitment as for their direct effects on legislation. Their actions expressed an idea whose time had come, and drove that idea more deeply into their hearts. The 1980s move toward inclusive language (by referring, say, to "human nature" rather than "man's nature") similarly strengthened as well as expressed less sexist attitudes.

BRAINWASHING

For many, the most dramatic human influence is brainwashing, a term first used to describe what happened to American prisoners of war (POWs) during the Korean war. Actually, the Chinese "thought-control" program was not nearly as irresistible as this term suggests. Still it was disconcerting that hundreds of prisoners cooperated with their captors, that twenty-one chose to remain after being granted permission to return to America, and that many of those who did return came home believing that "although communism won't work in America, I think it's a good thing for Asia" (Segal, 1954). Edgar Schein (1956) interviewed many of the POWs during their journey home and reported that the captors' methods included a gradual escalation of demands. The Chinese always started with trivial requests and gradually worked up to more significant ones. "Thus after a prisoner had once been 'trained' to speak or write out trivia, statements on more important issues were demanded." Moreover, they always expected active participation, be it just copying something or participating in group discussions, writing self-criticism, or uttering public confessions.

Once a prisoner had spoken or written a statement, he felt an inner need to make his beliefs consistent with his public acts. This often drove prisoners to persuade themselves of what they had done. This "start small and build" tactic was an effective application of the foot-in-the-door technique.

From these observations—of the effects of role playing, the foot-in-the-door experience, moral and immoral acts, interracial behavior, social movements, and brainwashing—is there not a powerful practical lesson? If we want to change ourselves in some important way, we'd best not depend exclusively on introspection and intellectual insight. Sometimes we need to act—to begin writing that paper, to make those phone calls, to go see that person—even if we don't feel like acting. Jacques Barzun (1975) recognized the energizing power of action in advising aspiring writers to engage in the act of writing even if passive contemplation has left them feeling uncertain about their ideas:

"One does what one is; one becomes what one does."
Robert Masil, Kleine Prosa, *1930*

"You can use small commitments to manipulate a person's self-image; you can use them to turn citizens into 'public servants,' prospects into 'customers,' prisoners into 'collaborators.'"
Robert Cialdini, Influence, *1988*

"If we wish to conquer undesirable emotional tendencies in ourselves we must assiduously, and in the first instance cold-bloodedly, go through the outward motions of those contrary dispositions we prefer to cultivate."
William James,
"What Is an Emotion?" *1884*

If you are too modest about yourself or too plain indifferent about the possible reader and yet are required to write, then you have to pretend. Make believe that you want to bring somebody around to your opinion; in other words, adopt a thesis and start expounding it. . . . With a slight effort of the kind at the start—a challenge to utterance—you will find your pretense disappearing and a real concern creeping in. The subject will have taken hold of you as it does in the work of all habitual writers. (pp. 173–174)

To say that what we do affects how we feel is not to say that the self-persuasion effect is irrational. That which prompts us to act may also prompt us to think. Writing an essay, or role-playing an opposing view, forces us to recall and think up arguments we otherwise might have ignored. What is more, we remember information best when we have actively explained it in our own terms. Gordon Bower and Mark Masling (1979) gave Stanford students a list of bizarre correlations, such as "As the number of fire hydrants in an area decreases the crime rate increases." Students who simply studied or were given explanations for these correlations recalled only about 40 percent of them when tested later. But students who invented their own explanations recalled 73 percent of the correlations. (Take a moment to conjecture an explanation for the fire hydrant–crime correlation, and in a later chapter I will test your recall of the relationship.)

The memorability of self produced information may be one reason we are most affected by information we have reformulated in our own terms (Greenwald, 1968; Petty et al., 1981). As one student wrote me, "it wasn't until I tried to verbalize my beliefs that I really understood them." As a teacher and a writer, I must therefore remind myself not always to lay out finished results. It is better to stimulate students first to think through the implications of a theory, thus making them active listeners and readers. Even taking notes deepens the impression through active expression. William James (1899) made the same point eighty years ago: "No reception without *reaction*, no impression without correlative expression—this is the great maxim which the teacher ought never to forget."

WHY DO OUR ACTIONS AFFECT OUR ATTITUDES?

We have seen that several independent streams of observation from laboratory experiments and social history merge to form one river: the effect of our overt actions on our inner attitudes. This conclusion is more clearly established than its explanation. Do these diverse observations contain any clues to *why* action affects attitude? The social-psychologist detectives suspect three possible culprits. **Self-presentation theory** assumes that for strategic reasons we express attitudes that make us *appear* consistent. **Cognitive dissonance theory** assumes that to reduce discomfort, we self-justify our actions. **Self-perception theory** assumes that our actions are self-revealing (when uncertain about our feelings or beliefs, we look to our behavior, much as anyone else would). Let's examine each.

SELF-PRESENTATION

The first explanation began as a simple idea: Who among us does not care what people think? We spend countless dollars on stylish clothes, diets, cosmetics, even plastic surgery—all because we worry about what others think of us. To make a good impres-

"*My not wearing a hairpiece indicates to others that I'm comfortable with myself.*"

Self-perception theory assumes that our actions are self-revealing.

sion is often to gain social and material rewards, to feel better about ourselves, even to become more secure in our social identities (Leary & Kowalski, 1989).

Indeed, none of us wants to look foolishly inconsistent. To avoid seeming so, we express attitudes in line with our actions. To *appear* consistent we may even feign attitudes we don't really hold. Even if it necessitates a little insincerity or hypocrisy, it can pay to manage the impression one is making. Or so *self-presentation theory* suggests.

Already we have seen evidence that people do engage in "impression management." They will adjust what they say toward their listener's position, to please rather than offend. Sometimes it may take a bogus pipeline to cut through the feigned attitudes. Moreover, people take longer to deliver news of failure (for example, signalling wrong answers on an IQ-type test) than news of success; but this effect occurs only if the news bearers can be identified and are therefore concerned about making a bad impression (Bond & Anderson, 1987).

For some people, the effort to make a good impression is a way of life. By continually monitoring their own behavior, and noting how others are reacting, they can adjust their social performance when it is not having the desired effect. In dozens of studies, those who score high on a scale of **self-monitoring** tendency (who, for example, agree that "I tend to be what people expect me to be") have acted like social chameleons—adjusting their behavior in response to external situations (Snyder, 1987). Being conscious of others, they are less likely to act on their own attitudes and, having attuned their behavior to the situation, are more likely then to espouse an attitude

Self-monitoring:
Being attuned to the way one presents oneself in social situations and adjusting one's performance to create the desired impression.

they don't really hold (Zanna & Olson, 1982). For high self-monitors, attitudes therefore serve a social adjustment function; they help people adapt themselves to new jobs, roles, and relationships (Snyder & DeBono, 1989; Snyder & Copeland, 1989).

Those who score low in self-monitoring care less about what others think. They are more internally guided and thus more likely to talk or act in line with what they feel and believe (McCann & Hancock, 1983). For low self-monitors, attitudes serve to express their own underlying values. Most of us fall somewhere between the high self-monitoring extreme of the con artist and the low self-monitoring extreme of stubborn insensitivity.

Might our eagerness to present a favorable image explain why expressed attitudes shift toward consistency with behavior? To some extent, yes—people exhibit a much smaller attitude change when a bogus pipeline inhibits their trying to make a good impression (Paulhus, 1982; Tedeschi et al., 1987). Moreover, ***self-presentation*** involves not just trying to impress others but also trying to express our ideals and identity and to establish a reputation that reflects them. We want to know ourselves, and to have others know us, as we really are (Schlenker, 1986, 1987; Baumeister, 1982, 1985).

So, the attitude changes we have reviewed seem partly due to self-presentation tactics. George Bush and Michael Dukakis's expressed attitudes were surely somewhat strategic. But there was likely more to them than that. For one thing, we express changed attitudes even to someone who is ignorant of how we have behaved. (There is no need to present a consistent attitude when talking to someone who is unaware of our behavior.) Furthermore, the changed attitudes can affect later behavior in new situations. Thus, our self-presentations are sometimes internalized as genuine attitude changes. To explain how this happens, consider two other theories.

SELF-JUSTIFICATION

One theory is that our attitudes change because we are motivated to rationalize our behavior. Such is the implication of Leon Festinger's (1957) ***cognitive dissonance theory.*** The theory is very simple, but its range of application is enormous. It assumes we feel tension "dissonance") when two of our thoughts or beliefs ("cognitions") are psychologically inconsistent—when we recognize that they don't fit together. Festinger furthermore argued that we adjust our thinking to reduce this tension. For example, Steven Sherman and Larry Gorkin (1980) aroused dissonance in their Indiana University students by giving them the following riddle:

> A father and his son are out driving. They are involved in an accident. The father is killed, and the son is in critical condition. The son is rushed to the hospital and prepared for the operation. The doctor comes in, sees the patient, and exclaims, "I can't operate, it's my son!" How could this be?

Although virtually all the students had previously indicated they strongly favored sexual equality and other feminist ideals, most failed to solve the riddle (by identifying the doctor as the son's mother). Believing that "I am nonsexist" yet now realizing that "I perceived this riddle with sexist assumptions" thus evoked dissonance. When later the students judged a case of alleged sex discrimination, how do you suppose those who had failed to solve the riddle reacted? They reacted with exceptionally strong support for the female complainant, thus reducing their dissonance and reaffirming their nonsexist self-image.

"Public opinion is always more tyrannical towards those who obviously fear it than towards those who feel indifferent to it."
Bertrand Russell,
The Conquest of Happiness, *1930*

Self-presentation:
Expressing oneself and behaving in ways designed either to create a favorable impression or an impression that corresponds to one's ideals. (Also called "impression management.")

Cognitive dissonance:
Feelings of tension that arise when one is simultaneously aware of two inconsistent cognitions. For example, dissonance may occur when we realize that we have, with little justification, acted contrary to our attitudes or made a decision favoring one alternative despite reasons favoring another.

Applications of dissonance theory pertain mostly to discrepancies between our behavior and our attitudes. We are aware of both. Thus if we sense an inconsistency, we feel pressure for change. So if you can persuade people to adopt a new attitude, their behavior should adjust accordingly; that's common sense. Or if you can induce a person to behave differently, dissonance may be reduced by attitude change; that's the self-persuasion effect we have been reviewing.

Insufficient Justification

Cognitive dissonance theory is noted for several surprising predictions. Perhaps you can reason them out. Imagine you are a subject in a famous experiment conducted by Festinger and J. Merrill Carlsmith (1959). For an hour the study requires you to perform dull tasks such as turning wooden knobs again and again. After you finish, the experimenter explains that the study concerns the effect of people's expectations upon their performance. The next subject, who is waiting outside, must be led to expect that this is going to be an interesting experiment. The experimenter then informs you that the assistant who usually creates this expectation was unable to attend this session: "So could you fill in and do this?" It's for science and you are being paid, so you agree to tell the next subject (who is actually the experimenter's real assistant) what a delightful experience you have just had. "Really?" responds the supposed subject. "A friend of mine was in this experiment a week ago and she said it was boring." "Oh, no," you respond, "it's really very interesting. You get good exercise while turning some knobs. I'm sure you'll enjoy it." Finally, before you leave the lab, someone else who is doing a study of how people react to experiments asks you to complete a questionnaire indicating how much you actually enjoyed your knob-turning experience.

According to cognitive dissonance theory, we become even more motivated to believe in what we've done when the justification for our actions—high pay, recognition, promise of future increased responsibility—is insufficient.

"I have no intention of retiring. Football has been very good to me."

Following a 1934 earthquake in India, there were rumors outside the disaster zone of worse disasters to follow. It occurred to me that these rumors might be "anxiety-justifying"—cognitions that would justify their lingering fears. From that germ of an idea, my theory of dissonance reduction—making your view of the world fit with how you feel or what you've done—developed.

Leon Festinger,
New School for Social Research

Now for the prediction: Under which condition would you be most likely to believe your little lie and say the experiment was indeed interesting? When paid $1 for doing so, as some of Festinger and Carlsmith's subjects were? Or when paid a generous $20, as others were? Contrary to the common notion that big rewards produce big effects, Festinger and Carlsmith reasoned that those paid just $1 would be most likely to adjust their attitudes to their actions. Having ***insufficient justification*** for their action, they would experience more discomfort (dissonance) and thus be more motivated to believe in what they had done. Those paid $20 had sufficient justification for what they did and hence should have experienced less dissonance. As Figure 2-4 indicates, their results fit this intriguing prediction.*

Insufficient justification effect: Reduction of dissonance by internally justifying one's behavior, when external inducements are "insufficient" to fully justify it.

Dozens of other experimenters have obtained similar results. In general, people are most likely to persuade themselves of the validity of an act when they feel some choice about doing it and when it has foreseeable consequences. If, as in some experiments, you agree for a measly $1.50 to help a researcher by writing an essay supporting something you don't believe in—say, tuition increase—you may begin feeling somewhat greater sympathy with the policy. This is especially so if something makes you face the inconsistency or if you think important people will actually be reading your essay with your name on it (Leippe & Elkin, 1987). Feeling responsible for statements you have made, perhaps for strategic reasons, you now believe them more strongly. Pretense can become reality.

In 1971 Oregon became the first state to pass a controversial "bottle bill" requiring a deposit and refund on soft drink and alcohol containers, and people have ever since been choosing to return bottles for a measly 5 cents each. Having done so, their attitudes toward recycling bottles have become very positive, and the policy is no longer controversial (Kahle & Beatty, 1987).

Earlier we noted the insufficient-justification principle working with punishments as well as rewards. Recall, for example, that children who were severely threatened to deter them from playing with an attractive toy devalued the toy less than those who, having received only a mild threat, had to struggle with themselves a bit. When

---

*There is a seldom-reported final aspect of this 1950s experiment. Imagine yourself finally back with the experimenter, who is truthfully explaining the whole study. Not only do you learn that you've been duped, but the experimenter asks for the $20 bill back. Do you comply? Festinger and Carlsmith note that all of their Stanford student subjects willingly reached into their pockets and gave back the money. This is a foretaste of some quite amazing observations of compliance and conformity to be discussed in Chapter 7. As we will see, when the social situation makes clear demands, people are usually very responsive.

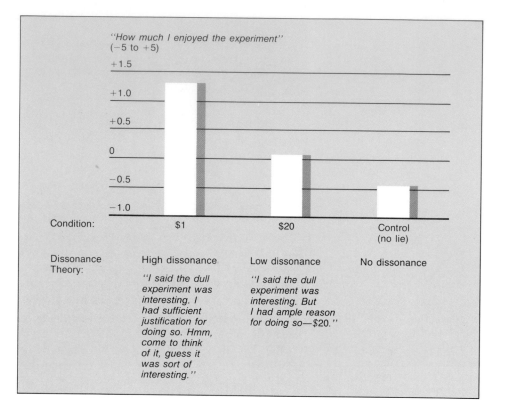

"How much I enjoyed the experiment"
(−5 to +5)

Condition:	$1	$20	Control (no lie)
Dissonance Theory:	High dissonance	Low dissonance	No dissonance
	"I said the dull experiment was interesting. I had sufficient justification for doing so. Hmm, come to think of it, guess it was sort of interesting."	"I said the dull experiment was interesting. But I had ample reason for doing so—$20."	

FIGURE 2-4

Insufficient justification: Dissonance theory predicts that when our actions are not fully explained by external rewards or coercion, we will experience dissonance, which can be reduced by coming to believe in what we have done. (Data from Festinger & Carlsmith, 1959.)

a parent says, "Clean up your room, Johnny, or I'll knock your block off," Johnny won't need to search inside himself for a justification for his cleaning his room. The severe threat is a fully adequate justification. Note that cognitive dissonance theory is concerned with what *induces* a desired action, rather than with the relative effectiveness of rewards and punishments administered *after* the act. It aims, for example, to have Johnny say, "I am cleaning up my room because I want a clean room," rather than "I am cleaning up my room only because my parents are making me." Business managers and college administrators take note: People are more likely to support rules if they share responsibility for them. Thus dorm residents who share responsibility for enforcing dorm rules are less tolerant of rule-breakers than are residents who have no control over their enforcement (Triplet et al., 1988).

Such implications of dissonance theory have led some to view it as an integration of humanistic and scientific perspectives. Authoritarian management will be effective, the theory predicts, only so long as the authority is present; behavior is not so likely to be internalized when there is little sense of choice. As Bree, a formerly enslaved talking horse in C. S. Lewis's *The Horse and His Boy* (1974), observes, "One of the worst results of being a slave and being forced to do things is that when there is no one to force you any more you find you have almost lost the power of forcing yourself" (p. 193). Dissonance theory is hardly permissive in its implications, for it insists that encouragements and inducements be enough to elicit desired action. But it does suggest that managers, teachers, and parents use only enough incentive to elicit the desired behavior. The principle: We accept responsibility for our behavior to the extent we have chosen it in the absence of obvious pressures and incentives.

Dissonance after Decisions

The emphasis on perceived choice and responsibility implies that making *decisions* will produce dissonance. When faced with an important decision—what college to attend, whom to date, which job to accept—we are sometimes torn between two equally attractive alternatives. Perhaps you can recall a time when, having committed yourself to one course of action, you become painfully aware of dissonant cognitions—the desirable features of what you had rejected and the undesirable features of what you had chosen. If you decided to live on campus, you may have realized you were forgoing the greater spaciousness and freedom of an apartment in favor of the cramped, noisy quarters of the dorm. If you elected to live off campus, you perhaps pondered that your decision entailed physical separation from campus and friends, as well as the necessity of cooking.

Experiments indicate that after making such important decisions we usually reduce dissonance by upgrading the chosen alternative and denigrating the option passed over. In the first published dissonance experiment (1956), Jack Brehm had University of Minnesota women rate eight products, such as a toaster, a radio, and a hair dryer. They were then shown two objects they had rated closely and told they could have whichever they chose. Later, when rerating the eight objects, the women increased their evaluation of the item they had chosen, and decreased their evaluation of the rejected item. It seems that when we've chosen our fate, the grass does *not* then grow greener on the other side of the fence. The fence is more likely to be entwined with sour grapes.

If you understand the principle you may be able to predict the result of one of the most recent dissonance experiments. Mark Zanna and Gerald Sande (1987) engaged one group of University of Waterloo students in evaluating the quality of information provided concerning two applicants for a new student housing project. A second group of students also made what they believed were *actual decisions* regarding which of the two applicants to admit. When, later, the students in both groups were asked to rate seven applicants, including the two they had closely scrutinized, how do you suppose the two groups rated the two candidates? The "no decision" group rated them not much differently; the group that made an actual decision now saw the chosen applicant as much superior to the unchosen one.

With simple decisions, this deciding-becomes-believing effect can occur very quickly. Robert Knox and James Inkster (1968) found that racetrack bettors who had just put down their money on a horse felt more optimistic about their bet than did those who were about to bet. In the few moments that intervened between standing in line and walking away from the betting window, nothing had changed—except for the decision that had been finalized and the person's feelings about it. Likewise, contestants in carnival games of chance feel more confident of winning right after agreeing to play than right before, and voters indicate more esteem and confidence in their candidate just after voting than just before (Younger et al., 1977). There may sometimes be but a slight difference between the two options, as I can recall in helping make faculty tenure decisions. The competence of one faculty member who barely makes it and that of another who barely loses out seem not very different—until after the decision is made and announced.

What all these experiments and examples suggest is that, once made, decisions tend to grow their own legs of support—self-justifying reasons why one's commitment was wise. Often, these new legs are strong enough that when one leg is pulled away—perhaps the original one—the decision does not collapse. Alison decides to take a trip

"Every time you make a choice you are turning the central part of you, the part of you that chooses, into something a little different from what it was before."
C. S. Lewis, Mere Christianity

home if it can be done for an air fare under $300. It can be, so she makes her reservation and begins to think of additional reasons why she is glad she is going. When she goes to buy the tickets, however, she learns there has been a fare increase to $350. No matter, she is now determined to go. As when being low-balled by a car dealer, it never occurs to people, reports Robert Cialdini (1984, p. 103), "that those additional reasons might never have existed had the choice not been made in the first place."

SELF-PERCEPTION

Although dissonance theory has inspired a tremendous amount of research, its phenomena have also been explained by an even simpler theory. Consider how we make inferences about other people's attitudes. We observe a person's behavior and the situation in which it occurs, and then we attribute the behavior either to the person's traits and attitudes or to environmental forces. If we see Mr. and Mrs. Jones coercing their little Sally into saying "I'm sorry," we attribute Sally's reluctant behavior to the constraints of the situation, not to her personal regret. If we see Sally apologizing with no apparent inducement, we are more likely to attribute the apology to Sally herself.

Self-perception theory (proposed by Daryl Bem, 1972) assumes that we make similar inferences when we observe our own behavior. When our attitudes are weak or ambiguous, we are in the same position as someone observing us from the outside. Just as we discern what people are really like by looking closely at their actions when they are free to act as they please, so do we decide what we ourselves are like. Hearing myself talk informs me of my attitudes; observing my actions provides clues to how strong my beliefs are, especially if my behavior is not easily attributable to external constraints. The acts we freely commit are sometimes quite self-revealing.

The philosopher-psychologist William James proposed a similar explanation for emotion a century ago. We infer our emotions, he suggested, by observing our bodies and our behaviors. A stimulus such as a growling bear confronts a woman in the forest. She tenses, her heartbeat increases, adrenaline is secreted, and she runs away. Observing all this, she then experiences fear. At a college where I was to lecture, I awoke before dawn and was unable to get back to sleep. Observing my wakefulness, I concluded that I must be anxious.

You may be skeptical of this idea; I was when I first heard it. However, some experiments support it. Research on the effects of facial expressions even suggests a way for you to experience the self-perception effect. For example, when James Laird (1974, 1984), induced college students to frown while electrodes were attached to their faces—"contract these muscles," "pull your brows together"—they reported feeling angry. It's more fun to try out Laird's other finding: Those induced to smile felt happier and found cartoons more humorous. Some of the facial muscle responses associated with emotions are more subtle, subtle enough to be imperceptible to observers (Cacioppo et al., 1988). People who are trained to control these muscles, such as by tensing the forehead muscles, can subtly alter their emotional responses (McCanne & Anderson, 1987). The effect may be physiological as well as cognitive. One theory holds that tensing certain muscles restricts blood flow from the brain, thus impeding the cooling of the brain and influencing release of the brain's emotion-arousing chemical messengers (Zajonc et al., 1988).

We have all experienced this self-perception phenomenon. We're feeling crabby, but then the phone rings or someone comes to the door and elicits from us warm, polite

Self-perception theory: The theory that when we are unsure of our attitudes we infer them much as would someone observing us—by looking at our behavior and the circumstances under which it occurs.

"Self-knowledge is best learned, not by contemplation, but action."
Goethe

"I can watch myself and my actions, just like an outsider."
Anne Frank,
The Diary of a Young Girl

"The free expression by outward signs of emotion intensifies it. On the other hand, the repression as far as possible, of all outward signs softens our emotions."
Charles Darwin, The Expression of the Emotions in Man and Animals

behavior. "How's everything?" "Just fine, thanks. How are things with you?" "Oh, not bad. . . ." If our irritableness is not intense, this warm behavior may change our whole attitude after we hang up. It's tough to smile and feel grouchy. When Miss America parades her smile she may, after all, be helping herself feel happy. Going through the motions can trigger the emotions.

Even your gait can affect how you feel. When you get up from reading this chapter, walk for a minute taking short, shuffling steps, with eyes downcast. Then walk for a minute taking long strides with your arms swinging and your eyes straight ahead. Can you, like the Skidmore College participants in an experiment by Sara Snodgrass (1986), feel the difference?

If our expressions influence our feelings, then would imitating others' expressions help us know what they are feeling? An experiment by Katherine Burns Vaughan and John Lanzetta (1981) suggests it would. They asked Dartmouth College students to observe someone receiving electric shock. Some of the observers were told to make

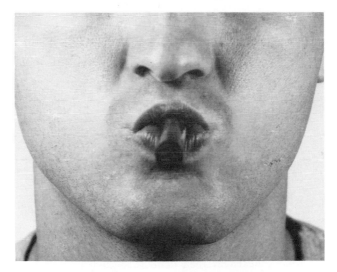

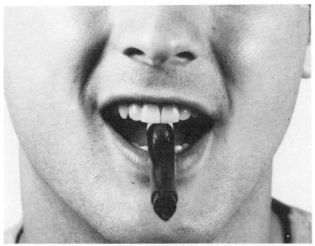

Motions and emotions. German psychologist Fritz Strack and his colleagues (1988) report that people find cartoons funnier while holding a pen with their teeth (which involves one of the smiling muscles) than while holding it with their lips (which activates muscles incompatible with smiling).

an expression of pain whenever the shock came on. Compared to other students who did not act out the expressions, these grimacing students perspired more and had a faster heart rate whenever they observed the person being shocked. Acting out the person's emotion apparently enabled the observers to feel more empathy. The implication: To sense how other people are feeling, let your own face mimic their expressions.

Our facial expressions also influence our attitudes. In a clever experiment, Gary Wells and Richard Petty (1980) had University of Alberta students "test headphone sets" by making either vertical or horizontal head movements while listening to a radio editorial. Who most agreed with the editorial? Those who had been nodding their heads up and down. Why? Wells and Petty surmised that positive thoughts are compatible with vertical nodding and incompatible with horizontal motion. Try it yourself when listening to someone: Do you feel more agreeable when nodding rather than shaking your head?

Overjustification and Intrinsic Motivation

Recall the insufficient justification effect—that the *smallest* incentive that will get people to do something is generally the most effective in getting them to like the activity and keep on doing it. Cognitive dissonance theory offers one explanation for this: When external inducements are not enough to justify our behavior we are more likely to *justify it internally.*

Self-perception theory offers another explanation: people explain their behavior by noting the conditions under which it occurs. Thus if we heard someone proclaiming the wisdom of a tuition increase after being paid $20 to do so, surely we would be less likely to accept the authenticity of that person's views than if we thought the person was expressing those opinions for virtually no pay. Perhaps we make similar inferences when observing ourselves.

Self-perception theory goes even a step further. Contrary to the notion that rewards always increase motivation, it suggests that unnecessary rewards sometimes have a hidden cost. Rewarding people for doing what they already enjoy may lead them to attribute their doing it to the reward, thus undermining their self-perception that they do it because they like it. Experiments by Edward Deci and Richard Ryan (1985, 1987), at the University of Rochester, by Mark Lepper and David Greene (1979) at Stanford, and by Ann Boggiano and her colleagues (1985, 1987) at the University of Colorado have confirmed this *overjustification effect.* People who are paid for playing with enjoyable puzzles subsequently play with the puzzles less than people who play without being paid; promising children a reward for doing what they intrinsically enjoy (for example, playing with magic markers) turns their play into work.

A folktale illustrates the overjustification effect. An old man lived alone on a street where boys played noisily every afternoon. The din annoyed him, so one day he called the boys to his door. He told them he loved the cheerful sound of children's voices and promised them each 50 cents if they would return the next day. Next afternoon the youngsters raced back and played more lustily than ever. The old man paid them and promised another reward the next day. Again they returned, whooping it up, and the man again paid them, this time 25 cents. The following day they got only 15 cents and the man explained that his meagre resources were being exhausted. "Please, though, would you come and play for 10 cents tomorrow?" The boys were disappointed and

Overjustification effect:
The consequence of bribing people to do what they already like doing; they may be led to see their action as externally controlled rather than intrinsically appealing.

told the man they would not be back. It wasn't worth the effort, they said, to play all afternoon at his house for only 10 cents.

As self-perception theory implies, an *unanticipated* reward afterward does *not* diminish intrinsic interest, apparently because people can still attribute their action to their own motivation (Bradley & Mannell, 1984). (It's like the heroine who, having fallen in love with the woodcutter, now learns that he's really a prince.) And if compliments for a good job make us feel more competent and successful, this can actually *increase* our intrinsic motivation. But if an unnecessary reward is offered beforehand in an obvious effort to control behavior, the overjustification effect is likely. So what matters is what a reward implies: Rewards and praise that *inform* people of their achievements (that make them feel "I'm very good at this") will likely *boost* their intrinsic motivation; rewards that seek to *control* people, that lead them to believe it was the reward that caused their effort ("I did it for the money"), will likely *diminish* the intrinsic appeal of an enjoyable task (Rosenfeld et al., 1980; Sansone, 1986).

But how then might we cultivate people's enjoyment of tasks that are not intrinsically appealing? Young Maria may find her first piano lessons frustrating. Tommy may not have an intrinsic love of fifth-grade science. Sandra may not look forward to making those first sales calls. In such cases, the parent, teacher, or manager should probably use some incentives to coax the desired behavior (Workman & Williams, 1980; Boggiano & Ruble, 1985). So, if we provide students with *just enough* justification to perform a learning task (and use such rewards to help them feel competent), we may help them maximize their enjoyment of it and their eagerness to pursue the subject on their own. When the justification is overly sufficient—as happens in classrooms where teachers dictate behavior and use rewards to control the children—child-driven learning may diminish (Deci & Ryan, 1985). My younger son eagerly consumed six or eight library books a week—until our library started a reading club which promised a party to those who read ten books in three months. Three weeks later he began checking out only one or two books during our weekly visit. Why? "Because you only need to read ten books, you know."

COMPARING THE THEORIES

We have seen one explanation of why our actions *seem* to affect our attitudes (self-presentation theory), and two explanations of why our actions *genuinely* affect our attitudes: (1) the dissonance-theory assumption that we are motivated to justify our behavior in order to reduce our internal discomfort, and (2) the self-perception-theory assumption that we calmly observe our behavior and make reasonable inferences about our attitudes from it, just as we do when observing other people.

The latter two explanations seem to contradict one another. So which is right? It's difficult to find a critical test that decides between them. In most instances they make the same predictions, and each theory can be bent to accommodate most of the findings we have considered (Greenwald, 1975). Daryl Bem (1972), the self-perception theorist, has even suggested it boils down to a matter of loyalties and aesthetics. This illustrates the subjectivity of scientific theorizing (see Chapter 1). Neither dissonance theory nor self-perception theory has been handed to us by nature. Both are products of human imagination—creative attempts to simplify and explain what we've observed.

It is not unusual in science to find that a principle (such as "attitudes follow behavior") is predictable from more than one theory. Physicist Richard Feynman (1967) marveled that "one of the amazing characteristics of nature" is the "wide range of beautiful ways" in which it can be described: "I do not understand the reason why it is that the correct laws of physics seem to be expressible in such a tremendous variety of ways" (pp. 53–55). Like different roads leading to the same place, different sets of assumptions can lead to the same principle. If anything, this *strengthens* our confidence in the principle. It becomes credible not only because of the data which support it, but also because it rests on more than one theoretical pillar.

Dissonance as Arousal

Can we say that one of our theories is more adequate than the other? On one key point strong support has emerged for dissonance theory. Recall that dissonance is, by definition, an aroused state of uncomfortable tension. To reduce this tension we supposedly change our attitudes. Self-perception theory says nothing about tension being aroused when our actions and attitudes are not harmonious. It assumes merely that when our attitudes are weak to begin with, we will use our behavior and its circumstances as a clue to our attitudes (like the person who said, "How do I know how I feel until I hear what I say?").

Are conditions that supposedly produce dissonance (for example, making decisions or acting contrary to one's attitudes) actually *arousing?* The accumulated evidence indicates that the answer is yes, providing that the behavior has *unwanted conse-*

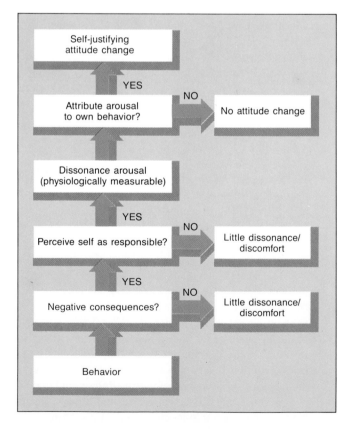

FIGURE 2-5
A revised version of dissonance theory: the sequence that leads from behavior to attitude change.

BEHIND THE SCENES

I have always been fascinated by cognitive dissonance theory's portrayal of people as rationalizers. The idea seems to capture something profoundly important—our relentless interest in explaining ourselves. Yet Festinger's idea about *why* we rationalize seems wrong. My research convinces me that the real goal of rationalization is not self consistency but a sense of self-adequacy. We find that people can easily tolerate inconsistency—if they are allowed to affirm their overall worth. Thus it is the war for global self-worth, not the battle against specific inconsistencies, that causes our rationalizations.

Claude Steele,
University of Michigan

quences for which the *person feels responsible* (Cooper & Fazio, 1984). If in the privacy of your closet you say something you don't believe, dissonance will be minimal. But it will be much greater if there are unpleasant consequences—if (as in the $1/$20 lie-telling experiment) someone hears and believes you, if the negative effects are irrevocable rather than something you can take back, and if the person harmed is someone you like rather than dislike. If, moreover, you feel responsible for these consequences— if you can't easily excuse your act because you freely agreed to it, and if you could foresee its consequences—then dissonance will be aroused (see Figure 2-5), and the arousal will likely be manifest as increased perspiration and heart rate (Cacioppo & Petty, 1986; Croyle & Cooper, 1983).

There is a fundamental reason why "volunteering" to say or do undesirable things is arousing, suggests Claude Steele (1988). Such acts are embarrassing. They make us feel foolish. They threaten our sense of personal competence and goodness. Justifying our actions and decisions is therefore self-protective; by so doing we affirm our sense of integrity and self-worth.

So what do you suppose happens if, after committing a self-contradictory act, people are offered some other way to reaffirm their sense of self-worth, such as by

Coerced behavior is rarely internalized.

"No, Hoskins, you're not going to do it just because I'm telling you to do it. You're going to do it because you believe in it."

doing a good deed? In several experiments, Steele found that, with their self-concepts secured, people felt much less need to justify their acts. Ergo, says Steele, people are aroused by their own desirable dissonant behaviors because such acts threaten their positive self-concepts. Had the Chinese used threats of torture to gain the POWs' compliance, the POWs would have had less need to justify their acts to themselves. You don't need to feel guilty about or justify forced acts.

So dissonance conditions do indeed arouse tension, especially when one's sense of self-worth is threatened. But is this arousal necessary for the "attitudes-follow-behavior" effect? There are indications that the answer is again yes. In experiments with University of Washington students, Steele and his colleagues (1981) found that when arousal was reduced by drinking alcohol the attitudes-follow-behavior effect disappeared. Students who had been induced to write an essay favoring a big tuition increase reduced their dissonance by adjusting their attitudes—*unless* after writing the unpleasant essay they imbibed alcohol, supposedly as part of a beer- or vodka-tasting experiment. Apparently, alcohol and other drugs can be a substitute way to reduce dissonance.

Self-Perceiving When Not Self-Contradicting

The evidence is clear and strong: Dissonance procedures are arousing, and arousal is an ingredient of the self-persuasive effects of acting contrary to one's attitudes. (Indeed, an arousal boost provided by taking an arousing amphetamine drug that one *thinks* is merely an inert placebo accentuates the attitude change.) But dissonance theory cannot explain all the findings. When people argue a position that is in line with their opinion, although a step or two beyond it, procedures that usually eliminate any arousal don't seem to reduce the change in attitudes (Fazio et al, 1977, 1979). Dissonance theory also does not explain the overjustification effect, since being paid to do what you like to do should not arouse great tension. And what about situations where the induced action really does not contradict any attitude—when, for example, people are induced to smile or grimace. Here, too, there should be no dissonance. In these cases, self-perception theory has a ready explanation.

In short, it appears that dissonance theory successfully explains what happens when we act contrary to our clearly defined attitudes (for example, regarding an election, or some hot campus issue): We feel tension, so we adjust our attitudes to reduce it. Dissonance theory, then, explains attitude *change*. In situations where our attitudes aren't well formed, self-perception theory explains the attitude *formation* that occurs as we act and reflect, thereby developing a more readily accessible attitude to guide our future behavior (Fazio, 1987).

SUMMING UP

DO OUR ATTITUDES DETERMINE OUR BEHAVIOR?

What is the relationship between our inner attitudes and our external actions? Social psychologists agree that attitudes and actions have a reciprocal relationship, each feeding the other. Popular wisdom stresses the impact of attitudes on action. Surprisingly, our attitudes—usually assessed as our feelings toward some object or person—are often quite poor predictors of our actions. Moreover, changing people's attitudes typically fails to produce much change in their behavior. These findings sent social psychologists scurrying to find out why we so often fail to play the game we talk. The answer now seems clear: Our attitude expressions and our behaviors are each subject to many influences. Our attitudes *will* predict our behavior (1) if these "other influences" are minimized, (2) if the attitude corresponds very closely to the predicted behavior (as in voting studies), and (3) if we are conscious of our attitudes (either because something reminds us of them or because we acquired them in a manner that makes them strong). Thus there *is* a connection between what we think and feel and what we do, even if that connection in many situations is looser than we'd like to believe.

DOES OUR BEHAVIOR DETERMINE OUR ATTITUDES?

The attitude-action relation works also in the reverse direction: We are likely not only to think ourselves into action, but also to act ourselves into a way of thinking. When we act, we amplify the idea lying behind what we have done, especially when we feel responsible for it. Many streams of evidence converge to establish this principle. The actions prescribed by social roles mold the attitudes of the role players. Research on the foot-in-the door phenomenon indicates that committing a small act (for example, agreeing to do a small favor) later makes people more willing to do a larger one. Actions also affect our moral attitudes: We tend to justify as right that which we have done. Similarly, our racial and political behaviors help shape our social consciousness: We seem not only to stand up for what we believe, but also to believe in what we have stood up for.

WHY DO OUR ACTIONS AFFECT OUR ATTITUDES?

Three competing theories explain *why* our actions affect our attitude reports. *Self-presentation theory* assumes that people, especially those who self-monitor their behavior hoping to create a good impression, will adapt their attitude reports to *appear* reasonably consistent with their actions. The available evidence confirms that people do adjust their attitude statements out of concern for what other people will think, but also indicates that some genuine attitude change occurs. Two theories propose that our actions trigger genuine attitude change. *Dissonance theory* explains this attitude change by assuming that we are motivated to justify our behavior in order to reduce the tension we feel when acting contrary to our attitudes or after making a difficult decision. It further proposes that the less external justification we have for an undesirable action, the more we will feel responsible for it, and thus the more dissonance will be aroused and attitudes will change. *Self-perception theory* assumes that when our attitudes are weak we simply observe our behavior and its circumstances and infer what our attitudes must be. One interesting implication of self-perception theory is the "overjustification effect": Rewarding people to do what they like doing anyway can turn their pleasure into drudgery (if the reward leads them to attribute their behavior to the reward). Evidence supports predictions from both theories, suggesting that each describes what happens under certain conditions.

FOR FURTHER READING

Cialdini, R. B. (1988). *Influence: Science and practice* (2nd ed.). Glenview, IL: Scott, Foresman/Little, Brown. An engrossing summary of six "weapons of influence," as revealed by social-psychological research and exploited in everyday situations. See, especially, Chapter 3, "Commitment and Consistency: Hobgoblins of the Mind."

Lindzey, G., & Aronson, E. (Eds.). (1985). *Handbook of social psychology* (3rd ed.) (Vols. 1–2). New York: Random House. (Distributed by Erlbaum.) Leading researchers provide authoritative overviews of research on attitudes and on every other major topic in social psychology.

Snyder, M. (1987). *Public appearances/Private realities: The psychology of self-monitoring*. New York: Freeman. Describes how people vary in their eagerness to create a good impression in each situation versus being true to themselves whatever the situation, and how this "self-monitoring" tendency affects their attitude-behavior consistency, their friendships and romantic relationships, and their jobs and careers.

CHAPTER
3

EXPLAINING BEHAVIOR

EXPLAINING BEHAVIOR

———

In September of 1983, the Soviet Union shot down Korean Airlines Flight 007, killing all 269 people on board. The U.S. reaction to the Soviet act was swift and harsh: The Soviets were condemned for their impulsive hostility in slaying the innocent people on board an obviously off-course civilian flight.

In July of 1988, the USS Vincennes, in battle with Iranian gunboats in the Persian Gulf, shot down Iran Airbus Flight 655, killing all 290 people on board. Now the Soviets condemned the Americans for their impulsive hostility in slaying the innocent people on board an on-course civilian flight.

Was each country right to attribute the other's action to evil intentions and to doubt the other's claim to have misidentified the oncoming plane? Or was each act an understandable response to recent events?—Were the Soviet perceptions clouded by incidents of border invasion and aircraft spying and were U.S. perceptions clouded by a battle with Iranian gunboats and by memory of the earlier air-launched missile damage done to a sister destroyer?

As these cases illustrate, our judgments of nations and people depend on how we explain their behavior. Depending on one's explanation, killing someone may be judged as murder, manslaughter, self-defense, or patriotism. Social psychologists are therefore devoting enormous energy to understanding how we go about explaining people's behavior. This quest to understand our everyday explanations is part of a larger effort, described in this and the next chapter, to discover how we process social information—how we take in, store, and recall information about the goings-on around us. For example, what factors influence the behaviors we notice and the way we interpret and remember them? And how, in turn, do our explanations of people's behavior influence the way we evaluate and react to them? Let's see.

ATTRIBUTING CAUSALITY:
TO THE PERSON OR THE SITUATION?

The airplane shootings are dramatic examples of a question we face daily. In trying to understand people—especially when they do something unpleasant or unexpected (Bohner et al., 1988)—we wonder *why* they act that way. When a salesperson says, "That outfit really looks nice on you," does this reflect a genuine feeling, or is it a ploy the salesperson is trained to use in such situations? If worker productivity declines, shall we presume it is because workers are getting lazier or because of changes in their work situation (for example, inefficiencies resulting from new regulations)? Does a young boy's lashing out at his school classmates mean he has a hostile personality, or is he responding to stressful circumstances?

HOW DO WE EXPLAIN OTHERS' BEHAVIOR?

We spend an enormous amount of time analyzing and discussing why things happen as they do, especially when something negative or unexpected occurs (Hamilton, 1989; Weiner, 1985). Amy Holtzworth-Munroe and Neil Jacobson (1985) report that married people often analyze their partners' behaviors, especially their negative behaviors. Cold hostility is more likely to leave the partner wondering "why?" than is a warm hug. Their characteristic answers—"she's a cold, crabby person" versus "she's frustrated because of how I acted" or "he's had a bad day"—are linked with their marriage satisfaction.

Indeed, our conclusions about why people act as they do are profoundly important. They determine our reactions to people and our decisions regarding them. For example, Antonia Abbey (1987) and her colleagues have repeatedly found that men are more likely than women to attribute a woman's friendliness to sexual interest. This misreading of warmth as a sexual come-on (an example of a "misattribution") can lead to inappropriate behavior and helps explain the greater sexual assertiveness exhibited by men across the world (Kenrick & Trost, 1987). Such misattributions can also contribute both to date rape and to the greater tendency of men in various cultures, from Boston to Bombay, to justify rape by blaming the victim's behavior (Kanekar & Nazareth, 1988; Muehlenhard, 1988; Shotland, 1988).

Attribution Theories

Attribution theory:
The theory of how people explain others' behavior—for example, by attributing it either to internal *dispositions* (enduring traits, motives, and attitudes) or to external *situations*.

Attribution theory analyzes how we make judgments about people. There are several distinct varieties of attribution theory. But they do share some common assumptions: that we seek to make sense of our world, that we often attribute people's actions either to internal or external causes, that we do so in fairly logical ways. Let us consider these assumptions.

Fritz Heider (1958), widely regarded as the originator of attribution theory, analyzed the "commonsense psychology" by which people explain everyday events. Heider concluded that people tend to attribute someone's behavior either to *internal* causes (for example, the person's disposition) or *external* causes (for example, something about the person's situation). Thus, a teacher may wonder whether a child's underachievement is due to lack of motivation and ability (a "dispositional attribution") or to physical and social circumstances, such as poor nutrition and family difficulties (a "situational attribution"). This distinction between internal (dispositional) and external (situational)

We tend to attribute someone's behavior or the outcome of an event either to *internal* (dispositional) or *external* (situational) causes.

"So! If it's good, it's Mister Coffee. If it's bad, it's me."

causes can become blurred. To say a schoolchild "is fearful" may be a short semantic leap from saying, "School frightens the child." Nevertheless, social psychologists have discovered that we quite freely attribute people's behavior to their dispositions rather than to their situations.

Inferring Traits

For example, Edward Jones and Keith Davis (1965) noted that people have a strong tendency to *infer* that people's intentions and dispositions *correspond* to their actions. If I observe Rick making a hurtful, sarcastic comment to Linda, I may infer that Rick is a hostile person. Jones and Davis's "theory of correspondent inferences" specifies the conditions under which such attributions are most likely. For example, normal or expected behavior tells us less about the person than does unusual behavior. If Rick is sarcastic in a job interview, where any candidate would normally be pleasant, this tells us more about Rick than were he to be sarcastic just after his new car was dented.

"Attribution theory is the most important development in social psychology."
Craig A. Anderson (1988)

Indeed, the ease with which we infer traits is remarkable. In experiments at New York University, James Uleman (1989) has found that, if given a statement to remember such as, "The librarian carries the old woman's groceries across the street," students will instantly, unintentionally, and unconsciously infer a trait. When later they are helped to recall the sentence, the most valuable clue word is not "books" (to cue librarian) or "bags" (to cue groceries) but "helpful"—the inferred trait that I suspect you, too, spontaneously attributed to the librarian.

Commonsense Attributions

As these examples suggest, people often make quite rational attributions. In further testimony to the reasonable ways in which we explain someone's behavior, attribution theorist Harold Kelley (1973) of UCLA has noted how people use information about "consistency," "distinctiveness," and "consensus" (see Figure 3-1). For example, when explaining someone's behavior (why Bob just tripped over the feet of his dancing partner, Lisa), most people appropriately use information concerning *consistency* (Does Bob often trip over Lisa's feet), *distinctiveness* (Does Bob trip over the feet of his other dance partners?), and *consensus* (Do others trip over Lisa's feet?) (McArthur, 1972). If we learn that Bob and Bob alone consistently stumbles over Lisa's feet—and, in fact, over the feet of all his dance partners—we will likely attribute the incident to Bob, as logically we should. So our commonsense psychology often explains behavior much as would a professional scientist. (Kelley does, however, find that in everyday explanation people often discount a contributing cause of someone's behavior if other

FIGURE 3-1
Harold Kelley's theory of attributions. Three factors—consistency, distinctiveness, and consensus—influence whether we attribute someone's behavior to internal or external causes.

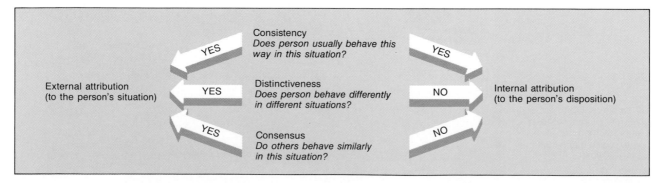

plausible causes are already known. If I can specify one or two reasons why a student might have done poorly on an exam, I may ignore or discount other possible reasons.)

Information Integration

Further evidence of the reasonable manner in which we form judgments of one another comes from research by Norman Anderson (1968, 1974) on "information integration." Anderson and his collaborators have discerned some logical rules by which we combine different pieces of information about a person into an overall impression. For example, suppose that you have an upcoming blind date with someone described as intelligent, daring, lazy, and sincere. Research on how people combine such information suggests that you would likely weigh each item of information according to its importance. If sincerity is especially important to you, you will give it more weight. If you are like the participants in experiments by Solomon Asch (1946), David Hamilton and Mark Zanna (1972), and Bert Hodges (1974), you may also give extra weight to information that comes first, and you may be more sensitive to negative than positive information. First impressions can color your interpretation of later information. Having first learned that someone is "intelligent," you may then interpret the person's being "daring" as meaning courageous rather than reckless. Negative information, such as "she is dishonest," also has extra potency, perhaps because it is more unusual. Once you have interpreted and weighed each piece of information, you then use your mental algebra to integrate the information. The result is your overall impression of your upcoming date.

Why We Study Attribution Errors

So far, so good. We form impressions of others and explain their behavior in some reasonable ways. More fascinating, though, are the predictable errors that distort our commonsense judgments. This chapter and the two that follow present new research on the foibles and fallacies of our social thinking. Reading these chapters may make it seem, as one student put it, that "social psychologists get their kicks out of playing tricks on people." Actually, the experiments are not an intellectual magic show designed to demonstrate "what fools these mortals be" (although some of the experiments are indeed amusing). Their purpose rather is to reveal *how* we think about ourselves and others. It is for the same reason that other psychologists study visual illusions — not just as mind-teasing demonstrations, but for what they reveal about how our visual system processes information.

If our capacity for illusion and self-deception seems shocking, remember that our modes of thought are generally adaptive. Our erroneous thinking is often a by-product of our mind's strategies for simplifying complex information. This parallels our perceptual mechanisms, which generally give us a useful image of the world, but will sometimes produce illusions.

A second reason for focusing upon the biases that penetrate our thinking is that we are generally unaware of them. My hunch is that you will find more surprises, more challenges, and more personal benefit in an analysis of our errors and biases than you would in a string of testimonies to what you are already aware of: our capacity for logical thought and intellectual achievement. This is also why classic epics of world literature so often portray pride and other human failings. Liberal education exposes us to fallacies of our thinking in hopes that we might improve it, by putting it more in touch with reality. The hope seems not in vain: Psychology students have been found to explain behavior less simplistically than equally able science students (Fletcher et al., 1986). So, remembering this overriding aim—*developing our capacity for critical thinking*—let us, in the remainder of this chapter and the two chapters that follow, see how the new research on social thinking can enhance our social reasoning.

THE FUNDAMENTAL ATTRIBUTION ERROR

As later chapters will reveal, social psychology's most important lesson concerns how much we are affected by our social environments. At any moment, what we say and do depends substantially on the situation, as well as on what we bring to the situation. In experiments, a slight difference between two situations sometimes produces great differences in the way people respond. I see this when I teach classes at both 8:30 A.M. and 7:00 P.M. Silent stares greet me at 8:30; at 7:00 o'clock it almost takes a bullhorn to break up the party. In each situation, some individuals are more talkative than others, but the difference between the two situations exceeds the individual differences.

Attribution researchers have found that we fail to appreciate this important lesson of social psychology. When explaining someone's behavior, we often underestimate the impact of the situation and overestimate the extent to which it reflects the person's characteristic traits and attitudes. Thus even knowing the effect of the time of day on classroom conversation, I may assume that the people in the 7:00 P.M. class are more extroverted than the "silent types" who enroll at 8:30 A.M.

Even Coerced Behavior Gets Attributed to the Actor

Fundamental attribution error: The tendency for observers to underestimate situational influences and overestimate dispositional influences upon others' behavior. (Also called "correspondence bias"—the assumption that people's dispositions correspond to their behavior.)

This discounting of situational effects, dubbed the *fundamental attribution error* by Lee Ross (1977), has been evident in many experiments. In the first such study, Edward Jones and Victor Harris (1967) had Duke University students read debaters' speeches supporting or attacking Cuba's leader, Fidel Castro. When the position taken was said to have been chosen by the debater, the students logically enough assumed it reflected the debater's attitude. But what happened when the students were told that the position had been assigned by the debate coach? Remarkably, even knowing that

FIGURE 3-2
The fundamental attribution error. When people read a debate speech supporting or attacking Fidel Castro, they attributed corresponding attitudes to the speech writer, even when the writer's position was known to have been assigned by the debate coach. (Data from Jones & Harris, 1967.)

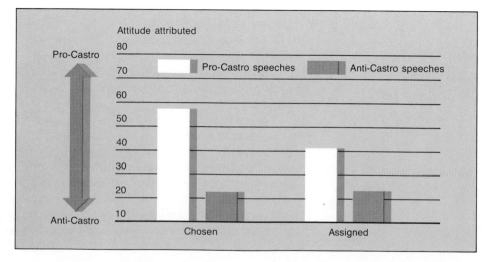

the debater was *assigned* a pro-Castro position did not prevent their inferring that the debater had some pro-Castro attitudes (see Figure 3-2; also Miller et al., 1981).

The effect is so irresistible that even when people themselves cause someone else's behavior, they still fail to recognize that the person's behavior is externally influenced. For example, if subjects dictate an opinion that someone else must then express, they still tend to see the person as actually holding that opinion (Gilbert & Jones, 1986). If subjects are asked to be either self-enhancing or self-deprecating during an interview, they are very aware of why they are acting so. But they remain just as *un*aware of the effect their behavior has on a fellow interviewee. If John feigns modesty, his naïve partner Bob will likely exhibit modesty as well. John will easily understand his own apparent modesty, but will think that poor Bob suffers low self-esteem (Baumeister et al., 1988).

The Fundamental Attribution Error in Everyday Situations

Does the fundamental attribution error also occur in everyday life? If we know the checkout cashier is programmed to say, "Thank you and have a nice day," will we nevertheless automatically conclude that the cashier is a friendly, grateful person? David Napolitan and George Goethals (1979) explored this question by having Williams College students talk with a supposed clinical-psychology graduate student who acted either warm and friendly or aloof and critical. Half the students were told beforehand that her behavior would be spontaneous. The other half were told that for purposes of the experiment she had been instructed to feign friendly (or unfriendly) behavior. The effect of this information? The students totally disregarded it. If she acted friendly, they inferred that she was really a friendly person, and if she acted unfriendly, they assumed she was an unfriendly person, regardless of why she acted as she did. As when viewing a dummy on the ventriloquist's lap, or a movie actor playing a scripted "good-guy" or "bad-guy" role, it is difficult to escape the illusion that the programmed behavior reflects an inner disposition. Perhaps this is why Leonard Nimoy, who played Spock on *Star Trek*, entitled his book, *I Am Not Spock*.

The discounting of social constraints was further revealed in a thought-provoking experiment by Lee Ross and his collaborators (Ross et al., 1977). The experiment recreated Ross's firsthand experience of moving from graduate student to professor. His doctoral oral exam had proved a humbling experience, as his apparently brilliant professors quizzed him on topics of *their* expertise. Six months later, *Dr.* Ross was himself an examiner, now able to ask penetrating questions on *his own* favorite topics. Ross's hapless candidate later confessed to feeling exactly as Ross had a half year before—dissatisfied with his ignorance and impressed with the apparent brilliance of the examiners, including the most junior of them.

Working with Teresa Amabile and Julia Steinmetz, Ross randomly assigned some Stanford University students to play the role of questioner and others to play the role of contestant in a simulated quiz game. They invited the questioners to make up difficult questions that would demonstrate their general wealth of knowledge. It's fun to imagine such questions: "Where is Bainbridge Island?" "What is the seventh book in the Old Testament?" "Who is the current editor of *Psychology Today?*" If even these few questions have you feeling a little uninformed, then you will appreciate the results of this experiment. Despite being fully aware that the roles randomly assigned to questioner and contestant guaranteed that the questioner would have the advantage, both the contestants and observers of the experiment succumbed to the erroneous impression that the questioners *really were* more knowledgeable than the contestants. (See

Have you ever noticed that the question-askers on TV game shows such as Jeopardy *seem more intelligent than their contestants?*

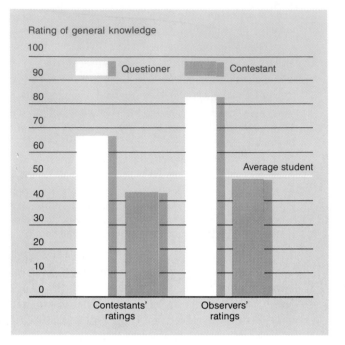

FIGURE 3-3
Both contestants and observers of a simulated quiz game assumed that a person who had been randomly assigned the role of questioner was actually far more knowledgeable than the contestant. This failure to appreciate the extent to which the assigned roles of questioner and contestant simply made the questioner *seem* more knowledgeable illustrates the fundamental attribution error. (Data from Ross, Amabile, & Steinmetz, 1977.)

Figure 3-3.) (Follow-up research indicates that the misimpressions are hardly a reflection of low social intelligence. If anything, intelligent and socially competent people are *more* likely to make the attribution error [Block & Funder, 1986].)

In real life, those with social power usually initiate and control conversation, often leading underlings to overestimate their superiors' knowledge and intelligence. Medical doctors, for example, are often presumed to be experts on all sorts of questions unrelated to medicine. Similarly, it has been my experience that students often overestimate the brilliance of their teachers. (Teachers are, as in the experiment, questioners on subjects of their special expertise.) When some of these students later become teachers, they are usually amazed to discover that teachers are not so brilliant after all.

We commit the fundamental attribution error when explaining *other people's* behavior. We often explain our own behavior in terms of the situation, while holding others responsible for their behavior. Thus we might think "John was hostile because he is an angry person" even when he would attribute his behavior to environmental factors ("I was angry because everything was going wrong"). Indeed, when referring to ourselves, we typically use verbs that describe our actions and reactions ("I get annoyed when . . ."); referring to someone else, we more often describe what that person is ("He is crabby") (McGuire & McGuire, 1986). Thus we typically describe ourselves in terms of our current thoughts and feelings but describe others in terms of their enduring traits (White & Younger, 1988).

Attributions of responsibility are at the heart of many judicial decisions (Fincham & Jaspars, 1980). In 1988, after Colonel Oliver North was indicted on charges of theft, fraud, and conspiracy, a controversy ensued: Was North accountable for illegal activity and should he therefore be jailed? Or was North acting under orders in the line of duty? The case exemplifies many judicial controversies: The prosecution argues, "You

In 1988 and 1989, a great controversy surrounded Colonel Oliver North's responsibility for the events that took place in the Iran-Contra affair. Should he, indeed, have been convicted of theft, fraud, and conspiracy, for which he was indicted? Or should he have been exonerated for having done what he had to, given the situation?

are to blame, for you could have done otherwise"; the defendant replies, "It wasn't my fault; I was a victim of the situation" or "under the circumstance I did right."

To illustrate attribution error most of us need look no further than our own experience. Determined to make some new friends, Bev plasters a smile on her face and anxiously plunges into a party. Everyone there seems quite relaxed and happy as they laugh and talk with one another. Bev wonders to herself, "Why is everyone else always so at ease in groups like this while I'm feeling shy and tense?" Actually, everyone else is feeling nervous, too, and making the same attributional error in assuming that Bev and the others *are* as they *appear*—confidently convivial.

WHY THE ATTRIBUTION ERROR?

So far we have seen an error in the way we explain other people's behavior: We often attribute it so much to their inner dispositions that we ignore powerful situational determinants. Why is there this tendency to underestimate the situational determinants of others' behavior, but not our own?

Focus of Attention

Attribution theorists point out, first, that we have a different perspective when observing than when acting (Jones & Nisbett, 1971; Jones, 1976). When we watch another person act, that *person* occupies the center of our attention and so seems to cause whatever happens. When we act, the environment commands our attention. If this is true, what might we expect if the perspectives were reversed—if somehow we could see ourselves as others see us and if we saw the world through their eyes? Should this not eliminate or even reverse the typical attribution error?

Using this reasoning, see if you can predict the result of a clever experiment conducted by Michael Storms (1973). If you were a subject in Storms's experiment you might have found yourself seated facing another student with whom you were to talk for a few minutes. Beside you is a TV camera that shares your view of the other student. Facing you from alongside the other student are an observer and another TV camera. Afterward, both you and the observer who faced you judge whether your behavior was caused more by your personal characteristics or by the situation you were reacting to.

Question: Which of you will attribute the least importance to the situation? Storms found it was the observer (another demonstration of the fundamental attribution error). Now what if we reverse your and the observer's points of view by having you each watch the videotape recorded from the other's perspective? (You now view yourself while the observer views what you saw.) This reverses the attributions: You now tend to see your behavior as emanating more from your person, while the observer now attributes it mostly to the situation you faced.

In another experiment, people viewed a videotape of a suspect confessing while being interviewed by a police detective. If they viewed the confession through a camera focused on the suspect, they perceived it as genuine. If they viewed it through a camera focused on the detective, they perceived it as more coerced (Lassiter & Irvine, 1986). So one reason we underestimate the impact of others' situations is that our attention is on *them* more than on their situation. Being the focus of our attention, the quarterback and ball carriers on a football team are likely (relative to the blockers) to be overly credited for victories and blamed for defeats.

Seeing ourselves on television is just one means of redirecting our attention to ourselves. Seeing ourselves in a mirror, hearing our tape-recorded voices, having our pictures taken, filling out biographical questionnaires—such experiences similarly focus our attention inward, making us *self*-conscious instead of *situation*-conscious.

Self-awareness:

A self-conscious state in which attention is focused on oneself. Makes people more sensitive to their own attitudes and dispositions.

Robert Wicklund, Shelley Duval, and their collaborators have explored the consequences of becoming ***self-aware*** by focusing upon oneself (Duval & Wicklund, 1972; Wicklund, 1979, 1982). Recall from the last chapter that inner attitudes often lie dormant unless attention is drawn to them; people who are made self-conscious by looking in a mirror act more in line with their attitudes (for example, they are less likely to cheat). When people's attention is focused upon themselves they also attribute more responsibility to themselves. Allan Fenigstein and Charles Carver (1978) demonstrated this by having their students at Kenyon College and the University of Miami (Florida) imagine themselves in some hypothetical situations. Those made self-conscious, by thinking they were hearing their heartbeats while pondering the situation, saw themselves as more responsible for the imaginary outcome than did those who thought they were just hearing extraneous noises. These investigators, along with Michael Scheier, have also found that some people are consistently more self-conscious than others. In experiments, people who report themselves as privately self-conscious (for example, who agree with statements such as "I'm generally attentive to my inner feelings") behave similarly to people whose attention has been self-focused with a mirror (Carver & Scheier, 1978). Thus, people whose attention is focused on themselves—either briefly during an experiment or because they are self-conscious persons—view themselves more as observers typically do; they attribute their behavior more to internal factors and less to the situation.

Here, then is one good reason for the attribution error: *Causality is found where our attention is drawn.* To see this in your own experience, consider: Would you say that your social psychology instructor is more a quiet or talkative person?

My guess is that you inferred that he or she is a fairly outgoing person. But consider further: Your attention is focused on your instructor while he or she behaves in a context that demands speaking. The instructor, on the other hand, observes his or her own behavior in many different situations, not only in the classroom but in meetings, at home, and so forth. Thus in answer to the same question, your instructor might say, "Me talkative? Well, it all depends on the situation. When I'm in class or with good friends I'm rather outgoing. But at conventions and in unfamiliar situations I feel and act rather shy."

If, indeed, we more readily see how our own behavior responds to particular situations, we should also see ourselves as less predictable and more variable than other people. And that is precisely what several recent studies found in the United States, Canada, and West Germany (Baxter & Goldberg, 1987; Kammer, 1982; Sande et al., 1988). Moreover, the less opportunity we have to observe people's behavior in context, the more we make attributions to their personalities. Thomas Gilovich (1987) explored this by showing people a videotape of someone and then having them describe the person's actions to other people. The secondhand impressions were more extreme. Similarly, people's impressions of someone they have often heard about from a friend are typically more extreme than their friend's firsthand impressions. The better you know someone the less prone you are to overgeneralized impressions—and whom do you know better than yourself?

Cultural Differences in Attributions

Other explanations for the attribution error have also been suggested (Ickes, 1980; Watson, 1982). For example, our western world view predisposes us to assume that people, not situations, are the source of what happens. Jerald Jellison and Jane Green (1981) report that among University of Southern California students internal explanations are more socially approved. "You can do it," we are assured by the pop psychology of our positive-thinking culture.

"You can do anything you want to if you just set your mind to it and go to work."
J. Danforth Quayle,
U.S. Vice-Presidential Debate,
October 5, 1988

This assumes that, with the right disposition and attitude, anyone can surmount almost any problem: you get what you deserve and deserve what you get. Thus bad behavior is often explained by labeling the person who does it as "sick," "lazy," or "sadistic." As children grow up in western culture they increasingly explain a person's behavior in terms of the person's personal characteristics (Ross et al., 1978; Ross, 1981; Ruble et al., 1979). As a first grader, one of my sons brought home an example of how this occurs. When he unscrambled the words "gate the sleeve caught Tom on his" into "The gate caught Tom on his sleeve," his teacher, applying the western cultural assumptions of the curriculum materials, marked this wrong. The "right" answer located cause within Tom, not the gate: "Tom caught his sleeve on the gate."

Some languages promote external attributions. Instead of "I was late," Spanish idiom allows one to say "The clock caused me to be late." In cultures that are less individualistic, people are less prone to perceiving people in terms of their personal dispositions (Zebrowitz-McArthur, 1988). When told of someone's actions, Hindus in India are less likely than are Americans to offer dispositional explanations ("She is kind") and are more likely to offer situational explanations ("Her friends were with her") (Miller, 1984). College students in Japan are less likely than students in the U.S.

to answer the question, "Who am I?," with psychological traits ("I am sincere," "I am confident") and are more likely to declare their social identities ("I am a Keio student") (Cousins, 1989).

HOW FUNDAMENTAL IS THE FUNDAMENTAL ATTRIBUTION ERROR?

Like most provocative ideas, the presumption that we're all prone to a fundamental attribution error has its critics. Granted, say some, there may be an attribution *bias*, but in any given instance this may or may not produce an "error," just as parents who are biased to believe their child does not drink or use drugs may or may not be in error (Harvey et al., 1981). One can be biased to believe what is true. Moreover, some everyday circumstances, such as being in church or on a job interview, are like the experiments we have been considering: They involve clear constraints which actors can detect more easily than observers. Hence the attribution error. But other settings—in one's room, at a park—allow people to exhibit their own individuality. In settings such as these, people may see their own behavior as *less* constrained, and as more internally directed, than do observers (Monson & Snyder, 1977; Quattrone, 1982). So it is probably an overstatement to suggest that in all settings observers underestimate situational influences.

Nevertheless, experiments reveal that the bias occurs even when we are aware of the situational forces—for example, even when reminded that an assigned debate position is really not a good basis for inferring someone's attitudes (Croxton & Morrow, 1984; Croxton & Miller, 1987; Reeder et al., 1989) or that the questioners' role in the quiz game gives them an advantage in displaying their knowledge (Johnson et al., 1984). It takes more mental effort to assess social effects on people's behavior than merely to attribute it to their disposition (Gilbert et al., 1988). It's as if the typical subject thinks, "This isn't a very good basis for making a judgment, but it's easy and about all I've got to go on." Still, it is sobering to think that you and I can know about a social process that distorts our thinking and still be susceptible to it.

The attribution error is *fundamental* because it can affect our attitudes and actions. Researchers in Britain, India, Australia, and the United States have found that people's attributions are linked with their attitudes toward the poor and unemployed (Feather, 1983; Furnham, 1982; Pandey et al., 1982; Wagstaff, 1983). Those who attribute poverty and unemployment to personal dispositions ("They're just lazy and undeserving") tend to adopt political positions that are less sympathetic to such people than are the positions of those who make external attributions ("If you or I were to have lived with the same overcrowding, poor education, and discrimination, would we be any better off?"). French investigators Jean-Leon Beauvois and Nicole Dubois (1988) report that "relatively privileged" middle-class people are more likely than less advantaged people to assume that people's behaviors have internal explanations. (Those who have "made it" tend to assume that you get what you deserve.) And in the laboratory, those who observe a quiz game not only judge the questioner as smarter than the contestant, they are also more likely to defer to the questioner on matters of general knowledge (Quattrone, 1982b). An error of attribution can become an error of action.

Remembering that our analysis of thinking errors has a constructive goal, how then might we benefit from being aware of the bias? Perhaps being sensitive to it can help us assess our reactions to people. Recently, I assisted with the interviewing of two candidates for a faculty position. The first candidate was interviewed by six of us

"Most poor people are not lazy. . . . They catch the early bus. . . . They raise other people's children. . . . They clean the streets. No, no, they're not lazy."
The Reverend Jesse Jackson, Address to the Democratic National Convention, July 1988.

at once, each of us having the opportunity to ask two or three questions. I came away thinking, "What a stiff, awkward person he is." The second candidate I met privately over coffee and we immediately discovered we had a close friend in common. As we talked, I became increasingly impressed by what a "warm, engaging, stimulating person she is." Only later did I remember the fundamental attribution error and reassess my confident analysis. I had attributed his stiffness and her warmth to their dispositions; in fact, I later realized, such behavior may have resulted partly from the formality versus informality of their interview situations. Had I been able to view these interactions through the perspective of their eyes, instead of my own, I would have been more understanding.

PERCEIVING AND EXPLAINING OURSELVES

We have considered how we explain others' behavior, paying special attention to the fundamental attribution error. Social psychologists are also now studying how we explain our own behavior, and how our conceptions of ourselves influence the way we select, interpret, and recall information. Indeed, during the 1980s no topic in psychology was more researched than the self. In 1988, the word "self" appeared in more than 5500 book and article summaries in *Psychological Abstracts*—almost triple the number fifteen years earlier. In Chapter 2, we saw examples of this focus on the self—in the theories of self-presentation, self-justification, and self-perception, and in research on self-monitoring and self-awareness.

Self-reference effect:
The tendency to process efficiently and remember well information related to oneself.

During the 1980s a new wave of research has revealed that our ideas about ourselves (our "self-schemas") powerfully affect our processing of social information. Our sense of self serves to organize our thoughts, feelings, and actions, thereby influencing how we perceive, remember, and evaluate both other people and ourselves (Markus & Wurf, 1987). One example is the ***self-reference effect:*** When information is relevant to our self-conceptions we process it more quickly and remember it better (Higgins & Bargh, 1987; Kihlstrom et al., 1988; Reeder et al., 1987). If asked whether specific words such as "outgoing" describe ourselves, we later remember those words better than if asked whether they describe someone else. If asked to compare themselves with a character in a short story, we remember that character better.

As we process self-relevant information, a potent bias enters. We readily attribute our failures to difficult situations, while taking credit for our successes. In this and other ways we maintain a generally favorable self-image, thereby enjoying the benefits of positive self-esteem while occasionally suffering the perils of self-righteous pride.

THE SELF-SERVING BIAS: "HOW DO I LOVE ME? LET ME COUNT THE WAYS."

Self-serving bias:
The tendency to perceive oneself favorably.

It is widely believed that most of us suffer the "I'm not OK—you're OK" problem of low self-esteem. For example, counseling psychologist Carl Rogers (1958) concluded that most people he has known "despise themselves, regard themselves as worthless and unlovable." As comedian Groucho Marx put it, "I'd never join any club that would accept a person like me." The evidence, however, indicates that writer William Saroyan was closer to the truth: "Every man is a good man in a bad world—as he himself knows." Although social psychologists are debating the reason for this ***self-serving bias,*** there is general agreement regarding its reality, its prevalence, and its potency.

Attributions for Positive and Negative Events

Time and again, experiments have found that people readily accept credit when told they have succeeded (attributing the success to their ability and effort), yet often attribute failure to such external factors as bad luck or the problem's inherent "impossibility" (Whitley & Frieze, 1985, 1986). Similarly, in explaining their victories, athletes commonly credit themselves, but are more likely to attribute losses to something else: bad breaks, bad officiating, the other team's super effort (Mullen & Riordan, 1988). And how much responsibility do you suppose car drivers tend to accept for their accidents? On insurance forms, drivers have described their accidents in words such as these: "An invisible car came out of nowhere, struck my car and vanished." "As I reached an intersection, a hedge sprang up, obscuring my vision and I did not see the other car." "A pedestrian hit me and went under my car" (*Toronto News*, 1977). Situations that combine skill and chance (for example, games, exams, job applications) are especially prone to the phenomenon: Winners can easily attribute their successes to their skill, while losers can attribute their losses to chance. When I win at Scrabble, it's because of my verbal dexterity; when I lose, it's because "Who could get anywhere with a Q but no U?" When gamblers win, they can attribute the outcome to their skill; when they lose, the outcome tends to be explained away, perhaps by a critical "fluke" play in a sporting event (Gilovich, 1983).

In experiments that require two people to cooperate in order to make money, most individuals blame their partner for failure (Myers & Bach, 1976). This follows a tradition established in the most ancient example of self-serving bias, Adam's excuse: "The woman whom thou gave to be with me, she gave me fruit of the tree, and I ate." Thus while managers usually blame poor performance on workers' lack of ability or effort, the workers are more likely to blame something external—inadequate supplies, excessive work load, difficult coworkers, ambiguous assignments (Rice, 1985).

When other people are blamed for their bad deeds while one's own are excused, open hostility is not far away. It happens in aggressive confrontations between police and citizens. It happens in parent-child relations. It happens in marriage (Harvey, 1987). Especially in times of conflict, each party sees its own "firmness" as reasonable but attributes the other's actions to a beastly disposition. After a quarrel, husband John attributes the biting words of wife Mary to her nastiness but sees his own anger as justified.

Similarly, when explaining their own problems to Ann Landers or Dear Abby, letter writers usually blame someone else ("Sidney is a drag on a trip—he has no interest in seeing new places or meeting new people"). When explaining someone else's problem, people are much less likely to externalize blame (Fischer et al., 1987). And compared to those who are happily married, unhappy couples exhibit far greater self-serving bias, by blaming rather than accepting the partner when problems arise (Fincham et al., 1987). In one survey, divorcing people were ten times more likely to blame the spouse for the breakup than to blame themselves (Kitson & Sussman, 1982).

Michael Ross and Fiore Sicoly (1979) observed another marital version of self-serving bias. They found that young married Canadians usually felt they took more responsibility for such activities as cleaning the house and caring for the children than their spouses were willing to credit them for. In a more recent survey of Americans, 91 percent of wives but only 76 percent of husbands credited the wife with doing most of the food shopping (Burros, 1988). Every night, my wife and I pitch our laundry at the foot of our bedroom clothes hamper. In the morning, one of us puts it in. When she suggested that I take more responsibility for this, I thought, "Huh? I already do

"Give them grace, when they hurt each other, to recognize and acknowledge their fault and to seek each other's forgiveness."
Marriage prayer from The Book of Common Prayer

it 75 percent of the time." So I asked her how often she thought she picked up the clothes. "Oh," she replied, "about 75 percent of the time."

Students exhibit this self-serving bias. Researchers Walter Stephan, Robert Arkin, Mark Davis, and others have consistently found that after receiving an examination grade, those who do well tend to accept personal credit by judging the exam a valid measure of their competence (for example, Arkin & Maruyama, 1979; Davis & Stephan, 1980; Gilmor & Reid, 1979; Griffin et al., 1983). Those who do poorly are much more likely to criticize the exam as a poor indicator.

Reading about these experiments, I cannot resist a satisfied "knew-it-all-along" feeling. But we college professors are not immune to self-serving bias. Mary Glenn Wiley and her co-workers (1979) asked 230 scholars who had submitted articles to sociology journals why their papers had been accepted or rejected. The scholars attributed their rejections mostly to factors beyond their control (for example, bad luck in the editor's choice of critic for the paper). As you can by now imagine, they did not equally attribute their acceptances to *good* luck in the editor's choice of critics, but rather to controllable factors like the quality of their article and the effort they put into it.

The experiments dealing with students' means of explaining their good and bad performances are complemented by experiments on teachers' ways of explaining their students' good and bad performances. When there is no need to feign modesty, those assigned the role of teachers tend to take credit for positive outcomes and blame failure on the student, especially when the student's performance reflects on them (Arkin et al., 1980; Davis, 1979; Tetlock, 1980). Teachers, it seems, are likely to think, "I helped Maria to be graduated with honors. But, despite all my help, Melinda flunked out."

Can We All Be Better Than Average?

These indications of a self-serving bias are reinforced by research studies that invite people to compare themselves to others. If the Chinese philosopher Lao-tzu was right that "At no time in the world will a man who is sane over-reach himself, over-spend himself, over-rate himself" (*The Way of Life*, sixth century B.C.), then most of us are a little insane. For in nearly any dimension that is both subjective and socially desirable most people see themselves as better than average. Consider:

- Most business people see themselves as more ethical than the average business person (Baumhart, 1968; Brenner & Molander, 1977), 90 percent of business managers rate their performance as superior to their average peer (French, 1968), and most managers see their leadership as more encouraging of openness and innovation than do their subordinates and neutral observers (Hollander, 1985).

- Most community residents see themselves as less prejudiced and as fairer than others in their communities (Fields & Schuman, 1976; Lenihan, 1965; Messick et al., 1985; O'Gorman & Garry, 1976).

- Most drivers—even most drivers who have been hospitalized for accidents—believe themselves to be safer and more skilled than the average driver (Svenson, 1981).

- Most Americans perceive themselves as more intelligent than their average peer (Wylie, 1979), and as better looking (*Public Opinion*, 1984).

- Even smog-breathing Los Angeles residents view themselves as healthier than most of their neighbors, and most college students believe they will outlive their actuarially predicted age of death by about ten years (Larwood, 1978; C. R. Snyder, 1978).

*"I dread to think of all the inaccuracies
there would be if you wrote my biography after I'm gone."*

Most Americans perceive themselves as more intelligent and better looking than their average peer.

Every community, it seems, is like Garrison Keillor's fictional Lake Wobegon, where "all the women are strong, all the men are good-looking, and all the children are above average."

• Perhaps one reason for this optimism is that although 12 percent of Americans feel old for their age and 22 percent feel their age, many more—66 percent—think they are young for their age (*Public Opinion*, 1984). All of which calls to mind Freud's joke about the man who told his wife, "If one of us should die, I think I would go live in Paris."

Periodically, the College Entrance Examination Board invites the 1 million high school seniors taking its Scholastic Aptitude Test to indicate "how you feel you compare with other people your own age in certain areas of ability." Judging from the students' responses, it appears that America's high school seniors are not wracked with inferiority feelings. In the year for which I obtained the data, 70 percent rated themselves as above average in "leadership ability," 2 percent as below average. In "ability to get along with others"—a trait dimension that is definitely both subjective and socially desirable—*zero* percent of the 829,000 students who responded rated themselves below average, 60 percent rated themselves in the top 10 percent, and 25 percent saw themselves among the top 1 percent!

Subjective dimensions (such as "getting along with others") trigger greatest self-serving bias because they give us so much leeway in constructing our own definitions of success (Dunning et al., 1989). Asked to rank my "neatness" I would think about my office, not my handwriting. Rating my athletic ability, I would likely ponder my basketball play, and not the agonizing weeks I spent as a Little League baseball player hiding in right field. By defining ambiguous criteria in our own terms, each of us can see ourselves as relatively successful.

Other Self-Serving Tendencies

These tendencies toward (1) self-serving attributions and (2) self-congratulatory comparisons are not the only indications of favorably biased self-perceptions. We will see in the following chapters that most of us (3) more readily believe flattering than self-deflating information, (4) overestimate how desirably we would act in a given situation, (5) evidence a "cognitive conceit" by overestimating the accuracy of our beliefs and judgments, and (6) misremember our own past in self-enhancing ways.

"How little we should enjoy life if we never flattered ourselves!"
La Rochefoucauld, Maxims, *1665*

Moreover, (7) if an undesirable act cannot be misremembered or undone, then, as we noted in Chapter 2, we may justify it. (8) The more favorably we perceive ourselves on some dimension (say, intelligence, persistence, or sense of humor), the more we use that dimension as a basis for judging others (Lewicki, 1983). (9) If a test or some other source of information flatters us, then not only do we believe it, we also evaluate positively both the test and any evidence which suggests that the test is valid (Pyszczynski et al., 1985; Tesser & Paulhus, 1983). (10) We tend to see ourselves as center stage; we overestimate the extent to which others' behavior is aimed at us and we see ourselves as responsible for happenings in which we played only a small part (Fenigstein, 1984). (11) Although some of these consequences may be negative, we tend to see our underlying motives as primarily good and others' motives as less good (Schlenker, 1984). (12) Judging from photos, we not only guess that attractive people have desirable personalities, we also guess that they have personalities more like our own than do unattractive people (Marks et al., 1981). (13) We like to associate ourselves with the glory of others' success, but if we find ourselves linked with (say, born on the same day as) some reprehensible person, we boost ourselves by softening our view of the rascal (Finch & Cialdini, 1989).

What is more, (14) many of us have what researcher Neil Weinstein (1980, 1982; Weinstein & Lachendro, 1982) terms "an unrealistic optimism about future life events." At Rutgers University, for example, students perceive themselves as far more likely than their classmates to experience positive events such as getting a good job, drawing a good salary, and owning a home, and as far less likely to experience negative events

Knowing that half of American marriages end in divorce, most young Americans nonetheless believe that their marital romance will last a lifetime.

THE ILLUSION OF INVULNERABILITY

In a 1942 Harvard Chapel Meditation, psychologist Gordon W. Allport (1978, pp. 19–20) described the perils of unrealistic optimism:

> Recently I examined two hundred life histories written by refugees from Nazi Germany. With scarcely an exception these people had found themselves blinded by their own hopes.
>
> Not one of them would at first believe that Hitlerism could bring such a catastrophe upon them.
>
> In 1932 they hoped and therefore believed that Hitler would never come to power.
>
> In 1933 they hoped and therefore believed that he could not put his threats into execution.
>
> In 1934 they hoped and therefore believed that the nightmare would soon pass.

> In 1938 the Austrians were certain that Hitler could never come to Austria, because they hoped that Austrians were different from Germans. . . .
>
> Another example comes from a study of college undergraduates who were asked to estimate their income in five years' and in ten years' time after leaving college. The results, I regret to report, are quite fantastic. Most of them picture themselves as well-to-do, quite overlooking probabilities.
>
> If they were headed for medicine they estimated their income within a range which only about 5 percent of the medical profession achieves. If they were to become airplane pilots they figured a salary above that obtained by any pilots.
>
> Hope based on ignorance may spring eternal, but it certainly spells a fall. It is more of a vice than a virtue.

such as developing a drinking problem, having a heart attack before age 40, or being fired.

Linda Perloff (1987) reasons that this "illusion of invulnerability" can actually make us more vulnerable. If we believe we are immune to misfortune, precautions will seem unnecessary. Most young Americans know that half of U.S. marriages end in divorce but persist in believing that *their* marital romance will be lifelong (Lehman & Nisbett, 1985). In a study of undergraduate women, Jerry Burger and Linda Burns (1988) found that those who were sexually active nevertheless perceived themselves, compared to other women at their university, as much *less* vulnerable to unwanted pregnancy, especially if they did *not* consistently use effective contraception. Those who cheerfully shun seat belts, deny the effects of smoking, and stumble into ill-fated relationships remind us that blind optimism, like pride, may go before a fall.

A dash of pessimism can also energize students, most of whcm exhibit excess optimism about upcoming exams (Sparrell & Shrauger, 1984). Students who are overconfident tend to underprepare, whereas their equally able but more anxious peers, fearing that they are going to bomb the upcoming exam, proceed to study furiously and get high grades (Goodhart, 1986; Norem & Cantor, 1986; Showers & Ruben, 1987). Success in school and beyond requires enough optimism to sustain hope and enough pessimism to motivate concern.

"O God, give us grace to accept with serenity the things that cannot be changed, courage to change the things which should be changed, and the wisdom to distinguish the one from the other."
Reinhold Niebuhr,
"The Serenity Prayer," 1943

Finally, (15) we have a curious tendency to enhance our self-image by over- or underestimating the extent to which others think and act as we do. On matters of *opinion*, we find support for our positions by overestimating the extent to which others concur (Marks & Miller, 1987; Mullen et al., 1985; Mullen & Hu, 1988). Likewise, when we behave undesirably or fail in a task, we reassure ourselves by thinking that such behaviors are commonplace. Not only do we tend to think and act as we perceive others do (see Chapter 7), we tend to guess that others think and act as we do. If we favor George Bush for president, cheat on our income taxes, or smoke, we are likely to overestimate the number of other people who do likewise. Overestimating the commonality of one's opinions, feelings, and negative behaviors is the ***false consensus***

False consensus effect:
The tendency to overestimate the commonality of one's opinions and one's undesirable or unsuccessful behaviors.

False uniqueness effect:
The tendency to underestimate the commonality of one's abilities and one's desirable or successful behaviors.

effect. Lance Shotland and Jane Craig (1988) suspect that this helps explain why males are quicker than females to perceive friendly behavior as sexually motivated: Men have a lower threshold for sexual arousal and are likely to assume that women share similar sexual feelings.

On matters of *ability* or when we behave desirably or successfully, a ***false uniqueness effect*** more often occurs (Mullen et al., 1988; Suls & Wan, 1987). We serve our self-image by seeing our talents and admirable behaviors as relatively unusual. Thus those who drink heavily but use seat belts *over*estimate (false consensus) the number of fellow heavy drinkers and *under*estimate (false uniqueness) the commonality of seat belt use (Suls et al., 1988). Simply put, one's failings are seen as normal, one's virtues as rare.

Self-Disparagement

Perhaps you have by now recalled times when someone was not self-praising but self-disparaging. On such occasions, there may still have been a self-serving process at work. For example, most of us have learned that putting ourselves down is often a successful technique for eliciting "strokes" from others. We know that a remark such as "I wish I weren't so ugly" will at the very least elicit a "Come now. I know a couple of people who are uglier than you."

There is another reason why people verbally disparage themselves and praise others. Think of the football coach who, before the big bowl game, extols the awesome strength of the upcoming opponent. Is the coach sincere? Robert Gould, Paul Brounstein, and Harold Sigall (1977; see also Bond, 1979) found that in a laboratory contest their University of Maryland students similarly aggrandized their anticipated opponent, but only when the assessment was made publicly. Those who indicated their assessments privately and anonymously credited their future opponent with much less ability. When coaches publicly exalt their opponents, they not only convey an image of modesty and good sportsmanship; they set the stage for a favorable evaluation no matter what the outcome. A win becomes a praiseworthy achievement; a loss, attributable to the opponent's "great defense." Modesty, said the seventeenth-century philosopher Francis Bacon, is but one of the "arts of ostentation." Sometimes people sabotage their chances for success by presenting themselves as shy, ill, or handicapped by past traumas. Far from being deliberately self-destructive, such behaviors typically have a self-protective aim (Arkin et al., 1986; Baumeister & Scher, 1988; Rhodewalt, 1987): "I'm not a failure—I'm okay except for this problem that handicapped me."

Taking this a step further, might people even handicap themselves with self-defeating behavior? Recall that people eagerly protect their self-images by attributing their failures to external factors rather than to themselves. Can you see why, *fearing failure*, people might therefore handicap themselves by partying half the night before a job interview, getting a headache the day of a big date, or shrugging off studying before a big exam? When one's self-image is tied up with one's performance, it can be more self-deflating to try hard and fail than to have a ready excuse. If we fail while working under a handicap we can cling to a sense of competence; if we succeed under such conditions, it can only heighten our self-image.

This analysis of ***self-handicapping,*** proposed by Steven Berglas and Edward Jones (1978), has been confirmed in experiments. For example, might you act as their Duke University students did in an experiment that was said to concern "drugs and intellectual performance"? Imagine yourself guessing answers to some horribly difficult

"Humility is often but a trick whereby pride abases itself only to exalt itself later."
La Rochefoucauld, Maxims

Self-handicapping:
Protecting one's self-image by creating a handy excuse for failure.

"Congratulations! I understand you're everybody's favorite."

By praising our competitors, we soften the blow of possible defeat and glorify the victories we may achieve.

aptitude questions and then being told, "Yours was one of the best scores seen to date!" Feeling incredibly lucky, you are then offered a choice between two drugs before answering more of these items. One drug is said to aid intellectual performance and the other to inhibit it. Which drug do you want? Most of their students wanted the drug that would supposedly disrupt their thinking, thus providing a handy excuse for their anticipated poorer performance.

Researchers have documented other ways in which people self-handicap. Fearing failure, people have been observed to minimize their preparing for important individual athletic events (Rhodewalt et al., 1984); not to try as hard as they could during a tough, ego-involving task (Hormuth, 1986; Pyszczynski & Greenberg, 1983); and to perform poorly at the beginning of a task in order not to create unreachable expectations (Baumgardner & Brownlee, 1987). After losing to some younger rivals, tennis great Martina Navritalova confessed that she was "afraid to play my best. . . . I was scared to find out if they could beat me when I'm playing my best because if they can, then I am finished" (Frankel & Snyder, 1987).

"With no attempt there can be no failure; with no failure no humiliation."
William James,
Principles of Psychology, *1890*

Why the Self-Serving Bias?

The self-serving bias has been explained in three ways. These parallel the three explanations considered in Chapter 2 for the effect of actions on attitudes.

Self-Presentation

Self-presentation theory, as you may recall, assumes that we like to present a good image both to an external audience (other people) and to an internal audience (ourselves). And that helps us understand why people will self-handicap when failure might make them look bad (Arkin & Baumgardner, 1985). It also explains why people express more modesty when their self-flattery is vulnerable to being debunked or when experts will be scrutinizing their self-evaluations (Arkin et al., 1980; Riess et al., 1981; Weary et al., 1982). Professor Smith will likely express less confidence in the significance of her work when presenting it to professional colleagues than when presenting it to students.

"The presented self is (usually) too good to be true [yet] is often genuinely believed."
Anthony Greenwald & Steven Breckler (1985)

Presenting oneself in ways that create a good impression is a very delicate matter. People want to be seen as able, but also as modest and honest (Carlston & Shovar, 1983). Because modesty generally creates a good impression (Forsyth et al., 1981; Schlenker & Leary, 1982), people often display *less* self-esteem than they privately feel (Miller & Schlenker, 1985). But there are some situations (for example, when you really have done extremely well) where false disclaimers ("I did well, but it's no big deal") may come across as boastful, and other situations (for example, on a job interview) where you may pay a price for too much modesty. Thus to consistently make a good impression—as modest yet competent—requires social skill. The tendency to self-present modesty may be especially great in cultures such as China's that value self-restraint (Wu & Tseng, 1985), but the self-serving bias is hardly restricted to North America. Self-serving perceptions have been noted with Dutch high school and university students, Belgian basketball players, Indian Hindus, Japanese drivers, Australian students and workers, Chinese students, and French people of all ages (de Vries & van Knippenberg, 1987; Liebrand & others, 1986; Lefebvre, 1979; Murphy-Berman & Sharma, 1986; Hagiwara, 1983; Feather, 1983; Ruzzene & Noller, 1986; Chan, 1987; and Codol, 1976, respectively).

Information-Processing

Why do people across the world perceive (if not always present) themselves in self-enhancing ways? One explanation is a variation on what Chapter 2 called self-perception theory; it sees the self-serving bias as springing not from any deep emotional need to enhance oneself, but simply as a by-product of the way we process and remember information about ourselves.

Recall the study by Michael Ross and Fiore Sicoly (1979) in which married people gave themselves more credit for household work than their spouses. Might this not be due, as Ross and Sicoly believe, to the greater ease with which we recall things we have actively done, compared with what we've not done or what we've observed others doing? I can easily picture myself picking up the laundry, but I have difficulty picturing myself absentmindedly overlooking it.

Self-Justification

But are the biased perceptions simply a perceptual error, an unemotional bent in how we process information? Or are there also self-serving *motives* involved? A third view—that we are motivated to protect and enhance our self-esteem—is akin to dissonance theory, which assumes a similar self-protective motive. As one theorist put it, "Dissonance-reducing behavior is ego-defensive behavior; by reducing dissonance, we maintain a positive image of ourselves—an image that depicts us as good, or smart, or worthwhile" (Aronson, 1984, p. 124).

Experiments of late confirm that emotions do indeed color our social thinking. A motivational engine powers our cognitive machinery. The feelings we have after success and failure motivate self-serving explanations, especially if we are ego-involved (Burger, 1986; Pyszczynski & Greenberg, 1987; Steele, 1988). We are not just cool information-processing machines.

For example, Abraham Tesser (1988) at the University of Georgia reports that a "self-esteem maintenance" motive predicts a variety of interesting findings, even friction among brothers and sisters. Do you have a sibling of the same sex who is close to you in age? If so, people probably compared the two of you as you grew up. Tesser presumes that if one of you is perceived as more capable than the other, the less able

Among sibling relationships, the threat to self-esteem is greatest for an older child with a highly capable younger brother or sister.

one will likely be motivated to act in ways that maintain his or her self-esteem. (Tesser thinks the threat to self-esteem is greatest for an older child with a highly capable younger sibling.) Tesser's data fit his theory of self-esteem maintenance. For example, a man with a brother who is different in level of ability typically recalls not getting along well with him; a man with a brother of similar ability is more likely to recall very little friction.

The self-presentation, information-processing, and self-justification views can stretch to cover most findings, which makes it hard to declare any one of the theories as victorious (Tetlock & Manstead, 1985). Likely, all three processes are at work, perhaps at different stages. Theorist Craig Anderson (1988) believes that self-justifying motives color what information we ponder—if we get a bad exam grade, well, how fair was the exam anyway?—but that we then dispassionately process information deemed to matter.

Reflections on Self-Serving Bias

No doubt many readers are finding all this either depressing or contrary to their own occasional feelings of inadequacy. To be sure, those of us who exhibit self-serving bias— and apparently that includes most of us—may still feel inferior to certain specific individuals, especially when we compare ourselves to someone who is a step or two higher on the ladder of success, attractiveness, or whatever.

"Narcissism, like selfishness, is an overcompensation for the basic lack of self-love."
Erich Fromm, Escape from Freedom

And not everyone has a self-serving bias. Some people *do* suffer from unreasonably low self-esteem. Are such people hungering for esteem and therefore more likely than people with high self-esteem to exhibit the self-serving bias? Is the self-serving bias just a boastful cover used by those plagued with low self-esteem? This is what some theorists, such as Erich Fromm, have proposed (Shrauger, 1975). And it's true: When we are really feeling good about ourselves, we seem to be less defensive (Epstein & Feist, 1988). In one experiment, those whose ego had recently been wounded were indeed more prone to self-serving attributions of success or failure than were those whose ego had recently received a boost (McCarrey et al., 1982). On the other hand, those who score highest on self-esteem tests (who say nice things about themselves) also say nice things about themselves when explaining their successes and failures (Ickes & Layden, 1978; Levine & Uleman, 1979; Rosenfeld, 1979), when describing their own traits (Roth et al., 1986), when evaluating their group (Brown et al., 1988), and when comparing themselves to others (Brown, 1986). Thus, in questionnaire studies, high self-esteem and self-serving bias go hand in hand.

In fact, making excuses—shifting attributions for bad events to something external to our sense of self (usually without awareness of doing so)—serves to support self-esteem, protect against anxiety and depression, and sustain health and ambition (Snyder & Higgins, 1988). As we will see in Chapter 5, although most people excuse their failures on laboratory tasks, or perceive themselves as being more in control than they are, depressed people are more accurate in their self-appraisals. Sadder but wiser.

And consider: Thanks to our reluctance to share negative impressions, most of us have difficulty gauging how strangers and casual acquaintances are really perceiving us (DePaulo et al., 1987; Kenny & Albright, 1987). Depressed people are less prone to illusions; they generally see themselves *as* other people see them (Lewinsohn et al., 1980). This prompts the unsettling thought that Pascal may have been right: "I lay it down as a fact that, if all men knew what others say of them, there would not be four friends in the world." And that truly is a depressing thought.

"No one speaks of us in our presence as in our absence."
Pascal, Pensees, 1670

Self-serving perceptions are not lies; they are self-deceptions, In fact, as the new research on depression suggests, there may be some practical wisdom in such pride: Self-deceptions may be adaptive and have survival value. Cheaters, for example, may give a more convincing display of honesty if they believe in their honesty. Belief in our superiority can also motivate us to achieve and can sustain our sense of hope in difficult times.

The self-serving bias is not always adaptive, however. Pride does indeed often go before a fall. People who blame others for their social difficulties are often less happy than people who can acknowledge their mistakes (Newman & Langer, 1981; Peterson et al., 1981; C. A. Anderson et al., 1982). Research by Barry Schlenker (1976; Schlenker & Miller, 1977a, 1977b) at the University of Florida has also shown how self-serving perceptions can poison a group. In nine different experiments Schlenker had people work together on some task. He then gave them false information that suggested their group had done either well or poorly. In every one of these studies the members of successful groups claimed more responsibility for their group's performance than did members of groups that supposedly failed at the task. Likewise, most presented themselves as contributing more than the others in their group when the group did well; few said they contributed less.

"Victory finds a hundred fathers but defeat is an orphan."
Count Galeazzo Ciano,
The Ciano Diaries

Such self-deception can lead individual group members to expect greater-than-average rewards when their organization does well, and less-than-average blame when it does not. If most individuals in a group believe they are underpaid and underappreciated, relative to their better-than-average contributions, disharmony and envy will likely rear their smug heads. College presidents and academic deans will readily recognize the phenomenon. Most college faculty members—94 percent in one survey at the University of Nebraska (Cross, 1977), 90 percent in a survey of the faculties of twenty-four institutions (Blackburn et al., 1980)—rate themselves as superior to their average colleague. It is therefore inevitable that when merit salary raises are announced and half receive an average raise or less, many will feel an injustice has been done them.

Biased self-assessments can also distort managerial judgment. When groups are comparable, people tend to consider their own group superior (Codol, 1976; D. M. Taylor & Doria, 1981; Zander, 1969). Thus, most corporation presidents predict more growth for their own firms than for their competition (Larwood & Whittaker, 1977). Similarly, production managers often overpredict their production (Kidd & Morgan, 1969). As Laurie Larwood (1977) noted, such overoptimism can produce disastrous consequences. If those who deal in the stock market or in real estate perceive their business intuition to be superior to their competitors, they may be in for some severe disappointments. Even the capitalist economist Adam Smith, normally a defender of people's economic rationality, foresaw that people overestimate their chances of gain, owing to "an absurd presumption in their own good fortune," which arises from "the overweening conceit which the greater part of men have of their own abilities" (Spiegel, 1971, p. 243).

Self-serving pride in group settings can become especially dangerous.

"Then we're in agreement. There's nothing rotten here in Denmark. Something is rotten everywhere else."

"Hubris is back in town."
W. C. Fields

The observation that people see and present themselves with a favorable bias is hardly new. In fact, research on the self-serving bias confirms some ancient wisdom about human nature. The tragic flaw portrayed in Greek drama was *hubris*, or pride. Like the subjects of our experiments, the Greek tragic figures were not self-consciously evil; they merely thought too highly of themselves. In literature, the pitfalls of pride are portrayed again and again. And in religion, pride has long been considered first among the "seven deadly sins."

If pride is akin to the self-serving bias, then what is humility? Is it self-contempt? Or can we be self-affirming and self-accepting without a self-serving bias? To paraphrase the English scholar-writer C. S. Lewis, humility surely is not handsome people trying to believe they are ugly and clever people trying to believe they are fools. False modesty can actually lead to an ironic pride in one's better-than-average humility. (Perhaps some readers have by now congratulated themselves on being unusually free of the self-serving bias.) True humility is more like self-forgetfulness than false modesty. It leaves people free to rejoice in their special talents and, with the same honesty, to recognize those of others.

SELF-EFFICACY

We have seen two potent biases recently uncovered by social psychologists: a tendency to ignore powerful situational forces when explaining others' behavior (the fundamental attribution error) and a tendency to perceive and present ourselves favorably (the self-serving bias). The first bias can dispose us to misunderstand others' problems (for example, by assuming that unemployed people are necessarily lazy or incompetent), and self-righteous pride can fuel conflict among people and nations who all see themselves as more moral and deserving than others.

"Half the truth is often a great lie."
Benjamin Franklin, Poor Richard

But is there not a danger if we stop here and say no more? Might we begin excusing people for misdeeds? Or, if we take an ax to our inflated selves, mightn't we lose what self-confidence we formerly had? As Pascal taught 300 years ago, no single truth is ever sufficient, because the world is not simple.

Studies of the fundamental attribution error and self-serving bias reveal some deep truths about human nature. But there is an important complement to these truths. High self-esteem—a sense of one's self-worth—is adaptive. Compared to those with

---

TO FEEL BETTER: INCREASE SUCCESS OR DECREASE PRETENSIONS

In his pioneering 1890 text, *Principles of Psychology*, the philosopher-psychologist William James offered a formula for self-esteem:

Our self-feeling in this world depends entirely on . . . a fraction of which our pretensions are the denominator and the numerator our success: Thus,

$$\text{Self-esteem} = \frac{\text{Success}}{\text{Pretensions}}.$$

Such a fraction may be increased as well by diminishing the denominator as by increasing the numerator. To give

up pretensions is as blessed a relief as to get them gratified; and where disappointment is incessant and the struggle unending, this is what men will always do. The history of evangelical theology, with its conviction of sin, its self-despair, and its abandonment of salvation by works, is the deepest of possible examples, but we meet others in every walk of life. . . . How pleasant is the day when we give up striving to be young—or slender! Thank God! we say, those illusions are gone. Everything added to the Self is a burden as well as a pride.

BEHIND THE SCENES

Our research on self-efficacy was an unanticipated result of our discovery that people who overcame phobias through mastery experiences, say by learning to deal with snakes, became more confident and venturesome in other areas of their life. The specific treatment, it seemed, had strengthened people's general sense of efficacy in managing events in their lives. From this realization came our further studies of how perceived self-efficacy affects various behaviors, from stress reactions to achievement strivings to career pursuits.

Albert Bandura,
Stanford University

Self-efficacy:
A sense that one is competent and effective. Distinguished from self-esteem, a sense of one's self-worth. A bombardier might feel high self-efficacy and low self-esteem.

low self-esteem, people with high self-esteem are happier, less neurotic, less troubled by ulcers and insomnia, less prone to drug and alcohol addictions (Brockner & Hulton, 1978). In experiments, people whose self-esteem is temporarily bruised—say, by being told they did miserably on an intelligence test—are more likely to disparage others. More generally, people who are negative about themselves tend also to be negative about others (Wills, 1981). Mockery says as much about the mocker as the one mocked.

Additional research on topics such as "locus of control" (see box), "learned helplessness," and "intrinsic motivation" confirms the benefits of seeing oneself as competent and effective. Albert Bandura (1986) merges much of this research into a concept of ***self-efficacy,*** a scholarly version of the wisdom behind the old "power of positive thinking." An optimistic yet realistic belief in our own possibilities pays dividends. People with strong feelings of self-efficacy are more persistent, less anxious and depressed, and more academically successful (Maddux & Stanley, 1986; Scheier & Carver, 1988).

LOCUS OF CONTROL

Which do you more strongly believe?

In the long run people get the respect they deserve in this world.	or	Unfortunately, an individual's worth often passes unrecognized no matter how hard he tries.
What happens to me is my own doing.	or	Sometimes I feel that I don't have enough control over the direction my life is taking.
The average person can have an influence in government decisions.	or	This world is run by the few people in power, and there is not much the little guy can do about it.

Do your answers to such questions (from Rotter, 1973) indicate that you believe you control your own destiny ("internal locus of control") or that chance or outside forces determine your fate ("external locus of control")? Compared to people with external locus of control, those who see themselves as internally controlled are more likely to do well in school, successfully stop smoking, wear seat belts, practice birth control, deal with marital problems directly, make lots of money, and delay instant gratification in order to achieve long-term goals (e.g., Findlay & Cooper, 1983; Lefcourt, 1982; Miller et al., 1986).

How competent and effective we feel depends on how we explain negative events. Perhaps you have known students who blame poor exam grades on things beyond their control—their feelings of stupidity or their "poor" teachers, texts, or tests. If such students are coached to adopt a more hopeful attitude—to believe that effort, good study habits, and self-discipline can make a difference—their grades tend to go up (Noel et al., 1987; Peterson & Barrett, 1987).

Successful people are more likely to see setbacks as a fluke or to think "I need a new approach." For example, new life insurance sales representatives who view failures as uncontrollable ("It's impossible for me, and there's nothing I can do to change things") sell fewer policies and are twice as likely to quit during their first year as their more optimistic colleagues (Seligman & Schulman, 1986). As we noted earlier, one can also be naïvely optimistic—like the Israeli soccer fans who before big games feel confident that *their* team is going to win, no matter which team they are rooting for (Babad, 1987). "It is therefore wise," remarked philosopher Bertrand Russell (1930) "to be not unduly conceited, though also not too modest to be enterprising" (p. 113).

Learned Helplessness versus Self-Determination

The benefits of a sense of personal efficacy have also been demonstrated in animal research. Dogs which learn a sense of helplessness (by being taught they cannot escape shocks) will later fail to take initiative in another situation when they *could* escape the punishment. By contrast, animals that are taught personal control (by allowing them to escape their first shocks successfully) adapt easily to a new situation. Researcher Martin Seligman (1975, 1977) notes similarities in human situations, such as when depressed or oppressed people become passive because they believe that their efforts have no effect. Helpless dogs and depressed people both suffer paralysis of the will, passive resignation, even motionless apathy.

Here is a clue to how institutions—whether malevolent, like concentration camps, or benevolent, like hospitals—can unwittingly dehumanize people. In hospitals, "good patients" don't ring bells, don't ask questions, don't try to control what's happening (S. E. Taylor, 1979). Such passivity may be good for hospital efficiency, but it is bad for patients. Feelings of efficacy, of an ability to control one's life, have been linked to health and survival. Losing control over what you do and what others do to you can make unpleasant events profoundly stressful (Pomperleau & Rodin, 1986). Several diseases are associated with feelings of helplessness and diminished choice. So is the rapidity of decline and death in concentration camps and nursing homes. Hospital patients who are induced to believe in their ability to control stress require fewer pain relievers and sedatives and are seen by nurses as exhibiting less anxiety (Langer et al., 1975).

In a related experiment, Langer and Judith Rodin (1976; Rodin & Langer, 1977) treated elderly patients in a high-rated Connecticut nursing home in one of two ways. With one patient group the benevolent care givers stressed "our responsibility to make this a home you can be proud of and happy in." These patients were treated as passive recipients of the normal well-intentioned, sympathetic care. Three weeks later, most were rated by themselves, by interviewers, and by nurses as further debilitated. Their experience must have been similar to that of James McKay (1980), an eighty-seven-year-old psychologist:

> I became a nonperson last summer. My wife had an arthritic knee which put her in a walker, and I chose that moment to break my leg. We went to a nursing home. It was all nursing

Feelings of self-efficacy and autonomy influence both our physical and psychological well-being.

and no home. The doctor and the head nurse made all decisions; we were merely animate objects. Thank heavens it was only two weeks. . . . The top man of the nursing home was very well trained and very compassionate; I considered it the best home in town. But we were nonpersons from the time we entered until we left.

Langer and Rodin's other treatment promoted self-efficacy. It stressed the patients' opportunities for choice, their possibilities for influencing nursing-home policy, and their responsibility "to make of your life whatever you want." These patients were also given small decisions to make and responsibilities to fulfill. Over the ensuing three weeks, 93 percent of this group showed improved alertness, activity, and happiness.

These research findings suggest that systems of governing or managing people which maximize their sense of self-efficacy will be most conducive to health and happiness (Deci & Ryan, 1987). When prisoners are given some control over their environments—by being able to move chairs, control TV sets, and switch the lights—they experience less stress, exhibit fewer health problems, and commit less vandalism (Ruback et al., 1986; Wener et al., 1987). When workers are given leeway in carrying out tasks and allowed to participate in decision making, their morale improves (Miller & Monge, 1986). If institutionalized residents are allowed choice in such matters as what to eat for breakfast, when to go to a movie, whether to sleep late or get up early, they may live longer and certainly will be happier than if these decisions are made for them.

Collective Efficacy

Although it is commonly thought that hopelessness breeds militant social action, the truth is that it more often breeds apathy. Protesting members of aggrieved groups generally have more self-pride and a stronger belief in their ability to influence events than do those who don't protest (Caplan, 1970; Forward & Williams, 1970; Lipset, 1966). In many countries, university students, not the most severely disadvantaged members of the society, spearhead political activism. Bandura (1982) writes:

> People who have a sense of collective efficacy will mobilize their efforts and resources to cope with external obstacles to the changes they seek. But those convinced of their inefficacy

"If my mind can conceive it and my heart can believe it, I know I can achieve it. Down with dope! Up with hope! I am somebody!"
Jesse Jackson, Civil Rights March on Washington, 1983

will cease trying even though changes are attainable through concerted effort. . . . As a society, we enjoy the benefits left by those before us who collectively resisted inhumanities and worked for social reforms that permit a better life. Our own collective efficacy will, in turn, shape how future generations will live their lives.

"Argue for your limitations, and sure enough they're yours."
Richard Bach, Illusions: Adventures of a Reluctant Messiah

Although this psychological research and comment on self-efficacy is new, the emphasis on taking charge of one's life and realizing one's potential dates way back. The you-can-do-it theme of Horatio Alger's rags-to-riches books is an enduring American idea, one expressed in Norman Vincent Peale's 1950s best-seller, *The Power of Positive Thinking* ("If you think in positive terms you will get positive results. That is the simple fact."), and more recently in many popular books and courses which urge people to succeed through positive mental attitudes. Bandura believes that self-efficacy grows not so much by self-persuasion ("I think I can, I think I can") as by undertaking challenging yet realistic tasks and succeeding. For example, students who experience academic success develop higher appraisals of their academic ability, which in turn often stimulates them to work harder and achieve more success (Felson, 1984). Nevertheless, insofar as research on self-efficacy gives us greater confidence in traditional virtues such as perseverance and hope, it performs no small service.

"Poised somewhere between sinful vanity and self-destructive submissiveness is a golden mean of self-esteem appropriate to the human condition."
Sanford Lyman, The Seven Deadly Sins: Society and Evil

Still, let us remember the point at which we began our consideration of self-efficacy: Any truth, separated from its complementary truth, is but a half-truth. The truth embodied in the concept of self-efficacy may encourage us not to resign ourselves to bad situations, to persist despite initial failures, to exert effort without being overly distracted by self-doubts. But lest the pendulum swing too far toward *this* truth, we had best remember that it, too, is not the whole story. If positive thinking can accom-

Confidence and feelings of self-efficacy are rooted in our successes.

"This gives my confidence a real boost."

plish anything, then, by implication, if we are unhappily married, poor, or depressed we have but ourselves to blame. Shame! If only we had tried harder, been more disciplined, less stupid. Failing to appreciate that people's difficulties sometimes reflect the oppressive power of social situations can tempt us to blame them for their difficulties, or even to blame ourselves too harshly for our own.

SUMMING UP

ATTRIBUTING CAUSALITY: TO THE PERSON OR THE SITUATION?

Attribution researchers study how we explain people's behavior. For example when will we attribute someone's behavior to internal causes, such as the person's disposition, and when to the situation? By and large we make quite reasonable attributions. However, we are consistently prone to two errors. When explaining people's behavior it is difficult to resist the *fundamental attribution error*. This is a tendency to attribute their behavior so much to their inner traits and attitudes that we discount situational constraints, even when these are obvious. We make this attribution error partly because when we watch someone act, that *person* is the focus of our attention. In general, we attribute causation to whatever our attention is focused upon. When *we* act, our attention is usually on what we are reacting to. Thus we are more sensitive to the situational influences upon ourselves.

PERCEIVING AND EXPLAINING OURSELVES

When perceiving ourselves, we are prone to another error: the *self-serving bias*. This is a tendency to blame the situation for our failures while taking credit for our successes, to see ourselves as generally "better than average," and in at least a dozen ways to protect and enhance our self-image. Even self-disparaging and self-handicapping behaviors can sometimes be understood as strategies for protecting or enhancing one's self-image. Three explanations have been offered for the self-serving bias. One is that we seek to *present* a positive image. The other two suggest that we genuinely perceive ourselves in self-enhancing ways, either as a by-product of how we *process information* (if good things more often happen to us than bad things, it is logical to blame unusual circumstances for the occasional bad outcomes) or as a result of a self-esteem *motivation*. The evidence suggests that we are indeed motivated to see ourselves favorably.

Research on these tendencies to ignore powerful situational forces when explaining others' behavior and to adopt an inflated view of ourselves is complemented by other research on the benefits of believing in our own potential and encouraging others to believe in theirs. People with a strong sense of *self-efficacy* cope better and achieve more than do people who lack a sense of their own competence and effectiveness.

FOR FURTHER READING

Bandura, A. (1986). *Social foundations of thought and action: A social-cognitive theory.* Englewood Cliffs, NJ: Prentice-Hall. Describes research on self-efficacy in the context of Bandura's theory of personality and social behavior.

Harvey, J. H., & Weary, G. (1981). *Perspectives on attributional processes.* Dubuque, IA: Brown. A clear introduction to theories of attribution and their applications in everyday life.

Heider, F. (1958/1980). *The psychology of interpersonal relations.* New York: Wiley. The influential, classic treatment of attribution—how people explain their own and others' behavior.

Snyder, C. R., Higgins, R. L., & Stucky, R. J. (1983). *Excuses: Masquerades in search of grace.* New York: Wiley. Shows how we use attributions and rationalizations to protect self-esteem, save face, and explain our behavior.

CHAPTER

4

SOCIAL BELIEFS

───────

here on the continuum between god-like apprehension and heads of straw are we? How deserving are we of our name, *homo sapiens*—wise humans?

The centuries-old debate over the dimensions of human wisdom and foolishness persists in an ongoing scientific controversy over human rationality. Those impressed by our cognitive powers point to the unimaginable complexity of our brains, which enable us to outstrip the smartest computers in recognizing patterns, handling language, and processing abstract information. Those impressed by our capacity for error point to the ways in which we form and sustain false beliefs about the social world (among which are three examples considered in earlier chapters—the I-knew-it-all-along phenomenon, the fundamental attribution error, and the self-serving bias).

Through much of its history, psychology has explored and emphasized the mind's facility at fabricating experiences—dreams, hallucinations, delusions, perceptual illusions. Sigmund Freud was fascinated by our capacity for creating a web of illusion. "Freud unmasked our hypocrisies, our phony ideas, our rationalization, our vanities," noted Calvin Hall (1978), "and not all the efforts of humanists and rationalists will restore the mask." More recently, brain researchers have discovered that patients whose two brain hemispheres have been surgically separated will instantly fabricate— and believe—explanations of puzzling behaviors (Gazzaniga, 1985). If the patient gets up and takes a few steps after the experimenter flashes the instruction "walk" to the patient's nonverbal right hemisphere, the verbal left hemisphere will instantly invent a plausible explanation ("I felt like getting a drink").

The most striking indications of illusory thinking come, however, not from the speculations of Freud or experiments on split-brain subjects, but from the vast new literature on how we take in, store, and retrieve information. Social psychologists of late have emphasized the points at which our information processing, though generally adaptive, can lead us astray. Just as perception researchers study visual illusions—for what they reveal about our normal perceptual mechanisms—so social psychologists study distortions in social thinking for what they reveal about normal information processing. They aim to give us a map of everyday social thinking, with the hazards clearly marked. As we examine some of these thinking hazards, bear in mind that demonstrations of how people create counterfeit beliefs hardly proves that all beliefs are counterfeit. Still, if you want to be wary of counterfeiting, it helps to know how it's done. So, continuing the discussion of Chapter 3, let's further explore how we naturally form ideas about ourselves and others, and where our information processing can go awry.

"People are good enough to get through life, poor enough to make predictable and consequential mistakes."
Baruch Fischhoff (1981)

WE OFTEN DO NOT KNOW WHY WE DO WHAT WE DO

"There is one thing, and only one in the whole universe which we know more about than we could learn from external observation," noted C. S. Lewis (1960, pp. 18–19). "That one thing is [ourselves]. We have, so to speak, inside information; we are in the know."

Indeed, some things we know best by intuition and personal experience. The *fallibility* of our self-knowledge is, however, considerably less self-evident; sometimes we *think* we are "in the know," but our inside information is demonstrably erroneous. This is the unavoidable conclusion of some fascinating recent research.

WE EASILY FORGET OUR PREVIOUS ATTITUDES

Five years ago, how did you feel about nuclear power? about South African apartheid? about your parents? If your attitudes have changed, are you aware of the extent of the change?

To answer such questions, experimenters have asked people whose attitudes have been altered to recall their preexperiment attitudes. The result is unnerving: People often insist that they have always felt much as they now feel. For example, Daryl Bem and Keith McConnell (1970) took a survey among Carnegie-Mellon University students. Buried in it was a question concerning student control over the university curriculum. A week later the students agreed to write an essay opposing student control. After doing so, their attitudes shifted toward greater opposition to student control. When asked to recall how they had answered the question a week previous, they "remem-

In the past five years, how much have your attitudes about the Soviet Union changed?

bered" holding the opinion that they *now* held and denied that the experiment had affected them.

After observing their Clark University students similarly denying their former attitudes, researchers D. R. Wixon and James Laird (1976) commented that "The speed, magnitude, and certainty" with which the students revised their own histories "was striking."

Cathy McFarland and Michael Ross (1985) have found that we even revise our recalled views of other people as our relationships with them change. They had university students evaluate their steady dating partners and then evaluate them again two months later. Students who were more in love than ever had some tendency to recall love at first sight, while those who had broken up were more likely to recall having recognized the partner as somewhat selfish and ill-tempered.

It's not that we are totally unaware of how we used to feel, just that when our memories are hazy we use our current feelings as a guide to how we used to feel. Parents of every generation bemoan the values of the next generation, partly because they misrecall their youthful values as closer to their current values.

WE READILY DENY REAL INFLUENCES UPON US

Why did you choose your college? Why did you lash out at your roommate? Why did you fall in love with your fiancé or spouse? Sometimes we know. Other times we don't actually know. Compelled to explain ourselves, we may therefore concoct a good but incorrect story.

Explaining Our Behavior

When asked why we have felt or acted as we have, we usually have ready answers. Yet, when the determinants are not obvious, our self-explanations often err. Factors that have big effects are sometimes reported as having little effect, and factors having little effect are sometimes perceived as having had a big effect.

Richard Nisbett and Stanley Schachter (1966) demonstrated this by asking Columbia University students to take a series of electric shocks of steadily increasing intensity. Beforehand, some of them were given a fake pill which, they were told, would produce feelings of heart palpitations, breathing irregularities, and butterflies in the stomach—the very symptoms that usually accompany being shocked. Nisbett and Schachter anticipated that the people would therefore attribute these symptoms of shock to the fake pill, rather than to the shock, and would thus be willing to tolerate more shock than people not given the pill. Indeed, the effect was enormous—people given the fake pill took four times as much shock. Afterwards, informed they had taken more shock than average, they were asked why. Not only did their answers make no reference to the pill, when pressed (and even after the experimenter explained the hypotheses of the experiment in detail) they denied any influence of the pill. They would usually say the pill likely did affect *others*, but not themselves; a typical reply was, "I didn't even think about the pill."

Other times people think they *have* been affected by something that has had no effect. For example, Nisbett and Timothy Wilson (1977) had some University of Michigan students evaluate a documentary film. While some of them watched, a power saw was run outside the room. Most people felt that this distracting noise affected their ratings. Actually, their ratings were indistinguishable from those of control subjects who viewed the film without distraction.

Even more thought-provoking are several studies that each asked people to record their mood every day for two or three months (Stone et al., 1985; Weiss & Brown, 1976; Wilson et al., 1982). The people also recorded factors that might affect their moods: the day of the week, the weather, the amount they slept, and so forth. At the end of each study, the people then judged how much each of the factors had affected their moods. Remarkably (given that their attention was being drawn to their daily moods) there was little relationship between their perceptions of how important a factor was and how well the factor actually predicted their mood. In fact, their estimates of how well the weather or the day of the week had predicted their mood were no better than estimates made by strangers. These findings raise a disconcerting question: How much insight do we have into what makes us happy or unhappy?

"There are three things extremely hard, Steel, a Diamond, and to know one's self."
Benjamin Franklin

Predicting Our Behavior

Finally, we often poorly predict our own future behavior. When asked whether they would comply with demands to deliver cruel electric shocks or would be hesitant to help a victim if several other people were present, people overwhelmingly deny their vulnerability to such influences. But as we will see, experiments have shown that many of us are vulnerable. Moreover, consider what Sidney Shrauger (1983) discovered when he had college students predict the likelihood of their experiencing dozens of different events during the ensuing two months (becoming romantically involved, being sick, and so forth): Their self-predictions were hardly more accurate than predictions based on the average person's experience. The surest thing we can say about your individual future is that it is hard for you to predict. The best advice for those who wish to predict their future behavior is to ponder their own past behavior in similar situations (Osberg & Shrauger, 1986).

The Wisdom and Delusions of Self-Analysis

To a striking extent, then, we often make false assertions about what we have felt in the past, what has influenced us, and what we will feel and do. Our intuitive "self-insights" are sometimes dead wrong. However, we must be careful not to overstate the matter. When the causes of behavior are conspicuous and the correct explanation fits our intuition, our self-perceptions can be accurate (Gavanski & Hoffman, 1987). For example, Peter Wright and Peter Rip (1981) found that California high school juniors *could* discern how their reactions to a college were influenced by such features as its size, tuition, and distance from home. It is when the causes of behavior are not obvious even to an observer that our self-explanations become more erroneous.

How little we actualize Thales' advice, "Know thyself," is reinforced by cognitive psychologists, who contend that we are unaware of much that goes on in our minds. Studies of perception and memory show that our awareness is mostly of the *results* of our thinking and not of the *process* of thinking. We have all experienced the results of our mind's unconscious workings—when we set an unconscious mental clock to record the passage of time and to awaken us at an appointed hour, or when we achieve a seemingly spontaneous creative insight after a problem has unconsciously "incubated." Similarly, creative scientists and artists often cannot report the thought process that produced their insights.

Social psychologist Timothy Wilson (1985) offers the bold idea that the mental processes that control our social behavior are distinct from the mental processes that are engaged when we consciously attempt to explain our behavior. Thus, to the extent that attitude reports are based on a rational self-analysis they may fail to reflect the underlying attitudes that actually guide our behavior. In nine experiments, Wilson and his co-workers (1989) found that people's expressed attitudes—toward things or toward other people—predicted their later behavior reasonably well, *unless* the people were asked before indicating their attitudes to analyze their feelings. For example, when dating couples filled out a scale indicating their happiness with the relationship, their expressed feelings were a reasonably good predictor of whether they were still dating several months later; but if before filling out the scale they first listed all the reasons they could think of why their relationship was good or bad, then their attitude reports were useless in predicting the future of the relationship! Apparently the process of dissecting the relationship drew people's attention to easily verbalized factors that actually were less important than other aspects of the relationship that were harder to verbalize. As Pascal discerned some 300 years ago, "The heart has its reasons which reason does not know."

Murray Millar and Abraham Tesser (1985, 1989) believe that Wilson overstates our self-ignorance. Their research suggests that, yes, drawing people's attention to *reasons* can diminish the usefulness of attitude reports in predicting behaviors that are driven by one's *feelings*. If instead of having people rationally analyze their romantic relationships Wilson had asked them to get more in touch with their feelings ("How do you feel when you are with and apart from your partner?") then maybe their subsequent attitude reports would have become *more* insightful. Other behavior domains—say choosing which school to attend based on considerations of cost, career advancement, and so forth—seem more cognitively driven. For these, an analysis of reasons rather than feelings may be most useful. So it seems that while the heart does have reasons of which the conscious mind is ignorant, sometimes the mind's own reasons are decisive.

To summarize, we easily forget our old attitudes and have difficulty identifying influences upon us. This research on the incompleteness of our self-knowledge offers at least two practical implications. The first is for psychological inquiry. The introspections of one's clients or research subjects may provide useful clues to their psychological processes, but these *self-reports are often untrustworthy*. People's errors in self-understanding place limits on the scientific usefulness of their subjective personal reports.

The second implication has ramifications for our everyday lives. The sincerity with which people report and interpret their experiences is no guarantee of the validity of these personal reports. Personal testimonies are powerfully persuasive, but they may also convey unwitting error. Perhaps keeping this potential for error in mind can help us to feel less intimidated by other people and to be less gullible.

OUR PRECONCEPTIONS CONTROL OUR INTERPRETATIONS AND MEMORIES

Experiments indicate that one of the most significant facts about our minds is the extent to which our preconceived notions guide the way we view, interpret, and remember the information that comes to us. Most of us do not need experiments to acknowledge that our existing beliefs affect how we interpret and recall events. Yet generally we fail to realize how great this effect is. Let's look at some recent experiments which suggest that the influence of our beliefs is indeed very great. Some of these experiments examine how *pre*judgments affect the way people perceive and interpret information they are then given. Other experiments plant a judgment in people's minds *after* they have been given information; these experiments study how after-the-fact ideas bias people's *recall*.

HOW WE PERCEIVE AND INTERPRET EVENTS

Evidence for the effects of our prejudgments and expectations is standard fare for introductory courses in psychology. Numerous demonstrations illustrate that what we see in a picture can be influenced by what we are led to expect. Recall the dalmatian dog in Chapter 1. Or consider this phrase:

A
BIRD
IN THE
THE HAND

Did you notice anything wrong with it? There is more to perception than meets the eye. This was tragically demonstrated when the crew of the *USS Vincennes* misjudged an Iranian airliner as an F-14, and then proceeded to misperceive radar information accordingly. In a Congressional hearing on the incident, social psychologist Richard Nisbett (1988) noted that "the effects of expectations on generating and sustaining mistaken hypotheses can be dramatic."

The same is true of social perception. As we noted in Chapter 1, the opposing fans in an aggressive athletic contest may each see the other side as the more villainous. Because social perceptions are very much in the eye of the beholder, even a simple stimulus may strike two people quite differently. Saying "Brian Mulroney is an average prime minister" may sound like a put-down to one of his ardent admirers and as positively biased to one who regards him with contempt.

An experiment by Robert Vallone, Lee Ross, and Mark Lepper (1985) reveals how powerfully our preconceptions can influence our social perceptions. They showed pro-Israeli and pro-Arab university students six network news segments describing the 1982 Beirut Massacre—the killing of civilian refugees at two camps in Lebanon. As Figure 4-1 illustrates, each group perceived the networks as hostile to its side and likely to sway nonpartisans toward the opposing view. The phenomenon is commonplace: Presidential candidates and their supporters view the news media as unsympathetic to their cause; sports fans perceive the referees as partial to the other side; people in conflict (married couples, labor and management, opposing racial groups) see impartial mediators as biased against them.

"As I am, so I see."
Ralph Waldo Emerson, Essays

Our shared assumptions about the world can even make contradictory evidence seem supportive. For example, Ross and Lepper assisted Charles Lord (1979) in showing two purported new research studies to Stanford University students. Half the students favored capital punishment and half opposed it. One study confirmed and the other disconfirmed the students' beliefs about the crime-deterring effectiveness of the death penalty. Both the proponents and opponents of capital punishment readily accepted the evidence that confirmed their belief but were sharply critical of the discon-

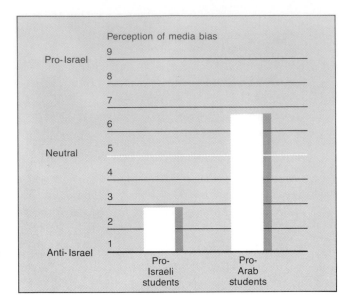

FIGURE 4-1
Pro-Israeli and pro-Arab students who viewed network news descriptions of the "Beirut Massacre" each viewed the coverage as biased against their point of view. (Data from Vallone, Ross, & Lepper, 1985.)

firming evidence. Showing the two sides an *identical* body of mixed evidence had therefore not narrowed their disagreement, but *increased* it. Each side had perceived the evidence as supporting its belief and now believed even more strongly.

Is this why, in politics, religion, and science, ambiguous evidence often fuels rather than extinguishes the fires of debate among people who hold strongly opposing opinions? The American presidential debates have served mostly to reinforce people's predebate opinions; by nearly a 10 to 1 margin, those who already favored one candidate or the other in the 1960, 1976, and 1980 debates perceived their candidate as having won (Kinder & Sears, 1985).

Scientists, too, are swayed by their own preconceptions. Recall from Chapter 1 the extent to which beliefs and values can penetrate science. Philosophers of science have therefore been reminding us that our observations of reality are always "theory-laden." There is an objective reality out there, but we are always viewing it through the spectacles of our beliefs, attitudes, and values. This is one reason our beliefs are so important; they shape our interpretation of everything else. Often, justifiably so. Your preconceptions of the editorial standards of certain tabloid newspapers probably justify your disregarding headlines proclaiming that "Computers talk with the dead." Such preconceptions are useful: The occasional biases they create are the price we pay for their helping us to efficiently filter and organize vast amounts of information.

That presuppositions affect both scientific and everyday thinking is now an accepted fact. Less well known are experiments that manipulate people's preconceptions, with astonishing effects upon how they interpret and recall what they observe. Myron Rothbart and Pamela Birrell (1977) had University of Oregon students assess the facial expression of "Kurt Walden," pictured here. Students told he was a racist leader in the Nazi Gestapo who was responsible for barbaric medical experiments on concentration camp inmates judged his expression in this picture to be cruel and frowning. (Can you see that barely suppressed sneer?) Those told he was a leader in the anti-Nazi underground movement whose courage saved thousands of Jewish lives judged the facial expression as more warm and kindly. (On second thought, look at those caring eyes and that almost smiling mouth.)

"Once you have a belief, it influences how you perceive all other relevant information. Once you see a country as hostile, you are likely to interpret ambiguous actions on their part as signifying their hostility."
Political scientist Robert Jervis (1985)

"The error of our eye directs our mind: What error leads must err."
Shakespeare, Troilus and Cressida

Kurt Walden: Would you judge this man to be cruel or kindly?

West German researcher Harald Wallbott (1988) has similarly controlled people's perceptions of emotion by manipulating the setting in which a face is observed. He notes that filmmakers know this as the "Kulechov effect," named after a Soviet film director who would skillfully guide viewers' inferences by manipulating their assumptions. Kulechov demonstrated the phenomenon by creating three short films that presented an actor's neutral expression after viewers had first been shown a dead woman, a dish of soup, or a girl playing—making the actor seem sad, thoughtful, or happy.

Belief Perseverance

To give you a feeling for the next set of experiments, can you remember the relationship reported near the end of Chapter 2 between fire hydrants and crime rate? Did you attempt to explain the relationship? (The point of the example was that people who actively explain something are the most likely to remember it.) Now let me clear the record by confessing that the investigators in that study actually had no information about the relationship between the number of fire hydrants in an area and its crime rate; they just made up the relationship. What do you suppose it really is? As the number of fire hydrants in an area goes up, does the crime rate tend to go up or down?

Experiments by Lee Ross, Craig Anderson, and their colleagues have similarly planted a falsehood in people's minds and then tried to discredit it. If a false idea biases people's processing of information, then, if the idea is later discredited, will its effects upon their thinking be erased? Imagine a baby sitter who surmises, during an evening with an infant who cries constantly, that bottle feeding produces colicky babies: "Come to think of it, cow's milk obviously is better suited to calves than babies." When, afterwards, it is discovered that the infant was suffering a high fever, will the sitter nevertheless persist in now presuming that bottle feeding causes colic (Ross & Anderson, 1982)?

The experiments reveal that it is indeed surprisingly difficult to demolish a falsehood, once the person has conjured up a rationale for it. In each experiment, first a belief was established, either by proclaiming it true (as with our fire hydrants and crime example) or else by inducing the person to conclude its truth after inspecting two sample cases. Then, people were asked to explain *why* it is true. Finally, the initial information was totally discredited—the person was told the truth, that the information was manufactured for the experiment and that half the people in the experiment were given opposing theory or data. Nevertheless, the new belief amazingly survived the discrediting about 75 percent intact, presumably because the people still retained their invented explanations for the belief. This phenomenon, named **belief perseverance,** shows that beliefs can take on a life of their own, by surviving the discrediting of the evidence that gave them birth.

For instance, Anderson, Lepper, and Ross (1980) asked people to decide whether people who take risks make good or bad firefighters. They were given only two concrete cases to inspect; one group was shown a risk-prone person being a successful firefighter and a cautious person an unsuccessful one. The other group was shown cases suggesting the opposite conclusion. After forming their theory that risk-prone people make better or worse firefighters, the people wrote an explanation for it—for example, that risk-prone people are brave, or that cautious people are careful. Once formed, each explanation could exist independently of the information that initially created the belief. Thus when that information was discredited, the people still held their self-generated explanations and therefore continued to believe that risk-prone people really *do* make better or worse firefighters.

These experiments also indicate that the more closely we examine our theories and explain how they *might* be true, the more closed we become to discrediting information. Once we consider why an accused person might be guilty, why someone of whom we have a negative first impression acts that way, or why a favored stock might rise in value, our explanations may survive challenging evidence (Jelalian & Miller, 1984).

When beliefs about ourselves survive discrediting, the consequence may be self-defeating behavior. Failure at the hands of an incompetent teacher can lead people to see themselves as incompetent, long after the circumstances that caused their failure are explained and removed (Lepper et al., 1986). But belief perseverance can work the other way: Consider those told by the "Famous Writers" correspondence school that they have great potential. After discovering that others answering the same ad received identical letters, might they nevertheless salvage reasons that the evaluation is correct in *their* case and embark on an ill-fated writing career (Slusher & Anderson, 1989)?

In summary, the evidence is compelling: Our beliefs and expectations have a powerful effect upon how we notice and interpret events. On the whole, we surely benefit from our preconceptions, just as scientists benefit from creating theories that guide them in noticing and interpreting events. But the benefits sometimes entail a cost; we become prisoners of our own thought patterns. Thus the canals that were so often "seen" on Mars turned out to indeed be the product of intelligent life—an intelligence on earth's side of the telescope.

Belief perseverance:
Clinging to one's initial conceptions, as when the foundation for one's belief is discredited but an explanation of why the belief might be true survives.

"No one denies that new evidence can change people's beliefs. Children do eventually renounce their belief in Santa Claus. Our contention is simply that such changes generally occur slowly, and that more compelling evidence is often required to alter a belief than to create it."
Less Ross & Mark Lepper (1980)

"Two-thirds of what we see is behind our eyes."
Chinese proverb

Do people who take risks make good or bad firefighters?

Is there any way we can restrain the belief perseverance phenomenon? Fortunately, a simple remedy exists: *explain the opposite*. Charles Lord, Mark Lepper, and Elizabeth Preston (1984) repeated the capital punishment study described earlier and added two variations. First, they asked some of their subjects to be *"as objective and unbiased* as possible" in evaluating the evidence. It was to no avail; those for and those against capital punishment who received this plea were just as biased in their evaluation of the evidence as those who did not. In the other variation the researchers asked a third group of subjects to consider the opposite point of view—to ask themselves "whether you would have made the same high or low evaluations had exactly the same study produced results on the *other* side of the issue." Having considered the possibility of opposite findings, these people were much less likely to be biased in their evaluations of the evidence for and against their views. Likewise, in his experiments Craig Anderson (1982; Anderson & Sechler, 1986) has consistently found that explaining why an opposite theory might be true—why a cautious rather than a risk-taking person might be a better firefighter—reduces or eliminates belief perseverance. So, to counteract belief perseverance force yourself to explain why an opposing belief might be true.

HOW WE RECALL EVENTS

Our beliefs control not only our perceptions and interpretations, but also our memories. Do you agree or disagree with this statement?

Memory can be likened to a storage chest in the brain into which we deposit material and from which we can withdraw it later if needed. Occasionally, something gets lost from the "chest," and then we say we have forgotten.

Memory Construction

About 85 percent of college students agree that memory is like a storage chest (Lamal, 1979). As a 1988 ad in *Psychology Today* magazine put it, "Science has proven the accumulated experience of a lifetime is preserved perfectly in your mind." Actually, psychological research has very nearly proven the opposite. Many memories are not copies of our past experience that remain on deposit in a memory bank. Rather, memories often are constructed at the time of withdrawal (Loftus, 1980b; Loftus & Loftus, 1980). Like a paleontologist inferring the appearance of a dinosaur from bone fragments, we may reconstruct our distant past from fragments of information. Thus we can easily (though unconsciously) revise our memories to suit our current knowledge. When one of my sons complained that "The June issue of *Cricket* magazine never came" and was shown where it was, he delightedly responded, "Oh good, I knew I'd gotten it."

Memory construction enables people to revise their own past histories. For example, Michael Ross, Cathy McFarland, and Garth Fletcher (1981) exposed some University of Waterloo students to a message convincing them of the desirability of toothbrushing. Later, in a supposedly different experiment, these students recalled brushing their teeth more often during the preceding two weeks than did other students who had not heard the message. Likewise, when representative samples of Americans are queried about their cigarette smoking and their reports are projected to the nation as a whole, at least a third of the 600 billion cigarettes sold annually are unaccounted for (Hall, 1985). Noting the similarity of such findings to happenings in George Orwell's *Nineteen Eighty-Four*—where it was "necessary to remember that events happened in the desired manner"—social psychologist Anthony Greenwald (1980) surmises that we all have "totalitarian egos" that continuously revise our pasts to suit our present views.

Sometimes our present view is that we have improved—in which case we may misrecall our past as more *un*like the present than it actually was. Such a tendency would help explain a puzzling pair of consistent findings: Research studies find that those who participate in self-improvement programs (diet programs, anti-smoking programs, exercise programs, psychotherapy) evidence only modest improvement on average, yet claim to have experienced considerable benefit (Myers, 1989). Michael Ross and Michael Conway (1985) suggest a partial solution to this puzzle. Having expended time, effort, and money on a self-improvement venture, people may conveniently think, "I may not be perfect now, but I was worse before; this did me a lot of good." This is precisely the sort of thinking that Conway and Ross (1984) found when they had the participants in one study-skills course report their study habits before and after the course. The participants emerged from the experience thinking their skills had improved, especially in comparison to their now biased memories about how terrible their study skills had been before the course. But despite their belittling of their past and their optimism about their academic future, the sad truth is that their grades did not change.

Studies of conflicting eyewitness testimonies further illustrate our tendency to recall the past with great confidence but meagre accuracy. Elizabeth Loftus and John Palmer (1973) showed University of Washington students a film of a traffic accident and then asked them questions about what they had seen. People who were asked "How fast were the cars going when they smashed into each other?" gave higher estimates than those asked "How fast were the cars going when they hit each other?" A week later they were also asked whether they recalled seeing any broken glass.

Although there was no broken glass in the accident, people who had been asked the question with "smashed into" were more than twice as likely as those asked the question with "hit" to report seeing broken glass. What is more, it is very difficult for untrained observers to distinguish between people's unreal memories (those constructed from suggestion) and memories based on actual experience (Schooler et al., 1986). Such experiments demonstrate how in constructing a memory we unconsciously use our general knowledge and beliefs to fill in the holes, thus organizing mere fragments from our actual past into a convincing memory.

You can demonstrate memory construction by recalling a scene from a favorite past experience. . . . Do you see yourself in the scene? If so, your memory must be a reconstruction, for in reality you did not see yourself.

This constructive memory process affects our recall of social as well as physical events. Jack Croxton, Timothy Eddy, and Nancy Morrow (1984) had students spend 15 minutes conversing with someone. Those who were afterward informed that this person reported liking both them and the experiment tended later to recall this person's behavior as relaxed, comfortable, and happy. Those informed that the person disliked them recalled the person as nervous, uncomfortable, and not so happy.

To understand why, it helps to have an idea how our memories work. We can think of memory fragments as being stored in a web of associations. To retrieve a memory, we need to activate one of the strands that leads to it, a process called ***priming*** (Bower, 1986). Priming is what the philosopher-psychologist William James described as the "wakening of associations." Often our associations are awakened, or primed, without our realizing it. Watching a scary movie while alone at home can prime our thinking—by activating frightening memories that cause us to interpret the creaking furnace as an intruder. In experiments, ideas that are planted in people's minds act like long-standing preconceptions: They automatically—unintentionally, effortlessly, and without awareness—influence how people interpret and recall events (Bargh, 1989).

Priming:
The activation of particular associations in memory.

In Chapter 5 we will see that psychiatrists and clinical psychologists are not immune to these unwitting human tendencies. Indeed, we all *selectively notice, interpret, and recall events in ways that sustain our ideas.*

WE OVERESTIMATE THE ACCURACY OF OUR JUDGMENTS

We have seen how easily we can form false impressions of (1) what we have thought and felt in the past, (2) why we do what we do, and (3) what we will do. And we have seen how our beliefs control our perceptions, interpretations, and memories. Unaware of such tendencies, we may sometimes also be unaware of our judgmental mistakes.

THE OVERCONFIDENCE PHENOMENON

The intellectual conceit evident in our judgments of our past knowledge (the I-knew-it-all-along phenomenon described in Chapter 1) extends to estimates of our current knowledge. For example, Daniel Kahneman and Amos Tversky (1979) gave people factual questions and asked them to fill in the blanks, as in: "I feel 98 percent certain that the air distance between New Delhi and Beijing is more than _____ miles but less than _____ miles."

Overconfidence phenomenon:
The tendency to be more confident than correct—to overestimate the accuracy of one's beliefs.

The people were overconfident: About 30 percent of the time, the correct answers lay outside the range about which they felt 98 percent confident. Baruch Fischhoff and his colleagues (1977) discovered that the same ***overconfidence phenomenon*** occurs when people indicate their certainty regarding answers they've given to multiple-choice questions ("Which is longer: [a] the Panama Canal, or [b] the Suez Canal?"). If people are 60 percent likely to answer such a question correctly, they will typically *feel* about 75 percent sure.

WHY ARE WE OVERCONFIDENT?

Overconfidence is an accepted fact of experimental psychology that extends to our predictions of people's social behavior (Fischhoff, 1982; Dunning et al., 1989). The issue now is what produces it. Why are we so confident of our judgments? Why does experience not lead us to a more realistic self-appraisal? There are a number of reasons (Klayman & Ha, 1987; Skov & Sherman, 1986). For one thing, people are not inclined to seek out information that might disprove what they believe. P. C. Wason (1960) demonstrated this, as you can, by giving people a sequence of three numbers—2, 4, 6—which conformed to a rule he had in mind (the rule was simply *any three ascending numbers*). To enable the people to discover the rule, Wason allowed each person to generate sets of three numbers. Each time Wason told the person whether the set did or didn't conform to his rule. When sure they had discovered the rule, the people were to stop and announce it. The result? Seldom right, but never in doubt: Twenty-three out of twenty-nine people convinced themselves of a wrong rule. They had formed some erroneous belief about what Wason's rule was (for example, counting by twos) and then searched for only *confirming* evidence (for example, 8, 10, 12) rather than attempting to *disconfirm* their hunches. Other experiments confirm that *it is hard for us to discard our ideas*. We are eager to verify our beliefs, but we are not inclined to seek evidence that might disprove our beliefs, a phenomenon known as the ***confirmation bias***.

This preference for confirming information helps explain why our self-images are so remarkably stable. In experiments at the University of Texas at Austin, William Swann and Stephen Read (1981a; 1981b) discovered that students rather consistently

"When you know a thing, to hold that you know it; and when you do not know a thing, to allow that you do not know it; this is knowledge."
Confucius, Analects

Confirmation bias:
A tendency to search for information that confirms one's preconceptions.

Overconfident decision makers can wreak havoc, as was the case when a team of NASA managers ordered the launch of the space shuttle Challenger despite engineers' reservations about its safety.

seek, elicit, and recall feedback that confirms their beliefs about themselves. Swann and Read liken their findings to how someone with a domineering self-image might behave at a party. Upon arriving, the person *seeks* those guests whom she knows acknowledge her dominance. In conversation she then presents her views in ways that *elicit* the respect she has come to expect. After the party, she has trouble recalling conversations in which her influence was minimal and more easily *recalls* her persuasiveness in the conversations that she dominated. Thus, she believes that her self-image has been strongly confirmed.

OVERCONFIDENCE IN EVERYDAY LIFE

In everyday life, what *actually* happens more readily catches our attention than what *doesn't* happen. For example, most people do reasonably well at their jobs. Therefore managers may feel confident of their ability to identify promising applicants; as they scan their employees, they are gratified by how well most are doing. The managers cannot examine those they did not hire, so it is difficult to imagine how managers could disconfirm any overconfidence in their hiring ability (Slovic, 1972). Similarly, stock experts, armed with the latest scoop, market their services with the confident presumption that they can beat the stock market average. But, incredible as it may seem, economist Burton Malkiel (1985) reports that mutual fund portfolios selected by investment analysts have not outperformed randomly selected stocks.

Editors' assessments of manuscripts also reveal the surprising amount of error in human judgment. In psychology, studies have revealed that there is usually a distressingly modest relationship between one reviewer's evaluation of a manuscript and a second reviewer's evaluation. But it's not true just of psychology. Writer Chuck Ross (1979), using a pseudonym, mailed a typewritten copy of Jerzy Kosinski's novel *Steps* to twenty-eight major publishers and literary agencies. All rejected it, including Random House, which had published the book in 1968 and watched it win the National Book Award and sell more than 400,000 copies. The novel came closest to being accepted by Houghton Mifflin, publisher of three other Kosinski novels: "Several of us read your untitled novel here with admiration for writing and style. Jerzy Kosinski comes to mind as a point of comparison. . . . The drawback to the manuscript, as it stands, is that it doesn't add up to a satisfactory whole."

As this example hints, overconfident decision makers can wreak havoc. It was a confident Lyndon Johnson who invested U.S. weapons and soldiers in the effort to salvage democracy in South Vietnam. It was a confident Ronald Reagan who believed that selling weapons to Iran would promote moderation and help liberate U.S. hostages in Lebanon. It was a confident team of NASA managers who ordered the launch of the space shuttle *Challenger* despite engineers' reservations about its safety.

REMEDIES FOR OVERCONFIDENCE

What constructive lessons can we draw from research on overconfidence? One might be to downplay other people's dogmatic statements. When people are absolutely sure that they are right, we might read it as an 85 percent chance of their being correct (Fischhoff, 1982).

In experiments, two techniques have successfully reduced the overconfidence bias. Training people by giving them prompt feedback on the accuracy of their judgments seems to help (Lichtenstein & Fischhoff, 1980). In everyday life, weather forecasters

The air distance between New Delhi and Beijing is 2500 miles. The Suez Canal is twice as long as the Panama Canal.

"The wise know too well their weakness to assume infallibility; and he who knows most, knows best how little he knows."
Thomas Jefferson, Writings

Regarding the atomic bomb: "That is the biggest fool thing we have ever done. The bomb will never go off, and I speak as an expert in explosives."
Admiral William Leahy to President Truman, 1945

and those who set the odds in horse racing both receive clear, daily feedback on the accuracy of their predictions—and experts in both of these groups do quite well at estimating the probable accuracy of their predictions (Fischhoff, 1982). Another way to reduce overconfidence is to get people to think of one good reason why their judgments might be wrong, thus forcing them to consider disconfirming information (Koriat et al., 1980). Perhaps managers could therefore foster more realistic judgments by insisting that all proposals and recommendations include reasons why they might not work.

Still, we should be careful lest we undermine people's self-confidence to a point where they spend too much time in self-analysis, or where self-doubts begin to cripple their decisiveness. In times when their wisdom is needed, those lacking self-confidence may shrink from speaking up or making tough decisions. *Over*confidence can cost us, but realistic self-confidence is adaptive.

WE OFTEN IGNORE USEFUL INFORMATION

A panel of psychologists interviewed a sample of thirty engineers and seventy lawyers, and summarized their impressions in thumbnail descriptions of those individuals. The following description has been drawn at random from the sample of thirty engineers and seventy lawyers:

Jack is a thirty-nine-year-old man.

Question: What is the probability that Jack is a lawyer rather than an engineer?

Given no more information than this about Jack, most people surmise that the chances of his being a lawyer are 70 percent, if indeed that is the frequency (or "base-rate") of lawyers in the sample from which he was drawn.

Now let's consider another example drawn from the same sample of engineers and lawyers.

Twice divorced, Frank spends most of his free time hanging around the country club. His clubhouse bar conversations often center around his regrets at having tried to follow his esteemed father's footsteps. The long hours he had spent at academic drudgery would have been better invested in learning how to be less quarrelsome in his relations with other people.

Asked to guess Frank's occupation, more than 80 percent of University of Oregon students surmised he was one of the lawyers (Fischhoff & Bar-Hillel, 1984). Fair enough. But how do you suppose their estimates changed when the sample description was changed to say that 70 percent were engineers? Not in the slightest. The students took no account of the base-rate of engineers and lawyers; in their minds Frank was more representative of lawyers, and that was all that seemed to matter.

Now, returning to Jack, what do you suppose would happen if we added some irrelevant anecdotal information?

Jack is a thirty-nine-year-old man. He is married with no children. A man of high ability and high motivation, he promises to be quite successful in his field. He is well liked by his colleagues.

This information contains no clues as to whether Jack is a lawyer or engineer. People know this, for they typically say that it's about 50-50 which he is—*regardless* of whether they were told his group was 70 percent lawyers or 30 percent lawyers (Kahneman & Tversky, 1973). This illustrates the extent to which we use useless anecdotal information and ignore abstract (for example, statistical) information.

OUR USE OF USELESS INFORMATION

Our willingness to ignore useful information and use useless information is also apparent in some amusing experiments. Consider the following two questions, adapted from an experiment by Henry Zukier (1982; Nisbett et al., 1981).

> Roberta is a university student who spends about three hours studying outside of classes in an average week. What would you guess her grade point average to be?

> Judith is a university student who spends about three hours studying outside of classes in an average week. Judith has four plants in the place she's living in now. On an average weekday, she goes to sleep around midnight. She has a brother and two sisters. Two months is the longest period of time she has dated one person. She describes herself as being often a cheerful person. What would you guess her grade point average to be?

The first question has but one bit of useful information. Those given it usually estimated low grades. People given questions such as the second did not believe there is any connection between how many plants one has and grade average. Yet, when such worthless information was added to the useful information about study time it diluted the impact of the useful information—so much so that it no longer made much difference whether the hypothetical student was said to study three or thirty-one hours per week! In attending to the useless information, people missed the crucial information.

Thomas Gilovich (1981) observed a similar use of useless information when he asked California sportswriters and football coaches to judge the professional potential of hypothetical college football players. Gilovich was amused to discover that judgments were affected not only by relevant information concerning the player's ability, but also by such trivia as whether the player came from the same hometown as a well-known professional player.

IGNORING BASE-RATE INFORMATION

As this last experiment indicates, specific, anecdotal information can have great persuasive power. Researchers Richard Nisbett and Eugene Borgida (Nisbett et al., 1976) explored the tendency to overuse anecdotal information by showing University of Michigan students videotaped interviews of people who were supposedly subjects in an experiment in which most subjects failed to assist a seizure victim. Being told how most subjects acted had almost no effect upon people's predictions of how the individual they observed acted. The apparent niceness of this individual was more vivid and compelling than the general truth about how most subjects really acted: "Ted seems so pleasant that I can't imagine him being unresponsive to another's plight." This illustrates the ***base-rate fallacy:*** Focusing upon the specific individual seemed to push into the background useful information about the population the person came from.

There is, of course, a positive side to viewing people as individuals and not merely as statistical units. But a problem arises when we formulate our beliefs about people

Base-rate fallacy:
The tendency to ignore or underuse base-rate information (information that describes most people), and instead to be influenced by distinctive features of the case being judged.

in general from our observations of particular persons; preoccupation with individuals can easily distort our perception of what is generally true. Our impressions of a group, for example, tend to be overly influenced by extreme members of the group, as when one man's attempt to assassinate President Reagan caused people to bemoan, "It's not safe to walk the streets anymore," and conclude that "There's a sickness in the American soul." As psychologist Gordon Allport put it, "Given a thimbleful of facts we rush to make generalizations as large as a tub."

It would be an overstatement to say that people are never sensitive to base-rate information. People will make use of the data when their relevance is obvious or when the people have been sensitized to the data's usefulness (Zukier & Pepitone, 1984; Ginossar & Trope, 1987). For example, if we are told that students taking a particular exam had a high rate of failure, we will infer that the exam was difficult and this will influence our judgment of how likely it is that a particular student passed the exam. Likewise, information that may apply to anyone in a sample, such as the frequency of apartment break-ins on a particular block, will be used when guessing the likelihood that a particular family has suffered a break-in.

"Examples work more forcibly on the mind than precepts."
Henry Fielding, Joseph Andrews

Nevertheless, the research does suggest a basic principle of human social thinking: People are slow to deduce particular instances from a general truth, but are remarkably quick to infer general truth from a vivid instance. One University of Michigan study presented students with a vivid welfare case—a magazine article about a ne'er-do-well Puerto Rican woman who had a succession of unruly children sired by a succession of common-law husbands. When this case was set against factual statistics about welfare cases—for example, information indicating that, contrary to this case, 90 percent of welfare recipients in her age bracket "are off the welfare rolls by the end of four years"—the facts had less effect on people's opinions about the laziness and hopelessness of most welfare recipients than did the single vivid case (Hamill et al., 1980). No wonder that after hearing and reading countless instances of rapes, robberies, and beatings, 9 out of 10 Canadians overestimate—usually by a considerable margin—the percentage of crimes that involve violence (Doob & Roberts, 1988).

Sometimes the vivid example is a personal experience. In one experiment, 85 percent of students at the University of Warsaw, Poland, who had interacted with a warm, friendly experimenter later chose from a pair of photos a woman who looked something like her as the friendlier one; students who had not first interacted with the friendly experimenter were virtually 50-50 in choosing which of the pair seemed friendlier (Lewicki, 1985). In a follow-up study, the experimenter acted *un*friendly toward half the subjects. When these subjects later had to turn in their data to one of two women, they nearly always avoided the one who looked a little like the experimenter. (Perhaps you, too, can recall a time when you reacted positively or negatively to someone who reminded you of someone else.)

"Testimonials may be more compelling than mountains of facts and figures (as mountains of facts and figures in social psychology so compellingly demonstrate)."
Mark Snyder (1988)

Before buying my new Honda I consulted the *Consumer Reports* survey of car owners and found the repair record of the Dodge Colt, which for a time I considered, to be quite good. A short while later, I mentioned my interest in the Colt to a student. "Oh no," he moaned, "don't consider a Colt. I worked in a gas station last summer and serviced two Dodge Colts that kept falling apart and being brought in for one thing after another." How did I use this information—and the glowing testimonies from two friends who were Honda owners? Did I simply increment the *Consumer Reports* surveys of Colt and Honda owners by an iota of two more each? Although I knew that, logically, that is what I should have done, it was nearly impossible to downplay my consciousness of these vivid accounts.

THE AVAILABILITY HEURISTIC

People's individual testimonies are more compelling than general information partly because vivid information more deeply etches itself upon the mind (Reyes et al., 1980). Consider these questions:

1. Does the letter *k* appear more often as the first letter of a word or as the third letter?
2. What percent of deaths in the U.S. each year are due to:
      _____ accidents
      _____ cardiovascular diseases (e.g., heart attacks and strokes)?

Availability heuristic:
An efficient but fallible rule-of-thumb that judges the likelihood of things in terms of their availability in memory. If instances of something come readily to mind, we presume it to be commonplace.

Likely your answers reflected the common human tendency to judge the likelihood of events in terms of how readily instances come to mind. If examples are readily *available* in our memory—as vivid examples, such as accidental deaths, tend to be—then we will tend to presume that the event is commonplace. Usually it is, so we are often well served by this cognitive rule of thumb, called the ***availability heuristic.*** (Heuristics are simple, efficient thinking strategies—rules of thumb.) But we are not always well served by this rule. Easy-to-imagine events, such as diseases with easy-to-picture symptoms, may seem more likely than diseases with harder-to-picture symptoms (Sherman et al., 1985).

The availability heuristic explains why perceived risk is often badly out of joint with the real risks of things. News footage of airplane crashes are readily available in people's memories. This misleads many to suppose that they are more at risk travelling somewhere in a commercial airplane than in their car. In actuality, U.S. travellers from 1980 through 1986 were 76 times more likely to die in a car crash than on a commercial flight covering the same distance. Likewise, many people who suppose that coal burning is a safer method of producing power than nuclear energy (which, in the United States, has yet to kill anyone—Lewis, 1985) take little account of the tens of thousands of people who quietly succumb each year to diseases related to coal mining and air pollution, to say nothing of the future consequences of the looming greenhouse

When viewing this scene from the Aloha Airlines disaster in 1988, many people perceived that the risk of flying is far greater than it actually is.

effect. The point: Dramatic events stick in our minds and we use ease of recall—the availability heuristic—when judging the likelihood of events.

In their research on energy conservation, Marti Gonzales and her coresearchers (1988) showed how the availability heuristic can be harnessed to good ends. They trained California home energy auditors to communicate their findings to homeowners with vivid, memorable images. Rather than simply pointing out small spaces around doors where heat is lost, the auditor would say, "If you were to add up all the cracks around and under the doors of your home, you'd have the equivalent of a hole the size of a football in your living room wall." With such remarks, and by eliciting the homeowners' active commitment in helping measure cracks and state their intentions to remedy them, the trained auditors triggered a 50 percent increase in the number of customers applying for energy financing programs.

ILLUSIONS OF CAUSATION, CORRELATION, AND PERSONAL CONTROL

Another influence on everyday thinking is our search for order in random events, a tendency that can lead to illusions of correlation and control.

ILLUSORY CORRELATION

Illusory correlation:
Perception of a relationship where none exists, or perception of a stronger relationship than actually exists.

It's easy to see a correlation where none exists. When we expect to see significant relationships we easily misperceive random events as significantly related—an ***illusory correlation.*** As part of their research with the Bell Telephone Laboratories, William Ward and Herbert Jenkins (1965) showed people the results of a hypothetical fifty-day cloud-seeding experiment. They told their subjects which of the fifty days the clouds had been seeded and which of the days it had rained. This information was nothing more than a random mix of results; sometimes it rained after seeding, sometimes it didn't. People nevertheless were convinced—in conformity with their intuitive supposition about the effects of cloud seeding—that they really had observed a relationship between cloud seeding and rain.

Other experiments confirm that people easily misperceive random events as confirming their beliefs (Crocker, 1981; Jennings et al., 1982; Troiler & Hamilton, 1986). When we believe a correlation exists between two things, we are more likely to notice and recall confirming than disconfirming instances. The joint occurrence of two unusual events—say the premonition of a strange event and the subsequent occurrence of that event—is especially likely to be noticed and remembered, far more than all the times those unusual events do not coincide. Hence, we easily overestimate the frequency with which these strange things happen. If, after we think about a friend, that friend calls us, we are far more likely to notice and remember this coincidence than all the times we think of a friend without any ensuing call, or receive a call from a friend about whom we have not been thinking.

Thomas Gilovich (1988) offers another familiar example: "Infertile" couples who adopt a child are more likely to conceive than similar couples who do not adopt. Couples who adopt, it is popularly theorized, finally relax—and conceive. But no such theory is necessary, because it ain't so. Although researchers have found no correlation between adoption and conception, our attention is drawn to couples who have conceived

FINDING ORDER IN RANDOM EVENTS

If someone were to flip a coin six times, would one of these sequences of heads (H) and tails (T) be more likely than the other two: HHHTTT or HTTHTH or HHHHHH?

Daniel Kahneman and Amos Tversky (1972) found that HTTHTH and its reverse *seem* more likely to people than the other possible sequences. Actually, any exact sequence of outcomes, given six flips, has a 1 in 64 chance of occurring.

"It ain't so much the things we don't know that get us in trouble. It's the things we know that ain't so."
Nineteenth-century American saying

after adopting (rather than to those who conceive before adopting or who don't conceive after adopting).

The difficulty we have recognizing coincidental, random events for what they are predisposes us to perceive order even when we are shown a purely random series of events (see box). During Germany's World War II bombing blitz on England, Londoners developed elaborate theories of where the Germans were aiming. However, when London was later divided up into small, geographic areas, bomb hits per area were seen to have occurred randomly (Feller, 1968). However, because random events tend to occur in bunches—flip a coin 20 times and you will get several runs of heads and of tails—*after* the bombings, people could "see" some order. Likewise, hospital staff sometimes "explain" runs of boys or girls in the sequence of births by concocting theories, such as boys being conceived under a certain phase of the moon. And basketball players and coaches perceive hot or cold shooting streaks and feed the ball accordingly—despite careful and extensive statistical analyses revealing that professional and college players are no more likely to make a basket after just making one than after just missing one (Gilovich, 1988). A 50 percent shooter will indeed have streaks of baskets made or missed, but no more than a coin tosser will have streaks of heads or tails.

This intense human desire to find order, even in random events, is what leads us to make attributions. By attributing events to one cause or another, we order our worlds and make things seem more predictable and controllable. Generally that tendency is adaptive, but occasionally it leads us astray.

ILLUSION OF CONTROL

Illusion of control:
Perception of uncontrollable events as subject to one's control or as more controllable than they are.

Our tendency to perceive random events as though they were related feeds the frequent illusion that chance events are subject to our personal control. During recent droughts in England and in the United States the news media reported several instances of rain dances, a few of which were followed by rain. During the 1988 summer drought, retired farmer Elmer Carlson arranged a rain dance by sixteen Hopi Indians in Audubon, Iowa. The next day it rained 1 inch. "The miracles are still here, we just have to ask for them," explained Carlson (Associated Press, 1988).

Perceived Control When Gambling

Ellen Langer (1977) has demonstrated the illusion of control with experiments on gambling behavior. People were easily seduced into believing they could beat chance. If they chose a lottery number for themselves they demanded four times as much money for the sale of their lottery ticket as people whose number was assigned by the experimenter. If they played a game of chance against an awkward and nervous person, they were willing to bet significantly more than when playing against a dapper, confident opponent. In these and other ways, Langer consistently observed that people act as if they can control chance events.

Observations of real-life gamblers have confirmed these experimental findings. Dice players often behave as if they could control the outcome by throwing softly for low numbers and hard for high numbers (Henslin, 1967). Putting the experimental results to practical use, Langer suggests that state lotteries can maximize betting by giving participants maximum choice on their tickets—letting people choose their own lucky numbers. The extent to which the gambling industry thrives because gamblers are susceptible to an illusion of control testifies that this phenomenon is resistant to reason. Gamblers' hopes that they can beat the laws of chance sustain their gambling. Wins are attributed to the gambler's skill and foresight, and losses become "near misses" that are often explained away by "flukes"—perhaps (for the sports gambler) a bad call by the referee or a freakish bounce of the ball (Gilovich & Douglas, 1986).

Another of Langer's studies indicates that if people experience some unusual early successes in a chance situation, later failures may be discounted (Langer & Roth, 1975). People predicted the outcomes of thirty coin tosses. Langer rigged the feedback so that some people experienced mostly wins during the first ten flips while others experienced either mostly losses or a random sequence of wins and losses. Across all thirty trials, however, each person accumulated the same total outcome: fifteen wins and fifteen losses. Nonetheless, those who started with a fairly consistent sequence of wins made inflated estimates of how many flips they had actually predicted and how many they could predict given another hundred trials. Likewise, those who experience early successes on an "ESP" task tend to recall themselves as more successful than do those who experience early failures, even when later results return overall performance to a mere chance level in both cases (Zenker et al., 1982). Whether trying to predict coin tosses or future events, those who experience early success evidently come to perceive themselves as skilled, and therefore discount later failures. Our propensity

The illusion of control takes many forms.

"The next dance you will see is for partly cloudy conditions with moderating temperatures."

to see events as controllable is apparently so strong that just a few early positive results can induce an illusion of control.

In my home we have occasionally flipped a coin to settle trivial disputes. At one point one of my sons began arguing that he always lost coin tosses. I reminded him that each flip is a 50-50 proposition. To my dismay, he suffered several more consecutive losses. No amount of rational persuasion could then convince him that he really had a 50-50 chance on the next toss. What makes Langer's results so striking is that her subjects were not ten-year-old boys, but educated Yale University students.

Regression Toward the Average

Regression toward the average: The statistical tendency for extreme scores or extreme behavior to return toward one's average.

Tversky and Kahneman (1974) have identified another way by which an illusion of control may arise: We fail to recognize the statistical phenomenon of *regression toward the average* even though it often occurs in real life. The phenomenon is simply illustrated: Because exam scores are imperfectly correlated, most students who have obtained extremely high scores on an exam will obtain lower scores on the next exam. Their first scores are at the ceiling and thus each student's second score is more likely to fall back ("regress") toward his or her own average than to push the ceiling even higher. (This is why a student who does consistently good work, even if never the best, will sometimes end a course at the top of the class.) Conversely, those who do worst on the first exam are likely to improve. Thus if those who scored lowest are tutored after the first exam, the tutors are likely to be rewarded for their efforts, even if the tutoring had no effect.

Likewise, a counselor who is visited by people at their most depressed is more likely to be gratified by their subsequent improvement than to observe further deterioration. When things are desperately bad we will try anything rather than sit passively, and whatever we try—going to a psychotherapist, starting a new diet-exercise plan, reading a self-help book—is more likely to be followed by improvement than by further deterioration. Thus it often seems effective, whether it actually had an effect or not.

Sometimes we do recognize that events are not likely to continue at an unusually good or bad extreme. Experience has taught us that when everything is going great, something will go wrong, and that when life is dealing us terrible blows we can usually look forward to things getting better. Often, though, we fail to recognize this regression effect. We puzzle at why baseball's rookie-of-the-year often has a more ordinary second year—did he become overconfident? Self-conscious? We forget that exceptional performance tends to regress toward normality. Imagine a volleyball coach who rewards her team with lavish praise and a light practice after their best match of the season and harasses them after an exceptionally bad match. She then wrongly concludes that rewards lead to poorer performance in the next game while punishments improve performance—failing to understand that because performance is not perfectly reliable, unusual performances tend to fall back toward the usual. Parents and teachers may reach the same mistaken conclusion after reacting to unusually good or bad behaviors.

To simulate the consequences of using praise and punishment, Paul Schaffner (1985) invited Bowdoin College students to train an imaginary fourth-grade boy, "Harold," to come to school by 8:30 each morning. For each school day of a three-week period, a computer would display Harold's arrival time, which was always between 8:20 and 8:40. The subjects would then select a response to Harold, ranging from strong praise to strong reprimand. As you might expect, they usually praised Harold when he arrived before 8:30 and reprimanded him when he arrived after 8:30. Because Schaffner had programmed the computer to display a random sequence of arrival times for Harold, his arrival time tended to improve (to regress toward 8:30) after being reprimanded. For example, if Harold arrived at 8:39 he was almost sure to be reprimanded, and his randomly selected next-day arrival time was likely to be earlier than 8:39. Thus, *even though their reprimands were having no effect*, most subjects ended the experiment believing that their reprimands had been effective. This experiment demonstrates Tversky and Kahneman's provocative conclusion: that nature operates in such a way that we often (erroneously) feel punished for rewarding others and rewarded for punishing them. In actuality, as every student of psychology knows, positive reinforcement for doing things right is usually more effective and has fewer negative side effects.

OUR ERRONEOUS BELIEFS MAY GENERATE THEIR OWN REALITY

Self-fulfilling prophecy: The tendency for one's expectations to evoke behavior that confirms the expectations.

One additional reason that beliefs are so resistant to disconfirmation is that our beliefs sometimes lead us to act in ways which elicit their apparent confirmation. In Chapter 3, we noted that this **self-fulfilling prophecy** effect applies to our beliefs about ourselves. People with a strong sense of self-efficacy—who believe in their competence and ability to achieve—do, in fact, achieve more than comparable people who have lower self-expectations. Our beliefs about other people can also be self-fulfilling. In his well-known studies of "experimenter bias," Robert Rosenthal (1984) demonstrated that research subjects sometimes live up to what is expected of them. For example, in one experiment, experimenters asked subjects to judge the successfulness of people in various photographs. Although all the experimenters read the same instructions to their subjects and showed them the same photos, those led to expect high ratings nevertheless obtained higher ratings than did experimenters who expected their subjects to see the photographed people as failures. Even more startling—and controversial—have been subsequent reports that teachers' beliefs about their students similarly serve as self-fulfilling prophecies.

DO TEACHERS' EXPECTATIONS AFFECT THEIR STUDENTS?

There is little doubt that teachers do have higher expectations for some students than for others. Perhaps you have detected this after having a brother or sister precede you in school, or from having received a label such as "gifted" or "learning disabled," or when sensing that the conversation in the teachers' lounge sent your reputation ahead of you, or upon learning that the teacher had scrutinized your school file or discovered your family's social status. Do teachers' expectations formed in such ways have any effect upon students? It's clear that teachers' evaluations are *correlated* with student achievement: Teachers think well of students who do well. But are teachers' evaluations more caused *by* or the cause *of* student performance? A study of 4300 British schoolchildren by William Crano and Phyllis Mellon (1978) suggests that the teachers' beliefs are as much a cause as a consequence of their students' performance. High evaluations (especially of the child's social development) were more likely to be followed by high academic performance than was high performance to be followed by high evaluations.

Could we test this conclusion experimentally? For example, pretend that a teacher is given an erroneous impression that Jane, Sally, Johnny, and Manuel, four randomly selected students, are unusually capable. Will the teacher then likely give special treatment to these four, thus eliciting superior performance from them? In a now famous experiment, Rosenthal and Lenore Jacobson (1968) reported precisely that. Randomly selected children in a San Francisco elementary school who were said (on the basis of a fictitious test) to be on the verge of a dramatic intellectual spurt did then spurt ahead in IQ score. Since this dramatic result seemed to suggest that the school problems of "disadvantaged" children might merely reflect their teachers' low expectations, the findings were soon publicized in the national media as well as in many college textbooks in psychology and education. But further analysis revealed the teacher-expectations effect to be not so powerful and reliable as this initial study had led many to believe. Some critics questioned the IQ measure and the statistical procedures used by Rosenthal and Jacobson (Thorndike, 1968; Elashoff & Snow, 1971). Moreover, by Rosenthal's own count, in only 36 percent of the 400 published experiments do teachers' expectations significantly affect students' performance (Rosenthal, 1985, 1987). Evidently, low expectations do not doom a capable child, nor do high expectations magically transform a slow learner into a valedictorian. Human nature is not so pliable.

Why do teachers' expectations *sometimes* affect students? Rosenthal and other investigators report that teachers look, smile, and nod more at "high-potential students." But the effect seems not entirely due to such nonverbal messages. Teachers also may teach more to their "gifted" students, set higher goals for them, call on them more, and give them more time to answer (Cooper, 1983; Harris & Rosenthal, 1985; Jussim, 1986).

Reading the experiments on teacher expectations has always made me wonder about the effect of *students'* expectations upon their teachers. You no doubt begin many of your courses well aware of student comments that "Professor Smith is interesting" and "Professor Jones is a bore." Recently, Robert Feldman and Thomas Prohaska (1979; Feldman & Theiss, 1982) demonstrated that such expectations can affect both student and teacher. Students in a learning experiment who expected to be taught by a competent teacher perceived their teacher (who was unaware of their expectations) as more competent and interesting than did students with low expectations; furthermore, the students actually learned more. In a follow-up experiment, Feldman and Prohaska videotaped teachers and had observers later rate their performance. Teachers who had been assigned a student who nonverbally conveyed positive expectations were judged most capable.

To see whether such effects might also occur in actual classrooms, a research team led by David Jamieson (1987) conducted an experiment with four Ontario high school classes taught by a just-transferred teacher. Students in two of the classes were told during individual interviews that both their fellow students and the research team rated the teacher very highly and that the teacher herself was very enthusiastic about the class. Compared to the control classes, whose expectations were not raised, these students subsequently paid better attention during class and at the end of the teaching unit got better grades and rated the teacher as clearer in her teaching. The attitudes that a class has toward its teacher are as important, it seems, as the teacher's attitude toward the students.

DO WE GET WHAT WE EXPECT FROM OTHERS?

So, the expectations of experimenters and teachers are occasionally self-fulfilling. How general is this self-fulfilling-prophecy effect? Do we tend to get from others what we expect of them? There are times when our negative expectations of someone lead us to be extra nice to them, which induces them to be nice in return—thus *dis*confirming our expectations. But the much more common finding in studies of social interaction is that, yes, we do tend to get what we expect (Miller & Turnbull, 1986).

In laboratory games, hostility nearly always begets hostility: People who *perceive* their opponents as noncooperative will readily induce them to *be* noncooperative (Kelley & Stahelski, 1970). Self-confirming beliefs abound in times of conflict. Each party's perception of the other as attacking, resentful, and vindictive induces the other to display these behaviors in self-defense, thus creating a vicious self-perpetuating circle. For example, married persons may act in ways that induce each other to confirm their perceptions. Whether I expect my wife to be in a bad mood or in a warm, loving mood may affect how I relate to her, thereby inducing her to confirm my belief.

Several experiments conducted by Mark Snyder (1984) at the University of Minnesota show how, once formed, erroneous beliefs about the social world can induce others to confirm those beliefs, a phenomenon called ***behavioral confirmation.*** In one study, Snyder, Elizabeth Tanke, and Ellen Berscheid (1977) had men students talk on the telephone with women they thought (from having been shown a picture) were either

Behavioral confirmation:
A type of self-fulfilling prophecy whereby people's social expectations lead them to act in ways that cause others to confirm their expectations.

In influencing classroom performance, the attitudes that a class has toward its teacher are as important as the teacher's attitude toward the students.

BEHIND THE SCENES

Our research on "when belief creates reality" suggests a reason why erroneous stereotypes stubbornly persist: Believing their stereotypes, people may treat others in ways that elicit the very behaviors they expect. Doubting their stereotypes, they may test them by selectively gathering confirming evidence. Thus, whether right or wrong, stereotypes may create and sustain their own reality.

Mark Snyder,
University of Minnesota

attractive or unattractive. Analysis of just the women's comments during the conversations revealed that the women who were presumed attractive did in fact speak in a more warm and likable way than the women who were presumed unattractive. The men's erroneous beliefs had become a self-fulfilling prophecy, leading them to act in a way that influenced the women to fulfill their stereotype that beautiful people are desirable people.

In another experiment, Snyder and William Swann (1978a) found that when people interacted with someone who expected them to be hostile, they responded by using a noise weapon more aggressively. When led to see their aggression as a reflection of themselves—for example, when told, "People's use of the noise weapon reflects the

THE SELF-FULFILLING PSYCHOLOGY OF THE STOCK MARKET

On the evening of January 6, 1981, Joseph Granville, a popular Florida investment adviser, wired his clients: "Stock prices will nose-dive; sell tomorrow." Word of Granville's advice soon spread, and January 7 became the heaviest day of trading in the previous history of the New York Stock Exchange. The Dow Jones average dropped 23 points. All told, stock values lost $40 billion.

Nearly a half-century ago, John Maynard Keynes likened such stock market psychology to the popular beauty contests then conducted by London newspapers. To win, one had to pick the six faces out of a hundred that were, in turn, chosen most frequently by the other newspaper contestants. Thus, as Keynes wrote, "Each competitor has to pick not those faces which he himself finds prettiest, but those which he thinks likeliest to catch the fancy of the other competitors."

In like fashion, investors have to pick not simply the stocks that touch their fancy, but the stocks that will find favor among other investors. The name of the game is to predict the behavior of others. As one Wall Street fund manager explained, "You may or may not agree with Granville's view—but that's usually beside the point." If you think his advice will cause others to sell, then you want to sell quickly, before prices drop more. If you expect others to buy, you buy now to beat the rush.

The self-fulfilling psychology of the stock market worked to an extreme on Monday, October 19, 1987, when the Dow Jones average crashed 508 points, causing people to lose—on paper—about 20 percent of the value of their stock investments. Part of what happens during such slides is that the media and rumor mill focus on whatever bad news is available to explain it. Once reported, the stories further diminish people's expectations, thereby causing declining prices to fall still lower—and vice-versa with the focus on good news when stocks are rising.

Note: Adapted from Steve Lohr (1981, January 13). The puzzling stock market. *The New York Times*, pp. D1, D9; and Berkley Rice, (1988, April) Boom & doom on Wall Street. *Psychology Today*, pp. 50–54.

type of person they are"—they subsequently were also more hostile to a naive person who had no prior knowledge about them. These experiments help us understand how social beliefs, such as stereotypes about handicapped people or about people of a particular race or sex, may be self-confirming. We help construct our own social realities. How others treat us reflects how we and others have treated them.

As with virtually every phenomenon of social behavior, the tendency of people to confirm others' expectations does have its limits. For one thing, people who are strongly motivated to form accurate rather than rapid impressions will indeed elicit more accurate information (Neuberg, 1989). For another, people who are told about another's expectation may work to overcome it (Darley et al., 1988; Swann, 1987). If Chuck knows that Jane thinks he's an airhead, he may strive to disprove her impression.

William Swann and Robin Ely (1984) report a third condition under which people's behavior tends not to confirm our expectations: when our expectations clash with a clear conception they have of themselves. For example, Swann and Ely found that when a strongly outgoing person was interviewed by someone who expected her to be introverted, it was the interviewer's perceptions and not the interviewee's behavior that changed. Interviewees who were unsure of themselves were more likely to live up to the interviewer's expectations.

As this last experiment suggests, our beliefs about others can be self-fulfilling, but so, too, can our beliefs about ourselves. In several experiments, Steven Sherman (1980) has found that people tend to fulfill predictions they make of their own behavior. For example, when Bloomington, Indiana, residents were called and asked to volunteer three hours to an American Cancer Society drive, only 4 percent agreed to do so. When a comparable group of other residents were called and asked to *predict* how they would react if they were to receive such a request, almost half predicted they would agree to help—and most of these did indeed agree to do so when later they were contacted by the Cancer Society. This not only illustrates a self-serving bias (people overestimated how desirably they would act were they to be approached unforewarned), it also illustrates the self-fulfilling consequences of predicting one's own behavior. Formulating a plan for how we would want to act in a given situation makes it more likely that we will really do it. This suggests several constructive applications. For example, if teenagers were asked, "What would you do if your friends pressured you to smoke?" might they be more self-determined when such a situation actually arises?

CONCLUSIONS

We could extend the list of thinking principles. But surely this much—when added to our previous discussions of hindsight bias, the fundamental attribution error, and self-serving bias—has been a sufficient glimpse of the ease and the manner with which people come to believe what may be untrue. The threat to our vanity posed by research on the limits and fallacies of human thought is amplified by the fact that most of the participants in these experiments were highly intelligent people, generally students at leading universities. Moreover, these predictable distortions and biases occurred even when people were motivated by money to think optimally. As one researcher concluded, the illusions "have a persistent quality not unlike that of perceptual illusions" (Slovic, 1972).

Research in cognitive social psychology thus mirrors the mixed review given humanity in literature, philosophy, and religion. On the one hand, many research psychologists have spent lifetimes exploring the awesome capacities of the human mind (see Manis, 1977). We are capable of great achievements and impressive insights into nature. We are smart enough to have cracked our own genetic code, to have invented talking computers, to have sent people to the moon. Yet our intuition is more vulnerable to error than we intuitively suspect. With rather incredible ease, we can form and sustain false beliefs.

But have these experiments just been playing intellectual tricks on their hapless participants, thus making their intuitions look worse than they are? Richard Nisbett and Lee Ross (1980) contend that, if anything, the laboratory procedures *overestimate* our intuitive powers. The experiments usually present people with clear evidence and forewarn them that their reasoning ability is being tested. Seldom does life say to us: "Here is some evidence. Now put on your intellectual Sunday best and answer these questions."

Often our everyday failings are inconsequential, but not always so. False impressions, interpretations, and beliefs can produce serious consequences. When making important social judgments—Why are so many people on welfare? Do the Russians desire peace or conquest? Does my friend love me, or my money?—even small biases can have profound social consequences. Since we know that errors even creep into sophisticated scientific thinking, it seems safe to conclude that none of us is exempt from them. Apparently human nature has not changed since 3000 years ago when the Psalmist observed that "no one can see his own errors." As Winston Churchill wryly observed, "Man will occasionally stumble over the truth, but most of the time he will pick himself up and continue on."

Lest we succumb to the cynical conclusion that *all* beliefs are absurd, I hasten now to balance the picture. The elegant analyses of the imperfections of our thinking are themselves a tribute to human wisdom. (Were one to argue that *all* human thought is illusory, the assertion would be self-refuting, for it, too, would be but an illusion. It would be logically equivalent to contending that "all generalizations are false, including this one.")

Just as medical science has found it a useful working assumption that any given body organ exists to serve a function, so have behavioral scientists found it useful to assume that *our modes of thought and behavior are generally adaptive* (Funder, 1987; Kruglanski & Ajzen, 1983; Swann, 1984). The rules of thought which produce so many false convictions and such striking deficiencies in our statistical intuition usually serve us well. Frequently, the errors are a by-product of our minds' strategies for simplifying the complex information our minds receive. We just misapply or overuse generally sensible strategies.

Herbert Simon (1957) was among the modern researchers who first described the bounds of human reason. Simon contends that to cope with reality we simplify it. Consider the awesome complexity of a chess game, for example. A game can unfold in an almost infinite variety of ways; the number of possible chess games is greater than the number of particles in the universe. How do we cope with such complexity? We adopt some simplifying rules of thumb—heuristics. These heuristics are imperfect— they sometimes lead us into defeat—but they do enable us to make efficient, snap judgments. For example, the availability heuristic—judging the likelihood of things in terms of their availability in memory—enables us to estimate speedily the frequency of an event, though it may also lead us to overestimate the commonality of vivid, easily remembered occurrences.

Illusory thinking can likewise spring from heuristics that are generally useful and may even facilitate our survival. The belief in our power to control events helps main-

"In creating these problems, we didn't set out to fool people. All our problems fooled us, too."
Amos Tversky (1985)

tain hope and effort where despair might otherwise prevail. If things are sometimes subject to control and sometimes not, we will maximize our outcomes by "positive thinking." Optimistic thinking pays dividends.

We might even say that our beliefs are like scientific theories—sometimes in error, yet useful as generalizations. To say that a theory (or a way of thinking) is imperfect is not to say it should be discarded. Yet, just as we constantly seek to improve our theories, might we not also work to reduce error in our social thinking? In school, math teachers teach, teach, teach, until the mind is finally trained to process numerical information accurately and automatically. We assume that such ability does not come naturally, else why bother with the years of training? Research psychologist Robyn Dawes (1980)—who is dismayed that "study after study has shown [that] people have very limited abilities to process information on a conscious level, particularly social information"—suggests that we should also teach, teach, teach how to process social information.

"The spirit of liberty is the spirit which is not too sure that it is right; the spirit of liberty is the spirit which seeks to understand the minds of other men and women; the spirit of liberty is the spirit which weighs their interests alongside its own without bias."
Learned Hand, The Spirit of Liberty

Richard Nisbett and Lee Ross (1980) believe that such education could indeed reduce our vulnerability to certain types of error. As a beginning, they propose that people first be trained to recognize likely sources of error in their own social intuition. Such is precisely the constructive intent of this chapter. Second, they advocate statistics courses that are geared to everyday problems of logic and social judgment. Given such training, people do in fact reason better about everyday events (Nisbett et al., 1987; Lehman et al., 1988). Third, they suggest that such teaching will be most effective when richly illustrated with concrete, vivid anecdotes and examples from everyday life. Finally, they suggest teaching memorable and useful slogans, such as:

"It's an empirical question." In other words, hunches need to be checked against the relevant data.

"Which hat did you draw that sample out of?" In other words, vivid but unrepresentative samples are suspect. Also: "You can lie with statistics, but a well-chosen example does the job better."

"Beware the fundamental attribution error." In other words, consider the actor's situation before jumping to conclusions about his disposition. Also: "What would you have done if you were in her shoes?"

"Rob the average man of his life-illusion, and you rob him also of his happiness."
Henrik Ibsen, The Wild Duck

Is research on pride and error *too* humbling? Are the researchers who uncover our susceptibility to error the modern counterpart to Gregers Werle in Henrik Ibsen's play *The Wild Duck?* (Werle demolished people's illusions, leaving them without hope or meaning.) Surely we can acknowledge the hard truth of our human limits and still sympathize with the deeper message that people are more than machines. Our subjective experiences are a large part of the stuff of our humanity—our art and our music, our enjoyment of friendship and love, our mystical and religious experiences.

The cognitive and social psychologists who explore illusory thinking are not out to remake us into unfeeling, logical machines. They would grant, or even insist, that intuition and feeling not only enrich human experience, but are an important source of creative ideas. They add, however, the humbling reminder that our susceptibility to error also makes clear our need for disciplined training of the mind. Norman Cousins (1978) calls this "the biggest truth of all about learning: that its purpose is to unlock the human mind and to develop it into an organ capable of thought—conceptual thought, analytical thought, sequential thought."

SUMMING UP

Research psychologists have for a long time explored the mind's awesome capacity for processing information. Recently, researchers in "cognitive social psychology" have turned their attention to the errors we typically make when processing information. Since we are generally unaware of how errors enter our thinking, an examination of our "illusory thinking" can be revealing and, if it helps improve our thinking, beneficial. This chapter described six ways in which we form and sustain false beliefs—"reasons for unreason," we might call them.

WE OFTEN DO NOT KNOW WHY WE DO WHAT WE DO

First, we often do not know why we behave the way we do. In experiments, people whose attitudes have been changed will often deny that they have been influenced; they will insist that how they feel now is how they have always felt. When powerful influences upon our behavior are not so conspicuous that any observer could spot them, we too can be oblivious to what has affected us.

OUR PRECONCEPTIONS CONTROL OUR INTERPRETATIONS AND MEMORIES

Second, our preconceptions strongly influence how we interpret and remember events. In experiments, people's prejudgments have striking effects upon how they perceive and interpret information. Other experiments have planted judgments or false ideas in people's minds *after* they have been given information. These experiments reveal that just as before-the-fact judgments bias our perceptions and interpretations, so do after-the-fact judgments bias our recall.

WE OVERESTIMATE THE ACCURACY OF OUR JUDGMENTS

Third, we have too much faith in our judgments. This "overconfidence phenomenon" seems partly due to the much greater ease with which we can imagine why we might be right than why we might be wrong. Moreover, people are more likely to search for information that can confirm their beliefs than information that can disconfirm them.

WE OFTEN IGNORE USEFUL INFORMATION

Fourth, when given compelling anecdotes or even useless information, we often ignore useful base-rate information. This is partly due to the later ease of recall ("availability") of vivid information.

ILLUSIONS OF CAUSATION, CORRELATION, AND PERSONAL CONTROL

Fifth, we are often swayed by illusions of correlation and personal control. It is tempting to perceive correlations where none exist ("illusory correlation") and to think we can control events which are really beyond our control (the "illusion of control").

OUR ERRONEOUS BELIEFS MAY GENERATE THEIR OWN REALITY

Finally, erroneous beliefs take on a life of their own. Studies of experimenter bias and teacher expectations indicate that at least sometimes an erroneous belief that certain people are unusually capable (or incapable) can lead one to give special treatment to those people. This may elicit superior (or inferior) performance, and therefore seem to confirm an assumption that is actually false. Similarly, in everyday social affairs we often get "behavioral confirmation" of what we expect.

These six sources of illusory thinking, plus three more considered previously (the I-knew-it-all-along phenomenon, the fundamental attribution error, and the self-serving bias), indicate our capacity for forming and sustaining false beliefs. Often these illusions of human thought are by-products of thinking strategies (heuristics) that usually serve us well, just as visual illusions are a by-product of perceptual mechanisms that help us organize sensory information. But they are errors nonetheless, errors that can warp our perceptions of reality and prejudice our judgments of persons.

FOR FURTHER READING

Goleman, D. (1985). *Vital lies, simple truths: The psychology of self-deception and shared illusions*. New York: Simon & Schuster. A gifted psychologist/writer examines how and why we fool ourselves.

Kahneman, D., Slovic, P., & Tversky, A. (Eds.). (1982). *Judgment under uncertainty: Heuristics and biases*. New York: Cambridge University Press. Influential researchers describe how we make social judgments and how our intuitions go awry.

Maital, S. (1982). *Minds, markets, and money: Psychological foundations of economic behavior*. New York: Basic Books. Insightfully applies social-psychological principles to people's beliefs and behavior regarding inflation, consumption, and the stock market.

Nisbett, R., & Ross, L. (1980). *Human inference: Strategies and shortcomings of social judgment*. Englewood Cliffs, NJ: Prentice-Hall. An insightful and delightful book on the pitfalls of social reasoning by two influential social psychologists.

CHAPTER
5

APPLICATION: SOCIAL THINKING IN THE CLINIC

CHAPTER

5

APPLICATION: SOCIAL THINKING IN THE CLINIC

If you are a typical college student you may at some point during this year be at least mildly depressed—feeling dissatisfied with your life, discouraged about the future, sad, lacking appetite and energy, unable to concentrate, perhaps even wondering if life is worth it. Maybe disappointing grades will jeopardize your career goals. Perhaps the breakup of a relationship will leave you despairing. And maybe your brooding self-focus at such times only worsens your feelings. For 5 to 10 percent of men and twice that many women, life's down times are not just temporary blue moods but one or more major depressive episodes that last for weeks at a time without any obvious cause.

Among the thriving areas of "applied social psychology" is one that applies research on social cognition (described in Chapters 2 to 4) to problems such as depression. This bridge-building research between social and clinical psychology is providing answers to three important questions: (1) How might the ways in which we think about ourselves and others feed problems such as depression, loneliness, anxiety, and even physical illness? (2) How might these maladaptive thought patterns be reversed? (3) As lay people or as professional psychologists, how might we improve the judgments and predictions we make regarding others? In this chapter, then, we will glimpse what social psychology has so far contributed to the *understanding* of psychological disorders such as depression, to their *treatment*, and to improving the process of clinical *judgment and prediction*.

Clinical psychology:
The study, assessment, and treatment of people with psychological difficulties.

SOCIAL COGNITION IN PROBLEM BEHAVIORS

One of psychology's most intriguing research frontiers concerns the cognitive processes that accompany psychological disorders. How do the attributions, expectations, and other thought patterns of troubled and untroubled people differ? In the case of depression, the most heavily researched disorder, dozens of new studies are providing some answers.

SOCIAL COGNITION AND DEPRESSION

As we all know from experience, depressed people are negative thinkers. When we are down, we view life through dark-colored glasses. Psychiatrist Aaron Beck (1982) reports that with seriously depressed people—those who are feeling worthless, lethargic, disinterested in friends and family, unable to sleep or eat normally—the negative thinking may become self-defeating. Their intensely negative outlook leads them to magnify bad experiences, minimize good ones, and become unrealistically pessimistic. One depressed young woman illustrates: "The real me is worthless and inadequate. I can't move forward with my work because I become frozen with doubt" (Burns, 1980, p. 29).

Negative Distortion or Depressive Realism?

Do all depressed people have an unrealistically negative view of things? To find out, Lauren Alloy and Lyn Abramson (1979) studied college students who had scored as mildly depressed or nondepressed on a depression inventory. They had the students observe whether their pressing a button or not was linked with whether or not a light came on. Surprisingly, the depressed students were quite accurate in estimating their

Depressive realism:
The tendency of mildly depressed people to make accurate rather than self-serving judgments, attributions, and predictions.

Note: Severely depressed people may indeed be unrealistically negative.

degree of control; it was the nondepressives whose judgments were distorted, by exaggerating the extent of their control. A string of later experiments consistently confirmed this phenomenon of ***depressive realism,*** also known as the "sadder-but-wiser effect": Nondepressed people overestimate the degree to which they are responsible for positive events and underestimate their responsibility for negative events; depressed people do not (Alloy & Abramson, 1988).

Although these studies have refuted the common presumption that depressed people are unrealistic, they have revealed a specific way in which depressed people think differently from those nondepressed. One difference lies in their attributions of responsibility. Consider: If you fail an exam and blame yourself, you may conclude that you are stupid or lazy and feel depressed. If you attribute the failure to an unfair exam or to other circumstances beyond your control, you are more likely to feel angry. In a hundred-plus studies involving 15,000 subjects (Sweeney et al., 1986), depressed people have been more likely than nondepressed people to exhibit a negative "attributional style" (see Figure 5-1). They are more likely to attribute failures and setbacks to causes that are *stable* ("It's going to last forever"), *global* ("It's going to affect everything I do"), and *internal* ("It's all my fault"). The result of this pessimistic, overgeneralized, self-blaming thinking, say Abramson and her colleagues (1989), is a depressing sense of hopelessness.

Compared to this depressive attributional style, self-serving illusions seem adaptive. If, in hindsight, this sounds obvious, consider how much more obvious would sound the familiar pronouncement that mental health is based on *accurate* perceptions of ourselves and the world. After amassing the available research, Shelley Taylor and Jonathon Brown (1988) say that, mental health derives, rather, from "overly positive self-evaluations, exaggerated perceptions of control or mastery, and unrealistic optimism." Thanks to our positive illusions, we are happier, more productive, and less self-preoccupied than are depressed realists.

Pride can also breed the problems noted in Chapters 3 and 4, such as the false optimism that doubts real perils and the "I'm-better-than-you" attitude that underlies social conflicts and prejudice. Still, we can understand how La Rochefoucauld could surmise "that Nature, which has so wisely constructed our bodies for our welfare, gave us pride to spare us the painful knowledge of our shortcomings" (*Maxims,* 1665).

"Life is the art of being well deceived."
William Hazlitt, 1778–1830

FIGURE 5-1
Depressive attributional style. Depression is linked with a negative, pessimistic way of explaining and interpreting failures.

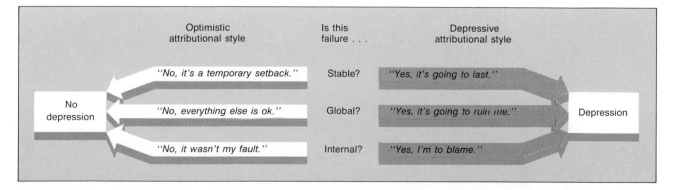

BEHIND THE SCENES

As graduate students we were shocked to discover that the popular and clinical lore that depressed people distort reality had never been tested. We were further surprised when our own studies revealed that *non*depressed people often distort reality—in an optimistic direction. This phenomenon of depressive realism—what we call the "sadder but wiser effect"— makes us wonder: Does realism about oneself and one's world make people more vulnerable to depression? Or is realism a consequence of depression?

Lauren Alloy, Northwestern University, and
Lyn Abramson, University of Wisconsin

Are Depressive Attributions a Cause or Result of Depression?

The cognitive accompaniments of depression raise a chicken-and-egg question: Is the attributional style of depressed people the cause or the consequence of their depressed mood?

Depressed Moods Cause Negative Thinking

Without doubt, our moods color our thinking. To West Germans enjoying their team's World Cup soccer victory (Schwarz et al., 1987) and to Australians emerging from a heartwarming movie (Forgas & Moylan, 1987), people seem goodhearted, life in general seems wonderful. Put in a happy mood, the world seems friendlier, decisions come more easily, good news more readily comes to mind (Johnson & Tversky, 1983; Isen & Means, 1983; Stone & Glass, 1986). When we *feel* happy, we *think* happy and optimistic thoughts.

Let our mood turn gloomy and our thoughts switch onto a different track. Off come the rose-colored glasses, on come the dark glasses. Now the bad mood primes our recollections of negative events (Bower, 1987; Johnson & Magaro, 1987). Whereas *formerly* depressed people recall their parents the same as do never-depressed people, *currently* depressed people recall their parents as having been rejecting and punitive (Lewinsohn & Rosenbaum, 1987). When a black mood strikes, our relationships seem to sour, our self-image takes a dive, our hopes for the future dim, people's behavior seems more sinister (Brown & Taylor, 1986; Mayer & Salovey, 1987).

You can get a feel for the effects of your mood by imagining yourself as a subject in one experiment that used hypnosis to put people in a temporary good or bad mood (Forgas et al., 1984). After being identified as a hypnotizable subject, you are invited to the Stanford University psychology laboratory for an interview. The next day you return and are put in a hypnotic state and asked to recall either a time when you felt unhappy, depressed, disappointed, let down, and rejected or a time when you were happy, successful, liked, and accepted. After imagining these recollections in a vivid, lifelike way, you find that the researcher asks you to watch a videotape of your earlier interview. If made to feel happy, you are generally pleased with what you see, and you are able to detect numerous instances of your poise, interest, and social skill. If

IDEAS TO REMEMBER

Vladimir Horowitz

In any academic field the results of tens of thousands of studies, the conclusions of thousands of investigators, the insights of hundreds of theorists, can usually be boiled down to a few overriding ideas. Biology offers us principles such as natural selection and adaptation. Sociology builds upon concepts such as social structure, cultural relativity, and societal organization. Music depends upon our ideas of rhythm, melody, and harmony.

If we were to distill this book's first section, Social Thinking, and its next, Social Influence, which concepts would be included on a short list of social psychology's big ideas? What fundamental principles are worth remembering long after you have forgotten most of what you learned while studying social psychology. My short list of "great ideas we ought never forget" includes these five:

Any attitude is but one determinant of any relevant behavior. Nevertheless, when it is highly relevant to the behavior and we are made keenly conscious of it, an attitude may be an important determinant. Our political attitudes influence our voting behavior. Our smoking attitudes influence our susceptibility to peer pressures to smoke. Our attitudes toward the victims of famine influence our contributions to famine relief. The persuasive forces that shape attitudes therefore warrant our close attention. Whether we view a persuasive appeal as "education" or as "propaganda," its impact may be considerable.

Ironically, another powerful influence over our attitudes is our own past actions. Whenever we act, and feel responsible for how we have acted, our attitudes tend to follow our action. This subtle, self-persuasive process enables all sorts of people—political campaigners, lovers, even terrorists—to believe more strongly in those things for which they have witnessed or suffered.

II. ONE OF THE MOST HUMAN OF TENDENCIES IS OUR URGE TO EXPLAIN BEHAVIOR, TO ATTRIBUTE IT TO SOME CAUSE, AND THEREFORE MAKE IT SEEM ORDERLY, PREDICTABLE, AND CONTROLLABLE.

As intuitive scientists, our attributions usually are made very efficiently and with sufficient accuracy for our daily needs. When someone's behavior is consistent and distincive, we infer the person has traits and attitudes that predispose such behavior. Usually that is true, so our common sense attributions generally serve us well. We know to avoid someone who is consistently heartless and ill-tempered, and to approach those who seem always to be warm and friendly. But . . .

III. IN WAYS WE ARE OFTEN UNAWARE, OUR EXPLANATIONS AND SOCIAL JUDGMENTS ARE VULNERABLE
TO ERROR.

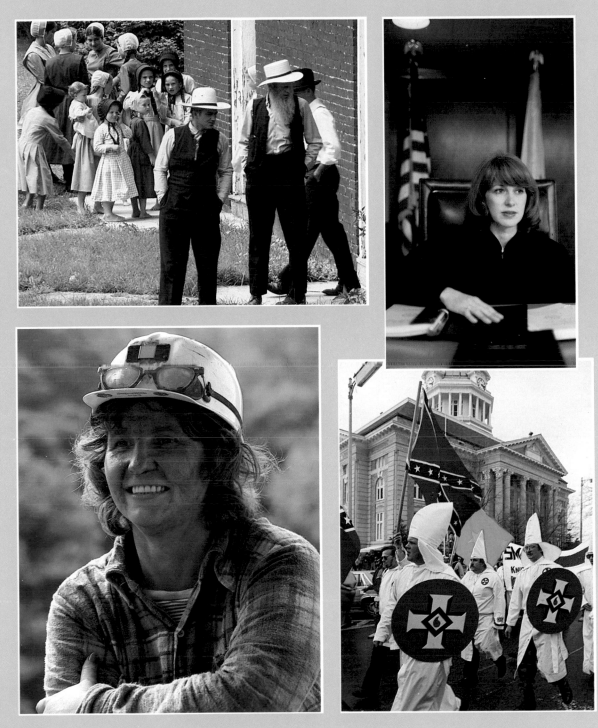

When observing others we are sometimes too prone to attribute their behavior to their dispositions (for example, to think that someone who acts strangely must *be* strange), to be biased by our preconceptions, to "see" illusory relationships and causes, to treat people in ways that trigger them to fulfill our expectations, to be swayed more by vivid anecdotes than by statistical reality. Failing to recognize such sources of error in our social thinking, we also are prone to overconfidence in our social judgments.

Our views of ourselves are similarly fragile containers of truth. Heeding the ancient admonition to "know thyself," we analyze our own behavior. Although we are better aware than others of how we adjust our behavior in response to different situations, we are hardly impartial observers of ourselves. Indeed, our human tendency to self-serving attributions is at times tragically evident in conflicts between married partners, management and labor, rich and poor. Each side views its motives alone as pure, its actions and expectations as beyond reproach; but so does its opposition, and so the conflict continues. On the other hand, to fail to believe in our efficacy or to make self-blaming attributions is a recipe for failure, loneliness, and depression.

Why do our actions not always mirror our attitudes? Because the enormous power of social situations sometimes overrides people's inner dispositions. There is wide-ranging evidence that most people are capable of a wide variety of behaviors. Faced with certain situations, most people are capable of acting kindly or brutally, independently or submissively, wisely or foolishly. Social behavior, then, is a product of both our internal social thinking and of external social forces.

Betty Freidan

Martin Luther King, Jr.

Although powerful situations may override individual differences, social psychologists do not view humans as passive tumbleweeds, blown this way and that by the social winds. When facing the same situation, different people may react differently, depending on their personality, cultural history, and so forth. Moreover, when people feel coerced by blatant social pressure, they will sometimes react in ways that restore their perception of freedom. Those in a numerical minority will also sometimes oppose and sway the majority, reminding us that we are not only the creatures of our social world, but also its creators.

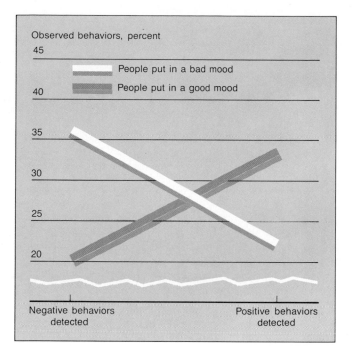

FIGURE 5-2
A temporary good or bad mood strongly influenced people's ratings of their videotaped behavior. Those in a bad mood detected many fewer positive behaviors. (Forgas et al., 1984.)

"When we are in a good mood others seem happy, the environment seems beneficent, life seems wonderful; when we are in a bad mood everything seems dark and gloomy. Yet we don't usually attribute these consequences to our mood—they seem to be 'out there.' The world really [seems] different."
Michael Ross and Garth Fletcher (1985, p. 85).

put in a bad mood, viewing the same tape seems to reveal a quite different you—one who is frequently stiff, nervous, and inarticulate (see Figure 5-2). Given the extent to which your mood colors your processing of information, you are relieved at how things seem to brighten when the experimenter hypnotically switches you to a happy mood before leaving the experiment.

The consequences of a depressed mood are not only cognitive but also behavioral. The person who is withdrawn, glum, and complaining does not elicit joy and warmth in others. Thus Stephen Strack and James Coyne (1983) found that depressed people were realistic in thinking that their behavior was not well accepted by others. Depressed behavior can trigger hostility, anxiety, and even reciprocal depression in others. College students who have depressed roommates tend to be a little depressed themselves (Burchill & Stiles, 1988; Howes et al., 1985).

Does Negative Thinking Cause Depression?

So, being depressed has cognitive and behavioral effects. Does it also have cognitive origins? It's perfectly normal to feel depressed over a *major* loss, such as losing your job, suffering a death in the family, or being rejected or abused. But why are some people so readily depressed by *minor* stresses? Results have been mixed, because negative thinking tends to wax and wane with depression (Barnett & Gotlib, 1988; Kuiper & Higgins, 1985). But new evidence suggests that a negative attributional style may contribute to depressive reactions: Colin Sacks and Daphne Bugental (1987) asked some young women to get acquainted with a stranger who sometimes acted cold and unfriendly, creating an awkward social situation. Unlike optimistic women, those with a more pessimistic explanatory style—who characteristically offer stable, global, and internal attributions for bad events—reacted to the social failure by becoming somewhat depressed. Moreover, they then behaved more antagonistically toward the next

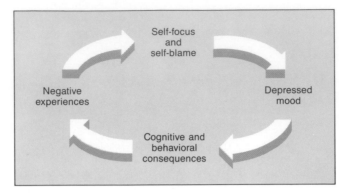

FIGURE 5-3
The vicious cycle of depression.

person they met. Thus their negative thinking predisposed a negative (depressed) mood response which predisposed negative behavior, thereby activating depression's vicious cycle (see Figure 5-3).

Outside the laboratory, studies of children, teenagers, and adults have confirmed that those with the pessimistic explanatory style are more likely to become depressed when bad things happen (Anderson et al., 1988; Brown & Siegel, 1988; Nolen-Hoeksema et al., 1986). If you are predisposed to see negative events—money problems, bad grades, social rejections—as uncontrollable, you are more likely to get depressed.

Depression researcher Peter Lewinsohn and his colleagues (1985) have assembled these findings into a coherent psychological understanding of depression. In their view, the negative self-image, attributions, and expectations of a depressed person are an essential link in a vicious cycle that is triggered by negative experience—perhaps academic or vocational failure, or family conflict, or social rejection. In those vulnerable to depression such stresses trigger a brooding, self-focused, self-blaming (Pyszczynski & Greenberg, 1987a), which creates a depressed mood that drastically alters the way a person thinks and acts, which then fuels further negative experiences, self-blame, depressed mood, and so forth. Thus depression is viewed as both a cause and a consequence of negative cognitions.

Martin Seligman (1988) believes that self-focus and self-blame help explain the near-epidemic levels of depression in America today. Compared to 50 years ago, rates of "unipolar" depression (the type most commonly experienced) have risen tenfold. Seligman believes that the decline of religion and family, and the growth of the individualistic "you can do it" idea can breed hopelessness; when the self stands alone, with nothing to fall back on, failed courses, careers, and marriages produce despair.

The insights gained by examining the thinking style linked with depression have encouraged social psychologists to study the thinking patterns associated with other problems. How do those who are plagued with excessive loneliness, shyness, or alcohol abuse view themselves relative to others? How well do they recall their successes and their failures, and to what do they attribute their ups and downs? To what extent is their attention focused on themselves rather than on others in the world around them? Although the research is still in its early stages, these are among the questions now being asked. Let us glimpse some of the emerging answers.

SOCIAL COGNITION AND LONELINESS

Loneliness, whether chronic or temporary, is a painful awareness that one's social relationships are less numerous or meaningful than one desires. Jenny de Jong-Gierveld

(1987) observed in her study of Dutch adults that people who are unmarried and un-attached are more likely to feel lonely, prompting her to speculate that the modern emphasis on individual fulfillment and the depreciation of marriage and family life may be "loneliness-provoking" (as well as depression-provoking). But loneliness need not coincide with aloneness. One can feel lonely in the middle of a party. And one can be utterly alone—as I am while writing these words in the solitude of an isolated turret office at a British university 5000 miles from home—without feeling particularly lonely. To feel lonely is to feel excluded from a group, unloved by those around you, unable to share your private concerns, or different and alienated from those in your surroundings (Beck & Young, 1978; Davis & Franzoi, 1986). Adolescents experience such feelings more commonly than do adults. When beeped by an electronic pager at various times during a week and asked to record what they were doing and how they felt, adolescents were more likely than adults to report feeling lonely when alone (Larson et al., 1982). Males and females feel lonely under somewhat different circumstances—males when isolated from group interaction, women when deprived of close one-to-one relationships (Berg & McQuinn, 1988; Stokes & Levin, 1986).

Like depressed people, chronically lonely people seem caught in a vicious cycle of self-defeating social cognitions and social behaviors. For one thing, they have some of the negative attributional style of the depressed—blaming themselves for their deficient social relationships (Anderson et al., 1983; Snodgrass, 1987). Moreover, they perceive others in negative ways as well. When paired with a stranger of the same sex or with a first-year college roommate, lonely students are more likely to harbor a negative perception of the other person (Jones et al., 1981; Wittenberg & Reis, 1986).

These negative perceptions may have a basis in reality *and* function as self-fulfilling

To feel lonely is to feel excluded from a group, unloved by those around you, or unable to share your private concerns.

prophecies. For lonely people often do find it hard to introduce themselves, make phone calls, and participate in groups (Rook, 1984; Spitzberg & Hurt, 1987). They tend to be self-conscious and low in self-esteem, and when talking with a stranger they have been observed to spend more time talking about themselves and to take less interest in their conversational partners than do non-lonely people (Jones et al., 1982). So it is not surprising that after such conversations, the new acquaintances often come away with more negative impressions of the lonely people (Jones et al., 1983). Believing in their social unworthiness and being rather pessimistic about others seems to inhibit lonely people from behaving in ways that would reduce their loneliness.

SOCIAL COGNITION AND SOCIAL ANXIETY

Being interviewed for a much-wanted job, dating someone for the first time, giving a speech or performance before an important audience, or stepping into a roomful of strangers can make almost anyone feel anxious. Some people—especially those who are shy or easily embarrassed—feel anxious in almost any situation in which they might be evaluated. For these people, anxiety may seem more a trait than a temporary state.

What causes us to feel anxious in social situations? Why are some people shackled in the prison of their own shyness? Barry Schlenker and Mark Leary (1982b, 1985; Leary, 1984, 1986; Maddux et al., 1988) help answer these questions by applying self-presentation theory. As you may recall from Chapters 2 and 3, self-presentation theory assumes that we are eager to present ourselves in ways that make a good impression and avoid making a bad impression. The implications of this for social anxiety are straightforward: *We feel anxious when we are motivated to impress others*, *but are doubting our ability to do so.* This simple principle helps explain a variety of research findings, each of which will probably ring true to your own experience: We feel most anxious

- when dealing with powerful, high-status people—people whose impressions matter
- when in an evaluative context, as when making a first impression on someone, such as one's fiance's parents
- when the interaction focuses on something that is central to our self-image rather than something unimportant, as when a college professor presents ideas before peers at a professional convention
- when in novel situations where we are unsure of the social rules, such as a first school dance or first formal dinner
- when we are self-conscious (as shy people often are), with our attention focused not on the other people but on ourselves and how we are coming across

The natural tendency in all such situations is to be cautiously self-protective: to talk less; to avoid topics that reveal one's ignorance; to be guarded about oneself; to be unassertive, agreeable, and smiling.

Shyness is a form of social anxiety characterized by self-consciousness and worry about being evaluated (Anderson & Harvey, 1988; Asendorpf, 1987; Carver & Scheier, 1986). People who are temporarily or chronically self-conscious are inclined to see incidental events as somehow relevant to themselves (Fenigstein, 1984). They over-personalize situations, a tendency that breeds anxious concern and, in extreme cases, paranoia. For example, highly self-conscious people (whose numbers include many

Meeting a person of high status—like Jesse Jackson—would make most people feel anxious.

normal teenagers) overestimate the extent to which other people are watching and evaluating them. If their hair won't comb right or they have a facial blemish, they assume everyone else notices and is judging them accordingly.

To reduce social anxiety, some people turn to alcohol. Alcohol lowers anxiety as it reduces self-consciousness (Hull & Young, 1983). As this implies, those who are chronically self-conscious are especially likely to drink following a failure. And if they become alcoholics they are more likely than those low in self-consciousness to relapse from treatment when experiencing stress and failure.

Symptoms as diverse as anxiety and alcohol abuse can also serve what Chapter 3 called a self-handicapping function. Labeling oneself as anxious, shy, depressed, or under the influence of alcohol can provide an excuse for failure (Snyder & Smith, 1986). Behind a barricade of symptoms, the person's ego stands secure. "Why did I do poorly on the test? I knew the material, but I just get all tensed up and can't think when taking the exam." "Why don't I date? Because I'm shy, so people don't easily get to know the real me." The symptom is a guise, an unconscious strategic ploy that explains away negative outcomes.

So, what if we were to remove the need for such a guise—by providing people with a handy alternative explanation for their anxiety and therefore for possible failure? Would, say, a shy person then no longer need to be shy? That is precisely what Susan Brodt and Philip Zimbardo (1981) found when they brought shy and not-shy college women to the laboratory and had them converse with a handsome male who posed as a fellow subject. Prior to the conversation, the women were cooped up in a small chamber and blasted with loud noise. Some of the shy women (but not others) were told that the noise would leave them with a pounding heart, a common symptom of social anxiety. Thus when these shy women later talked with the man they were able to attribute their pounding heart and any difficulties in the conversation to the noise rather than to their shyness or social inadequacy. Compared to the shy women who were not given this handy explanation for their pounding heart, these shy women were no longer so shy. Like the non-shy women, they talked fluently once the conversation got going and asked questions of the man. In fact, unlike the other shy women (whom the man could easily spot as shy), these shy women were to him indistinguishable from the not-shy women.

SOCIAL COGNITION AND PHYSICAL ILLNESS

Health Psychology

During the health-conscious 1980s, reports by the National Academy of Sciences and other agencies informed us that half of all deaths are linked with people's behavior—with their consuming cigarettes, alcohol, drugs, and harmful foods; with their reactions to stress; with their lack of exercise and nonadherence to doctor's orders. Efforts to study and modify these behavioral contributions to illness helped create a new indisciplinary field of **behavioral medicine.** Psychology's contribution to this interdisciplinary science is its new subfield, **health psychology.** The American Psychological Association's division of health psychology, formed in 1979, mushroomed to 2900 members in its first ten years, including many of the estimated 3000 psychologists now working in U.S. medical schools.

Among health psychology's questions, and tentative answers, are the following:

Behavioral medicine:
An interdisciplinary field that integrates and applies behavioral and medical knowledge regarding health and disease.

Health psychology:
A subfield of psychology that provides psychology's contribution to behavioral medicine.

1. Do our characteristic emotions, and our ways of responding to stressful events, predict our susceptibility to heart disease, stroke, cancer, and other ailments?
   - Heart disease has been linked with a competitive, impatient, and—the aspect that matters—*anger-prone* "Type A personality" (e.g., Dembroski & Costa, 1987). Under stress, reactive, anger-prone people secrete more of the stress hormones believed to accelerate the buildup of plaque on the walls of the heart's arteries.
   - Sustained stress appears to suppress the disease-fighting immune system, leaving us more vulnerable to infections and malignancy (e.g., Weinberger et al., 1987). Experiments reveal that the immune system's activity can also be influenced by conditioning.
2. How can we control or even reduce stress?
   - Health psychologists are exploring the benefits of aerobic exercise (which seems an effective antidote to mild depression and anxiety), relaxation training (to help control tension-related ailments such as headaches and high blood pressure), and supportive close relationships (which can help buffer the impact of stress).
3. How do people decide whether they are ill, and what can be done to ensure that they seek needed medical help and will then follow a treatment regimen?
   - We decide or worry that we are sick when symptoms fit one of our existing "schemas" for disease (e.g., Bishop, 1987). (Does the small cyst match our idea of a malignant lump? Is the stomachache bad enough to be appendicitis? Is the pain in the chest area merely—as many heart attack victims suppose—a muscle spasm?)
   - Patients are more willing to follow treatment instructions when they have a warm

relationship with their doctor, when they help plan their treatment regimen, and when treatment options are framed attractively—people are more likely to elect an operation when given "a 40 percent of surviving" than when given "a 60 percent chance of not surviving" (e.g., Wilson et al., 1987).

4. What life-style changes would prevent illness and promote health, and how might such changes be encouraged?
   - Psychologists are exploring the social influences that motivate adolescents to start smoking and have pioneered effective smoking prevention techniques (see p. 263).
   - New explorations of internal and external influences on body weight explain why the obese have difficulty losing weight permanently but also how they can best modify eating and exercise (e.g., Polivy & Herman, 1985).

Social psychologists have helped provide answers to all these questions. To illustrate their work, let's look more deeply at one question: How do our styles of explaining events and our feelings of control affect our vulnerability to illness?

Optimism and Health

Stories abound of patients who take a sudden turn for the worse when something makes them lose hope or who suddenly improve when hope is renewed. As cancer attacks the liver of 9-year-old Jeff, his doctors fear the worst. But Jeff remains optimistic. He is determined to grow up to be a research scientist who will search for cancer's cure.

One day Jeff is elated with the news that a specialist who has taken a long-distance interest in his case is planning to stop off while on a cross-country trip. There is so much Jeff wants to tell the doctor and to show him from the diary he has kept since he got sick.

On the anticipated day, fog blankets his city. The doctor's plane is diverted to another city, from which the doctor flies on to his final destination. Hearing the disappointing news, Jeff cries quietly. The next morning, pneumonia and fever have developed, and Jeff lies listless. By evening he is in a coma. The next afternoon he dies (Visintainer & Seligman, 1983).

Understanding the links between attitudes and disease requires more than dramatic true stories such as this, however. Even if, say, hopelessness coincides with cancer, is it just that cancer breeds hopelessness, or does hopelessness also hinder resistance to cancer? To resolve this chicken-and-egg riddle, researchers have (1) experimentally created hopelessness by subjecting organisms to uncontrollable stresses and (2) correlated the hopeless explanatory style with future illnesses.

Stress and Illness

The clearest indication of the effects of hopelessness—what Chapter 3 termed *learned helplessness*—comes from experiments that subject animals to mild but uncontrollable electric shocks, loud noises, or crowding. Such experiences seem not to *cause* diseases such as cancer but rather to lower the body's disease resistance. Rats injected with live cancer cells are much more likely to develop and die of tumors if they also receive inescapable shocks than if they receive escapable shocks or no shocks. Moreover, compared to juvenile rats given controllable shocks, those given uncontrollable shocks are twice as likely to develop tumors when given cancer cells and another

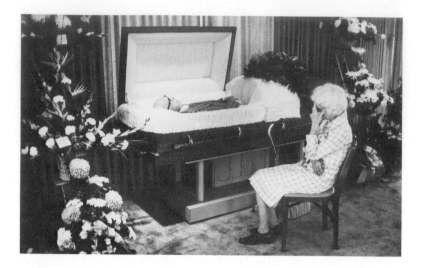

A lowering of tolerance in the immune system has been associated with the onset of extreme stress, such as that caused by the death of a spouse.

round of either escapable or inescapable shocks as adults (Visintainer & Seligman, 1985). Animals that have learned helplessness react more passively, and blood tests reveal their immune responses to be weakened.

It's a big leap from rats to humans. But a growing body of evidence reveals that people who undergo highly stressful experiences similarly become more vulnerable to disease. The death of a spouse, the stress of a space flight landing, even the strain of an exam week have all been associated with depressed immune defenses (Jemmott & Locke, 1984). In one experiment, even a temporary stress magnified the severity of symptoms experienced by volunteers who were knowingly infected with a cold virus (Dixon, 1986).

Pessimistic Explanatory Style and Illness

If uncontrollable stress affects health by generating a passive, hopeless resignation, then will people who exhibit such attitudes be more vulnerable to illness? Several studies have confirmed that a pessimistic style of explaining bad events—saying "It's my responsibility, it's going to last, and it's going to undermine everything"—makes illness more likely. Christopher Peterson and Martin Seligman (1987) studied the press quotes of ninety-four old or deceased members of baseball's Hall of Fame and gauged the extent to which they offered pessimistic (stable, global, internal) explanations for bad events, such as losing big games. Those who routinely did so tended to die at somewhat younger ages, whereas optimists—who offered stable, global, and internal explanations for *good* events—tended to live longer.

Peterson, Seligman, and George Valliant (1988) offer other findings: Harvard graduates who expressed the least pessimism when interviewed in 1946 were healthiest when restudied in 1980; Virginia Tech introductory psychology students who offered stable and global explanations for bad events suffered more colds, sore throats, and flus a year later. Michael Sheier and Charles Carver (1987) similarly report that those with a generally optimistic outlook (who agree, for example, that "I usually expect the best") are less often bothered by various illnesses and recover better from coronary bypass surgery. Even cancer patients appear somewhat more likely to survive if their attitude is hopeful and determined rather than pessimistic and stoical (Levy et al., 1988; Pettingale et al., 1985). Blood tests provide a reason, by linking the pessimistic explanatory style with weaker immune defenses (Kamen et al., 1988).

From their own studies, researchers Howard Tennen and Glenn Affleck (1987) agree that a positive, hopeful attributional style is generally good medicine. But they also remind us that every silver lining has a cloud. Optimists, as we noted in Chapter 3, may see themselves as invulnerable and thus fail to take sensible precautions. And when things go wrong in a big way—when the optimist has a Down's syndrome child or encounters a devastating illness—the adversity can be shattering. Optimism *is* good for health. But we'd best acknowledge its limits, remembering that even optimists have a mortality rate of 100 percent.

"You are dust, and to dust you shall return."
Genesis 3:19

SOCIAL-PSYCHOLOGICAL APPROACHES TO TREATMENT

So far we have considered patterns of social thinking that are linked with problems in living, ranging from serious depression to everyday shyness to physical illness. Does the emerging understanding of maladaptive thought patterns suggest any guidelines for treating such difficulties? There is no single social-psychological method of therapy. But social psychologists are now suggesting how their principles might be integrated into existing treatment techniques. Building on what we have already learned, let's consider three examples.

INDUCING INTERNAL CHANGE THROUGH EXTERNAL BEHAVIOR

In Chapter 2, "Behavior and Attitudes," we reviewed the wide-ranging evidence for a simple but powerful principle: Our actions affect our attitudes. The roles we play, the things we say and do, and the decisions we make help form who we are. When we act, we amplify ideas that are consistent with what we have done, especially when we feel some responsibility for our action. The behaviors that we choose to commit have self-persuasive aftereffects.

Consistent with the attitudes-follow-behavior principle, several psychotherapy techniques prescribe action. If we cannot directly control our feelings by sheer will power, we can influence them indirectly, through our behavior. Behavior therapists attempt to shape behavior and, if they care about inner dispositions at all, assume that these will tag along after the behavior has changed. Assertiveness training employs the same foot-in-the-door procedure that we saw to have an influence upon attitudes: The individual first role-plays being assertive in a supportive context and then gradually becomes assertive in everyday life. Rational-emotive therapy assumes that we generate our own emotions; its clients are given "homework" assignments to act in new ways that will generate new emotions. Encounter groups subtly induce participants to behave in novel ways in front of the group—to express anger, cry, act with high self-esteem, express positive feelings.

Experiments confirm that the things we say about ourselves can affect how we inwardly feel. In one experiment, students were induced to write self-laudatory essays (Mirels & McPeek, 1977). Compared to students who wrote essays about a current social issue, those who had presented themselves as intelligent, caring, and sensitive later expressed higher self-esteem when privately rating themselves for a different experimenter. In several more experiments, Edward Jones and his associates (1981; Rhodewalt and Agustsdottir, 1986) influenced students to present themselves to an interviewer in either self-enhancing or self-deprecating ways. Again, the students' public displays—whether upbeat or downbeat—carried over to their later private responses on a test of actual self-esteem. Saying is believing, even when talking about oneself. This was especially true when the students were made to feel responsible for how they presented themselves.

The importance of perceived choice is also apparent in an experiment by Pamela Mendonca and Sharon Brehm (1983). They invited one group of overweight children who were about to begin a treatment program to choose which treatment they preferred and then periodically reminded them that they had chosen their treatment. Compared to no-choice children who simultaneously experienced the same eight-week weight-loss program, those who felt responsible for their treatment had lost more weight when reweighed at the end of the eight weeks and three months later.

BREAKING THE VICIOUS CYCLES OF DEPRESSION AND SOCIAL ANXIETY

We have seen that depression, loneliness, and social anxiety tend to maintain themselves in a vicious cycle of negative experiences, negative thinking, and self-defeating behavior. On the brighter side, it should therefore be possible to break the cycle at any of several points—by changing the environment, by training the person to behave more constructively, by reversing one's self-blame and negative attributions and expectations. Not surprisingly, several different therapy methods have been found effective in helping people break free of problems such as depression, and even without therapy most people eventually manage to break out of the cycle.

Social Skills Training

As we have seen, problems such as depression, loneliness, and shyness are not just problems in one's mind. To be around a depressed person for weeks on end can be irritating and even depressing, reactions which the depressed person then uses to justify the depression. Lonely and shy people may indeed come across poorly in social situations, and know it. In such cases, social skills training may help. By observing and then practicing needed social behaviors in safe situations, the person may develop the confidence required to behave more effectively in other situations.

As the person begins to behave more skillfully and to enjoy the rewards of doing so, the result may also be a more positive self-perception. Frances Haemmerlie and Robert Montgomery (1982, 1984, 1986) have demonstrated this in several heartwarming studies with shy, anxious college students. Drawing upon self-perception theory (see p. 58) they surmised that those who seldom date and are nervous around those of the other sex infer that "I don't date much, so I must be socially inadequate, so I shouldn't try reaching out to anyone." To reverse this negative self-perception, Haemmerlie and Montgomery enticed such students into some altogether pleasant interactions with people of the other sex. In one experiment, college men completed social anxiety questionnaires and then came to the laboratory on two different days. Each day they enjoyed 12-minute conversations with six young women. The men thought the women were fellow subjects; actually, the women had been asked simply to carry on a natural, positive, friendly conversation with each of the men.

The effect of these 2½ hours of conversation was remarkable. As one subject wrote afterwards, "I had never met so many girls that I could have a good conversation with. After a few girls, my confidence grew to the point where I didn't notice being nervous like I once did." Such comments were supported by a variety of measures. Unlike men in a control condition, those who experienced the conversations reported considerably less female-related anxiety when they were re-tested one week and six months later. Placed alone in a room with an attractive female stranger, they also became much more likely to initiate conversation. And outside the laboratory they actually began occasional dating. Haemmerlie and Montgomery note that not only did all this occur without any counseling, it may very well have occurred *because* there was no counseling. Having behaved successfully on their own, the subjects could now perceive themselves as more socially competent. Although seven months later the researchers did debrief the subjects, by that time the men had presumably enjoyed sufficient social success on their own to maintain their internal attributions for success. "Nothing succeeds like success," concludes Haemmerlie (1987), "as long as there are no external factors present that the client can use as an excuse for that success!"

Attributional Style Therapy

The vicious cycles that maintain depression, loneliness, and shyness can be broken not only by training in more effective social skills and by positive experiences that alter self-perceptions, but also by directly modifying negative thought patterns. Some people actually have quite adequate social skills, but their experiences with hypercritical friends and family have convinced them they do not. For such people it may be enough to help them reverse their negative beliefs about themselves and their futures. Among the cognitive therapies having this aim is an "attributional style therapy" proposed by social psychologists (Abramson, 1988; Försterling, 1986).

In one such program for teaching depressed college students to change their typical attributions, Mary Anne Layden (1982) first explained the advantages of making attributions more like those of the typical nondepressed person (by accepting credit for successes and seeing how circumstances can make things go wrong). After assigning a variety of tasks, she helped the people to see how they typically interpreted success and failure.

Finally, there came the treatment phase: Layden instructed each person to keep a diary of daily successes and failures, making special note of how they contributed to their own successes and of external reasons for their failures. When retested after a month of this attributional retraining and compared with an untreated control group, the people's self-esteem had risen and their attributional style had become more normal. In fact, the more their attributional style improved, the more their depression had lifted. By changing their social cognitions they had changed their emotions.

MAINTAINING CHANGE THROUGH INTERNAL ATTRIBUTIONS FOR SUCCESS

Two of the principles considered so far—that internal change may follow changes in external behavior, and that changed self-perceptions and self-attributions can help break a vicious cycle—converge on a corollary principle: Once achieved, improvements are most likely to be maintained if people attribute them to internal factors under their continued control rather than to external factors such as the temporary treatment program.

As a general rule, coercive therapy techniques trigger the most immediate behavior changes (Brehm & Smith, 1986). By making the unwanted behavior extremely costly or embarrassing and the "healthy" behavior extremely rewarding, a therapist may achieve quick and dramatic results. The problem, as thirty years of social-psy-

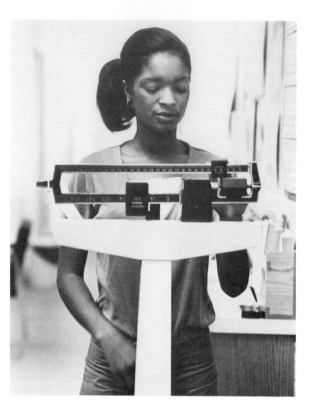

Once achieved, an ideal weight is most likely to be maintained if dieters attribute their success to internal factors under their control rather than to external factors such as a temporary treatment program.

chological research reminds us, is that coerced behavior changes tend not to endure.

To appreciate why not, consider the experience of Martha, who is concerned with her mild obesity and frustrated with her inability to do anything about it. Martha is therefore considering several different commercial weight-control programs, each of which claims that "it" achieves the best results. She chooses one and is ordered onto a strict 1,200-calorie-a-day diet. Moreover, she is required to record and report her calorie intake each day and to come in once a week and be weighed so she and her instructor can know precisely how she is doing. Confident of the program's value and not wanting to embarrass herself, Martha strictly adheres to the program and is delighted to find the unwanted pounds gradually disappearing. "This unique program really does work!," Martha tells herself as she reaches her target weight.

Sadly, however, after graduating from the program, Martha's experience repeats that of most weight-control graduates (Wing & Jeffry, 1979): She regains her lost weight. On the street, she sees her weight-control instructor approaching. Embarrassed, she moves to the other side of the sidewalk and looks away. Alas, she is recognized by the instructor, who warmly invites her back into "the program." Admitting that the program achieved good results for her the first time, Martha grants her need of it and agrees to return, beginning a second round of the loss/gain cycle.

Although Martha is fictional, her experience represents that of the participants in several weight-control experiments, including one by Janet Sonne and Dean Janoff (1979). Half of the participants were led, like Martha, to attribute their changed eating behavior to the program. The others were led to credit their own abilities and efforts. Both groups lost weight during the program, but those in the self-control condition had best maintained the weight loss when reweighed eleven weeks later. These people, like those in the shy-man-meets-women study described earlier, illustrate the benefits of what Albert Bandura calls self-efficacy (see p. 93). Having learned to cope successfully and believing it was they themselves who did it, they now felt more confident and effective and behaved accordingly.

Having emphasized what changed behavior and thought patterns can accomplish, we do well to remind ourselves of their limits. Social skill training, positive thinking, and other such factors cannot transform us into consistent winners who are loved and admired by everyone. What is more, temporary depression, loneliness, and shyness are perfectly appropriate responses—to profoundly sad events. It is only when such feelings exist chronically and without any discernible cause that there is reason for concern and a need to know how best to reverse the self-defeating thoughts and behaviors.

MAKING CLINICAL JUDGMENTS

Clinical psychologists seek not only to understand and treat psychological disorders but also to make accurate judgments, recommendations, and predictions. Is Susan suicidal? Should John be committed to a mental hospital? If released, will Tom be a homicide risk?

Clinical psychologists are not the only ones who analyze people. Employers and personnel managers scrutinize people during interviews; they select certain questions, see and hear particular things, and file some things away in memory. The net result is their impression of the person and their intuitive prediction of how competent and reliable the person would be as an employee. For that matter, all of us all the time are forming impressions of others and analyzing their behavior. Why did she act that way toward me? Is he as weird as he looks? If I criticize her how will she take it?

Such judgments of personality illustrate basic principles of social judgment introduced in Chapter 4. By alerting mental-health workers, judges, interviewers, and the like to how people form impressions and *mis*impressions, our hope is that misjudgments can be averted. So let's identify some of the ways in which personality judgments can be led astray, whether made by lay people or by mental-health professionals.

"To free a man of error is to give, not to take away. Knowledge that a thing is false is a truth."
Arthur Schopenhauer, 1788–1860

AMATEUR PSYCHOLOGIZING

Judging Others

As Chapter 4 indicated, we often lack self-insight. Richard Nisbett and Nancy Bellows (1977) have shown that this sometimes renders us unaware of what has influenced our judgments of others. They had University of Michigan students rate a female job applicant. While perusing her folder, the students read that the woman (1) was physically attractive, (2) had an excellent academic record, (3) had spilled coffee during her interview, (4) had been in a car accident, and/or (5) would later be introduced to them. When later they were asked how much each of the five factors had influenced their ratings, the students were surprisingly ignorant of how much each factor had swayed them. For example, the students felt more liking for interviewees who spilled coffee, yet the students denied that the coffee spilling had influenced them.

There are several additional reasons why our everyday assessments of people are prone to error. We all have what researchers call "implicit personality theories": "Salespeople are extroverted," "Show people are egocentric," "Scholars are reclusive." Once formed, these theories and stereotypes are easily perpetuated in ways usually unnoticed. For example, Chapter 11 will reveal how easily we slip into overestimating the uniformity of people we group within a particular category (football players, racial minorities, and so forth).

Judging Ourselves

Illusory thinking also contaminates our judgments of ourselves. Consider the "Barnum effect"—named in honor of circus entrepreneur P. T. Barnum, who said, "There's a sucker born every minute," and remarked that a good circus had a "little something for everybody." Read the following, which is intended to be a description that fits most people. How well does it fit you?

> You have a strong need for other people to like you and for them to admire you. You have a tendency to be critical of yourself. You have a great deal of unused energy which you have not turned to your advantage. While you have some personality weaknesses, you are generally able to compensate for them. Your sexual adjustment has presented some problems for you. Disciplined and controlled on the outside, you tend to be worrisome and insecure inside. At times you have serious doubts as to whether you have made the right decision or done the right thing. You prefer a certain amount of change and variety and become dissatisfied when hemmed in by restrictions and limitations. You pride yourself on being an independent thinker and do not accept other opinions without satisfactory proof. You have found it unwise to be too frank in revealing yourself to others. At times you are extroverted, affable, sociable, while at other times you are introverted, wary, and reserved. Some of your aspirations tend to be pretty unrealistic. (Forer, 1949)

In many experiments, researchers have shown people such descriptions (this one was constructed from a horoscope book). Told, as were you, that the information is true of most individuals, people usually indicate that it fits so-so. But if told that the description is designed specifically for them on the basis of their psychological tests or astrological data, people usually say the description is very accurate. In fact, given a choice between a fake description and an actual test-based description of themselves, people tend to judge the phony description as equally or more accurate (Dickson & Kelly, 1985; Standing & Keays, 1986). And that helps explain why people as prominent as Nancy and Ronald Reagan continue to take astrologers' opinions seriously, despite overwhelming evidence that astrology doesn't work (birth dates are uncorrelated with traits, astrologers can't beat chance when trying to identify someone of a given birth date from a line-up of personality descriptions, and people don't recognize their own horoscope in a set of horoscopes—Carlson, 1985).

Graphologists—people who make predictions from handwriting samples—have similarly been found to do no better than chance when trying to guess people's occupations, based on several pages of their handwriting.
(Ben-Shakhar et al., 1986)

People also are more inclined to accept false results supposedly derived from projective tests (like the Rorschach inkblots) than from an objective personality test. And having accepted the phony results, they express increased confidence in psychological testing and in the skill of their clinician. Richard Petty and Timothy Brock (1979) have found that people also live up to assessments provided by a psychologist. Ohio State University students who were told, "You are an open-minded person. You have the ability to see both sides of an issue," later wrote a fairly balanced assessment of two issues. Those told that "You are not a wishy-washy person. . . . You can take a strong stand on one side and defend it," wrote one-sided assessments of the issues.

Finally people see these Barnum descriptions as more true of themselves than of

A Barnum description relies on information that is true of most individuals.

"Ah-ha! You are not happy."

people in general, especially when the description is positive. Within reason, the more favorable a description is, the more people believe it and the more likely they are to perceive it as unique to themselves (Ruzzene & Noller, 1986; Schlenker et al., 1979; Shavit & Shouval, 1980). Joel Johnson and his colleagues (1985) report that this self-serving bias occurs even when people are not deceived into thinking the descriptions were designed for them. His subjects were able to recognize negative statements as being as applicable to themselves as anyone else. But as Figure 5-4 indicates, they judged paragraphs built of positive descriptions ("finds it easy to be open and demonstrative") as much more true of themselves than of their casual acquaintances.

In summary, when judging others we do well to remember that we are:

- Unaware of what has influenced our assessments of others,
- Prone to perceive people in line with our stereotypes, and
- Susceptible to the "Barnum effect" (accepting worthless diagnoses).

PROFESSIONAL PSYCHOLOGIZING

Professional clinical judgment is a type of social judgment, subject to the principles of social thinking (Leary & Maddux, 1987). Thus these findings raise some disconcerting implications for psychiatry and clinical psychology. Regardless of whether a particular diagnosis has any validity, the recipient is likely to stand in awe of it, especially after expending effort and money to receive it. The Barnum effect suggests a recipe for

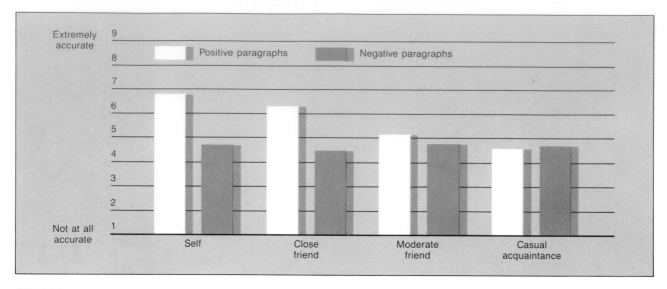

FIGURE 5-4

"If it's positive, it sounds like me (and my best friend)." Subjects judged that favorable paragraphs were not especially accurate descriptions of their casual acquaintances but were more accurate descriptions of their good friends and even better descriptions of themselves. (From Johnson et al., 1985.)

impressing clients: Give people a subjective test; make them think that its interpretation is unique to them; and drawing upon things true of most people, tell them something that is positive, though somewhat ambiguous. Such an approach should increase your clients' faith in your clinical skills—even if what they have been told has no diagnostic validity.

Illusory Correlations

Consider the following court transcript in which a seemingly confident psychologist (Psy) is being questioned by an attorney (Att):

ATT: You asked the defendant to draw a human figure?

PSY: Yes.

ATT: And this is the figure he drew for you? What does it indicate to you about his personality?

PSY: You will note this is a rear view of a male. This is very rare, statistically. It indicates hiding guilt feelings, or turning away from reality.

ATT: And this drawing of a female figure, does it indicate anything to you; and, if so, what?

PSY: It indicates hostility toward women on the part of the subject. The pose, the hands on the hips, the hard-looking face, the stern expression.

ATT: Anything else?

PSY: The size of the ears indicates a paranoid outlook, or hallucinations. Also, the absence of feet indicates feelings of insecurity. (Jeffery, 1964)

The assumption here, as in so many clinical judgments, is that test results reveal something important. But do they? There is a simple way to decide. Have one clinician administer and interpret the test, have another clinician assess the same person's symptoms, and repeat this process over many people. The proof is in the pudding: Are the test outcomes indeed correlated with the reported symptoms? Some tests are indeed predictive. With other tests, such as the Draw-a-Person test discussed above, the correlation is far weaker than its users suppose. Why, then, do many clinicians such as the one above continue to have such apparently unwarranted confidence?

Pioneering experiments by Loren Chapman and Jean Chapman (1969, 1971) help us see why. They invited both college students and professional clinicians to study patients' test performances and diagnoses. If they expected a particular association, they generally were able to perceive it, regardless of whether the data confirmed their expectations. For example, clinicians who believed that suspicious people draw peculiar eyes on the Draw-a-Person test perceived such a relationship—even when shown cases in which suspicious people drew peculiar eyes *less* often than nonsuspicious people. It's a familiar phenomenon: To believe is to see. Believing a relationship exists between two things, they were more likely to notice confirming than disconfirming instances.

In fairness to clinicians, I hasten to add that the shortcomings we are considering could also be shown at work among political analysts, historians, sportscasters, personnel directors, stockbrokers, and many other professionals, including the research psychologists who point them out. As a researcher I have often been blind to the shortcomings of my theoretical analyses. I am so eager to presume that my idea of truth is *the* truth that no matter how hard I try, I cannot see my own error. This has been especially evident from the editorial review process that precedes any research publication. During the last twenty years I have read dozens of reviews of my own submitted manuscripts and have been a reviewer for dozens of others. My experience is that it is far easier to spot someone else's sloppy thinking than to perceive my own equally sloppy thinking.

"No one can see his own errors."
Psalms 19:12

Hindsight and Overconfidence

If someone we know commits suicide, how, in hindsight, do we react? One common reaction is to think that we, or those close to the person, should have been able to predict and therefore to prevent the suicide. In retrospect, one can see the suicidal signs and the pleas for help. "We should have known." Indeed, in one experiment those who were given a summary of a case and told the person committed suicide were more likely to say they "would have expected" the suicide than were those given the same case information without the suicide being mentioned (Goggin & Range, 1985). Moreover, if told of the suicide, their reactions to the victim's family members were more negative. Thus, after a tragedy the I-knew- (or should-have-known-) it-all-along phenomenon can leave family, friends, and therapists feeling judgmental or guilty. Perhaps if this phenomenon were more widely understood, people could be more accepting of themselves and others in such times.

"Undergraduate psychology can, and I believe should, seek to liberate the student from ignorance, but also from the arrogance of believing we know more about ourselves and others than we really do."
David L. Cole (1982)

Hindsight bias afflicts professionals' judgments, too, as Hal Arkes and his colleagues (1988) discovered when they asked neuropsychologists to diagnose a man described as suffering a tremor and deteriorating memory. For each of three groups, one of three possible diagnoses was said to be correct. Given a supposed diagnosis, nearly half of the neuropsychologists thought they, too, would have made the same diagnosis. But Arkes also found a way to minimize this hindsight bias: Ask the professionals to give a reason why one of the other diagnoses *might* have been correct.

Perhaps the most striking example of potential error in after-the-fact explanations was provided by David Rosenhan (1973) and seven of his Stanford University associates. To test mental health workers' clinical insights they each made an appointment with a different mental hospital admissions office and complained of "hearing voices."

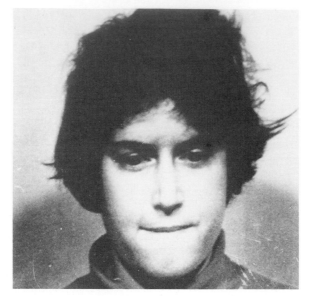

In hindsight, we tell ourselves that we "should have known" something would happen after it does, but often never think it will before the event occurs. When babysitter Laurie Dann shot and killed several schoolchildren in Winnetka, Illinois, in 1988, many psychologists said experts "should have known" she might have done this based on her psychological history.

Apart from giving false names and vocations, they otherwise reported honestly their life histories and emotional states and exhibited no further symptoms. Most got diagnosed as schizophrenic and remained hospitalized for two to three weeks. With this diagnosis in mind, the clinicians searched for and easily found incidents in the pseudopatients' (normal) life histories and hospital behavior that "confirmed" and "explained" the diagnosis. For example, Rosenhan tells of one pseudopatient who truthfully explained to the interviewer that he

> had a close relationship with his mother but was rather remote from his father during his early childhood. During adolescence and beyond, however, his father became a close friend, while his relationship with his mother cooled. His present relationship with his wife was characteristically close and warm. Apart from occasional angry exchanges, friction was minimal. The children had rarely been spanked.

The interviewer, "knowing" the person was "schizophrenic," "explained" the problem this way:

> This white 39-year-old male . . . manifests a long history of considerable ambivalence in close relationships, which begins in early childhood. A warm relationship with his mother cools during his adolescence. A distant relationship to his father is described as becoming very intense. Affective stability is absent. His attempts to control emotionality with his wife and children are punctuated by angry outbursts and, in the case of the children, spankings. And while he says that he has several good friends, one senses considerable ambivalence embedded in those relationships also.

Rosenhan later told some mental hospital staff members (who had heard about his controversial experiment but doubted such mistakes could occur in their hospital) that during the ensuing three months one or more pseudopatients would seek admission to their hospital. After the three months, he asked the staff to guess which of the 193 patients admitted during that time were really pseudopatients. Of the 193 new patients, 41 were accused by at least one staff member of being normal; actually, *none* were pseudopatients.

Self-Confirming Diagnoses

People can also be induced to give information that fulfills their clinician's expectations. In a clever series of experiments at the University of Minnesota, Mark Snyder (1984), in collaboration with William Swann and others, gave interviewers hypotheses to test concerning possible personal traits of individuals. To get a feel for their experiments, imagine yourself on a blind date with someone who has been told that you are an uninhibited, outgoing person. To see whether this is true, your date slips questions into the conversation, such as, "Have you ever done anything crazy in front of other people?" As you answer such questions, will your date meet a different "you" than if you were probed for times you were shy and retiring?

Snyder and Swann found that people tend to test for a trait by looking for information that would confirm it. If trying to find out if someone is an extrovert, the questions they select often solicit instances of extroversion ("What would you do if you wanted to liven things up at a party?") If testing for introversion they are more likely to ask "What factors make it hard for you to really open up to people?" This style of questioning led those being tested for extroversion to behave more sociably and those being tested for introversion to reveal a more shy and reserved self.

At Indiana University, Russell Fazio and his coresearchers (1981) reproduced this finding and also discovered that those asked the "extroverted questions" later perceived themselves as actually more outgoing than those asked the introverted questions. Moreover, they really became noticeably more outgoing. An accomplice of the experimenter later met each subject in a waiting room, and 70 percent of the time correctly guessed from the subject's outgoingness which condition the subject had come from. When given the structured list of questions to choose from, even experienced psychotherapists prefer the extroverted questions when testing for extroversion and unwittingly trigger more extroverted behavior among their interviewees (Dallas & Baron, 1985; Snyder & Thomsen, 1988). Here, then, is more evidence that our erroneous beliefs may generate their own reality.

In subsequent experiments, Snyder and his colleagues attempted several techniques to induce people to search for behaviors that would *disconfirm* the trait they were testing. In one experiment, they (Snyder et al., 1982) actually told the interviewers that "it is relevant and informative to find out ways in which the person . . . may not be like the stereotype." In another experiment Snyder (1981a) even offered "$25 to the person who develops the set of questions that tell the most about . . . the interviewee." Still, people resisted asking "introverted questions" when testing for extroversion. This illustrates the confirmation bias discussed in Chapter 4: When testing our beliefs (for example, that Blacks are good athletes), we are more likely to seek information that would verify them (for example, athletic superstars who are Black) than to seek disconfirming information (for example, poorly coordinated people who are Black).

As often happens, these provocative findings triggered new research that reveals their limits. When lay people or psychotherapists are invited to make up *their own* questions to test whether someone is extroverted, they are less likely to seek confirmation (Dallas & Baron, 1985; Trope et al., 1984). Indeed, many of their questions seem quite appropriate for distinguishing extroverted from introverted people. But other studies indicate that when interviewers have definite ideas of their own, these ideas *will* influence questions they make up (Lalljee et al., 1984; Swann & Giuliano, 1987). Recall, for example, that when teachers questioned the young "cyranoids" described on p. 2, their behavior, too, confirmed the surmise of poet Robert Browning:

> As is your sort of mind,
> So is your sort of search:
> you'll find
> What you desire.

Based on Snyder's experiments, can you imagine why the behaviors of people undergoing psychotherapy come to fit the theories of their therapists (Whitman et al., 1963)? Snyder (1981a) explains:

> The psychiatrist who believes (erroneously) that adult gay males had bad childhood relationships with their mothers may meticulously probe for recalled (or fabricated) signs of tension between their gay clients and their mothers, but neglect to so carefully interrogate their heterosexual clients about their maternal relationships. No doubt, any individual could recall some friction with his or her mother, however minor or isolated the incidents.

For example, when a psychologist and a psychiatrist, Harold Renaud and Floyd Estess (1961), conducted life history interviews of 100 healthy, successful adult men they were startled to discover that the childhood experiences of these men were loaded with "traumatic events," tense relations with certain people, and less-than-optimal handling by their parents—the very factors usually invoked to explain psychiatric problems.

Clinical Versus Statistical Prediction

Given these hindsight- and diagnosis-confirming tendencies, it will probably come as no surprise that most clinicians and interviewers express considerably more confidence in their intuitive assessments than in statistical data. Indeed, if they are pressed for evidence, we may expect that interviewers will readily recall examples that confirm their interviewing ability. Yet when intuitive prediction is matched against statistical prediction (for example, predicting graduate school success using a formula that includes grades and aptitude scores), the latter usually does as well or better (Meehl, 1954; Sawyer, 1966; L. R. Goldberg, 1968). Statistical predictions are indeed unreliable, very unreliable, but human intuition—even expert intuition—is even more unreliable (Cocozza & Steadman, 1978; Faust & Ziskin, 1988).

Three decades after demonstrating the superiority of statistical over intuitive prediction, Paul Meehl (1986) says the evidence is stronger than ever:

> There is no controversy in social science which shows [so many] studies coming out so uniformly in the same direction as this one. . . . When you are pushing 90 investigations, predicting everything from the outcome of football games to the diagnosis of liver disease and when you can hardly come up with a half dozen studies showing even a weak tendency in favor of the clinician, it is time to draw a practical conclusion. . . .

> Surely we all know that the human brain is poor at weighting and computing. When you check out at a supermarket, you don't eyeball the heap of purchases and say to the clerk, "Well it looks to me as if it's about $17.00 worth; what do you think?"

"The effect of Meehl's work on clinical practice in the mental health area can be summed up in a single word: Zilch. He was honored, elected to the president of [the American Psychological Association] at a very young age in 1962, recently elected to the National Academy of Sciences, and ignored."
Robyn M. Dawes (1989)

So, why do so many clinicians continue to interpret Rorschach inkblot tests and offer intuitive predictions about future parolees, suicide risks, and likelihood of child abuse? Partly out of sheer ignorance, says Meehl, but also partly out of "mistaken conceptions of ethics":

> If I try to forecast something important about a college student, or a criminal, or a depressed patient by inefficient rather than efficient means, meanwhile charging this person or the taxpayer 10 times as much money as I would need to achieve greater predictive accuracy, that is not a sound ethical practice. That it feels better, warmer, and cuddlier to me as predictor is a shabby excuse indeed.

Such words are shocking. Surely Meehl and the other researchers underestimate our skills of intuition. To see why such findings are apparently true, consider the assessment of human potential by graduate admissions interviewers. University of Oregon researcher Robyn Dawes (1976) illustrates why statistical prediction is so often superior to an interviewer's intuition when predicting certain outcomes such as graduate school success:

> What makes us think that we can do a better job of selection by interviewing (students) for a half hour, than we can by adding together relevant (standardized) variables, such as undergraduate GPA, GRE score, and perhaps ratings of letters of recommendation. The most reasonable explanation to me lies in our overevaluation of our cognitive capacity. And it is really cognitive conceit. Consider, for example, what goes into a GPA. Because for most graduate applicants it is based on at least 3½ years of undergraduate study, it is a composite measure arising from a minimum of 28 courses and possibly, with the popularity of the quarter system, as many as 50. . . . Yet you and I, looking at a folder or interviewing someone for a half hour, are supposed to be able to form a better impression than one based on 3½ years of the cumulative evaluations of 20–40 different professors. . . . Finally, if we do wish to ignore GPA, it appears that the only reason for doing so is believing that the candidate is particularly brilliant even though his or her record may not show it. What better evidence for such brilliance can we have than a score on a carefully devised aptitude test? Do we really think we are better equipped to assess such aptitude than is the Educational Testing Service, whatever its faults?

Statistical assessment of candidates for job openings usually determines aptitude better than a job interview—the typical measure of possible future performance.

A PHYSICIAN LOOKS AT SOCIAL PSYCHOLOGY

Reading this book helps me understand the human behaviors I observe in my work as a cancer specialist and as medical director of a large staff of physicians. A few examples:

Reviews of medical records illustrate the "I-knew-it all-along phenomenon." Physicians looking at cases in hindsight often believe *they* would have more quickly recognized and treated problems such as cancer and appendicitis. Once you know the correct diagnosis, it's easy to look back and interpret the early symptoms accordingly.

For many physicians I have known, the intrinsic motives behind their entering the profession—to help people, to be scientifically stimulated—soon become "overjustified" by the high pay. Before long, the joy is lost. The extrinsic rewards become the reason to practice, and the physician, having lost the altruistic motives, works to increase "success," measured in income.

"Self-serving bias" is ever present. We physicians gladly accept personal credit when things go well. When they don't—when the patient is misdiagnosed or doesn't get well or dies—we attribute the failure elsewhere. We were given inadequate information or the case was ill-fated from the beginning.

I also observe many examples of "belief perseverance." Even when presented with the documented facts about, say, how AIDS is transmitted, people will strangely persist in wrongly believing that it is just a "gay" disease or that they should fear catching it from mosquito bites. It makes me wonder: How can I more effectively persuade people of what they need to know and act upon?

Indeed, as I observe medical attitudes and decision making I feel myself submerged in a giant practical laboratory of social psychology. To understand the goings-on around me, I find social psychological insights invaluable and would strongly advise premed students to study the field. *(Burton F. VanderLaan, Chicago, Illinois.)*

> *" 'I beseech ye in the bowels of Christ, think that ye may be mistaken.' I shall like to have that written over the portals of every church, every school, and every courthouse, and, may I say, of every legislative body in the United States."*
> *Judge Learned Hand, 1951, echoing Oliver Cromwell's 1650 plea to the Church of Scotland*

In summary, the evidence suggests that, although the value of psychotherapy is being established (Smith et al., 1980; Elkin, 1986), there can be problems with clinical judgments. Professional clinicians

- Can easily convince clients of worthless diagnoses,
- Are frequently the victims of illusory correlation,
- Are too readily convinced of their own after-the-fact analyses,
- Fail to appreciate how erroneous diagnoses can be self-confirming.

Implications

The implications for mental health workers are more easily stated than practiced: Be mindful that clients' verbal agreement with what you say does not prove its validity. Beware of the tendency to see relationships that you expect to see or that are supported by striking examples readily available in your memory. Recognize that after-the-fact psychologizing is seductively convincing, leading clinicians sometimes to feel overconfident of their judgments and sometimes to judge themselves too harshly for not having foreseen outcomes that, in hindsight, seem predictable. Guard against the tendency to ask questions that assume your preconceptions are correct; consider opposing ideas and test them, too.

Actually, the research on illusory thinking that we have considered in this unit on social thinking has implications not only for mental health workers but for all psychologists. What Lewis Thomas (1978) has said of biology may as justly be said of psychology:

The solidest piece of scientific truth I know of, the one thing about which I feel totally confident, is that we are profoundly ignorant about nature. Indeed, I regard this as the major discovery of the past 100 years of biology. . . . It is this sudden confrontation with · the depth and scope of ignorance that represents the most significant contribution of 20th century science to the human intellect. We are, at last, facing up to it. In earlier times, we either pretended to understand how things worked or ignored the problem, or simply made up stories to fill the gaps.

Psychology has crept only a little way across the edge of insight into our human condition. Ignorant of their ignorance, some psychologists are tempted to invent glib stories to fill the gaps in our understanding. If these stories are not rigorously checked against objective reality, they will be resilient to disconfirmation. What is more, intuitive observation will support them, even if they are mutually contradictory. Research on illusory thinking therefore beckons psychologists to a new humility concerning the truth of their unchecked speculation. It reminds research psychologists why, in the true spirit of science, they must test their preconceptions before propounding them as truth. To seek the hard facts, even if they threaten one's cherished illusions—that is the ideal of every science.

"One thing I have learned in a long life: that all our science, measured against reality, is primitive and childlike—and yet it is the most precious thing we have."
Albert Einstein, in B. Hoffman & H. Dukes, Albert Einstein: Creator and Rebel

Do not misunderstand: I am *not* arguing that the scientific method can answer all human questions. There are questions which it cannot address and ways of knowing which it cannot capture. But science *is* one means for examining claims about nature, human nature included. Propositions that imply observable consequences are best evaluated by systematic observation and experiment—which is the whole point of social psychology. To be sure, inventive genius is also required, lest researchers test only trivialities. But whatever unique and enduring insights psychology can offer will be hammered out by research psychologists sorting through competing truth claims. Science always involves an interplay between intuition and rigorous test, between creative hunches and skepticism.

Psychology will never be as exact a science as chemistry. But psychology's distinct contribution is its careful observations and experiments. For reasons that are obvious, psychological investigations must not rely exclusively upon people's subjective reports of the working of their minds or of why they acted or felt as they did. We must gather information in a way analogous to how we assess our personal health. If we are having doubts about our health we will utilize at least two sources of information about our condition: Our intuitive feelings *plus* what the lab technician's microscope may detect, even if our unaided observation could not. The experimental method is the research psychologist's microscope.

"Science is the great antidote to the poison of enthusiasm and superstition."
Adam Smith, Wealth of Nations

Knowing the enormity of illusory thinking therefore points not to the cynical conclusion that all beliefs are arbitrary, but to the need for a science of human thought and behavior, a science that will restrain our imagination by subjecting our speculations to empirical scrutiny.

SUMMING UP

To review and apply principles of social cognition discussed in previous chapters, we have considered some of social psychology's contributions to clinical understanding, treatment, and judgment.

SOCIAL COGNITION IN PROBLEM BEHAVIORS

Social psychologists are actively exploring the attributions and expectations of depressed, lonely, socially anxious, and physically ill people. Without doubt, depressed people have a negative attributional style. Compared to nondepressed people, they engage in more self-blame, they interpret and recall events in a more negative light, and they are less hopeful about the future. Despite their more negative judgments, in laboratory tests mildly depressed people tend to be surprisingly realistic. Depressed thinking has consequences for the depressed person's behavior, which in turn helps maintain a self-defeating cycle. Much the same can be said of those who suffer chronic loneliness and states of social anxiety such as extreme shyness. The mushrooming new field of health psychology is exploring, among other things, the links between the illness and stress, and a pessimistic explanatory style.

SOCIAL-PSYCHOLOGICAL APPROACHES TO TREATMENT

Among the social-psychological principles that may be usefully applied in treatment are these three: (1) Internal change can be triggered by changes in external behavior. (2) A self-defeating cycle of negative attitudes and behaviors can be broken by training more skillful behavior, by positive experiences that alter self-perceptions, and by directly modifying negative thought patterns. (3) Improved states are most likely to be maintained after treatment if people attribute their improvement to internal factors under their continued control rather than to the treatment program itself.

MAKING CLINICAL JUDGMENTS

From their studies of how people form judgments and misjudgments of others, social psychologists also offer warnings regarding how judgments, recommendations, and predictions can be led astray. As we judge others we are sometimes unaware of what has influenced our assessments of them and we are inclined to perceive them in line with our stereotypes. When judging ourselves we are susceptible to the "Barnum effect" (accepting worthless diagnoses), especially when the feedback is positive.

Psychiatrists and clinical psychologists are not immune to illusory thinking. As they diagnose and treat their clients, they are often the victims of illusory correlations. After-the-fact explanations of people's difficulties are easy, sometimes too easy. Indeed, the very act of explaining can breed overconfidence in one's clinical judgment. When interacting with clients, erroneous diagnoses are sometimes self-confirming, because interviewers tend to seek and recall information that illustrates and verifies whatever they are looking for.

Research on the errors that so easily creep into our intuitive judgments documents the need for rigorous testing of our intuitive conclusions. The scientific method cannot answer all questions and is itself vulnerable to bias. Thankfully, however, it can help us sift truth from falsehood.

FOR FURTHER READING

Abramson, L. Y. (Ed.). (1988). *Social cognition and clinical psychology: A synthesis.* New York: Guilford. Various experts explore the implications of research on social thinking for psychological health and psychotherapy.

Alloy, L. B. (Ed.). (1988). *Cognitive processes in depression*. New York: Guilford. Essays by seasoned scholars examine depression from the social/cognitive perspective.

Leary, M. R., & Miller, R. S. (1986). *Social psychology and dysfunctional behavior: Origins, diagnosis, and treatment*. New York: Springer-Verlag. Uses concepts from social psychology to illuminate assorted problems, including anxiety, shyness, and insomnia, and to propose new ideas for treatment.

Maddux, J. E., Stoltenberg, C. D., & Rosenwein, R. (Ed.). (1988). *Social processes in clinical and counseling psychology*. New York: Springer-Verlag.

Seligman, M. E. P. (1990). *Learned optimism*. New York: Alfred Knopf. Researcher Seligman summarizes the roots and fruits of an optimistic attributional style.

PART TWO

SOCIAL INFLUENCE

S ocial psychology is the science that studies not only how we *think about* one another—our topic in the preceding chapters—but also how we *influence* and *relate* to one another. In chapters 6 through 10 we therefore probe social psychology's central concern: the powers of social influence.

What are these unseen social forces that push and shove us? And how powerful are they? Research on social influence helps illuminate the invisible strings by which our social worlds tug us this way and that. This unit reveals these subtle powers, especially the cultural sources of our attitudes and behavior (Chapter 6), the forces of social conformity (Chapter 7), the principles of persuasion (Chapter 8), the consequences of our participation in groups (Chapter 9), and how all these social influences operate together in everyday situations. In Chapter 10, we will take a close look at the social influences at work in a specific setting—the courtroom.

Seeing these influences, we may better understand why people feel and act as they do. And we may ourselves become freer—less vulnerable to unwanted social manipulation and more adept at pulling our own strings.

CULTURAL INFLUENCES

―――――

What we eat and drink, what we believe, what music we enjoy, depend largely upon our culture. We all know this. Yet, given how readily most of us accept our way as *the* way, the diversity of human cultures is remarkable. Sociologist Ian Robertson (1987) notes that

> Americans eat oysters but not snails. The French eat snails but not locusts. The Zulus eat locusts but not fish. The Jews eat fish but not pork. The Hindus eat pork but not beef. The Russians eat beef but not snakes. The Chinese eat snakes but not people. The Jalé of New Guinea find people delicious. (p. 67)

The range of dress habits is just as great. If you were a traditional Muslim woman you would cover your entire body, even your face, and be thought deviant if you didn't. If you were a North American woman you would expose your face, arms, and legs, but you would cover your breasts and pelvic region, and be thought deviant if you didn't. If you were a Tasaday tribe woman in the Philippines you would go about your daily activities naked, and be thought deviant if you didn't.

Culture has a similarly strong impact upon our social behavior. This chapter first illustrates cultural differences, and how social norms and roles help perpetuate such differences. Then the chapter probes the most pervasive role—one's gender role. Analyzing this one role allows us to explore some fascinating research, to appreciate the complexity of trying to disentangle biological and cultural influences upon human behavior, and to reflect on issues that pertain to our lives as men and women.

NORMS

American males may feel uncomfortable when Middle Eastern heads of state greet the U.S. president with their familiar kiss upon the cheek. A West German student at a university where "Herr Professor" is seldom talked with outside the lecture hall considers it strange that at my institution most faculty office doors are open and students stop by freely. An Iranian student on her first visit to an American McDonald's restaurant fumbles around in her paper bag looking for the eating utensils until, astonished, she notes the other customers eating their French fries with, of all things, their hands. Likewise, in many corners of the globe *your* best manners are a serious breach of etiquette. Oxford social psychologist Michael Argyle (1988) notes that foreigners visiting Japan anxiously struggle to master the rules of the social game—when to take their shoes off, how to pour the tea, when to give and open gifts, how to act toward someone higher or lower in the social hierarchy.

Norms:
Rules for accepted and expected behavior. Norms prescribe "proper" behavior.

As these examples illustrate, all cultures—be they juvenile gangs, remote tribes, or nations—have their own accepted ideas about appropriate behavior. Often, these social expectations, or ***norms,*** are viewed negatively, as a force that imprisons us all in its blind effort to perpetuate tradition. Norms restrain and control us so successfully and so subtly that we hardly sense their existence. Like fish in the ocean, we are so totally immersed in the ideas and behaviors of our culture that we must leap out of it in order to understand it. There is no better way to learn the norms of our culture than to visit another culture and see that its members do things *that* way, while we do them *this* way. I tell my children that while, yes, Europeans eat meat with the fork facing down in the left hand, we Americans consider it good manners to cut the meat and then transfer the fork to the right hand: "I admit it's inefficient. But it's the way *we* do it."

All cultures—be they juvenile gangs, remote tribes, or nations—have their own accepted ideas about appropriate behavior. For instance, females in America have a range of acceptable dress habits; whereas females in the Middle East must adhere to somewhat more stringent rules.

NORMS GREASE THE SOCIAL MACHINERY

Cultural norms may seem arbitrary and confining. However, just as a play moves smoothly when the actors know their lines, so our everyday social behavior occurs smoothly to the extent that people perform expected behaviors. Consider Michael Argyle's description of five stages that transpire when a British family moves into a home and the wife is visited by the woman next door (D. Cohen, 1980). First, the greetings, after which the visitor enters. Next, the visitor admires the house. During the third stage, the newcomer serves coffee and cookies and the women exchange information—mainly about their husbands. The fourth stage smooths any feelings that may have been ruffled during stage three (such as if one woman said her husband was a labor union executive while the other said her husband was in management). Stage five is the farewells.

Argyle notes that for the social interaction to proceed smoothly both persons must recognize each of the five stages. The rare visitor who arrives at the house and blurts out "My man's with IBM" or the householder who immediately thrusts coffee and cookies on the visitor reveals a lack of social skill. Indeed, many awkward, embarrassing moments are caused by our unintentionally violating social norms: walking into the wrong restroom, arriving at the party in coat and tie to find everyone else in jeans, clapping at a pause during a symphony.

Norms not only grease the social machinery, they also liberate us from preoccupation with what we are saying and doing. In strange situations, the norms may be unclear, so we carefully monitor others' behavior and adjust our own accordingly. But in familiar situations, our words and acts come effortlessly. Well-learned, ritualistic ways of interacting free us to concentrate on other matters.

BEHIND THE SCENES

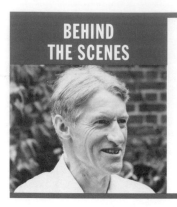

In my youth I knew one or two people who were very shy, and who were obviously made unhappy by this. What were they doing wrong? I studied psychology at Cambridge, but psychology didn't seem to have the answer. However, after meeting scholars who were working on human skills I realized that social behaviour was a kind of skill, too. With Adam Kendon and my other collaborators at Oxford, I became aware that social skill requires correctly producing and receiving nonverbal messages. Moreover, we came to believe that social skills, like motor skills, can be trained.

Michael Argyle,
Oxford University

NORMS VARY WITH CULTURE

Cultural norms vary greatly. Thus a person whose roots are in an expressive Mediterranean culture may be perceived by someone from a more formal northern European culture as "warm, charming, inefficient, and time-wasting," while the northern European may be perceived as "efficient, cold, and overconcerned with time" (Triandis,

*"Women kiss women good night. Men kiss women good night.
But men do not kiss men good night—especially in Armonk."*

1981). Latin American business executives who arrive late for a dinner engagement may be mystified by how uptight their American counterparts are about punctuality.

Cultures also vary in their norms for ***personal space,*** a sort of portable bubble or buffer zone that we like to maintain between ourselves and others. As the situation changes, the bubble varies in size. With strangers we maintain a fairly large personal space, keeping a distance of 4 feet or more between us. On uncrowded buses, or in restrooms or libraries, we protect our space and respect others' space. We let friends come closer, often within 2 or 3 feet. As poet W. H. Auden observed, "Some 30 inches from my nose, the frontier of my person goes."

Some people prefer more personal space than others. Although the research evidence is still hazy (Hayduk, 1983), studies suggest that adults maintain more distance than children, that men keep more distance from one another than do women, and that Americans, the British, and Scandinavians prefer more distance than do Arabs, the French, and Latin Americans (H. W. Smith, 1981; Sommer, 1969; Stockdale, 1978).

To see the effect of encroaching on another's personal space, you can do as researchers have and play space invader. Stand or sit but a foot or so from a friend and strike up a conversation. Does the person fidget, look away, back off, show other signs of discomfort? Such are among the signs of arousal noted by researchers (Altman & Vinsel, 1978). One controversial experiment even observed that men require more time to begin urination and less time to complete the act (known symptoms of mild emotional arousal) when another man is standing at an adjacent urinal (Middlemist et al., 1976, 1977).

A UNIVERSAL NORM

Despite the enormous cultural variation in norms for eating, punctuality, personal space, and many other behaviors, we humans do hold some norms in common. Best known is the taboo against incest: Parents are not to have sexual relations with their children, nor siblings with one another. (Although the taboo is apparently violated more often than psychologists used to believe, the norm is still universal). Harvard social psychologist Roger Brown (1965) described a less well known but equally universal norm. His description of this norm caused me to respond with: "Ah yes, I've seen-it-all-along. Why did I never notice it?"

Brown's "universal norm" concerns how people of unequal status relate to one another. Every society has its hierarchy: Based on lineage, wealth, occupation, or whatever, some people are recognized as higher and some as lower on the status ladder. One can detect this status hierarchy in the ways people address each other and initiate relationships. Have you ever noticed that the distant, respectful way people speak to a superior (for example, title and last name) is also the way they speak to a stranger? And that the familiar address (for example, first name) often used in speaking to subordinates is also used in speaking to intimate friends? Our building custodian, "Steve," addresses the faculty as "Dr. So and So." A student and a professor will similarly address one another in a nonmutual way, as will doctors and patients, and other dyads occupying roles with clearly unequal status.

Most languages have two forms of the English pronoun "you": a respectful form and a familiar form (for example, *Sie* and *du* in German, *vous* and *tu* in French, *usted* and *tu* in Spanish). Norms for the use of these pronouns often express the inequality of status. The familiar form is used with one's intimates and with those perceived as inferior (for example, not only with close friends and family members but also in speaking to children and dogs). Thus a German child's respect receives a boost when

Personal space:
The buffer zone we like to maintain around our bodies. Its size depends upon our familiarity with whomever is near us.

Dyad:
A group of two.

Despite the enormous cultural variation in norms, we humans do hold some norms in common.

"Look, everyone here loves vanilla, right? So let's start there."

In The Female Eunuch, *Germaine Greer notes how the language of affection reduces women to foods and baby animals—honey, lamb, sugar, sweetie-pie, kitten, chick.*

strangers begin addressing the child as "Sie" instead of "du." Nouns, too, can express assumed social inequalities. Hence Americans have been known to label people as Black "boys" and White "men," as the "girls" in the secretarial pool and the "women" of the faculty. Even among faculty studied by Rebecca Rubin (1981), young female professors were far more likely than young male professors to have students call them by their first names.

This first aspect of Brown's universal norm—that *forms of address communicate not only social distance, but also social status*—is closely correlated to the second aspect. In Europe, where most dyads begin a relationship with the polite, formal "you" and may eventually progress to the more intimate "you," someone obviously has to initiate the increased intimacy. Who do you suppose does so? *Advances in intimacy are usually suggested by the higher-status person.* On some congenial occasion, the elder, or richer, or more distinguished of the two may say, "Why don't we say *du* to one another?" This norm extends beyond language to every type of advance in intimacy. It is more acceptable to borrow a pen from or put a hand on the shoulder of one's intimates and subordinates than to behave in such a casual way with strangers or superiors. Similarly, the president of my college invites faculty to his home before they invite him to theirs. In general, then, the higher status person is the pacesetter in the progression toward intimacy.

Universal norms are intriguing because they would seem to reflect some universal aspect of human nature or some universal requirement of human social life. If it is indeed universally true that advances in intimacy are initiated by persons of higher status, then who initiates with whom will indicate relative social status. For example, on your campus who initiates dates? When I attended college in the early 1960s, except for specially designated weeks or for sorority parties the women never did. Since then, the feminist movement has affected the self-perceived status of millions of women, including many who do not consider themselves feminists. Although the male-initiated date is still far more frequent, women now feel freer to initiate a casual date.

ROLES

All the world's a stage,
And all the men and women merely players:
They have their exits and their entrances;
And one man in his time plays many parts. . . .

William Shakespeare

Role theorists presume, as did William Shakespeare, that social life is like acting on a theatrical stage, with all its scenes, masks, and prescribed scripts. Like the role of Jaques, who speaks the above lines in *As You Like It*, social roles, such as parent, student, and friend, outlast those who play them. And, as Jaques says, these roles allow some freedom of interpretation to those who act them out; great performances are defined by the particular way the role is played. However, some aspects of any role *must* be performed. Jaques must utter the above lines. A student must at least show up for exams, turn in papers, and maintain some minimum grade point average.

When only a few norms are associated with a social category (for example, pedestrians should keep to the right and not jaywalk), it is not customary to regard the position as a social role. A *role* is defined by a substantial group of norms. For example, I could readily generate a long list of norms prescribing my activities as a professor or as a father. Although I may acquire my particular image by violating the least important norms (I ride a bike to campus even in the snow), violating my role's most

Role:
A set of norms that defines how people in a given social position ought to behave.

In some cultures, the parameters defining the personal space between friends become smaller and smaller as friendships strengthen.

important norms (failing to meet my classes, abusing my children) could lead to my expulsion from it. From their studies conducted in Britain, Italy, Hong Kong, and Japan, Michael Argyle and Monika Henderson (1985) noted several cultural variations in friendship norms (in Japan it's especially important not to embarrass a friend with public criticism). But there are also some apparently universal norms: Respect the friend's privacy, make eye contact while talking, don't divulge things said in confidence. These are among the rules of the friendship game. Break them and the game is over.

EFFECTS OF ROLE PLAYING

In Chapter 2, we briefly considered evidence that we tend to absorb our roles. On a first date or on a new job, we may act the role self-consciously. However, as the role is internalized, self-consciousness subsides. What was unreal becomes real.

"Nowhere is social psychology further apart from public consciousness," noted Philip Brickman (1978), "than in its understanding of how things become real for people." Take the case of kidnapped heiress Patricia Hearst. While held by some young revolutionaries who called themselves the Symbionese Liberation Army, she renounced her former life, her wealthy parents, and her fiancé. Announcing that she had joined her captors, she asked that people "Try to understand the changes I've gone through." Twelve days later a bank camera recorded her participation in an armed holdup. Eventually, Hearst was apprehended and, after "deprogramming," resumed her role as an heiress. Today, she is a suburban Connecticut housewife and mother who devotes much of her time to charitable causes (Johnson, 1988). Had Patricia Hearst really been a dedicated revolutionary all along or had she only pretended to cooperate with her captors, people could have more readily comprehended her actions. What they could not understand (and what therefore helped make this one of the biggest news stories of the 1970s) was, as Brickman wrote, "that she could really be an heiress, really a revolutionary, and then perhaps really an heiress again." It's mind-blowing. Surely, this could not happen to you or me—or could it?

The last section of this chapter will reassure us. Our actions not only depend on the social situation but also on our dispositions. Not everyone responds in the same way to intense social pressures. You and I might have handled the predicament Patricia Hearst was in differently than she. Nevertheless, some social situations can move most "normal" people to behave in "abnormal" ways. This is clear from some experiments that have put well-intentioned people in an evil situation to see whether good or evil prevails. To a dismaying extent, evil wins. Nice guys often don't finish nice.

An illustration: Consider the effect of participating in a role that necessitates destructive behavior. Role "playing" often ceases to be play as the role becomes absorbed into one's traits and attitudes. Combat soldiers typically develop degrading images of their enemy. Or picture some prisoners and prison guards. Is your image positive? Negative? Perhaps you can recall images of prison riots, such as the 1980 rampage in the New Mexico State Penitentiary near Santa Fe. There, thirty-three prisoners died, many were beaten with clubs, savagely burned with blowtorches, doused with gasoline and set on fire, or dismembered with homemade knives.

Roles That Dehumanize

Does prison brutality occur because the dispositions of those involved are cruel? (Former Georgia governor Lester Maddox was once asked if there was any way to

"If only it were all so simple! If only there were evil people somewhere insidiously committing evil deeds, and it were necessary only to separate them from the rest of us and destroy them. But the line dividing good and evil cuts through the heart of every human being."
Aleksandr Solzhenitsyn, The Gulag Archipelago

improve prisons. "What we need," he replied, "is a better class of prisoner.") Could prison reform occur by employing better people as guards and by isolating sadistic prisoners? Or do prisons dehumanize people because the institutional roles of guard and prisoner tend to embitter and harden even the most compassionate of people—that is, does the person make the place violent, or does the place make the person violent?

The debate continues between those who say the evil resides solely in the individuals (reform the guards, rehabilitate the prisoners) and those who see evil in the inherent dynamics of prison life. Debate of this kind endures because we typically start with the acknowledged problem and work backwards, speculating about causes. Because personality and situational factors are intertwined, we can make a case for either. Recognizing this dilemma, Philip Zimbardo assigned similar groups of people to differing roles. In a simulated prison constructed in the basement of the psychology department at Stanford University, he subjected some decent, intelligent college men to important features of the prison situation. Among this volunteer group, half, by a flip of a coin, were designated guards. They were given uniforms, billy clubs, and whistles, and instructed to enforce certain rules. The other half, the prisoners, were locked in barren cells and forced to wear humiliating outfits.

After little more than a day of role "playing," the guards and prisoners, and even the experimenters, got caught up in the situation. The guards devised cruelly degrading routines; the prisoners broke down, rebelled, or became apathetic; and the experimenters worked overtime to maintain prison security. There developed, reported Zimbardo (1972b), a "growing confusion between reality and illusion, between role-

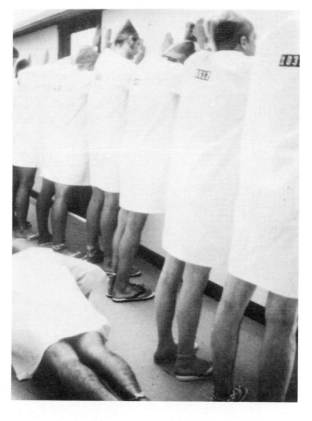

Guards and prisoners in the Stanford prison simulation quickly absorbed the roles they played.

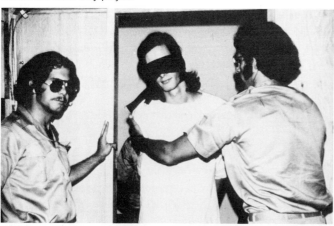

playing and self-identity. . . . This prison which we had created . . . was absorbing us as creatures of its own reality." The simulation was planned to last two weeks. But:

> At the end of only six days we had to close down our mock prison because what we saw was frightening. It was no longer apparent to us or most of the subjects where they ended and their roles began. The majority had indeed become "prisoners" or "guards," no longer able to clearly differentiate between role-playing and self. There were dramatic changes in virtually every aspect of their behavior, thinking and feeling. In less than a week, the experience of imprisonment undid (temporarily) a lifetime of learning; human values were suspended, self-concepts were challenged, and the ugliest, most base, pathological side of human nature surfaced. We were horrified because we saw some boys ("guards") treat other boys as if they were despicable animals, taking pleasure in cruelty, while other boys ("prisoners") became servile, dehumanized robots who thought only of escape, of their own individual survival, and of their mounting hatred of the guards. (Zimbardo, 1971, p. 3)

The most fundamental demonstration of this controversial simulation has not to do with real prisons, which certainly differ from the simulated one. Nor does it even have to do with the many real-life situations which may involve similarly destructive role relations. Rather, it demonstrates how that which was unreal (an artificial role) can evolve into that which is real. To make this insight concrete, consider the roles of master and slave. Imagine playing the role of slave—not just for six days, but for decades. If a few days altered the behavior of those in Zimbardo's "prison," then decades of a subservient behavior is bound to have substantial corrosive effects upon the slave's traits and self-concept. The master may be even more profoundly affected, because the master's role is chosen. Frederick Douglass, a former slave, recalls his slave mistress's transformation as she absorbed her role:

> My new mistress proved to be all she appeared when I first met her at the door,—a woman of the kindest heart and finest feelings. She had never had a slave under her control previously to myself, and prior to her marriage she had been dependent upon her own industry for a living. She was by trade a weaver; and by constant application to her business, she had been in a good degree preserved from the blighting and dehumanizing effects of slavery. I was utterly astonished at her goodness. I scarcely knew how to behave towards her. She was entirely unlike any other white woman I had ever seen. I could not approach her as I was accustomed to approach other white ladies. My early instruction was all out of place. The crouching servility, usually so acceptable a quality in a slave, did not answer when manifested toward her. Her favor was not gained by it; she seemed to be disturbed by it. She did not deem it impudent or unmannerly for a slave to look her in the face. The meanest slave was put fully at ease in her presence, and none left without feeling better for having seen her. Her face was made of heavenly smiles, and her voice of tranquil music.
>
> But, alas! this kind heart had but a short time to remain such. The fatal poison of irresponsible power was already in her hands, and soon commenced its infernal work. That cheerful eye, under the influence of slavery, soon became red with rage; that voice, made all of sweet accord, changed to one of harsh and horrid discord; and that angelic face gave place to that of a demon. (Douglass, 1845, pp. 57–58)

Burnout:
Hostility, apathy, or loss of idealism resulting from prolonged stress or from conflict between those in antagonistic roles.

Burnout

The transforming power of a new role is often experienced by human service professionals in the **burnout** of their initial idealism. A New York City police officer described the experience: "You change when you become a cop—you become tough and hard and

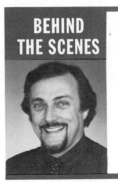

BEHIND THE SCENES

W e've taken the message of our simulated prison study—the corrupting power of the prison situation—to prison officials, judges, lawyers, and committees of the U.S. Senate and House. That "good people" could be so vulnerable to the "evil forces" in a simulated prison environment challenges us to reevaluate assumptions about the causes of social and personal pathology.

Philip Zimbardo,
Stanford University

cynical. You have to condition yourself to be that way in order to survive on this job. And sometimes, without realizing it, you act that way all the time, even with your wife and kids" (Maslach & Jackson, 1979). Similarly, ward attendants in institutions for the mentally retarded often start to refer to residents with derogatory labels such as "biter," "soiler," and "brat"; and the initial idealism of social workers, like that of Frederick Douglass's slave mistress, is often transformed into an impersonal, demeaning attitude (Wills, 1978).

And the clients? They often view the staff workers as cold and callous. One young man, recovering from the amputation of his leg, went with his mother to the social security office to request information about aid for the disabled. After the caseworker accused them of trying to rip off the government, they went home and cried for three hours. Of course, not all police officers, ward attendants, and caseworkers become so insensitive. Yet the wide range of personalities who experience burnout suggests we might usefully view burnout as being caused by bad situations rather than by inherently bad people.

Christina Maslach (1978, 1982) has identified how role relations between staff and clients create burnout. The norms of the caseworker role (some of them formalized as rules and regulations) require the caseworker to ask the client very personal questions, yet restrict the caseworker's freedom to offer aid. This produces a tense relationship and induces the caseworker to keep an emotional distance. Informal norms dictate that the caseworker be assertive, the client passive and dependent. As a result, the caseworker may unknowingly come to view the clients as objects. Moreover, the situation dictates that clients bring them feedback when things go wrong, but not when things go right. And, if the casework does not bring gratifying results, to what will the professional helper likely attribute client complaints and minimal success? To the clients' dispositions, of course: "If they can't change after all I've done for them, then let's face it—there's something basically wrong with them."

Recall the fundamental attribution error from Chapter 3. When professional helpers are selectively exposed to clients' problems and negative behaviors, do they attribute these problems to the clients' dispositions rather than to their situations?

ROLE REVERSAL

Thus far we have dealt primarily with role playing's negative effects. But role playing can also be used for good. By intentionally playing a new role, people can sometimes change themselves or empathize with people whose roles differ from their own. "Psychodrama," a form of psychotherapy, uses role playing for just this purpose. In George Bernard Shaw's *Pygmalion*, Eliza Doolittle, the uncouth flower vendor, discovers that if she plays the role of a lady, and is viewed by others as a lady, then she in fact is a lady. What wasn't real now is.

"Great Spirit, grant that I may not criticize my neighbor until I have walked for a moon in his moccasins."
Old Indian Prayer

Roles often come in pairs—parent and child, husband and wife, teacher and student, doctor and patient, employer and employee, police and citizen. To help each understand the other, role reversals can help. The problem with much human conversation and argument, observed La Rochefoucauld, "is that a man pays more attention to his own utterances than to giving an exact answer to questions put to him. Even the most charming and clever do little more than appear attentive, while in their eyes one may see a look of bewilderment as one talks, so anxious are they to return to their own ideas" (1665, No. 139). A negotiator or group leader can therefore create better communication by having the two sides reverse roles, each arguing the other's position. Alternatively, each side can be asked to restate the other party's point (to the other's satisfaction) before replying. The next time you get into a difficult argument with a friend or parent, try to stop it in the middle and have each of you restate the other's perceptions and feelings before going on with your own. Likely, your mutual understanding will increase.

ROLE CONFLICT

Roles are sets of norms, and norms are expectations for how one ought to behave. Sometimes people's expectations conflict, as when new mothers and fathers disagree about how much of the housework and childcare each should do (Ruble et al., 1988). There are three types of role conflict, each requiring its own method of resolution.

Conflict between Person and Role

Conflict between person and role:
Tension between one's personality or attitudes and the expectations of one's role.

Surely you have sometimes found your own personality or attitudes incompatible with the expectations of an assigned role. Perhaps you were elected president of a group, but found the role a strain, given your normally unassertive nature. Or perhaps you took a job that required you to act in accord with rules that you disagreed with. There was an uncomfortable difference between the role and the real you.

Among people new to an occupational role, such conflicts are common. Young professors frequently chafe under the expectations of the professor role and what it requires of them in order to achieve tenure. Young Catholic priests surveyed by sociologist Mary Ellen Reilly (1978) expressed widespread disagreement with church positions on birth control, divorce, and clerical celibacy—positions priests are expected to support. With time will their attitudes shift to become more like those of priests aged fifty-five and older, more than 90 percent of whom agreed with the church's position on these issues? If so, this would illustrate one way of resolving the conflict of person versus role: adjusting one's traits and attitudes to fit the role.

Intrarole Conflict

Have you ever been torn by conflicting expectations for how you ought to behave in a given role? The college administration may expect students serving as dormitory advisers to enforce regulations and report violations; the advisers' fellow students, however, may expect them to hold what they learn in confidence. Most professors have felt the anguish of having some of their students wish they would stick closer to the text, while others in the very same class complain that the lectures are based too much on the text. Among the young Catholic priests surveyed by Reilly, two-thirds experienced "great differences" between the expectations of the older priests and those of their younger peers.

Intrarole conflict:
Tension created by contradictory expectations about how a given role should be played.

Intrarole conflicts can be difficult to resolve. Sometimes it is possible to have the parties with the conflicting expectations seek greater consensus. Other times the conflict can be dealt with by attaching more importance to some expectations than others. Thus the young priests indicated they were most interested in the expectations of their young peers.

Interrole Conflict

You have likely experienced conflicts between the expectations of two different roles. Perhaps you have presented one "self" to your parents as you play the role of dutiful son or daughter, and quite another "self" in your role as college student. The manners, talk, and attitudes of home and campus can be kept comfortably separate, as long as the two roles are acted on separate stages. But when the stages overlap—say, on parents' weekend or when you take friends home—you face role conflict. If two sets of expectations sharply conflict, we usually resolve the ***interrole conflict*** by keeping them separate. Thus students may breathe sighs of relief as their parents complete the campus inspections and drive home.

Interrole conflict:
Tension between the requirements of two roles that must be played at once.

Despite the tensions associated with role conflict, occupying multiple roles has its blessings. Patricia Linville (1987) reports that those who occupy several roles and therefore have multiple identities—as parent, spouse, worker, amateur athlete, community leader, or whatever—feel their whole sense of self less threatened by problems

If two sets of expectations in our lives conflict, we usually resolve the interrole conflict by separating the roles as required by the situation.

"I don't mind your acting as your own attorney, but would you please stop hopping on and off that damned chair?"

in any given area. When, say, facing a possible divorce, the one who can think "Despite my marital problems, I am a good parent" (or a skilled and appreciated worker) is not so likely to be devastated.

Keeping this introduction to cultural norms and roles in mind, let us now consider, as an in-depth illustration, one cultural role on which recently there has been much research.

GENDER ROLES

The power of socially prescribed roles to shape our attitudes, our behavior, and even our sense of self is nowhere more evident than in society's implanting ideas about masculinity and femininity and how men and women should behave. But before considering gender-role indoctrination, let's first briefly consider what there is to explain: How different are men and women?

HOW DO MALES AND FEMALES DIFFER?

"In 1970, the field, psychology of women, had not been defined. Today . . . the study of women and gender has entered the mainstream within social psychology."
Barbara Strudler Wallston (1987)

In the last twenty years, *Psychological Abstracts* has indexed more than 20,000 articles on "human sex differences." So what have we learned from these studies comparing hundreds of thousands of males and females?

First, their similarities are considerable. In age of teething and walking, in overall generosity, helpfulness, and intelligence, and in many other ways, males and females are not noticeably different (E. Maccoby, 1980). Even in physical abilities, where the gender gap is greatest, the overlap between the sexes is considerable. In the annual Boston Marathon, the average man finishes about a half hour ahead of the average woman, but some women finish ahead of most of the superbly conditioned men. Don Schollander's world-record-setting 4 minutes 12.2 seconds in the 400-meter swim at the 1964 Olympic Games would have placed him last against the eight women racing in the 1988 Olympics and a full 8.35 seconds behind winner, Janet Evans.

With psychological traits, the gender similarities are even greater. The English scholar Samuel Johnson recognized the much greater variation *within* than between the sexes when asked whether man or woman was more intelligent. His reply: "Which man? Which woman?"

Gender similarities, however, rouse much less interest and publicity than gender-related differences. The difference in, say, males' and females' average scores on the SAT math test elicit much more attention than their similar average scores on the SAT verbal test. Differences excite scientific curiosity and draw media attention and for that reason may exaggerate our perceptions of the differences between women and men, who are assuredly not of "*opposite*" sex, notes Lauren Harris (1979): "Neither in any physiological nor in any psychological sense are males and females contrary or antithetical in nature or tendency. . . ." Moreover, as we will see, *believing* that certain differences exist may lead men and women both to perceive and to enact expected differences, thereby fulfilling the prophecy.

What, then, are these small gender differences in social behavior? Among them are differences in aggressiveness, empathy and nonverbal sensitivity, sexual initiative, and social power.

The world's fastest woman in 1988 would have been the world's fastest human being in 1928. Percy Williams' Olympic gold-medal winning time in the 1928 men's 100-meter dash would have left him trailing Florence Griffith Joyner by three-tenths of a second in the 1988 women's 100-meter dash.

Aggression

Aggression:
Physical or verbal behavior intended to hurt someone. In laboratory experiments, this might mean delivering electric shocks or saying something likely to hurt another's feelings. By this social psychological definition, one can be socially assertive without being aggressive.

By **aggression,** psychologists refer not to assertiveness but to behavior that intends to hurt. Throughout the world, hunting, fighting, and warring are primarily men's activities. In surveys, men admit to more aggression than do women. In laboratory experiments, men indeed exhibit more physical aggression, for example by administering what they believe are hurtful electric shocks (Eagly & Steffen, 1986; Hyde, 1986). In the United States, men are arrested for violent crimes eight times more often than women—a trend found in every society that has kept crime records (Kenrick, 1987).

Criminal violence is extreme and unusual behavior; this year 99 + percent of people will *not* be arrested for murder or assault. It is a curious feature of statistical distributions that even a small difference between the averages of two groups—say between the overlapping distributions of male and female aggressiveness—can create noticeable differences at the extremes. Only 5 percent of the variation in individuals' activity levels is attributable to gender (Eaton & Enns, 1986), but that's all it takes to make extreme activity—diagnosed as hyperactivity—three times more common in boys than girls. In other words, observing the extremes—say, the preponderance of males among the criminally violent, the hyperactive, and the junior high math whiz kids—can mislead us into exaggerated perceptions of differences between groups.

Empathy and Sensitivity

Empathy:
The vicarious experience of another's feelings; putting oneself in another's shoes.

There is no doubt that the average female *reports* being more empathic, more able to feel what another feels—"to rejoice with those who rejoice, and weep with those who weep." This is especially true when in surveys women and men describe their emotional responses. To some extent it is also true in laboratory studies, in which women have been more likely to cry and to report feeling distressed at another's distress (Eisenberg & Lennon, 1983).

"In the different voice of women lies the truth of an ethic of care."
Carol Gilligan (1982, p. 173)

Moreover, many investigators report that women are less competitive and more cooperative than men and more concerned with social relationships (Gilligan, 1982; Knight & Dubro, 1984). Compared to their friendships with men, both men and women report their friendships with women to be higher in intimacy, enjoyment, and nurturance (Sapadin, 1988). Judith Hall (1984) found that in 94 percent of published studies of adult smiling, females smiled more than males. More recent studies outside the laboratory confirm that women's generally greater warmth is frequently expressed as smiling. When Marianne LaFrance (1985) analyzed 9000 college yearbook photos, and when Amy Halberstadt and Martha Saitta (1987) studied 1100 magazine and newspaper photos and 1300 people in shopping malls, parks, and streets, they consistently found that females were more likely to smile. In groups, men contribute more task-oriented behaviors, such as giving information, and women contribute more positive social-emotional behaviors, such as giving help or showing support (Eagly, 1987).

One explanation for this male/female difference in expressed empathy is that women tend to be better at reading others' emotions. In her analysis of 125 studies of men's and women's sensitivity to nonverbal cues, Hall (1984) has discerned that women are generally superior at decoding others' emotional messages. For example, when shown a two-second silent film clip of the face of an upset woman, women tend to guess more accurately whether she is angry or discussing a divorce. Women also are more skilled at expressing emotions nonverbally, reports Hall.

Sexual Attitudes and Behavior

Susan Hendrick and her colleagues (1985) report that many studies, including their own, reveal a gender gap in sexual attitudes: Women are "moderately conservative" about casual sex, and men are "moderately permissive." The American Council on Education's recent survey of a quarter million first-year college students is illustrative. "If two people really like each other, it's all right for them to have sex even if they've known each other for only a very short time," agreed 66 percent of men but only 39 percent of women (Astin et al., 1987).

The gender difference in sexual attitudes carries over to behavior. Across the world, males are more likely to initiate sexual relations and to be less selective about their partners, a pattern that characterizes most animal species (Hinde, 1984; Kenrick & Trost, 1987). Not only in sexual relations, but also in courtship, self-disclosure, and touching, males tend to take more initiative (Hendrick, 1988; Kenrick, 1987).

Social Power

In both modern and traditional societies around the globe, people perceive men to be more dominant, driven, and aggressive, women to be more submissive, nurturant, and affiliative (Williams & Best, 1986). And in every known society, men *are* socially dominant. Iftikhar Hassan (1980) of Pakistan's National Institute of Psychology explains the status of the average Pakistani woman:

> She knows that parents are not happy at the birth of a girl and she should not complain about parents not sending her to school as she is not expected to take up a job. She is taught to be patient, sacrificing, obedient. . . . If something goes wrong with her marriage she is the one who is to be blamed. If any one of her children do not succeed in life, she is the main cause of their failure. And in the rare circumstance that she seeks a divorce or receives a divorce her chances of second marriage are very slim because Pakistani culture is very harsh on divorced women.

In the United States, which prides itself on being more egalitarian than most cultures, women comprise 51 percent of the population, but 5 percent of the 1989 Congress and 3.4% of corporate boards of directors (Boyd, 1988). In Canada's 1989 National Parliament, 13 percent are women; in Britain, 6 percent are women. When

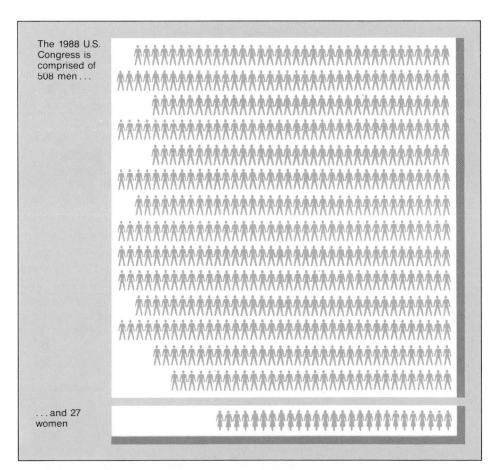

The 1988 U.S. Congress is comprised of 508 men . . .

. . . and 27 women

FIGURE 6-1

In the United States, as in every known society, men exert greater social power than do women.

salaries are paid, those in traditionally male occupations receive more. When asked what pay they deserve, women often expect less than do similarly qualified or competent men (Major, 1987). When juries are formed, 90 percent of foremen—though only half of all jurors—are men (Kerr et al., 1982).

Studies of the links between gender and communication style reveal that men tend to talk more assertively, interrupt more, and look people more directly in the eyes (Hall, 1987; Henley, 1977). Such are also the behaviors of the more dominant or expert person, as when a professor talks with a student (Dovidio et al., 1988a,b; Ellyson & Dovidio, 1985). Stating the same result from a female perspective, we could say that women's speech tends to be perceived like that of less powerful and warmer people—as less interruptive, more sensitive, less cocky.

Aware of such findings, Nancy Henley (1977) has argued that women should stop feigning smiles, averting their eyes, and tolerating interruptions, and should instead look people in the eye and speak assertively. Judith Hall (1984), however, values women's less autocratic communication style, and therefore objects to the idea

> that women should change their nonverbal style so as to appear more affectively distant and insensitive. . . . What would be sacrificed is the deeper value to self and society of a behavioral style that is adaptive, socially wise, and likely to facilitate positive interaction, understanding, and trust. . . . Whenever it is assumed that women's nonverbal behavior is undesirable, yet another myth is perpetuated: that male behavior is "normal" and that it is women's behavior that is deviant and in need of explanation. (pp. 152–153)

WHY DO MALES AND FEMALES DIFFER?

These male-female differences in social behavior may be modest, but they provoke interest. Just as detectives are interested in crimes, not in law-abiding behavior, so psychological detectives are intrigued by differences, not similarities. In the case of the male-female differences in aggression, empathy, sexual initiative, and power, the causes for the "crimes" are still under investigation. Preliminary inquiry has identified two suspected culprits: biology and culture.

Biology

Men have penises, women have vaginas. Men produce sperm, women eggs. Men have the muscle mass to throw a spear far, women can breastfeed. Are biological sex differences limited to these obvious distinctions in reproduction and physique? Or do men's and women's genes, hormones, and brains differ in ways that also contribute to their behavioral differences? Social scientists have recently been giving increased attention to biological influences on social behavior. Consider the "biosocial" view of gender differences.

The Evolution of the Sexes

Since Darwin, most biologists have assumed that for millions of years organisms have competed to survive and leave descendants. Genes that increase the odds of an organism's leaving descendants will naturally become more abundant. If those lacking such genes leave few descendants, their genes will fade from the species. In the snowy Arctic environment, for example, polar bear genes programming a thick coat of camouflaging fur have won the genetic competition and now predominate.

Sociobiology:
The study of the emergence of social behavior using the principles of evolutionary biology.

Simplified, Darwin assumed that the way organisms evolve is adaptive, otherwise they wouldn't be here. Organisms that are well adapted to their environment are more likely to contribute their genes to posterity. The controversial new field of *sociobiology* studies how this evolutionary process may predispose not just physical traits, such as polar bear coats, but also social behaviors.

The theory offers a ready explanation for why the males of most mammalian species exert more sexual initiative. Sociobiologist Edward O. Wilson explains:

> During the full period of time it takes to bring a fetus to term, from the fertilization of the egg to the birth of the infant, one male can fertilize many females but a female can be fertilized by only one male. Thus if males are able to court one female after another, some will be big winners and others will be absolute losers, while virtually all healthy females will succeed in being fertilized. It pays males to be aggressive, hasty, fickle, and undiscriminating. In theory it is more profitable for females to be coy, to hold back until they can identify males with the best genes. (p. 125)

"The fact seems inescapable that men and women do differ genetically, physiologically, and in many important ways psychologically. This should not be surprising to us, since as a species we have a long biological history of having two sexual forms and have had a sexual division of labor dating back perhaps several million years."
Doreen Kimura (1985)

In other words, past reproductive successes should, over time, spread the genes of sexually assertive males, thereby predisposing more sexual initiative in males than in females.

Wilson and other sociobiologists (Barash, 1979) have also argued that today's men and women bear the imprint of the ancestral division of labor. Men were hunters and warriors; women were food gatherers and bore and nursed the children. Thus natural selection favored the emergence of differing physical traits in males and females, and also of differing psychological traits—aggressiveness in males, and empathy, sensitivity, and nurturance in females.

As you can well imagine, these ideas have provoked controversy. Some assume that sociobiologists are suggesting that women are biologically suited to domestic tasks and men to work outside the home. Actually, even Wilson believes that males and females are but modestly bent by genetic predispositions. Culture, he thinks, more greatly bends the genders.

Without disputing the principle of natural selection—that nature tends to select physical and behavioral traits that contribute to the survival of one's genes—the critics see two problems with sociobiological explanations. First, they are troubled that sociobiological explanation so often starts with an effect (such as the male-female difference in aggression or sexual initiative) and then works backward to conjecture an explanation for it. This approach is reminiscent of "functionalism," psychology's dominant theory during the 1920s. "Why does that behavior occur? Because it serves such and such a function." The theorist can hardly lose at this game. Attributing behavior to social norms—after you know what behavior has occurred—is similarly sure to succeed. When one begins by knowing what there is to predict, hindsight almost guarantees a successful "explanation."

Recall that the way to prevent the hindsight bias is to imagine things turning out otherwise. Let's try it. If *women* were the stronger and more aggressive sex, could we conjecture why natural selection might have made it so? I have a hunch we could. After all, since they are the primary caretakers of the young, strong and aggressive women would more successfully protect their young. Thus natural selection maximized strength and aggressiveness in women. Except, of course, it did not.

Or if human males were never known to have extramarital affairs, might we not see the sociobiological wisdom behind their fidelity? After all, males who are loyal to their mates and offspring will more successfully ensure that their young survive to

Across cultures, mothers' roles always include a close bond with their infants. Fathers' roles range from indifference in some cultures to tender loving care in others.

"Sex differences in behavior may have been relevant to our ancestors gathering roots and hunting squirrels on the plains of Northern Africa, but their manifestations in modern society are less clearly 'adaptive.' Modern society is information oriented—big biceps and gushing testosterone have less direct relevance to the president of a computer firm."
Douglas Kenrick (1987)

perpetuate their genes. (This is, in fact, a sociobiological explanation for why humans, and certain other species whose young require a heavy parental investment, tend to pair off.)

A hunch is a hunch and mine may well be wrong. Perhaps the male-female differences that exist can be more plausibly explained than their imagined opposites. Even so, as the sociobiologist would remind us, evolutionary wisdom is *past* wisdom. It tells us what behaviors were adaptive in times past. Whether such tendencies are still adaptive and commendable is quite a different question.

Critics also note that while sociobiology might explain some of our commonalities and even some of our differences (a certain amount of diversity can aid survival), our common evolutionary heritage does not predict, say, the enormous cultural variation in human marriage patterns (from one spouse to a succession of spouses to multiple wives to multiple husbands to spouse-swapping). Nor does it explain cultural changes in behavior patterns over mere decades of time. The most significant trait that nature has endowed us with, it seems, is our human capacity to adapt—to learn and to change.

In response to such criticisms, the defenders of sociobiology respond that their ideas are not merely speculations based on hindsight. Rather, they evaluate their hypotheses with data from the behavior of animals, from people in various cultures, and from hormonal and genetic studies. Moreover, as sociobiology's influence in psychology grows, predictions are being introduced that enable its hypotheses to be confirmed or refuted. As the debate continues, the one thing everyone can agree upon is that sociobiology is one of the most provocative theories in social psychology today.

Hormones

The results of architectural blueprints can be seen in physical structures. The effects of genetic blueprints can be seen in bodily structures, such as the sex hormones that differentiate males and females. To what extent do hormonal differences contribute to psychological differences?

Infants have built-in abilities to suck, grasp, and cry. Do mothers have a corresponding built-in predisposition to respond? Advocates of the biosocial perspective, such as sociologist Alice Rossi (1978), argue that they do. Behaviors critical to survival, such as the attachment of nursing mothers to their dependent infants, tend to be innate and culturally universal. For example, an infant's crying and nursing stimulates in the mother the secretion of oxytocin, the same sex hormone that causes the nipples to erect during lovemaking. For most of human history, the physical pleasure of breast feeding probably helped forge the mother-infant bond. Thus Rossi finds it not surprising that, while many cultures expect men to be loving fathers, *all* cultures expect women to be closely attached to their young children. Likely, she would also not be surprised that in one study of more than 7000 passers-by in a Seattle shopping mall, teenage and young adult women were more than twice as likely as similar-age men to pause to look at a baby (Robinson et al., 1979).

A universal behavior pattern—one found in every known society—likely has some biological predisposition. In a book that helped rekindle interest in *The Psychology of Sex Differences*, Eleanor Maccoby and Carol Jacklin (1974) enumerated reasons for supposing that the culturally universal male-female aggression difference is partly biological: It appears in subhuman primates (from an early age, male monkeys are more aggressive than females); it appears early in life (before cultural pressures would have much effect); and it can be influenced by sex hormones. In monkey experiments, females given male hormones become as aggressive and dominant as males. Moreover, human females who receive excess male hormones during fetal development (due to a glandular malfunction or to injections their mothers received) tend as prepubertal children to be aggressive and "tomboyish" (Money, 1987). None of these lines of evidence is by itself conclusive (perhaps the tomboyish girls were treated differently). But taken together, they do convince most scholars that sex hormones make a difference.

Culture

Gender role:
A set of behavior expectations (norms) for males or females.

No one disputes culture's enormous impact on ***gender roles.*** Our whole sense of what it means to be male or female is socially constructed. From birth onward culture teaches us the importance of sex as a social category. People's first question—"Is it a boy or a girl?"—helps them know how to categorize and relate to the newborn. Infants are dressed as girls or boys, preschoolers are given either girls' or boys' toys, schoolchildren are often seated, lined up, and engaged in play as girls or boys. But do such cultural practices create gender differences or merely reflect them? Cultural variations in gender roles, supplemented by experiments on gender roles, leave no doubt that culture helps construct our gender categories.

Cultural Differences in Gender Roles

We've already noted a few cultural universals: Virtually all societies are patriarchal—ruled by men. Men fight the wars and hunt large game; women gather food and tend the children (a division of labor that makes evolutionary sense to a sociobiologist). In their book, *The Longest War*, Carol Tavris and Carole Wade (1984) illustrate another universal. See if you can detect and state it:

Among the Toda of India, men do the domestic chores; such work is too sacred for a mere female. If the women of a tribe grow sweet potatoes and men grow yams, yams will be the tribe's prestige food, the food distributed at feasts. . . . And if women take over a formerly all-male occupation, it loses status, as happened to the professions of typing and teaching in the United States, medicine in the Soviet Union, and cultivating cassavas in Nigeria. (p. 21)

The rule is this, say Tavris and Offir: Men's work, no matter what it is, is most prestigious.

So there are cross-cultural similarities. But cultural differences are more numerous. In nonwesternized regions, agricultural food-accumulating societies tend to restrict women to child-related activities and men tend to regard such activities with contempt. In more nomadic hunting-gathering societies, women have greater freedom and gender-role distinctions are not so sharp (Van Leeuwen, 1978). Moreover, although every culture distinguishes masculinity from femininity, the traits and jobs assigned men in one culture are, in another, sometimes those assigned women. In some tribes, men do the weaving; in other tribes, weaving is a woman's work.

In the United States, most physicians and dentists are men. In Denmark, dentistry is predominantly a woman's occupation, as is medicine in the Soviet Union. A biological explanation of the U.S. male predominance in these occupations would require human biology to be different in Denmark and the Soviet Union. Plainly, such is not the case. Even in the United States, secretaries, nurses, and teachers used to be mostly men. Has the biological suitability of men for these occupations somehow lessened?

Cultures vary not only in the tasks and occupations deemed suitable for women and men but in the sexes' social behavior. In the United States, males have less intimate same-sex friendships than do females, especially after marrying (Tschann, 1988). In India, men need not be rugged individualists. Thus men and women are equally free to share intimate feelings and worries with their best friends (Berman et al., 1988).

Experiments on Gender Roles

The discussion of cultural variation has asked a simple question: If we hold biology constant but vary cultural expectations, what do we get? Answer: A big effect of culture. Social psychologists ask the same question when they experimentally explore the social origins of gender differences. In the laboratory, too, social factors significantly affect how males and females behave.

Recall from Chapters 4 and 5 that our social ideas are often self-confirming. People expected to be hostile, extraverted, or gifted may actually exhibit hostility, extraversion, or high achievement. Mark Zanna and his colleagues wondered whether being stereotyped in a gender role would, similarly, lead one to fulfill the stereotype. In one experiment, Zanna and Susan Pack (1975) had Princeton University undergraduate women answer a questionnaire on which they described themselves to a tall, unattached, senior man they expected to meet. Women led to believe that the man's ideal woman was "traditional" (deferent to her husband, emotional, home-oriented) presented themselves as more conventionally feminine than did women expecting to meet a man who supposedly liked independent, competitive, ambitious women. Moreover, when given a problem-solving test, those expecting to meet the nonsexist man behaved more intelligently: They solved 18 percent more problems than those expecting to meet the man with the traditional views. This adapting of themselves to fit the man's image was much less pronounced if the man was less desirable—a short, already attached freshman.

Do you ever present one self to members of your own sex and a different self to members of the other sex?

BEHIND THE SCENES

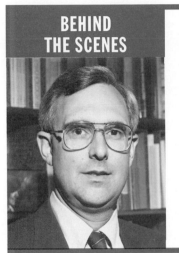

When I began my career at Princeton in 1970, the first group of female undergraduates had just enrolled at this formerly all-male bastion. These pioneers were incredibly bright and very ambitious. Indeed, the majority intended to become doctors, lawyers, or professors! It was Susan Pack's intuition that, despite the great capabilities and high achievement motivation of her female peers, they still "acted dumb" when confronted with the typical attractive, though chauvinistic, Princeton male. Susan's undergraduate honors thesis, designed to test this notion, demonstrated that Princeton females "acted dumb" or "acted smart" depending, in part, on whether they believed an attractive Princeton male held chauvinistic or liberated attitudes about women. I wonder: would these results hold today at Princeton? At other colleges? Would males, too, act to fulfill the gender stereotypes of attractive females?

Mark Zanna, *University of Waterloo*

Aware that three-fourths of television's roles are played by men (Gerbner et al., 1986), and that women have played stereotyped roles on programs and in ads, social psychologists have questioned such portrayals. For example, Florence Geis and her colleagues (1984) had their University of Delaware students view either re-creations of four typical sex-stereotyped commercials or the same commercials with the gender roles reversed (for example, a little man proudly serves a delicious package dinner to his hungry wife, who is just home from work). When the women viewers then wrote essays about what they envisioned their lives to be "ten years from now," those who viewed the nontraditional commercials were more likely to express career aspirations. A follow-up experiment revealed that women who viewed the nontraditional commercials were also less conforming in a laboratory test and more self-confident when delivering a speech (Jennings et al., 1980).

If viewing but four vivid commercials has even a temporary effect on women's aspirations and behavior, one must wonder about the cumulative effect of the 350,000 commercials commonly viewed during the growing-up years and of the many more instances of gender stereotyping in television's programs. Recent experiments by Christine Hansen (1988; Hansen & Hansen, 1988) show that viewing rock music videos can color people's impressions of other social interactions. After viewing images of a macho man and sexually acquiescent woman, subjects tended to view a woman whom they observed as more submissive and sexual.

Biology and Culture

The cultural variations in gender roles and the experiments on gender roles illustrate this chapter's central message: Cultural norms subtly but powerfully affect our attitudes and behavior. But they needn't do so independent of biology. What biology initiates, culture may accentuate. If males' genes and hormones predispose them to be more physically aggressive than females, culture may amplify this difference by socializing males to be tough and females to be the kinder, gentler sex.

Biology and culture may also *interact.* In humans, biological traits influence how the environment reacts. People respond differently to a Sylvester Stallone than to a Woody Allen. Men, being 8 percent taller and averaging almost double the proportion

Interaction:
The effect of one factor (such as biology) depends on another factor (such as environment).

FIGURE 6-2
A social-role theory of gender differences in social behavior. Various influences, including childhood experiences and biological factors, bend males and females toward differing roles. It is the expectations and the skills and beliefs associated with these differing roles that affect men's and women's behavior. (Adapted from Eagly, 1987.)

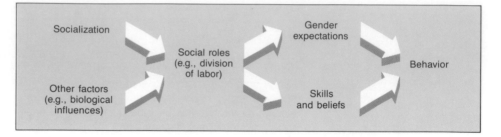

of muscle mass, may likewise have different experiences than women (Kenrick, 1987). Or consider this: There is a very strong cultural norm dictating that males should be taller than their female mates. In one recent study, only 1 in 720 married couples violated this norm (Gillis & Avis, 1980). With hindsight, we can speculate a psychological explanation: Perhaps being taller (and older) helps men perpetuate their social power over women. But we can also speculate biological wisdom that might underlie the cultural norm: If people preferred partners of the same height, tall men and short women would often be without partners. As it is, biology dictates that men tend to be taller than women, and culture dictates such within couples. So the height norm might well be biology *and* culture, hand in hand.

In her book on *Sex Differences in Social Behavior*, Alice Eagly (1987) theorizes a process by which biology and culture interact (see Figure 6-2). She believes that a variety of factors, including biological influences and childhood socialization experiences, have traditionally predisposed a sexual division of labor. In adult life the immediate causes of gender differences in social behavior are the *roles* that reflect this sexual division of labor. Given that men tend to be found in roles demanding social and physical power, and women in more nurturant roles, each sex tends to exhibit the behaviors expected of those who fill such roles. As they do so their skills and beliefs are shaped accordingly. Thus the effects of biology and socialization may be important insofar as they influence the social roles that people are playing in the here and now.

CHANGING GENDER ROLES

From the perspective of evolution, Act I of the human drama may be drawing to a close. Gender roles that were biologically adaptive in ages when women were pregnant both often and unpredictably may be less adaptive now that most women spend far more time working outside the home than mothering. Let us see how gender roles have changed in recent years and then ponder how they might change in the future.

Gender roles are converging. In 1962, only a third of women in the metropolitan Detroit area disagreed with the statement, "Most of the important decisions in the life of the family should be made by the man of the house." Fifteen years later, more than two-thirds disagreed. And three-fourths disagreed that some work is meant for men and other work for women (Thornton & Freedman, 1979).

But as noted in the Chapter 2 discussion of attitudes and actions, people don't always act out the attitudes they express. It's one thing for a man to say he approves "the changes in women's roles" (which, according to a Louis Harris poll, most men say they do); it's another for him to cook dinner. As one well-known actress remarked, "I've been married to a fascist and married to a Marxist, and neither one of them took out the garbage" (Tavris & Wade, 1984, p. 366).

"Can man be free if woman be a slave?"
Percy Bysshe Shelley,
The Revolt of Islam

Traditional gender roles: "It's OK for both husband and wife to work, but only until one or the other gets pregnant."
Sam Levenson

"I enjoy housework. To 'liberate' me from such is to 'enslave' me to an assigned task and call it employment."
A soon-to-be-married bachelor

In some ways, however, behavior *is* changing. Between 1965 and 1985, American women were spending progressively less time in household tasks, men progressively more time—thus raising the total proportion of housework done by men from 15 to 33 percent (Robinson, 1988). From 1947 to 1989 the proportion of U.S. women in the labor force rose from 32 to 57 percent. When the class of 1991 began college in 1987, one-third of the women—five times the percentage of twenty years earlier—were intending to pursue careers in business, law, medicine, or engineering (Astin et al., 1987a,b). During these same two decades, the percentage of first-year students agreeing that "The activities of married women are best confined to the home and family" plunged from 57 to 26 percent. As Figure 6-3 shows, for increasing numbers of women the dream of a doctoral degree has become a reality.

Assuming the continuation of these trends, imagine eventually reaching a point where nearly all men and women have full-time jobs. If such occurs, will gender roles—for better or for worse—disappear? Carol Tavris and Carole Wade (1984) have analyzed societies where, already, nearly all women are employed. For example, based on the Marxist ideology of the equality of the sexes, the communist governments in the Soviet Union and China revolutionized the roles of women. Similarly, Israel's communal kibbutz communities have consciously liberated women from housework. Yet each of these social experiments in equality has failed to achieve its egalitarian goals. In all three societies, women have less political and social power than men. In the Soviet Union, for example, women have made up nearly half the work force but only 5 percent of the Communist Party's Central Committee. As Nikita Khrushchev once admitted, "It

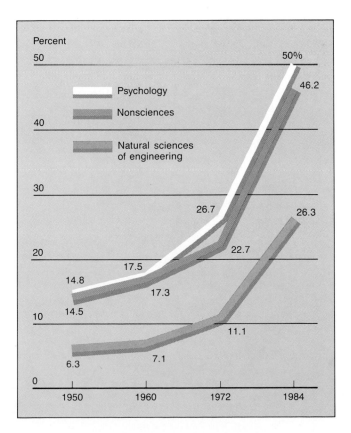

FIGURE 6-3
Percentage of American doctorates earned by women. (From Howard & others, 1986.)

turns out that it is men who do the administering and women who do the work" (1980, p. 65). And when you ask, "Who works in the communal child-care nurseries?" and "Who cooks dinner?" the answers are usually as predictable as those given in the United States. Women may share increasingly in the breadwinning, but they still do most of the bread baking. Thus Tavris and Wade conclude that while

> increasing numbers of women are taking their place alongside men in the working world, men are not taking their place alongside women in the nursery and the kitchen. No country has given the question top priority. Until they do the hand that rocks the cradle will be too tired to rule the world. (p. 366)

"Wherever a man may happen to turn, whatever a man may undertake, he will always end up by returning to that path which nature has marked out for him."
Goethe, Autobiography, *1811*

Why is it easier to prescribe than to practice the elimination of sex roles? The answer again lies with the controversy of biology versus culture. "Aha!" some say, "this feminist attempt to abolish gender roles goes against our natural state. Sure, with enough effort, some people can overcome biological dispositions for awhile, but once they slack off, they go right back to their biologically prescribed maleness or femaleness." Others point to the existence of enormous cultural variation, and suggest, "In just one or two generations you can't possibly expect to overturn a long history of male supremacy."

However, in at least one sense, men may now actually be the *less* liberated sex: Male gender roles, some researchers believe, are the more rigidly defined. Consider some instances: Both parents and children are more tolerant of girls playing "like a boy" than boys playing "like a girl" (Carter & McCloskey, 1983–84; O'Leary & Donoghue, 1978). Better a tomboy than a sissy. Moreover, women feel freer to become doctors than men to become nurses. And social norms now allow married women

"Mr. Edwards, this is your secretary, Melissa. When you have a moment, would you run down and get me a regular coffee and a pineapple Danish?"

"If women are to be free to choose to pursue a career as well as marriage, they must also be free to choose the making of a home and the nurture of a family as their vocation."
Madeleine L'Engle, Walking on Water, *1980*

increased freedom to choose whether or not to have a paying vocation; men who shun a job and assume the domestic role are "shiftless" and "lazy." In these areas, at least, it is men who are more predictable, more locked into their role.

SHOULD THERE BE GENDER ROLES?

Describing traditional gender roles does not make them wrong and another set of norms right. A description of what *is* needn't provide a prescription of what *ought* to be. Nevertheless, many of the social scientists who study human norms have strong personal convictions about what ought to be. Most favor eliminating or modifying gender roles so all persons can develop their own potentialities, unhindered by consideration of their sex.

There are at least three ways in which we might minimize gender roles: by (1) socializing females to behave more like males (such as through assertiveness training); (2) socializing males to exhibit traditional feminine qualities (sensitivity, nurturance, cooperativeness); or (3) socializing everyone to become **androgynous**—to develop both "masculine" and "feminine" traits, so they may draw upon whichever are appropriate in given situations.

Androgyny (andros, *man*, + gyne, *women*): Possession of both "masculine" and "feminine" psychological traits. The androgynous person is said to be high in both traditionally masculine qualities (for example, independence, assertiveness, competitiveness) and traditionally feminine qualities (for example, warmth, tenderness, compassion).

In research studies, androgynous subjects are those who describe themselves as having both "masculine" assertiveness, independence, and so forth, *and* "feminine" warmth, compassion, and so forth. Some initial reports suggested that androgynous people feel better about themselves than do gender-typed masculine men and feminine women. But dozens of follow-up studies, from North American to India, revealed that, for both men and women, masculine qualities were associated with high self-regard (Orlofsky & O'Heron, 1987; Sethi & Bala, 1983; Whitley, 1985).

For personal relationships, however, traditional feminine qualities make for greater satisfaction (Ickes, 1985; Kurdek & Schmitt, 1986). William Ickes and Richard Barnes (1978) discovered this when they arranged brief blind dates in the laboratory for forty couples. Ten of the couples were composed of a masculine male and feminine female, the rest included at least one androgynous person. Did "opposites attract" in the ten couples with complementary masculine/feminine qualities? Hardly. During their 5 minutes, the macho-man-meets-sweet-woman couples did less talking, mutual gazing, smiling, and laughing than did the other couples. And as Figure 6-4 shows, afterward they expressed much less attraction for each other.

Strong masculine qualities seem to interfere with intimacy. In a study of 108 married couples in Sydney, Australia, John Antill (1983) found that when either the wife or husband had traditionally feminine qualities such as gentleness, sensitivity, and affectionateness—or better yet, when *both* did—marital satisfaction was higher. Having the personal attributes of Rambo may be good for self-esteem, but both husbands and wives report that it's much more satisfying to be married to someone who is nurturant, sensitive, and emotionally supportive.

Such a relationship contributes not only to a happy marriage but to a satisfying life. Grace Baruch and Rosaline Barnett (1986) of the Wellesley College Center for Research on Women report that for women what influences overall happiness is not so much which roles a woman occupies—as paid worker, wife, and/or mother—but the quality of her experience in those roles. Happiness is having work that fits your interests and provides a sense of competence and accomplishment; having a partner who is a close, supportive companion; having loving children of whom you feel proud.

So, should gender roles be eliminated? Some say that biological gender differences

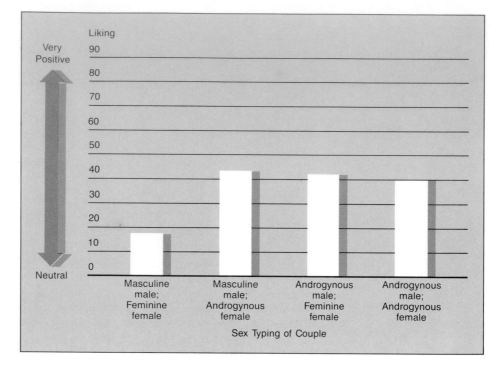

FIGURE 6-4
Do masculine men and feminine women make the most compatible couples? After spending five minutes alone with someone of the other sex, University of Wisconsin students indicated their liking for this person whom they had just met. The masculine male–feminine female couples indicated much less attraction to one another than did other types of couples. (Data from Ickes & Barnes, 1978.)

make social differences inevitable. Sociologist Alice Rossi (1978) has warned that "We cannot just toss out the physiological equipment that centuries of adaptation have created. [Our vision of equality should be] respectful of natural body processes and of the differences between individuals. . . ." Concern also exists that making androgyny the ideal—one person having to be all things—takes Western individualism to the extreme (Sampson, 1977; Wallston, 1981). Might it therefore be better to accept and value our differences? Two people, like two sides of a coin, can be different yet equal.

Others, like Sandra Bem (1987), grant there may be some "biologically based sex

"Men and women are different. What needs to be made equal is the value placed upon these differences.
Diane McGuinness and Karl Pribram (1978)

Working as equals, males and females can use their differences to achieve common goals effectively and harmoniously.

"We're a great team, Sash—you with your small and large motor skills, me with my spatial awareness and hand-eye coördination."

differences in behavior," but believe that culture's version of gender greatly exaggerates the small sex differences that exist naturally. If, given social conditions that do not restrain people because of their sex,

> it turns out that more men than women become engineers or that more women than men decide to stay at home with their children, I'll live happily with those sex differences as well as with any others that emerge. But I am willing to bet that the sex differences that emerge under those conditions will not be nearly as large or as diverse as the ones that currently exist in our society.

THE GREAT LESSON OF SOCIAL PSYCHOLOGY: PERSONS AND SITUATIONS

Food for thought. If Bohr's statement is a great truth, what is its opposite?

"There are trivial truths and great truths," declared the physicist Niels Bohr. "The opposite of a trivial truth is plainly false. The opposite of a great truth is also true." Each chapter in this unit on social influence teaches us about a great truth: the power of the social situation. This great truth about the power of external pressures would sufficiently explain our behavior if we were passive, like tumbleweed. But unlike tumbleweed, we are not just blown here and there by the environment. We act, we react; we respond, and we get responses; we can resist the social situation, and sometimes even change it. Thus each of these "social influence" chapters concludes by calling attention to the opposite of the great truth: the power of the person.

Yet, even with this recognition of our own power, perhaps this chapter's stress on the power of culture leaves you somewhat uncomfortable. Most of us resent any suggestion that external forces determine our behavior. We want to think of ourselves as free beings, as the originators of our actions (well, at least of our good actions). We sense that believing in social determinism can lead to what philosopher Jean-Paul Sartre called "bad faith"—evading responsibility by blaming something or someone for one's fate.

"The words of truth are always paradoxical."
Lao-Tsze, The Simple Way

Actually, social control (the power of the situation) and personal control (the power of the person) compete no more with one another than do biological and cultural explanations. Social and personal explanations of our social behavior are both valid, for at any moment we are both the creatures and the creators of our social worlds. We may well be the products of our genes and environment. But it is also true that the future is coming, and it is our job to decide where it is going. Our choices today determine our environment tomorrow.

Social situations do profoundly influence individuals. But individuals also influence the social situation. The two *interact*. Thus asking whether people's behavior is determined by their external situations or their inner dispositions is like asking whether the area of a field is determined by its length or its width.

The interaction occurs in at least three ways (Snyder & Ickes, 1985). First, a given social situation often affects different people somewhat differently. Because our minds do not see reality identically, we each respond to a situation as we perceive it. And some people are more sensitive and responsive to social situations than others (M. Snyder, 1983). Japanese people, for example, have been found more responsive to the situation than British people (Argyle et al., 1978).

Interaction between persons and situations also occurs because people can choose to be part of a particular situation. Given a choice, sociable people elect situations that evoke social interaction (Gormly, 1983). When you chose your college you were also choosing to expose yourself to a specific set of social influences. Ardent political liberals are unlikely to settle in Orange County, California, join the Chamber of Commerce, or read *U.S. News and World Report*. They are more likely to live in San Francisco, join Common Cause, and read the *New Republic*—in other words, to choose a social world that reinforces their liberal inclinations.

Finally, people often create their situations. Recall again that our preconceptions can be self-fulfilling: If we expect someone to be extraverted, hostile, feminine, or sexy, our actions toward the person may induce the very behavior we expect. What, after all, composes a social situation, but the people in it? A liberal political environment is one created by political liberals. What takes place at the Elks Club bar is created by the patrons. The social environment is not like the weather—something that just happens to us. It is more like our homes—something we have made for ourselves.

This reciprocal causation (between social situations and persons) allows us to see people as either *reacting to* or *acting upon* their environment. Each perspective is correct, for we are both the products and the architects of our social worlds. However, to be practical, is one perspective wiser? Even that question is complex, for in one sense, it is wise to see ourselves as the creatures of our environments—lest we become too proud of our achievements and too self-blaming for our problems—and to see others as free actors—lest we become paternalistic and manipulative.

However, perhaps we would do well to assume more often the reverse—to view ourselves as free agents and to view others as influenced by their environments. Thus we would assume self-efficacy as we view ourselves, and seek understanding and social reform as we relate to others. (If we view others as influenced by their situations we are more likely to understand and empathize than smugly to pronounce unpleasant behavior as that chosen by "immoral," "sadistic," or "lazy" persons.) Interestingly, most religions similarly encourage us to take responsibility for ourselves but to refrain from judging others. Does religion teach this because our natural inclination is to excuse our own failures while blaming others for theirs?

> "*If we explain poverty, or emotional disorders, or crime and delinquency, or alcoholism, or even unemployment, as resulting from personal, internal, individual defects . . . then there simply is not much we can do about prevention.*"
> George Albee (1979)

SUMMING UP

NORMS

The remarkably wide diversity of attitudes and behaviors from one culture to another indicates the extent to which we are the products of cultural norms. Norms restrain and control us, but they also lubricate the social machinery: social behavior occurs with more ease when everyone knows what is both expected and accepted.

Despite their distinct differences, cultures share some norms in common. One apparently universal norm concerns how people of unequal status relate to one another. The more formal way we communicate with strangers is the same way we communicate with superiors. Moreover, increased intimacy (for example, a social invitation) is usually initiated by the person with higher status.

ROLES

A role is a set of norms associated with a given social position. We tend to assimilate the roles we play. Thus our playing a destructive role can be corrupting, as illustrated in observations of students playing the role of prison guard. Parallels to these laboratory results are found in daily life, such as in the "burnout" often experienced by police officers, ward attendants, and social workers. But role playing can also be used constructively. By reversing roles intentionally for a time, we can develop empathy for another.

The expectations associated with a role sometimes conflict. If one's personality or attitudes clash with the role one must play, the result is the conflict of person and role. Intrarole conflict arises when there is disagreement about how a given role should be played. Interrole conflict occurs when there is an incompatibility between the requirements of two different roles.

GENDER ROLES

These basic principles of role theory are perhaps best illustrated in the most pervasive, most heavily researched social roles: the roles of male and female. As do other sets of norms, gender roles vary widely from culture to culture. Yet some cultural norms are universal (for example, that men are warriors and women care for the young children). Gender roles help create gender differences: Men often behave more aggressively, take more sexual initiative, exhibit less empathy and sensitivity to nonverbal cues, and exert more social power. These differences are small, and are certainly outnumbered by the ways men and women are alike. But differences, not similarities, catch the eye and provoke the mind.

Biological sex differences may contribute to behavioral differences. Sociobiologists speculate how evolution might have created a sexual division of labor. The evidence is clearer, however, that hormonal sex differences help create aggressiveness in males and a mother-infant bond in females.

The effect of culture on gender roles is unambiguous. Biology cannot explain the striking variations in gender roles from culture to culture. Also, laboratory experiments document that in day-to-day social interaction and in the media, gender-role stereotypes tend to be self-fulfilling. These cultural and experimental lines of research all indicate that if biology is held constant while cultural expectations are varied, the cultural effects are pronounced.

However, biological and cultural explanations need not be contradictory. Indeed, they interact, biological factors operating within a cultural context and culture being built upon a biological foundation.

In industrialized nations such as the United States, gender roles are converging. People are beginning to accept more similar roles for men and women, and women's employment rates have increased dramatically. Yet in no culture have gender roles been eliminated.

Should they be? This is an ideological rather than a scientific question. Many social psychologists who study gender roles advocate their elimination, or at least their modification. Some advocate androgyny, the combination of feminine and masculine traits. They feel that, freed from rigid gender roles, the ideal androgynous person can, as appropriate, be "masculine" one moment and "feminine" the next. Other social psychologists question this ideal. Either they argue that it ignores biological differences, or they question the individualism of expecting each person to be all things.

PERSONS AND SITUATIONS

The great truth about the power of social influence is but half the truth if separated from its complementary truth: the power of the person. Persons and situations interact in at least three ways. First, social situations influence individual persons, yet individuals vary in how they interpret and react to a given situation. Second, people choose many of the situations that influence them. Third, social situations are created by people. Thus power resides both in persons and in situations. We create and are created by our social worlds.

FOR FURTHER READING

Basow, S. A. (1986). *Gender stereotypes: Traditions and alternatives*, 2nd ed. Pacific Grove, CA: Brooks/Cole. A helpful interdisciplinary look at gender differences and their social origins.

Bond, M. (Ed.). (1989). *The cross-cultural challenge to social psychology.* Newbury Park, CA: Sage. Social psychologists examine cultural influences on social processes and debate the necessity of cross-cultural research.

Eagly, A. H. (1987). *Sex differences in social behavior: A social-role explanation.* Hillsdale, NJ: Erlbaum. How and why are men and women alike and different in aggressiveness, altruism, influenceability, and nonverbal behavior? Eagly digests all the available research studies and cogently explains the outcomes.

Tavris, C., & Wade, C. (1984). *The longest war: Sex differences in perspective* (2nd. ed.). San Diego, CA: Harcourt-Brace-Johanovich. A wise and witty introduction to the social psychology and biology of gender.

CHAPTER 7

CONFORMITY

CHAPTER

7

CONFORMITY

———

I t was a long-awaited May afternoon. Three thousand family members and friends had gathered for the celebration. One cue, 400 Hope College seniors rose to hear the college president declare, "I hereby confer upon each of you the degree of Bachelor of Arts, with all the rights and privileges appertaining thereto." The declaration finished, the 25 new alumni in the first row began filing forward to receive their diplomas. As they did so, the other 375 eyed one another nervously, each thinking: "Weren't we instructed to sit down now and await our row's turn?" But no one sat. The seconds ticked by. Half the first row now had diplomas in hand. Outwardly, the standing herd kept its cool. But inside each head thoughts were buzzing: "We could be standing here for a half hour before it is our row's turn. . . . We're blocking the view of spectators seated behind us. . . . Why doesn't someone sit down?" Still, no one sat. Now two minutes had elapsed. The graduation marshal, whose instructions at the graduation rehearsal were being ignored, strode up to the first standing row and subtly signaled it to sit down. No one sat. So he moved to the next row and audibly ordered it to "Sit down!" Within two seconds, 375 much-relieved people were happily relaxing in their chairs.

Witnessing this scene raised in my mind three sets of questions. First, why, given the great diversity of individuals among that large group, was their behavior so uniform? Is social pressure sometimes powerful enough to obliterate individual differences? Where were the rugged individualists?

Second, 25 percent of those graduates had been my students in social psychology. Although it was the furthest thing from their minds at the moment, they knew about conformity. When studying the topic, many of them had privately assured themselves that they would never be so docile as were subjects in the famous conformity experiments. But here they were, participating in one of life's parallels to the laboratory experiments. In everyday life is the heroic individualistic act always more easily fantasized than performed? Are we more susceptible to social influence than we realize? Does learning about social influence not liberate us from it?

Third, is conformity as bad as my description of this docile "herd" implies: Should I have been dismayed at their "mindless conformity" or instead pleased at their "group solidarity" and "social sensitivity"?

Let us take the last question first. Is conformity good or bad? This is another of those questions that has no scientific answer. But assuming the values most of us share, two things can be said. First, conformity is at times bad (for example, when it leads someone at a party to drink before driving home), at times good (for example, when it inhibits people from cutting in front of us in a theater line), and at times relatively inconsequential (for example, when it disposes us to wear white when playing tennis).

Second, the very term "conformity" does nevertheless carry a negative value judgment. How would you feel if you overheard someone describing you as a "real conformist"? I suspect you would feel hurt, because in western cultures the trait of going along with peer pressure is generally not prized. Hence American and European social psychologists more often give it negative labels (conformity, submission, compliance) than positive ones (communal sensitivity, responsiveness, cooperative team play). We choose labels to suit our judgments. In retrospect, I view the U.S. senators who cast unpopular votes against the Vietnam war as "independent" and "inner-directed," and those who cast unpopular votes against civil rights legislation as "eccentric" and "self-centered."

Labels both describe and evaluate. They are, however, inescapable. We cannot discuss the phenomena of this chapter without labels. So let us be clear on the meanings of the following labels: conformity, compliance, acceptance.

When, as part of a crowd, you rise to cheer a game-winning touchdown, are you conforming? When, along with millions of others, you drink milk, are your conforming? When you and everyone else agree that men look better with combable hair than with crewcuts, are you conforming? Maybe, maybe not. The key is whether or not your behavior and beliefs would be the same apart from the group. Would you rise to cheer the touchdown if you were the only fan in the stands? Conformity is not just acting as other people act, it is being affected by how they act. It is acting differently from the way you would act if you were alone. Thus Charles Kiesler and Sara Kiesler (1969) defined **_conformity_** as "a change in behavior or belief . . . as a result of real or imagined group pressure" (p. 2).

Sometimes we conform without really believing in what we are doing. We put on the mandatory necktie, though we dislike doing so. This insincere outward conformity is called **_compliance._** We comply primarily to reap a reward or avoid a punishment. If our compliance is with an explicit command, the compliance is called obedience.

Other times we genuinely believe in what the group has convinced us to do. We may join millions of others in drinking milk because we have been convinced that milk is nutritious. This sincere inward conformity is called **_acceptance_**.

Compliance and acceptance are often related. As Chapter 2 emphasized, attitudes follow behavior. Thus compliance can breed acceptance. Unless we feel no responsibility for our behavior, we usually become sympathetic to what we have stood up for.

Researchers who study conformity have constructed some fascinating miniature social worlds—laboratory microcultures that simplify and simulate important features of everyday social influence. Let us begin our scrutiny to conformity research by examining three noted sets of these experiments, each of which has provided a method that others could use to study conformity, and some startling findings.

Conformity:
A change in behavior or belief as a result of real or imagined group pressure.

Compliance:
Publicly acting in accord with social pressure while privately disagreeing.

Acceptance:
Both acting and believing in accord with social pressure.

Sometimes it is difficult to avoid conforming.

The American People Finally Speak Up

CLASSIC STUDIES

SHERIF'S STUDIES OF NORM FORMATION

The first of the three "classics" provides a bridge between the last chapter's discussion of the power of culture to create and perpetuate arbitrary norms and this chapter on conformity. Muzafer Sherif (1937) wondered whether one could observe in the laboratory the emergence of a social norm. Much like a biologist seeking to isolate a virus in the laboratory where it might then be experimented upon, Sherif wanted to isolate and then experiment with the social phenomenon of norm formation.

Were you a participant in one of Sherif's experiments, you might find yourself seated in a dark room. Fifteen feet in front of you a pinpoint of light appears. After the few seconds it remains on, you must guess how far it moves. At first nothing happens. Then it moves erratically and finally disappears. Since the dark room leaves no guide for distance you squirm before offering an uncertain "6 inches." The procedure is repeated. This time you say "10 inches." With further repetitions your estimates continue to average about 8 inches.

The next day you return, joined by two others who the day before had the same experience. When the light goes off for the first time, the other two people offer their best guesses from the day before. "One inch" says one. The other states, "2 inches." A bit taken aback, you nevertheless guess "8 inches." Do you think that with successive repetitions of this group experience, both this day and for the next two days, your responses will change? The Columbia University men whom Sherif tested changed their estimates markedly. As Figure 7-1 illustrates, a group norm typically emerged. (The norm was false. Why? The light never moved! Sherif had taken advantage of a perceptual illusion called the ***autokinetic phenomenon.***)

Sherif and others after him used this technique to answer questions about people's suggestibility. For example, when a year later people were retested alone would their estimates again diverge or would they continue to state the group norm? Remarkably,

The autokinetic phenomenon: Self (*auto*) motion (*kinetic*). The apparent movement of a stationary point of light in the dark. Perhaps you have experienced this when thinking you have spotted a moving satellite in the sky, only to realize later that it was merely an isolated star.

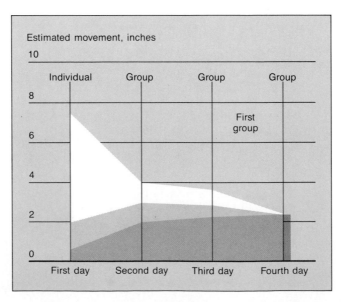

FIGURE 7-1
A sample group from Sherif's study of norm formation. Three individuals converge as they give repeated estimates of the apparent movement of a point of light. (Data from Sherif & Sherif, 1969, p. 209.)

they continued to support the group norm (Rohrer et al., 1954). (Does this suggest compliance or acceptance?)

Struck by what seems to be culture's power to perpetuate false beliefs, Robert Jacobs and Donald Campbell (1961) wondered whether such could be demonstrated and studied in their Northwestern University laboratory. Using the autokinetic phenomenon, they had a **confederate** plant an inflated estimate of how far the light moved. The confederate then left the experiment and was replaced by another real subject who was in turn replaced by a still newer member. The inflated illusion nevertheless persisted for five generations. These people had become "unwitting conspirators in perpetuating a cultural fraud." The lesson of these experiments: Because we are influenced by those around us, our views of reality are not ours alone.

In everyday life the consequences of suggestibility are sometimes amusing. In late March of 1954, Seattle newspapers reported damage to car windshields in a city 80 miles to the north. On the morning of April 14, similar windshield damage was reported 65 miles away, and later that day only 45 miles distant. By nightfall, the windshield-pitting agent had reached Seattle. Before April 15 passed, the Seattle police department received complaints of damage to over 3000 windshields (Medalia & Larsen, 1958). That evening the mayor of Seattle called on President Eisenhower for help.

I was an eleven-year-old Seattleite at the time. I can recall searching our windshield, having been frightened by the explanation that an H-bomb, which had recently been tested in the Pacific, was raining its fallout upon Seattle. However, on April 16 the newspapers hinted that actually the culprit might well be mass suggestibility. After April 17 there were no more complaints. A later analysis of the pitted windshields concluded that the cause was ordinary road damage. What had we been doing that we had not done before the report? Given the suggestion, we had looked carefully *at* our windshields instead of *through* them.

Suggestibility in real life is not always so amusing. Hijackings, UFO sightings, and even suicides tend to come in waves. Sociologist David Phillips (1985) reports that fatal auto accidents, private airplane crashes, and overt suicides increase after well-publicized suicides. For example, following Marilyn Monroe's August 6, 1962, suicide, there were 200 more August suicides in the United States than normal. Moreover, the fatalities increase only in areas where the suicide story is publicized. And the more newspaper inches given the story, the greater the increase in subsequent fatalities. Phillips believes that this indicates both the power of suggestion and that many car and plane "accidents" may in fact be suicides.

ASCH'S STUDIES OF GROUP PRESSURE

Participants in the autokinetic experiments were faced with an ambiguous reality, one with no obviously correct answer. Social psychologist Solomon Asch (1956) suspected that intelligent people would not conform in situations where they could readily see the truth for themselves. To test his hunch and to examine factors he thought might affect conformity, Asch created a clever experimental situation.

Imagine yourself as one of Asch's volunteer subjects. You are seated sixth in a row of seven people. After explaining that you will be taking part in a study of perceptual judgments, the experimenter then asks you to indicate which of the three lines in Figure 7-2 is identical to the standard line. You can easily see that it's line 2. So, you are hardly surprised when the five people responding before you all say "line 2."

The next comparison proves just as easy for everyone. You think "ho hum" and settle in to endure politely a boring experiment. But on the third trial you are startled.

Confederate:
An accomplice of the experimenter.

"Why doth one man's yawning make another yawn?"
Robert Burton, Anatomy of Melancholy

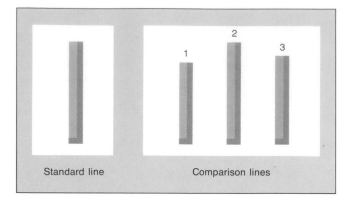

FIGURE 7-2
Sample comparison from Solomon Asch's conformity procedure. The participants were asked to judge which of three comparison lines was equal to the standard.

Standard line   Comparison lines

Although the correct answer seems just as clearcut, the first person gives what seems to you to be a wrong answer. When the second person gives the same answer, you sit up in your chair and stare at the cards. The third person agrees with the first two. Your jaw drops; you start to perspire. "What is this?" you ask yourself. "Are they blind? Or am I?" The fourth and fifth people concur with the others. And then the experimenter looks to you. Now you are experiencing an "epistemological nightmare":

In one of Asch's conformity experiments, the subject, number 6, experienced uneasiness and conflict after hearing incorrect responses from the five persons who answered a question before him.

"How am I to know what is true? Is it what my peers tell me or what my eyes tell me?"

Dozens of college students experienced this conflict when they participated in Asch's experiments. Those who answered alone were correct more than 99 percent of the time. Asch wondered: If several others (confederates who had been coached by the experimenter) gave identical wrong answers, would this prompt people to call true what they would otherwise have declared false? Although some people never conformed, most did so at least once, and, all told, 37 percent of the responses were conforming. Of course, that means 63 percent of the time people did not conform. Despite the independence shown by many of his subjects, Asch's (1955) feelings about the conformity were as clear as the correct answers to his questions: "That reasonably intelligent and well-meaning young people are willing to call white black is a matter of concern. It raises questions about our ways of education and about the values that guide our conduct."

Asch's procedure became the standard for hundreds of later experiments. Such experiments lack what Chapter 1 called the "mundane realism" of everyday conformity, but they do have "experimental realism." People get emotionally involved in the experience. Some may even find it stressful. However, the procedure is expensive and difficult to control because it requires a troupe of confederates who must act with near-perfect consistency from subject to subject. Richard Crutchfield (1955) remedied this by automating Asch's experiment. Five participants—each a real subject—sit in adjacent booths and view questions projected on the wall across the room. Each booth has a panel of lights and switches that allows the subjects to indicate their judgments and to see how others are responding. After a few warm-up trials, all subjects find themselves responding last after observing the purported responses of the other four.

The technique also enables one to present a variety of questions. For example, Crutchfield tested military officers by presenting a circle and a star side by side. The area of the circle was one-third greater. But when each officer thought the others had

Ethical note: Professional ethics usually dictate explaining the experiment afterward (see Chapter 1). Pretend you were an experimenter who just finished a session with a fully conforming participant. Could you explain the deception without making the participant feel gullible and spineless?

Which is bigger?

a)   b)

FIGURE 7-3
Richard Crutchfield's conformity-testing procedure. People sit in adjacent booths and answer questions presented on the wall in front of them after witnessing others' purported answers. (Drawing by Anne Canevari Green.)

judged the star as larger, 46 percent of them denied their senses and voted with the group. When a sample of the officers were tested privately, each one rejected the statement, "I doubt whether I would make a good leader." Of course—these *were* leaders. Yet, believing other officers all accepted the statement, almost 40 percent did so.

Even positions which were ideologically objectionable (to people questioned individually) have been approved when the group approves. Not long before the 1960s free-speech movement surfaced at the University of California, Berkeley, Crutchfield and his colleagues found 58 percent of the students they tested there willing to go along with the group and agree that, "Free speech being a privilege rather than a right, it is proper for a society to suspend free speech when it feels itself threatened" (Krech et al., 1962).

"It is too easy to go over to the majority."
Seneca, Epistulae ad Lucilium

The Sherif, Asch, and Crutchfield results are startling because in none of them is there any explicit pressure to conform—no promised rewards for "team play," no threatened punishments for individuality. One wonders: If people are this compliant in response to such minimal pressure, how much more compliant might they be if directly coerced? Could the average North American be coerced into performing the types of cruelties performed in Germany under Nazi rule? I would have guessed no: North Americans' democratic and individualistic values would make them resistant to such pressure. And besides, the easy verbal pronouncements of these experiments are a giant step away from compliance with pressure to harm someone. You and I would never yield to coercion to hurt another. Or would we? Stanley Milgram wondered.

MILGRAM'S OBEDIENCE EXPERIMENTS

Milgram's (1965, 1974) experiments on what happens when the demands of authority conflict with the demands of conscience have become the most famous and controversial experiments in all of social psychology. "Perhaps more than any other empirical contributions in the history of social science," notes Lee Ross (1988), "they have become part of our society's shared intellectual legacy—that small body of historical incidents, biblical parables, and classic literature that serious thinkers feel free to draw on when they debate about human nature or contemplate human history."

Picture the scene: Two men come to Yale University's psychology laboratory to participate in a study of learning and memory. They are met by a stern experimenter in a gray technician's coat who explains that this is a pioneering study of the effect of punishment on learning. The experiment requires one of them to teach a list of word pairs to the other and to punish errors by delivering shocks of increasing intensity. To designate the roles, they draw slips out of a hat. One of the men, a mild-mannered forty-seven-year-old accountant who is the experimenter's confederate, pretends that his slip says "learner" and is ushered into an adjacent room. The "teacher" (who has come in response to a newspaper ad) takes a mild sample shock and then looks on as the learner is strapped into a chair and has an electrode attached to his wrist.

The teacher and experimenter then return to the main room where the teacher takes his place before a "Shock Generator" with switches ranging in 15-volt increments from 15 to 450 volts. The switches are given labels such as, "Slight Shock," "Very Strong Shock," "Danger: Severe Shock," and so forth. Under the 435 and 450 volt switches is printed simply "XXX." The teacher is told to "move one level higher on the shock generator" each time the learner gives a wrong answer. With each flick of a switch, lights flash, relay switches click, and one hears an electric buzzing sound.

If the teacher complies with the experimenter's requests he hears the learner grunt at 75, 90, and 105 volts. At 120 volts the learner shouts that the shocks are painful. And at 150 volts he cries out, "Experimenter, get me out of here! I won't be in the experiment anymore! I refuse to go on!" By 270 volts his protests have become screams of agony and he continues insisting he be let out. At 300 and 315 volts he screams his refusal to answer. After 330 volts he falls silent. In answer to the teacher's inquiries and pleas to terminate the experiment, the experimenter states that the learner's nonresponses should be treated as wrong answers. To keep the teacher going he uses but four verbal prods:

PROD 1: Please continue (*or* Please go on).
PROD 2: The experiment requires that you continue.
PROD 3: It is absolutely essential that you continue.
PROD 4: You have no other choice, you *must* go on.

Were you a "teacher" in this experiment, how far would you go? Milgram described the experiment to 110 psychiatrists, college students, and middle-class adults. People in all three groups guessed that they would disobey by about 135 volts; none expected to go beyond 300 volts. Recognizing that self-estimates may reflect self-serving bias, Milgram asked them how far they thought *other* people would go. Virtually no one expected anyone to proceed to the end of the shock panel. (The psychiatrists guessed about one in a thousand.)

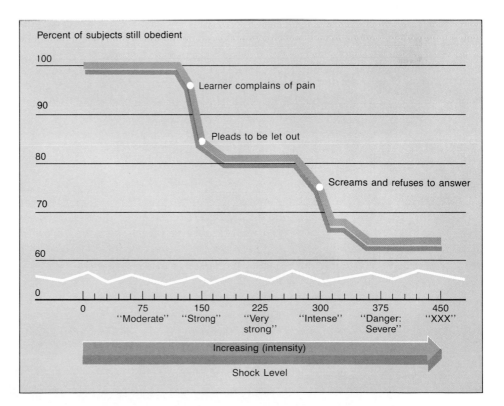

FIGURE 7-4
The Milgram obedience experiment. Percentage of subjects complying despite the learner's cries of protest and failure to respond. (From Milgram, 1965.)

But when Milgram conducted the experiment with forty men—a vocational mix of twenty- to fifty-year-olds—twenty-five of them (63 percent) went clear to 450 volts. In fact, all who reached 450 volts complied with a command to *continue* the procedure until, after two further trials, the experimenter called it to a halt. Given this disturbing result, Milgram made the learner's protests even more compelling. As the learner was strapped into the chair, the teacher heard him mention his "slight heart condition" and heard the experimenter's reassurance that "although the shocks may be painful, they cause no permanent tissue damage." The learner's subsequent anguished protests (see box) were to little avail; of forty new men in this experiment, twenty-six (65 percent) fully complied with the experimenter's demands (see Figure 7-4).

The obedience of his subjects disturbed Milgram. The procedures he used equally disturbed many social psychologists (Miller, 1986). Although the "learner" in these experiments actually received no shock (he disengaged himself from the electric chair and turned on a tape recorder that delivered his protests), some critics nevertheless said that, ironically, Milgram did to his subjects what they did to their victims: stress

THE LEARNER'S SCHEDULE OF PROTESTS IN MILGRAM'S "HEART DISTURBANCE" EXPERIMENTS

75 volts	Ugh!
90 volts	Ugh!
105 volts	Ugh! (*louder*)
120 volts	Ugh! Hey this really hurts.
135 volts	Ugh!!
150 volts	Ugh!!! Experimenter! That's all. Get me out of here. I told you I had heart trouble. My heart's starting to bother me now. Get me out of here, please. My heart's starting to bother me. I refuse to go on. Let me out.
165 volts	Ugh! Let me out! (*shouting*)
180 volts	Ugh! I can't stand the pain. Let me out of here! (*shouting*)
195 volts	Ugh! Let me out of here. Let me out of here. My heart's bothering me. Let me out of here! You have no right to keep me here! Let me out! Let me out of here! Let me out! Let me out of here! My heart's bothering me. Let me out! Let me out!
210 volts	Ugh!! Experimenter! Get me out of here. I've had enough. I won't be in the experiment any more.
225 volts	Ugh!
240 volts	Ugh!
255 volts	Ugh! Get me out of here.
270 volts	(*Agonized scream.*) Let me out of here. Let me out of here. Let me out of here. Let me out. Do you hear? Let me out of here.
285 volts	(*Agonized scream.*)
300 volts	(*Agonized scream.*) I absolutely refuse to answer any more. Get me out of here. You can't hold me here. Get me out. Get me out of here.
315 volts	(*Intensely agonized scream.*) I told you I refuse to answer. I'm no longer part of this experiment.
330 volts	(*Intense and prolonged agonized scream.*) Let me out of here. Let me out of here. My heart's bothering me. Let me out, I tell you. (*Hysterically*) Let me out of here. Let me out of here. You have no right to hold me here. Let me out! Let me out! Let me out! Let me out of here! Let me out! Let me out!

Note: From *Obedience to Authority* by Stanley Milgram. New York: Harper & Row, 1974, pp. 56–57.

An obedient subject in the "touch" condition forces the victim's hand onto the shock plate. Usually, however, teachers were more compassionate to victims who were close at hand.

them against their will. Indeed, many of the teachers did experience agony. They sweated, trembled, stuttered, bit their lips, groaned, or even broke into uncontrollable nervous laughter. A *New York Times* reviewer complained that the cruelty that the experiments "inflict upon their unwitting subjects is surpassed only by the cruelty that they elicit from them" (Marcus, 1974). Critics also argued that the participants' self-concepts may have been altered. One participant's wife told him, "You can call yourself Eichmann" (referring to Nazi death camp administrator Adolf Eichmann).

In his own defense, Milgram pointed not only to the lessons his nearly two dozen experiments have taught us, but also to the support he received from the participants after the deception was revealed and the experiment explained. When surveyed afterwards, 84 percent said they were glad to have participated; only 1 percent regretted volunteering. A year later, a psychiatrist interviewed forty of those who had suffered most and concluded that, despite the temporary stress, none was harmed. Ironically, people told about Milgram's experiment seem not to be troubled by what he did if told that only 10 percent of the subjects both obeyed and became temporarily upset; somehow a lower result makes the procedures seem more ethical (Schlenker & Forsyth, 1977).

Milgram did more than reveal the extent to which people will obey an authority; he also examined the conditions that breed obedience. In further experiments he varied the social conditions and obtained compliance ranging from 0 percent fully obedient to 93 percent. The determining factors were these four.

Emotional Distance of the Victim

Milgram's teachers acted with least compassion when their learners could not be seen (and could not see them). When the victim was remote and no complaints were heard, nearly all participants obeyed calmly to the end. When the learner was brought into the same room, "only" 40 percent obeyed to 450 volts. And full compliance dropped to 30 percent when teachers were required to force the learner's hand into contact with a shock plate.

PERSONALIZING THE VICTIMS

Innocent victims trigger more compassion if personalized. In a week when a soon-forgotten earthquake in Iran kills 3000 people, a lone boy dies, trapped in a well-shaft in Italy, and the whole world grieves. The projected death statistics of a nuclear war are impersonal to the point of being incomprehensible. So international law professor Roger Fisher proposed a way to personalize the victims:

> It so happens that a young man, usually a navy officer, accompanies the President wherever he goes. This young man has a black attache case which contains the codes that are needed to fire nuclear weapons.
>
> I can see the President at a staff meeting considering nuclear war as an abstract question. He might conclude, "On SIOP Plan One, the decision is affirmative. Communicate the Alpha line XYZ." Such jargon keeps what is involved at a distance.
>
> My suggestion, then, is quite simple. Put that needed code number in a little capsule and implant that capsule right next to the heart of a volunteer. The volunteer will carry with him a big, heavy butcher knife as he accompanies the President. If ever the President wants to fire nuclear weapons, the only way he can do so is by first, with his own hands, killing one human being.
>
> "George," the President would say, "I'm sorry, but tens of millions must die." The President then would have to look at someone and realize what death is—what an *innocent* death is. Blood on the White House carpet: it's reality brought home.
>
> When I suggested this to friends in the Pentagon, they said, "My God, that's terrible. Having to kill someone would distort the President's judgment. He might never push the button."

Note: Adapted from "Preventing Nuclear War" by Roger Fisher, *Bulletin of the Atomic Scientists*, March, 1981, pp. 11–17.

In everyday life, too, it is easiest to abuse someone who is distant or depersonalized. Executioners depersonalize those being executed by placing hoods over their heads. The ethics of war allow one to bomb a helpless village from 40,000 feet but not to shoot an equally helpless villager. Even in combat with an enemy they can see, many soldiers either do not fire or do not aim. Such disobedience is rare among those who are ordered to kill with the more distant artillery or aircraft weapons (Padgett, 1986).

On the positive side, people act most compassionately toward those who are personalized. This is why those appealing on behalf of the unborn or the hungry and impoverished nearly always personalize the target group with a compelling photograph or description. Lacking such, most people are not much aroused by great tragedies. In his 1790 *Theory of Moral Sentiments*, Scottish economist Adam Smith imagined that "the great empire of China, with all its myriads of inhabitants, was suddenly swallowed up by an earthquake." Your average European, he guessed, would on hearing the news "express very strongly his sorrow for the misfortune of that unhappy people, would make many melancholy reflections upon the precariousness of human life, . . . and when all this fine philosophy was over [would resume] his business or his pleasure . . . as if no such accident had happened."

If it were in your power to prevent either a tidal wave that would kill 25,000 people in Pakistan, a crash that would kill 250 people at your local airport, or a car accident that would kill a close friend, which would you prevent?

Closeness and Legitimacy of the Authority

Milgram found that obedience was affected by the physical presence of the experimenter. When he gave the commands by telephone, full obedience dropped to 21 percent (although many lied and said they were obeying). Other studies of compliance have similarly found that when the one making the request is physically close, compliance increases. For example, if given a light touch on the arm, people are more likely to lend a dime, sign a petition, or sample a new pizza (Kleinke, 1977; Willis & Hamm, 1980; Smith et al., 1982).

Moreover, the authority must be perceived as legitimate. In another twist on the basic obedience experiment, the experimenter received a rigged telephone call that required him to leave the laboratory. He said that since the equipment recorded data automatically, the teacher should just go ahead on his own. After the experimenter left, another subject who had been assigned a clerical role (actually a second confederate) assumed command. He "decided" that the shock should be increased one level for each wrong answer and commanded the teacher accordingly.

With this authority of lower status, 80 percent of the teachers refused to comply fully. The confederate, feigning disgust at this defiance, then came and sat down in front of the shock generator and tried to take over the teacher's role. At this point most of the defiant participants protested. Some tried to unplug the generator. One large man lifted the zealous shocker from his chair and threw him across the room. This rebellion against an illegitimate authority contrasted sharply with the deferential politeness usually shown the experimenter.

It also contrasts with the behavior of hospital nurses who in one study were called by an unknown physician and ordered to administer an obvious overdose of a drug (Hofling et al., 1966). One group of nurses and nursing students were told about the experimental procedure and asked how they would react; nearly all said they would not have given the medication as ordered. One explained that she would have replied, "I'm sorry, sir, but I am not authorized to give any medication without a written order, especially one so large over the usual dose and one that I'm unfamiliar with. If it were possible, I would be glad to do it, but this is against hospital policy and my own ethical standards." Nevertheless, when twenty-two other nurses were actually given the phoned-in overdose order, all but one proceeded to comply without delay (until being intercepted on their way to the patient). Although not all nurses are so compliant (Rank & Jacobson, 1977), these nurses were following a well-practiced script: Doctor (a legitimate authority) orders and nurse obeys.

Institutional Authority

If the prestige of the authority is this important, then perhaps the institutional prestige of Yale University had helped legitimize the experimenter's commands. In postexperimental interviews, many participants volunteered that had it not been for Yale's reputation for integrity and excellence, they would not have shocked the learner. To see whether this was true, Milgram moved the experiment to Bridgeport, Connecticut, and dissociated it from Yale. He set himself up in a somewhat run-down commercial building as the "Research Associates of Bridgeport," an organization of unknown character. When the usual "heart disturbance" experiment was run with the same personnel, what percentage of the men do you suppose fully obeyed? Though reduced, the rate remained remarkably high—48 percent.

The Liberating Effects of Group Influence

These classic experiments give us a negative view of conformity. Can conformity be constructive? Perhaps you can recall a time you felt justifiably upset with an unfair teacher, or with your peers for their inappropriate behavior, but were hesitant to object. Then one or two others objected, and you followed their example. Milgram captured this liberating effect of conformity by placing the teacher with two confederate teachers who were to collaborate in conducting the procedure. During the experiment, both defied the experimenter, who then ordered the real subject to continue by himself. Did these teachers obey? No. Ninety percent liberated themselves by conforming to the defiant confederates.

REFLECTIONS ON THE CLASSIC STUDIES

The most common response to Milgram's results is to note their counterparts in recent history: in the "I was only following orders" defenses—of Adolf Eichmann; of Lieutenant William Calley, who directed the unprovoked slaughter of hundreds of Vietnamese villagers in My Lai; and of the participants in various government scandals. Soldiers are trained to obey superiors. In the United States, the military acknowledges that even Marines should disobey inappropriate orders, but soldiers are not trained to recognize an illegal or immoral order (Staub, 1989). Thus one participant in the My Lai massacre recalled,

> [Lieutenant Calley] told me to start shooting. So I started shooting, I poured about four clips into the group. . . . They were begging and saying, 'No, no.' And the mothers were hugging their children and. . . . Well, we kept right on firing. They was waving their arms and begging. . . . (Wallace, 1969)

"If the commander-in-chief tells this lieutenant colonel to go stand in the corner and sit on his head, I will do so."
Oliver North, 1987

The obedience experiments differ from the other conformity experiments in the strength of the social pressure: Compliance is explicitly commanded, not merely the result of noncoerced imitation. Without the experimenter's coercion, people were not disposed to act cruelly. Yet all these experiments, from Sherif to Milgram, share certain commonalities. They all demonstrate how compliance can take precedence over one's moral sense. They all provoked people to abdicate their inner standards in response to group pressure. They all do more than teach us an academic lesson; they sensitize us to analogous conflicts in our own lives. And they all illustrate and affirm certain social psychological principles discussed in earlier chapters. Let us recall some of these.

Behavior and Attitudes

In Chapter 2 we noted that one reason our attitudes often fail to determine our behavior is that, as vividly demonstrated by these classic experiments, external influences sometimes override inner convictions. When responding in the absence of others, Asch's subjects could nearly always give the correct answer. But it was another matter when they stood alone against a group. In the obedience experiments, a powerful social pressure (the experimenter's commands) overcame a weaker one (the remote victim's pleas). Torn between the pleas of the victim and the orders of the experimenter, between the desire to avoid doing harm and the desire to be a good subject, a surprising number chose to obey. As Milgram explained,

> Some subjects were totally convinced of the wrongness of what they were doing . . . and felt that—within themselves, at least—they had been on the side of the angels. What they failed to realize is that subjective feelings are largely irrelevant to the moral issue at hand so long as they are not transformed into action. Political control is effected through action. . . . Tyrannies are perpetuated by difficult men who do not possess the courage to act

BEHIND THE SCENES

While working for Solomon E. Asch, I wondered whether his conformity experiments could be made more humanly significant. First, I imagined an experiment similar to Asch's except that the group induced the person to deliver shocks to a protesting victim. But a control was needed to see how much shock a person would give in the absence of group pressure. Someone, presumably the experimenter, would have to instruct the subject to give the shocks. But now a new question arose: Just how far *would* a person go when ordered to administer such shocks? In my mind, the issue had shifted to the willingness of people to comply with destructive orders. It was an exciting moment for me. I realized that this simple question was both humanly important and capable of being precisely answered. (Abridged from the original for this book, with permission of Alexandra Milgram.)

Stanley Milgram (1933–1984),
City University of New York

out their beliefs. Time and again in the experiment people disvalued what they were doing but could not muster the inner resources to translate their values into action. (Milgram, 1974, p. 10)

Why were the participants unable to disengage themselves? How had they become trapped? Imagine yourself as the teacher in yet another version of Milgram's experiment, one he never conducted. Assume that when the learner gives the first wrong answer the experimenter asks you to begin at 330 volts. After flicking the switch, you hear the learner agonizingly scream, complain of a heart disturbance, and plead again and again for mercy. Would you continue?

I think not. Recall the step-by-step entrapment of the foot-in-the-door phenomenon (Chapter 2) as we compare this hypothetical experiment to what Milgram's teachers experienced. The teacher's first commitment was a mild one—15 volts—and it elicited no protest. Surely you, too, would agree to do that much. By the time he had administered 75 volts and had heard the learner's first groan, he already had complied five times. On the next trial he was asked to commit an act only slightly more extreme than what he had already repeatedly committed. By the time he had administered 330 volts, the teacher, after twenty-two acts of compliance, had surely managed to reduce some of the dissonance. He was thus probably in a vastly different psychological state from that of a person who might have begun the experiment at that point. As Chapter 2 emphasized, one's external behavior and internal disposition can feed one another, sometimes in a spiraling escalation.

During the early 1970s, this stepwise process was used by the military junta then in power in Greece to train torturers (Haritos-Fatouros, 1988; Staub, 1989). In Greece, as in the training of SS officers in Nazi Germany, future torturers were initially selected based on their respect for and submission to authority. But such tendencies alone do not a torturer make. Thus the trainee would first be assigned to guard prisoners, then to participate in arresting squads, then ordered to occasionally hit prisoners, then to observe torture, and only then to practice it. Step by step, an obedient but otherwise decent person evolved into an agent of cruelty. Compliance bred acceptance.

"Men's actions are too strong for them. Show me a man who has acted and who has not been the victim and slave of his action."
Ralph Waldo Emerson,
Representative Men: Goethe

The "blame-the-victim" mode of self-justification discussed in Chapter 2 was one such type of acceptance. Milgram reports that

> Many subjects harshly devalue the victim *as a consequence* of acting against him. Such comments as "He was so stupid and stubborn he deserved to get shocked," were common. Once having acted against the victim, these subjects found it necessary to view him as an unworthy individual, whose punishment was made inevitable by his own deficiencies of intellect and character. (Milgram, 1974, p. 10)

The Power of the Situation

The most important lesson of Chapter 6—that cultures powerfully shape our lives—and the most important lesson of this chapter—that current social forces are similarly powerful—point to the awesome potency of social situations. To feel such for yourself, imagine violating some less than earthshaking norms: standing up in the middle of a class; singing out loud in a restaurant; greeting some distinguished senior professors with their first names; wearing shorts to church; playing golf in a suit; munching Cracker Jack at a piano recital. In trying to break with social constraints one suddenly realizes how strong they are.

Some of Milgram's own students learned this lesson when he and John Sabini (1983) asked their help in studying the effects of violating a simple social norm, by asking riders on the New York City subway system for their seats. To their surprise, 56 percent gave up their seats, even when no justification was given. The students' own reactions to making this request were just as interesting: Most found it agonizingly difficult. Frequently, the words got stuck in their throats and they had to withdraw. Once having made a request and received a seat, they sometimes pretended sickness in order to make their norm violation seem justifiable. Such is the power of the unspoken rules governing our public behavior.

There is also a lesson here about evil. Evil is not just the result of a few bad apples that need to be replaced with good ones. It also results from social forces—from the heat, humidity, and disease that help make a whole barrel go bad. As these experiments demonstrate, powerful situations can induce people to conform to falsehoods or capitulate to cruelty. Thus, like the seductive power of the ring in J. R. R. Tolkien's *Lord of the Rings*, evil situations have enormous corrupting power. This is especially true when, as happens often in complex societies, the vilest of evils evolve from a sequence of small evils. Nazi leaders were surprised at how easily they got German civil servants to handle the paperwork of the Holocaust. They were not killing Jews, of course. They were merely pushing paper (Silver & Geller, 1978). When fragmented, evil becomes easier. Milgram studied this compartmentalization of evil by involving yet another forty men more indirectly. Rather than trigger the shock, they had only to administer the learning test. Thirty-seven of the forty fully complied.

And so it is in our everyday lives: The drift toward evil usually comes in small increments, without any conscious commitment to do evil. Procrastination involves a similar unintended drift toward self-harm (Sabini & Silver, 1982). A student knows weeks ahead the deadline for a term paper. Each diversion from work on the paper—a video game here, a TV program there—seems harmless enough. Yet the student gradually veers toward not doing the paper without ever consciously deciding not to do it.

"When you think of the long and gloomy history of man, you will find more hideous crimes have been committed in the name of obedience than in the name of rebellion."
C. P. Snow

The Fundamental Attribution Error

Why have some of us been so startled by the results of these classic experiments? Is it not because we expect people to act in accord with their dispositions? We are not startled when a surly person commits a heinous act, but we expect those with pleasing dispositions to be kind. Bad people do bad things; good people do good things.

"Eichmann did not hate Jews, and that made it worse, to have no feelings. To make Eichmann appear a monster renders him less dangerous than he was. If you kill a monster you can go to bed and sleep, for there aren't many of them. But if Eichmann was normality, then this is a far more dangerous situation."
Hannah Arendt,
Eichmann in Jerusalem

When you read about Milgram's experiments, what impressions did you form of the teachers? Most people attribute negative dispositions to them. When told about one or two of the obedient subjects, people judge them aggressive, cold, and unappealing—even after being informed that their behavior was typical of other subjects (A. G. Miller et al., 1973). Cruelty is presumed to be inflicted by the cruel at heart.

Günter Bierbrauer (1979) tried to eliminate this underestimation of social forces (in Chapter 3 termed the fundamental attribution error). He had university students either observe a vivid reenactment of the experiment or play the role of obedient teacher themselves. Even so, they still predicted that their friends would, in a repeat of Milgram's experiment, be only minimally compliant. Bierbrauer concluded that although social scientists accumulate evidence that our behavior is a product of our social history and current environment, most people "remain unmoved by these facts." They continue to believe that people's inner qualities reveal themselves—"that only good men do good and merit praise and that only evil men do evil and deserve punishment."

"The assaulting quality of the Milgram experiment is really a valuable attack on the denial and indifference of all of us. Whatever upset follows facing the truth, we must eventually face up to the fact that so many of us are, in fact, available to be genociders or their assistants."
Israel W. Charny (1981)
Executive Director, International Conference on the Holocaust and Genocide

It is tempting to presume that Eichmann and the Auschwitz camp commanders were uncivilized monsters. But after a hard day's work, the Auschwitz commanders would relax, listening to Beethoven and Schubert. Eichmann himself has been described as bland, outwardly indistinguishable from common people with ordinary jobs (Arendt, 1963). And so it was in the obedience research. Milgram's conclusion makes it harder to attribute the Holocaust to unique character traits in the German people: "The most fundamental lesson of our study," he noted, is that "ordinary people, simply doing their jobs, and without any particular hostility on their part, can become agents in a terrible destructive process" (Milgram, 1974, p. 6). As Mister Rogers often reminds his preschool television audience, "Good people sometimes do bad things." Perhaps, then, we should be more wary of political leaders whose genial and charming dispositions lull us into supposing that they would never do evil.

The classic conformity experiments answered some questions, but, as often occurs, raised others: (1) Sometimes people conform; sometimes they do not. When do they? (2) Why do people conform? Why don't people ignore the group and "to their own selves be true"? (3) Is there a type of person who is most conforming? Let us take these questions one at a time.

WHEN DO PEOPLE CONFORM?

Social psychologists wondered: If even Asch's noncoercive, unambiguous situation could elicit a conformity rate of 37 percent, might other settings produce even more? Researchers soon discovered that conformity was indeed heightened if the judgments were difficult or if the subjects were led to feel incompetent. The more insecure we are about our judgments, the more influenced we are by others. Researchers have also found that the nature of the group has an important influence. Conformity is highest . . .

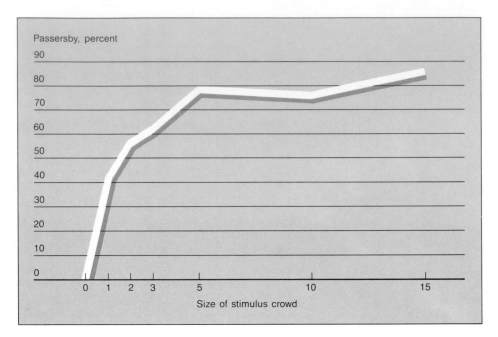

FIGURE 7-5
Group size and conformity. The percentage of passers-by who imitated a group looking upward increased as group size increased to five persons. (Data from Milgram, Bickman, & Berkowitz, 1969.)

WHEN THE GROUP IS:

Three or More People

In laboratory experiments a group need not be large to have a large effect. Asch and other researchers found that three to five people will elicit much more conformity than just one or two. However, increasing the number of people beyond five yields diminishing returns (Rosenberg, 1961; Gerard et al., 1968). In a field experiment, Milgram, Leonard Bickman, and Lawrence Berkowitz (1969) had one, two, three, five, ten, or fifteen people pause on a busy New York City sidewalk and look up. As Figure 7-5 indicates, the percentage of passers-by who also looked up increased as the number looking up increased from one to five persons.

Bibb Latané (1981) accounts for the diminishing returns of increases in group size with his "social impact theory." The theory proposes that social influence increases with the immediacy and size of the group. But as the number of influencing persons increases, the increments in social impact decrease: the second person has less effect than the first, and the nth person has less effect than the $(n - 1)$th.

The way the group is "packaged" also makes a difference. Researcher David Wilder (1977) gave University of Wisconsin students a jury case. Before giving their own judgments, the students watched videotapes of four confederates giving their judgments of the case. When presented as two independent groups of two people, the participants conformed more than when the four confederates presented their judgments as a group. Similarly, two groups of three people elicited more conformity than one group of six, and three groups of two people elicited even more. Evidently, the concurrence of several small groups makes a position more credible than does that of a single large group.

Unanimous

Imagine yourself in a conformity experiment where all but one of the people responding before you give a wrong answer. Would the example of this one nonconforming confederate be as liberating as it was for the subjects in Milgram's obedience experiment? Several experiments have found that when a group's unanimity is punctured, so also is its social power (Asch, 1955; Allen & Levine, 1969; Morris & Miller, 1975). As Figure 7-6 illustrates, subjects will nearly always voice their convictions, if but one other person has also done so. Interestingly, the subjects in such experiments often later say they felt warm toward and close to their nonconforming ally, but deny that the ally influenced them: "I would have answered just the same if he weren't there."

It is difficult to be a minority of one, to stand alone against a group. Few juries are hung because of the persistence of but one dissenting juror. Thus, these experiments teach the practical lesson that it is easier to stand up for something if you can find someone else to stand up with you. Many religious groups recognize this. Following the example of Jesus, who sent his disciples out in pairs, the Mormons, for example, always send two missionaries into a neighborhood together. The support of but one comrade greatly increases a person's social courage.

Observing someone else's dissent—even when it is wrong—can increase our own independence in similar situations. Charlan Nemeth and Cynthia Chiles (1988) discovered this after having people observe a lone individual in a group of four misjudge blue stimuli as green. Although the dissenter erred, observing him enabled the observers later to exhibit their own form of independence. In a followup experiment, 76 percent of the time they correctly labelled red slides "red" even when everyone else was calling them "orange." Lacking this model of courage, 70 percent of the time observers went along with the group in calling red "orange."

"My opinion, my conviction, gains infinitely in strength and success, the moment a second mind has adopted it."
Novalis, Fragment

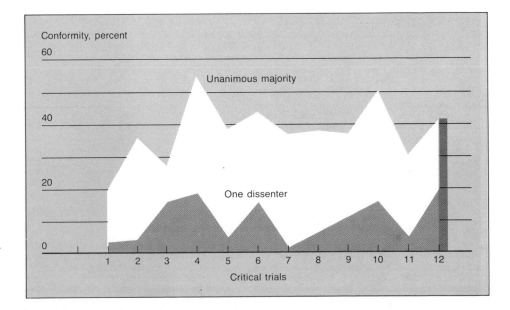

FIGURE 7-6
The effect of unanimity on conformity. When the group's unanimity was punctured by the presence of one confederate who gave correct answers, subjects conformed only one-fourth as often. (From Asch, 1955.)

Cohesive

Cohesiveness:
A "we feeling"—the extent to which members of a group are bound together, such as by attraction for one another.

A minority opinion from someone outside of the groups we identify with—say from someone at another college or of a different religion—sways us less than the same minority opinion from someone within our group (Clark & Maass, 1988, 1989). Thus we may expect that a heterosexual arguing for gay rights would more effectively sway heterosexuals than would a homosexual. The more *cohesive* a group is, the more power it seems to have over its members. In college sororities, friends tend to share binge-eating tendencies, especially as they grow more close-knit (Crandall, 1988).

In experiments, too, group members who feel or are led to feel attracted to the group are more responsive to the group's influence (Berkowitz, 1954; Lott & Lott, 1961; Sakurai, 1975). Perhaps the people we are attracted to are more credible to us. Disagreeing with such people probably disturbs us. Because we do not want to be rejected by the people we like, we may allow them to have a certain power over us. In his *Essay Concerning Human Understanding* the seventeenth-century philosopher John Locke recognized the cohesiveness factor: "Nor is there one in ten thousand who is stiff and insensible enough to bear up under the constant dislike and condemnation of his own club."

High in Status

As you might suspect, higher-status people tend to have somewhat more impact (Mullen, 1985). Studies of jaywalking behavior, conducted with the unwitting aid of nearly 24,000 pedestrians, reveal that the baseline jaywalking rate of 25 percent is decreased to 17 percent in the presence of a nonjaywalking confederate and increased to 44 percent in the presence of a jaywalker (Mullen et al., 1988). The nonjaywalker does most to discourage jaywalking when well-dressed (although, strangely, jaywalking confederates do not trigger more jaywalking when well-dressed). Clothes seem to "make the person" in Australia, too. Michael Walker, Susan Harriman, and Stuart Costello (1980) found that Sydney pedestrians were more compliant when approached by a well-dressed survey taker than one poorly dressed.

Milgram (1974) reports that in his obedience experiments people of lower status tended to accept the experimenter's commands more readily than people of higher status. For example, after administering 450 volts, one subject, a thirty-seven-year-old welder, turned to the experimenter and deferentially asked, "Where do we go from here, Professor?" (p. 46). Another subject, a divinity school professor, disobeyed at 150 volts, and after objecting, "I don't understand why the experiment is placed above this person's life," treated the experimenter as an unthinking technician, plying him with questions about "the ethics of this thing" (p. 48).

WHEN THE RESPONSE IS:

Public

One of the first questions researchers raised was this: Would people conform more in their public responses than in their private opinions? Or would they be more readily swayed in their private opinions but unwilling to publicly conform, lest they appear wishy-washy? The answer is now clear: In experiments, people conform more when they must respond in the presence of others than when allowed to write down their answer privately. For example, Asch's subjects, after hearing others respond, were less influenced by group pressure if they could write an answer that would be seen

"If you worry about missing the boat—remember the Titanic."
Anonymous

only by the experimenter. It is much easier to stand up for what we believe in the privacy of the voting booth than in front of a group of dissenters.

Made Without Prior Commitment

In 1980, Genuine Risk became only the second filly to win the Kentucky Derby. In her next race, the Preakness, she came off the last turn gaining on the leader, Codex, a colt. As they came out of the turn they were neck and neck. Codex then moved sideways toward Genuine Risk, causing her to hesitate and giving him a narrow victory. Had Codex brushed Genuine Risk? Had his jockey even whipped Genuine Risk in the face? The race referees huddled. After a brief deliberation they judged that no foul had occurred, confirming Codex as the winner. The decision caused an uproar. On the televised instant replays, it appeared that Genuine Risk, the sentimental favorite, had indeed been brushed. A protest was filed. In the days that followed, the decision was reconsidered. But it was not changed.

Did the race officials' commitments immediately after the race affect their openness toward reaching a different decision later? We will never know. However, we can put people through a laboratory version of this event—with and without the immediate commitment—and observe whether the commitment makes a difference. Again, imagine yourself in an Asch-type experiment. The experimenter displays the lines and asks you to respond first. After you have given your judgment and then heard everyone else disagree, the experimenter offers you an opportunity to reconsider. In the face of such group pressure do you back down? In experiments, people almost never do (Deutsch & Gerard, 1955). Once having made a public commitment they stick to it. The most they will do is adjust their judgments in later situations (Saltzstein & Sandberg, 1979). Thus, for example, we may expect that judges of diving contests will seldom change their rating of a dive after observing the other judges' ratings, although they might adjust their ratings of later dives.

Prior commitment: Once they have committed themselves to a position, people seldom yield to social pressure. Contrary to this cartoon, real umpires and referees rarely reverse their initial judgments.

MANKOFF

"All right! Have it your own way. It was a ball."

Prior commitments restrain persuasion, too. In experiments on decision making by simulated juries, hung verdicts are more likely in tight cases when jurors are polled by a show of hands rather than by secret ballot (Kerr & MacCoun, 1985). Making a public commitment leads people to attribute responsibility for such action to themselves, which in turn makes them hesitant to back down (Mayer et al., 1980). Smart persuaders know this. They ask questions that prompt us to make statements for rather than against what they are marketing. Textbook salespeople are more likely to ask professors what they do *not* like about their competitors' books than what they *do* like about them. Religious evangelists invite people "to get up out of your seat," knowing that people are more likely to hold to their newfound faith if they have made a public commitment to it.

Public commitment may reduce conformity not only because people are more accepting of what they have made a commitment to, but also because they hate to appear wishy-washy. A. R. Allgeier and his collaborators (1979) found that, compared to people whose attitudes were stable, those whose attitudes changed were viewed as less decisive and reliable. People who "wander, waver, waffle, and wiggle," as President Ford said contemptuously of candidate Jimmy Carter in 1976, lose respect.

On the other hand: "Those who never retract their opinions love themselves more than they love truth."
Joubert, Pensees

WHY CONFORM?

Here I was, a native American attending my first lecture during an extended visit at a West German university. As the lecturer finished, I lifted my hands to join in the clapping. But rather than clap, the other people began rapping the tables with their knuckles. What did this mean? Were they disapprovingly "knocking" the speech? Surely, not everyone would so overtly rebuke the visiting dignitary. Nor did their faces indicate displeasure. No, I decided, this must be a German ovation. Whereupon, I added my knuckles to the chorus.

What prompted this conformity? Why had I not remained true to myself and clapped even while the others rapped? There are two possibilities: A person may bow to the group either to be accepted and avoid rejection, or because the group provides important information. Morton Deutsch and Harold Gerard (1955) named these two possibilities **normative** social influence and **informational** social influence.

Normative influence:
Conformity based on a person's desire to be accepted by the group.

Normative conformity is "going along with the crowd" to avoid rejection, to stay in people's good graces, or to gain their approval. In the laboratory and in everyday life, groups often reject those who consistently deviate (Schachter, 1951; Miller & Anderson, 1979). Can you recall such an experience? As most of us know, social rejection is painful. Hence when we deviate from group norms we often pay a price in anxiety, if not in rejection. Darrin Lehman and Alan Reifman (1987) believe that explains their finding that in 1984–1985 games involving the Los Angeles Lakers, National Basketball Association referees called fewer fouls on star players when they were playing at home (2.4 fouls per game) than when they were playing away (3.1 fouls per game). (Nonstar players were called for the same number of fouls at home and away.)

Sometimes the high price of deviation compels people to support what they do not believe in. Some of the soldiers at My Lai performed abhorrent acts out of fear of being court-martialed for disobedience. Thus, normative influence most commonly leads to compliance. This is especially true for people seeking to climb a group's status ladder

"Do as most do and men will speak well of thee."
Thomas Fuller, Gnomologia

Informational influence:
Conformity that results from accepting evidence about reality provided by other people.

(Hollander, 1958). As John F. Kennedy (1956) recalled, " 'The way to get along,' I was told when I entered Congress, 'is to go along' " (p. 4).

Informational influence, on the other hand, leads people to accept others' views. When reality is ambiguous, as it was for subjects in the autokinetic situation, other people can be a valuable source of information. The subject may reason, "I can't tell how far the light is moving. But this guy seems to know." Others' responses may also affect how we interpret ambiguous stimuli. People who witness others agreeing that "free speech should be limited" may infer a different meaning to the statement than those who witness others disagreeing (Allen & Wilder, 1980). In short, normative influence is motivated by concern for one's social image and outcomes; informational influence is motivated by the desire to be correct.

In day-to-day life, normative and informational influence often occur together. I was not about to be the only person in the room clapping (normative influence), yet the others' behavior also clued me how to show my appreciation (informational influence).

Some of the experiments on "when people conform" have isolated either normative or informational influence. Consider: Conformity is greater when responses take place in the presence of the group; this surely reflects normative influence (because subjects receive the same information whether they respond publicly or privately). What is more, the larger the group, the greater the difference between public and private responding (Insko et al., 1985). On the other hand, conformity is greater when participants feel incompetent, when the task is difficult, or when the subjects are concerned with being right. So, why do we conform? Either because we want to be liked and approved or because we want to be right.

WHO CONFORMS?

Are some people generally more susceptible (or should I say, more *open?*) to social influence? Among your friends, can you identify some who are "conformists" and others who are "independent"? I suspect that most of us can. Researchers are exploring several areas in their search for the conformer. Let us look briefly at three.

MALES VERSUS FEMALES

Although Milgram's subjects (1974) were nearly all men — some 1000 in all — forty women subjects did experience the "heart-disturbance" obedience procedure. Milgram assumed that women were generally more compliant, yet also more empathic and less aggressive. What he found was no difference: 65 percent were fully compliant.

Among Americans tested in group-pressure situations during the last thirty years, there has been a slight tendency for women to conform more than men. Alice Eagly and Linda Carli (1981; Becker, 1986) discerned this by statistically combining results from the dozens of available studies. They describe the effect as "barely visible to the naked eye." Studies reporting women to be more conforming tend to be those in which participants' responses are witnessed by the other group members (as in the Asch experiment), and tend to have been conducted by men some years ago (Eagly et al., 1981; Cooper, 1979; Sohn, 1980). Newer conformity experiments and those conducted by women have less often found females more conforming. [Most other gender differences in social behavior appear uninfluenced by the sex of the investigator, reports Eagly (1987).]

But is labeling this small effect a "conformity difference" a negative judgment upon the women "conformers"? Remember, our label for the phenomenon is somewhat

I began my work on gender and social influence in the early 1970s. Like many feminist activists of the day, I initially assumed that, despite negative cultural stereotypes about women, the behavior of women and men is substantially equivalent. Over the years, my views have evolved considerably in response to research on sex differences and gender stereotypes. I have found that women and men do behave somewhat differently, especially in relatively unstructured situations in which gender roles become important. Although most of these differences are gender-stereotypic, feminists should not assume that these differences reflect unfavorably on women. Women's tendencies to be more attuned to other people's concerns and to treat others more democratically are assets in many situations, and people recognize these desirable qualities of women's behavior. In fact, my recent research on gender stereotypes shows that, if we take both negative and positive qualities into account, the stereotype of women is currently more favorable than the stereotype of men.

Alice Eagly, *Purdue University*

arbitrary. Perhaps we should instead call the difference a "greater people orientation." (Recall from Chapter 6 that women are slightly more empathic and socially sensitive.) Perhaps, then, we should say that women are slightly more flexible, more open and responsive to their social environment, more concerned with interpersonal relations. Such language carries quite different connotations from saying that women are more conforming.

To say that women are slightly more influenceable because they are more concerned with interpersonal relations attributes the difference to personality. Eagly and Wendy Wood (1985) believe that gender differences in conformity may instead be a product of the social roles that men and women have typically occupied. Recall from Chapter 6 that male-female differences are not just gender differences, but also (or instead) status differences. In everyday life, men tend to occupy positions of greater status and power than do women, so we often see men exerting influence and women accepting influence. This explains why people *perceive* a much greater gender difference in conformity than has been found in experiments (in which men and women are assigned identical roles). It also may explain why some of the gender difference in social power carries over into the laboratory. Knowing only the sex of a man and a woman, people tend to assume that the man is of higher status (Eagly & Wood, 1982). This assumption may create a self-fulfilling prophecy that the man is more powerful.

PERSONALITY

The history of social-psychological thinking about the relationship between personality traits and social behavior parallels the history of thinking about attitudes and behavior (Sherman & Fazio, 1983). During the 1950s and early 1960s it was generally believed that people's actions expressed their inner motives and dispositions. For example, several studies found that people who described themselves as having a strong need for social approval were more conforming (Snyder & Ickes, 1985).

"Wait! Wait! Listen to me! . . . We don't HAVE to be just sheep!"

A group's unanimity, versus nonunanimity, has a stronger impact on behavior than each individual's personality.

Then, during the late 1960s and 1970s, other attempts to link personal characteristics with social behaviors such as conformity found only weak connections (W. Mischel, 1968). In contrast to the demonstrable power of situational factors, such as the group's unanimity versus nonunanimity, people's personality scores did not strongly predict their behavior. The rule seemed to be that if you wanted to know how conforming or aggressive or helpful someone was going to be, you were better off knowing the details of the situation than the person's scores on a battery of psychological tests. As Milgram (1974) concluded, "I am certain that there is a complex personality basis to obedience and disobedience. But I know we have not found it" (p. 205). Reflecting on his prison simulation (p. 194) and other experiments, Philip Zimbardo argued that the ultimate message

is to say what it is we have to do to break through your egocentricism, to say you're not different, anything any human being has ever done cannot be alien to you, you can't divorce it! We must break through this "we-they" idea that our dispositional orientation promotes and understand that the situational forces operating on a person at any given moment could be so powerful as to override everything prior—values, history, biology, family, church. (Bruck, 1976)

More recently, during the 1980s, the implication that our personal dispositions make little difference has prompted personality researchers to identify the circumstances under which our traits do predict our behavior. Their research has affirmed a principle that we met in Chapter 2—that while internal factors (attitudes, personality traits) seldom precisely predict a specific action, they better predict a person's behavior in general, across many situations (Epstein, 1980; Rushton et al., 1983). An analogy may help: Just as your response to a single test item is hard to predict, so is your behavior in a single situation. And just as your total score across the many items of a test is more predictable, so too your total conformity (or outgoingness or aggressiveness) across many situations is more predictable.

Personality also predicts behavior better when the people being studied are diverse, when the trait is specific to a situation (such as "speech anxiety" rather than anxiety in general), and when the social influences are weak. Like many other laboratory studies, Milgram's obedience experiments created "strong" situations; they made clear-cut demands on people that made it difficult for personality differences to operate. William Ickes (1982) and Thomas Monson and colleagues (1982) report that in "weak" situations—such as when two strangers are simply left alone together in a waiting room with no cues to guide their behavior—their individual personalities are freer to shine. If we compare two similar personalities in powerfully different situations, the situational effect will overwhelm the personality difference. But if we compare a group of Charles Manson types with a group of Mother Teresa types in a smattering of everyday situations, the personality effect will look much stronger.

It is interesting to note how the pendulum of professional opinion swings. Without discounting the undeniable power of social forces, the pendulum is now swinging back toward a recognition of the consequences of an individual's personality. Like the attitude researchers whom we considered earlier, personality researchers are clarifying and reaffirming the connection between who we are and what we do. As a result of their efforts, virtually every social psychologist today would agree with the dictum of theorist Kurt Lewin (1936), that "Every psychological event depends upon the state of the person and at the same time on the environment, although their relative importance is different in different cases" (p. 12).

CULTURAL DIFFERENCES

Does knowing people's cultural background help us predict how conforming they are? Indeed. James Whittaker and Robert Meade (1967) repeated Asch's conformity experiment in several countries and found similar conformity rates in most—31 percent in Lebanon, 32 percent in Hong Kong, 34 percent in Brazil—but 51 percent conformity among the Bantu of Zimbabwe, a tribe with strong punishments for nonconformity. When Milgram (1961) used a different conformity procedure to compare Norwegian and French students, he consistently found the Norwegian students to be the more conforming. However, cultures may change. Subsequent replications of Asch's experiment with university students in Britain and the United States triggered less conformity than Asch had observed two decades previous (Larsen, 1974; Nicholson et al., 1985; Perrin & Spencer, 1981).

When the obedience experiments were repeated by researchers in West Germany, Italy, South Africa, Australia, Spain, and Jordan, how do you suppose the results compared to those obtained with American subjects? The obedience rates were gen-

Children raised in other cultures may learn different values. For instance, in Asian cultures, behaving in a way that perpetuates the honor of one's group, or family, rather than the honor of oneself, is the most important personal goal.

erally similar, or even higher—85 percent in Munich (Mantell, 1971; Meeus & Raaijmakers, 1986; Milgram, 1974).

In a study of "administrative obedience," Wim Meeus and Quinten Raaijmakers (1986) ordered Dutch adults who had volunteered for an experiment to disrupt a job applicant who was taking an employment test, causing the applicant to fail the test and supposedly remain unemployed. In the guise of an experiment on the effects of stress, the subjects had to trigger fifteen derogatory computer messages that caused the applicant to become progressively more upset. As the applicant's tension turned to irritation and finally to despair, the subjects felt the procedure unfair and found their task disagreeable. Yet, by shifting responsibility to the experimenter, 90 percent fully complied.

So, conformity and obedience are universal phenomena but vary by culture (Bond, 1989; Triandis et al., 1988). Those of us who grow up in Euro-American cultures are generally taught individualism: You are responsible for yourself. Follow your own conscience. Be true to yourself. Define your unique gifts. Meet your own needs. Respect one another's privacy—even as yours has been respected, perhaps by the granting of a private bedroom and by knocking on your territorial door before entering.

"I don't want to get adjusted to this world."
Woody Guthrie

Those of us who grow up in Asian cultures are more likely to be taught communalism: Your family or clan is responsible for its individual members, whose actions therefore reflect shame or honor upon it. So bring honor to your group. Be true to your traditions. Show respect for your elders and superiors. Cultivate harmony and do not criticize another publicly. Be loyal to your family, company, and nation. Live communally, without assuming that you have a private self separate from your social context.

The effect of such cultural assumptions was apparent in a cross-cultural comparison of individualism in 12-year-olds (Garbarino & Bronfenbrenner, 1976; Shouval et al., 1975). The international team of researchers assessed conformity to conventional

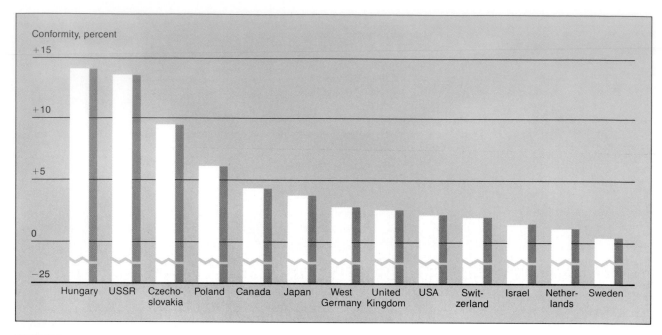

FIGURE 7-7
Conformity of 12-year-olds to moral standards of adult authorities. (Data from Garbarino & Bronfenbrenner, 1976.)

standards by having children predict their behavior in a variety of situations. As Figure 7-7 shows, children from more individualistic Western nations were considerably more likely to admit to disobedient, mischievous tendencies than children from more collectivist countries such as the U.S.S.R., where both home and school emphasize "obedience and propriety." The children in the collectivist countries described themselves as more compliant with adult expectations and less likely to join their peers in defying adult expectations.

EuroAmerican individualism has intensified during this century. In Italy, England, Germany, and the United States, parents prize independence and self-reliance; forty years ago and more they were more likely to value obedience (see Figure 7-8). The downside of this individualism, as we noted on page 140, is an accompanying rapid rise in depression. When facing failure or loss, the self-reliant individual has nowhere to turn for hope. And consider: If a 1982 ad for *Fortune* magazine was right in proclaiming the American Dream—that you can "make it on your own," on "your own drive, your own guts, your own energy, your own ambition"—then whose fault is it if you *don't* make it on your own?

RESISTING SOCIAL PRESSURE

This chapter, like the one preceding, has emphasized the power of social forces. It is therefore fitting that we conclude by again reminding ourselves of the power of the person. Unlike passive billiard balls, we act in response to the forces upon us. Knowing that someone is trying to coerce us may even prompt us to react in the *opposite* direction.

"To do just the opposite is also a form of imitation."
Lichtenberg, Aphorisma, *1764–1799*

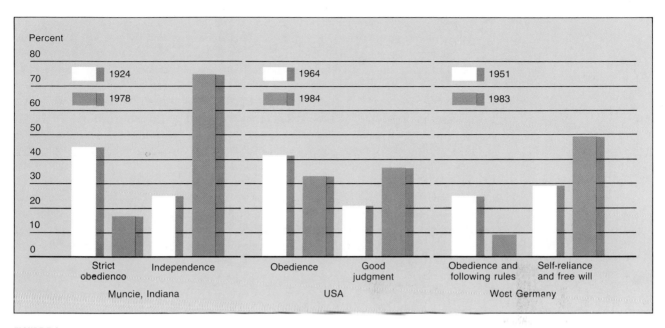

Percent

FIGURE 7-8
Repeated surveys of mothers in Muncie, Indiana, 54 years apart, and of West German adults, illustrate the growth of individualistic values during this century. (Data from Alwin, 1989, and Remley, 1988.)

Reactance:
A motive to protect or restore one's sense of freedom. Reactance is aroused when freedom of action is threatened.

REACTANCE

People value their sense of freedom and like to protect an image of self-efficacy (Baer et al., 1980). Consequently, when social pressure becomes so blatant that it threatens their sense of freedom, they often rebel. Think of Romeo and Juliet, whose love for one another was intensified by their parents' opposition. Or think of children asserting their freedom and independence by doing the opposite of what their parents ask. Savvy parents therefore often offer their children choices instead of commands. Such phrasing allows the child to maintain a sense of freedom: "It's time to clean up: Do you want a bath or a shower?"

The theory of psychological **reactance**—that people do indeed act to protect their sense of freedom—is supported by experiments showing that attempts to restrict a person's freedom often produce a reactive "boomerang effect" (Brehm & Brehm, 1981). Suppose someone stops you on the street and asks you to sign a petition that advocates something you mildly support. While considering the petition you are told that someone else believes "people absolutely should not be allowed to distribute or sign such petitions." Reactance theory predicts that such obvious attempts to limit people's freedom would actually increase the likelihood of their signing. When Madeline Heilman (1976) staged this experiment on the streets of New York City, that is precisely what she found. Clinical psychologists, too, sometimes use the reactance principle, by ordering resistant clients to act out the to-be-eliminated behavior (Seltzer, 1983; Brehm, 1986). By resisting the therapist, these clients get better.

William Swann and his colleagues (1988) report that people who are highly certain of their beliefs are hard to persuade, but may persuade themselves if challenged to defend a belief even more extreme than their own. They discovered this when asking conservative University of Texas women (who agreed, for example, that "I would expect my husband to be head of the house") to defend extremely conservative statements. Asked, "Why do you think men always make better bosses than women?," or "Why do you sympathize with the feelings of some men that women are better kept barefoot and pregnant?," the women reacted by distancing themselves from such ideas.

Reactance can escalate into social rebellion. Like obedience, rebellion can be produced and observed in experiments. William Gamson, Bruce Fireman, and Steven Rytina (1982) posed as a commercial research firm. They recruited people from towns near the University of Michigan to come to a hotel conference room for "a group discussion of community standards." Once there, the people learned that the discussions were to be videotaped on behalf of a large oil company seeking to win a legal case against a local station manager who had spoken out against high gas prices. In the first discussion, virtually everyone sided with the station manager. To convince the court that people in the local community were on its side, the supposed company representative then began to tell more and more of the group members to defend the company. In the end, everyone was instructed to attack the station manager and asked to sign an affadavit giving the company permission to edit the tapes and use them in court.

By leaving the room from time to time, the experimenter gave the group members repeated opportunities to interpret and react to the injustice they were being asked to comply with. Most groups rebelled, objecting to and resisting the demand that they misrepresent their opinions in order to help the oil company. Some groups even mobilized themselves to stop the whole effort. They made plans to go to a newspaper, the Better Business Bureau, a lawyer, or the court.

By creating and observing the unfolding of small social rebellions, the researchers glimpsed how a revolt occurs. They found that successful resistance often begins soon. The more a group unquestioningly complies with the unjust demands, the more trouble it later has breaking free. And someone must be willing to seed the process by expressing the reservations that others are feeling.

These demonstrations of reactance reassure us that people are not puppets. Sociologist Peter Berger (1963) expressed the point vividly:

> We see the puppets dancing in their miniature stage, moving up and down as the strings pull them around, following the prescribed course of their various little parts. We learn to understand the logic of this theater and we find ourselves in its motions. We locate ourselves in society and thus recognize our own position as we hang from its subtle strings. For a moment we see ourselves as puppets indeed. But then we grasp a decisive difference between the puppet theater and our own drama. Unlike the puppets, we have the possibility of stopping in our movements, looking up and perceiving the machinery by which we have been moved. In this act lies the first step towards freedom. (p. 176)

ASSERTING OUR UNIQUENESS

Imagine a world of complete conformity, where there were no human differences. Would there be happiness in such a world? If nonconformity can create discomfort, can sameness create comfort?

People feel uncomfortable when they appear too different from others. But they are also discomfited by appearing exactly like everyone else. As experiments by C. R. Snyder and Howard Fromkin (1980; see also Duval, 1976) have shown, people feel better when they see themselves as unique and will act in ways that set them apart and maintain their sense of individuality. In one experiment (Snyder, 1980), Purdue University students were led to believe that their "10 most important attitudes" were either distinct from or nearly identical to the attitudes of 10,000 other students. When they then participated in a conformity experiment, those who had been deprived of their feeling of uniqueness were most likely to assert their individuality by nonconformity. In another experiment, people who heard others express attitudes that were identical to their own actually altered their positions in order to maintain their sense of uniqueness.

So it seems that while we do not like being greatly deviant, we are all alike in wanting to feel distinctive. But as research on self-serving bias (Chapter 3) makes clear, it is not just any kind of distinctiveness we seek, but distinctiveness in the right direction. Our quest is not merely to be different from the average, but better than average.

The tendency to see oneself as unique is also evident in people's "spontaneous self-concepts." William McGuire and his Yale University colleagues (McGuire & Padawer-Singer, 1978; McGuire et al., 1979) report that when children are invited to "tell us about yourself," they are most likely to mention their distinctive attributes. Foreign-born children are more likely than others to mention their birthplace; redheads are more likely than black- and brown-haired children to volunteer their hair color; light and heavy children are the most likely to refer to their body weight; minority children are the most likely to mention their race. Likewise we become more keenly aware of our gender when we are with people of the other sex (Cota & Dion, 1986). The principle, says McGuire, is that "one is conscious of oneself insofar as, and in the ways that, one is different." Thus "If I am a Black woman in a group of White women, I tend to think of myself as a Black; if I move to a group of Black men, my blackness loses salience and I become more conscious of being a woman" (McGuire et al., 1978). This insight can help us understand why any type of minority group tends to be conscious of its distinctiveness and how the culture is relating to it, and also why the majority group is sometimes bewildered by what it perceives as the "hypersensitivity" of the minority group.

"There are no exceptions to the rule that everybody likes to be an exception to the rule."
Malcolm Forbes, Forbes Magazine

"Self-consciousness, the recognition of a creature by itself as a 'self,' [cannot] exist except in contrast with an 'other,' a something which is not the self."
C. S. Lewis,
The Problem of Pain, *1940*

SUMMING UP

Conformity—changing one's behavior or belief as a result of group pressure—comes in two forms. *Compliance* is outwardly going along with the group while inwardly disagreeing. *Acceptance* is believing as well as acting in accord with social pressure. Both types have been explored in laboratory experiments that ask: (1) To what extent do people conform? (2) When do people conform? (3) Why do people conform? (4) Who conforms most?

CLASSIC STUDIES

Three classic sets of experiments illustrate how conformity is studied and how conforming people can be. Muzafer Sherif observed that people's estimates of the illusory movement of a point of light were easily influenced by the judgments of others. Norms for "proper" answers emerged and were perpetuated over both long periods of time and succeeding generations of subjects. This laboratory demonstration of suggestibility parallels suggestibility in real life.

Solomon Asch used a task that was as clear-cut as Sherif's was ambiguous. Asch had people listen to others judge which of three comparison lines was equal to a standard line and then make the same judgment themselves. When the others unanimously gave a wrong answer, the subjects conformed 37 percent of the time.

Sherif's procedure elicited acceptance; Stanley Milgram's obedience experiments, on the other hand, elicited an extreme form of compliance. Under optimum conditions— a legitimate, close-at-hand commander, a remote victim, and no one else to exemplify disobedience—65 percent of his adult male subjects fully obeyed instructions to deliver what were supposedly traumatizing electric shocks to a screaming innocent victim in an adjacent room.

These classic experiments demonstrate the potency of social forces and the ease with which compliance can begin to breed acceptance. Evil is not just the product of bad people in a nice world, but also the product of powerful situations that induce people to conform to falsehoods or capitulate to cruelty.

WHEN DO PEOPLE CONFORM?

Using conformity testing procedures such as these, many subsequent experiments explored the circumstances that are conducive to conformity. Conformity is affected by the characteristics of the group: People conform most when confronted by the unanimous reports of three or more attractive, high-status people. People also conform most when their responses are public (in the presence of the group) and when they are made without prior commitment.

WHY CONFORM?

Experiments reveal two reasons why people conform at all. *Normative influence* results from a person's desire to be accepted by the group. *Informational influence* results from others' providing evidence about reality. For example, the tendency to conform more when responding publicly reflects normative influence, and the tendency to conform more on difficult decision-making tasks reflects informational influence.

WHO CONFORMS?

This question has produced fewer definitive answers. In experiments, females have, on the average, been slightly more conforming than males. (If this sounds negative it is because labels such as "conformity" evaluate as well as describe behavior. Call the trait "openness" or "communal sensitivity" and it takes on a more positive connotation.) Although global personality scores are poor predictors of specific acts of conformity, these scores can better predict genderal tendencies to conformity (and other social behaviors), especially in "weak" situations where social forces do not overwhelm individual differences. Although conformity and obedience are universal, cultural differences indicate that people can be socialized to be more or less socially responsive.

RESISTING SOCIAL PRESSURE

The chapter's emphasis on the power of social pressure must not be separated from a complementary emphasis on the power of the person. We are not puppets. When attempts at social coercion become blatant, people often experience *reactance*—a motivation to defy the coercion in order to maintain their sense of freedom. When group members simultaneously experience reactance the result may be rebellion. People are not comfortable being too different from a group, but neither do they want to appear the same as everyone else. Thus, they will act in ways that preserve their sense of uniqueness and individuality. And in a group, they tend to be most conscious of their differences from the others.

Finally, a comment on the experimental method used in conformity research. Conformity situations in the laboratory differ from those in everyday life: How often are we asked to judge lines or administer shock? Much as combustion is similar for a burning match and a forest fire, the psychological processes engaged in the laboratory and everyday life are assumed to be similar (Milgram, 1974). One must be careful in generalizing from the simplicity of a burning match to the complexity of a forest fire. Yet, just as controlled experiments on burning matches can give us insights into combustion that we cannot gain by observing forest fires, so also can the social-psychological experiment offer insights into behavior not readily revealed in everyday life. The experimental situation is unique, but so too is every social situation. By testing with a variety of unique tasks, and by repeating experiments in different times and places, researchers probe for the common principles that lie beneath the surface diversity.

FOR FURTHER READING

Kelman, H. C., & Hamilton, V. L. (1988). *Crimes of obedience: Toward a social psychology of authority and responsibility*. New Haven, CT: Yale University Press. Social psychologist Kelman and sociologist Hamilton analyze crimes ordered by authority (the My Lai massacre, Watergate, the Iran-Contra affair) and the public's response to them.

Milgram, S. (1974). *Obedience to authority*. New York: Harper & Row. The complete but simply written account of the experiments that, in the words of Milgram's biographer, now belong "to the self-understanding of literate people in our age."

Miller, A. G. (1986). *The obedience experiments: A case study of controversy in social science*. New York: Praeger. A skillful review of the nearly two dozen obedience experiments conducted by Stanley Milgram and of the replications, critiques, and controversies that ensued. As one reviewer notes, this is a book that "any serious student of social psychology would profit from reading."

Staub, E. (1989). *Roots of evil: The psychological and cultural sources of genocide*. New York: Cambridge University Press. How can human beings kill and brutalize other human beings? This book powerfully analyzes the social psychological roots of human torture and slaughter as practiced in Turkey, Nazi Germany, Argentina, Cambodia, Russia, and Greece.

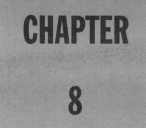

CHAPTER 8

PERSUASION

Our social behavior is influenced not only by the immediate situation (as we saw in Chapter 7) but also by our attitudes. Those who wish to influence our behavior may therefore seek to change those attitudes.

Consider Joseph Goebbels, Nazi Germany's minister of "popular enlightenment" and propaganda. Given the control of Germany's publications, radio programs, motion pictures, and the arts, he undertook to persuade Germans to accept Nazi ideology. His fellow Nazi, Julius Streicher published *Der Stürmer*, a weekly anti-Semitic (anti-Jewish) newspaper with a circulation of 500,000 and the only paper said to have been read cover to cover by Streicher's intimate friend, Adolf Hitler. Streicher also published anti-Semitic children's books and spoke at rallies attended by hundreds of thousands. How effective were Goebbels, Streicher, and other Nazi propagandists? Did they, as the Allies alleged at Streicher's Nuremberg trial, "inject poison into the minds of millions and millions"? (Bytwerk, 1976). Most Germans were not persuaded to feel raging hatred for the Jews. But some were, others became sympathetic to anti-Semitic measures, and most of the rest became either sufficiently uncertain or intimidated to permit the Holocaust.

Powerful persuasive forces are at work also in the United States. In the wake of publicized research on the physical and social consequences of marijuana use, adolescent attitudes have changed rapidly. Among the 16,000 high school seniors surveyed annually by the University of Michigan, the proportion who believe there is "great risk" to regular marijuana use has doubled in ten years—from 36 percent in 1977 to 74 percent in 1987 (Johnston et al., 1988). During the same ten-year period support for the legalization of marijuana dropped sharply among the quarter of a million new college students surveyed annually by the American Council on Education—from 53 percent to 19 percent (Astin et al., 1987a,b). Behavior changed, too—marijuana use within the month preceding the survey dropped from 36 percent of high school seniors to 21 percent. This follows a similar decline in cigarette smoking—from 45 percent of Americans in 1958 to 31 percent in 1986. Of entering college students only 8 percent smoke (Gallup, 1986; Astin et al., 1987). [The earlier rise in cigarette smoking, particularly among women since the 1920s, was itself the result of a campaign of persuasion (Cunningham, 1983).] As we saw in Chapter 6, Americans' attitudes regarding women's roles also have shifted dramatically, with the majority now overwhelmingly favoring roles for women that three decades ago the majority overwhelmingly opposed.

But then again, not all persuasive efforts succeed. Shortly after taking office, President Carter declared that America's response to the energy crisis should be "the moral equivalent of war" and urged people to conserve. The following summer Americans consumed more gas than ever before. Governmental efforts to persuade people to use seat belts have been equally unsuccessful. After one massive effort had no discernible effect on seat-belt use (seven carefully designed cable TV messages were broadcast 943 times during prime time to 6,400 households), psychologist Paul Slovic (1985) thought he and his colleagues might do better. Their hunch was that a mere 10 percent of the people use seat belts because nonusers perceive themselves to be invulnerable. Although it is true that only one trip in 100,000 produces an injury, the fact that we take about 50,000 trips in an average lifetime means that for many people the feeling of safety eventually turns out to be what Chapter 3 called an "illusion of invulnerability."

With the support of the National Traffic Safety Administration, Slovic and his colleagues produced twelve messages designed to persuade people of the risks of driving without seat belts. After pretesting with hundreds of people, six polished TV

"Remember that to change thy mind and to follow him that sets thee right, is to be none the less a free agent."
Marcus Aurelius Antoninus, Meditations

"A fanatic is one who can't change his mind and won't change the subject."
Winston Churchill, 1954

236

messages were evaluated by several thousand people at a "screening house" and the three best messages were repeatedly presented to yet another group of people. Alas, the messages had no effect on their seat-belt use. Because each safe trip reinforces people's nonuse of seat belts, concluded Slovic, "there seems to be no form of educational campaign or message that will persuade more than a small percentage of American motorists to voluntarily wear seat belts." Given that people fail to appreciate the cumulative risk and to protect themselves, the only available remedy is a law that requires seat belt use.

As these examples show, efforts to persuade are sometimes diabolical, sometimes salutary; sometimes effective, sometimes futile. Persuasion is neither inherently good nor bad. It is usually the persuasive message's content that elicits our judgments of good or bad. The bad we call "propaganda." The good we call "education." Of course, some messages are, in fact, true, some false. True education is more factually based and less coercive than mere propaganda. Yet, generally, we call it "education" when we believe it, "propaganda" when we don't (Lumsden et al., 1980). To most Americans, the Boy Scouts promoting American virtues is education; the Red Guard promoting Communist virtues is propaganda.

Our opinions have to come from somewhere. So, as long as we have opinions, persuasion—whether it be education or propaganda—is inevitable. Social psychologists therefore seek to understand what makes a message effective: What factors effectively influence us? And how, as persuaders, can we most effectively "educate" others?

Social psychologists usually study persuasion the way some geologists study erosion—by observing the effects of various factors in brief controlled experiments. The effects produced are on a small scale and are most potent with attitudes not strongly linked to one's values (Johnson & Eagly, 1989). Yet they enable one to better understand how, given enough time, such factors could produce big effects.

Thus far, four factors have received the most study: (1) the communicator, (2) the message, (3) how the message is communicated, and (4) the audience. In other words, *who* says *what* by *what means* to *whom?*

"To swallow and follow, whether old doctrine or new propaganda, is a weakness still dominating the human mind."
Charlotte Perkins Gilman,
Human Work

EFFECTIVE PERSUASION

WHO SAYS? THE EFFECT OF THE COMMUNICATOR

Imagine the following scene: I. M. Wright, a middle-aged American, is watching the evening news. In the first segment, a small group of radicals is shown tearing down an American flag. As they do, one shouts through a bullhorn that whenever any government becomes oppressive, "it is the Right of the People to alter or to abolish it. . . . It is their right, it is their duty, to throw off such government!" Angered, Mr. Wright mutters to his wife, "It's sickening to hear them spouting that Communist line." In the next segment, a presidential candidate speaking before an antitax rally declares, "Thrift should be the guiding principle in our government expenditure. It should be made clear to all government workers that corruption and waste are very great crimes." An obviously pleased Mr. Wright relaxes and smiles: "Now that's the kind of good sense we need. That's my kinda guy."

Now switch the scene. Imagine Mr. Wright hearing the same revolutionary line at a July 4 oration of the Declaration of Independence (from which the line comes),

Effective persuaders know how to convey a message effectively.

"If I seem excited, Mr. Bolling, it's only because I know that I can make you a very rich man."

and hearing a Communist speaker read the thrift lines from *Quotations from Chairman Mao Tsetung* (from which they come). Would the two speeches now affect Mr. Wright differently? Social psychologists have found that who says something makes a big difference. In one experiment, when the Socialist and Liberal leaders in the Dutch parliament argued identical positions using the same words, each was most effective with members of his own party (Wiegman, 1985). But precisely what is it that makes one communicator more persuasive than another? It is to this question that researchers have directed their attention.

Credibility

All of us, I suspect, would find a statement about the benefits of exercise more believable if attributed to the National Academy of Sciences rather than to a testimonial in the *National Enquirer*. Such effects of a source's credibility may diminish after a month or so. If a message is persuasive, but with time its source is forgotten or dissociated from the message, then the impact of a high-credibility communicator may decrease as time passes. The impact of a low-credibility communicator may correspondingly *increase* over time (if the message is remembered better than the reason for discounting it)—a phenomenon called the **sleeper effect** (Cook & Flay, 1978; Gruder et al., 1978; Pratkanis et al., 1988).

Sleeper effect:
A delayed impact of a message; occurs when the message is remembered but a reason for discounting it is forgotten.

Credible communicators are both *expert* and *trustworthy*. How does one become "expert"? One way, obviously, is to be viewed as *knowledgeable* on the topic. A message about toothbrushing from "Dr. James Rundle of the Canadian Dental Association" is much more convincing that the same message from "Jim Rundle, a local high school student who did a project with some of his classmates on dental hygiene" (Olson & Cal, 1984). After more than a decade spent studying high school marijuana use, the University of Michigan researchers (Backman et al., 1988) acknowledge that scare messages from unreliable sources failed to dissuade marijuana use during the 1960s and 1970s. But "when communicated by a credible source," scientific reports of the biological and psychological consequences of long-term marijuana use "can play an important role in reducing . . . drug use."

"Believe an expert."
Virgil, Aeneid

Another way to appear credible is to *speak confidently*. Bonnie Erickson and her collaborators (1978; also Lee & Ofshe, 1981) had University of North Carolina students evaluate courtroom testimony given either in the straightforward manner said to be characteristic of "men's speech" (see Chapter 6) or in the hesitating manner of "women's speech." For example:

> **QUESTION:**   "Approximately how long did you stay there before the ambulance arrived?"
>
> **ANSWER:**   (*Straightforward*) "Twenty minutes. Long enough to help get Mrs. David straightened out."
> (*Hesitating*) "Oh, it seems like it was about uh, twenty minutes. Just long enough to help my friend Mrs. David, you know, get straightened out."

Witnesses who were straightforward were rated as considerably more competent and credible than those whose speech was hesitant.

Speech style affects a speaker's apparent trustworthiness, too. Gordon Hemsley and Anthony Doob (1978) found that if, while testifying, videotaped witnesses looked their questioner straight in the eye instead of gazing downward, they impressed people as more believable.

Norman Miller and his colleagues (1976) at the University of Southern California have found that both trustworthiness and credibility are increased by talking fast. People in the Los Angeles area who listened to tape-recorded messages on topics such as "the danger of coffee drinking" rated fast speakers (about 190 words per minute) as more objective, intelligent, and knowledgeable than slow speakers (about 110 words per minute). It is not surprising, then, that they also found the more rapid speakers more persuasive.

But is it speed alone that makes rapid speakers more persuasive? Or is it something that accompanies rapid speech, like higher intensity or pitch? Marketing researcher James MacLachlan (1979; MacLachlan & Siegel, 1980) electronically compressed radio and television commercials without altering the speaker's pitch, inflection, and intensity. (This is done by deleting minute segments, about 1/50th of a second in length, from all parts of the speech.) He found that speed itself does seem to be a factor. When the commercials were speeded up by 25 percent, listeners comprehended just as well, rated the speakers as more knowledgeable, intelligent, and sincere, and found the messages more interesting. In fact, the normal 140- to 150-word-per-minute speech rate can be almost doubled before comprehension begins to drop abruptly (Foulke & Sticht, 1969). John F. Kennedy, who was regarded as an exceptionally effective public speaker, sometimes spoke in bursts approaching 300 words per minute.

Trustworthiness is also higher if the audience believes the communicator is not trying to persuade them. In an experimental version of what later became the "hidden-camera" method of television advertising, Elaine Hatfield and Leon Festinger (Walster and Festinger, 1962) had some Stanford University undergraduates eavesdrop on the conversation of graduate students. (What they actually heard was a tape recording.) When the conversational topic was relevant to the eavesdroppers (for example, having to do with campus regulations), the students were more influenced when the speakers were supposedly unsuspecting than when the speakers were said to be aware that someone was listening. After all, if people do not know they are being overheard, why would they be less than fully honest?

Similarly, people who argue against their own self-interest or who argue a position that is bound to cost them popularity are perceived as more sincere than those who offer self-serving arguments. Alice Eagly, Wendy Wood, and Shelly Chaiken (1978) presented University of Massachusetts students with a speech attacking a company's pollution of a river. When the speech was said to have been given either by a political candidate with a business background or to an audience of company supporters, it seemed more unbiased and was more persuasive than when the same antibusiness speech was supposedly given by a proenvironment politician to a group of environmentalists. In the latter case, one could attribute the politician's arguments to personal bias or to the effect of the audience.

As if aware of this study, candidate Jimmy Carter in 1976 announced his support of amnesty for Vietnam draft resisters before, of all places, the American Legion convention. It was like advocating lower wages to a convention of labor leaders, but it did help convince the larger public of his sincerity. Being willing also to suffer on behalf of one's beliefs—which many greater leaders have done—has a similar effect (Knight & Weiss, 1980).

These experiments all point to the importance of attribution: To what do we attribute a speaker's position—to the speaker's bias and selfish motives or to the factual evidence? Wood and Eagly (1981) report that when a speaker argues an *unexpected* position we are more likely to attribute the message to compelling evidence, and thus to be persuaded by it. Similarly, Joel Wachtler and Elizabeth Counselman (1981) found that students at Hobart and William Smith Colleges were most persuaded by arguments for generous compensation in a personal-injury case when the arguments came from a stingy, Scrooge-type person. Arguments for stingy compensation were most persuasive when they came from a normally warm, generous person. We might speculate, therefore, that an arms-limitation treaty between the U.S. and the Soviet Union would be most trusted by Americans if negotiated by a conservative, promilitary president.

Credibility:
Believability. A credible communicator is perceived as both expert and trustworthy.

Some television ads are obviously constructed to make the communicator appear both expert and trustworthy. Drug companies peddle pain relievers using an unhesitating white-coated speaker, such as Pernell Roberts (known to TV watchers as "Trapper John, M.D."), who declares that most doctors recommend their ingredient (the ingredient, of course, is aspirin). Yet there are other ads that do not seem to use the credibility principle. Is Bill Cosby really a trustworthy expert on Jell-O desserts? And are you and I more likely to drink Coke because Michael Jackson recommends it?

Attractiveness

Most people deny that endorsements by star athletes and entertainers affect them. Everyone knows that these stars are seldom if ever really knowledgeable about the products. Besides, we know the intent is to persuade us; we don't just accidentally eavesdrop on Cosby lapping Jello. But such ads are predicated upon another characteristic of an effective communicator: attractiveness. We may think that we are not influenced by how attractive or likeable the person is, but researchers have found otherwise.

Attractiveness varies in several ways. *Physical appeal* is one. Experimenters have sometimes found that arguments, especially emotional ones, are more influential when they come from beautiful people (Chaikin, 1979; Dion & Stein, 1978; Pallak et al., 1983). *Similarity* is another. As Chapter 13 will emphasize, we tend to like people who are similar to us; contrary to the old proverb, opposites generally do *not* attract. Not only do we like people who are similar to us, but we are also influenced by them. For example, Theodore Dembroski, Thomas Lasater, and Albert Ramirez (1978) gave Black junior high students in St. Petersburg, Florida, and Birmingham, Alabama, a taped

Michael J. Fox for America's Libraries

We may think people's attractiveness does not influence how we receive their message, but researchers have found otherwise.

Attractiveness:
Having qualities which appeal to an audience. An appealing communicator (often someone similar to the audience) is most persuasive on matters of subjective preference.

appeal for proper dental care. When a dentist assessed the cleanliness of their teeth the next day, those who had heard the appeal from a Black dentist had cleaner teeth than those who had heard the same appeal from a White dentist.

Is similarity more important than credibility? Sometimes yes, sometimes no. Timothy Brock (1965) found paint store customers more influenced by the testimony of an inexpert person who had recently bought the same amount of paint they planned to buy than by an expert who had recently purchased twenty times as much. But recall that a leading dentist (a dissimilar but credible source) was more persuasive on the topic of dental hygiene than a student (a similar but inexpert source).

Seemingly contradictory findings such as this bring out the detective in the scientist. They suggest that an undiscovered factor is at work—that similarity is more important given factor X and credibility is more important given not-X. But what is factor X? George Goethals and Eric Nelson (1973) suggest that it is whether the topic is one of *subjective preference* or *objective reality*. When the choice concerns matters of personal value, taste, or way of life, similar communicators will be most influential. But on judgments of fact—Does Seattle have more rainfall than London?—confirmation of our belief by a *dissimilar* person does more to boost our confidence. After all, a dissimilar person provides a more independent judgment. In a laboratory test, Goethals and Nelson confirmed this idea that similar communicators are much more effective on matters of value and preference than on judgments of fact.

There is, however, one known circumstance under which attractive communicators are *less* effective even on matters of preference. When an attractive source gets you to *do* something that is rather unpleasant you can justify your action by your liking for the person. When a nasty, unattractive source gets you to do the same thing, you cannot so easily attribute your compliance to your liking for the person. (This fits both self-perception and dissonance theories, as discussed in Chapter 2.) For example, Army reservists who ate fried grasshoppers at the request of a stern, unfriendly experimenter ended up liking the insects *more* than those asked by a warm, polite experimenter (Smith, 1977). It was as if they thought, "I'm not eating them because I like the experimenter, so I must be eating them because I like them."

WHAT IS SAID? THE CONTENT OF THE MESSAGE

Persuasion is affected not only by who says a thing, but also by *what* that person says. If you were to help organize an appeal to get people to vote for school taxes, or to stop smoking, or to contribute money to world hunger relief, you might grapple with several practical questions concerning the content of your appeal. Common sense can be made to argue on either side of these questions: (1) Is a message more persuasive if it is carefully reasoned, or if it arouses emotion? (2) How discrepant (different) should the message be from the audience's existing opinions: Do you get more opinion change by advocating a position only slightly discrepant from the listeners' existing opinions? Or by advocating a more extreme point of view? (3) Should the message express your side only, or should it acknowledge and attempt to refute opposing views? (4) If both sides are to be presented, say in successive talks at a community meeting, is there an advantage to going first or last? Let's take these questions one at a time.

Appeal to Reason versus Emotion

"The truth is always the strongest argument."
Sophocles, Phaedra

Suppose you were campaigning in support of world hunger relief. Would you best itemize your arguments and cite an array of impressive statistics? Or would you be more effective with an emotional approach, say by presenting the compelling story of one starving child? Of course, an argument need not be unreasonable to arouse emotion. Still, which is more influential—reason or emotion? Was Shakespeare's Lysander right when he said, "The will of man is by his reason sway'd"? Or was Lord Chesterfield's advice wiser: "Address yourself generally to the senses, to the heart, and to the weaknesses of mankind, but rarely to their reason"?

"Opinion is ultimately determined by the feelings and not by the intellect."
Herbert Spencer, Social Statics

The answer seems to depend on whom you are speaking to. Well-educated or analytical people are more responsive to rational appeals than are less educated or unanalytical people (Cacioppo et al., 1983; Hovland et al., 1949). Similarly, highly involved audiences are more responsive to reasoned arguments; audiences that care little devote little time to thinking through the arguments and so are more affected by simply how much they like the communicator (Chaiken, 1980; Petty et al., 1981). To judge from their responses during interviews prior to the 1980 U.S. presidential election, many voters were not very involved, for their voting preferences were more predictable from emotional reactions to the candidates (for example, whether Ronald Reagan ever made them feel happy) than by their beliefs about the candidates' traits and likely behaviors (Abelson et al., 1982). Again in 1988, many people who agreed more with Michael Dukakis nevertheless *liked* George Bush more and therefore voted for Bush.

Advertising research, as in one study of the persuasiveness of 168 television commercials (Agres, 1987), reveals that the most effective ads invoke both reasons ("You'll get whiter whites with Detergent X") and emotions ("the brand to use if you care about your family").

Messages also become more persuasive through association with good feelings. Irving Janis and his colleagues (1965; Dabbs & Janis, 1965) found that Yale students were more convinced by persuasive messages if allowed to enjoy peanuts and Pepsi while reading them (see Figure 8-1). Similarly, Mark Galizio and Clyde Hendrick (1972) found Kent State University students more persuaded by folk-song lyrics that were accompanied by pleasant guitar music than by lyrics that were sung or spoken without

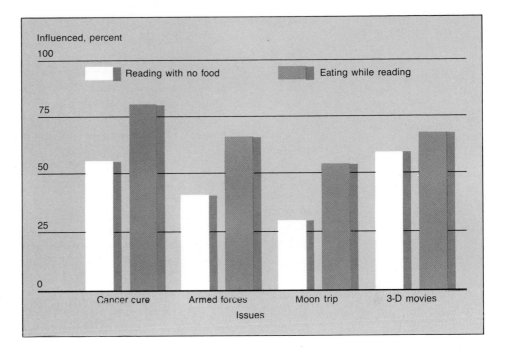

Influenced, percent

Reading with no food   Eating while reading

Cancer cure   Armed forces   Moon trip   3-D movies

Issues

FIGURE 8-1
People who read while snacking were more persuaded than those who read without eating. (Data from Janis, Kaye, & Kirschner, 1965.)

the accompaniment. Those who like conducting business over sumptuous lunches with soft background music can celebrate these results.

Messages also can be effective by evoking negative emotions. In trying to convince people to cut down on smoking, brush their teeth more often, get a tetanus shot, or drive carefully, a fear-arousing message can be potent. Showing cigarette smokers the horrible things that sometimes happen to people who smoke too much adds to the persuasiveness of a message. But how much fear should be aroused? Should you evoke just a little fear, lest people become so frightened that they tune out your painful message? Or should you try to scare the daylights out of them? Several experiments by Howard Leventhal (1970) and his collaborators at the University of Wisconsin and by Ronald Rogers and his collaborators at the University of Alabama (Robberson & Rogers, 1988) reveal that, generally, the more frightening or negative a communication is, the more potent it is.

The effectiveness of fear-arousing communications is being applied in ads against the use of cigarettes, alcohol, and other drugs. For example, Dawn Wilson and her colleagues (1987, 1988) had doctors send a letter to their patients who smoked. Of those who received a positively framed message (explaining that by quitting they would live longer) 8 percent tried to quit smoking. Of those who received a fear-framed message (explaining that by continuing to smoke they would likely die sooner) 30 percent tried to quit. Similarly, researcher Claude Levy-Leboyer (1988) found that attitudes toward alcohol and drinking habits among French youth were most effectively changed by fear-arousing pictures, leading the French government to incorporate fear-arousing information into its TV spots.

But increasing listeners' fear won't always make a message more potent. If people are not instructed how to avoid the danger—as the hellfire-and-brimstone preacher typically does—frightening messages can be too much to cope with (Leventhal, 1970; Rogers & Mewborn, 1976). Such messages are more likely to be effective if people not only are led to fear the severity and likelihood of a threatened event (say, a lung cancer death due to cigarette smoking), but also to believe that there is an effective protective strategy that they are capable of following (Maddux & Rogers, 1983). Polls during the mid-1980s revealed that some 40 percent of Americans believed that a nuclear war is "fairly" or "very" likely and that it would likely annihilate them and most of the population (Fiske, 1987; Fox & Schofield, 1989; Fuld & Nevin, 1988). Because they felt incapable of doing anything effective, most of these people were, however, doing nothing actively to prevent a nuclear holocaust. Fear without feelings of self-efficacy breeds only inactive concern.

Political propaganda often exploits fear arousal. Streicher's *Der Stürmer* aroused fear with hundreds upon hundreds of unsubstantiated anecdotes about Jews who were said to have ground rats to make hash, seduced and corrupted non-Jewish women, and cheated families out of their life savings. Streicher's appeals, like most Nazi propaganda, were emotional, not logical. The appeals also gave clear, specific instructions on how to combat "the danger": They listed Jewish businesses so readers would avoid them, encouraged readers to submit for publication the names of Germans who patronized Jewish shops and professionals, and directed readers to compile lists of Jews in their area (Bytwerk & Brooks, 1980). This was vivid propaganda, hard to forget. The negative campaign ads that dominated the 1988 U.S. presidential campaign also played on fears—fears of a possible "President Quayle" should George Bush die in office, fears of "soft-on-crime" candidate Dukakis cultivated with TV ads depicting a Massachusetts convict who, while out on a prison furlough, committed a heinous crime.

The potency of fear-arousing information is also apparent in recent research. Vividly imagined diseases seem more likely than hard-to-picture diseases (Sherman et al., 1985). Frightening films can also be influential. When several teams of researchers sampled the 100 million Americans before and again several weeks after their viewing of the 1983 nuclear-war television film "The Day After," they found that viewers' concern over nuclear war had risen (Oskamp et al., 1985; Schofield & Pavelchak, 1985). Another study revealed that the television series *AMERIKA*, which portrayed disastrous consequences of a Soviet occupation of the United States, heightened viewers' hostility toward the Soviet Union (Olguin et al., 1988). When it comes to persuasion, an emotional picture can be worth a thousand words.

In general, then, emotional appeals seem more effective than might be implied by the view that human beings are preeminently rational animals. Communicators who evoke or are associated with good feelings tend to be persuasive. So, too, do strong fear appeals, especially when the listener is given effective ways to reduce the fear.

"If those who have studied the art of writing are in accord on any one point, it is on this: the surest way to arouse and hold the attention of the reader is by being specific, definite, and concrete."
William Strunk and E. B. White, The Elements of Style, 1979

Discrepancy

Picture the following scene: Wanda arrives home on spring vacation, hoping to convert her portly middle-aged father to her new "health-fitness lifestyle." She runs 5 miles a day, while her father chuckles that his idea of exercise is "pushing the button on my garage door opener and turning pages of the *Wall Street Journal*." Wanda ponders: "Would I be more likely to get Dad off his duff by urging him to try a modest exercise program, say a daily walk, or by trying to get him involved in something strenuous, say a program of calisthenics and running? Maybe if I asked him to take up a rigorous exercise program he would compromise and at least take up something worthwhile. But then again maybe he'd think I'm crazy and do nothing."

Like Wanda, social psychologists have been able to reason either way. Disagreement produces discomfort, and discomfort prompts people to change their opinions

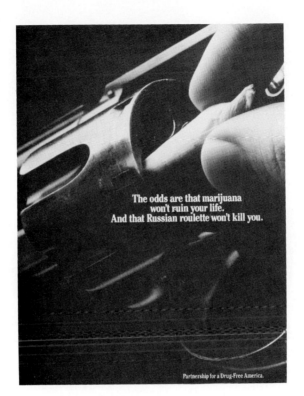

The odds are that marijuana won't ruin your life. And that Russian roulette won't kill you.

Partnership for a Drug-Free America.

A picture is worth a thousand words.

(recall from Chapter 2 the effects of dissonance). So perhaps wider disagreement will produce more change. But then again, a communicator who proclaims a discomfiting message may get discredited. One study found that the more people disagreed with conclusions drawn by a newscaster, the more biased, inaccurate, and untrustworthy they believed the newscaster to be (Zanna et al., 1976). So perhaps wider disagreement will produce *less* change.

Given these considerations, Elliot Aronson, Judith Turner, and Merrill Carlsmith (1963) reasoned that a highly credible source would elicit most opinion change by advocating a position greatly discrepant from the position held by the recipient, but that a communicator with little credibility probably would be dismissed for doing so. Sure enough, when T. S. Eliot was said to have offered high praise for a poem that people initially disliked, they changed their opinion more than when he offered faint praise for the same poem. But when "Agnes Stearns," "a student at Mississippi State Teachers College," evaluated a disliked poem, faint praise was as persuasive as high praise. Thus, as Figure 8-2 shows, discrepancy and credibility *interact:* The effect of large versus small discrepancy depends upon whether or not the communicator is credible.

So the answer to Wanda's question—"Should I argue an extreme position?"—is, "It depends." Is Wanda in her adoring father's eyes a highly prestigious, authoritative source? If so, Wanda should push for the most complete fitness program. If not, Wanda would be wise to make a more modest appeal.

The answer also depends on how involved her father is in the issue. Those highly involved in an issue tend to accept a narrow range of views. Thus a moderately discrepant message may seem foolishly radical to one who is highly involved, especially if the message differs from one's opinion rather than being a more extreme view of

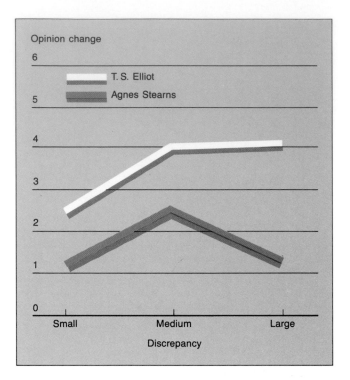

FIGURE 8-2
Discrepancy interacts with communicator credibility. Only a highly credible communicator maintains effectiveness when arguing an extreme position. (Data from Aronson, Turner, & Carlsmith, 1963.)

what one already agrees with (Rhine & Severance, 1970; Pallak et al., 1972; Petty & Cacioppo, 1979). So if Wanda's father has not yet thought or cared much about the exercise question, she can profitably take a more extreme position than if he is strongly committed to not exercising.

One-Sided versus Two-Sided Appeals

Another practical issue faced by persuaders is whether to acknowledge and refute opposing arguments. Once again, common sense offers no clear answer. Acknowledging the opposing arguments might confuse the audience, thus weakening the case. On the other hand, a message might seem fairer, might be more disarming, if it anticipated the opposition's arguments.

After Germany's defeat in World War II, the U.S. Army did not want soldiers to be overconfident that Japan now would be easily vanquished. So Carl Hovland and his colleagues (1949) in the Army's Information and Education Division designed two radio broadcasts arguing that the war in the Pacific would last at least two more years. One broadcast was one-sided; it failed to acknowledge the existence of contradictory arguments such as the advantage of fighting only one enemy instead of two. The other broadcast was two-sided; it mentioned and responded to the opposing arguments. As Figure 8-3 illustrates, which message was most effective depended on the listener. Those who already agreed were strengthened more by a one-sided appeal; those disagreeing were more likely to be persuaded by an appeal that acknowledged opposing arguments.

Subsequent experiments revealed that if people are aware of opposing arguments (as well-informed people are likely to be) or are likely later to hear the other side, then

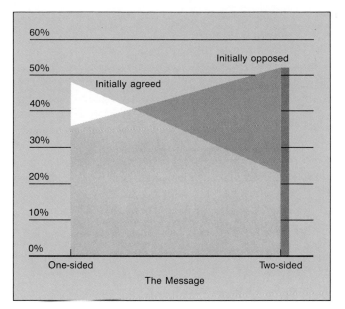

FIGURE 8-3
The interaction of initial opinion with one- versus two-sidedness. American World War II soldiers initially opposed to a message suggesting that Japanese would not be easily defeated were more persuaded by a two-sided communication. Soldiers initially agreeing with the message were strengthened more by a one-sided message. (Data from Houland, Lumsdaine, & Sheffield, 1949.)

"Opponents fancy they refute us when they repeat their own opinion and pay no attention to ours."
Goethe, Maxims and Reflections, *early nineteenth century*

a two-sided presentation is more persuasive and enduring (Lumsdaine & Janis, 1953; Jones & Brehm, 1970). Apparently, a one-sided message stimulates an informed audience to think of counter-arguments and to view the communicator as biased. Thus, a political candidate speaking to a politically informed group would be wise to respond to the opposition. Social psychologist Ralph White (1988) illustrates, by showing how a peace activist might respond to questions with two-sided answers, such as:

> *Question:* What about the Russians—I mean the Russian leaders? Are't they tough, ruthless aggressors, like Adolf Hitler? Aren't they out to conquer the world? It seems to me that we need a lot of strength and a lot of courage to stand up to Soviet aggression, if we want to keep the free world free.

> *Possible answer:* They are tough and ruthless, yes. And the last thing I'd want to do is to defend the Communist system. It's a poor system. But if we really want peace, I think we need to make a clear distinction between the Communist system and the attitudes of the Russians on war and peace. We all know the devastation and the suffering they went through in World War II. *Twenty million* dead. We lost a third of a million. For every one man we lost in that war, they lost 60! And they remember it, vividly—practically every Western person who has been to Russia comes back testifying to that. It's not because the Russians are nice guys that they want peace; it's a matter of self-interest and self-preservation. I would go so far as to say that the Soviet people, and their leaders, want peace fully as much as we do.

Primacy versus Recency

Imagine yourself a consultant to a prominent politician who must soon debate another prominent politician on the issue of a proposed nuclear arms limitation treaty. Three weeks before the treaty is voted upon, each politician is to appear on the nightly news and present a brief statement (previously prepared so that the second speaker will not be able to rebut the first). By the flip of a coin, your side has been given the choice whether to speak first or last. Knowing that you are a former social psychology student, everyone looks to you for advice.

Quickly, you mentally scan your old textbooks and lecture notes. Would going first be best? People's preconceptions control their interpretations, and a belief, once formed, is difficult to discredit (Chapter 4). So going first could give people ideas that would bias in your favor how they would perceive and interpret the second speech. And besides, people may pay most attention to what comes first. But then again, people remember recent things best, so might it be more effective to speak last?

Your first line of reasoning predicts what is most commonly found, a ***primacy effect:*** Information presented early is most persuasive. First impressions *are* important. For example, can you feel a difference between these two descriptions?

Primacy effect:
Other things being equal, information presented first usually has the most influence.

- John is intelligent, industrious, impulsive, critical, stubborn, and envious.
- John is envious, stubborn, critical, impulsive, industrious, and intelligent.

When Solomon Asch (1946) gave these sentences to college students in New York City, those who read the adjectives in the intelligent→envious order rated the person more positively (for example, as more sociable, humorous, and happy) than those given the envious→intelligent order. Evidently, the early-encountered information governed their interpretation of the later information, thus producing the primacy effect. Similarly, in experiments involving a task on which people must guess, when people succeed 50 percent of the time and fail 50 percent of the time, those whose successes come early are ultimately perceived as more able than those whose successes come mostly after early failures (Jones et al., 1968; Langer & Roth, 1975; McAndrew, 1981).

Does this indicate that primacy is also the rule in persuasion? Norman Miller and Donald Campbell (1959) gave Northwestern University students a condensed transcript from an actual trial of a civil suit. The plaintiff's testimony and arguments were placed in one block, those for the defense in another. The students read both blocks. When they returned a week later to indicate their opinions, most sided with the information they had read first. Gary Wells, Lawrence Wrightsman, and Peter Miene (1985) found a similar primacy effect when they varied the timing of a defense attorney's opening statement in the transcript of an actual criminal case. The statement was more effective if presented before the prosecution's presentation of the evidence, rather than after (as some experts advise).

Recency effect:
Sometimes information presented last has the most influence. Recency effects are less common than primacy effects.

What about the opposite possibility? Will our better memory for recent information ever create a ***recency effect?*** We know from our experience (as well as from memory experiments) that today's events can temporarily outweigh more significant events of the past. To test this, Miller and Campbell gave another group of students one block of testimony to read. A week later the researchers had them read the second block, immediately after which they were to indicate their opinions. Now the results were just the reverse of those from before—a recency effect. Apparently the first block of arguments, being a week old, had largely faded from memory. In general, then, it seems that forgetting creates the recency effect (1) when sufficient time separates the two messages, *and* (2) when the audience does not make a commitment after the first message but must decide soon after the second message. When the two messages are back-to-back, followed by a time gap, the primacy effect will likely occur (see Figure 8-4). So, what advice would you give to the political debater?

FIGURE 8-4

Primacy effect versus recency effect. When two persuasive messages are heard back-to-back and the audience then responds at some later time, the first message tends to have the advantage (primacy effect). When the two messages are separated in time and the audience responds soon after the second message, the second message tends to have the advantage (recency effect).

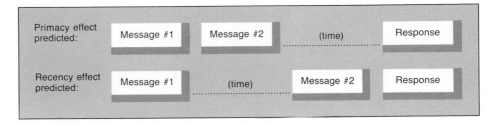

| Primacy effect predicted: | Message #1 | Message #2 | (time) | Response |

| Recency effect predicted: | Message #1 | (time) | Message #2 | Response |

HOW IS IT SAID? THE CHANNEL OF COMMUNICATION

Active Experience or Passive Reception?

In Chapter 2 we noted that our actions powerfully shape who we are. When we act, we amplify the idea lying behind what we've done, especially when we feel responsible for having committed the act. We also noted that attitudes rooted in our own direct experience—rather than learned secondhand—are more likely to endure and to affect our subsequent behavior. Compared to attitudes based on experience, those formed passively are held with less certainty, are unstable, and are vulnerable to attack.

Commonsense psychology nevertheless places enormous faith in the power of written words. How do we try to get people out to a campus event? Post notices. How do we get drivers to slow down and keep their eyes on the road? Put "Drive Carefully" messages on billboards. How do we try to prevent trash from being dropped on campus? Litter the campus bulletin boards and mailboxes with antilitter messages.

Are people that easy to persuade? Consider two well-intentioned efforts that suggest not. At Scripps College in California, a week-long anti-litter campaign urged students, "Keep Scripps' campus beautiful," "Let's clean up our trash," and so forth. Such slogans were placed in students' mailboxes each morning and displayed in prominent posters across the campus. On the day before the campaign began, social psychologist Raymond Paloutzian (1979) placed litter near a trash can along a well-traveled sidewalk and then stepped back to record the behavior of 180 passersby. No one picked up anything. On the last day of the campaign the test was repeated with 180 more passersby. Did the pedestrians now race one another in their zeal to comply with the appeals? Hardly. Only two of the 180 picked up trash.

Are spoken appeals any more persuasive? Not necessarily. Those of us who do public speaking, as teachers or persuaders, become so easily enamored of our spoken words that we are tempted to overestimate their power. Ask college students what aspect of their college experience has been most valuable or what they remember from their freshman year, and few, I am sad to say, recall the brilliant lectures that we faculty remember giving. Thomas Crawford (1974) and his associates evaluated the impact of the spoken word by going to the homes of people from twelve churches shortly before and after they heard sermons opposing racial bigotry and injustice. When asked during the second interview whether they had heard or read anything about racial prejudice or discrimination since the previous interview, only 10 percent spontaneously recalled the sermons. When the remaining 90 percent were asked directly whether their clergyman had "talked about prejudice or discrimination in the last couple of weeks," more than 30 percent denied hearing such a sermon. It is therefore hardly surprising that the sermons had no impact on racial attitudes.

When you stop to think about it, the preacher has so many hurdles to surmount

---

Channel of communication:
How the message is delivered—whether face to face, in writing, on film, or in some other way.

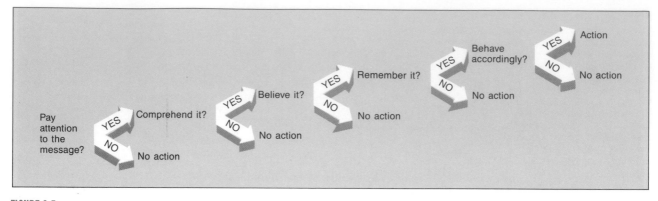

FIGURE 8-5
To elicit action, a persuasive message must clear several hurdles. As we shall see, what is crucial is not so much remembering the message itself as remembering one's own thoughts in response. (Adapted from McGuire, 1978.)

it's a wonder that preaching affects as many people as it does. As Figure 8-5 indicates, persuasive speakers must deliver a message that not only gets their attention but is also understandable, convincing, memorable, and compelling. A carefully thought-out appeal must consider each of these steps in the persuasion process.

However, passively received appeals are not always futile. When Ultra-Brite toothpaste was introduced with a massive "boost your sex appeal" advertising campaign, it quickly became the third leading seller. My drugstore sells two brands of aspirin, one heavily advertised and one unadvertised. Apart from slight differences in how fast each tablet crumbles in your mouth, any pharmacist will tell you the two brands are identical. Aspirin is aspirin. Our bodies cannot tell the difference between them. But our pocketbooks can. The advertised brand sells for three times the price of the unadvertised brand. And sell it does, to millions of people. Such is the power of the media.

With such power, can the media enable a wealthy political candidate to buy an election? Joseph Grush (1980) analyzed candidate expenditures in all the 1976 Democratic presidential primaries and found that those who spent the most in any election usually got the most votes. As Grush notes, the effect of this exposure was often to make an unfamiliar candidate into a familiar one. (This parallels laboratory experiments in which mere exposure to unfamiliar stimuli breeds liking—see Chapter 13.) Would the media be as potent with familiar candidates and issues? Likely not. Researchers have time and again found little effect of political advertising on voters' attitudes in the general presidential election (although, of course, even a small effect could swing a close election) (Kinder & Sears, 1985; McGuire, 1986).

Since passively received appeals are sometimes effective and sometimes not, can we specify in advance the types of topics on which a persuasive appeal is most likely to be successful? One general rule seems to be that persuasion decreases as the significance and familiarity of the issue increases. On minor issues, such as which brand of aspirin to buy, it is easy to demonstrate the media's power. On more familiar and important issues, such as racial attitudes in racially tense cities, persuading people is like trying to push a piano uphill. It is not impossible, but one "shove" won't do it.

Personal versus Media Influence

Studies of persuasion have demonstrated that the major influence upon our most important beliefs and attitudes is not the media but our direct contact with people. Two field experiments illustrate the strength of personal influence. Some years ago, Samuel Eldersveld and Richard Dodge (1954) studied political persuasion in Ann Arbor, Michigan. Citizens intending not to vote for a revision of the city charter were divided into three groups. Of those exposed only to what they saw and heard in the mass media, 19 percent voted for the revision on election day. A second group received four mailings in support of the revision. Forty-five percent voted for it. People in a third group were personally visited and given the appeal face to face. Seventy-five percent of these people cast their votes for it.

In a more recent field experiment, a research team led by John Farquhar and Nathan Maccoby (1977; Maccoby & Alexander, 1980; Maccoby, 1980) tried to reduce the frequency of heart disease among middle-aged adults in three small California cities. To ascertain the relative effectiveness of personal and media influence, they interviewed and medically examined some 1200 people both before the project began and at the end of each of the following three years. Residents of Tracy, California, received no persuasive appeals other than those usually occurring in their media. In Gilroy, California, a two-year multimedia campaign used TV, radio, newspapers, and direct mail to teach people about coronary risk and what they could do to reduce it. In Watsonville, California, this media campaign was supplemented by personal contacts with two-thirds of those whose blood pressure, weight, age, and so forth put them in a high risk category. Using behavior-modification principles, the researchers helped people set specific objectives and reinforced their successes. As Figure 8-6 indicates, after one, two, and three years the high-risk people in Tracy (the control town) were about as much at risk as before. High-risk people in Gilroy, which was deluged with media appeals, improved their health habits and were now somewhat less at risk. Those in Watsonville, who also received the personal contacts, changed most of all.

I suspect college students will have little trouble recognizing in their own experience the potency of personal influence. In retrospect, most say they learned more

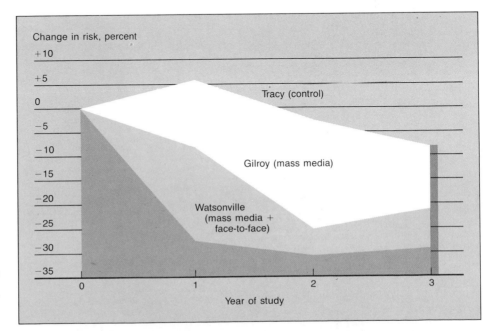

FIGURE 8-6
Percentage change from baseline (0) in coronary risk after one, two, or three years of health education. (Data from Maccoby, 1980.)

from their friends and fellow students than from their contact with "books" or "professors." Educational researchers have confirmed the students' intuition: Out-of-class personal relationships powerfully determine how students change during college (Astin, 1972; Wilson et al., 1975).

Although face-to-face influence is usually greater than that of the media, we should not underestimate the media's power. Those whose personal influence on our opinions is considerable must get their ideas somewhere. Oftentimes their sources are the media. Elihu Katz (1957) observed that much of the media's effects operate in a ***two-step flow of communication***—from media to opinion leaders to those of us in the rank and file. If I want to evaluate stereo equipment, I defer to the opinions of my oldest son, who gets some of his ideas from the printed page.

By itself, the two-step flow model is an oversimplification. The media also communicate directly with mass audiences. In Britain, people get much of their health-related information through the newspapers. Connie Kristiansen and Christian Harding (1988) think it more than a mere coincidence that, compared to those who read the quality newspapers, those who read the tabloids receive much less informative news about health—and are more likely to die prematurely. But the two-step model does remind us that the influences of media can penetrate the culture subtly. Even if the media had little direct effect upon people's attitudes, they could still have a big effect, indirectly. Those rare children who grow up without watching television do not grow up apart from television's influence. Unless they live as hermits, they will likely join in TV-imitative play on the school ground and ask their parents for the TV-related toys that their friends have.

Our lumping together all media from mass mailings to television is surely also an oversimplification. Studies comparing different media find that the more lifelike the medium, the more persuasive its message. Thus the order of persuasiveness seems to be: live, videotaped, audiotaped, and written. But to add to the complexity, Shelly Chaiken and Alice Eagly (1978) and Barrie Gunter and others (1986) note that re-

Two-step flow of communication:
Media influence often occurs through opinion leaders, who in turn influence others.

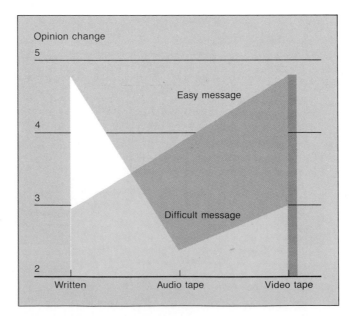

FIGURE 8-7
Easy-to-understand messages were most persuasive when videotaped. Difficult messages were most persuasive when written. Thus the difficulty of the message interacted with the medium to determine persuasiveness. (Data from Chaiken & Eagly, 1978.)

searchers have found that messages are best *comprehended* and *recalled* when written. Comprehension is one of the first steps in the persuasion process (see Figure 8-5). So Chaiken and Eagly reasoned that if a message is difficult to comprehend, persuasion, too, might actually be greatest when the message is written. They gave University of Massachusetts students easy or difficult messages in writing, on audiotape, or videotape. Figure 8-7 displays their results: Difficult messages were indeed most persuasive when written, easy messages when videotaped. By drawing attention to the communicator and away from the message itself, the TV medium also makes the communicator's characteristics more important than they otherwise would be (Chaiken & Eagly, 1983).

TO WHOM IS IT SAID? THE AUDIENCE

As we saw in Chapter 7, there are several reasons why people's measurable traits seem to bear no strong, straightforward relation to their responsiveness to social influence. Regarding one's susceptibility to persuasion, such is true for an additional reason: A particular trait may contribute to one step in the persuasion process (Figure 8-5), but work against another. For example, if intelligent people quickly comprehend but slowly yield to a message, then we cannot state a simple relationship between intelligence and persuasibility. Instead, we might expect personality to interact with particular aspects of the communication. A difficult message is most persuasive with intelligent people (who apparently understand it better). Less intelligent people are more persuaded by a simple message; once they understand the message, they more readily yield to it without counterarguing (McGuire, 1968).

What the Audience Is Thinking

In thinking about persuasive messages, it is easy to forget what's crucial, which is not the message itself but what responses it evokes in a person's mind. Our minds are not mere sponges that soak up whatever messages pour over them. If the message summons favorable thoughts, we will probably be persuaded. If it provokes us to counterargue—to think up contrary arguments—we will remain unpersuaded.

Forewarned Is Forearmed—If You Care Enough to Counterargue

What circumstances breed counterarguing? One is a communicator of low credibility propounding a disagreeable message (Perloff & Brock, 1980). Another is a *forewarning* that someone is going to try to persuade you. If you had to tell your parents that you wanted to drop out of school, you would likely anticipate their trying to persuade you to stay. So, you might develop a list of arguments to counter every conceivable argument they might make. Jonathan Freedman and David Sears (1965) demonstrated the difficulty of trying to persuade someone under such circumstances. They forewarned one of two large groups of California high school seniors that they were going to hear a talk entitled "Why Teenagers Should Not Be Allowed to Drive." Those forewarned were hardly persuaded at all; those not forewarned were persuaded.

Follow-up research confirmed that sneak attacks on people's attitudes are especially useful with people who are involved in the issue. If given several minutes' forewarning, such people will prepare their defenses (Petty & Cacioppo, 1977, 1979). But when people regard an issue as trivial, even blatant propaganda (as that for most aspirin and toothpaste) can be effective. Few bother to construct counterarguments.

"To be forewarned and therefore forearmed . . . is eminently rational if our belief is true; but if our belief is a delusion, this same forewarning and forearming would obviously be the method whereby the delusion rendered itself incurable."
C. S. Lewis,
Screwtape Proposes a Toast, 1965.

Similarly, when a premise is subtly slipped into a conversation—"Why was Sue hostile to Mark?"—people tend simply to accept the premise (in this instance, that Sue was, in fact, hostile) (Swann, Giuliano, & Wegner, 1982).

Distraction Disarms Counterarguing

Verbal persuasion can also be increased by distracting people with something that attracts their attention enough to inhibit their counterarguing, yet is not so powerful that the message gets ignored (Festinger & Maccoby, 1964; Osterhouse & Brock, 1970; Keating & Brock, 1974). Political ads often employ this technique. While the words promote the candidate, the visual images of the candidate in action restrain our ana-lyzing what is being said. Distraction is especially effective when the message is simple or easily refuted; with difficult messages, distraction interferes with thoughtful reflec-tion (Regan & Cheng, 1973; Harkins & Petty, 1981a).

This research on how persuasion increases as counterarguing decreases makes me wonder: Are fast talkers more persuasive partly because they leave us less time to counterargue? Are easy messages less persuasive when written because readers pace themselves and can therefore pause to counterargue? And does television shape im-portant attitudes more through its subtle or hidden messages (for example, concerning gender roles) than through its explicit persuasive appeals? After all, if we do not notice a message, we cannot counterargue it.

Uninvolved Audiences Use Peripheral Cues

Out of this research on audience reactions there has emerged a much-needed theory of persuasion. Time and again in this chapter I have explained that the effect of some factor, such as a communicator's credibility, depends on (interacts with) some other factor. It would be nice if all effects were simple ones, but the reality is that human beings are not simple, and describing a pretzel-shaped reality requires pretzel-shaped principles. Still, as the list of not-very-general generalizations grows and be-comes hard to remember, we wish for a theory of persuasion that would serve the functions of any good theory—by organizing and making sense of the bewildering array of facts and by generating predictions and practical applications.

Richard Petty and John Cacioppo (1986) propose such a theory, which they call the "elaboration likelihood model." Simply stated, it contends that when people are highly involved in an issue or analytically inclined, they are more likely to *think* about a message (mentally elaborate upon it) and so to be influenced by the favorability of their own thoughts. When people are uninterested or unable to think about the mes-sage, they will rely on peripheral cues such as the attractiveness of the communicator, the mere number of arguments in the message, and the pleasantness of the surround-ings, (see Figure 8-8).

Shelly Chaiken (1987) derived and confirmed a similar idea from research on heu-ristics. Because there is insufficient time to think every issue through carefully, we economize by using simple decision rules on minimally relevant issues. Residents of my community were recently asked to vote on a complicated issue involving the legal ownership of our local hospital. Having insufficient interest and time to study this question myself—I had this book to write—I noted that the supporters of the refer-endum were people whom I either liked or regarded as experts. So I used a simple rule-of-thumb heuristic—friends and experts can be trusted—and voted accordingly.

This basically simple theory—that what you think in response to a message is crucial, *if* you are motivated and able to think about it—helps us understand some of

"People are usually more convinced by reasons they discover themselves than by those found by others."
Blaise Pascal, Pensees, *1620*

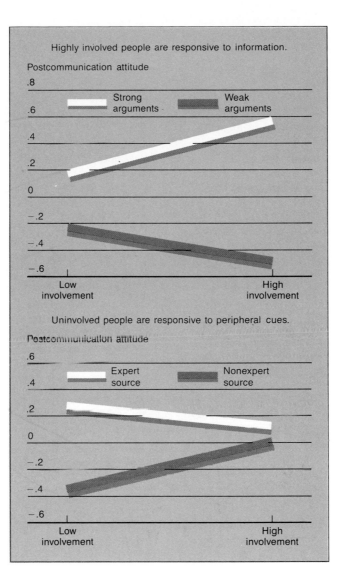

FIGURE 8-8

Central versus peripheral routes to attitude change. When college students were given an *involving* persuasive message (advocating that they be required to pass an exam in their major before being allowed to graduate), they were unpersuaded by weak arguments but found strong arguments convincing (top panel). Whether the source was an expert (Princeton professor of education) or not (a high school student) made little difference. However, when the same message was *uninvolving* (advocating that the exam policy begin in 10 years), the quality of the arguments made little difference, but the expertise of the source was an important determinant of agreement (bottom panel). (From Petty, Cacioppo, & Goldman, 1981.)

the findings we have so far encountered. For example, expert communicators tend to be more readily believed because when people trust the source they are more likely to think favorable thoughts and less likely to counterargue. When they mistrust a communicator, they are more likely to inwardly defend their preconceptions by refuting the disagreeable message.

The theory has also generated many predictions, most of which have been confirmed in experiments by Petty, Cacioppo, and others (Axsom et al., 1987; Leippe & Elkin, 1987; Harkins & Petty, 1987). Many of the experiments have explored ways to stimulate people's thinking—by using rhetorical questions when people are uninterested in the issue, by presenting multiple speakers (for example, having three speakers each give one argument instead of one speaker giving three), by making people feel responsible for evaluating the message, by using relaxed rather than standing postures, by repeating the message, and by getting people's undistracted attention. Their consistent finding: Each of these techniques for stimulating thinking tends to make strong messages even more persuasive and (because of counterarguing) weak messages less persuasive.

"Psychotherapy can be viewed as a branch of applied social psychology."
Stanley Strong (1978, p. 101)

The theory also has practical implications for everyday arenas of human influence, such as advertising (Petty et al., 1983; Haugtvedt et al., 1988) and psychotherapy (Petty et al., 1984; Heesacker, 1986a,b). Effective communicators will be concerned not only with their images and their messages but also with how the recipients are likely to react. How they will react depends not only on their interest in the issue, but also on their dispositions—their analytical inclinations, their tolerance for uncertainty, their need to be true to themselves (Cacioppo et al., 1986; Sorrentino et al., 1988; Snyder & DeBono, 1987). Leila Worth and Diane Mackie (1987; Mackie & Worth, 1988) report that strong moods also make a difference. Being in a good rather than a neutral mood makes people more sensitive to peripheral cues and thus likely to be swayed as much by an expert's poor as good arguments.

So, are the consumers or counselees likely to think and remember thoughts that favor the persuader's point-of-view? If yes, quality arguments will likely be persuasive. During the closing days of his 1980 presidential campaign, Ronald Reagan effectively used rhetorical questions to stimulate desired thoughts in the voters' minds. His summary statement in the presidential debate began with two rhetorical questions that were repeated often during the remaining week of the campaign: "Are you better off than you were four years ago? Is it easier for you to go and buy things in the stores than it was four years ago?" Most people answered no, and voted for Reagan.

To repeat, if people are not motivated to invest cognitive energy in analyzing an issue, then peripheral cues such as the communicator's expertise and likeability will determine their opinion. But if the relevance of the message or their own analytical bent motivates thoughtfulness, then the thoughts triggered by the arguments—and not peripheral cues—will determine opinion.

Age

As is well known, today's older people tend to have different social and political attitudes than younger people. There are at least two plausible explanations for this generation gap. One is a *life-cycle explanation:* Attitudes change (for example, become more conservative) as people grow older. The other is a *generational explanation:* The attitudes young people adopted in earlier generations have persisted largely unchanged; since these attitudes are different from those being adopted by today's young people, a generation gap has developed. Which explanation strikes you as more correct?

David Sears (1979, 1986) reports that the evidence supports the generational explanation. In surveying and resurveying groups of younger and older people over several years, and in studying the extent to which younger and older people change after moving into new situations, it is almost always found that the attitudes of older people change less than do those of young people. As Sears puts it, researchers have "almost invariably found generational rather than life cycle effects. . . ."

The point is not that older adults are inflexible; people now in their fifties and sixties do generally have more liberal sexual and racial attitudes than they had in their thirties and forties (Glenn, 1980, 1981). The point is that the teens and early twenties are important formative years. The attitudes formed then tend to be stable thereafter. (If you are an 18- to 25-year-old, you may, therefore, want to choose intentionally your own social influences—the groups you join, the books you read, the roles you adapt.)

BEHIND THE SCENES

Our research over more than a decade reveals that when we are vitally interested in an issue, we process persuasive arguments carefully. When an issue seems irrelevant, our opinions are more influenced by simple cues, such as a speaker's credibility. Yet people differ: some of us—those high in "need for cognition"—are unimpressed by weak arguments from an impressive source. Such naturally critical people seem to enjoy thinking things through for themselves.

Richard E. Petty and
John T. Cacioppo,
Ohio State University

CASE STUDIES IN PERSUASION: CULT INDOCTRINATION

In one survey of over 1000 San Francisco area high school students, 54 percent reported having had at least one contact with a cult recruiter.
Philip G. Zimbardo & Cynthia F. Hartley (1985)

The persuasion principles described in this chapter are being applied, whether consciously or not, in ways that indicate their power. Consider the social influences that have caused hundreds of thousands of Americans to join one of 2500 religious cults (Singer, 1979a; West & Singer, 1980). Hare Krishna chanters, Moonies, Jonestown suicide victims—how are they persuaded to adopt beliefs radically different from those they had previously held? Do their experiences illustrate the dynamics of human persuasion?

Bear two things in mind: First, this is hindsight analysis. It uses persuasion principles as categories for explaining a fascinating social phenomenon. If the principles

Hundreds of thousands of Americans in recent years have been recruited by members of some 2500 religious cults, but seldom through an abrupt decision.

"You go on home without me, Irene. I'm going to join this man's cult."

seem applicable, this analysis will illustrate them, but it will not prove their impact. With hindsight, almost any type of analysis can seem valid.

Second, explaining *why* people have been convinced to believe something says nothing about the *truth* of their beliefs. That is a logically separate issue. A psychology of religion that could tell us *why* a theist believes in God and an atheist disbelieves would not answer the question of who is right. Explaining either belief does not explain it away. Thus when someone tries to discount your beliefs by saying "You just believe that because . . . ," you might recall the reply of Archbishop William Temple. After giving an address at Oxford, a questioner opened the discussion with a challenge: "Well, of course, Archibishop, the point is that you believe what you believe because of the way you were brought up." To which the Archbishop replied: "That is as it may be. But the fact remains that you believe I believe what I believe because of the way I was brought up, because of the way you were brought up."

Cult:
A group typically characterized by (1) the distinctive ritual of its devotion to a god or a person, (2) isolation from the surrounding "evil" culture, and (3) a living charismatic leader.

In the eyes of the public two troubling and mystifying **cults** have been Sun Myung Moon's Unification Church and Jim Jones's Peoples Temple. The Reverend Moon's curious mixture of Christianity, anticommunism, and glorification of Moon himself as a new messiah has attracted a worldwide following. In response to Moon's declaration, "What I wish must be your wish," many have committed themselves and their incomes to the Unification Church. How are they persuaded to do so?

In 1978, 911 followers of the Reverend Jones shocked the world when they complied with his order to drink cupfuls of strawberry drink laced with tranquilizers, painkillers, and a lethal dose of cyanide. How could such a thing happen? What persuaded these people to give Jones such total allegiance? In hindsight, it looks as if the attitude-change principles have been at work.

ATTITUDES FOLLOW BEHAVIOR

Compliance Breeds Acceptance

As Chapter 2 indicated over and again, a commitment that is voluntarily chosen, substantial, made public, and repeated, is likely to be internalized. Cult leaders seem to know this. Their new converts soon learn that membership is no trivial matter. They are quickly made active members of the team, not mere spectators. Disciplined rituals within the cult community and canvassing and fund raising for the cult in public strengthen the initiates' identities as cult members. Just as the participants in social-psychological experiments come to believe in those things for which they have suffered and witnessed (Aronson & Mills, 1959; Gerard & Mathewson, 1966), so do the cult's initiates: The greater the personal commitment, the more the need to justify it.

The Foot-in-the-Door Phenomenon

How are we induced to make substantial commitments? Seldom by an abrupt, conscious decision. One does not just one day up and decide, "I'm through with mainstream religion. I'm gonna find a cult." Nor do cult recruiters approach people on the street with, "Hi. I'm a Moonie. Care to join us?"

In actuality, the recruitment strategy skillfully applies the foot-in-the-door principle. Unification Church recruiters may invite people to a dinner and then to a weekend of warm fellowship and discussions of philosophies of life. At the weekend retreat, they encourage the attenders to join in songs, activities, and discussion. Once potential

"Listen—just take one of our brochures and see
what we're all about. ... In the meantime, you
may wish to ask yourself, 'Am I a happy cow?'"

Some persuasive techniques are
particularly difficult to resist.

converts are identified, they are urged to sign up for longer training retreats. Eventually the activities become more arduous—soliciting contributions and attempting to convert others.

Jim Jones used this foot-in-the-door technique (see Chapter 2) with his Peoples Temple members. At first, monetary offerings were voluntary. He next inaugurated a required 10-percent-of-income contribution, which soon increased to 25 percent. Finally, he ordered members to turn over to him everything they possessed. Workloads also became progressively more demanding. As ex-member Grace Stoen recalls,

> Nothing was ever done drastically. That's how Jim Jones got away with so much. You slowly gave up things and slowly had to put up with more, but it was always done very gradually. It was amazing, because you would sit up sometimes and say, wow, I really have given up a lot. I really am putting up with a lot. But he did it so slowly that you figured, I've made it this far, what the hell is the difference? (Conway & Siegelman, 1979, p. 236).

PERSUASIVE ELEMENTS

The Communicator

Nearly every successful cult has a charismatic leader—someone who can attract and direct the support of the members. As in experiments on persuasion, a credible communicator is someone the audience perceives as an expert and worthy of their trust—for example, as "Father" Moon.

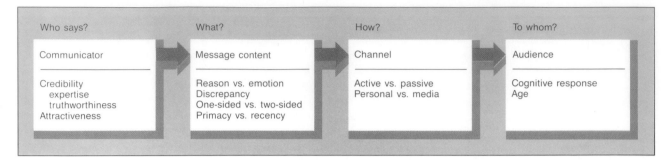

FIGURE 8-9
Summary of variables known to affect the impact of persuasive communications. In real life, these variables may interact; the effect of one variable may depend on the level of another.

Jim Jones reportedly used devious "psychic readings" to establish his powerful credibility. Newcomers were asked to identify themselves as they entered the church before Jones's services. Then one of his aides would call the person's home and say "Hi. We're doing a survey and we'd like to ask you some questions." Later, one ex-member recalls, with this information in hand Jones would call out the person's name and say,

> Have you ever seen me before? Well, you live in such and such a place, your phone number is such and such, and in your living room you've got this, that, and the other, and on your sofa you've got such and such a pillow. . . . Now do you remember me ever being in your house? (Conway & Siegelman, 1979, p. 234)

Trust is another aspect of credibility. Cult researcher Margaret Singer (1979b) noted that middle-class Caucasian youths are more vulnerable because they are more trusting. They lack the "street smarts" of lower-class youths (who know how to resist a hustle) and the wariness of upper-class youths (who have been warned of kidnappers since childhood). Also, many cult members have been recruited by their own friends or relatives, people whom they have come to trust (Stark & Bainbridge, 1980).

The Message

To people who are lonely and depressed, the vivid, emotional messages and the warmth and acceptance with which they are showered by the group can be strikingly appealing: Trust the master, join the family; we have the answer, the "one way." The message echoes through channels as varied as lectures, small-group discussions, and direct social pressure.

The Audience

Who is most receptive to the message? New recruits are disproportionately young—people under twenty-five, those still at that comparatively open age before attitudes and values become stable. Some, such as the followers of Jim Jones, are less educated people who are attracted by the simplicity of the message and who find it difficult to counterargue. More are well-educated and middle class, but these too may be so caught up in the ideals that they overlook the contradictions in those who profess selflessness and practice greed, who pretend concern and behave indifferently.

Potential converts tend also to be at a turning point in life or facing a personal crisis. They have needs; the cult offers them an answer (Singer, 1979b; Lofland & Stark, 1965). Times of social and economic upheaval are therefore especially conducive to an Ayatollah or a "Father" who can make what appears to be simple sense out of the confusion (O'Dea, 1968; Sales, 1972).

GROUP ISOLATION

Cults illustrate a major topic of the next chapter: the power of a group to shape its members' views. Members are usually separated from their previous social support systems and isolated with a group of fellow cultists. There may occur what Rodney Stark and William Bainbridge (1980) call a "social implosion": External ties weaken until the group socially collapses inward, each person engaging only with other group members. Cut off from families and former friends, they begin to lose their access to counterarguments. The group now defines reality. And since disagreements are frowned upon—or in the case of the Peoples Temple even punished—the apparent consensus helps eliminate lingering doubts.

These techniques—binding behavior commitments, persuasion, and group isolation—do not have unlimited power. As Jim Jones made his demands more extreme, he increasingly had to control his people with intimidation. He used threats of harm to any who fled the community, beatings for noncompliance, and drugs to neutralize disagreeable members. By the end, he was as much an arm twister as a mind bender.

Still, cult techniques of social influence are disconcerting because of their power and their similarity to techniques used by groups more familiar to us. Fraternity and sorority members, for example, have reported that the initial "love bombing" of potential cult recruits is not unlike their own "rush" period, during which prospective pledges are lavished with warm attention and made to feel special. During the subsequent "pledge" period, new members are somewhat isolated, cut off from old friends who did not pledge. They spend time studying the history and rules of their new group, they suffer and commit time on its behalf, and they are expected to comply with all demands. Not surprisingly, the end result is usually a committed new member. Terrorist organizations, too, exploit some of these principles in recruiting and indoctrinating members (McCauley & Segal, 1987).

I chose the example of fraternities and sororities not to disparage them but to illustrate two concluding observations. First, if we attribute cult indoctrination to the leader's mystical force or to the followers' peculiar weaknesses, we may delude ourselves into thinking ourselves immune to such powers of social control. In truth, as the fraternity and sorority example suggests, our own groups—and countless salespeople, political leaders, and other persuaders—successfully use many of the same influence tactics on us. Second, that Jim Jones abused the power of persuasion does not mean that the power is itself intrinsically bad. Nuclear power can be used to light up homes or to blacken cities. Sexual power can be used to express and celebrate committed love or to use and abuse people for selfish gratification. Persuasive power can be used to enlighten or to deceive. That these powers can be exploited for evil purposes should warn us to guard against their immoral use. The powers themselves are neither inherently evil nor good. How we use them determines whether they are constructive or destructive.

RESISTING PERSUASION: ATTITUDE INOCULATION

I hope that recognizing how your attitudes can be manipulated has provoked you to consider how to *resist* unwanted persuasion. If, because of an aura of credibility, the repairperson's uniform and doctor's title have intimidated us into unquestioning agreement, we can rethink our habitual responses to authority. We can seek more information before committing our time or money. We can question what we don't understand.

STRENGTHENING PERSONAL COMMITMENTS

In Chapter 7, we saw another way to resist: Before encountering others' judgments, make a public commitment to your position. Once people have stood up for their convictions, they are less susceptible (or should we say less "open"?) to what others have to say.

Challenging Beliefs

How can people be stimulated to commit themselves in everyday situations? From his experiments, Charles Kiesler (1971) offers one possible way: Mildly attack their position. Kiesler found that when people who were already commited to a position were attacked strongly enough to cause them to react, but not so strongly as to overwhelm them, they became even more committed. Kiesler explains it this way:

> When you attack a committed person and your attack is of inadequate strength, you drive him to even more extreme behaviors in defense of his previous commitment. His commitment escalates, in a sense, because the number of acts consistent with his belief increases (p. 88).

Perhaps you can recall a time when this happened in an argument, as those involved escalated their rhetoric, committing themselves to increasingly extreme positions.

Developing Counterarguments

Inoculation:
Exposing people to weak attacks upon their attitudes, so that when stronger attacks come they will have refutations available.

"The SLA . . . read me news items they clipped from the newspapers almost every day. Some of their stories were indisputable, sometimes I did not know what to believe. It was all very confusing. I realized that my life prior to my kidnapping had indeed been very sheltered; I had taken little or no interest in foreign affairs, politics, or economics."
Patricia Campbell Hearst,
Every Secret Thing

There is a second reason why a mild attack might build resistance. Since people can resist persuasion by counterarguing, a mild attack can elicit counterarguments that will then be available should a stronger attack come. William McGuire (1964) documented this in a series of experiments on *attitude inoculation.* McGuire wondered: Could we inoculate people against persuasion much as we inoculate them against a virus? Consider what happens when you receive polio vaccine. You subject yourself to a weak polio virus, thus stimulating your body's defenses in preparation for a strong polio virus. Might a similar technique be used to ward off undesired persuasion? Could we take people raised in a "germ-free ideological environment"—people who hold some unquestioned belief—and stimulate their mental defenses by subjecting them to a small "dose" of belief-threatening material?

That is what McGuire did. First, he found some cultural truisms—statements people wholeheartedly agreed with, such as "It's a good idea to brush your teeth after every meal if at all possible." McGuire then found that people were vulnerable to a massive, credible assault upon these truisms (for example, prestigious authorities were said to have discovered that too much toothbrushing can damage one's gums). If, however, prior to having their belief attacked they were "immunized" by first receiving a small challenge to their belief, and if they read or wrote an essay in refutation of this mild attack, then they were better able to resist the subsequent powerful attack.

CASE STUDIES: LARGE-SCALE INOCULATION PROGRAMS

Inoculating Children Against Peer Pressure to Smoke

In a clear demonstration of how laboratory research findings can lead to practical application, a research team led by Alfred McAlister (1980) had high school students "inoculate" seventh graders against peer pressures to smoke. For example, the seventh graders were taught to respond to advertisements implying that liberated women smoke by saying, "She's not really liberated if she is hooked on tobacco." They also acted in role plays in which, for example, after being called "chicken" for not taking a cigarette, they answered with statements like "I'd be a real chicken if I smoked just to impress you." After several such sessions during the seventh and eighth grades, the inoculated students were half as likely to begin smoking as uninoculated students at a sister junior high school that had an identical parental smoking rate (see Figure 8-10).

Other research teams have confirmed that education-inoculation procedures can indeed substantially reduce the teenage smoking rate (Evans et al., 1984; Flay et al., 1985). Not only do their programs inoculate sixth or seventh graders against "dares" and other peer pressures to experiment with cigarettes, but they also package several other persuasive tactics, such as using attractive peers to communicate information, triggering the students' own cognitive processing ("Here's something you might want to think about"), and getting the students to make a public commitment (by making a rational decision about smoking and then announcing it, along with their reasoning, to their classmates). These smoking-prevention programs require only two to six one-hour class sessions, using prepared curricular materials or videotapes. Thus any school district or teacher wishing to implement the social-psychological approach to smoking

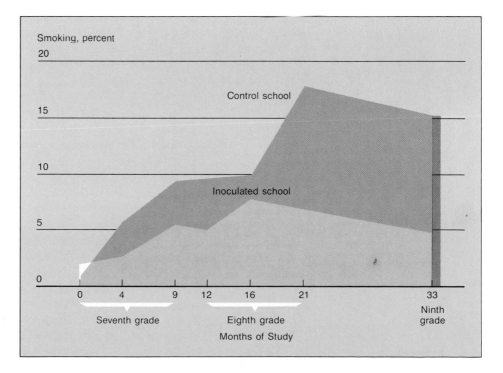

FIGURE 8-10
The percentage of cigarette smokers at an "inoculated" junior high school was much less than at a matched control school using a more typical smoking education program. (Data from McAlister et al., 1980; Telch et al., 1981.)

prevention can do so easily, inexpensively, and with the hope of significant reductions in future smoking rates and associated health costs.

Inoculating Children Against Advertising Influence

Researchers are also now studying how to immunize young children so they can more effectively analyze and evaluate television commercials. This research is prompted partly by studies indicating that children, especially those under eight years, (1) have trouble distinguishing commercials from programs and fail to grasp their persuasive intent, (2) trust television advertising rather indiscriminately, and (3) desire and badger their parents for whatever products are advertised (Adler et al., 1980; S. Feshbach, 1980; Palmer & Dorr, 1980). Children, it seems, are an advertiser's dream: the gullible, vulnerable, easy sell. Moreover, approximately half of the 20,000 ads the typical child sees in a year are for low-nutrition, often sugary foods. Armed with such data, citizens groups have given the advertisers of such products a chewing out (Moody, 1980): "When a sophisticated advertiser spends millions to sell unsophisticated, trusting children an unhealthy product, this can only be called exploitation. No wonder the consumption of dairy products has declined since the advent of television, while soft-drink consumption has almost doubled." On the other side are the commercial interests, who claim that such ads allow parents to teach their children consumer skills and, more important, finance children's television programs. In the United States, the Federal Trade Commission has been in the middle, pondering both research findings and political pressures while deciding whether to place new constraints on TV ads aimed at young children.

A currently debated question: What is the cumulative effect on children's materialism of witnessing some 350,000 commercials during their growing-up years?

Meanwhile, researchers have wondered whether children might be taught how to resist deceptive ads. In one such effort, a team of investigators led by Norma Feshbach (1980; S. Cohen, 1980) gave small groups of elementary school children in the Los Angeles area three half-hour lessons that sought to stimulate their abilities to analyze commercials. The children were inoculated by viewing ads and discussing them. For example, after viewing a toy ad they were immediately given the toy and challenged to make it do what they had just seen on the television. Such experiences helped breed a more realistic understanding of the credibility of certain commercials.

INOCULATION AND ITS IMPLICATIONS

This inoculation research also has some provocative implications. It suggests that the best way to build resistance to brainwashing may not be, as some senators thought after the Korean war, to introduce more courses on patriotism and Americanism. Teachers might be better advised, suggested McGuire, to inoculate—to challenge somewhat the concepts and principles of democracy, helping their students to develop defenses.

For the same reason, religious educators should be wary of creating a "germ-free ideological environment" in their churches and schools. For example, Daniel Batson (1975) observed that teenage churchgoers who rejected a belief-threatening message actually *intensified* their belief commitment. An attack refuted is apparently more likely to solidify one's position than to undermine it, particularly if the threatening material can be examined with some like-minded others. Cults apply this principle by forewarning members of how their families and friends will dispute the cult's beliefs. When the expected attack comes, the member is armed with counterarguments.

Another implication is that, for the persuader, an ineffective appeal can be worse than none at all. Why? Those who reject an appeal are thereby inoculated against

BEHIND THE SCENES

I confess to having felt like Mr. Clean when doing this immunization work because I was studying how to help people resist being manipulated. Then, after our research was published, an advertising executive called and said, "Very interesting, Professor: I was delighted to read about it." Somewhat righteously, I replied, "Very nice of you to say that Mr. Executive, but I'm really on the other side. You're trying to persuade people, and I'm trying to make them more resistant." "Oh, don't underrate yourself, Professor," he said. "We can use what you're doing to diminish the effect of our competitors' ads." And sure enough, it has become almost standard for advertisers to mention other brands and deflate their claims.

William McGuire, Yale University

further such appeals. This seemed evident in an experiment in which Susan Darley and Joel Cooper (1972) invited students to write essays advocating a strict dress code. Since this was against the students' own positions and the essays were to be published, all chose *not* to write the essay—even those offered money to do so. The interesting finding was that the students who turned down the money then became even more extreme and confident in their anti-dress-code opinions. Having now made an overt decision against the dress code, they became even more resistant to it. Similarly, those who have rejected initial appeals to quit smoking may become immune to further appeals. So it seems that ineffective persuasion, by stimulating the listener's defenses, may be counterproductive—"hardening the heart" against subsequent appeals.

Perhaps inoculation research has a personal implication, too. Do you want to build up your resistance to persuasion without becoming closed to valid messages? Be an active listener. Force yourself to counterargue. After hearing a political speech, discuss it with others. In other words, don't just listen; react. If the message cannot withstand careful analysis, so much the worse for it. If it can, its effect on you will be the more enduring for having done so.

Many children, especially those under age 8, have difficulty distinguishing commercials from television programs.

SUMMING UP

EFFECTIVE PERSUASION

What makes for effective persuasion? Four factors have been extensively researched: the communicator, the message, the channel by which the message is communicated, and the audience.

The Communicator

Credible communicators are perceived as trustworthy experts. People who speak unhesitatingly, who talk fast, and who look listeners straight in the eye are more credible. So also are people who are overheard without their knowledge or who argue against their own self-interest. An attractive communicator—for example, someone appealing or similar to the audience—also tends to be effective. An exception is when an unattractive communicator succeeds in getting people to do something unpleasant; because doing so cannot be justified by the attractiveness of the communicator, people may improve their opinion of the act to explain their compliance.

The Message

Emotional factors can play a role. Associating a message with the good feelings one has while eating, drinking, or listening to music makes it more convincing. Some types of messages that arouse fear can also be effective, perhaps because they are vivid and memorable.

How discrepant should a message be from the audience's existing opinions? That depends on the communicator's credibility. Highly credible people are able to elicit the greatest changes in opinion when they argue a relatively extreme position; less credible people are more successful when they advocate positions closer to those of the audience.

Is a message most persuasive when it presents only its position or when it introduces the opposing side as well? This depends on the listeners. When the audience already agrees with the message, is unaware of opposing arguments, and is unlikely later to be subjected to the opposition, then a one-sided appeal is most effective (although perhaps not most ethical). With more sophisticated audiences or with those not already agreeing, two-sided messages are most successful.

If two sides of an issue are to be presented, do the arguments presented first or second have the advantage? The most common finding is what is called a primacy effect: Information presented early is most potent, especially when it affects one's interpretation of the later information. However, if a time gap separates the two sides, the effect of the early information diminishes; if a decision is made right after hearing the second side, which is therefore still fresh in the mind, the result will likely be a recency effect.

The Channel

Another important consideration is *how* the message is communicated. Attitudes developed from actual experience are usually stronger than those shaped by appeals passively received. Nevertheless, although not as potent as face-to-face personal influence, the mass media can be effective when the issue is minor (such as which brand of aspirin to buy) or unfamiliar (such as deciding between two otherwise unknown political candidates). Some of the media's effect may, however, be transmitted in two steps: directly to opinion leaders and then on to others through their personal influence.

The Audience

Finally, it matters *who* receives the message. Traits such as intelligence bear no simple relation to persuasibility, apparently because a trait that contributes to one's receiving and comprehending a message will often work against yielding to it. More crucial is what the audience thinks while receiving a message. Do they think agreeing thoughts? Do they counterargue? Forewarning an audience that a disagreeable message is coming reduces persuasion by stimulating counterarguments. On the other hand, distracting people while they hear a disagreeable message can increase persuasion by interfering with their counterarguing. Highly involved or analytically minded people are more likely to be affected by the quality of the arguments than by peripheral cues such as the communicator's attractiveness.

The age of the audience also makes a difference. Researchers who have resurveyed people over time find that older people's attitudes are more stable. Apparently, we form most of our basic attitudes and values when young and then carry them through adulthood. As succeeding generations form new attitudes, generation gaps result.

CASE STUDIES IN PERSUASION: CULT INDOCTRINATION

The successes of religious cults, such as the Unification Church and the Peoples Temple, provide an opportunity to see powerful persuasion processes at work. It appears that their success has resulted partly by their eliciting behavior commitments (as described in Chapter 2), by applying principles of effective persuasion (this chapter), and by isolating members in like-minded groups (to be discussed in Chapter 9).

RESISTING PERSUASION: ATTITUDE INOCULATION

How do people resist persuasion? A prior public commitment to one's own position, stimulated perhaps by a mild attack on the position, breeds resistance to later persuasion. A mild attack can also serve as an inoculation, stimulating one's attitudinal defenses to develop counterarguments that will then be available if and when a strong attack comes. This implies, paradoxically, that one way to strengthen existing attitudes is to challenge them, though not so strongly as to overwhelm them.

FOR FURTHER READING

Cialdini, R. B. (1988). *Influence: Science and practice.* Glenview, IL: Scott, Foresman. A tremendously entertaining and informative description of how and why people agree to things. Cialdini explains how skillful car salespeople, Tupperware dealers, realtors, and cult recruiters exploit the "weapons of influence."

Petty, R. E., & Cacioppo, J. T. (1986). *Communication and persuasion: Central and peripheral routes to attitude change.* New York: Springer-Verlag. An important recent book on persuasion by two influential researchers; presents a theory that organizes many separate findings from attitude-change research.

CHAPTER

9

GROUP INFLUENCE

Our world contains not only 5 billion individuals, but also 200 nation-states, 4 million local communities, 20 million economic organizations, and hundreds of millions of other formal and informal groups—couples on dates, families, churches, housemates in bull sessions. How do such groups influence their individual members? Consider some concrete examples of the group influences studied by social psychologists:

- *Social facilitation:* Wanda is wearily nearing the end of her daily jog. Her head prods her to keep pushing it; her body begs her to walk it in. She compromises and slogs home. The next day's conditions are identical, except that a friend runs with her. Wanda runs her route two minutes faster. She wonders: "Wow! Did I run better merely because Gail was with me?"

- *Social loafing:* In a team tug-of-war, will eight people on a side exert as much force as the sum of their best efforts in individual tugs-of-war? A century ago, French engineer Max Ringelmann (reported by Kravitz & Martin, 1986) found that the collective effort of such teams was but half the sum of the individual efforts. Were the participants coasting on the group's effort? If so, does such loafing also occur in work groups or on team projects that are group graded?

- *Deindividuation:* In preparation for battle, warriors in some tribal cultures are depersonalized with body and face paints or special masks. After the battle, some cultures kill, torture, or mutilate any remaining enemies; other cultures take prisoners alive. Robert Watson (1973) scrutinized anthropological files and discovered that the cultures with depersonalized warriors are also the cultures that are brutal to the enemy. Are people in modern cultures ever depersonalized by their own groups? If so, how, and with what results?

- *Group polarization:* Educational researchers have detected a curious "accentuation phenomenon." Initial attitude differences among students in different colleges tend to become accentuated as they progress through college. Likewise, attitude differences between those who belong to a fraternity or a sorority and those who do not are modest at the freshman level, more pronounced in the senior year. Does this phenomenon occur because group interaction among like-minded people accentuates their initial leanings? If so, why?

- *Groupthink:* The executives of a soft-drink company enthusiastically discuss plans for their new asparagus-flavored soda pop. The group invites no contrary opinions and, because group members who harbor doubts hesitate to puncture the group's enthusiasm, the group deludes itself that all endorse the product and overestimates its probable success. In real social situations, do group influences often work against optimal decisions? If so, what group forces are hampering the decision making and how can they be avoided?

- *Minority influence:* The movie *12 Angry Men* opens at a murder trial as twelve wary jurors file into the juryroom. It is a hot day; they are tired, close to agreement, and eager for a quick verdict convicting a teenage boy of killing his father with a knife. But one maverick, played by Henry Fonda, refuses to vote guilty. As the heated deliberation proceeds, all the jurors, one by one, change their verdicts until consensus is reached: "Not guilty." In real juries, a lone individual seldom sways the entire group. Yet, history is made by minorities that sway majorities. What helps make a minority—or a leader—persuasive?

We will examine these seven intriguing phenomena of group influences one at a time. But first things first: What is a group, and why do groups exist?

WHAT IS A GROUP?

The answer seems self-evident—until several people compare their definitions. Are Wanda and her jogging partner a group? Are the passengers on an airplane a group? Is a group a set of people who identify with one another, who sense they belong to one another? Is it people who share common goals and rely on one another? Does a group form when a number of individuals become organized? When their relationships with one another continue over time? Such are among the characteristics that various social psychologists have used to define a group (McGrath, 1984).

Group:
Two or more people who, for longer than a few moments, interact with and influence one another, and perceive one another as "us."

Group dynamics expert Marvin Shaw (1981) argues that all groups have one thing in common: Their members interact. He therefore defines a ***group*** as two or more people who interact with and influence one another. Moreover, notes Australian social psychologist John Turner (1987), groups perceive themselves as "us" in contrast to "them." So Wanda and her jogging companion might indeed be considered a group. And most certainly the fraternity and sorority members and corporate decision makers would be members of groups. Such groups may exist for several reasons—to meet one's need to belong, to provide information, to supply rewards, to accomplish goals.

By Shaw's definition, the passengers on a routine airplane flight would seem *not* to be a group. Although physically together, they are more a collection of individuals than a true, interacting group. But the distinction between simple collective behavior among unrelated individuals on a plane and the more influential group behavior among interacting individuals sometimes blurs. For example, people who are merely in one another's presence do sometimes influence one another and may indeed perceive themselves as, say, "us" fans in contrast with "them" who root for the other team. In this chapter we will first consider three examples of such collective influence: social facilitation, social loafing, and deindividuation. These phenomena transpire in situations that involve minimal interaction and hence only border on group behavior. Then we will consider three examples of social influence in interacting groups: group polarization, groupthink, and minority influence. These phenomena indisputably involve group behavior.

SOCIAL FACILITATION

Let's begin with social psychology's most elementary question: How are we affected by the mere presence of other people? "Mere presence" means people are not competing, do not reward or punish, and in fact do nothing except be present as a passive audience or as ***co-actors.*** Would the mere presence of other people affect your jogging, eating, typing, or exam performance? The search for the answer is a delightful scientific mystery story.

Co-actors:
A group of people working simultaneously and individually on a noncompetitive task.

THE PRESENCE OF OTHERS CAN BOOST PERFORMANCE

Almost a century ago, Norman Triplett (1898), a psychologist interested in bicycle racing, noticed that cyclists' times were faster when racing together than when racing

The presence of others can boost well-learned performance.

alone against the clock. Before he peddled his hunch (that the presence of others boosts performance), Triplett conducted one of social psychology's early laboratory experiments. Children told to wind string on a fishing reel as rapidly as possible wound faster when they worked with co-actors than when working alone.

Subsequent experiments in the early decades of this century found that the presence of others also improves the speed with which people do simple multiplication problems and cross out designated letters, and improves the accuracy with which people perform simple motor tasks such as keeping a metal stick in contact with a dime-size disc on a moving turntable (F. W. Allport, 1920; Dashiell, 1930; Travis, 1925). This **social-facilitation** effect, as it came to be called, also occurs with animals. In the presence of others of their species, ants excavate more sand and chickens eat more grain (Bayer, 1929; Chen, 1937).

THE PRESENCE OF OTHERS CAN HURT PERFORMANCE

On the other hand, some studies conducted about the same time revealed that the presence of others could also hinder performance on certain tasks. In the presence of others, cockroaches, parakeets, and greenfinches learn mazes more slowly than when alone (Allee & Masure, 1936; Gates & Allee, 1933; Klopfer, 1958). This disruptive effect also occurs with people. The presence of others diminishes people's efficiency at learning nonsense syllables, completing a maze, and performing complex multiplication problems (Dashiell, 1930; Pessin, 1933; Pessin & Husband, 1933).

Saying that the presence of others sometimes facilitates performance and sometimes hinders it is about as satisfying as a weather forecast predicting that it might be sunny, but then again it might rain. Consequently, by 1940, research activity in this area fizzled. For twenty-five years it lay dormant until awakened by the touch of a new idea.

THE GENERAL RULE

Can these seemingly contradictory findings be reconciled by a general rule? Social psychologist Robert Zajonc (pronounced *Zy-ence*, rhymes with *science*), wondered. As often happens at creative moments in science, Zajonc (1965) used one field of research to illuminate another. In this case the illumination came from a well-established principle in experimental psychology: Arousal enhances whatever response tendency is dominant. That is, on easy tasks [for which the most likely ("dominant") response is the correct one], increased arousal enhances performance. People solve easy anagrams, such as *akec*, fastest when they are anxious. On complex tasks (for which the correct answer is not the dominant response), increased arousal promotes *in*correct responding. Thus on harder anagrams people do worse when anxious.

Could this principle solve the mystery of social facilitation? It seemed reasonable to presume that people are more aroused or energized in the presence of others. (Most of us can recall feeling more tense or excited when before an audience.) If social arousal facilitates dominant responses, it should boost performance on easy tasks and hurt performance on difficult tasks. Looking back at the confusing results, everything seemed to fit. Winding fishing reels, doing simple multiplication problems, and eating were all easy tasks for which the observed responses were well-learned or naturally dominant. And sure enough, having others around boosted performance. On the other hand, learning new material, doing a maze, or solving complex math problems were more difficult tasks for which the correct responses were initially less probable. And sure enough, the presence of others increased the number of *incorrect* responses on these tasks. The same general rule—arousal facilitates dominant responses—seemed to work in both cases. Suddenly, what had been assumed to be contradictory results were now recognized as not contradictory at all.

Zajonc's solution, so simple and elegant, left other social psychologists thinking what Thomas H. Huxley thought after first reading Darwin's *Origin of Species:* "How

Social facilitation:
(1) Original meaning—the tendency of people to perform simple or well-learned tasks better when others are present.
(2) Current meaning—the strengthening of dominant (prevalent, likely) responses due to the presence of others.

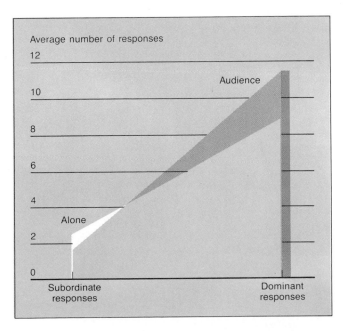

FIGURE 9-1

Social facilitation of dominant responses. People responded with dominant words (practiced sixteen times) more frequently, and subordinate words (practiced but once) less frequently, when observers were present. (Data from Zajonc & Sales, 1965.)

"Discovery consists of seeing what everybody has seen and thinking what nobody has thought."
Albert Axent-Gyorgyi,
The Scientist Speculates

extremely stupid not to have thought of that!" It seemed obvious—once Zajonc had pointed it out. Perhaps, however, the pieces appeared to merge so neatly only because they were being viewed through the spectacles of hindsight. Would the solution survive direct experimental tests?

Indeed, after almost 300 studies conducted with the help of more than 25,000 volunteer subjects, it has survived (Bond & Titus, 1983; Guerin, 1986). First, several experiments in which Zajonc and his associates manufactured an arbitrary dominant response confirmed that an audience enhanced this response. In one, Zajonc and Stephen Sales (1966) asked people to pronounce various nonsense words between one and sixteen times. The people were then told that the same words would be flashed on a screen, one at a time. Each time, they were to guess which had appeared. When the people were actually shown only random black lines for 1/100 second, they "saw" mostly the words they had pronounced most frequently. These words had become the dominant responses. Thus people who took the same test in the presence of two others were even more likely to guess the dominant words (see Figure 9-1).

Subsequent experiments have confirmed this effect—the facilitation of dominant responses—in various ways. Peter Hunt and Joseph Hillery (1973) found that in the presence of others, University of Akron students took less time to learn a simple maze and more time to learn one that was complex (just as the cockroaches did in the experiment previously cited). And James Michaels and his collaborators (1982) found that good pool players in the Virginia Polytechnic Institute student union (who had made 71 percent of their shots while being unobtrusively observed) did even better (80 percent) when four observers came up to watch them play. Poor shooters (who had previously averaged 36 percent) did even worse (25 percent) when closely observed.

We have seen that people do respond to the presence of others. But are people really aroused by the presence of observers? In times of stress, a comrade can be

The arousal created by a large number of spectators tends to enhance well-learned, automatic behaviors.

comforting. However, researchers have occasionally found that with others present, people perspire more, breathe faster, tense their muscles more, and have higher blood pressure and a faster heart rate (Geen & Gange, 1983; Moore & Baron, 1983).

CROWDING: THE PRESENCE OF MANY OTHERS

The effect of other people increases with their number (Jackson & Latane, 1981; Knowles, 1983). Sometimes the arousal and self-conscious attention created by a very large number of people interfere with well-learned, automatic behaviors such as speaking. Stutterers tend to stutter more in front of larger audiences than when speaking to just one or two people (Mullen, 1986). College basketball players have been observed to become slightly *less* accurate in their free-throw shooting when highly aroused by a packed fieldhouse (Sokoll & Mynatt, 1984). In baseball's World Series, home teams have won 60 percent of the first two games, but only 40 percent of the final games (Baumeister & Steinhilber, 1984). The arousal created by playing before the home fans helps to a point—two-thirds of college basketball games are won by the home team (Hirt & Kimble, 1981)—but when the pressure of a World Series final game is added, the home team players sometimes choke, and so have made double the number of fielding errors in final games as in games 1 and 2.

Being *in* a crowd also intensifies people's normally positive or negative reactions. Thus when they sit very close, friendly people are liked even more, *un*friendly people are *dis*liked even more (Schiffenbauer & Schiavo, 1976; Storms & Thomas, 1977). In experiments both with students at Columbia University and with visitors to the Ontario Science Center, Freedman and his co-workers (1979; 1980) had an accomplice listen to a humorous tape or watch a movie with other subjects. When all sat close together, the accomplice could more readily induce them to laugh and clap. As theater directors and sports fans know, and as other researchers have confirmed (Aiello et al., 1983; Worchel & Brown, 1984), a "good house" is a full house. Perhaps you've noticed that a class of thirty-five students feels more warm and lively in a room that seats just thirty-five than when spread around a room that seats 100. This occurs partly because when others are close by we are more likely to notice and join in their laughter or clapping. But crowding also enhances arousal, as Gary Evans (1979) found. He tested ten-person groups of University of Massachusetts students, either in a room 20 by 30 feet or in one 8 by 12 feet. Compared to those in the large room, those in the one densely packed had higher pulse rates and blood pressure (indicating arousal), and though their performance on simple tasks did not suffer, on difficult tasks they made more errors. In their study with university students in India, Dinesh Nagar and Janak Pandey (1987) similarly found that crowding hampered performance only on complex tasks, such as solving difficult anagrams.

WHY ARE WE AROUSED IN THE PRESENCE OF OTHERS?

To this point we have seen that what you do well, you will likely be energized to do best in front of others (unless you become hyperaroused and self-conscious). What you find difficult may seem impossible when others are watching. Deodorant producers certainly have capitalized on this social arousal. Their advertising depicts its bodily effect. What is it about other people that causes arousal? Is it their mere presence? The answers are still being debated. However, there is evidence to support three possible factors, each of which may play a role.

Evaluation Apprehension

Evaluation apprehension:
Concern for how others are
evaluating oneself.

Nickolas Cottrell surmised that observers make us apprehensive because we wonder how they are evaluating us. To test whether this *evaluation apprehension* exists, Cottrell and his associates (1968) repeated Zajonc and Sales's nonsense-syllable study at Kent State University and added a third condition. In this "mere presence" condition the observers, supposedly in preparation for a perception experiment, were blindfolded in order to prevent them from evaluating the subjects' performance. In contrast to the effect of the watching audience, the mere presence of these blindfolded people did *not* boost well-practiced responses. Other experiments confirmed Cottrell's conclusion: The enhancement of dominant responses is strongest when people think they are being evaluated. In one experiment, joggers on a University of California at Santa Barbara jogging path sped up as they came upon a woman seated on the grass—*if* she was facing them rather than sitting with her back turned (Worringham & Messick, 1983).

Evaluation apprehension also helps explain some other findings, such as why people perform best when their co-actor is slightly superior (Seta, 1982), why socially anxious people who worry about others' evaluations are the ones most affected by their presence (Gastorf et al., 1980; Geen & Gange, 1983), and why social facilitation effects are greatest when the others are unfamiliar and hard to keep an eye on (Guerin & Innes, 1982). The self-consciousness we feel when being evaluated by others can also interfere with behaviors that are best performed automatically—without thinking about how we're doing them (Mullen & Baumeister, 1987). If self-conscious basketball players analyze their body movements while shooting the game's critical free throws, they are more likely to miss.

Driven by Distraction

Glenn Sanders, Robert Baron, and Danny Moore (1978; Baron, 1986) carry evaluation apprehension a step further. They theorize that people who are concerned with how co-actors are doing on the task or how an audience is reacting get distracted from the task at hand. Their experiments suggest that this *conflict* between paying attention to others and paying attention to the task makes people even more aroused. Evidence that people are indeed "driven by distraction" comes from experiments in which social facilitation is produced not just by the presence of another person, but by even a nonhuman distraction, such as bursts of light (Sanders, 1981a; 1981b).

Mere Presence

Zajonc, however, believes that the mere presence of others does produce some arousal even when there exists no evaluation apprehension or conflict. For example, people's color preferences are stronger when they make judgments with others present (Goldman, 1967). On such a task, there is no "good" or "right" answer for others to evaluate, hence no reason to be concerned with their reactions.

The fact that facilitation effects also occur with animals, which probably are not consciously worrying about how other animals are evaluating them, hints at some type of innate social arousal mechanism running through much of the zoological world. I think that Wanda, our jogger, would agree. Most joggers feel energized when jogging with someone else, even one who neither competes nor evaluates.

This is a good time to remind ourselves of the purpose of a theory. As we noted in Chapter 1, a good theory is a scientific shorthand: It simplifies and summarizes a

FIGURE 9-2
In the "open office plan" people work in the presence of others. How might this affect worker efficiency? (Photo courtesy of Herman Miller Inc.)

variety of observations. Social facilitation theory does this well. It is a simple summary of many research findings. A good theory also offers clear predictions that can be used (1) to confirm or modify the theory, (2) to generate new exploration, and (3) to suggest practical application. Social facilitation theory has definitely generated the first two types of prediction: (1) the basics of the theory (that the presence of others is arousing, and that this social arousal enhances dominant responses) have been confirmed, and (2) the theory has brought new life to a long dormant field of research. Does it also suggest (3) some practical applications?

Application is properly the last phase of research. In their study of social facilitation, researchers have yet to work much on this. That gives us the opportunity to speculate on what some applications might be. For example, as Figure 9-2 illustrates, many new office buildings are replacing private offices with large, open areas divided by low partitions. Might the resulting awareness of others' presence help energize the performance of well-learned tasks, but disrupt creative thinking on complex tasks? Can you think of other possible applications?

SOCIAL LOAFING

The social facilitation effect we've been examining usually occurs in situations where people are working toward individual goals and where their efforts, whether winding fishing reels or solving math problems, can be individually evaluated. These situations parallel some everyday work situations, but not those situations that require cooperative effort, where people pool their efforts toward a *common* goal and where individuals are *not* accountable for their efforts. A team tug-of-war provides one such example. The effects of organizational fund-raising might well be another. People on a work crew might be yet another. On such "additive tasks"—tasks where the group's achievement depends on the sum of the individual efforts—will team spirit boost productivity? Will bricklayers lay bricks faster when working as a team than when working alone?

One way to attack a question such as this is with laboratory simulations. Like the aeronautical engineer's wind tunnel, a controlled miniature reality can enable researchers to isolate and study important variables.

MANY HANDS MAKE LIGHT WORK

Contrary to the common notion that "in unity there is strength," the tug-of-war experiment mentioned on p. 270 suggested that group members may actually be *less* motivated when performing additive tasks. However, Ivan Steiner (1972) noticed a problem with the tug-of-war experiment. Perhaps the group's poor performance stemmed from poor coordination—people pulling in slightly different directions at slightly different times. A group of Massachusetts researchers led by Alan Ingham (1974) cleverly eliminated this problem by making individuals think others were pulling with them, when in fact they were pulling alone. Blindfolded participants assigned the first position in the apparatus shown in Figure 9-3 and told to "pull as hard as you can" pulled 18 percent harder when they knew they were pulling alone than when they believed that behind them from two to five people were also pulling.

At Ohio State University, researchers Bibb Latané, Kipling Williams, and Stephen Harkins (1979; Harkins et al., 1980) kept their ears open for other ways to investigate this phenomenon, which they labeled **social loafing.** They observed that the noise produced by six people shouting or clapping "as loud as you can" was less than three times that produced by one person alone. However, like the tug-of-war task, noise-making is vulnerable to group inefficiency. So Latané and his associates followed Ingham's example by leading participants to believe others were shouting or clapping with them, when in fact they were doing so alone.

Their method was to blindfold six people, seat them in a semicircle, and have them put on headphones, over which they were blasted with the sound of people shouting or clapping. People could not even hear their own shouting or clapping, much less that of others. On various trials they were instructed to shout or clap either alone or along with the group. Other people told about the experiment guessed the subjects would shout louder when with others, because they would be less embarrassed (Harkins, 1981). The actual result? Once again, social loafing: When the participants believed five others were also either shouting or clapping, they produced one-third less noise than

Social loafing:
The tendency for people to exert less effort when they pool their efforts toward a common goal than when they are individually accountable.

FIGURE 9-3
The rope-pulling apparatus. People in the first position pulled less hard when they thought people behind them were also pulling. (Data from Ingham, Levinger, Graves, & Peckham, 1974.) (Photo by Alan G. Ingham.)

when they thought themselves alone. It is interesting that those who clapped both alone and in groups did not view themselves as loafing; they perceived themselves clapping equally in both situations. This cheering effect even occurs when the subjects are high school cheerleaders who believe themselves to be cheering together or alone (Hardy & Latané, 1986).

John Sweeney (1973), a political scientist interested in the policy implications of social loafing, obtained similar results in an experiment at the University of Texas. He found that students pumped exercise bicycles more energetically (as measured by electrical output) when they knew they were being individually monitored than when they thought their output was being pooled with that of other riders. In the group condition, people were tempted to ***free ride*** on the group effort.

In this and some four dozen other studies (see Figure 9-4), we see a twist on one of the psychological forces that contributes to the social facilitation effect: evaluation apprehension. In the experiments dealing with social loafing, individuals believe they are evaluated only when acting alone. The group situation (rope pulling, shouting, and so forth) *decreases* evaluation apprehension; when individuals are not accountable and cannot evaluate their own efforts, responsibility is diffused across all group members (Kerr & Bruun, 1981; Harkins & Jackson, 1985). By contrast, the social facilitation experiments *increased* the individual's vulnerability to evaluation. When made the center of attention, people more self-consciously monitor their behavior (Mullen & Baumeister, 1987). Similar effects of self-attentiveness can occur when people evaluate themselves compared with some standard, such as how other people are doing (Harkins & Szymanski, 1987, 1988). So the principle is the same: when being observed *increases* evaluation concerns, social facilitation occurs; when being lost in a crowd *decreases* evaluation concerns, social loafing occurs.

To motivate group members, one strategy is therefore to make their performances

Free riders:
People who benefit from the group but give little in return.

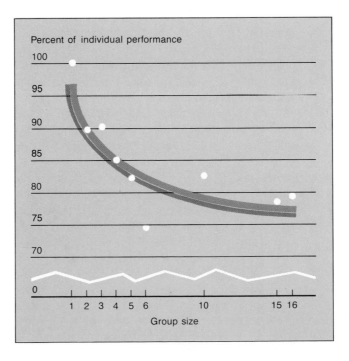

FIGURE 9-4
A statistical digest of forty-nine studies involving more than 4000 participants, revealed that effort decreases (loafing increases) as the size of the group increases. Each dot represents the aggregate data from one of these studies. (From Jackson & Williams, 1988.)

individually identifiable. Some football coaches do this by individually filming and evaluating each lineman. The Ohio State researchers did the same by having group members wear individual microphones while engaged in group shouting (Williams et al., 1981). They found that, whether they were in a group or not, people exerted more effort when their outputs were individually identifiable.

SOCIAL LOAFING IN EVERYDAY LIVING

How widespread is social loafing? In the laboratory, the phenomenon has been observed not only among people who are pulling ropes, cycling, shouting, and clapping, but also among those who are pumping water or air, evaluating poems or editorials, producing ideas, typing, and detecting signals. But can the results of these experiments be generalized to worker productivity in everyday situations? We can, at this point, only speculate, noting situations that at least superficially parallel the laboratory phenomenon.

On their collective farms, Russian peasants have worked one field one day, another field the next, with little direct responsibility for any given plot. For their own use, they were given small private plots. In one analysis, the private plots occupied but 1 percent of the agricultural land yet produced 27 percent of the Soviet farm output (H. Smith, 1976). In Hungary, private plots account for only 13 percent of the farmland, but have produced one-third of the produce (Spivak, 1979). In China, where farmers are now allowed to sell food grown in excess of that owed to the state, food production has been increasing 8 percent a year since 1978—2½ times the rate in the preceding 26 years (Church, 1986).

In America, workers who do not pay dues or volunteer time to their union or professional association nevertheless are usually happy to accept its benefits. This hints at another possible explanation of social loafing. When rewards are divided equally, regardless of how much one contributes to the group, any individual gets more reward per unit of effort by free riding on the group. Hence, people may be motivated to slack off when their efforts are not individually monitored and rewarded. In a pickle factory the key job is picking the right size dill-pickle halves off the conveyor belt and stuffing them in jars. Unfortunately, workers are temped to stuff any size pickle in, since their output is not identifiable (the jars go into a common hopper before reaching the quality-control section). Williams, Harkins, and Latané (1981) note that research on social loafing suggests "making individual production identifiable, and raises the question: 'How many pickles could a pickle packer pack if pickle packers were only paid for properly packed pickles?' "

But surely, collective effort does not always lead group members to slack off. Sometimes the goal is so compelling, and maximum output from everyone is so essential, that team spirit can at least maintain effort if not intensify it. In an Olympic crew race, will the individual rowers in an eight-person crew pull their oars with less effort than those in a one- or two-person crew? In the Hope College class rope pulling competition pictured at the front of this chapter does social loafing occur? My hunch is not. Similarly, Latané notes that Israel's communal kibbutz farms have actually outproduced Israel's noncollective farms (Leon, 1969), and Williams (1981) and Loren Davis and his associates (1984) report that groups of friends loaf less (if they loaf at all) than do groups of strangers. Perhaps, then, the cohesiveness of the kibbutz organization somehow intensifies effort. If so, then will social loafing not occur in less individualistic, more group-centered cultures? To find out, Latané and his co-researchers headed for

Social loafing: People who pool their efforts toward a common goal without being individually accountable tend to exert less effort than when performing the same task alone.

Asia where they repeated their sound production experiments in Japan, Thailand, Taiwan, India, and Malaysia. Their findings? Social loafing was evident in all these countries, too.

Other experiments show that people in groups loaf less when the task is *challenging, appealing,* or *involving* (Brickner et al., 1986; Jackson & Williams, 1985). On challenging tasks, people may perceive their efforts as indispensable—a perception known to minimize loafing (Harkins & Petty, 1982; Kerr, 1983; Kerr & Bruun, 1983). People will also work near their maximum if they believe fellow group members are doing likewise (Zaccaro, 1984).

Some of these findings parallel those from studies of everyday work groups. When groups are given challenging objectives, when they are rewarded for group success, and when there is a spirit of commitment to the "team," group members tend to work hard (Hackman, 1986). So while social loafing is a common occurrence when group members work collectively and without individual accountability, many hands need not always make light work.

DEINDIVIDUATION

DOING TOGETHER WHAT WE WOULD NOT DO ALONE

Experiments on social facilitation indicate that groups can arouse people. Social loafing experiments indicate that groups can diffuse responsibility. When high levels of arousal are combined with diffused responsibility, one's normal inhibitions may diminish. The result may be acts ranging from a mild lessening of restraint (throwing food in the dining hall, snarling at a referee, screaming during a rock concert) to impulsive self-gratification (group vandalism, orgies, thefts) to destructive social explosions (riots, lynchings, torturings). In a 1967 incident, 200 University of Oklahoma students gathered to watch a disturbed fellow student threatening to jump from a tower. They began to chant "Jump. Jump. . . ." The student jumped to his death (UPI, 1967).

Deindividuation:
Loss of self-awareness and evaluation apprehension; occurs in group situations that foster anonymity and draw attention away from the individual.

"*A mob is a society of bodies voluntarily bereaving themselves of reason.*"
Ralph Waldo Emerson,
"Compensation," Essays, First Series

One thing these unrestrained behaviors have in common is that they are somehow provoked by the power of a group. It is hard to imagine a single rock fan screaming deliriously at a private rock concert, or a single Oklahoma student trying to coax someone to suicide. In group situations people are more likely to abandon their normal restraints, to lose their sense of individuality, to become what Leon Festinger, Albert Pepitone, and Theodore Newcomb (1952) labeled **deindividuated.** What circumstances elicit this psychological state?

A Group

A group not only has the power to arouse its members, but also to render them unidentifiable. The snarling crowd protects the snarling basketball fan from accountability. A lynch mob enables its members to believe that they will not be prosecuted; the action is perceived as the *group's*. Rioters, made faceless by the mob, are freed to loot. In an analysis of twenty-one instances in which crowds were present as someone threatened to jump from a building or bridge, Leon Mann (1981) found that when the crowd was small and exposed by daylight, people usually did not try to bait the person. But when a large crowd or the cover of night gave people anonymity, the crowd usually baited and jeered. Brian Mullen (1986) reports a similar effect of lynch mobs: The bigger the mob, the more its members lose self-awareness and become willing to commit atrocities, such as burning, lacerating, or dismembering the victim. In each of these examples, from sports crowds to lynch mobs, evaluation apprehension plummets. And because "everyone is doing it," all can attribute their behavior to the situation rather than to their own choices.

Philip Zimbardo (1970) speculated that the mere immensity of crowded cities contributes to anonymity and thus to norms that permit vandalism. He once purchased two 10-year-old cars and left them with the hoods up and license plates removed, one on a street near the old Bronx campus of New York University and one near the Stanford University campus in Palo Alto, a much smaller city. In New York the first auto strippers arrived within ten minutes, taking the battery and radiator. After three days and twenty-three incidents of theft and vandalism by neatly dressed White people, the car was reduced to a battered, useless hulk of metal. By contrast, the only person observed to touch the Palo Alto car in over a week was a passerby who lowered the hood when it began to rain.

Physical Anonymity

How can we be sure that the crucial difference between the Bronx and Palo Alto is greater anonymity in the Bronx? We can't. But we can experiment with anonymity to see if it actually lessens inhibitions. In one such experiment, Zimbardo (1970) dressed New York University women in identical white coats and hoods, making them resemble members of the Ku Klux Klan (see Figure 9-5). Asked to deliver electric shocks to a woman, they pressed the shock button twice as long as did women who were visible and wearing large name tags.

A research team led by Edward Diener (1976) cleverly demonstrated the effect both of being in a group *and* of being physically anonymous. At Halloween, they observed 1352 Seattle children trick-or-treating. As the children, either alone or in groups, approached one of twenty-seven homes scattered throughout the city, an experimenter greeted them warmly, invited them to "take *one* of the candies," and then left the room. Hidden observers noted that children in groups were more than twice

FIGURE 9-5
Anonymous, although obviously poised, women delivered more shock to helpless victims than did identifiable women. (Photo courtesy of Philip Zimbardo.)

as likely to take extra candy as those alone. Also, children left anonymous were more than twice as likely to transgress as those who had been asked their names and where they lived. The transgression rate thus varied dramatically with the situation, from 8 percent among children alone and identified up to 80 percent among anonymous children.

These experiments make me wonder about the effect of wearing uniforms. In Zimbardo's prison simulation the guards and prisoners were dressed in depersonalizing common outfits (see Chapter 6). Did this contribute to the depraved behavior that followed? Recall, too, the discovery by Robert Watson that warriors wearing depersonalizing masks or face paints treat their victims more brutally. Does becoming physically anonymous always unleash our worst impulses?

Fortunately, no. For one thing, the situations in which some of these experiments took place had clear antisocial cues. Robert Johnson and Leslie Downing (1979) point out that the Klan-like outfits worn by Zimbardo's subjects may have been cues that encouraged hostility. So, in an experiment at the University of Georgia, they had women put on nurses' uniforms before deciding how much shock someone should receive. When those wearing the nurses' uniforms were made anonymous, they became *less* aggressive in administering shock than when their names and personal identities were stressed. Evidently being anonymous makes one less self-conscious and more responsive to cues present in the situation, whether negative (for example, Klan uniforms) or positive (for example, nurses' uniforms).

This helps explain why wearing black uniforms—which are traditionally associated with evil and death—can have an effect opposite to that of wearing a nurse's uniform. Mark Frank and Thomas Gilovich (1988) report that, led by the Los Angeles Raiders and the Philadelphia Flyers, black-uniformed teams consistently ranked near the top of the National Football and Hockey Leagues in penalties assessed between 1970 and 1986. Their follow-up laboratory research suggests that just putting on a black jersey can trigger aggressive behavior.

Even if anonymity does unleash our impulses, as well as make us more responsive to social cues, we must remember that not all our impulses are sinister. Consider the heart-warming outcome of an experiment conducted by Swarthmore College researchers Kenneth Gergen, Mary Gergen, and William Barton (1973). Imagine that, as a subject in this experiment, you are ushered through double doors into a totally darkened environmental chamber, where you will spend the next hour (unless you choose to leave) with seven strangers of both sexes. You are told that "There are no rules as to what you should do together. At the end of the time period you will be escorted from the room alone, and will subsequently depart from the experimental site alone. There will be no opportunity to [formally] meet the other participants."

Control participants, who spent the hour in a lighted room with more conventional expectations, chose simply to sit and converse the whole time. By contrast, the experience of being anonymous in the dark room with unclear expectations "unleashed" intimacy and affection. People in the dark talked less, but they talked more about "important" things. Ninety percent purposefully touched someone; 50 percent hugged another. Few disliked the anonymity; most deeply enjoyed it and volunteered to return without pay. Anonymity had "freed up" intimacy and playfulness.

Activities that Arouse and Distract

Aggressive outbursts by large groups are often preceded by minor actions that arouse and divert people's attention. Group shouting, chanting, clapping, or dancing serve both to hype people up and to reduce their self-consciousness. One Moonie observer recalls how the "choo-choo" chant helped deindividuate:

> All the brothers and sisters joined hands and chanted with increasing intensity, choo-choo-choo, Choo-choo-choo, CHOO-CHOO-CHOO! YEA! YEA! POWW!!! The act made us a group, as though in some strange way we had all experienced something important together. The power of the choo-choo frightened me, but it made me feel more comfortable and there was something very relaxing about building up the energy and releasing it. (Zimbardo et al., 1977, p. 186)

In William Golding's (1962) *Lord of the Flies*, a group of marooned boys gradually descended into savagery. The boys sometimes preceded their savage acts by group activities, such as dancing in a circle and chanting "*Kill the beast! Cut his throat! Spill his blood!*" By so doing, the group became "a single organism" (p. 182).

Edward Diener's experiments (1976; 1979) at the University of Washington and the University of Illinois have shown that such activities as throwing rocks and group singing can set the stage for more disinhibited behavior. There is a self-reinforcing pleasure in doing an impulsive act while observing others doing it also. For one thing, when we see others act as we are acting, we may think they feel as we do, and so be reinforced in our own feelings (Orive, 1984). Moreover, impulsive group action absorbs our attention. When we yell at the referee we are not thinking about our values; we are reacting to the immediate situation. Consequently, when we stop to think about what we have done or said, we sometimes feel chagrined. Sometimes. Not always. For at other times we intentionally seek deindividuating group experiences—dances, worship experiences, group encounters—where we can enjoy intense positive feelings and a sense of closeness with others.

"The use of self-control is like the use of brakes on a train. It is useful when you find yourself going in the wrong direction, but merely harmful when the direction is right."
Bertrand Russell,
Marriage and Morals

"Attending a service in the Gothic cathedral, we have the sensation of being enclosed and steeped in an integral universe, and of losing a prickly sense of self in the community of worshippers."
Yi-Fu Tuan (1982, p. 127)

As in *Lord of the Flies*, group shouting, chanting, clapping, or dancing both hype people up and reduce their self-consciousness, turning them into a "single organism."

DEINDIVIDUATION AS DIMINISHED SELF-AWARENESS

Group experiences that diminish people's self-consciousness tend to disconnect their behavior from their attitudes. Experiments by Steven Prentice-Dunn and Ronald Rogers (1980, 1989) and Ed Diener (1980) reveal that unself-conscious, deindividuated people are less restrained, less self-regulated, more likely to act without thinking about their own values, more responsive to the immediate situation. These findings complement and reinforce the experiments on *self-awareness* considered in Chapters 2 and 3. Self-awareness is the other side of the coin from deindividuation. Those made self-aware, say by acting in front of a mirror or TV camera, exhibit *increased* self-control, and their actions are more strongly rooted in their attitudes. People made self-aware are less likely to cheat when given a convenient chance to do so (Diener & Wallbom, 1976; Beaman et al., 1979), as are those who generally have a strong sense of themselves as distinct and independent (Nadler et al., 1982). People who are self-conscious, or who are made so, exhibit greater consistency between their words outside a situation and their deeds in it.

Therefore, we may expect that circumstances that diminish self-awareness (as alcohol consumption does—Hull et al., 1983) will increase deindividuation. On the other hand, deindividuation should be lessened by circumstances that increase self-awareness: mirrors and cameras, small towns, bright lights, large name tags, undistracted quiet, individual clothes and houses (Ickes et al., 1978). When a teenager leaves for a party a parent's parting advice could well be, "Have fun, and remember who you are"—in other words, enjoy the group, but be self-aware; don't become deindividuated.

GROUP POLARIZATION

Which effects—good or bad—does group interaction more often have? On the one hand, mob violence demonstrates the destructive potential of groups. On the other, group therapists, management consultants, and educational theorists proclaim the benefits of group experiences, and leaders of social and religious movements urge their followers to strengthen their identities by fellowship with like-minded others.

Recent research helps clarify our understanding of such effects. From studies of people in small groups, a principle has emerged that helps explain both apparently destructive and constructive outcomes: In general, group discussion strengthens group members' initial inclinations, good or bad—a phenomenon called "group polarization." The unfolding of this research literature illustrates beautifully the very process of inquiry—how an interesting discovery often leads researchers to hasty and erroneous conclusions, which are ultimately replaced with better conclusions and new ideas for research. This research on group polarization is one scientific mystery I can discuss firsthand, having been one of the detectives. So let us take the story from the beginning.

THE STORY BEGINS: "RISKY SHIFT"

A research literature of more than 300 studies originated in a surprising finding by James Stoner (1961), then an MIT graduate student. For his master's thesis in industrial management, Stoner decided to compare risk-taking by individuals and groups. He wanted to test the commonly held belief that groups are more cautious than individuals. Stoner's procedure, which was followed in dozens of later experiments, posed some decision dilemmas to people by themselves. Each problem described a decision faced by a fictional character. The participant's task was to advise the character how much risk to take. Put yourself in the participant's shoes: What advice would you give the character in this item?

> Henry is a writer who is said to have considerable creative talent but who so far has been earning a comfortable living by writing cheap westerns. Recently he has come up with an idea for a potentially significant novel. If it could be written and accepted it might have considerable literary impact and be a big boost to his career. On the other hand, if he is not able to work out his idea or if the novel is a flop, he will have expended considerable time and energy without remuneration.
>
> Imagine that you are advising Henry. Please check the *lowest* probability that you would consider acceptable for Henry to attempt to write the novel.
>
> Henry should attempt to write the novel if the chances that the novel will be a success are at least:
> _____ 1 in 10
> _____ 2 in 10
> _____ 3 in 10
> _____ 4 in 10
> _____ 5 in 10
> _____ 6 in 10
> _____ 7 in 10
> _____ 8 in 10
> _____ 9 in 10

_____ 10 in 10 (Place a check here if you think Henry should attempt the novel only if it is certain that the novel will be a success.)

After making your decision, guess what the average reader of this book would advise.

After marking their advice on a dozen items similar to this one, five or so individuals would then gather in a group to discuss and reach agreement on each item. How do you suppose the group decisions compared to the average of the decisions made prior to the discussions? Were the groups likely to take greater risks? Were they more cautious? About the same?

Much to everyone's amazement, the decisions chosen by the group were by and large *riskier* than those selected before discussion. This finding was immediately dubbed the "risky shift" phenomenon, and it set off a wave of investigations into group risk-taking. These studies revealed that this effect occurs not only when a group makes a unanimous decision; after a brief discussion individuals, too, will alter their decisions. What is more, Stoner's finding was successfully repeated in a dozen different nations with people of varying ages and occupations.

People's opinions did converge during discussion. However, it was curious that the point toward which they converged was usually a lower (riskier) number than their initial average. Here was a delightful puzzle, for the risky shift effect, while not huge, was nevertheless reliable, unexpected, and without any immediately obvious explanation. What group influences produce such an effect? And how widespread is the effect? Do discussions in juries, business committees, and military organizations also tend to promote risk-taking?

After about five years of speculation and research on groups being more prone to take risks, indications surfaced that the risky shift was not as universal as first thought. One could write decision dilemmas that did *not* yield a reliable risky shift, or on which people even became more *cautious* after discussion. One such dealt with "Roger," a young married man with two school-age children and a secure but low-paying job. Roger can afford life's necessities, but few of its luxuries. He hears that the stock of a relatively unknown company may soon either triple in value, if its new product is favorably received, or decline considerably if it does not sell. Roger has no savings. So in order to invest in the company, he is considering selling his life insurance policy.

Is there a general principle that will predict both the tendency to give riskier advice after discussing Henry's situation, and more cautious advice after discussing Roger's? Yes. If you are like most, you would likely advise Henry to take greater risk than Roger, even before talking with others. It turns out that there is a strong tendency for discussion to accentuate these initial leanings.

Investigators therefore began to realize that this group phenomenon was *not*, as originally assumed, a consistent shift to risk, but perhaps rather a tendency for group discussion to *enhance* the group's initial leanings. This idea led investigators to postulate a ***group polarization*** phenomenon: The average inclination of group members before discussion is generally strengthened by discussion.

Group polarization:
Group-produced enhancement of members' preexisting tendencies. Refers to a strengthening of the members' *average* tendency, not to a split within the group.

DO GROUPS INTENSIFY OPINIONS?

Experiments on Group Polarization

This new view of the changes induced by discussion prompted experimenters to have people discuss statements that most of them favored or most of them opposed. Will

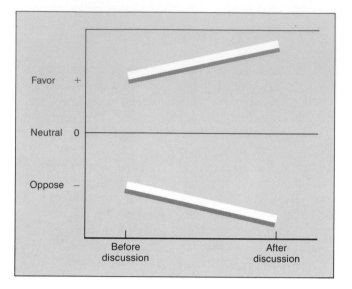

FIGURE 9-6
The group-polarization hypothesis predicts that an attitude shared by group members will usually be strengthened by discussion. For example, if people initially tend to favor risk on a life dilemma question (such as that concerning Henry), they tend to favor it even more after discussion. If initially they tend to oppose risk (as in the case of Roger's decision about selling his life insurance), they tend to oppose it even more after discussion.

talking in groups enhance their initial inclinations as it did with the decision dilemmas? The group polarization hypothesis predicts that, yes, the initial average position will be strengthened (see Figure 9-6).

Group polarization has been confirmed in dozens of studies. For example, Serge Moscovici and Marisa Zavalloni (1969) observed that discussion enhanced French students' initially positive attitude toward their Premier and negative attitude toward Americans. Likewise, Mititoshi Isozaki (1984) found that the guilty verdicts that Japanese university students were inclined to give in a traffic accident case became even stronger after they discussed the case.

Another research strategy has been to pick issues on which opinions are divided and then isolate people who hold the same view. Does discussion with like-minded people strengthen their shared views? Does it magnify the attitude gap that separates them from those on the other side of the issue?

George Bishop and I decided to pursue this question. We set up groups of relatively prejudiced and unprejudiced high school students and asked them to respond—both before and after discussion—to issues involving racial attitudes, such as property rights versus open housing (Myers & Bishop, 1970). We found that the discussions among like-minded students did indeed increase the initial gap between the two groups (see Figure 9-7).

Naturally Occurring Group Polarization

There is plenty of evidence that in everyday life people associate mostly with others whose attitudes are similar to their own (see Chapter 13). Most of us need only look at our circle of friends to illustrate this point. So, does group interaction in everyday situations also intensify shared attitudes? In naturally occurring events, it is difficult to disentangle cause and effect, but the laboratory phenomenon does seem to have real-life parallels.

One such parallel is what education researchers call the "accentuation phenomenon": Initial differences among college-student groups are accentuated with time in

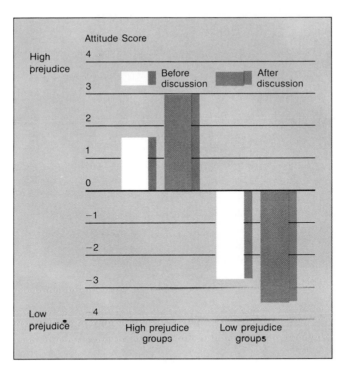

FIGURE 9-7
Discussion increased polarization between homogeneous groups of high- and low-prejudice high school students. (Data from Myers and Bishop, 1970.)

college. For instance, if the students at college X are initially more intellectual than the students at college Y, that difference will likely expand as they progress through college. Researchers believe this results partly from group members reinforcing their shared inclinations (Feldman & Newcomb, 1969; Chickering & McCormick, 1973; Wilson et al., 1975).

Another parallel comes from observations of societal polarization. During community conflicts, like-minded people increasingly associate with one another, thus amplifying their shared tendencies. Similarly, investigators of gang delinquency have observed a process of mutual reinforcement within neighborhood gangs whose members have a common socioeconomic and ethnic background (Cartwright, 1975). From their analysis of terrorist organizations around the world, Clark McCauley and Mary

GROUP POLARIZATION

Shakespeare portrayed the polarizing power of the like-minded group in this dialogue of Julius Caesar's followers:

ANTONY: Kind souls, what weep you when you but behold Our Caesar's vesture wounded? Look you here, Here is himself, marr'd, as you see, with traitors.

Note: From *Julius Caesar* by William Shakespeare, Act III, Scene III, ll. 199–209.

FIRST CITIZEN: O piteous spectacle!

SECOND CITIZEN: O noble Caesar!

THIRD CITIZEN: O woeful day!

FOURTH CITIZEN: O traitors, villains!

FIRST CITIZEN: O most bloody sight!

SECOND CITIZEN: We will be revenged!

ALL: Revenge! About! Seek! Burn! Fire! Kill! Slay! Let not a traitor live!

Segal (1987) note that terrorism does not erupt suddenly. Rather, it arises among people whose shared grievances bring them together. As they interact in isolation from moderating influences, they become progressively more extreme.

EXPLAINING GROUP POLARIZATION

Why polarization takes place at all became a tantalizing puzzle for a number of social psychologists: Why do groups of people seem to adopt stances more exaggerated than the average opinions of their individual members? Researchers hoped that solving the mystery of group polarization might provide new insights into social influence. Solving small puzzles sometimes provides clues for solving larger ones.

Among several proposed theories of group polarization, two have survived scientific scrutiny. One deals with the arguments presented during a discussion, the other with how members of a group view themselves vis-à-vis the other members. Recalling two important concepts introduced in Chapter 7, the first idea is an example of informational influence (influence that results from accepting evidence about reality), the second of normative influence (influence based on a person's desire to be accepted or admired by a group).

Informational Influence

According to the best supported explanation, group discussion elicits a pooling of ideas, most of which favor the dominant viewpoint. These ideas may include persuasive arguments that some group members had not previously considered. When discussing Henry the writer, for example, someone may cogently observe that "Henry should go for it, because he has little to lose—if his novel flops he can always go back to writing cheap westerns." But such statements combine information about the person's *arguments* regarding the issue with cues concerning the person's *position* on the issue. Disentangling these two factors, it has been found that when people hear relevant arguments without learning the specific stands that other people assume, they still shift their positions (Burnstein & Vinokur, 1977; Hinsz & Davis, 1984). *Arguments*, in and of themselves, are apparently a principal factor in polarizing attitudes.

Researchers have also found that *active verbal participation* in discussion elicits more changes in attitude than does passive listening. Both participants and observers hear the same ideas, but when participants put them into their own words the resulting verbal commitment seems to magnify the impact of the discussion. This finding parallels attitude research showing that people remember best and are most influenced by a message if they have actively put it in their own words (Greenwald, 1978; Tesser, 1978). It also illustrates a point made in Chapter 8: People's minds are not just blank tablets for persuaders to write on; what people *think* in response to a message is crucial. Indeed, just thinking about an issue for a couple minutes can make people's opinions more emphatic (Millar & Tesser, 1986). Even just *expecting* to discuss an issue with an equally expert person of an opposing view can motivate people to marshal their arguments, and thus to adopt an even more extreme position (Fitzpatrick & Eagly, 1981).

Normative Influence

In the second explanation of polarization, social comparison with others plays an important role. As Leon Festinger (1954) argued in his influential theory of *social com-*

Social comparison:
Evaluating one's opinions and abilities by comparing oneself to others.

parison, it is human nature to want to evaluate our opinions and abilities, something we can do by comparing our views with those held by other people like ourselves. Moreover, people want to be perceived favorably, so they may express stronger opinions if they discover that other people share their views more than they had supposed.

Perhaps you can recall a time when you and others were guarded and reserved in a group, until someone broke the ice and said, "Well, to be perfectly honest, I think . . . ," and soon you were all surprised to discover strong support for views you had each assumed were not widely shared. Sometimes when a professor asks if anyone has any questions, no one will respond, leading each student to infer that he or she is the only one confused. All believe that fear of embarrassment explains their own silence, but that everyone else's silence means they understand the material. Dale Miller and Cathy McFarland (1987) bottled this familiar phenomenon in a laboratory experiment, by asking people to read an incomprehensible article and to seek help if they ran into "any really serious problems in understanding the paper." Although none of the subjects sought help, they presumed that *other* subjects would not be similarly restrained by fear of embarrassment. Thus they wrongly inferred that people who didn't seek help must have understood it. To overcome such **pluralistic ignorance,** someone must break the ice, enabling people to reveal and reinforce their shared but secret reactions.

Pluralistic ignorance:
A false impression of how other people are thinking, feeling, or responding.

When people are asked (as you were earlier) to predict how others would respond to items such as the "Henry" dilemma, they typically exhibit pluralistic ignorance: They guess that others' opinions are less supportive of the socially preferred tendency (in this case, writing the novel) than is their own opinion. A typical person will advise writing the novel even if its chance of success is only 4 in 10, but estimate that most other people would require 5 or 6 in 10. Thus, when the discussion begins, many group members will soon discover that they are not outshining the others as they had supposed; in fact, some of the others are already out ahead of them, having taken an even stronger position on behalf of writing the novel. No longer restrained by a misperceived group norm, they will now be liberated to give stronger expression to their preferences. What is more, people tend to admire as most sincere and competent those persons who are on their side of an issue but who are more extreme (Eisenger & Mills, 1968). This, too, may contribute to polarization. (Note: if learning others' views actually changes one's own view of reality, then informational rather than normative influence is at work.)

This finding is reminiscent of the self-serving bias (Chapter 3): People tend to view themselves as better-than-average embodiments of socially desirable traits and attitudes.

This social comparison theory prompted a series of experiments that exposed people to others' positions without exposing them to others' arguments. This is roughly the experience we have when reading the results of an opinion poll. When people learn others' positions—without opportunity for discussion—will they adjust their responses so as to maintain a favorable position relative to others? When people have not already made a prior commitment to a particular response, seeing others' responses does indeed stimulate a small polarization (Sanders & Baron, 1977; Goethals & Zanna, 1979). (See Figure 9-8 for an example.) The polarization is usually not as great as that produced by a lively discussion. Still, it surprised researchers that instead of simply conforming to the group average, people more often go it one better. Are people seeking to "one-up" the observed norm in order to differentiate themselves from the group? Is this another indication of what some researchers (see Chapter 7) believe is our need to feel unique? Roger Brown (1974) believes so: "To be virtuous, in any of an indefinite number of situations, is to be different from the [average]—in the right direction and to the right degree."

The research on group polarization illustrates a characteristic of social-psycholog-

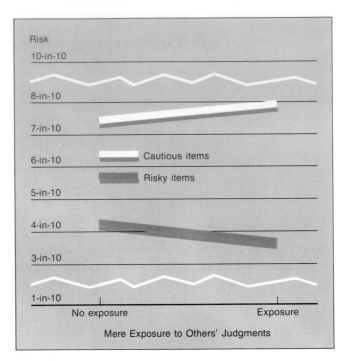

FIGURE 9-8
On "risky" dilemma items (such as the case of Henry), mere exposure to others' judgments enhanced individuals' risk-prone tendencies. On "cautious" dilemma items (such as the case of Roger), exposure to others' judgments enhanced their cautiousness. (Data from Myers, 1978.)

ical inquiry. Much as we like our explanations to be simple, more often than not no one explanation of a phenomenon can by itself account for all the data. Because people are complex, more than one factor frequently influences a phenomenon. In group discussions, persuasive arguments predominate on issues that have a factual element (is she guilty of the crime?), and social comparison sways responses on value-laden judgments (how long a sentence should she serve?) (Kaplan & Miller, 1987). On the many issues that have both factual and value-laden aspects, the two factors work together: Discovering that others share one's feelings (social comparison) can unleash arguments (informational influence) supporting what everyone secretly favors.

GROUPTHINK

Are the social-psychological phenomena that we have been considering in these first nine chapters evident in highly sophisticated decision-making groups? In a corporate boardroom or a meeting of the President's Cabinet is there likely to be self-justification? Self-serving bias? A cohesive "we feeling" provoking conformity and rejection of nonconformers? Public commitment producing resistance to change? Group polarization? Social psychologist Irving Janis (1971; 1982a) wondered whether such phenomena might help explain good and bad group decisions made by recent American presidents and their advisers. To find out, he analyzed the decision making procedures that led to several major fiascos, such as:

• **Pearl Harbor.** In the weeks preceding the 1941 Pearl Harbor attack, military commanders in Hawaii were fed a steady stream of information about Japan's preparations for attack—somewhere. Then military intelligence lost radio contact with Japanese aircraft carriers, which had begun moving full-steam straight for Hawaii. Air reconnaissance could have spotted the carriers, or at least provided a few minutes' warning of the impending attack. But the complacent commanders decided against such precautions. Thus, no alert was sounded until the Japanese were directly attacking the virtually defenseless ships and airfields.

- **The Bay of Pigs invasion.** "How could we have been so stupid?" asked President John Kennedy after he and his advisers learned the disastrous outcome of their 1961 attempt to overthrow Castro by sending into Cuba 1400 CIA-trained Cuban exiles. Nearly all the invaders were soon killed or captured, the United States was humiliated, and Cuba allied itself even closer to the U.S.S.R.

- **The Vietnam war.** From 1964 to 1967 President Lyndon Johnson and his "Tuesday lunch group" of policy advisers escalated the Vietnam war on the assumption that U.S. aerial bombardment, defoliation, and search and destroy missions were likely to bring North Vietnam to the peace table while maintaining the appreciative support of the South Vietnamese populace. The escalation decisions were made despite warnings from government intelligence experts as well as from leaders of nearly all U.S. allies. The resulting disaster cost 56,500 American and more than one million Vietnamese lives, drove the President from office, and created huge budget deficits that helped fuel inflation in the 1970s.

Groupthink:
The mode of thinking that persons engage in when concurrence-seeking becomes so dominant in a cohesive ingroup that it tends to override realistic appraisal of alternative courses of action."
Irving Janis (1971)

During President Johnson's "Tuesday Lunch Group" weekly meetings, more time was spent maintaining the group's harmony by rationalizing its past actions than reflecting upon their outcomes.

Janis believes that these blunders were bred by the tendency of these decision-making groups to suppress dissent in the interests of group harmony, a phenomenon he calls *groupthink*. The soil from which groupthink sprouts includes an amiable, cohesive group, relative isolation of the group from contrary viewpoints, and a directive leader who signals what decision he or she favors. For example, when planning the ill-fated Bay of Pigs invasion, the newly elected President Kennedy and his advisers

enjoyed a strong esprit de corps; arguments critical of the plan were suppressed or excluded; and the President himself soon indicated his endorsement of the invasion.

SYMPTOMS OF GROUPTHINK

From historical records and the memoirs of participants and observers, Janis identified eight symptoms of groupthink that ran through these bad decisions.

1 An Illusion of Invulnerability

The groups Janis studied all developed an excessive optimism that blinded them to warnings of danger. When told that radio contact with the Japanese carriers had been lost, Admiral Kimmel, the chief naval officer at Pearl Harbor, joked about their possibly being about to round Honolulu's Diamond Head. Kimmel's laughing at the idea was a way of dismissing the very possibility of its being true. Jerome Frank (1984), an observer of psychological ingredients of international relations, believes that today's leaders suffer a similar group illusion:

> The military and political establishments of the nuclear powers are able to maintain the curious delusion that their nation could prevail in a nuclear confrontation because their members form a closed communication system that continually reinforces this belief. Persons cannot join the inner circles of decision makers unless they already share the same world view.

2 Rationalization

The groups discounted challenges to their past decisions by collectively justifying them. President Johnson's Tuesday lunch group spent far more time rationalizing (explaining and justifying) than reflecting upon and rethinking their prior decisions to escalate. Each of their initiatives became an action to be defended and justified.

3 Unquestioned Belief in the Group's Morality

Group members assume the inherent morality of their group, ignoring ethical and moral issues. Although the Kennedy group knew that adviser Arthur Schlesinger, Jr., and Senator J. William Fulbright had moral reservations about invading a small, neighboring country, the group never entertained or discussed these moral qualms.

4 Stereotyped View of Opponent

Participants in these groupthink tanks appeared to consider their enemies too evil to negotiate with, or so weak and unintelligent that they could not possibly defend themselves against the planned initiative. The Kennedy group convinced itself that Castro's military was so weak and his popular support so shallow that a mere brigade could easily overwhelm his regime.

5 Conformity Pressure

Dissent was not appreciated. Group members who raised doubts about the group's assumption and plans were readily refuted, at times not by argument but by personal sarcasm. Once, when President Johnson's assistant Bill Moyers arrived at a meeting, the President derided him with "Well, here comes Mr. Stop-the-Bombing." To avoid disapproval, most people fall into line when faced with such ridicule.

6 Self-Censorship

Since disagreements were often discomforting and the groups seemed in consensus, the members tended to withhold, even discount, their own misgivings. In the months following the Bay of Pigs invasion, Arthur Schlesinger (1965) reproached himself

> for having kept so silent during those crucial discussions in the Cabinet Room, though my feelings of guilt were tempered by the knowledge that a course of objection would have accomplished little save to gain me a name as a nuisance. I can only explain my failure to do more than raise a few timid questions by reporting that one's impulse to blow the whistle on this nonsense was simply undone by the circumstances of the discussion. (p. 255)

7 Illusion of Unanimity

Self-censorship and pressure against puncturing a group's apparent consensus can lead to an illusion of unanimity. What is more, the apparent consensus appears to validate the group's decision. This appearance of consensus was evident in the three fiascos, and in other fiascos before and since. Albert Speer (1971), an adviser of Adolf Hitler,

"All those in favor say 'Aye.'"
"Aye."   "Aye."   "Aye."
"Aye."   "Aye."

Self-censorship can contribute to an illusion of unanimity.

describes the atmosphere around Hitler as one where pressure to conform suppressed all deviation. The absence of dissent created an illusion of unanimity that seemed to justify the most heinous acts.

> In normal circumstances people who turn their backs on reality are soon set straight by the mockery and criticism of those around them, which makes them aware they have lost credibility. In the Third Reich there were no such correctives, especially for those who belonged to the upper stratum. On the contrary, every self-deception was multiplied as in a hall of distorting mirrors, becoming a repeatedly confirmed picture of a fantastical dream world which no longer bore any relationship to the grim outside world. In those mirrors I could see nothing but my own face reproduced many times over. No external factors disturbed the uniformity of hundreds of unchanging faces, all mine. (p. 379)

8 Mindguards

Some members protect the group from information that would dispute the effectiveness or morality of its decisions. Prior to the Bay of Pigs, Robert Kennedy took Schlesinger aside and told him "Don't push it any further," and Secretary of State Dean Rusk withheld diplomatic and intelligence experts' warnings against the invasion. By so doing they served the President as what we might call "mindguards," parallel to bodyguards but protecting him from disagreeable facts rather than from physical harm.

GROUPTHINK IN ACTION

Janis believes that these groupthink symptoms cause several defects in making decisions. As summarized in Figure 9-9, these involve a failure to seek and discuss contrary information and alternative possibilities.

Such failure was tragically evident in the decision process by which NASA decided to launch the space shuttle Challenger on its fateful mission. Engineers at the Morton Thiokol Co., which makes the shuttle's rocket boosters, and at Rockwell International, which manufactures the orbiter, had opposed the launch because of dangers posed by the subfreezing temperatures. The Thiokol engineers feared that the cold would make the rubber seals at the joints between the rocket's four main segments too brittle to contain the rocket's superhot gases. Several months before the doomed mission, the company's top expert had warned in a memo that it was a "jump ball" as to whether

FIGURE 9-9
Theoretical analysis of groupthink. (Data from Janis & Mann, 1977, p. 132.)

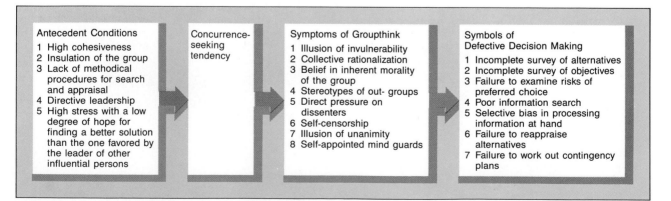

Antecedent Conditions	Concurrence-seeking tendency	Symptoms of Groupthink	Symbols of Defective Decision Making
1 High cohesiveness 2 Insulation of the group 3 Lack of methodical procedures for search and appraisal 4 Directive leadership 5 High stress with a low degree of hope for finding a better solution than the one favored by the leader of other influential persons		1 Illusion of invulnerability 2 Collective rationalization 3 Belief in inherent morality of the group 4 Stereotypes of out-groups 5 Direct pressure on dissenters 6 Self-censorship 7 Illusion of unanimity 8 Self-appointed mind guards	1 Incomplete survey of alternatives 2 Incomplete survey of objectives 3 Failure to examine risks of preferred choice 4 Poor information search 5 Selective bias in processing information at hand 6 Failure to reappraise alternatives 7 Failure to work out contingency plans

the seal would hold, and that if it failed "the result would be a catastrophe of the highest order" (Magnuson, 1986).

In a group discussion via telephone the night before the launch, the engineers argued their case with their uncertain managers and with NASA officials, who were eager to proceed with the already delayed launch. One Thiokol official later testified that "We got ourselves into the thought process that we were trying to find some way to prove to them [the booster] wouldn't work. We couldn't prove absolutely that it wouldn't work." Thus it was that an *illusion of invulnerability* was maintained. *Conformity pressures* also operated, as when one of the NASA officials complained, "My God, Thiokol, when do you want me to launch, next April?" and when the top Thiokol executive declared that "we have to make a management decision" and then asked his engineering vice-president to "take off his engineering hat and put on his management hat." To create an *illusion of unanimity*, this same executive then proceeded to poll only the management officials, ignoring the engineers. The group go-ahead decision now made, one of the engineers belatedly pleaded with a NASA official to reconsider: "If anything happened to this launch," he said prophetically, "I sure wouldn't want to be the person that had to stand in front of a board of inquiry to explain why I launched." Thanks, finally, to *mindguarding*, the top NASA executive who made the final decision to launch was never told about the engineers' concerns, nor about the reservations of the Rockwell officials. Protected from the disagreeable information, he confidently gave the go-ahead to launch the Challenger on its tragic flight.

"There was a serious flaw in the decision-making process."
Report of the Presidential Commission on the Space Shuttle Challenger Accident, *1986*

PREVENTING GROUPTHINK

Does this bleak analysis imply that group decision making is inherently defective? To pose the question with contradictory proverbs, do too many cooks always spoil the broth or can two or more heads sometimes be better than one?

TEN PRESCRIPTIONS FOR PREVENTING GROUPTHINK

1. Tell group members about groupthink, its causes and consequences.
2. The leader should be impartial, should not endorse any position.
3. The leader should instruct everyone to critically evaluate, should encourage objections and doubts.
4. One or more members should be assigned the role of "devil's advocate."
5. From time to time subdivide the group. Have the subgroups meet separately and then come together to air differences.

6. When the issue concerns relations with a rival group, take time to survey all warning signals and identify various possible actions by the rival.
7. After reaching a preliminary decision, a "second-chance" meeting should be called at which each member is asked to express remaining doubts.
8. Outside experts should attend meetings on a staggered basis and be asked to challenge the group's views.
9. Each group member should air the group's deliberations with trusted associates and report their reactions.
10. Several independent groups should work simultaneously on the same question.

Note: Adapted from "Counteracting the Adverse Effects of Concurrence-Seeking in Policy-Planning Groups: Theory and Research Perspectives" by I. L. Janis. In H. Brandstätter et al. (Eds.), *Group Decision Making*. New York: Academic Press, 1982, pp. 477–501.

Group insights often are better. Patrick Laughlin (1980; Laughlin & Adamopoulos, 1980) has demonstrated this with various "intellective" tasks. For instance, consider this analogy problem: *Assertion* is to *disproved* as *action* is to (*hindered, opposed, illegal, precipitate,* or *thwarted*). Most college students miss this question when answering alone, but answer correctly after discussion. (See the marginal note below for the answer.) Moreover, Laughlin finds that if but two members of a six-person group are initially correct, two-thirds of the time they convince all the others; however, if but one person is correct, this "minority of one" almost three-fourths of the time fails to convince the wayward group. Dell Warnick and Glenn Sanders (1980) confirmed that several heads can be better than one when they studied the accuracy of eyewitnesses' reports of videotaped crime. Groups of eyewitnesses gave accounts that were far more accurate than those provided by the average isolated individual.

Janis also analyzed two highly successful group decisions: the Truman administration's formulation of the Marshall Plan for getting Europe back on its feet after World War II and the Kennedy administration's handling of Russia's attempts to install missile bases in Cuba. Janis's recommendations for preventing groupthink (see box) incorporate many of the effective group procedures used by both the Marshall Plan and the missile-crisis groups. These suggestions attempt to remedy the defects that characterize groupthink by ensuring that the group seeks information from all sides and improves its evaluation of possible alternatives.

GROUPTHINK ILLUSTRATES GROUP INFLUENCE PRINCIPLES

In general terms, the "symptoms of groupthink" seem to fit and illustrate the previously discussed findings pertaining to self-justification, self-serving bias, and conformity. Ivan Steiner (1982) believes the hypothesized groupthink processes coincide also with previous research on group influence. For example, researchers have noted that problem-solving groups have a strong tendency to converge on a single solution. This convergence phenomenon (which Janis calls concurrence seeking) is also evident in the group polarization experiments: A group's average position may polarize, but its members also converge.

Experiments on group problem-solving document self-censorship and biased discussion. Once a margin of support for one alternative develops, better ideas have little chance of being accepted. Likewise, reports Steiner, descriptions of mob lynchings reveal that once a lynching was suggested, misgivings, if not immediately expressed, were drowned out. Drawing on biased information is evident in group polarization experiments. The arguments that surface in group discussion tend to be more one-sided than those volunteered by individuals privately. When asked to write whatever arguments relevant to "Henry the writer" come to mind, individuals typically volunteer almost twice as many reasons for attempting the novel as opposing it. In discussion, this tendency is magnified; the expressed arguments average about 3 to 1 in favor of attempting the novel. Thus group discussion typically exacerbates natural tendencies toward overconfidence (see page 113), thereby heightening an illusion of judgmental accuracy (Dunning & Ross, 1988).

Based on previous research, Steiner does, however, suggest that it is probably not cohesiveness per se that breeds groupthink. Highly cohesive groups (for example, a secure married couple) may provide their members with freedom to disagree. Steiner argues that the prime determinant of groupthink is instead *desire for cohesion*. Group members are likely to suppress disagreeable thoughts when they are striving to build or maintain good group feeling, or looking to the group for acceptance and approval.

"Like the child who first remarked on the Emperor's lack of clothes, minorities may be effective mainly when majorities have blinded themselves to naked reality. If the Emperor were in fact dressed, the child would, of course, be ignored."
Bibb Latane and Sharon Wolf (1981)

The answer to the question above is thwarted.

Social psychology is sometimes severely criticized for basing its findings mostly on North American college students. Certainly, it would be worthwhile knowing whether, say, the fundamental attribution error occurs among elderly Brazilians, Saudi secretaries, and Eskimo hunters, and, despite language barriers, cross-cultural knowledge is accumulating: Social psychological research around the world reveals that in some ways our behaviors differ, and in other ways people are genuinely similar.

If, as social psychology proclaims, our behaviors are shaped by social influences, then different cultures *should* have different impacts. Indeed, your standards regarding promptness, frankness, and nudity depend upon your culture. Whether you engage in premarital sex depends greatly on whether you are European (highly likely), North American (moderately likely), or Chinese (unlikely). Whether you equate beauty with

slimness or shapeliness depends on when and where in the world you live. Whether you define social justice as equality (all receive the same) or as equity (those who earn more receive more) depends on whether your ideology has been shaped by a Marxist or capitalist culture. Whether you tend to be expressive or reserved, casual or formal, hinges partly on

whether you have been reared in Black, Caucasian, or Asian culture. Whether you are focused primarily on yourself—your personal needs, desires, and morality—or on your family, clan, and communal groups hangs on how much you are a product of Western individualism.

If our differences display the impact of culture, our similarities display our kinship as brothers and sisters within one human family. What people in various cultures call physically attractive varies, yet there are social consequences to our shared biological heritage: Across the world men tend to favor female features that imply youth and health—and therefore good reproductive potential. Sexual standards vary, yet within any culture women tend to be less promiscuous than men. Points of comparison vary, yet around the world people like those whose attitudes and characteristics are similar rather than disimilar to their own. Nonverbal gestures vary, yet people from opposite corners of the globe know how to read one another's frowns and smiles.

Our kinship extends to our less admirable traits. The tendency to stereotype those outside one's group, and the resulting tendencies toward in-group favoritism and out-group prejudice, are universal. Hostility toward out-groups is worldwide, a phenomenon well known to Catholics and Protestants in Northern Ireland, Arabs and Israelis in the Middle East, Blacks and Whites in South Africa, and warring tribes in New Guinea. Even genocide has afflicted peoples worldwide—American Indians, Tasmanian natives, European Jews, and Cambodians among them.

   We also mark ourselves as one species through other basic phenomena of our social behavior. Humans everywhere affiliate, conform, and form hierarchies of status or dominance. Humans everywhere play sports and games, dance and feast, have music and religion. Humans everywhere live in families and form groups. Humans everywhere communicate through languages that share deep principles of grammar.
   "The more things change, the more they remain the same." As social psychologists we are not so much interested in listing cultural differences—those are a focus of anthropology—as in discovering universal principles that materialize in culturally specific ways. Our aim is what cross-cultural researcher Walter Lonner (1989) calls "a universalistic

psychology—a psychology that is as valid and meaningful in Omaha and Osaka as it is in Rome and Botswana." Attitudes and behaviors will always vary with culture, but the processes by which attitudes influence behavior vary much less. Social roles are defined differently in Japan than in North America, but in both cultures role expectations guide social relations. G. K. Chesterton had the idea nearly a century earlier: When someone "has discovered why men in Bond Street wear black hats he will at the same moment have discovered why men in Timbuctoo wear red feathers."

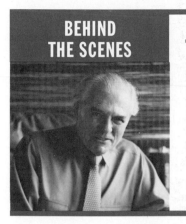

BEHIND
THE SCENES

The idea of *groupthink* hit me while reading Arthur Schlesinger's account of how the Kennedy administration decided to invade the Bay of Pigs. At first, I was puzzled: How could bright, shrewd people like John F. Kennedy and his advisers be taken in by the CIA's stupid, patchwork plan? I began to wonder whether some kind of psychological contagion had interfered, such as social conformity or the concurrence-seeking that I had observed in cohesive small groups. Further study convinced me that subtle group processes had hampered their carefully appraising the risks and debating the issues. When I then analyzed other U.S. foreign policy fiascos and the Watergate coverup, I found the same detrimental group processes at work.

Irving Janis,
Santa Rosa, California

MINORITY INFLUENCE

Each of the chapters so far in this unit on social influence has concluded with a reminder of our power as individuals. We have seen that while cultural situations mold us, we also help create and choose these very situations; that while pressures to conform sometimes overwhelm our better judgment, blatant pressure nevertheless can motivate us to assert our individuality and freedom; and that while persuasive forces are indeed powerful, we can still resist persuasion by making public commitments to our positions and by anticipating persuasive appeals. This chapter has emphasized group influences upon the individual. It is therefore fitting that we conclude it with a look at how individuals can influence their groups.

At the beginning of most social movements, a small minority will sometimes sway, and then even become, the majority. "All history," wrote Ralph Waldo Emerson, "is a record of the power of minorities, and of minorities of one." Think of Copernicus and Galileo, of Martin Luther, of the suffragettes. Technological history is also made by innovative minorities. As Robert Fulton developed his steamboat—"Fulton's Folly"—he endured constant derision: "Never did a single encouraging remark, a bright hope, a warm wish, cross my path" (Cantril & Bumstead, 1960).

What makes a minority persuasive? What might Arthur Schlesinger have done to get the group deliberating the Bay of Pigs invasion to consider seriously his misgivings? Experiments initiated by Serge Moscovici in Paris have identified several determinants of minority influence.

CONSISTENCY

"If the single man plant himself indomitably on his instincts, and there abide, the huge world will come round to him."
Ralph Waldo Emerson, Nature, Address, and Lectures: The American Scholar

More influential than a minority that wavers is a minority that unswervingly sticks to its position. Moscovici and his associates (1969, 1985) have found that if a minority consistently judges blue slides as green, members of the majority will occasionally agree; but if the minority wavers, saying blue to one-third of the blue slides and green to the rest, virtually no one in the majority will ever concur with the "green" judgments. Still being debated is the nature of this influence (Maass et al., 1987; Levine & Russo, 1987). Moscovici believes that a minority's going along with the majority usually reflects mere public compliance, but that a majority's being influenced by a minority more likely demonstrates genuine acceptance—for example, really recalling the blue slide as greenish. A minority influences by making us think more deeply; a majority can influence by intimidating us from disagreeing, by giving us a rule-of-thumb for deciding truth ("All those smart cookies can't be wrong"), or also by making us think more deeply (Burnstein & Kitayama, 1989; Mackie, 1987).

Experiments show—and experience confirms—that nonconformity, especially persistent nonconformity, is often painful (Levine, 1989). If you set out to be Emerson's minority of one, prepare yourself for ridicule. When Charlan Nemeth (1979) planted a minority of two within a simulated jury and had them oppose the majority's opinions, the duo was inevitably disliked. Nevertheless, the majority acknowledged that the persistence of the two did more than anything else to make them rethink their positions. In so doing, a minority may also stimulate creative thinking on problem-solving tasks (Nemeth, 1986). One need not win friends to influence people.

A persistent minority is influential, even if not popular, partly because it soon becomes the focus of debate (Schachter, 1951). Being the center of conversation allows one to contribute a disproportionate number of arguments. And Nemeth reports that in experiments on minority influence, as in the studies dealing with group polarization, the position supported by the most arguments usually wins. Talkative group members tend to be influential (Stein & Heller, 1979).

SELF-CONFIDENCE

Consistency and persistence in one's positions convey an image of self-confidence. Furthermore, Nemeth and Joel Wachtler (1974) reported that any behavior by a minority that conveys self-confidence—for example, taking the head seat at the table—will tend to raise self-doubts among the majority. By being reasonably firm and forceful, the minority's apparent self-assurance may prompt the majority to reconsider its position and consider other alternatives.

DEFECTIONS FROM THE MAJORITY

A persistent minority will at the very least puncture any illusion of unanimity that the group might otherwise have had. When a minority consistently doubts the majority wisdom, members of the majority who might otherwise have self-censored their own doubts will feel freer to express them, and may even switch to the minority position. In research with University of Kansas students, Charles Kiesler and Michael Pallak (1975) found that those in the majority disliked defectors, but had their own self-doubts accentuated by the defection. John Levine and his colleagues (1980) obtained similar results with University of Pittsburgh students; in fact, they found that a minority person who defected from the majority was even more persuasive than one who consistently voiced the minority position. And in her jury-simulation experiments, Nemeth found that once defections begin, others often soon follow, thus initiating a "snowball" effect. As President Carter slipped in the polls in the months preceding the 1980 election, some of his former supporters began to yearn for another alternative and called for an "open" Democratic National Convention. Speculating from the experiments, we might surmise that observing these defections aroused self-doubts among the President's remaining supporters.

Are these factors that strengthen minority influence unique to minorities? Sharon Wolf and Bibb Latané (1985; Wolf, 1987) believe not. They argue that the same social forces work for both majorities and minorities. If consistency, self-confidence, and defections from the other side contribute to the strength of a minority, such variables likely contribute to the strength of a majority also. The social impact of any position—whether held by a majority or a minority—depends on the strength, immediacy and number of those who support it. Thus minorities have less influence than majorities, because they are smaller. However, Anne Maass and Russell Clark (1984, 1986) agree with Moscovici that minorities are more likely to convert people to accepting their views, giving them as much influence as majorities in some situations. Nemeth (1986) also believes that the stress of being in the minority differs from the more relaxed reflection of the majority. And from their analyses of how groups evolve over time, John Levine and Richard Moreland (1985) conclude that new recruits to a group may exert a different type of minority influence than do longtime members. For example, while newcomers may be able to exert influence because of the attention they receive and the group awareness they trigger in the oldtimers, established members may feel freer to dissent and to exert leadership.

There is a delightful irony in this new emphasis on how individuals can influence the group. Until recently, the idea that the minority could sway the majority was itself a minority view in social psychology. Nevertheless, by arguing consistently and forcefully, Moscovici, Nemeth, and others have convinced the majority of group-influence researchers that minority influence is indeed a phenomenon worthy of study.

IS LEADERSHIP MINORITY INFLUENCE?

Leadership:
The process by which certain group members motivate and guide the group.

One example of the power of individuals is **leadership,** the process by which certain individuals mobilize and guide their groups. Some leaders are formally appointed or elected, others emerge informally as the group interacts. What makes for good leadership often depends on the situation—the best person to lead the engineering team may not make the best leader of the sales force. For example, some people excel at *task leadership*—at organizing work, setting standards, and focusing on the attainment of goals. Others excel at *social leadership*—at building teamwork, mediating conflicts, and being supportive.

Task leaders often have a directive style—one that can work well if the leader is bright enough to give good orders (Fiedler, 1987). Being goal-oriented, such leaders also keep the group's attention and effort focused on its mission. Many experiments indicate that the combination of specific, challenging goals and periodic progress reports help motivate high achievement (McCaul et al., 1987; Mento et al., 1987; Tubbs, 1986).

Women more than men tend to be democratic in their leadership style (Eagly, 1988).

Social leaders often have a democratic style—one that delegates authority and welcomes input from team members. Many experiments indicate that such leadership is good for morale. Group members usually feel more satisfied when they participate in making decisions (Spector, 1986; Vanderslice et al., 1987). Given control over their tasks, workers also become more motivated to achieve (Burger, 1987). People who value good group feeling and take pride in achievement therefore thrive under democratic leadership.

The once-popular "great person theory of leadership"—that all great leaders share certain traits—has fallen into disrepute. Effective leadership styles, we now know, vary with the situations. Recently, however, social psychologists have again wondered if there might be qualities that mark a good leader in many situations (Mumford, 1986). British social psychologists Peter Smith and Monir Tayeb (1989) report that studies

BEHIND THE SCENES

As a female raised Roman Catholic in the 1940s and 1950s, I was acutely aware of my minority status, and the expectations people had of me, as I struggled to achieve in both athletic and intellectual endeavors. However, this also made me aware of the contributions one can make by viewing things as an outsider. This perspective, heightened by my exposure to the conflict and violence of the late 1960s in Chicago, made me eager to understand the influence processes that enable social control and social change. I focused on the ways in which minorities exercised influence, but my ultimate concern is how social influence can improve social conditions by enlightening and educating us.

Charlan Jeanne Nemeth,
University of California, Berkeley

done in India, Taiwan, and Iran have found that the most effective supervisors in coal mines, banks, and government offices score high on tests of *both* task and social leadership. They are sensitive to the individual and group needs of their subordinates *and* actively concerned for how work is progressing.

Studies also reveal that many effective leaders of laboratory groups, work teams, and large corporations exhibit the behaviors that make for minority influence. They engender trust by consistently sticking to their goals. And they often exude a self-confident "charisma" that kindles the allegience of their followers (Bennis, 1984; House & Singh, 1987). Charismatic leaders typically have a compelling *vision* of some desired state of affairs, an ability to *communicate* this to others in clear and simple language, and enough optimism and faith in their group to *inspire* others to follow.

To be sure, groups also influence their leaders. Sometimes those at the front of the herd have simply sensed where it is already heading. Political candidates know how to read the opinion polls. A leader who deviates too radically from the group's standards may be rejected; thus smart leaders usually remain with the majority and spend their influence prudently. Nevertheless, effective individual leaders can some-

Consistency, vision, self-confidence, optimism, and the ability to communicate with others all define charismatic leaders, such as Franklin Delano Roosevelt, who effectively inspire others to believe in them.

times exhibit a type of minority influence—by mobilizing and guiding the energies of the group's majority.

SUMMING UP

We spend much of our lives in groups—with family members, friends, fellow students, coworkers, etc. What influences do such groups have upon their individual members? This chapter examined six phenomena of group influence.

SOCIAL FACILITATION

Perhaps the most elementary issue in social psychology concerns how we are affected by the mere presence of others. Some early experiments on this question found that one's performance improved when either observers or co-actors were present (social facilitation). Other experiments found that the presence of others can hurt one's performance. Robert Zajonc reconciled these seemingly contradictory findings by applying a well-known principle from experimental psychology: Arousal facilitates dominant responses. If we assume that the presence of others is arousing (an assumption confirmed by later research), it follows that the presence of observers or co-actors should boost performance on easy tasks (for which the correct response is dominant) and hinder performance on difficult tasks (for which incorrect responses are dominant). Such is precisely what has consistently been found, both in the earlier experiments that Zajonc sought to reconcile and in newer ones.

But why are we aroused by others' presence? Experiments suggest that the arousal stems partly from "evaluation apprehension" and partly from a conflict between paying attention to others and concentrating on the task. Other experiments, including some with animals, suggest that the presence of others can be somewhat arousing even when the actor is not being evaluated or distracted.

SOCIAL LOAFING

Social-facilitation researchers study people's performance on tasks where they can be individually evaluated. However, in many work situations people pool their efforts and work toward a common goal without individual accountability. Experiments indicate that group members often work less hard when performing such "additive tasks." This finding seems to parallel everyday situations in which responsibility is diffused, tempting individual group members to free ride on the group's effort.

DEINDIVIDUATION

When high levels of social arousal are combined with diffused responsibility, people may both abandon their normal restraints and lose their sense of individuality. Such "deindividuation" is especially likely when, after being aroused and distracted, people can assume anonymity by being in a large group or wearing indistinct garb. The net result? Diminished self-awareness and self-restraint and, therefore, increased responsiveness to the immediate situation, be it negative or positive. On the other hand, circumstances that *increase* self-awareness reduce one's being controlled by the situation by increasing one's self-control.

GROUP POLARIZATION

The potentially positive and negative results of group interaction can also be explained by findings from research on the effects of group discussion. While trying to understand the curious finding that group discussion enhanced risk taking, investigators discovered that discussion actually tends to strengthen whatever is the initially dominant point of view, whether risky or cautious, whether for or against a position on some attitudinal issue. Observations of naturally occurring social polarization suggest that in everyday situations, too, group interaction tends to intensify opinions.

The group polarization phenomenon provided a window through which researchers could observe the influence of a group. Experiments have confirmed the presence of two social influences: informational and normative. The information gleaned from a discussion mostly favors the initially preferred alternative, thus reinforcing people's support for it. Moreover, people may go further out on the limb when, after they have compared their positions, they discover surprising support for their initial inclinations.

GROUPTHINK

Analysis of the decisions that led to several international fiascos indicates that a group's desire for harmony can override its realistic appraisal of contrary views. This is especially true when group members strongly desire unity, when they are isolated from opposing ideas, and when the leader signals what he or she wants from the group. Symptomatic of this overriding concern for harmony, labeled "groupthink," are (1) an illusion of invulnerability, (2) rationalization, (3) unquestioned belief in the group's morality, (4) stereotyped views of the opposition, (5) pressure to conform, (6) self-censorship of misgivings, (7) an illusion of unanimity, and (8) "mindguards" who protect the group from unpleasant information.

However, both in experiments and in actual history, groups do sometimes make intelligent decisions. The circumstances under which such have been made suggest remedies for groupthink. By taking steps to ensure that the group seeks information from all sides and improves its evaluation of possible alternatives, the group can benefit from the combined insights of its members.

MINORITY INFLUENCE

It is important also to examine how individuals can influence their groups. If minority viewpoints were always impotent, history would be more static than it is. Experiments indicate that a minority is most influential when it is consistent and persistent in its views, when its actions convey self-confidence, and when it begins to elicit some defections from the majority. And, even if such factors do not persuade the majority to adopt the minority's views, they will likely increase the majority's self-doubts and prompt it to consider other alternatives more seriously.

Through their task and social leadership, formal and informal group leaders exert disproportionate influence. Those who consistently press toward their goals and exude a self-confident charisma often engender trust and inspire others to follow.

FOR FURTHER READING

Janis, I. L. (1982). *Groupthink: Psychological studies of policy decisions and fiascoes.* Boston: Houghton Mifflin. An informative and captivating analysis of the group decision processes that led to several historical fiascoes, from the failure to anticipate the Pearl Harbor attack to the Watergate cover-up.

Janis, I. L. (1989). *Crucial decisions: Leadership in policy making and crisis management.* New York: Free Press. Janis draws upon social psychological research and his close study of policymakers' mistakes in formulating guidelines for better executive and managerial decisions. Includes a profile of twenty effective leadership practices.

Paulus, P. B. (Ed.). (1989). *The psychology of group influence* (2d ed.). Hillsdale, NJ: Erlbaum. Experts provide state-of-the-art reviews of recent research on group influence. Includes further information on many of the topics discussed in this chapter.

CHAPTER

10

APPLICATION: SOCIAL PSYCHOLOGY IN COURT

Newspapers called it the "Preppy Murder Case." Robert Chambers, a 19-year-old prep-school graduate, acknowledged killing 18-year-old Jennifer Levin with his bare hands just before dawn in New York City's Central Park. In the 1988 trial that followed, the defense argued that Levin, sexually aggressive and inebriated after a night of drinking at a trendy bar where the two had met, hurt Chambers while molesting him, causing him in self-defense to flip her over and accidentally crush her throat with his arm. The victim's family was outraged: Not only did Chambers take her life, now he was attempting to murder her character as well. To blame the victim is the time-honored way of excusing sexual assault, noted the prosecution, a way that has effectively intimidated many victims from pressing charges. But could one blame this victim for the bruises on her legs and face?

For nine days the jury deliberated without reaching consensus. Were they biased by the defendant's attractiveness and social status? Did they heed the judge's instructions to ignore inadmissible remarks about the victim's sexual history? Were the jurors swayed by their own personal characteristics and their attitudes and beliefs about men's and women's behavior in such circumstances? After deliberations began, how did the jurors influence one another? Such questions are of great interest to lawyers, judges, and defendants. And they are questions to which social psychology can suggest answers, as some 100 American law schools have recognized by hiring one or more professors of "law and social science" (Melton et al., 1987).

We can think of a courtroom as a miniature social world, one that magnifies everyday social processes with major consequences for those involved. Here, as elsewhere, people think about and influence one another. Thus there exists a long list of topics pertinent to social psychology and law. Among such influences are the norms and judicial roles of a country's legal system and the cultural tradition embodied in its legal precedents. If a culture, say, views women as responsible for child rearing and for enticing men's sexual responses, such attitudes will likely be reflected in child custody decisions and in the scrutiny given rape victims.

In criminal cases, psychological factors may influence decisions involving arrest, interrogation, prosecution, plea bargaining, sentencing, and parole. Of criminal cases disposed of in U.S. District Courts during 1979, 83 percent never came to trial (U.S. Department of Justice, 1980). Much of the trial lawyer's work therefore "is not persuasion in the courtroom but bargaining in the conference room" (Saks & Hastie, 1978, pp. 119–120). Even in the conference room, decisions are made based on speculations about what a jury or judge might do. Sensing a hung jury and likely retrial in the Chambers murder case, the prosecution and defense struck a bargain. Chambers pled guilty to a reduced charge of first-degree manslaughter and went to prison, where he resides until at least 1993.

So, whether a case reaches a jury verdict or not, the social dynamics of the courtroom play an important role. Let's therefore consider two sets of factors that have been heavily researched: (1) features of the courtroom drama that can influence jurors' judgments of a defendant and (2) the characteristics of both the jurors and their deliberations.

JUDGING THE EVIDENCE

As the courtroom drama unfolds, jurors hear testimony, form impressions of the defendant, listen to instructions from the judge, and render a verdict. Let's take these steps one at a time, seeing what research reveals about jurors' reactions.

Such research explores two fundamental questions: First, when and how much do biases erode fair judgments? Second, given that jurors are not dispassionate computing machines, what reforms could minimize bias? Through its oaths, opposing attorneys, and cross-examinations, the judicial system aims to guarantee impartiality. Let's see how careful research might suggest ways to further that aim.

EYEWITNESS TESTIMONY

How Persuasive Is Eyewitness Testimony?

In Chapter 4 we noted that anecdotes and personal testimonies, being vivid and concrete, can be powerfully persuasive, often more so than information that is logically compelling but abstract. Especially when spoken in the unhesitating straightforward style of "men's speech" (Chapter 6), vivid accounts are hard to resist. There's no better way to end an argument than to say "I saw it with my own eyes!" Seeing is believing.

At the University of Washington, Elizabeth Loftus (1974; 1979a) found that those who had "seen" were indeed believed, even when their testimony was known to be essentially useless. When students were presented with a hypothetical robbery-murder case with circumstantial evidence but no eyewitness testimony, only 18 percent voted for conviction. Others received the same information but with the addition of a single eyewitness testimony; now 72 percent, knowing that someone had declared "That's the one!" voted for conviction. A third group received the same information as this second group, except that the testimony was discredited by the defense attorney (the witness had but 20/400 vision and was not wearing glasses at the moment of the crime). To what extent did this discrediting reduce the effect of the testimony? Hardly at all—68 percent still voted for conviction.

Follow-up experiments have found that, although discrediting reduces the number of guilty votes, a discredited eyewitness is more convincing than no eyewitness at all (Whitley, 1987). Unless contradicted by another eyewitness (Leippe, 1985), a vivid eyewitness picture of what transpired seems difficult to erase from jurors' minds. That helps explain why, compared to actual criminal cases lacking eyewitness testimony, court cases involving eyewitness testimony are more likely to produce convictions (Visher, 1987).

Ah, but can jurors not spot erroneous testimony? To find out, Gary Wells, R. C. L. Lindsay, and their colleagues staged hundreds of eyewitnessed thefts of a University of Alberta calculator. Afterward, they asked each eyewitness to identify the culprit from a photo lineup. Other people, acting as jurors, observed the eyewitnesses being questioned and then evaluated their testimony. Are eyewitnesses who make incorrect identifications believed less often than those who are accurate? To the contrary, both correct and incorrect eyewitnesses were believed 80 percent of the time (Wells et al., 1979). This led the researchers to speculate "that human observers have absolutely no ability to discern eyewitnesses who have mistakenly identified an innocent person" (Wells et al., 1980).

In a follow-up experiment, Lindsay, Wells, and Carolyn Rumpel (1981) staged the theft under conditions that sometimes allowed witnesses a good, long look at the thief and sometimes not. The jurors believed the questioned witnesses more when witnessing conditions were good. But even when witnessing conditions were so poor that two-thirds of the witnesses had actually misidentified an innocent person, 62 percent of the jurors still usually believed the witnesses.

In yet another experiment, Wells and Michael Leippe (1981) found that jurors

*"As it turned out, my battery of lawyers was no
match for their battery of eyewitnesses."*

*Eyewitnesses' recall of detail is
sometimes impressive. When
John Yuille and Judith Cutshall
(1986) studied accounts of a
midafternoon murder on a busy
Burnaby, British Columbia
street, they found that
eyewitnesses' recall for detail
was 80 percent accurate.*

were more skeptical of eyewitnesses whose memory for trivial details had been tested
in cross-examination. However, the cross-examination did most to discredit the *accurate* witnesses, whose memories of trivial details actually were poorer than the memories of those who had misidentified the culprit. Jurors are impressed by an eyewitness's
recall of trivial details (Bell & Loftus, 1988). They think that a witness who could
remember that there were three pictures hanging in the room must have "really been
paying attention." Actually, as other researchers have also found (Cutler et al., 1987),
those who paid attention to such details were *less* likely to have paid attention to the
culprit's face.

Though the lesson of this research is predictable from our earlier consideration of
the persuasive power of vivid information, it is nonetheless sobering that jurors find
eyewitnesses quite persuasive, even those whose testimony is inaccurate.

How Accurate Are Eyewitnesses?

Are eyewitness testimonies, in fact, often inaccurate? Stories abound of innocent people
who have wasted years in prison because of the erroneous testimony of eyewitnesses—
witnesses who were sincere, but sincerely wrong (Brandon & Davies, 1973). In the
United States alone, eyewitnesses accuse some 75,000 people a year of crimes (Goldstein et al., 1989). So even dozens of such cases wouldn't establish that eyewitness
accounts are not to be trusted. Whether assessing the accuracy of eyewitness recollections or psychics' predictions, one needs to ascertain their overall "hit" and "miss"
rates. One way to gather such information is to stage crimes comparable to those in
everyday life and later solicit eyewitness reports.

This has now been done many times, sometimes with encouraging results (Sanders
& Chiu, 1988), but often with disconcerting results. For example, at the California
State University, Hayward, 141 students witnessed an "assault" on a professor. Seven
weeks later, when Robert Buckhout (1974) asked them to identify the assailant from
a group of six photographs, 60 percent chose an innocent person. So it's not surprising
that eyewitnesses to actual crimes sometimes disagree about what they witnessed.

BEHIND THE SCENES

As I began testing people's ability to discriminate accurate from false eyewitness testimony, I barely considered the possibility that people would be incapable of discriminating. My excitement grew as the experiments progressed and it became clear that a centuries-old assumption of the criminal justice system was unsupported. Such research is one way in which social psychologists help criminal-justice officials clarify and revise their assumptions, many of which remain untested. And that is the fascination of social psychology in court.

Gary Wells, Iowa State University

"Certitude is not the test of certainty."
Oliver Wendell Holmes,
Collected Legal Papers

Of course, some witnesses are more confident than others. And Wells and his colleagues report that it's the confident witnesses whom jurors find most believable. Thus it is disconcerting that unless witnessing conditions are very favorable, eyewitnesses' "certainty" is virtually unrelated to their accuracy (Bothwell et al., 1987; Wells & Murray, 1984). Incorrect witnesses are virtually as self-assured as correct witnesses. Although two to four eyewitnesses questioned together are somewhat more accurate, they are also more confident, even when wrong (Stephenson et al., 1983, 1986a,b). Even when comparing different statements by the same witness, self-assured statements are nearly as likely to be wrong as less confident statements (Smith et al., 1989).

This repeated finding would surely come as a surprise to members of the 1972 U.S. Supreme Court. In a judgment that established the position of the U.S. judiciary system regarding eyewitness identifications, the Court declared that among the factors to be considered in determining accuracy is "the level of certainty demonstrated by the witness" (Wells & Murray, 1983). In fact, we now know that mistaken eyewitnesses are no less willing to testify, hardly less confident, and no less persuasive than accurate eyewitnesses.

Sources of Error: How Memories Are Constructed

Errors sneak into our perceptions and our memories because our minds are not videotape machines. Rather, we construct our memories, based partly on what we perceived at the time and partly on our expectations, beliefs, and current knowledge. (See Figures 10-1 and 10-2.)

MISTAKEN IDENTITY

Fifty years ago, Yale law professor Edwin Borchard (1932) documented sixty-five convictions of people whose innocence was ultimately established beyond a doubt. Most resulted from mistaken identifications of the culprit by eyewitnesses. Borchard observed that in several of the cases the convicted prisoner, later proved innocent, was saved from hanging or electrocution by a hairbreadth. Only by rare good fortune were some of the sentences of hanging and electrocution commuted to life imprisonment, so that the error could still be corrected. How many wrongfully convicted persons have actually been executed, it is impossible to say.

FIGURE 10-1
Sometimes believing is seeing. Cultural expectations affect perceiving, remembering, and reporting. In a 1947 experiment on rumor transmission, Gordon Allport and Leo Postman showed people this picture of a White man holding a razor blade and then had them tell a second person about it, who then told a third person, and so on. After six tellings, the razor blade in the White man's hand usually shifted to the Black man's. (From "Eyewitness Testimony" by Robert Buckhout. Copyright © 1974 by Scientific American, Inc. All rights reserved.)

Suggestive questions   Elizabeth Loftus and her associates (1978) provided a dramatic demonstration of memory construction. University of Washington students were shown thirty slides depicting successive stages of an automobile-pedestrian accident. One critical slide showed a red Datsun, stopped either at a stop or at a yield sign. (See Figure 10-3.) Afterward, half the students were asked among other questions, "Did another car pass the red Datsun while it was stopped at the stop sign?" The other half were asked the same question but with the words "stop sign" replaced by "yield sign." Later, when shown both slides in Figure 10-3 and asked which one they had previously seen, those previously asked the question consistent with what they had seen were 75 percent correct. But those previously asked the misleading question were only 41 percent correct; more often than not, they denied seeing what they had actually seen and instead "remembered" the picture with an object they had never seen! In other experiments, Loftus (1979a) has found that after suggestive questioning, witnesses

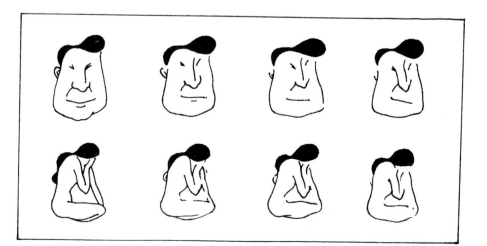

FIGURE 10-2
Expectations affect perception. Is the drawing on the far right a face or figure? (From Fisher, 1968, adapted by Loftus, 1979.) (Drawing by Anne Canevari Green.)

FIGURE 10-3
When shown one of these two pictures and then asked a question suggesting the sign from the *other* photo, most people later "remembered" seeing the sign they had never actually seen. (From Loftus, Miller, & Burns, 1978.) (Photos courtesy of Elizabeth Loftus.)

"A leading question is simply one that, either by its form or content, suggests to the witness what answer is desired or leads him to the desired answer. . . . While the rules of evidence and other safeguards provide protection in the courtroom, they are absent in the backroom of the precinct station."
Ernest Hilgard & Elizabeth Loftus (1979)

may believe that a red light was actually green or that a robber had a mustache when he didn't. When interrogating eyewitnesses, police and attorneys commonly ask questions that are framed by their own understanding of what transpired. So it is troubling to discover how easily witnesses incorporate misleading information into their memories, especially when they believe the questioner to be well-informed (Smith & Ellsworth, 1987). When the eyewitnesses are children, jurors and attorneys are more suspicious that recall may reflect suggestion (Leippe & Romanczyk, 1988; Leippe et al., 1988). Although information that children recall on their own is not notably error-prone, they are indeed more susceptible to misleading questions (Ceci et al., 1987).

Retelling Retelling events commits people to their recollections, whether accurate or not. Thus an accurate retelling helps people later resist misleading suggestions

(Bregman & McAllister, 1982). Other times, the more we retell a story the more we convince ourselves of a falsehood. Wells, Ferguson, and Lindsay (1981) demonstrated this by having some eyewitnesses to a staged theft rehearse their answers to questions before taking the witness stand. Doing so increased the confidence of those who were inaccurate, and thus made jurors who heard their false testimony more likely to vote the innocent person guilty.

Chapter 2 noted that people tend to adjust what they say to please their listeners and, having done so, often come to believe their altered message. Keeping this in mind, imagine that you witness an argument that erupts into a fight in which one person injures the other. Afterward, the injured party sues the other, and prior to the trial a smooth lawyer for one of the two parties interviews you. Might you slightly adjust your testimony, giving a version of the fight that tends to support this lawyer's client? If you did so, might your later recollections in court be similarly slanted? Blair Sheppard and Neil Vidmar (1980) report that the answers to these questions are yes. At the University of Western Ontario, they had some students serve as witnesses to a fight and others as lawyers and judges. When interviewed by lawyers for the defendant rather than the plaintiff, the witnesses later gave the judge testimony that was more favorable to the defendant. In a follow-up experiment, Vidmar and Nancy Lair (1983) noted that witnesses did not omit important facts from their testimony. They just changed their tone of voice and choice of words depending on whether they thought they were a witness for the defendant or the plaintiff. But even this was enough to bias the impressions of those who heard the testimony. So it's not only suggestive questions that can distort eyewitness recollections, but also their own retellings, which may be subtly adjusted to suit their audience.

Reducing Error

Given these error-prone tendencies, what constructive steps can be taken to increase the accuracy of eyewitnesses and jurors? Eyewitness experts have several ideas.

Train police interviewers   When Ronald Fisher and his coworkers (1987) examined tape-recorded interviews of eyewitnesses conducted by experienced Florida police detectives, they found a typical pattern. Following an open-ended beginning ("Tell me what you recall"), the detectives would occasionally interrupt with follow-up questions before asking a series of questions eliciting terse answers ("How tall was he?"). Fisher and Edward Geiselman concur that such interviews should begin by allowing eyewitnesses to offer their own unprompted recollections. But they note that such recollections will be most complete if the interviewer uses memory-jogging questions, such as by first guiding people to reconstruct the setting. One might have them visualize the scene and what they were thinking and feeling at the time. Even showing pictures of the setting—of, say, the store check-out lane with a clerk standing where she was robbed—can promote accurate recall (Cutler & Penrod, 1988). After being given ample, uninterrupted time to report everything that comes to mind, the witness's memories can still be jogged with evocative questions ("Was there anything unusual about the voice?" "Was there anything unusual about the person's appearance or clothing?"). When Fisher and his colleagues (1989) trained detectives in such questioning, the information they elicited from eyewitnesses increased by 50 percent.

However, interviewers must be careful to keep questions free of hidden assumptions. For example, Loftus and Guido Zanni (1975) report that questions such as "Did you see the broken headlight?" trigger twice as many "memories" of nonexistent events as did questions without the hidden assumption: "Did you see a broken headlight?" Likewise, flooding eyewitnesses' minds with an array of mugshots reduces their accuracy in later identifying the culprit (Brigham & Cairns, 1988).

Minimize false lineup identifications   The case of Ron Shatford illustrates how the composition of a police lineup can promote misidentification (Doob & Kirshenbaum, 1973). After a suburban Toronto department store robbery, the cashier involved could only recall that the culprit was not wearing a tie and was "very neatly dressed and rather good looking." When the good-looking Shatford was placed in a lineup with eleven unattractive men, all of whom wore ties, the cashier readily identified him as the culprit. Only after Shatford served fifteen months of a long sentence did another person confess, allowing Shatford to be retried and found not guilty. As this case illustrates, many eyewitnesses are prone to identify a lineup member who *most resembles* the culprit.

Gary Wells (1984; Wells & Turtle, 1986) reports that one way to reduce such misidentifications is first to lure unreliable eyewitnesses with a lineup that contains no suspects. After screening out those who make false identifications, those who remain are less likely to make false identifications when given the actual lineup. False identifications can also be reduced by having witnesses simply make individual yes/no

"That's him! *That's* the one! ... I'd recognize that silly little hat *any*where!"

judgments in response to a sequence of people (Cutler & Penrod, 1988; Lindsay & Wells, 1985). (If witnesses view a group of photos simultaneously, they are more likely to choose whoever most resembles the culprit.)

False identifications can also be minimized with instructions that acknowledge that the offender may not be in the lineup (Malpass & Devine, 1984). Compared to lineups of several suspects, a lineup composed of one suspect and several known-innocent people further reduces the chances that a suspect will be falsely identified (Wells & Turtle, 1986). Such lineups enable police to disregard eyewitnesses who make known errors; with all-suspect lineups, there is no opportunity to weed out witnesses who are guessing.

Educate jurors about eyewitness testimony   Do jurors critically evaluate eyewitness testimony? Do they intuitively understand how the circumstances of a lineup identification determines its reliability? Whether to take an eyewitness's self-confidence into account? How memory can be influenced by previously asked misleading questions, by stress at the time of the incident, by the time interval until being questioned, by whether the suspect is the same or a different race, by whether recall of other details is sharp or hazy? Studies in Canada, Britain, and the United States reveal that lay people are insensitive to most of these factors known to influence eyewitness testimony (Cutler et al., 1988; Noon & Hollin, 1987; Wells, 1986, 1987).

To educate jurors, experts are now frequently asked (usually by defense attorneys) to testify regarding eyewitness testimony. Their aim is to offer jurors the sort of information that you have been reading, helping them critically evaluate the testimony of both prosecution and defense witnesses. They explain that eyewitnesses often perceive events selectively, that subsequent discussions about the events can alter or add to their memories, that research using staged crimes has shown that witnesses often choose a wrong person from a lineup, that eyewitnesses are especially prone to error when trying to identify someone of another race (see Chapter 11), and that jurors should disregard the confidence with which an eyewitness offers testimony. Experiments (Loftus, 1980; Maass et al., 1985; Wells et al., 1980) show that such testimony can prompt jurors to analyze eyewitness reports more skeptically and discuss them more fully. And if taught the conditions under which eyewitness accounts *are* trustworthy, jurors become somewhat more likely to trust such testimony (Cutler et al., 1988; Wells, 1986).

THE DEFENDANT'S CHARACTERISTICS

"Jurymen seldom convict a person they like, or acquit one they dislike. The main work of the trial lawyer is to make a jury like his client, or at least to feel sympathy for him." So said the famed trial lawyer, Clarence Darrow (1933). Was he right? Is jurors' liking or disliking the defendant crucial? And is it true, as Darrow also said, that "facts regarding the crime are relatively unimportant"?

Darrow overstated the matter. One study of more than 3500 criminal cases and some 4000 civil cases found that four times in five the judge concurred with the jury's decision (Kalven & Zeisel, 1966). Although both may have been wrong, the evidence usually is clear enough that jurors can set aside their biases, focus on the evidence, and agree on a verdict (Saks & Hastie, 1978; Visher, 1987). Darrow was too cynical. Facts matter.

Nevertheless, when making arguable social judgments—would the defendant commit such an offense? intentionally?—facts are not all that matter. As we noted in

Chapter 8, communicators are more persuasive if they seem credible and attractive. Jurors can't help forming first impressions of the defendant's credibility and attractiveness. Can they then lay these preconceptions aside and decide the case based on the facts alone? To judge from the more lenient treatment often received by high-status defendants (McGillis, 1979), one suspects that some cultural bias may linger. But actual cases vary in so many ways—in the type of crime, in the status, age, sex, and race of the defendant—that it's hard to isolate the factors that influence jurors. Experimenters have therefore controlled such factors by giving people the same basic facts of a case while varying, say, the defendant's attractiveness or similarity to the jurors.

Physical Attractiveness

As we will see in Chapter 13, there exists a physical attractiveness stereotype: Beautiful people are perceived as good people. Michael Efran (1974) wondered whether this stereotype might bias students' judgments of another student who was accused of cheating. He asked some of his University of Toronto students whether attractiveness should affect one's presumption of guilt. Their answer: "No, it shouldn't." But did it? Yes. When Efran gave other students a description of the case with a photograph of either an attractive or an unattractive defendant, the accused who were most attractive were judged least guilty and recommended for least punishment.

Other experimenters have confirmed that when the evidence is meagre or ambiguous, justice is not blind to a defendant's looks (Cash, 1981; Stewart, 1980, 1983). Such is what Diane Berry and Leslie Zebrowitz-McArthur (1988) discovered when they asked people to judge the guilt of baby-faced and mature-faced defendants. Baby-faced adults (with large, round eyes and small chin) seemed more naive and so were found guilty more often of crimes of negligence and less often of intentional criminal acts. If convicted, unattractive people also strike people as more dangerous, especially if they are sexual offenders (Esses & Webster, 1988).

Other things being equal, physically appealing defendants may be judged more leniently.

"And so I ask the jury ... is that the face of a mass murderer?"

Similarity to the Jurors

If Clarence Darrow was even partially right in his declaration that one's liking for a defendant colors one's judgments, then other factors that influence one's liking for a person should also have an impact in the courtroom. Among such influences is the principle, noted in Chapter 8, that likeness (similarity) leads to liking. So it probably will not surprise you that when people pretend they are jurors, they are more sympathetic to a defendant who shares their attitudes, religion, race, or (in cases of sexual assault) gender (Towson & Zanna, 1983; Ugwuegbu, 1979; Selby et al., 1977). When Paul Amato had Australian students read evidence concerning a left- or right-wing person accused of a politically motivated burglary, they judged him less guilty if his political views were similar to their own. When Cookie Stephan and Walter Stephan (1986) had English-speaking people judge someone accused of assault, they were more likely to think the defendant not guilty if his testimony was in English, rather than translated from Spanish or Thai.

To see why similarity might breed sympathy, recall from Chapter 3 the fundamental attribution error—the tendency when explaining *other's* behavior to discount situational influences. When judging our own behavior, we are more sensitive to situational factors that explain our mistakes. Perhaps, then, people are more sympathetic toward a defendant with whom they can identify. If we think *we* wouldn't have done that criminal act, we may presume that someone like us would also have been unlikely to do it.

Ideally, jurors should leave such biases outside the courtroom door and begin a trial with blank minds. So implies the Sixth Amendment to the U.S. Constitution: "the accused shall enjoy the right to a speedy and public trial by impartial jury." In its concern for objectivity, the judicial system is similar to science: Both scientists and judges and jurors are to sift evidence free of bias; both the courts and science have rules about what evidence is relevant; both keep careful records and assume that others given the same evidence would decide similarly.

When the evidence is clear and jurors focus on it (as when they reread and debate the meaning of testimony), their biases are indeed minimal (Kaplan & Schersching, 1980). The quality of the evidence matters more than the prejudices of the jurors. To minimize juror bias in cases where the evidence is ambiguous, Daniel McGillis (1979) suggests forewarning jurors of sources of bias during their orientation sessions. Judges, too, commonly instruct jurors to ignore biasing information. But is it enough for the judge to remind jurors that "the issue is not whether you like or dislike the defendant, but whether the defendant committed the offense"?

THE JUDGE'S INSTRUCTIONS

All of us can recall courtroom dramas in which an attorney exclaimed, "Your honor, I object!" whereupon the judge sustained the objection and ordered the jury to ignore the other attorney's suggestive question or the witness's remark. For example, nearly all states in the U.S. now have "rape shield" statutes that prohibit or limit testimony concerning the victim's prior sexual activity. [Such testimony, though deemed irrelevant to the case at hand, tends to make jurors more sympathetic to the accused rapist's claim that the woman consented to sexual relations (Borgida, 1981; Cann et al., 1979).] If such unreliable, illegal, or prejudicial testimony is nevertheless slipped in by the defense or blurted out by a witness, will jurors follow a judge's instruction to ignore it?

Very possibly not. Several experimenters report that it is hard for jurors to ignore damaging pretrial publicity or inadmissible evidence such as the defendant's previous convictions. In one study, Stanley Sue, Ronald Smith, and Cathy Caldwell (1973) gave University of Washington students a description of a grocery store robbery-murder and a summary of the prosecution's case and the defense's case. When the prosecution's case was weak, no one judged the defendant guilty. When a tape recording of an incriminating phone call made by the defendant was added to the weak case, about one-third judged him guilty. The judge's instructing jurors that the tape was not legal evidence and should be ignored did nothing to erase this effect of the damaging testimony.

Reactance:
The desire to assert one's sense of freedom (see p. 229).

Indeed, in an experiment at Duke University, Sharon Wolf and David Montgomery (1977) found that a judge's order to ignore testimony—"It must play no role in your consideration of the case. You have no choice but to disregard it"—can even boomerang, adding to the testimony's impact. Perhaps such statements create reactance in the jurors. Or perhaps they sensitize jurors to the inadmissible testimony, much as happens when I warn you *not* to look at your nose as you finish this sentence.

We should not overstate these results: On some matters the judge's credibility does clearly influence the jury (Archer et al., 1979; Kerr et al., 1976). Indeed, one analysis of municipal court judges' behavior during videotaped trials revealed that their pretrial opinions of the case influenced their nonverbal behaviors during the trial—the tone of their instructions, their head nods, their frowns—which in turn related to the jury's later verdict (Blank et al., 1985). But the available research on how people form impressions of others indicates limits on the judge's powers of influence. It surely is easier for a judge to strike inadmissible testimony from the court records than from the jurors' minds. As trial lawyers sometimes say, "You can't unring a bell."

To minimize the effects of inadmissible testimony, judges had best *forewarn* jurors that certain types of evidence, such as a rape victim's sexual history, are irrelevant.

It is not always easy for jurors to erase inadmissible testimony from memory.

"The jury will disregard the witness's last remarks."

Once jurors form impressions based on such evidence, a judge's admonitions have much less effect (Borgida & White, 1980; Kassin & Wrightsman, 1979).

Better yet, judges could eliminate inadmissible testimony before the jurors hear it—by videotaping testimonies and removing the inadmissible parts. If, as some experiments suggest, live and videotaped testimony have much the same impact (Miller & Fontes, 1979), then perhaps more and more courtrooms will have life-size television monitors. Critics object that the procedure prevents jurors from observing how the defendant and others react to the witness. Proponents argue that videotaping not only enables the judge to edit out inadmissible testimony but also speeds up the trial and allows witnesses to talk about crucial events before their memories fade further.

Thus far we have considered three courtroom factors—eyewitness testimony, the defendant's characteristics, and the judge's instructions. Researchers are also studying the influence of many other factors. For example, at Michigan State University, Norbert Kerr (1978a; 1978b; 1981; 1982) has researched such issues as: Might a severe potential punishment (for example, a death penalty) make jurors less willing to convict? Do experienced jurors' judgments differ from those of novice jurors? Are defendants judged more harshly when the *victim* is attractive or has suffered greatly? Kerr's research suggests that the answer to all three questions is yes.

THE JURY

These courtroom influences upon "the average juror" are worth pondering. But most jurors are not "the average juror." They carry into the courthouse their individual

TESTING JURORS' COMPREHENSION

For a judge's instructions to be effective, they must first be understood. Study after study has found that many people do not comprehend the standard legalese of judicial instructions. Depending on the type of case, a jury may be told that the standard of proof is a "preponderance of the evidence," "clear and convincing evidence," or "beyond a reasonable doubt." Such statements may have one meaning for the legal community and different meanings in the minds of jurors (Kagehiro & Stanton, 1985). In one study of Nevada criminal instructions, viewers of videotaped instructions could answer only 15 percent of 89 questions posed to them about what they had heard (Elwork et al., 1982).

In studies at the University of California, Irvine, William Thompson and Edward Schumann (1987) discovered that people also easily misunderstand statistical information presented during trials. If told that a defendant's automobile has features like the one used in a hit-and-run accident—features characteristic of only 1 in 100 cars—some people will wrongly presume that the defendant is 99 percent likely to be guilty. (This ignores that there are many such cars and that the defendant was accused because hers happened to be one of them.) However, imagine being told that blood found on a beaten victim matches that of a defendant and that the incidence of this blood type is 5 percent. Three in five people will give this relevant evidence *no* weight if told by a clever defense attorney that 5 percent of the city's half million residents equals 2500 people—making the odds 1 in 2500 that the defendant is guilty. (This ignores that nearly all the 2500 cannot reasonably be considered suspects.)

Understanding how jurors misconstrue judicial instructions and statistical information is a first step toward better juror decisions. The next step is devising and testing clearer, more effective ways to present information—a task on which several social psychologists are currently at work.

attitudes and personalities, and when deliberating they influence one another. A key question is, how are their verdicts influenced by their individual dispositions and by their working together as a group?

THE JURORS AS INDIVIDUALS

Jury Selection

Given the variations among individual jurors, could trial lawyers use the jury selection processes to stack a jury in their favor? Often attorneys are severely limited in what questions they may ask prospective jurors. Nevertheless, legal folklore suggests they can sometimes "stack the jury." One president of the Association of Trial Lawyers of America boldly proclaimed, "Trial attorneys are acutely attuned to the nuances of human behavior, which enables them to detect the minutest traces of bias or inability to reach an appropriate decision" (Bigam, 1977).

Mindful of how error-prone people's subjective assessments of others tend to be (see Chapter 5), social psychologists are skeptical of the claim that attorneys come equipped with fine-tuned social Geiger counters. In several celebrated trials, survey researchers therefore assisted attorneys by using "scientific jury selection" to weed out potential jurors likely to be unsympathetic. For example, in a famous trial involving two of President Nixon's former cabinet members, conservatives John Mitchell and Maurice Stans, a survey revealed that from the defense's point of view the worst possible juror was "a liberal, Jewish, Democrat who reads the *New York Times* or the *Post*, listens to Walter Cronkite, is interested in political affairs, and is well-informed about Watergate" (Zeisel & Diamond, 1976). In nine trials where the defense is known to have relied on such methods, it has won seven (Wrightsman, 1978; Hans & Vidmar, 1982).

Despite the excitement—and ethical concern—about scientific jury selection, experiments reveal that jurors' attitudes and personal characteristics are actually poor predictors of their verdicts. There are "no magic questions to be asked of prospective jurors, not even a guarantee that a particular survey will detect useful attitude-behavior or personality-behavior relationships," report Steven Penrod and Brian Cutler (1987). Researchers Michael Saks and Reid Hastie (1978) concur: "The studies are unanimous in showing that evidence is a substantially more potent determinant of jurors' verdicts than the individual characteristics of jurors" (p. 68). In courtrooms, jurors' public pledge of fairness and the judge's instruction to "be fair" strongly commit most jurors to the norm of fairness. In experiments, it's only when the evidence is made ambiguous that researchers find jurors' personalities and general attitudes having much effect. Variations in the situation, especially in the evidence, generally have more effect. Saks and Hastie believe that "what this implies about human behavior, on juries or off, is that while we are unique individuals, our differences are vastly overshadowed by our similarities. Moreover, the range of situations we are likely to encounter is far more varied than the range of human beings who will encounter them" (p. 69).

"Death-Qualified" Jurors

A *close* case can, however, be decided by *who* gets selected for the jury. In criminal cases, people who do not oppose the death penalty—and who therefore are eligible to serve in cases where a death sentence is possible—are more prone to favor the prosecution, to feel that courts coddle criminals, and to oppose protecting the constitutional

"The kind of juror who would be unperturbed by the prospect of sending a man to his death . . . is the kind of juror who would too readily ignore the presumption of the defendant's innocence, accept the prosecution's version of the facts, and return a verdict of guilty."
Witherspoon v. Illinois, *1968*

rights of defendants (Bersoff, 1987). Simply put, those who favor the death penalty are more concerned with crime control and less concerned with due process of law. Thus when a court dismisses potential jurors who have moral scruples against the death penalty, it will likely also be composing a jury that is more likely to vote guilty. The research record is "unified," reports Phoebe Ellsworth (1985, p. 46): "Defendants in capital-punishment cases do assume the extra handicap of juries predisposed to find them guilty." What is more, conviction-prone jurors tend also to be more authoritarian—more rigid, punitive, and contemptuous of those with lower status (Gerbasi et al., 1977; Moran & Comfort, 1982; Werner et al., 1982).

Because the legal system operates on tradition and precedent, such research findings only slowly alter judicial practice. In 1986, the U.S. Supreme Court in a split decision overturned a lower court ruling that "death qualified" jurors are indeed a biased sample.

THE JURY AS A GROUP

Imagine a jury that, having finished a trial, has entered the jury room to begin its deliberations. Jury researchers Harry Kalven and Hans Zeisel (1966) report that chances are about 2 in 3 that the jurors will initially *not* agree on a verdict. Yet, after discussion, the odds reach almost 95 percent that they will emerge with a consensus. Obviously, group influence has transpired.

Juries are decision-making groups. Are they therefore subject to the social influences that mold other decision groups—to patterns of majority and minority influence, to group polarization, to groupthink? Let's start with a simple question: If we knew the jurors' initial leanings, could we predict their verdict?

The law prohibits observation of actual juries. Therefore, to create their own "mock juries," researchers simulate the jury process by presenting a case to groups of people and having them deliberate as would a real jury. In a series of such studies at the University of Illinois, James Davis, Robert Holt, Norbert Kerr, and Garold Stasser tested various mathematical schemes for predicting group decisions, including decisions by mock juries (Davis et al., 1975, 1977; Kerr et al., 1976). Will some mathematical combination of people's initial decisions predict their eventual group decision? Davis and his colleagues found that the scheme which predicts best varies according to the nature of the case. But in several experiments, a "two-thirds majority" scheme fared best: The group verdict was usually the alternative favored by at least two-thirds of the jurors at the outset. The lack of such a majority was likely to result in a hung jury.

The experimental findings of Davis and his collaborators fit well the survey findings of Kalven and Zeisel, who report that 9 out of 10 juries reach the verdict favored by the majority on the first ballot. Although you or I might fantasize about someday being the courageous lone juror who sways the majority, the fact is it seldom happens.

Minority Influence

Minority influence:
See pages 299–303.

Seldom, yet sometimes, the initial minority does prevail. In the Mitchell-Stans trial the four jurors who favored acquittal persisted and eventually prevailed. From the research on minority influence we can speculate that jurors in the minority will be most persuasive when they are consistent, persistent, and self-confident, especially if they can begin to trigger some defections from the majority.

Ironically, the most influential minority juror in the Mitchell-Stans trial, Andrew Choa, was a well-educated *New York Times* reader—someone who did not fit the survey profile of someone likely to be sympathetic to the defense. But Choa was also a dedicated supporter of Richard Nixon and a bank vice-president who ingratiated himself with the other jurors through various favors, such as taking them to movies in his bank's private auditorium (Zeisel & Diamond, 1976). Choa also illustrates a finding from jury experiments—that jurors who are male and of high social status tend to be most influential (Gerbasi et al., 1977).

Group Polarization

Group polarization:
See pages 286–292.

Jury deliberation seems to shift people's opinions in some other intriguing ways as well. In different experiments, jurors' initial sentiments have been magnified by their deliberation. For example, Robert Bray and Audrey Noble (1978) had University of Kentucky students listen to a thirty-minute tape of a murder trial and then, assuming the defendant was found guilty, recommend a prison sentence. Groups of high authoritarians initially recommended strong punishments (fifty-six years) and after deliberation were even more punitive (sixty-eight years). The low authoritarian groups were initially more lenient (thirty-eight years) and after deliberation became more so (twenty-nine years). Such findings hint that group polarization can occur in juries.

Confirmation that group polarization can occur in juries comes from an ambitious study in which Reid Hastie, Steven Penrod, and Nancy Pennington (1983) composed 69 twelve-person juries from Massachusetts citizens on jury duty. Each jury was shown a reenactment of an actual murder case, with roles played by an experienced judge and actual attorneys, and then given unlimited time to deliberate the case in a jury room. As Figure 10-4 shows, the evidence was incriminating: Four out of five jurors voted guilty prior to deliberation, but felt unsure enough that a weak verdict of manslaughter was their most popular preference. After deliberation, nearly all jurors agreed the accused was guilty, and most now preferred a stronger verdict—second degree murder. Through deliberation, the initial leanings had grown stronger.

Leniency

In many experiments, one other curious effect of deliberation has surfaced: Especially when the evidence is not highly incriminating, as it was in the experiment just described, jurors after deliberating tend to become more lenient (MacCoun & Kerr, 1988). This qualifies the "two-thirds-majority-rules" finding, for if even a bare majority initially favors acquittal, it usually will prevail (Stasser et al., 1981). Moreover, a minority that favors acquittal stands a better chance than one that favors conviction. And once again, a survey of actual juries confirms the laboratory results: Kalven and Zeisel (1966) report that in those cases where the majority does not prevail it usually shifts to acquittal (as in the Mitchell-Stans trial), and that when a judge disagrees with the jury's decision, it is usually because the jury acquits someone whom the judge would have convicted.

"It is better that ten guilty persons escape than one innocent suffer."
William Blackstone (1769)

Might "informational influence" (stemming from others' persuasive arguments) account for the increased leniency? The "innocent-unless-proved-guilty" and "proof-beyond-a-reasonable-doubt" rules put the burden of proof on those who favor conviction, perhaps making evidence of the defendant's innocence more persuasive than that for conviction. Or perhaps "normative influence" creates the leniency effect, as jurors

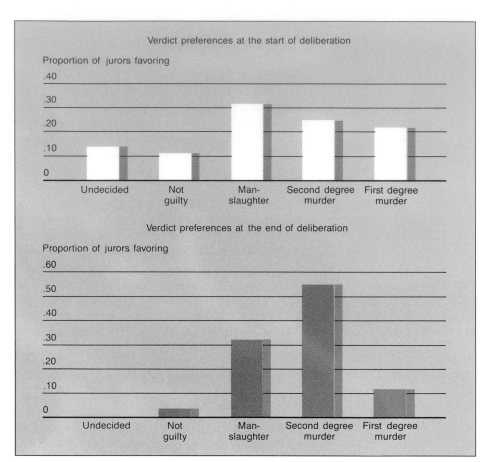

FIGURE 10-4
Group polarization in juries. In highly realistic simulations of a murder trial, 828 Massachusetts jurors indicated their initial verdict preferences, then deliberated the case for periods ranging from three hours to five days, and afterward indicated their verdicts. Initial tendencies, which favored the prosecution, were strengthened by the deliberation. Thus more people favored a murder verdict after deliberation than before. (From Hastie et al., 1983.)

who view themselves as fair-minded confront other jurors who are even more concerned with protecting a possibly innocent defendant.

Are Twelve Heads Better Than One?

In Chapter 9 we saw that on thought problems where there is an objective right answer, group rather than individual judgments are more often right. Does such hold true in juries? When deliberating, jurors not only exert normative pressure, trying to budge others' judgments by the sheer weight of their own, they also share information, thus enlarging one another's knowledge of the case. To the extent that informational influence moves jurors, we can hope that a jury's collective judgment will indeed be superior to that of its average member.

The evidence, though meagre, is encouraging. Some of the biases that contaminate the judgments of individual jurors have much less effect after the jurors have deliberated (Kaplan & Schersching, 1980). Deliberation seems not only to cancel out certain biases, but also to draw jurors' attention away from their own prejudgments, and to the evidence.

Are Six Heads as Good as Twelve?

In keeping with their British heritage, juries in the United States and Canada have traditionally been composed of twelve people whose task is to reach consensus. How-

"In France, a majority of eight out of twelve is sufficient to convict an accused."
Charlan Nemeth (1984)

ever, in several cases appealed during the early 1970s, the U.S. Supreme Court declared that in civil cases and state criminal cases not potentially involving a death penalty, courts could use six-person juries. Moreover, the court affirmed a state's right to allow less than unanimous verdicts, even upholding one Louisiana conviction based on a 9 to 3 vote (Tanke & Tanke, 1979). There is no reason to suppose, argued the court, that smaller juries, or juries not required to reach consensus, will deliberate or ultimately decide differently from the traditional jury.

The court's assumptions triggered an avalanche of criticism from both legal scholars and social psychologists (Saks, 1974). Some criticisms were matters of simple statistics. For example, if 10 percent of a community's total jury pool is Black, then 72 percent of twelve-member juries, but only 47 percent of six-member juries, may be expected to have at least one Black representative. So smaller juries are less likely to embody a community's diversity. And if, in a given case, one-sixth of the jurors initially favor acquittal, that would be a single individual in a six-member jury and two people in a twelve-member jury. The court assumed that, psychologically, the two situations would be identical. But as you may recall from our discussion of conformity, resisting group pressure is generally far more difficult for a minority of one than for a minority of two. Not surprisingly, then, 12-person juries are more likely than 6-person juries to have hung verdicts (Kerr & MacCoun, 1985).

Other criticisms were based on experiments by Michael Saks (1977), Charlan Nemeth (1977), and James Davis and others (1975). In these mock jury experiments, the overall distribution of verdicts from small or nonunanimous juries did not differ much from the verdicts pronounced by unanimous twelve-member juries, although verdicts from the smaller juries were slightly more inconsistent and unpredictable. There are, however, greater effects on the jury's deliberation. A smaller jury has the advantage of greater and more evenly balanced participation per juror, but the disadvantage of eliciting less total deliberation. Moreover, once juries realize that the necessary majority has been achieved, those not required to reach consensus seem to discuss minority views rather superficially (Davis et al., 1975; Foss, 1981; Hastie et al., 1983; Kerr et al., 1976).

"We have considered [the social science studies] carefully because they provide the only basis, besides judicial hunch, for a decision about whether smaller and smaller juries will be able to fulfill the purposes and functions of the Sixth Amendment."
Justice Harry Blackmun
(Ballew v. Georgia, 1978)

In 1978, after some of these studies were reported, the Supreme Court rejected the state of Georgia's five-member juries (although it still retains the six-member jury). Announcing the Court's decision, Justice Harry Blackmun drew upon both the logical and the experimental data to argue that five-person juries would be less representative, less reliable, less accurate (Grofman, 1980). Ironically, many of these data actually involved comparisons of *six-* versus twelve-member juries, and thus also argued against the six-member jury. But, having made and defended a public commitment to the six-member jury, the Court was not convinced that the same arguments apply (Tanke & Tanke, 1979).

SIMULATED JURIES AND REAL JURIES

Perhaps while reading this chapter you have wondered what some critics (Vidmar, 1979; Tapp, 1980) have wondered: Is there not an enormous gulf between college students discussing a simplified hypothetical case and real jurors deliberating a real person's fate? Indeed there is. It is one thing to ponder a pretend decision given minimal information, and quite another to agonize over the complexities and profound consequences of an actual case. So Reid Hastie, Martin Kaplan, James Davis, Eugene Borgida, and others have asked their participants, who sometimes are drawn from actual juror pools, to view enactments of actual trials. In some cases, participants have even been known to forget that a trial they are watching on television was not real, but staged (Thompson et al., 1981).

The usefulness of jury research was debated by the U.S. Supreme Court (1986) in its decision regarding the use of "death-qualified" jurors in capital punishment cases. The dissenting judges argued that a defendant's constitutional "right to a fair trial and an impartial jury whose composition is not biased toward the prosecution" is violated when only those not opposed to the death penalty are allowed to serve. Their argument, they said, was based chiefly on "the essential unanimity of the results obtained by researchers using diverse subjects and varied methodologies." The majority of the judges, however, declared their "serious doubts about the value of these studies in predicting the behavior of actual jurors." To which the dissenting judges replied that it is the courts themselves that have not allowed experiments with actual juries; thus "defendants claiming prejudice from death qualification should not be denied recourse to the only available means of proving their case."

Researchers also defend the laboratory simulations, by noting that the laboratory offers a practical, inexpensive method for studying important issues under controlled conditions (Bray & Kerr, 1982; Dillehay & Nietzel, 1980). What is more, as researchers have begun testing them in more realistic situations, findings from the laboratory jury studies have often held up quite well. Besides, no one contends that the simplified world of the jury experiment mirrors the complex world of the courtroom. Rather, the experiments help us formulate theories, theories that can be used to interpret the complex world.

Come to think of it, are these jury simulations any different from social psychology's other experiments, all of which create simplified versions of complex realities? By varying just one or two factors at a time in this simulated reality, the experimenter can pinpoint how changes in these one or two aspects can affect us. And that is the essence of the experimental method in social psychology.

SUMMING UP

In hundreds of recent experiments, courtroom procedures have been on trial. Social psychologists have conducted these experiments believing that the courtroom offers a natural context for studying how people form judgments, and that social psychology's principles and methods can shed new light on important judicial issues.

JUDGING THE EVIDENCE

During a trial, jurors hear testimony, form impressions of the defendant, and listen to the judge's instructions. At each of these stages, subtle factors may influence their judgments:

Eyewitness Testimony

Experiments reveal that both witnesses and jurors readily succumb to an illusion that a given witness's mental recording equipment functions free of significant error. But in fact, as witnesses construct and rehearse memories of what they have observed, errors creep in easily. Research suggests ways to alleviate such error, both in eyewitness reports and in jurors' use of such reports.

The Defendant's Characteristics

The facts of a case are usually compelling enough that jurors can lay aside their biases and render a fair judgment. But when the evidence is ambiguous, jurors are more likely to interpret it with the aid of their preconceived biases and to feel sympathetic to a defendant who is attractive or similar to themselves.

The Effectiveness of the Judge's Instructions

When jurors are exposed to damaging pretrial publicity or to inadmissible evidence, will they follow a judge's instruction to ignore it? In simulated trials, the judge's orders were sometimes followed, but often, especially when the judge's admonition came *after* the impression was made, they were not.

THE JURY

What matters is what happens not only in the courtroom, but also within and among the jurors themselves.

The Jurors as Individuals

In a close case, the jurors' own characteristics can influence their verdicts. For example, jurors who favor capital punishment or who are highly authoritarian appear more likely to convict certain types of defendants. Thus lawyers, sometimes with the aid of survey researchers, seek to identify and eliminate potential jurors likely to be unsympathetic to their side. Nevertheless, what matters most is not the jurors' personalities and general attitudes, but rather the situation that they must react to.

The Jury as a Group

Juries are groups, groups that are swayed by the same influences that bear upon other types of groups—patterns of majority and minority influence, group polarization, information exchange. Researchers have also examined and questioned the assumptions underlying several recent U.S. Supreme Court decisions permitting smaller juries and nonunanimous juries.

    Simulated juries are not real juries, so we must be cautious in generalizing these findings to actual courtrooms. Yet, like all experiments in social psychology, laboratory jury experiments can help us formulate theories and principles that we can use to interpret the more complex world of everyday life.

FOR FURTHER READING

Hans, V. P., & Vidmar, N. (1986). *Judging the jury.* New York: Plenum. A graceful review of the history of the jury, of two decades of jury research, of important court decisions, and of highly publicized trials. Examines issues involved in insanity, rape, and death penalty cases.

Kassin, S. M., & Wrightsman, L. S. (1988). *The American jury on trial: Psychological perspectives.* New York: Hemisphere. An easy-to-read and authoritative review of the entire process of trial by jury, from jury selection to verdict.

PART THREE

SOCIAL RELATIONS

Having explored how we *think about* (Part One) and *influence* (Part Two) one another, we come finally to social psychology's third facet—how we *relate* to one another. Our feelings and actions toward people are sometimes negative, sometimes positive. Chapters 11 (Prejudice) and 12 (Aggression) will examine the unpleasant aspects of human relations: Why do we dislike, even despise, one another? Why and when do we hurt one another? Then in Chapters 13 (Attraction) and 14 (Altruism) we will explore the more pleasant aspects: Why do we like or love particular people? When will we offer help to friends or strangers? Lastly in Chapter 15 (Conflict and Peacemaking) we will consider how social conflicts develop and how they can often be justly and amicably resolved.

329

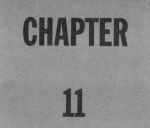

CHAPTER

11

PREJUDICE:
DISLIKING OTHERS

Prejudice comes in many forms—prejudices against people with AIDS, against "Northeastern liberals" or "Southern rednecks," against people who are short, fat, or homely. Consider a few actual occurrences of prejudice:

Shortly after World War II a Canadian social scientist simultaneously mailed 100 Ontario resorts two letters asking for room reservations for the same dates. In response to one letter, signed by "Mr. Lockwood," 93 percent of the resorts offered accommodations. In response to the other, signed by "Mr. Greenberg" (a frequently Jewish name), 36 percent offered accommodations. (Wax, 1948)

Several years ago, a group of homosexual students at the University of Illinois announced that the motto for one spring day would be: "If you are gay, wear blue jeans today." When the day dawned, many students who usually wore jeans woke up with an urge to dress up in a skirt or slacks. The homosexual group had made its point—that attitudes toward homosexuals are such that many would rather give up their usual clothes lest anyone suspect. . . . (*RCAgenda*, 1979)

Yoshio, one of a group of Japanese university students visiting an American college, matter-of-factly reveals to his Japanese peers that he is a "Burakumin," one of Japan's "ghetto-people" whose ancestors had an occupation regarded as polluting. Their response: Hands come to the mouth and brows furrow, revealing their shock and astonishment. For though physically indistinguishable from other Japanese, the Burakumin have for generations been segregated in Japan's slums, considered eligible only for the most menial occupations and unfit for intermarriage with other Japanese. So, how could it be that this obviously bright, attractive, ambitious student was a Burakumin?

WHAT IS PREJUDICE?

Prejudice, stereotyping, discrimination, racism, sexism. The terms often overlap. So, before seeking to understand prejudice, let's first sharpen our vocabulary by clarifying the terms. Each of the situations described above involved people harboring or acting upon bad feelings toward a group. And that is the essence of ***prejudice***: an unjustifiable negative attitude toward a group and its individual members. Prejudice involves pre-judgment; it biases us against a person based solely on the person's membership in a particular group.

Prejudice is an attitude. As we saw in Chapter 2, an attitude is a distinct combination of feelings, inclinations to act, and beliefs. This combination we called the ABC of attitudes: *a*ffect (feelings), *b*ehavior tendency (inclination to act), and *c*ognition (beliefs). A prejudiced person might therefore *dislike* the Burakumin and be inclined to *behave* in a discriminatory manner, *believing* them ignorant and dangerous.

The beliefs out of which prejudicial feelings grow are called ***stereotypes***. To stereotype is to generalize. In attempts to simplify the world, people often generalize: The British are reserved; Americans are outgoing; professors are absentminded; women who assume the title of Ms. are more assertive and ambitious than those who call themselves Miss or Mrs. (Dion, 1987). Such shorthand summaries of the world can sometimes be helpful. The problem with stereotypes arises when they are inaccurate, or *over*generalized, or resistant to change. Thus, if you told me I was about to meet Mike, an avid organic gardener, I might form an image of someone in bib overalls sporting a neatly trimmed beard and driving a van displaying a "Ban Handguns" bumper sticker. Certainly I would not expect someone to pull up in a Cadillac and

Prejudice:
An unjustifiable negative attitude toward a group and its individual members.

Stereotype:
A generalization about a group of people that distinguishes those people from others. Stereotypes can be overgeneralized, inaccurate, and resistant to new information.

emerge wearing a vested blue suit with a "We Need Nukes" lapel button. My stereotype of organic gardeners may contain a kernel of truth. Yet it is likely an overgeneralization. There may well be some conservatively dressed, Cadillac-driving organic gardeners. Were I to meet one I might just shrug it off by telling myself, "The exception proves the rule."

Discrimination:
Unjustifiable negative behavior toward a group of its members.

Racism:
(1) Individual's prejudicial attitudes and discriminatory behavior toward people of a given race, or (2) institutional practices (even if not motivated by prejudice) that subordinate people of a given race.

Sexism:
(1) Individual's prejudicial attitudes and discriminatory behavior toward people of a given sex, or (2) institutional practices (even if not motivated by prejudice) that subordinate people of a given sex.

Prejudice is a negative *attitude;* **discrimination** is negative *behavior.* And discriminatory behavior, though it often erupts from prejudicial attitudes, does not always do so. As Chapter 2 emphasized, attitudes and behavior are often loosely linked, partly because our behavior is influenced not only by our inner convictions but also by the requirements of particular situations. Prejudiced attitudes need not breed hostile acts, nor does all oppression spring from prejudice. **Racism** and **sexism,** for example, refer not only to individuals' prejudicial attitudes, but also to institutional practices that discriminate, even when there is no prejudicial intent.

Imagine a state police force that set a height requirement of 5 feet 10 inches for all its officers. If this institutional requirement were irrelevant to on-the-job effectiveness but tended to exclude Hispanics, Asians, and women, the requirement might then well be labeled racist and sexist. Note also that one could fairly make this allegation even if such discrimination were not intended. Similarly, if the word-of-mouth hiring practices in an all-White business had the effect of excluding employees different from those presently employed, the practice could be called racist, even if the employer were open-minded and intended no discrimination. In this chapter we will explore the sources and consequences of prejudiced attitudes, leaving it to sociologists and political scientists to explore racism and sexism in their institutional forms.

HOW PERVASIVE IS PREJUDICE?

Is prejudice inevitable? Can it be eradicated? As a case example, let's look at prejudice in the United States, examining trends in both racial and gender prejudice.

RACIAL PREJUDICE

In the context of the world, every race is a minority. Non-Hispanic Whites, for example, are but 1 in 5 people and will be but 1 in 8 within another half century. Thanks to mobility and migration during the past two centuries the world's races now intermingle, with relations that are sometimes hostile, sometimes amiable. A case in point: To judge from what Americans tell survey takers, racial prejudice toward Black Americans has plummeted since the early 1940s. In 1942, a majority of Americans agreed that "there should be separate sections for Negroes on streetcars and buses" (Hyman & Sheatsley, 1956); today, the question would seem bizarre. In 1942, fewer than a third of all Whites (only 1 in 50 in the south) supported school integration; in 1980, support for it was 90 percent. Considering what a thin slice of history is covered by the years since 1942, or even since slavery was an accepted practice, the changes are dramatic.

Psychologists continue to use the familiar terms Black and White, but capitalize them to emphasize that these are race labels and not literal color labels for persons of African and European ancestry.

Black Americans' attitudes also have changed since the 1940s, when Kenneth Clark and Mamie Clark (1947) demonstrated that Black Americans held anti-Black prejudices. In making its historic 1954 decision declaring segregated schools unconstitutional, the Supreme Court found it noteworthy that, when the Clarks gave African-American children a choice between Black dolls and White dolls, most chose the White. In studies from the 1950s through the 1970s, Black children were increasingly likely to prefer

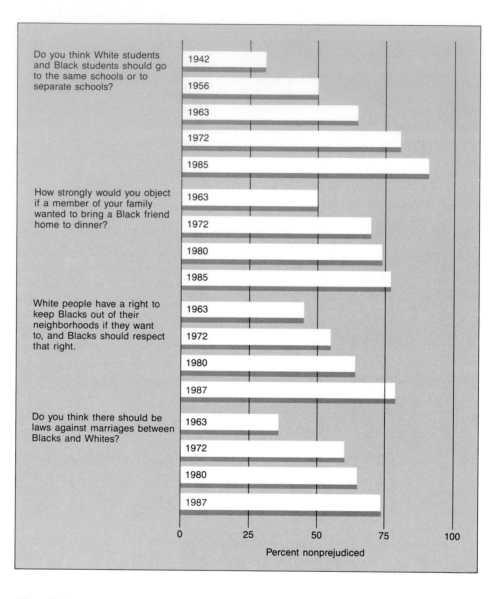

FIGURE 11-1
Expressed racial attitudes of White Americans from 1942 to 1985. (Data from Condran, 1979; Hyman & Sheatsley, 1956, 1964; National Opinion Research Center, 1980 to 1987.)

Black dolls. Among adults, Blacks have come to view Blacks and Whites as essentially equal in traits such as intelligence, laziness, and dependability (Jackman & Senter, 1981; Smedley & Bayton, 1978).

So, shall we conclude that racial prejudice is extinct in the United States? Although prejudice is no longer fashionable, there are several indications that racial prejudice still exists underground, surfacing when it is safe.

First, prejudice is evident in the residue of White Americans who, as Figure 11-1 indicates, unabashedly dislike Blacks. Their attitudes are mirrored by a smaller percentage of Black Americans who similarly dislike and avoid Whites (Farley et al., 1978).

Second, while variations on the question, "Should America oppress Blacks?" no longer detect prejudice, questions concerning more intimate interracial contacts do. "I would probably feel uncomfortable dancing with a Black person in a public place," is a more sensitive detector of racial feelings than "I would probably feel uncomfortable riding a bus with a Black person." In one recent survey, only 3 percent of Whites said they wouldn't want their child to attend an integrated school, but 57 percent acknowledged they would be unhappy if their child married a Black person (*Life*, 1988). Students in middle-schools with desegregated classrooms typically resegregate themselves when they socialize in the lunchroom (Sagar & Schofield, 1980b; Schofield, 1982, 1986). This phenomenon of *greatest prejudice in the most intimate social realms* seems to be a universal law of behavior. In India, people who accept the prejudices of the caste system will typically allow someone from a lower caste into their home but would not consider marrying such a person (Sharma, 1981).

Third, when racial attitudes are measured using techniques that minimize people's simply stating what they think is socially desirable, prejudice reappears. In Chapter 2, we saw what happens when White university students indicate their racial attitudes while hooked to an elaborate machine that supposedly acts as a lie detector: they often admit to more prejudice than do students responding under normal conditions. Other researchers have invited people to evaluate someone's behavior, that someone being either White or Black. Birt Duncan (1976) had White University of California, Irvine, students observe on a TV screen what they thought was a live confrontation between two men. The men's conversation developed into an argument that culminated with one of the two lightly shoving the other. When a White shoved a Black man, only 13 percent of the observers rated the act as "violent behavior." They more often interpreted the action as "playing around" or "dramatizing." Not so when a Black shoved a White man: Then, 73 percent of the observers said the act was "violent."

Fourth, many experiments have subtly assessed people's actual behavior toward Blacks and Whites. As we will see in Chapter 14, researchers have found that White Americans are as likely to aid a Black person (say, one who has dropped groceries) as a White—except when the person in need is remote (for example, a wrong number caller who needs a phone message relayed). Likewise, when asked to use electric shocks to "teach" a task to either a White or a Black person, White people are unaffected by the recipient's race—except when this aggressive behavior is safe, because the recipient can't retaliate or know who did it (Crosby et al., 1980). And in an experiment at the University of Alabama, Ronald Rogers and Steven Prentice-Dunn (1981) found that nonangered Whites administered less shock to a Black victim than a White victim, but that *angered* Whites behaved quite differently. When the victim had insulted them, they responded with *more* shocks when he was Black than when he was White (see Figure 11-2). The unavoidable conclusion: Discriminatory behavior surfaces not when a behavior would *look* prejudicial but when it can hide behind the screen of some other apparent motive.

Finally, attitude researchers similarly report that prejudicial attitudes, though no longer so blatant, still exist in subtle forms (Dovidio & Gaertner, 1988; Kinder, 1986; Pettigrew, 1985). One such form can be opposition to school busing to achieve better racial balance. If busing is serenely accepted when it transfers students between two White schools but vehemently resisted when it includes a school with a substantial minority enrollment, then one suspects that something more is involved than a commitment to neighborhood schools. John McConahay (1982, 1983) in surveying residents of the Louisville, Kentucky, area, found that people who strongly opposed busing for desegregation also exhibited other signs of subtle prejudice—for example, agreeing that "Over the past few years the government and news media have shown more respect to Blacks than they deserve." And Donald Kinder and David Sears (1981) found

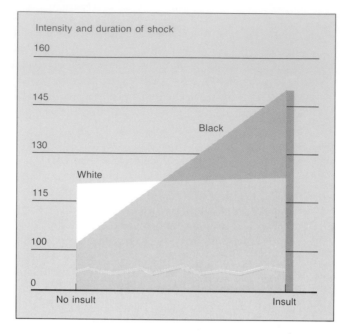

FIGURE 11-2
Does anger trigger latent prejudice? When White students administered electric shock, supposedly as part of a "behavior-modification experiment," they behaved less aggressively toward an agreeable Black victim than toward a White victim. But when the victim objected to the shocks and insulted the subjects, they responded with more aggression toward the Black victim. (Data from Rogers & Prentice-Dunn, 1981.)

that Whites in the Los Angeles area who exhibited subtle prejudice (for example, strong opposition to busing) were unlikely to vote for a prominent Black mayoral candidate.

Few are immune to subtle prejudice. Patricia Devine (1989) reports that seemingly unprejudiced people, like more prejudiced people, are aware of cultural stereotypes. Indeed, those low and high in prejudice often have similar automatic reactions, but the low-prejudice person will then consciously suppress these prejudicial thoughts and

If busing is accepted when it transfers students between White schools but resisted when it includes a school with a substantial minority enrollment, then we can suspect that something more is involved than a commitment to neighborhood schools.

feelings. It's like consciously breaking a bad habit, says Devine. Thomas Pettigrew (1987, p. 20) illustrates: "Many southerners have confessed to me . . . that even though in their minds they no longer feel prejudice toward Blacks, they still feel squeamish when they shake hands with a Black. These feelings are left over from what they learned in their families as children."

To summarize: The good news—during the past four decades blatant prejudice against Black Americans has plunged. White racial attitudes are far more egalitarian than a generation ago. The bad news pertains to all people of color [including American Indians and Hispanics (Trimble, 1988; Ramirez, 1988)]: Though now camouflaged by a more pleasant exterior, resentments and partiality still lurk.

PREJUDICE AGAINST WOMEN

How pervasive is prejudice against women? In Chapter 6, we examined gender-role norms—people's ideas about how women and men *ought* to behave. Here we first consider gender *stereotypes*—people's beliefs about how women and men *do* behave.

Gender Stereotypes

"All the pursuits of men are the pursuits of women also, and in all of them a woman is only a lesser man."
Plato, Republic

From research on stereotypes, two conclusions are indisputable: Strong gender stereotypes exist, and, as often happens, members of the stereotyped group accept the stereotypes. Men and women agree that you *can* judge the book by its sexual cover. Analyzing responses from a University of Michigan survey of adult Americans, Mary Jackman and Mary Senter (1981) found that gender stereotypes were much stronger than racial stereotypes. For example, only 22 percent of men thought the two sexes equally "emotional." Of the remaining 78 percent, those who believed females were more emotional outnumbered those who thought males were by 15 to 1. And what did the women believe? To within 1 percentage point, their responses were identical to those of the men.

When Inge Broverman, Paul Rosenkrantz, and their colleagues (Rosenkrantz et al., 1968; Broverman et al., 1972) surveyed New England college students and adults, they too found men and women in striking agreement: Males were seen as generally more competent (independent, dominant, decisive, ambitious) and females as warmer and more expressive (aware of others' feelings, tactful, gentle, exhibiting tender feelings). More recently, Natalie Porter, Florence Geis, and Joyce Jennings (Walstedt) (1983) found that women were not likely to be seen as leaders. They showed students pictures of "a group of graduate students working as a team on a research project" (see Figure 11-3). Then they gave them a test of "first impressions," asking them to guess which member contributed most to the group. When the group was either all-male or all-female, the students overwhelmingly chose the person at the head of the table. When the group was mixed-sex, a man occupying the head position was again overwhelmingly chosen. But a woman occupying that position was usually ignored. Each of the men in Figure 11-3 received more of the leadership choices than all three women combined. This stereotype of men as leaders seemed to operate unconsciously, for it was true not only of women as well as men, but also of feminists as well as nonfeminists. How pervasive are gender stereotypes? Quite pervasive.

It is important to remember that stereotypes are simply generalizations about a group of people, and as such may be true, false, or overgeneralized but based on a kernel of truth. How males and females *actually* differ was a topic of Chapter 6. There,

FIGURE 11-3
Which one of these people would you guess is the strongest contributor to the group? Shown this picture, college students usually guessed one of the two men, despite the fact that in same-sex groups the person at the head of the table is the most commonly guessed.

we noted that the average man and woman do differ somewhat in aggressiveness, empathy, sexual attitudes, and social power. So, might we conclude that gender stereotypes are accurate?

At best, they are probably overgeneralizations. Carol Lynn Martin (1987) surmised as much after asking visitors to the University of British Columbia to indicate which traits described themselves and to estimate what percentage of North American males and females have each trait. Males were *slightly* more likely than females to describe themselves as assertive and dominant and were slightly less likely to describe themselves as tender and compassionate. But as stereotypes these differences were greatly exaggerated: Their Canadian sample perceived North American males as almost twice as likely as females to be assertive and dominant and roughly half as likely to be tender and compassionate. So, self-perceived differences between the sexes are small, as are actual behavioral differences, but stereotypes are strong.

Stereotypes (beliefs) are not prejudices (attitudes). Stereotypes may support prejudice. But then again one might believe, without prejudice, that men and women are "different yet equal." Let us therefore see how researchers have probed for gender prejudice.

Gender Attitudes

Judging from what Americans tell survey researchers, attitudes toward women have changed as rapidly as racial attitudes. In 1937, one-third of Americans said they would vote for a qualified woman whom their party nominated for President; in 1988, 9 in 10 said they would. In 1967, 56 percent of first year American college students agreed that "The activities of married women are best confined to the home and family"; by 1987, only 26 percent agreed (Astin et al., 1987a, 1987b). In 1970, Americans were split 50-50 on whether they favored or opposed "efforts to strengthen women's status." By the end of the decade, this fundamental tenet of the women's movement was favored by better than 2 to 1. (See Figure 11-4.) And should there be "equal pay for women and men when they are doing the same job?" (NBC, 1977b). Yes, say both men and women—by a 16 to 1 margin, as close to absolute consensus as Americans ever get. From the days in which they were legally relegated to second-class citizenship and denied the right to vote, women have indeed come a long way.

And there is more good news for those who are upset by sex bias. One heavily publicized finding of prejudice against women seems no longer to hold true. In one study, Philip Goldberg (1968) gave women students at Connecticut College several short articles, asking them to judge the value of each. Sometimes a given article was attributed to a male author (for example, John T. McKay), other times to a female author (for example, Joan T. McKay). In general, the articles received lower ratings when attributed to a female. The historic mark of oppression—self-deprecation—surfaced again. Women were prejudiced against women.

Eager to demonstrate the subtle reality of gender prejudice, I obtained Goldberg's materials and repeated the experiment for the benefit of my own students. They showed no such tendency to deprecate women's work. So, working with Janet Swim and colleagues (1989), I searched the literature and corresponded with investigators to learn all I could about studies of gender bias in the evaluation of men's and women's work. To our surprise, the biases that occasionally surfaced were as often against men as women. But the most common result across 104 studies involving almost 20,000 people was *no difference*. On most comparisons, people's judgments of someone's work were not significantly affected by whether the work was attributed to a female or a male.

FIGURE 11-4

Prejudice against women: an idea whose time has passed? The percentage of Americans who say they favor efforts to strengthen women's status and would vote for a qualified woman candidate for president has steadily increased since the mid-1930s. (Data from Tom Smith, personal communication, and *Public Opinion*, September–October 1978, p. 36; January–February 1979, p. 36; and December–January 1980, pp. 33–34. Copyright American Enterprise Institute.)

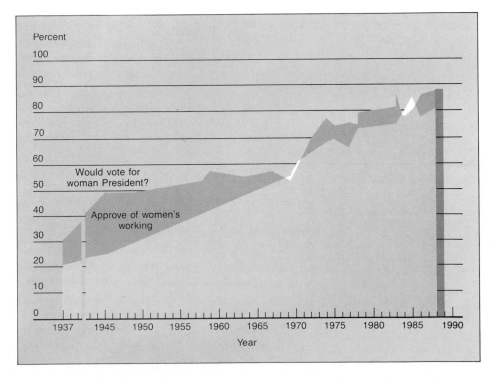

Gender prejudice can be expressed subtly in many ways.

"And just why do we always call my income the second income?"

The attention given highly publicized studies or prejudice against women's work illustrates once more a point emphasized in Chapter 1: Social scientists' values often penetrate their conclusions. This comment is not directed at the researchers who conducted the publicized studies; they did as they should in reporting their findings. However, as often happens, my colleagues and I more readily accepted, generalized, and proclaimed the findings supporting our preconceived biases than those opposing them.

So, can Americans congratulate themselves that gender bias is fast becoming extinct? Has the women's movement nearly completed its work? No. Despite the above findings, other research indicates that while blatant gender prejudice is dying, subtle bias still lives. For example, the bogus pipeline method has elicited admissions of bias. As we noted in Chapter 2, men led to believe an experimenter could read their true attitudes with a sensitive lie detector expressed less-than-usual sympathy toward women's rights.

Bias can also be subtly measured by having people evaluate the behavior of someone whose gender is irrelevant to that behavior. In experiments at Purdue University, Kay Deaux and her colleagues (1984) had people each evaluate only one person, thus hiding the experiment's purpose. In one experiment, students observed a fellow student succeeding on a perceptual task and were asked to explain it. When the task involved recognizing masculine objects (for example, a tire jack), a male's success was generally attributed to his ability; equivalent success by a female was attributed less to her ability, more to luck. However, with feminine objects, the student observers showed no such tendency to explain female success differently from male success (see Figure 11-5). Apparently, the students believed that anyone could perform the feminine tasks, but it took a man's skill (or else good luck) to perform the masculine tasks. In other experiments, females said to have succeeded in traditionally masculine activities—by becoming a successful physician, or by heroically helping police apprehend a gunman—were seen as less competent than a similarly successful male, but more highly motivated or deserving of a reward. However, men who succeeded in feminine tasks were not similarly considered as highly deserving (Feldman-Summers & Kiesler, 1974; Taynor & Deaux, 1973, 1975). In short, women who succeed in a "man's world" are

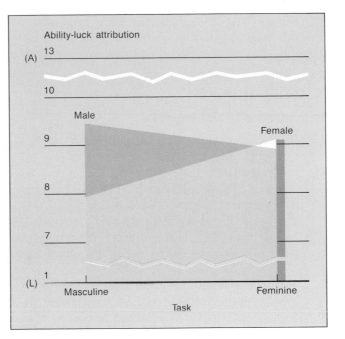

Ability-luck attribution

FIGURE 11-5
Explanations for the successes of male and female performers. On masculine tasks, male success was more likely to be attributed to ability than was female success. With feminine tasks, very little bias existed. (Data from Deaux & Emswiller, 1974.)

Question: "Misogyny" is the hatred of women; What is the corresponding word for the hatred of men? Answer: In most dictionaries, no such word exists.

often viewed as either uncommonly lucky or highly motivated, thus offsetting their presumed lesser abilities.

So, overt prejudice against racial minorities and women is far less prevalent today than it was just four decades ago. Although stereotypes remain, blatant racial and gender prejudices have largely disappeared. Nevertheless, techniques that are sensitive to subtle prejudice still detect widespread bias.

Most women know this. They believe that sex discrimination affects most working women, as shown by the lower salaries for women and for jobs such as child care worker that are filled mostly by women. Yet, curiously, Faye Crosby and her colleagues (1989) have repeatedly found that most women deny feeling personally discriminated against. Discrimination, they believe, is something faced by *other* women. *Their* employer is not villainous. They are doing better than the average woman. And, hearing no complaints, their managers—even in organizations where discrimination is occurring—can persuade themselves that justice prevails. Similar widespread denials of personal disadvantage, while perceiving discrimination against one's group, have been found among Blacks, unemployed people, and out-of-the-closet lesbians.

We have seen that prejudice, though often obscured, is real. What, then, causes prejudice? Let's examine its social, cognitive, and emotional sources.

SOCIAL SOURCES OF PREJUDICE

Prejudice springs from several factors, because prejudice, like other attitudes, serves several functions (Herek, 1986, 1987). Prejudicial attitudes may express our sense of who we are and gain us social acceptance; they may defend our sense of self against anxiety that arises from insecurity or inner conflict; and they may promote our well-being by supporting things that bring us pleasure and opposing things we believe are detrimental. Consider first how prejudice functions to defend the self-esteem and self-righteousness of those who are high or rising on the social and economic ladder.

SOCIAL INEQUALITIES

Prejudice Rationalizes Inequalities

"Prejudice is never easy unless it can pass itself off for reason." William Hazlitt (1778–1830), "On Prejudice"

A principle to remember: Unequal status breeds prejudice. Slaves are likely to be viewed by their masters as lazy, irresponsible, lacking ambition—as having just those traits that justify the existing social structure: slavery. Historians debate the forces that created the unequal status. But once inequalities exist, prejudice can be used to justify the economic and social superiority of those who have wealth and power. Thus, although prejudice and discrimination are but modestly associated—one often occurs without the other—they do support each other: Discrimination breeds prejudice, and prejudice legitimizes discrimination (Pettigrew, 1980).

Examples abound of prejudice rationalizing unequal status. Until recently, prejudice was greatest in regions of the U.S. where slavery had been practiced. Nineteenth-century European politicians and writers justified their imperial expansion by describing the exploited, colonized people as "inferior," "requiring protection," and a "burden" to be borne altruistically (G. W. Allport, 1958, pp. 204–205). Four decades ago, sociologist Helen Mayer Hacker (1951) noted how stereotypes of Blacks and women helped rationalize the inferior status of each: Both groups were viewed as being inferior in intelligence, as being emotional and primitive, and as "contented" with their subordinate role. Blacks were "inferior," women were "weaker." Blacks were all right in their place; women's place was in the home.

That attitudes easily adjust themselves to existing social relations is also evident in times of conflict. One often views one's enemies as subhuman and depersonalizes them with a label. Thus during World War II the Japanese people became the "sly Japs," and then after the war was over they became the "intelligent" Japanese whom Americans today are more likely to admire. Attitudes are amazingly adaptable.

In Chapter 2, we noted laboratory experiments revealing that oppressive acts breed negative attitudes. Harming an innocent victim typically leads aggressors to disparage their victims, thus helping to justify the hurtful behavior. For example,

Racial prejudice often begins during times of conflict, as during World War II when Japanese-Americans were sent to internment camps. Today, prejudice still exists. In Japan, racially stereotypical dolls indicate views some Japanese may have of Caucasians and Blacks.

Stephen Worchel and Virginia Andreoli (1978) found that, compared to students whose task was to reward someone for right answers on a learning task, those who instead gave shocks for wrong answers dehumanized their subject. They were less able to recall his unique characteristics (such as his name and physical characteristics) and better able to recall attributes such as race and religion that served to depersonalize the victim by identifying him with his groups. Thus, cruelty begets cruel attitudes and corrodes the aggressor's personal sensitivities.

Religion and Prejudice

Those who benefit from social inequalities, yet avow that "all are created equal," may especially need to construct self-serving justifications for the way things are. And what more powerful justification than to believe that God has ordained the existing social order? For all sorts of cruel deeds, noted William James, "Piety is the mask" (1902, p. 264)—the mask that sometimes portrays lovely expressions while hiding ugly motives.

In almost every country, religion is invoked on significant national occasions to sanctify the present order. In a remarkable turnabout, Father George Zabelka (1980), chaplain to the aircrews that bombed Hiroshima, Nagasaki, and other civilian targets in Japan, years later came to regret that he had provided religion's blessing upon these missions of devastation. "The whole structure of the secular, religious, and military society told me clearly that it was all right to 'let the Japs have it.' God was on the side of my country."

That religion can easily be used to justify injustice is one possible explanation of a remarkably consistent pair of findings concerning Christianity, the majority religion of North America: (1) American church members are more racially prejudiced than nonmembers, and (2) those professing traditional Christian beliefs are more prejudiced than those whose beliefs are less traditional (Batson et al., 1985; Gorsuch, 1988). These findings have been repeatedly observed no matter where and when the study was conducted or what type of racial prejudice was studied.

Although these findings are well-established, it is not clear what they mean. Knowing the correlation between two variables—religion and prejudice—tells us nothing about their causal connection. There might be no causal connection at all. Perhaps, for example, people with less education are more fundamentalist in their beliefs and also, for reasons having nothing to do with religion, more prejudiced in their attitudes. Or perhaps prejudice causes religion, by leading people to create religious ideas that support their prejudices. Or perhaps religion causes prejudice, by leading people to believe that since all persons possess free will, impoverished minorities have no one but themselves to blame for any perceived lack of virtue or achievement.

If indeed religion causes prejudice, then the more religious one is, the more prejudiced one would be. But three other findings consistently indicate this plainly is not so. First, among church members, faithful church attenders are, in twenty-four out of twenty-six comparisons, less prejudiced than irregular attenders (Batson & Ventis, 1982). Second, Gordon Allport and Michael Ross (1967) found that those for whom religion is an end in itself (those who agree, for example, with the statement, "My religious beliefs are what really lie behind my whole approach to life") express less prejudice than those for whom religion is more a means to other ends (for example, those who agree with the statement "A primary reason for my interest in religion is that my church is a congenial social activity"). Intrinsically religious people also are more likely to reflect their denomination's teachings regarding, say, whether homosexuals should be viewed with tolerance or hostility (Herek, 1987). And those for whom religion is an open-ended quest (not an attachment to pat answers) exhibit relatively little prejudice (Batson et al., 1986). Third, Protestant ministers and Roman Catholic priests have generally been far more supportive of civil rights efforts than have lay people (Hadden, 1969; Fichter, 1968). So all in all it's clear that some types of deeply religious people are far less prejudiced than more superficially religious people.

So, what is the relationship between religion and prejudice? As we have now seen several times in this chapter, the answer one gets depends on *how* one asks the question. If religiousness is defined in terms of church membership (not attendance) or willingness to agree at least superficially with traditional beliefs, then the more religious are the more racially prejudiced—hence the Ku Klux Klan, who rationalize bigotry with the aid of religion. However, if intensity of religious commitment is assessed in any of several other ways, then the very devout seem, on the average, less prejudiced than the nominally religious—hence the religious roots of the modern civil rights movement, among whose leaders were many ministers and priests. As Gordon Allport concluded, "The role of religion is paradoxical. It makes prejudice and it unmakes prejudice" (1958, p. 413).

Discrimination's Impact: The Self-Fulfilling Prophecy Lurks Again

Attitudes may coincide with the social order not only as a rationalization for it, but also because discrimination hurts its victims. "One's reputation," wrote Gordon Allport, "cannot be hammered, hammered, hammered into one's head without doing something to one's character" (1958, p. 139). In his classic book, *The Nature of Prejudice*, Allport catalogued 15 possible effects of victimization. Allport believed these reactions were reducible to two basic types—those that involve blaming oneself (for example, withdrawal, self-hate, aggression against one's own group), and those that involve blaming external causes (for example, fighting back, suspiciousness, increased group pride). If the net results are negative—for example, higher rates of illegitimacy, broken families, and delinquency—they can be used to justify continuing the prejudice and discrimination that help maintain them: "If we let those people in our nice neighborhood, property values will plummet."

But does discrimination affect its victims as this analysis supposes? We must be careful not to overstate the point, lest we feed the idea that the "victims" of prejudice are of necessity socially deficient. The soul and style of Black culture is for many a proud heritage and not just a response to victimization (Jones, 1983). Cultural differences need not imply social deficits. At the same time, social psychology has repeatedly demonstrated (recall Chapters 4, 5, and 6) that people's beliefs about others tend to be self-confirming. In laboratory experiments, for example, people's sex stereotypes can lead them to treat others in ways that create the reality fantasized (Skrypnek & Snyder, 1982).

That even subtle discrimination can affect its victims was evident in a clever pair of experiments by Carl Word, Mark Zanna, and Joel Cooper (1974). In the first experiment, White Princeton University men interviewed White and Black job applicants. When the applicant was Black, the interviewers sat farther away, terminated the interview 25 percent sooner, and made 50 percent more speech errors than when the applicant was White. Imagine yourself being interviewed by someone who sat at a distance, stammered, and ended the interview rather quickly. Would it affect your performance or your feelings about the interviewer? To find out, the researchers con-

"We have just enough religion to make us hate, but not enough to make us love one another."
Jonathan Swift,
Thoughts on Various Subjects.

"It is understandable that the suppressed people should develop an intense hostility towards a culture whose existence they make possible by their work, but in whose wealth they have too small a share."
Sigmund Freud,
The Future of an Illusion, *1927*

ducted a second experiment in which trained interviewers treated students as the interviewers in the first experiment had treated either the White or Black applicants. When videotapes of the students being interviewed were later rated, those who had been treated as were the Blacks in the first experiment were judged more nervous and less effective. Moreover, those being interviewed could themselves sense a difference; those treated as were the Blacks judged their interviewers as less adequate and less friendly. The experimenters concluded "that the 'problem' of black performance resides not entirely within the Blacks, but rather within the interaction setting itself."

The idea that victims need not be blameworthy is gaining acceptance. Nearly 3 of 4 White Americans now *disagree* that the reason "poor Blacks have not been able to rise out of poverty [is] mainly the fault of Blacks themselves," believing instead that "generations of slavery and discrimination have created conditions that make it difficult for blacks to work their way out of the lower class" (Dovidio et al., 1989).

INGROUP AND OUTGROUP

The social definition of who you are—your race, religion, sex, academic major—can also imply a definition of who you are not. The circle that includes "us" excludes "them." Thus, the mere experience of people's being formed into groups, quite apart from any relationship between the groups, may promote *ingroup bias*. Ask children, "Which are better, the children in your school or the children at (another school nearby)?" Virtually all will say their own school has the better children.

In a series of experiments, British social psychologists Henri Tajfel and Michael Billig (1974; Tajfel, 1970, 1981, 1982) found that even when the us–them distinction is inconsequential, people still immediately favor their own group. In one study, British teenagers evaluated modern abstract paintings and then were told that they and some others had favored the art of Paul Klee over that by Wassily Kandinsky. Then, without ever meeting the other members of their group, they were asked to divide some monetary awards among members of both groups. In experiment after experiment, when groups were defined even in this trivial way, favoritism toward one's group resulted. Researcher David Wilder (1981) summarizes the typical result: "When given the opportunity to divide 15 points [worth money], subjects generally award 9 or 10 points to their own group and 5 or 6 points to the other group." This bias occurs with both sexes and people of all ages and nationalities, though especially with people from individualistic cultures (Gudykunst, 1989). (People in communal cultures seem somewhat more disposed to identify with all their peers and so to treat everyone the same.)

Other researchers report that members of one's artificial group are also more positively rated (Brewer, 1979). In fact, some researchers report that even forming conspicuous groups on *no* logical basis—say, merely by composing groups X and Y with the flip of a coin—is sufficient to produce ingroup bias (Brewer & Silver, 1978; Billig & Tajfel, 1973; Locksley et al., 1980). In Kurt Vonnegut's novel *Slapstick*, computers gave everyone a new middle name; all "Daffodil-11's" then felt unity with one another and distance from "Raspberry-13's." The self-serving bias (Chapter 3) again surfaces, enabling people to achieve a more positive social identity: "We" are better than "they," even when "we" and "they" are alike. Because we evaluate ourselves partly in terms of our group memberships, seeing our own groups as superior helps us feel good about ourselves.

When our group has actually been successful, we can also make ourselves feel better by more strongly identifying with it. When queried after their school's football

"If we foresee evil in our fellow man, we tend to provoke it; if good, we elicit it."
Gordon Allport,
The Nature of Prejudice, 1958

Ingroup:
A group of people who share a sense of belonging, a feeling of common identity.

Outgroup:
A group that is perceived as distinctively different from or apart from the ingroup.

"There is a tendency to define one's own group positively in order to evaluate oneself positively."
John C. Turner (1984, p. 528).

Sometimes, anything favored by those we consider to be in the "outgroup" is cast in a negative light in our eyes.

"Uh-oh! They seem to have loved it!"

team has been victorious, college students frequently report that *"we* won." When questioned after their team has been defeated, they are somewhat more likely to report that *"they* lost." This tendency to bask in the reflected glory of a successful ingroup is especially strong among those who have just experienced an ego blow, such as learning they did poorly on a "creativity test" (Cialdini et al., 1976). We can also bask in the reflected glory of a friend's achievement, except when the friend outperforms us on something that is pertinent to our identity (Tesser et al., 1988). If you think of yourself as an outstanding psychology student, you will likely take more pleasure in a friend's excelling in mathematics than in psychology.

Ingroup bias:
The tendency to favor one's own group.

Ingroup bias is the favoring of one's group. Such relative favoritism could reflect (1) liking for the ingroup, or (2) dislike for the outgroup, or some combination of the two. If both, the implication would be that loyalty to one's group is generally accompanied by a devaluing of other groups. Is that true? Is ethnic pride conducive to prejudice? Does women's solidarity with other women stimulate them to dislike men? Does enthusiastic loyalty to a particular fraternity or sorority lead its members to deprecate independents and members of other fraternities and sororities? Results from experiments reveal support for both explanations, especially for the first: Apparently ingroup bias results primarily from perceiving that one's own group is good (Brewer, 1979), and to a lesser extent from a sense that other groups are bad (Rosenbaum & Holtz, 1985). Although, as always, we must be cautious about generalizing from laboratory experiments, it seems that positive feelings for our own groups need not be mirrored by equally strong negative feelings for outgroups. Granted, there appears to be some tendency for devotion to one's own race, religion, and social groups to be accompanied by a devaluation of other races, religions, and social groups, but the combination is not a given.

In everyday life, ingroup bias gets magnified by the tendency for people to interact primarily with the members of their own groups. When group members interact mostly with each other, their group feeling often gets intensified. For example, segregation was devised to confine feelings of sympathy and equality to those in the group (G. W. Allport, 1958, p. 205). Also, when interaction occurs mostly within group lines it frequently leads to exaggerated stereotyping of outgroups; to vested interests in maintaining the group's separation; and to thinking, feeling, and acting in ways unique to each group. Thus, ingroup bias is often amplified by patterns of interaction that further widen the gap between the groups.

CONFORMITY

Once established, prejudice is maintained largely by its own social inertia. If prejudice is a social norm—if it is expected—then many people will follow the path of least social resistance: They will conform to the social fashion. They will act not so much out of a need to hate as from a need to be liked and accepted (Pettigrew, 1980).

Studies by Thomas Pettigrew (1958) of Whites in South Africa and the American south revealed that during the 1950s those who conformed most to other social norms were also most prejudiced; those who in general were less conforming mirrored less of the surrounding prejudice. That nonconformity can exact a price was painfully evident to the ministers of Little Rock, Arkansas, where the Supreme Court's 1954 school desegregation decision was first implemented. Most ministers favored integration, but usually only privately; they knew that if they were to advocate it vigorously they would risk losing members and contributions (Campbell & Pettigrew, 1959). Or consider the Indiana steelworkers and West Virginia coal miners of the same era. In the mills and the mines, integration was accepted. However, in the neighborhood, the norm was rigid segregation (Reitzes, 1953; Minard, 1952). Prejudice was clearly *not* a manifestation of "sick" personalities, but more simply of the norms that operated in one situation but not another.

Conformity also maintains other prejudices. "If we have come to think that the nursery and the kitchen are the natural sphere of a woman," wrote George Bernard Shaw in an 1891 essay, "we have done so exactly as English children come to think that a cage is the natural sphere of a parrot—because they have never seen one anywhere else." Children who *have* seen women elsewhere—children of employed women, for example—tend to have less stereotyped views of men and women (Broverman et al., 1972; Hoffman, 1977). In short, it appears that people's attitudes are formed partly as mirrored images of surrounding attitudes, be those attitudes of "White pride," "Black pride," "male superiority," or "feminist consciousness."

In all this, there is a message of hope. If much prejudice is not deeply ingrained in one's personality, then as fashions change and new norms evolve, prejudice can diminish. And so it has.

INSTITUTIONAL SUPPORTS

Segregation is but one way that social institutions (schools, government, the media) bolster widespread prejudice. Prejudice also may be supported by political leaders, leaders who tend not only to reflect the prevailing attitudes but also to legitimize and

BEHIND THE SCENES

One's best ideas in social psychology often evolve from direct experience. As a White Southerner, I realized when reading *The Authoritarian Personality* as an undergraduate that the book did not explain most of what I thought I knew about antiBlack prejudice in the South. I knew many people who were racially prejudiced but did not appear to be authoritarian personalities. To explain the discrepancy, I needed only to recall the times I had been expelled from the public schools of Richmond, Virginia, for opposing the traditional racial norms. These ideas led directly to my research on how societal pressures to conform shape individual attitudes and behavior.

Thomas Pettigrew, University of California, Santa Cruz, and University of Amsterdam

reinforce them. When Arkansas' Governor Faubus barred the doors of Central High School in Little Rock, he was doing more than representing the majority of his constituents; he was helping to perpetuate their views.

Schools too reinforce dominant cultural attitudes. One analysis of stories in 134 children's readers written prior to 1970 found that stories focusing on boys outnumbered those on girls by better than 2 to 1 and men characters outnumbered women 3 to 1 (Women on Words and Images, 1972). Who was portrayed as showing initiative,

Much prejudice results not from "sick" personalities but simply from conforming to the norms with which we are raised.

bravery, and competence? In an old children's reader, the answer was vividly illustrated. Jane, sprawled out on the sidewalk, her roller skates beside her, listened as Mark explained to his mother:

"She cannot skate," said Mark.
"I can help her.
I want to help her.
Look at her, mother.
Just look at her.
She's just like a girl.
She gives up."

Not until the 1970s, not until our changing ideas about males and females fostered new perceptions of such portrayals, was this blatant stereotyping widely noticed. The institutional supports for prejudice are often unnoticed. Usually, they are not deliberately hateful attempts to oppress a group; more often they simply reflect how a culture at that time assumes things to be.

Are there contemporary examples of institutionalized biases that go as unnoticed by us as was the sexism of Mark and Jane a generation ago? Here is one that most of us have never noticed, although it is frequently right before our eyes: By examining 1750 photographs of people in magazines and newspapers, Dane Archer and his associates (1983) discovered that about two-thirds of the average male photo, but less than half of the average female photo, is devoted to the face. As they explored more widely, they found that this "face-ism" is widespread. They found it in the periodicals of eleven other countries, in 920 portraits gathered from the art work of six centuries, and in the amateur drawings of their students at the University of California, Santa Cruz. Georgia Nigro and her colleagues (1988) recently observed the face-ism phenomenon in more magazines, including *Ms.* The visual prominence given men's faces and women's bodies both reflects and perpetuates sex bias, the researchers suspect, because people whose faces are prominent in photos tend to be judged as more intelligent, ambitious, and attractive.

Many films and television programs also embody and reinforce prevailing cultural attitudes. The stupid, wide-eyed Black butlers and maids in the old Shirley Temple movies helped perpetuate the stereotypes they reflected. On radio and in the early years of television, the popular *Amos 'n' Andy* show provoked Americans to laugh at a portrayal of irresponsible, fun-loving Blacks. Today, most would find such images offensive, yet might fail to notice stereotyped portrayals of "savage" Indians (Trimble, 1988) or of the stereotyping and underrepresentation of women, whom men have outnumbered 3 to 1 in prime-time television and 9 to 1 as narrators of commercials (Bretl & Cantor, 1988; Gernber et al., 1986).

"The main reason that people think that women and men differ in their personal qualities is that the two sexes tend to be observed in different social roles."
Alice Eagly (1984)

EMOTIONAL SOURCES OF PREJUDICE

Although prejudice is usually bred by social situations, emotional factors often add fuel to the fire.

FRUSTRATION AND AGGRESSION: THE SCAPEGOAT THEORY

As we will see in Chapter 12, pain and frustration can evoke hostility. When the cause of our frustration is too intimidating or too vague, we often redirect our hostility. This

"And now at this point in the meeting I'd like to shift the blame away from me and onto someone else."

Scapegoats are used as a focus for our hostilities—no matter how unwarranted or displaced this aggression may be.

"Whoever is dissatisfied with himself is continually ready for revenge."
Nietzsche, The Gay Science, 1882–1887

phenomenon of "displaced aggression" may have contributed to the lynchings of Black people in the U.S. south. Between 1882 and 1930, there was a tendency for more lynchings to occur in years when the cotton price was low and economic frustration was therefore presumably high (Hovland & Sears, 1940; Hepworth & West, 1988).

Our targets for displaced aggression vary. Following their defeat in World War I and their country's subsequent economic chaos, many Germans treated Jews as villains. Long before Hitler came to power, one German leader explained, "The Jew is just convenient. . . . If there were no Jews, the anti-Semites would have to invent them" (quoted by G. W. Allport, 1958, p. 325). In earlier centuries hostilities were vented on witches. More recently, people who watched inflation or tax increases devour their wage increases could hardly direct their anger at the whole complex economic system. Some simplistic target more often bore the wrath, be it "lazy welfare bums" or "greedy corporations."

A famous experiment by Neal Miller and Richard Bugelski (1948) conducted with college-age men working at a summer camp confirmed the scapegoat theory. The men were asked to state their attitudes toward Japanese and Mexicans, both before and after being forced to stay in camp to take tests rather than attend a long-awaited free evening at a local theatre. Compared to a control group that did not undergo this frustration, the deprived group displayed increased prejudice following the frustration.

One source of frustration is competition. When two groups compete for jobs, housing, or social prestige, one group's goal fulfillment can become the other group's goal frustration. An ecological principle, Gause's law, states that maximum competition will exist between those species with identical needs. Similarly, researchers have consistently detected the strongest anti-Black prejudice among Whites who are closest to Blacks on the socioeconomic ladder (Greeley & Sheatsley, 1971; Tumin, 1958; Pettigrew, 1978; Vanneman & Pettigrew, 1972). When interests clash, prejudice pays, for some people. Certainly prejudice paid the White men who, for most of this century, managed to protect their own interests by excluding women and minorities from their trade. During the late 1980s, similar voices began calling for limits on the number of admissions and merit scholarships granted by competitive universities to high-achiev-ing Asian-Americans. Some Whites who are offended by quotas or goals for Black student admissions are less offended by the idea of guaranteeing places for themselves.

PERSONALITY DYNAMICS

Two people, with equal reason to feel frustrated or threatened, will often not be equally prejudiced. This suggests that prejudice serves other functions besides advancing our competitive well-being. Sometimes, suggested Sigmund Freud, people hold to beliefs and attitudes that satisfy their unconscious needs.

Needs for Status and Group Identification

Status is relative: To perceive ourselves as having status, we need people below us. Thus one psychological benefit of prejudice, or of any status system, is the feeling of superiority it offers. Most of us can recall a time when we took secret satisfaction in another's failure—perhaps when seeing a sibling reprimanded, or upon hearing of a classmate's difficulty on a test. From such comparisons our own esteem derives a boost. Is this why those low or slipping on the socioeconomic ladder and those whose positive self-image is being threatened tend to be more prejudiced (Lemyre & Smith, 1985; Thompson & Crocker, 1985)? In one study at Northwestern University, members of lower status sororities were more disparaging of other sororities than were members of higher-status sororities (Crocker et al., 1987). Perhaps people whose status is secure have less need to feel superior to others.

But other factors associated with low status could also account for prejudice. Imagine yourself as one of the Arizona State University students who took part in an experiment by Robert Cialdini and Kenneth Richardson (1980). You are walking alone across campus. Someone approaches you and solicits your participation in a five-minute survey. You agree. After the researcher gives you a brief "creativity test," he deflates you with the news that "you have scored relatively low on the test." The researcher then completes the survey by asking you some evaluative questions about either your school or its traditional rival, the University of Arizona. Would your feelings of failure affect your ratings of either school? Cialdini and Richardson found that, compared with those in a control group whose self-esteem was not threatened, the students who experienced failure gave higher ratings to their own school, lower ratings to their rival. Apparently, boasting of one's own group and denigrating outgroups can boost one's ego. Likewise, James Meindl and Melvin Lerner (1984) found that a humiliating experience—accidentally knocking over a stack of someone's important computer cards—provoked English-speaking Canadian students to express increased hostility toward French-speaking Canadians. And Teresa Amabile and Ann Glazebrook (1982) found that when Dartmouth College men were made to feel insecure, they judged others' work more harshly.

All this suggests that a man who doubts his own strength and independence might, by proclaiming women to be pitifully weak and dependent, boost his masculine image. Indeed, when Joel Grube, Randy Kleinhesselink, and Kathleen Kearney (1982) had Washington State University men view young women's videotaped job interviews, men with low self-acceptance disliked strong, nontraditional women. But men with high self-acceptance tended to be more attracted to *non*traditional than traditional women.

"By exciting emulation and comparisons of superiority, you lay the foundation of lasting mischief; you make brothers and sisters hate each other."
Samuel Johnson, quoted in James Boswell's Life of Samuel Johnson

A despised outgroup serves yet another need: the need to belong to an ingroup. As we will see in Chapter 15, the perception of a common enemy can serve as powerful cement for any group. School spirit is seldom so strong as when the game is with the arch-rival. The sense of comradeship among workers is often highest when they all feel a common antagonism toward management. To solidify the Nazi hold over Germany, Hitler used the "Jewish menace." Despised outgroups can strengthen the ingroup.

The Authoritarian Personality

Ethnocentrism:
A belief in the superiority of one's own ethnic and cultural group, and a corresponding disdain for all other groups.

The emotional needs that contribute to prejudice are said to predominate in the "authoritarian personality." In the 1940s, a group of University of California, Berkeley, researchers, two of whom had fled from Nazi Germany, set out on an urgent research mission—to uncover the psychological roots of an anti-Semitism so poisonous that it slaughtered millions of Jews and turned many millions of others into indifferent spectators. In studies of American adults, the researchers discovered that hostility toward Jews often coexisted with hostilities toward other minorities as well (Adorno et al., 1950). Morover, these *ethnocentric* people seemed to share authoritarian tendencies— an intolerance for weakness, a punitive attitude, and a submissive respect for their ingroup's authorities, as reflected in their agreement with statements such as "Obedience and respect for authority are the most important virtues children should learn."

The Berkeley researchers also found that frequently authoritarians had been harshly disciplined as children. This apparently led them to repress their own hostilities and impulses and to "project" such onto outgroups. Also, the insecurity of the authoritarian child was believed to predispose an excessive concern with power and status and an inflexible right-wrong way of thinking that made ambiguity difficult to tolerate; therefore, such people tended to be submissive to those with power over them and aggressive toward those beneath them.

The research on authoritarian personality has been criticized on several counts: (1) Perhaps mere lack of education accounted for the simplistic prejudices of authoritarian individuals. (2) The Berkeley researchers, by focusing on right-wing authoritarianism, seemed to overlook dogmatic authoritarianism of the left. (3) The democratic values of these researchers were hardly disguised: The contemptibly "rigid" authoritarian character which they described was strikingly similar to the "stable" character identified by psychologists in pre-Nazi Germany. Personal values thus determined whether such personalities were to be condemned for their "ethnocentrism" (American psychologists' label) or praised for their strong "ingroup loyalty" (German psychologists' label) (Brown, 1965).

Still, the main conclusion of this ambitious research has survived: There *are* individuals whose self-righteous hostilities surface as prejudice (Altemeyer, 1988). Feelings of moral superiority may go hand in hand with brutality toward one's perceived inferiors. Although the prejudices that maintain apartheid arise from social inequalities, socialization, and conformity (Louw-Potgieter, 1988), the South Africans who *most* strongly favor segregation tend to have authoritarian attitudes (van Staden, 1987). In repressive regimes across the world, people who become torturers typically have an authoritarian liking for hierarchical chains-of-command and contempt for those who are weak or resistant (Staub, 1989). Moreover, different forms of prejudice—toward Blacks, homosexuals, women, old people—*do* tend to coexist in the same individuals (Bierly, 1985; Snyder & Ickes, 1985).

COGNITIVE SOURCES OF PREJUDICE

Much of the foregoing explanation of prejudice could have been written in the 1960s. Not so what follows. This new look at prejudice supplements the established ideas by applying what has been learned from the explosion of research on social thinking. The basic point is this: Stereotyped beliefs and prejudiced attitudes exist not only because of social conditioning; not only because they serve an emotional function, enabling people to displace and project their hostilities; but also as by-products of our normal thinking processes. One should not assume that stereotypes always spring from malice. Rather, stereotypes are often a price we pay for simplifying our complex world. Stereotypes, by this view, are roughly analogous to perceptual illusions, a price we often pay for the benefits we derive from our perceptual knack for simplifying.

CATEGORIZATION

One way we simplify our worlds is to "categorize"—to organize the world by clustering objects into groups. A biologist organizes the world by classifying plants and animals. Once we have organized people into categories, we can more easily think and remember information about them. To the extent that persons in a group are similar, knowing their group enables us to predict better their individual behavior. Customs inspectors and airplane antihijack personnel are therefore taught "profiles" of individuals to suspect (Kraut & Poe, 1980). Such are categorization's benefits—providing useful information with a minimum amount of effort. However, the benefits exact a cost.

We have already considered one social cost: the ingroup bias. Merely dividing people into groups can trigger discrimination. There are other costs as well. When decisions must be made quickly, the use of efficient but oversimplified stereotypes increases (Kruglanski & Freund, 1983). Moreover, ethnicity and sex are, in our current world, powerful ways of categorizing people. Imagine Tom, a forty-year-old, Black real estate agent in New Orleans. I suspect that your image of "Black male" predominates over the categories "middleaged," "business person," and "southerner." By itself such categorization is not prejudice. But, as we will see, categorization does provide a foundation for prejudice.

Perceived Similarities within Groups, Differences Between Groups

Picture the following objects: apples, chairs, pencils. There is a strong tendency to see objects within a group as being more uniform than they really are. Were your apples all red, your chairs all straight-backed, your pencils all yellow? Similarly, once people are assigned to groups—athletes, theatre majors, math professors—we are prone to exaggerate the similarities within the groups and the differences between them (S. E. Taylor, 1981; Wilder, 1978). Consequently, mere division into groups can create a sense that members of another group are "all alike" but different from oneself and one's own group (Allen & Wilder, 1979). Because we generally like people we think are similar to us and dislike those we perceive to be different, this could provide a basis for the ingroup bias (Byrne & Wong, 1962; Rokeach & Mezei, 1966; Stein et al., 1965).

The mere fact of a group decision can also lead outsiders to overestimate the unanimity of group members. If a conservative wins a national election by a slim majority, observers infer that "the people have turned conservative." Should a liberal

Most sorority sisters and fraternity brothers see themselves as individuals in a diverse group, but they see those in other campus sororities and fraternities as homogenous.

have won by a similarly slim margin the people's attitudes would hardly have differed, but observers would have instead attributed a "liberal mood" to the country's voters. Whether the decision is made by majority rule or by a designated group executive, people tend to presume that it reflects the group members' attitudes (Allison & Messick, 1985, 1987; Mackie & Allison, 1987; Worth et al., 1987).

The tendency to see people in a group as more similar to one another than they really are is less true of perceptions of one's own group. Many non-Europeans see the Swiss as a fairly homogeneous people. But to the people of Switzerland, the Swiss are a diverse group, encompassing French-, German-, and Italian-speaking people. White Americans readily identify "Black leaders" who supposedly can speak for Black Americans and White reporters sometimes find it newsworthy that the "Black community is divided" on an issue. Whites apparently presume that their own racial group is more diverse, for they do not assume that there are "White leaders" who can speak for White America nor is it newsworthy that not all Whites agree on an issue. Similarly, to University of Oregon students, those of the other sex are perceived as having more uniform gender-related attributes than those of one's own sex; likewise, sorority sisters perceive the members of any other sorority as more homogeneous than the mix of women in their own sorority (Park & Rothbart, 1982).

"Women are more like each other than men [are]."
Lord (not *Lady*) Chesterfield

This "they are alike, we are diverse" phenomenon is especially potent among groups that are competing (Judd & Park, 1988). Moreover, the smaller the outgroup, the more people see it as unified (Mullen & Hu, 1988). Whether they are more homogeneous or not, the members of a small sorority will probably seem more alike.

Perhaps you have noticed that "they"—the members of any racial group other than your own—even look alike. Many of us can recall being embarrassed by having confused two people of another racial group, prompting the person we've misnamed to surmise, "You think we all look alike." A number of recent experiments, by John Brigham, June Chance, Alvin Goldstein, and Roy Malpass in the U.S. and by Hayden Ellis in Scotland, reveal that people of other races do in fact appear to look more alike than do people of one's own race (Brigham & Williamson, 1979; Chance & Goldstein, 1981; Ellis, 1981). For example, when White students are shown faces of a few White and a few Black individuals and then asked to pick these individuals out of a photographic lineup, they more accurately recognize the White faces than the Black.

I am White. When I first read this research I thought, of course: White people *are* more physically diverse than Blacks. But my reaction was apparently just an

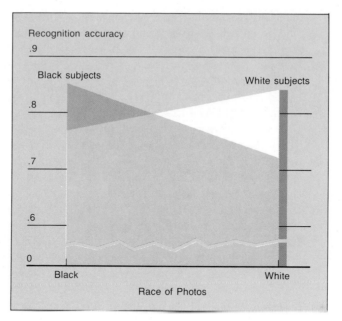

FIGURE 11-6
The own-race bias. White subjects more accurately recognize the faces of Whites than of Blacks; Black subjects more accurately recognize the faces of Blacks than of Whites. (From Devine & Malpass, 1985).

The term "own-race" bias is a misnomer in the case of Anglo/Hispanic identifications. Both ethnic groups are classified as Caucasians.

illustration of the phenomenon. For if my reaction were correct, Black people, too, would better recognize a White face among a lineup of Whites than a Black face in a lineup of Blacks. But in fact the opposite appears true: As Figure 11-6 illustrates, Blacks more easily recognize a fellow Black than they do a White (Bothwell et al., 1989). And Hispanics more readily recognize a fellow Hispanic whom they saw a couple hours earlier than they do an Anglo (Platz & Hosch, 1988).

This intriguing "own-race bias" appears to be an automatic cognitive phenomenon, for it is usually unrelated to the perceiver's racial attitudes (Brigham & Malpass, 1985). But experience may play a role. June Chance (1985) reports that White students have enormous difficulty recognizing individual Japanese faces (despite the fact that Japanese facial features are actually as varied as those of White faces); but White students become markedly better at recognizing Japanese faces if over several training sessions they view pairs of Japanese faces, which they must learn to differentiate. Chance's hunch is that experience enables people to become attuned to the types of faces they frequently encounter. And that perhaps explains why to me all Cabbage Patch dolls look alike, though not to my 9-year-old daughter and her friends.

THE PERSUASIVE POWER OF DISTINCTIVE STIMULI

Distinctive People Draw Attention

Other ways we perceive our worlds also breed stereotypes. Distinctive people and vivid or extreme occurrences often capture our attention and distort our judgments.

Have you ever found yourself working or socializing in a situation in which you were the only person present of your sex, race, or nationality? If so, there is a good chance your difference from the others made you more noticeable and the object of more attention. A Black in an otherwise White group, a man in an otherwise female group, or a woman in an otherwise male group tends to be perceived as more prominent and influential and to have his or her good and bad qualities exaggerated in people's minds (Crocker, 1984; S. E. Taylor & et al., 1979). This occurs because when someone in a group is made salient (conspicuous), we tend to see that person as causing whatever happens (Taylor & Fiske, 1978). If we are positioned to focus our attention on Joe, an average member of a group, Joe will seem to have a greater than average influence upon the group.

In an experiment at Harvard, Ellen Langer and Lois Imber (1980) found that students watching a videotape of a man reading paid closer attention when they were led to think he was out of the ordinary—a cancer patient, a homosexual, or a millionaire. They detected characteristics of the man that were ignored by other viewers, and their evaluation of him was more extreme. For example, those who thought the man a cancer patient noticed his distinctive facial characteristics and bodily movements, and thus perceived him as much more "different from most people" than did the other viewers. So the extra attention paid to distinctive people can create an illusion that such people differ more from others than they really do. If people thought you had the IQ of a genius, they would likely notice things about you that otherwise would pass unnoticed.

However, it is possible for people to perceive others reacting to their distinctiveness when actually they aren't. At Dartmouth College, researchers Robert Kleck and Angelo Strenta (1980) discovered this when they led college women to feel disfigured. The women thought the purpose of the experiment was to assess how another woman student would react to a facial scar that was created with theatrical makeup on the first woman's right cheek, running from the ear to the mouth. Actually, the purpose was to see how the women themselves, when made to feel deviant, would perceive others' behavior toward them. After applying the makeup, the experimenter gave each subject a small hand mirror so she could see the authentic-looking scar. When she put the mirror down, he then applied some "moisturizer" to "keep the makeup from cracking." What the "moisturizer" really did was remove the scar.

The scene that followed was poignant. A young woman, feeling terribly self-conscious about her supposedly disfigured face, is talking with another woman who sees no such disfigurement and knows nothing of what has gone before. If you have ever felt similarly self-conscious—perhaps about a physical handicap, adolescent acne,

When suffering from a physical handicap, we often perceive patronizing reactions from others which, in fact, may not exist. The result can be crippling. An exception, fashion model Marla Hanson turned her violent and tragic disfigurement into a testament of true courage as she confidently faced the press while recovering in the hospital.

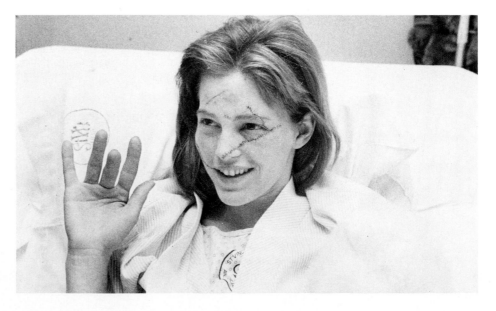

The self-consciousness created by being a token minority—say, a man in a group of women or a woman in a group of men—can also disrupt one's normal thinking and memory processes, thereby making the token person seem inept (Lord & Saenz, 1985).

even just "awful-looking hair"—then perhaps you can sympathize with the self-conscious woman. Compared to women in a control condition, who were led to believe their conversational partner merely thought they had an allergy, the "disfigured" women became acutely sensitive to how their partners were looking at them; they rated their partners as more tense, distant, and patronizing. But in fact, observers who later analyzed videotapes of how the "disfigured" persons were treated could find no such differences in treatment. Speculating from these results, it would seem that if we are self-conscious about being different, we may misinterpret mannerisms and comments that we would otherwise not notice.

Vivid, Distinctive Cases Get Remembered

Our minds also use distinctive cases as a shortcut to judging groups. Are Blacks good athletes? "Well, there's Carl Lewis and Florence Griffith Joyner and Mike Tyson. And look at the professional basketball teams. Yeah, I'd say so." Note the thought processes at work here: One recalls instances of a particular category and, based on those recalled, forms a generalization, which may or may not be correct. Hence the tourist who concluded, "All Indians walk single file. At least the one I saw did." The problem, as noted in Chapter 4, is that vivid instances, though persuasive because of their greater impact on memory, are seldom representative of the larger group. Exceptional athletes, though distinctive and memorable, are not the best basis for judging the distribution of athletic talent among an entire race.

Two experiments demonstrate how distinctive cases fuel stereotypes. In one, Myron Rothbart and his colleagues (1978) had University of Oregon students view fifty slides, each of which stated the man's height. For one group of students, ten of the men were said to be slightly over 6 feet (up to 6 feet 4 inches). For other students, these ten men were well over 6 feet (up to 6 feet 11 inches). When asked later how many of the men were over 6 feet, those given the moderately tall instances recalled 5 percent too many, while those given the extreme instances recalled 50 percent too many. In a follow-up experiment, students were given descriptions of the actions of fifty men, ten of whom had performed either nonviolent crimes such as forgery or violent crimes such as rape. Those shown the list with the violent crimes most overestimated the number of criminal acts.

Because distinctive, extreme cases are most easily remembered—and because they alone are newsworthy—they dominate our images of various groups. Ask some people to picture a person who opposes South African apartheid and you are more likely to call up televised images of protestors carrying placards than of the many ordinary people who oppose apartheid in less distinctive ways. The attention-getting power of distinctive, extreme cases helps explain why middle-class people so greatly exaggerate the dissimilarities between themselves and the underclass. Contrary to people's stereotypes of "welfare queens" driving Cadillacs, people living in poverty generally share the aspirations of the middle class and would rather provide for themselves than accept public assistance (Cook & Curtin, 1987).

That we are prone to overgeneralize from vivid cases is indisputable. The question has become, when are we most likely to do so? George Quattrone and Edward Jones (1980) report that the tendency to form stereotypes from the behavior of a single person is especially strong when one's prior expectations are weak and when the person is a member of an unfamiliar group. They showed Princeton and Rutgers students a videotape of a student who was said to attend either Princeton or Rutgers, and who decided, in one version of the tape, to wait alone for an experiment or, in another version of the tape, to wait with others. When the students were asked to guess what most other students would decide, they guessed that most students would choose as did the one they saw on the tape. But viewing a single student deciding whether to listen to rock or classical music—an area in which students have stronger expectations about other students' preferences—had less effect on their guesses of what most students would choose. Moreover, the tendency to generalize from the single case was much greater when the student was said to be from the other university, not one's own. Rutgers students who saw a supposed Princeton student choosing to wait alone thus ended up with an impression of Princeton students as rather solitary; those who saw the Princeton student choosing to be with others formed a more sociable impression of Princeton students. In other words, the less knowledge we have about a group and its behavior, the more likely we are to be influenced by a vivid case or two. To see is to believe.

Distinctive Events Produce Illusory Correlations

Stereotypes assume a correlation between people's group membership and their characteristics ("Italians are emotional," "Jews are shrewd," "Accountants are perfectionists"). Even under the best of conditions, our attentiveness to unusual occurrences can create *illusory correlations*. Because we are sensitive to distinctive events, the co-occurrence of two such events is especially noticeable—more noticeable than each of the times the unusual events do not occur together.

Illusory correlation:
A false impression that two variables, say gender and intelligence, are associated. See Chapter 4, p. 120.

David Hamilton and Robert Gifford (1976) demonstrated this in a clever experiment with students at Southern Connecticut State College. The students were shown slides on which various people, members of "Group A" or "Group B," were said to have done something desirable or undesirable. For example, "John, a member of Group A, visited a sick friend in the hospital." Twice as many statements described members of Group A as Group B, but both groups were associated with nine desirable behaviors for every four undesirable behaviors. Since both Group B and the undesirable acts were less frequent, their co-occurrence—for example, "Allen, a member of Group B, dented the fender of a parked car and didn't leave his name"—was an infrequent combination that caught people's attention. The students therefore overestimated the frequency with which the "minority" group (B) acted undesirably; consequently, they judged Group B more harshly.

Remember, Group B members actually committed undesirable acts in the same proportion as Group A members. Moreover, the students had no preexisting biases for or against Group B, and they received the information more systematically than daily experience ever offers it. Follow-up studies have confirmed the phenomenon and its explanation—that the joint occurrence of two distinctive events grabs attention (Hamilton & Sherman, 1989; Mullen & Johnson, 1988). Moreover, the negative impression may generalize to other domains (Acorn et al., 1988). Thus illusory correlation provides yet another source for the formation of racial stereotypes.

The mass media reflect and feed this phenomenon. For instance, when a self-described homosexual murders someone, homosexuality often gets mentioned. When a heterosexual person murders someone, this is a less distinctive event; thus the person's sexual orientation is seldom mentioned. Likewise, when an ex-mental patient shoots a victim such as John Lennon or President Reagan, the person's mental history commands attention. Assassins and mental hospitalization are both relatively infrequent, making their combination especially newsworthy. Such reporting can add to the illusion of a large correlation between (1) homosexuality or mental hospitalization and (2) violent tendencies.

Unlike those who judged Groups A and B, we often have preexisting biases. Further research by David Hamilton and Terrence Rose (1980) reveals that our preexisting stereotypes can lead us to "see" correlations that aren't there. They had University of California, Santa Barbara, students read sentences in which the members of different occupational groups were described by various adjectives (for example, "Doug, an accountant, is timid and thoughtful"). In actuality, each occupation was described equally often by each adjective; accountants, doctors, and salespeople were equally often reported to be timid, wealthy, and talkative. However, the students *thought* they had more often read descriptions of timid accountants, wealthy doctors, and talkative salespeople. Their stereotyping led them to perceive correlations that weren't there, thus helping to perpetuate the stereotypes (McArthur & Friedman, 1980). To believe is to see.

ATTRIBUTION: IS IT A JUST WORLD?

Fundamental attribution error:
See Chapter 3, p. 74.

In explaining others' actions, we frequently commit the fundamental attribution error. We attribute their behavior so much to their inner dispositions that we discount important situational forces. The error occurs partly because our attention is focused on the persons themselves, not on the constraints of their situations. For example, the race or sex of a person is vivid and attention-getting; the role requirements or situational forces working upon the person are more invisible. In the last century, even slavery was generally overlooked as an explanation for certain behaviors of slaves. Rather, their behavior was attributed to their own nature. Until recently, the same was true of how we explained the perceived differences between women and men. Since gender-role constraints were hard to see, we were more likely to attribute men's and women's behavior to their innate dispositions.

The Ultimate Attribution Error

The ultimate attribution error: Granting the benefit of the doubt to members of one's own group, but not to members of other groups. Thus negative behavior by out-group members is attributed to their dispositions, positive behavior explained away. (Also called "group-serving bias.")

Thomas Pettigrew (1979, 1980) argues that this fundamental attribution error becomes the ***ultimate attribution error*** when people explain the actions of people in groups. Members of one's own group are granted the benefit of the doubt: "She donated because she has a good heart; he refused because he had to under the circumstances." Members of other groups are less often given the benefit of the doubt; more often the worst is assumed: "He donated to gain their favor; she refused because she's selfish." Hence, as we noted earlier in this chapter, the shove that is perceived by Whites as mere "horsing around" when done by a fellow White man becomes a "violent gesture" when done by a Black. However, positive behavior by outgroup members is more likely to be dismissed, in one of several ways: as a "special case" ("He is certainly bright and hardworking—not at all like other Hispanics"), as due to luck or some special advantage ("She probably got admitted just because her med school had to fill its quota for women applicants"), as demanded by the situation ("Under the circumstances, what could the cheap Scot do but pay the whole check?"), or by attributing it to extra effort ("Jewish students get better grades because they're so compulsive"). Groups that stress modesty, such as the Chinese, or that have a comparatively disadvantaged status seem to exhibit less of this "group-serving bias," as the phenomenon is also known (Hewstone & Ward, 1985; Fletcher & Ward, 1989).

Earlier we noted that laying blame on the victim can be a way to justify one's own superior status. Now we see that can occur as people attribute the failures of an outgroup to the flawed dispositions of its members: "They fail because they're stupid; we fail because we didn't try" (Hewstone et al., 1982; Whitehead et al., 1982). If women, Blacks, or Jews have been abused, they must somehow have brought it on themselves. When the British marched a group of German civilians around the Belsen concentration camp at the close of World War II, one German responded, "What terrible criminals these prisoners must have been to receive such treatment."

The Just-World Phenomenon

Notice in the previous example that the person blaming the victim had done the victim no harm. In a series of experiments conducted at the Universities of Waterloo and Kentucky, Melvin Lerner and his colleagues (Lerner & Miller, 1978; Lerner, 1980) learned that merely *observing* another person being innocently victimized is enough to make the victim seem less worthy. Imagine that you along with some others are participating in a study on the perception of emotional cues (Lerner & Simmons, 1966). One of the participants, a confederate, is selected by lottery to perform a memory task. This person receives painful shocks whenever she gives a wrong answer. You and the others note her emotional responses. After watching the victim receive a number of these apparently painful shocks, you are asked to evaluate her. How would you respond? With compassionate sympathy? We might legitimately expect such. As Ralph Waldo Emerson wrote, "The martyr cannot be dishonored." But on the contrary, the experiments reveal that when observers were powerless to alter the victim's fate, they, by and large, rejected and devalued the victim. Juvenal, the Roman satirist, anticipated these results: "The Roman mob follows after Fortune . . . and hates those who have been condemned."

Just-world phenomenon: The tendency of people to believe the world is just and that therefore people get what they deserve and deserve what they get.

Lerner (1980) suggests that such disparaging of hapless victims results from our need to believe, "I am a just person living in a just world, a world where people get what they deserve." From early childhood, he argues, we are taught that good is rewarded and evil punished. Hard work and virtue pay dividends; laziness and immorality do not. From this it is but a short leap to assuming, furthermore, that those who are rewarded must be good and those who suffer must likewise deserve their fate. The classic illustration of such thinking is found in the Old Testament story of Job. Job's friends surmise that, this being a just world, Job must have done something wicked to elicit such terrible suffering.

All this suggests that one reason why people may seem indifferent to social injustice is not because they are unconcerned for justice, but because they *see* no injustice. What is more, believing in a just world—believing, as many people do, that rape victims must have behaved seductively (Borgida & Brekke, 1985), that battered spouses have provoked their beatings (Summers & Feldman, 1984), that poor people don't deserve better (Furnham & Gunter, 1984), that sick people are responsible for their illness (Gruman & Sloan, 1983)—enables successful people to reassure themselves that they, too, have gotten what they deserve. The wealthy and healthy can see their good fortune, and the misfortune of others, as justly deserved. Linking good fortune with virtue and misfortune with moral failure thus enables the fortunate to feel pride in their achievements and to shuck off responsibility toward the misfortunate.

People loathe a loser even when the loser's misfortune quite obviously stems from mere bad luck. People *know* that gambling outcomes are just good or bad luck and

IS IT A JUST WORLD? BLAMING THE RAPE VICTIM

The 21-year-old divorced mother had been drinking and socializing in Big Dan's bar in New Bedford, Massachusetts. But had she invited her fate? Egged on by one another, several male patrons men seized her, tore off most of her clothes, and gang-raped her on the barroom floor and then on the pool table while others in the bar applauded and cheered. In this and several other such incidents, dramatized in the 1988 movie, *The Accused*, many people condemned the victims as having "deserved it." "She had no business being in a bar," said one elderly woman. "She should have been home with her kids instead of destroying men's lives!"

This case, in both its actual and dramatized versions,

illustrates our human readiness not only to credit people for their successes but to blame them for their misfortunes. In one national survey, 33 percent of British people agreed that women who have been raped are usually to blame for it (Wagstaff, 1982). In a recent experiment, those given a description of a woman's friendly behavior with a man judged her actions as appropriate. Others, who were also told she was subsequently raped by the man, judged the *same* behavior as inappropriate—as having invited the rape (Janoff-Bulman et al., 1985). If it's a just world, then victims can be blamed for their fates. But is the world always just?

should not affect their evaluations of the gambler. Still, they can't resist playing Monday-morning quarterback—judging people by their results. Ignoring that reasonable decisions can bring bad results, they judge losers as less competent (Baron & Hershey, 1988). Lawyers and stock market speculators may similarly judge themselves by their outcomes, thus becoming smug after several successes and self-reproachful after failures. Talent and initiative are not unrelated to success. But the problem with the "It's-a-just-world" type of thinking is that it discounts the uncontrollable factors that leash one's best efforts.

On a more hopeful note, our yearning to see and to have a just, equitable world lies waiting to be tapped. The same motive that leads us to disparage life's losers when

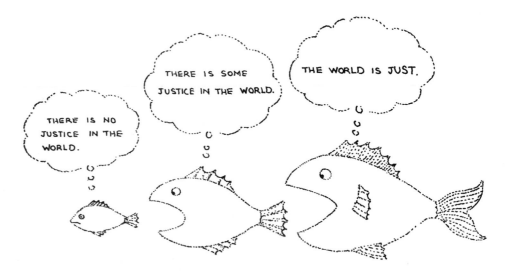

The just-world phenomenon.   MANKOFF

we can do little to help, can, when we finally recognize injustice, lead us to act (D. T. Miller, 1977). Once we perceive injustice, we are not indifferent to it.

COGNITIVE CONSEQUENCES OF STEREOTYPES

Stereotypes Are Self-Perpetuating

Prejudice is prejudgment. Prejudgments are inevitable. None of us is a dispassionate bookkeeper of social happenings, tallying evidence for and against our biases. Rather, our prejudgments influence how we interpret and process information (Bodenhausen, 1988).

Whenever a member of a group behaves as expected, the fact is duly noted; the prior belief is confirmed. When a member of the group behaves inconsistently with the observer's expectation, the behavior may be explained away as due to special circumstances (Crocker et al., 1983); or it may be misinterpreted, leaving the prior belief intact. Recall, for example, the teachers' underestimates of the "cyranoids" described on the first page of this book.

Perhaps you, too, can recall a time when, try as you might, you could not overcome someone's opinion of you, a time when no matter what you did you were misinterpreted. Such misinterpretations are likely when someone is anxiously expecting an unpleasant encounter with you (Wilder & Shapiro, 1989). William Ickes and his colleagues (1982) demonstrated this in an experiment with pairs of college-age men. Upon arrival, one member of each pair was falsely forewarned by the experimenters that the other subject was "one of the unfriendliest people I've talked to lately." The two were then introduced and left alone together for five minutes. As did students in another condition, who were led to think the other subject was exceptionally friendly, those who expected him to be *un*friendly went out of their way to be friendly to him, and their smiles and other friendly behaviors elicited a warm response from him. But unlike the positively biased students, those expecting an unfriendly person apparently attributed this reciprocal friendliness to their own "kid-gloves" treatment of him. Thus they afterward expressed more mistrust and dislike for the person and rated his behavior as less friendly. It seemed that, despite their partner's actual friendliness, the negative bias had induced these students to "see" hostilities lurking beneath his "forced smiles." As researcher David Hamilton (1981) quipped, "I wouldn't have seen it if I hadn't believed it!"

It would be an overstatement to say that we are absolutely blind to disconfirming facts. When Hamilton and George Bishop (1976) interviewed suburban Connecticut homeowners several times during the year following the arrival of a first Black neighbor, they found initial opposition melting. Fears that the new Black neighbors would not take care of their property or that property values would decline apparently proved groundless, thus partially disconfirming the negative stereotypes. Indeed, when these neighborhoods were later compared with nonintegrated neighborhoods, the researchers found no evidence that the presence of the Black neighbor had any effect upon property turnover rates, property values, or the race of subsequent home buyers in the neighborhood (Hamilton et al., 1984). The initial fears had been disconfirmed.

Still, it is fair to say that people's negative ideas about a person or a group are hard to disconfirm (Rothbart & John, 1985). For one thing, a positive image—that one is gentle, sincere, or dependable—is easily reversed by just a few behaviors to the contrary. An unfavorable image—that one is deceitful, hostile, or unethical—is not so easily countered (Rothbart & Park, 1986). Genuine friendliness is easily misinterpreted as superficial smoothness. The resistance of negative stereotypes to disconfirming facts was evident in congressional testimony given by then Governor of California Earl Warren regarding potential Japanese subversion during World War II: "I take the view that this [lack of subversive activity] is the most ominous sign in our whole situation. It convinces me more than perhaps any other factor that the sabotage we are to get [is] timed just like Pearl Harbor was timed . . ." (Daniels, 1975).

Although information that is strikingly inconsistent with a stereotype can be hard to misinterpret and forget, the stereotype can still be retained by splitting off a new category that accommodates the disconfirming cases (Brewer, 1988; Weber & Crocker, 1983). Homeowners who have desirable Black neighbors can form a new stereotype of "professional, middle-class" Blacks. This subgroup stereotype can help them still maintain the larger stereotype that *most* Blacks make irresponsible neighbors. Likewise, one who believes that women are basically passive and dependent can split off a new stereotype category of "aggressive feminist" to handle women who don't fit the basic female stereotype (S. E. Taylor, 1981). Similarly, people's images of the elderly seem to be split into stereotypes of the "grandmotherly" type, the "elder-statesman" type, and the inactive "senior-citizen" type (Brewer & Lui, 1984).

margin quote:

"There are no good women climbers. Women climbers either aren't good climbers or they aren't real woman."
Anonymous climber (cited by Rothbart & Lewis, 1988)

Do Stereotypes Bias Our Judgments of Individuals?

There is an upbeat note on which we can conclude our chapter. Anne Locksley, Eugene Borgida, and Nancy Brekke have found that, once someone knows a person, "stereotypes may have minimal, if any, impact on judgments about that person" (Locksley et al., 1980, 1982; Borgida et al., 1981). They discovered this by giving some University of Minnesota students anecdotal information about recent incidents in the life of "Nancy." In a supposed transcript of a telephone conversation, Nancy told a friend how she responded to three different situations (for example, being harassed by a seedy character while shopping). Some of the students read transcripts portraying Nancy responding assertively (telling the seedy character to leave); others read a report of passive responses (simply ignoring the character until he finally drifted away). Still other students received the identical information, except that the person was named "Paul" instead of Nancy. A day later the students predicted how Nancy (or Paul) would respond to other situations. Did knowing the person's sex have any effect on these predictions? None at all. Their expectations of how assertive the person would be were affected solely by what they had learned about that individual the day before. Even their judgments of the person's masculinity and femininity were unaffected by knowing the person's sex. Gender stereotypes had been left on the shelf; Nancy and Paul were evaluated as individuals.

The explanation for this finding is implied by an important principle discussed in Chapter 4. Given (1) general (base-rate) information about a group from which someone comes and (2) rather trivial, though vivid, anecdotal information about a particular person in that group, the vivid information usually overwhelms the general information when making judgments about that person. For example, after being told how most people in an experiment actually behaved and then viewing a brief interview with one of the supposed subjects, the typical viewer guesses the person's behavior from the interview, ignoring the base-rate information concerning how most people actually behaved.

Stereotypes are general beliefs about the distribution of traits in groups of people. For example, "assertiveness is found more often in men, passiveness in women." Such stereotypes are often believed, yet, like other general knowledge, are at times ignored when in competition with vivid, anecdotal information. Thus many people seem to believe that "politicians are crooks" but "our Senator Jones has integrity." Similarly, the bigot may hold extreme stereotypes and yet claim, "One of my best friends is. . . ." Borgida, Locksley, and Brekke explain: "People may sustain general prejudices while simultaneously treating individuals with whom they frequently interact in a nonprejudicial manner." Indeed, sometimes stereotypes can produce a contrast effect: A woman who rebukes someone cutting in front of her in a movie line ("Shouldn't you go to the end of the line?") may be regarded as more assertive than a man who reacts similarly (Manis et al., 1988).

These findings may resolve a puzzling set of findings considered early in this chapter. Recall the evidence indicating that gender stereotypes (1) are strong, yet (2) seem to have very little effect on people's judgments of particular pieces of writing attributed to a man or a woman, or of individual male or female mental health clients. Now we see why. Mental health workers may have strong gender stereotypes, yet ignore them when confronted with a particular individual.

That stereotypes may not be as pervasive as feared should not allay our concern. Sometimes stereotypes are so strong that they do color our judgments of individuals. Given information that categorizes a person (say, told that someone they are about to meet is schizophrenic), people tend to use it to form quick impressions of how much they would like the person. Lacking such information, they take more time to examine the person's individual characteristics (Fiske & Pavelchak, 1986). Also, sometimes we make judgments about someone, or begin interacting with someone, with little to go on but our stereotype. It is in such cases that stereotypes most strongly bias our interpretations and memories of people (Crocker & Park, 1985; Krueger & Rothbart, 1988).

Such bias was evident in an experiment by John Darley and Paget Gross (1983). Princeton University students viewed a videotape of a fourth-grade girl, Hannah, depicting her either in a depressed urban neighborhood, supposedly the child of lower-class parents, or in an affluent suburban setting, the child of professional parents. Asked to guess Hannah's ability level in various subjects, both groups of viewers refused to use Hannah's class background to prejudge her ability level; each group rated her ability level at her grade level. Other students were also shown a second videotape in which Hannah took an oral achievement test, getting some questions right, some wrong. Now, those who had previously been introduced to "high class" Hannah judged her answers as indicating high ability, and later recalled her getting most questions right; those who had met "lower class" Hannah judged her ability as below grade level, and recalled her missing almost half the questions. But remember: This second videotape was *identical* for both groups. So we see that when stereotypes are strong, and the information about someone is ambiguous (unlike the cases of Nancy and Paul), stereotypes can *subtly* bias our judgments of individuals.

Stereotypes more surely bias our judgments of groups. Sometimes, such as when we vote, we make judgments about groups as a whole. On such occasions, that "One of my best friends is . . ." becomes trivial; what matters, what shapes public policy toward a large group of people, is our impression of the group as a whole. So, though once we come to know a particular person we are often able to set aside our stereotypes and our prejudices, both still remain potent social forces.

Social psychologists have more successfully explained than alleviated prejudice. Because prejudice results from many interrelated factors, it has no simple remedy. Nevertheless, we can now anticipate some techniques for reducing prejudice (to be discussed further in Chapters 13 and 15): If unequal status breeds prejudice, then we can seek to create cooperative, equal-status relationships; if prejudice often rationalizes discriminatory behavior, then we can mandate nondiscrimination; if social institutions support prejudice, then we can pull out those supports (for example, have the media model interracial harmony); if outgroups seem more unlike one's own group than they really are, then we can make efforts to personalize their members. Such are among the prescribed antidotes for the poison of prejudice.

Since World War II, some of these antidotes have begun to be applied, and racial and gender prejudices have indeed diminished. It now remains to be seen whether, during the remaining years of this century, this progress will continue, or whether, as could easily happen in an age of diminishing resources, antagonisms will again erupt.

SUMMING UP

HOW PERVASIVE IS PREJUDICE?

Stereotypical beliefs, prejudicial attitudes, and discriminatory behavior have long poisoned our social existence. Judging by what Americans have told survey researchers during the last four decades, prejudice against Blacks and women has plunged. Nevertheless, subtle survey questions, and indirect methods for assessing people's attitudes and behavior, still reveal strong gender stereotypes and a fair amount of disguised racial and gender bias. Prejudice, though less obvious, yet lurks.

Prejudice arises from an intricate interplay of social, emotional, and cognitive sources.

SOCIAL SOURCES OF PREJUDICE

The social situation breeds and maintains prejudice in several ways. A group that enjoys social and economic superiority will often justify its standing with prejudicial beliefs. Moreover, prejudice can lead people to treat others in ways that trigger expected behavior, thus seeming to confirm the view one holds. Experiments also reveal that prejudice, or more specifically an ingroup bias, may arise from the mere fact of people's being divided into groups. Once established, prejudice is maintained partly through the inertia of conformity, and partly through institutional supports, such as the mass media.

EMOTIONAL SOURCES OF PREJUDICE

It has long been thought that prejudice has emotional roots, too. Frustration breeds hostility, which is sometimes vented on scapegoats, and sometimes expressed more directly against competing groups that are perceived as responsible for one's frustration. Prejudice, by providing a feeling of social superiority, may also help cover one's feelings of inferiority. Research has revealed that different types of prejudice are often found together in those who have an "authoritarian" attitude.

COGNITIVE SOURCES OF PREJUDICE

During the last decade, a new look at prejudice has emerged. This new research shows how the stereotyping that underlies prejudice can be a byproduct of the normal ways by which we simplify the world. First, clustering people into categories tends to make those within a group seem more uniform than they really are and to exaggerate the seeming differences between groups. Once in a group, there is also a tendency when viewing another group to perceive that "they act and look alike, we don't." Second, there is a compelling quality to anyone who is distinctive, such as a lone minority person in a group. Distinctive people draw our attention, making us aware of differences that we would otherwise not notice. We also better remember distinctive, extreme occurrences. Thus, knowing little about another group, one may even form a stereotype based on but a vivid case or two. The co-occurrence of two distinctive events—say a minority person committing an unusual crime—can also help create the illusion of a correlation between such people and such behavior. Finally, the tendency to attribute others' behavior to their dispositions can lead to the ultimate attribution error: attributing the undesirable behavior of outgroup members to their natural character, while explaining away their positive behaviors. Such blaming of the victim also results from the common presumption that this is a just world in which people get what they deserve.

Stereotypes have cognitive consequences as well as cognitive sources. By directing our interpretations and our memories, they lead us to "find" supportive evidence, even when none exists. Stereotypes are therefore resistant to disconfirmation. Yet, when people get to know an individual, they seem quite able to set aside their stereotypes of the individual's group and to judge the person individually. Stereotypes are more potent when judging unknown individuals and when judging and making decisions about whole groups.

FOR FURTHER READING

Altemeyer, B. (1988). *Enemies of freedom: Understanding right-wing authoritarianism.* San Francisco: Jossey-Bass. The complete report of a prize-winning analysis of why some people—notably those with self-righteous, authoritarian tendencies—belittle and brutalize socially disparaged outgroups.

Dovidio, J. F., & Gaertner, S. L. (Eds.). (1986). *Prejudice, discrimination, and racism.* Orlando, FL: Academic Press. The foremost researchers provide comprehensive summaries of recent research on prejudice, especially that involving White/Black relationships.

Katz, P. A., & Taylor, D. A. (1988). *Eliminating racism: Profiles in controversy.* New York: Plenum. Experts document the reality of prejudice against Blacks, Hispanics, Japanese Americans, American Indians, and women and examine the fruitfulness of various remedies, such as desegregation, cooperative behavior, and affirmative action.

Taylor, D. M., & Moghaddam, F. M. (1987). *Theories of intergroup relations: International social psychological perspectives.* New York: Praeger. A skillful summary and evaluation of major theories of prejudice and group attitudes.

CHAPTER

12

AGGRESSION:
HURTING OTHERS

___

CHAPTER

12

AGGRESSION:
HURTING OTHERS

umanity's potential for inhumanity is frightening. The *Bulletin of the Atomic Scientists* (1988) reports that the world has 55,000 nuclear weapons, each averaging 15 times more destructive power than the bomb that destroyed Hiroshima. Thanks to the 1988 arms reduction treaty, the United States will dismantle 520 nuclear warheads between 1989 and 1991, but during the same period will build 4800 new ones. Spending for arms and armies approaches $3 billion per *day*, or approximately $200 per year for every person on earth—hundreds of millions of whom never receive $200 in one year (see Figure 12-1).

Those who have trouble comprehending the threat of annihilation have no difficulty understanding the threat of violent crime. After several decades of rapid increase in rates of murder, rape, robbery, and assault, the rate of violent crime in the United States has finally leveled off (Figure 12-2), thanks partly to the lowered birthrate and therefore the lower proportion of teen and young adult males. Although Woody Allen's prediction that "by 1990 kidnapping will be the dominant mode of social interaction" has not been fulfilled, social violence remains at an historically high level.

But is barbarism unique to the late twentieth century? The *Guiness Book of World Records* suggests not. Consider:

- Bloodiest war: World War II, which during the 1940s killed 55 million people (counting both battle and civilian deaths).
- Bloodiest battle: The First Battle of the Somme in World War I, June 24 to November 13, 1916, which took more than one million lives.
- Bloodiest civil war: The T'ai-p'ing rebellion in China about the time of the American Civil War, in which 20 to 30 million people were slaughtered.
- Greatest mass killings: 26 million Chinese are reported to have been liquidated in the first sixteen years of Mao Tse-tung's regime. Stalin's purge of 1936 to 1938 is estimated to have killed 8 to 10 million Russians.

FIGURE 12-1
World military expenditures and gross national product, in constant dollars (adjusted for inflation, with 1960 spending set at 100). Note that military expenditures are 2.5 times the level of 1960, far outstripping economic gains. (From Sivard, 1987.)

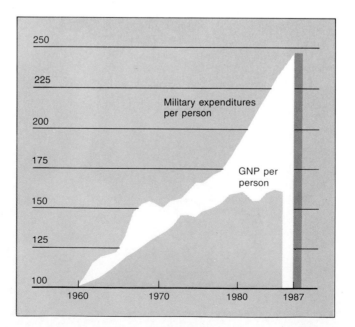

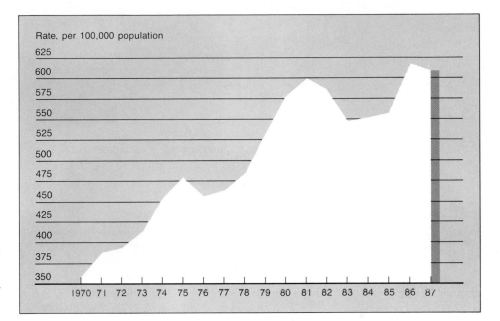

FIGURE 12-2
Violent crime in the United States between 1970 and 1987. (Rate per 100,000 of murder, forcible rape, robbery, and aggravated assault.) (Data from *FBI Uniform Crime Reports,* 1971–1988.)

"Our behavior toward each other is the strangest, most unpredictable, and most unaccountable of all the phenomena with which we are obliged to live. In all of nature, there is nothing so threatening to humanity as humanity itself."
Lewis Thomas (1981)

Or consider the fate of the native Americans who, having welcomed Columbus ashore, were described by him as "ever sweet and gentle," or the fate of the native Americans who generously saved the English from starvation after their 1620 landing in Plymouth. Except for those sold into slavery, both Indian groups were almost completely exterminated by the White invaders—a fate that was eventually to befall all but a fourth of the native population (Brown, 1971).

Cultural sophistication does not exempt one from inhumanity. Camp commanders at Auschwitz—where up to 6000 people a day were exterminated—would spend their evenings relaxing to the music of Beethoven and Schubert. The potential for inhumanity seems present among all peoples, whether "cultured" or not, whether Red or Yellow, Black or White.

Why this propensity to aggress? Is it because we, like the mythical Minotaur, are half human, half beast? What circumstances prompt aggressive outbursts? Can aggression be controlled? If so, how? In this chapter, these are our questions. However, let us first clarify this term, "aggression."

WHAT IS AGGRESSION?

The term is nebulous. We use it in many ways, for many reasons. Clearly, the original "Thugs," members of a former murdering fraternity in northern India, were aggressing when between 1550 and 1850 they strangled more than 2 million people. But when "aggressive" is used to describe a dynamic salesperson or a straight-talking woman, it takes on a different meaning. Social psychologists debate how to define aggression. But on this much they agree: We should sharpen our vocabulary by distinguishing between self-assured, energetic, go-getting behavior and behavior that hurts, harms, or destroys. The former can be called assertion. The latter clearly and surely is ***aggression***.

Aggression:
Physical or verbal behavior intended to hurt someone.

Chapter 6 defined aggression as physical or verbal behavior that is intended to hurt someone. This excludes painful auto accidents, dental treatments, and sidewalk collisions. But it does include a wide variety of actions aimed at hurting someone, whether such acts succeed or not. Thus gossipy "digs" about a person are usually considered aggressive. Researchers have struggled to find appropriate ways to study aggression in laboratory experiments. As we will see, they typically measure aggression by having people decide how much to hurt someone, such as by having them choose how much electric shock to impose.

Hostile aggression:
Aggression driven by anger and performed as an end in itself.

Instrumental aggression:
Aggression that is a means to some other end.

Our definition encompasses two distinct types of aggression. ***Hostile aggression*** springs from anger. Its goal is to injure. ***Instrumental aggression*** also aims to hurt, but only as a means to some other end (Feshback, 1970; Buss, 1971). Many wars, for example, have been undertaken not out of cruel desire to harm the enemy, but because the nation has seen the war as instrumental (useful) in gaining new territory or resources. Hostile aggression is "hot"; instrumental aggression is "cool." Distinguishing between hostile and instrumental aggression is sometimes difficult. What begins as a cool, calculating act can ignite hostility. Still, social psychologists find the distinction useful. Most murders are hostile. They are impulsive, emotional outbursts—which explains why data from 110 nations show that enforcing the death penalty has not resulted in fewer homicides (Wilkes, 1987). But some murders are instrumental. Chicago's more than 1000 murders since 1919 by mobster "hit men" have most likely been calculated to attain specific goals.

The distinction between people's hostile and instrumental aggression is paralleled by the distinction between animals' "social aggression," characterized by displays of rage, and "silent aggression," as when a predator stalks its prey. As further evidence of this distinction, Peter Marler (1974) reports that these two types of animal aggression involve separate brain regions.

THE NATURE OF AGGRESSION

Social psychologists have analyzed three primary ideas about aggression's cause: (1) There is an *inborn* aggressive drive, (2) aggression is a natural response to *frustrating* experiences, and (3) aggressive behavior, like other social behaviors, is *learned*. Because hostile and instrumental aggression may well have different causes, a combination of these major ideas about the nature of aggression could well be valid.

IS AGGRESSION INBORN?

Philosophers have long debated whether our human nature is fundamentally that of a benign, contented "noble savage" or that of a potentially explosive brute. The first view, popularly associated with the eighteenth-century philosopher Jean-Jacques Rousseau, blames society, not human nature, for the evils of human existence. The second, associated often with the philosopher Thomas Hobbes (1588–1679), sees society's restrictions as necessary to restrain and control the human brute. In this century, the "brutish" view—that aggressive drive is inborn and thus inevitable—has been most prominently argued by Sigmund Freud and by Konrad Lorenz.

Instinctive behavior:
An innate, unlearned behavior pattern exhibited by all members of a species.

Instinct Theory

Freud, the pioneering psychoanalyst, speculated that human aggression springs from our redirecting toward others the energy of a primitive death urge (which, loosely

Humanity has armed its capacity for destruction without comparably arming its capacity for the inhibition of aggression.

"Of course, we'll never actually <u>use</u> it against a potential enemy, but it will allow us to negotiate from a position of strength."

"Some say the world will end in fire, Some say in ice. From what I've tasted of desire I hold with those who favour fire."
Robert Frost,"Fire and Ice" in The Poetry of Robert Frost, *New York: Holt, Rinehart and Winston, 1969*

speaking, he called the "death instinct"). Lorenz, an observer of animal behavior, saw aggression as an adaptive rather than a self-destructive motivation. But they agreed that aggressive energy is instinctual and that, if not discharged, it builds up until it explodes or is "released" by an appropriate stimulus, much as a mouse releases the pent-up energy of a mousetrap. Although Lorenz (1967) also argued that we have innate mechanisms for inhibiting aggression (such as making oneself defenseless), he feared the implications of our having armed our "fighting instinct" without comparably arming our inhibitions.

This idea that aggressive energy instinctively wells up from within, quite apart from one's encounters with the environment, has been sharply criticized by social psychologists. Among animals, aggression is more modifiable than the instinct theory suggests. Among humans, aggressiveness varies widely, from the relatively gentle inhabitants of some South Sea islands, to the warring South American Yanomamo Indians, nearly half of whose surviving adult males have been involved in a killing (Chagnon, 1988); from the peaceful Iroquois Indians before the White invaders to the Iroquois warriors after the White invasion (Hornstein, 1976); from the nonviolence of Norway, where murder is rare, to the killings of Northern Ireland (see Figure 12-3). What is more, the use of "instincts" to explain social behavior fell into disrepute after sociologist Luther Bernard scanned books by 500 social scientists and in 1924 compiled a list of 5759 supposed human instincts (Barash, 1979, p. 4). What the social scientists had tried to do was *explain* social behavior by *naming* it. It is terribly tempting to play this explaining-by-naming game: "Why do sheep stay together?" "It's because of their herding instinct." "How do you know they have a herding instinct?" "Just look

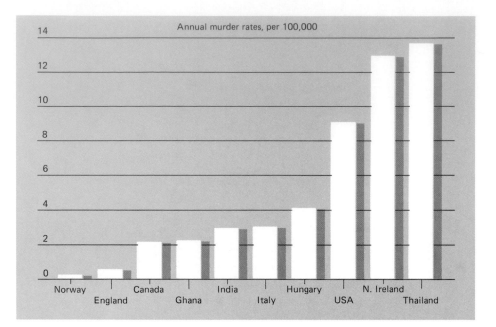

FIGURE 12-3

Aggression varies by culture, as indicated by the sharp country by country differences in homicide rates during the early 1970s. (Data from Archer & Gartner, 1984.)

at them: They're always together!" Such circular explanation is, of course, no explanation at all.

Biological Influences upon Aggression

Neural Influences

Although the human propensity to aggress may not qualify as an instinct, aggression *is* biologically influenced. Because aggression is a complex behavior, we cannot expect it to be controlled by any single, precise spot in the brain. But in both animals and humans, researchers have found complex neural systems that facilitate aggression. When these areas in the brain's inner core are activated, hostility increases; when activity in them is blocked, hostility decreases. Docile animals can thus be provoked into rage, and raging animals into submission. Similar effects have been observed with human patients. After receiving electrical stimulation in her amygdala (a part of the brain core), one woman smashed her guitar against the wall, barely missing her psychiatrist's head (Moyer, 1976).

Genetic Influences

The individual members of any species vary in the sensitivity of their neural systems controlling aggression. One source of differing sensitivity is heredity. Animals of many species have been bred for aggressiveness. At times, this is done for practical purposes (for example, the breeding of fighting cocks). Sometimes, breeding is done for purposes of research. Kirsti Lagerspetz (1979), a Finnish psychologist, took normal albino mice and bred the most aggressive ones with one another and the least aggressive ones with one another. After repeating this for twenty-six generations she had one set of fierce mice and one set that was placid.

The pit bull, like several other kinds of animals, is genetically predisposed to be aggressive.

Aggressiveness similarly varies among primates and humans (Asher, 1987; Olweus, 1979). The characteristic reactiveness of our temperaments—for example, how intense and reactive we are—is partly something we bring with us into the world, influenced by the reactivity of our sympathetic nervous system (Kagan, 1988). A person's temperament, observed in infancy, tends to endure (Larsen & Diener, 1987; Wilson & Matheny, 1986). Thus, identical twins, who come into the world with similar physical make-ups, are more likely than fraternal twins to agree, when asked separately whether they have "a violent temper" (Rushton et al., 1986).

Biochemical Influences

Blood chemistry is another influence upon the neural system's sensitivity to aggressive stimulation. Both laboratory experiments and police data indicate that when people are provoked, alcohol can diminish restraints on aggression (Taylor & Leonard, 1983). The U.S. Department of Justice estimates that nearly a third of the nation's 523,000 state prisoners drank heavily before committing rapes, burglaries, and assaults (Desmond, 1987). Alcohol enhances aggressiveness by reducing people's self-awareness and their ability to think through the potential negative consequences of their actions (Hull & Bond, 1986; Steele & Southwick, 1985). The result is a deindividuated and disinhibited state.

There are other biochemical influences, too. Low blood sugar can boost aggressiveness. And in males, aggressiveness can be influenced by the injection of the male sex hormone, testosterone (Moyer, 1983). Although hormonal influences appear much stronger in lower animals than in humans, drugs that diminish testosterone levels in violent human males will sometimes subdue their aggressive tendencies. Interestingly,

A 1985 soccer riot in Brussels left thirty-eight dead after English fans, aroused by the intense competition, deindividuated by their anonymity in the crowd, and loaded with alcohol, attacked Italian fans who, upon retreating, were crushed against a wall.

though perhaps coincidentally, after age twenty-five testosterone and rates of violent crime both decrease. Among both male and female prisoners convicted of unprovoked violent crimes, testosterone levels tend to be higher than among those imprisoned for nonviolent crimes (Dabbs et al., 1988).

So, there exist important neural, genetic, and biochemical influences on aggression. But is it aggression so much a part of human nature as to make peace unattainable? To counter such pessimism, the Council of Representatives of the American Psychological Association and the directors of the International Council of Psychologists have joined other organizations in unanimously endorsing a 1986 "statement on violence" developed by scientists from a dozen nations (Adams et al., 1987). "It is scientifically incorrect," declares the statement, to say that "war or any other violent behavior is genetically programmed into our human nature," or that "war is caused by 'instinct' or any single motivation." Thus there are, as we will see, ways to reduce human aggression.

IS AGGRESSION A RESPONSE TO FRUSTRATION?

It is a warm evening. Tired and thirsty after two hours of studying, you borrow some change from a friend and head for the nearest soft drink machine. As the machine devours the change, you can almost taste the cold, refreshing cola. But when you push the button, nothing happens. You push it again. Then you flip the coin return button. Not even your investment is returned. Your throat is now feeling parched. Again, you hit the buttons. You slam them. And finally you shake and whack the machine. You stomp back to your studies, empty-handed and short-changed. Should your roommate beware? Are you now more likely to say or do something hurtful?

One of the first psychological theories of aggression, the popular frustration-aggression theory, answers yes, yes indeed. In fact, John Dollard and several of his

Yale colleagues (1939) went so far as to propose that "aggression is always a conse-quence of frustration" and "frustration always leads to some form of aggression" (p. 1). One cannot occur without the other.

Frustration:
The blocking of goal-directed behavior.

Frustration, said Dollard and his colleagues, is anything (such as the malfunc-tioning vending machine) that blocks one's attaining a goal. Frustration is especially pronounced when one's motivation to achieve a goal is very strong, when one expected gratification, and when the blocking is complete.

As Figure 12-4 suggests, the aggressive energy need not be released directly against its source. We are taught to inhibit direct retaliation, especially when others might disapprove or punish; we learn instead to *displace* our hostilities to safer targets. *Displacement* is illustrated in an anecdote about a man who, having been humiliated by his boss, berates his wife, who yells at their son, who kicks the dog, which bites the mail carrier.

Displacement:
Redirecting aggression to a target other than the source of the frustration. Generally, the new target is a safer target, one that is less likely to retaliate or against whom aggression is more socially accepted.

Note that frustration-aggression theory is designed to explain hostile aggression, not instrumental aggression.

Frustration-Aggression Theory Revised

Laboratory tests of the frustration-aggression theory have produced mixed results: Sometimes frustration increases aggressiveness, sometimes not. For example, if the frustration is understandable—if, as in one experiment by Eugene Burnstein and Philip Worchel (1962), a confederate disrupts a group's problem solving because his hearing aid malfunctions (rather than just because he failed to pay attention)—then aggression does not increase.

Knowing that the original theory overstated the frustration-aggression connection, Leonard Berkowitz (1978, 1988) revised the theory. Berkowitz theorized that frustra-tion produces anger, an emotional readiness to aggress. Anger is especially likely when someone who frustrates us could have chosen to act otherwise (Weiner, 1981; Averill, 1983). And a frustrated person is presumed especially likely to lash out when there are aggressive cues that, so to speak, pull the cork, thus releasing the bottled-up anger. Sometimes the cork will blow without such cues, but when stimuli associated with aggression are present they amplify aggression.

Black clothing, which is often associated with aggression and death, can serve as an aggressive cue. Mark Frank and Thomas Gilovich (1988) report that, led by the Los Angeles Raiders and the Philadelphia Flyers, black-uniformed teams consistently ranked near the top of the National Football and Hockey Leagues in penalties assessed

FIGURE 12-4
Summary of the classic frustra-tion-aggression theory. Frustra-tion creates a motive to aggress. Fear of punishment or disap-proval for aggressing against the source of one's frustration may cause the aggressive drive to be displaced against some other tar-get or even redirected against oneself. (Based on Dollard et al., 1939, and Miller, 1941.)

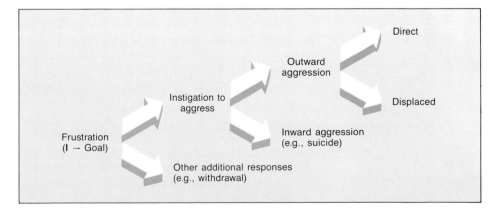

In several studies, the mere sight of a gun heightened aggressive impulses.

between 1970 and 1986. In the laboratory, just putting on a black jersey can trigger the wearer to act more aggressively.

Berkowitz (1968, 1981b) and others have found that the sight of a weapon—an obvious aggressive cue—also can heighten aggression. In one experiment, children who had just played with toy guns became more willing to knock down another child's blocks. In another experiment, angered University of Wisconsin men gave more electric shocks to their tormenter when a rifle and a revolver were nearby (supposedly having been left from a previous experiment) than when badminton racquets had been left behind (Berkowitz & LePage, 1967). Some experiments have failed to replicate this "weapons effect." But enough have replicated it that Berkowitz is unsurprised that over half of all U.S. murders are committed with handguns and that handguns in homes are far more likely to kill household members than intruders: "Guns not only permit violence, they can stimulate it as well. The finger pulls the trigger, but the trigger may also be pulling the finger."

To be sure, there are other reasons why countries that ban handguns have a much lower murder rate than does the United States [Britain, for example, has one-fourth as many people and one-sixteenth as many murders. Vancouver, British Columbia, and Seattle, Washington, have similar populations, climates, economies, and rates of criminal activity and assault—except that Vancouver, which carefully restricts handgun ownership, has one-fifth as many handgun murders as Seattle and thus a 40 percent lower overall murder rate (Sloan et al., 1988).] One additional reason for the handgun-murder link is the psychological distance provided by a gun. As Milgram's obedience studies taught us, cruelty is facilitated by remoteness from the victim. A knife attack can kill someone just as effectively but is more brutal and therefore more difficult than merely pulling a trigger while standing at a distance.

The Distinction between Frustration and Deprivation

"I would say a person is deprived if he lacks a goal object people generally regard as attractive or desirable, but is frustrated only when he had been anticipating the pleasure to be gotten from this object and then cannot fulfill this expectation."
Leonard Berkowitz (1972)

Picture someone feeling extremely frustrated—economically, or sexually, or politically. My hunch is that most will imagine someone economically, or sexually, or politically *deprived*. Ironically, however, frustration often is unrelated to deprivation. The most sexually frustrated people are probably not those who are celibate. The most economically frustrated people are probably not the impoverished residents of Jamaican shantytowns. In fact, the 1969 National Commission on the Causes and Prevention of Violence concluded that economic advancements may even exacerbate frustration and escalate violence. Let's pause to examine this paradoxical conclusion.

Prior to Detroit's 1967 riot, in which 43 people were killed and 683 structures damaged or destroyed by fire, I watched Michigan's Governor George Romney boast on television's *Meet the Press* about his state's leadership in civil rights legislation and about the $367 million in federal aid pumped into Detroit during the five preceding years. No sooner were his words ringing across televisionland, than a large Black neighborhood in Detroit exploded into this century's worst U.S. civil disorder. People were stunned. Why Detroit? Although things were still bad there, relative to the general affluence of the White populace, the injustices were even greater in some other American cities. The National Advisory Commission on Civil Disorders, established to answer the question, concluded that an immediate psychological cause was the frustration of expectations that had been fueled by the legislative and judicial civil rights victories of the 1960s. When there occurs a "revolution of rising expectations," as happened in Detroit and elsewhere, frustrations may escalate, even while conditions improve.

"Evils which are patiently endured when they seem inevitable become intolerable when once the idea of escape from them is suggested."
Alexis de Tocqueville, 1856
Sigmund Freud,
The Future of an Illusion, 1927

The principle works internationally. The political scientist–social psychologist team of Ivo and Rosaline Feierabend (1968, 1972) applied the frustration-aggression theory in a study of political instability within eighty-four nations. They found that when people in rapidly modernizing nations become urbanized and when their literacy improves, they then become more aware of material improvements. However, since the growing affluence of a nation usually diffuses slowly, the increasing gap between aspirations and achievements tends to intensify frustration. Expectation outstrips reality. Even as people's deprivation diminishes, their frustration and political aggression may therefore nevertheless escalate.

The point is not that actual deprivation and social injustice are irrelevant to social unrest. (Injustice can be a root cause, even if not the immediate psychological cause.) The point is simply this: Frustration is created by the *gap* between our expectations and our attainments.

Does Money Buy Happiness?

The principle "frustration equals expectations minus attainments" also can help us understand why our own feelings of economic satisfaction and frustration fluctuate. Consider the following rather bewildering set of facts: Fact 1: Americans at every income level, except the very top, insist that just 10 or 20 percent more income would make them happier (Strumpel, 1976). More money would relieve their financial woes

Deprivation without hope produces apathy.

and buy more happiness, they believe. Fact 2: During the late 1980s, the average American was enjoying a disposable income (corrected for inflation and taxes) double that of the mid-1950s. Given that most Americans believe money increases happiness, and that Americans do, in fact, have more money today than in decades past, they must be happier, right?

Wrong. Americans in recent years have been no more likely than those of the 1950s to report feeling happy and satisfied with their lives. In 1957, for example, 35 percent reported themselves "very happy." In 1987, after two decades of growing affluence, how many now declared themselves "very happy"?—32 percent (see Figure 12-5).

Within a given country there is a slight tendency for the wealthy to be happier than the poor; abject poverty can mean misery. Yet people in wealthier countries are not noticeably happier than those in poorer countries. Interviews with more than 160,000 Europeans since the mid-1970s reveal that the Danes, Swiss, Irish, and Dutch report themselves happier and more satisfied with life than do the French, Greeks, Italians, and West Germans (Inglehart & Rabier, 1986). These puzzling national differences are unexplained by differing standards of living, on which, for example, the West Germans rank much higher than the Irish.

Why are we not happier with our economic circumstances? Why all the commiserating about financial woes among people whose affluence has doubled? And why do yesterday's luxuries—color television, microwave ovens, stereo sound systems—become today's necessities, leading people always to feel their needs are greater than their incomes can provide? (One national survey revealed that two-thirds of Americans labeled a TV set, a clothes dryer, and aluminum foil as each a "necessity" rather than a "luxury you could do without" *Public Opinion*, 1984.)

Parkinson's second law:
Expenditures rise to meet
income.

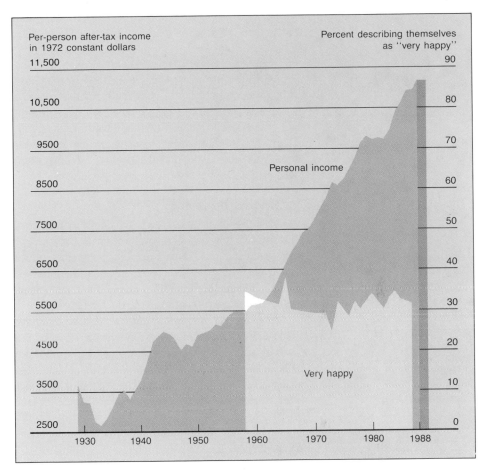

FIGURE 12-5
Money. Does it buy happiness? It can surely enable us to evade or overcome certain types of pain. Yet, although buying power has doubled since the 1950s, self-reported happiness has not increased. [Income data from *Historical Statistics of the U.S.* (data for 1929–1970) and *Economic Indicators*, May 1988. Happiness data cited by Smith (1979) and in personal communications.]

Adaptation-level phenomenon: The tendency to adapt to a given level of stimulation and thus to notice and react to changes from that level.

The Adaptation-Level Phenomenon

Two principles developed by research psychologists help explain people's rising expectations and therefore their continuing frustrations. The *adaptation-level phenomenon* implies that our feelings of success and failure, satisfaction and dissatisfaction, are relative to our prior achievements. Therefore, if our current achievements fall below what we previously accomplished, we feel dissatisfied, frustrated; if they rise above, we feel successful, satisfied.

If we continue to achieve, however, we soon adapt to the success. What we formerly felt positive about then registers as neutral, and what formerly felt neutral is now perceived as negative. This helps explain why, despite the rapid increase in real income during the past several decades, the average American is no happier. Donald Campbell (1975b) surmised that we humans will never create a social paradise on earth. If we did achieve such, we would soon redefine "utopia" and would once again feel sometimes pleased, sometimes deprived, sometimes neutral.

Most of us have experienced the adaptation-level phenomenon. Increased material goods, academic achievement, or social prestige provide an initial surge of pleasure. Yet, all too soon the feeling wanes. Now, we need an even higher level to give us another surge of pleasure. "Even as we contemplate our satisfaction with a given accomplishment, the satisfaction fades," noted Philip Brickman and Donald Campbell

(1971), "to be replaced finally by a new indifference and a new level of striving." And that is why, as an old Chinese proverb declares, "Man is never happy for a thousand days."

A study of state lottery winners illustrates the adaptation-level principle. Brickman and his colleagues, Dan Coates and Ronnie Janoff-Bulman (1978), found that at first the winners typically felt elated: "Winning the lottery was one of the best things that ever happened to me." Yet their self-reported overall happiness did not increase. In fact, the ordinary activities they had previously enjoyed, activities such as reading or eating a good breakfast, actually became less pleasurable. Winning the lottery was apparently such an emotional high that, by comparison, their ordinary pleasures paled.

Relative Deprivation

"A house may be large or small; as long as the surrounding houses are equally small, it satisfies all social demands for a dwelling. But let a palace arise beside the little house, and it shrinks from a little house into a hut."
Karl Marx

Relative deprivation:
The perception that one is less well off than others to whom one compares oneself.

The dissatisfactions bred by adapting to new attainments often become compounded when we compare ourselves with others. Ephraim Yuchtman (1976) observed that feelings of well-being, especially among white-collar workers, are closely connected with whether their compensation is equitable compared to others in their line of work. For instance, a salary raise for a city's police officers, while temporarily lifting their morale, may deflate that of the firefighters.

In everyday life, when people increase in affluence, or status, or achievement, they similarly raise the standards by which they evaluate their own attainments. When climbing the ladder of success, people look up, not down (Gruder, 1977; Suls & Tesch, 1978; Wheeler et al., 1982). They attend to where they are aspiring, often neglecting where they have come from. This "upward comparison" is conducive to feelings of *relative deprivation* (Crosby, 1982; Williams, 1975). Such feelings have been found to predict the reactions to perceived inequities by minority groups in the U.S. and Canada (Dion, 1985) and to explain why women who make less than men working in the same occupations feel underpaid only if they compare themselves with male rather than female colleagues (Zanna et al., 1987). There are different versions of the relative deprivation principle, one of which emphasizes that social protest erupts not from feelings of *personal* deprivation but the feeling that one's *group* is relatively deprived (Walker & Mann, 1987). But all versions agree that feelings of deprivation are determined not just by our objective situation but relative to some standard of comparison. Researchers are studying how we make those comparisons—how we decide with whom to compare ourselves and how such comparisons affect us (Levine & Moreland, 1987; Olson et al., 1986).

The term relative deprivation was coined by researchers studying the satisfaction felt by American soldiers in World War II (Merton & Kitt, 1950; Stouffer et al., 1949). Ironically, those in the Air Corps, where promotions were rapid and widespread, were *more* frustrated about their own rate of promotion than those in the Military Police, for whom promotions were slow and unpredictable. In retrospect, we can see that because the Air Corps' promotion rate was rapid and because most Air Corps personnel probably perceived themselves as better than the average Air Corps member (the self-serving bias), their aspirations likely soared higher than their achievements. The result? Frustration. And where there is frustration, aggressive tendencies often follow.

One possible source of such frustration is the affluence depicted in television. Karen Hennigan and her coworkers (1982) analyzed crime rates in American cities around the time that television was introduced. In thirty-four cities where television ownership became widespread in 1951, the 1951 larceny theft rate (for crimes such as shoplifting

Could Lucy ever experience enough "ups"? Not according to the adaptation-level phenomenon.

and bicycle stealing) took an observable jump. In thirty-four other cities, where a government freeze had delayed the introduction of television until 1955, a similar jump in the theft rate occurred—in 1955. Why? Hennigan and her colleagues believe that

> television caused younger and poorer persons (the major perpetrators of theft) to compare their life-styles and possessions with (a) those of wealthy television characters and (b) those portrayed in advertisements. Many of these viewers may have felt resentment and frustration over lacking the goods they could not afford, and some may have turned to crime as a way of obtaining the coveted goods and reducing any "relative deprivation."

The principles of adaptation-level and relative deprivation have a thought-provoking implication: Seeking satisfaction through material achievement requires continually expanding affluence merely to maintain the same level of satisfaction. "Poverty," said Plato, "consists not in the decrease of one's possessions, but in the increase of one's greed."

"All our wants, beyond those which a very moderate income will supply, are purely imaginary."
Henry St. John,
Letter to Swift, *1719*

Fortunately, the adaptation-level phenomenon also can enable us to adjust downward, should we choose or be forced to adopt a simplified way of life. If our buying power shrinks we initially feel some pain. But eventually most of us will adapt to the new reality. In the aftermath of the 1970s gas price hikes, North Americans managed to substantially reduce their "need" for large, gas-slurping cars. Even paraplegics, the blind, and other people with severe handicaps generally adapt to their tragic situation and eventually find a normal or near-normal level of life satisfaction (Brickman et al., 1978; Schulz & Decker, 1985). Victims of traumatic incidents surely must envy those who are not paralyzed, as many of us envy those who have won a state lottery. Yet, after a period of adjustment, none of these three groups differs appreciably from the others in moment-to-moment happiness. Human beings have an enormous capacity to adapt.

"However great the discrepancies between men's lots, there is always a certain balance of joy and sorrow which equalizes all."
La Rochefoucauld, Maxims, *1665*

Finally, experiences that lower our comparison standards can renew our contentment. A research team led by Marshall Dermer (1979) put a number of University of Wisconsin-Milwaukee women through some imaginative exercises in deprivation. After viewing depictions of how grim life was in Milwaukee in 1900, or after imagining and then writing about various personal tragedies, such as being burned and disfigured, the women expressed a greater sense of satisfaction with the quality of their own lives. In another experiment, Jennifer Crocker and Lisa Gallo (1985) found that those who five times completed the sentence "I'm glad I'm not a . . ." afterwards felt less depressed and more satisfied with life than did those who had completed sentences beginning "I wish I were a. . . . For this reason, people who are facing a severe personal threat often search for a silver lining by comparing downward (Taylor, 1983; Gibbons, 1986). As Abraham Maslow (1972) noted,

All you have to do is to go to a hospital and hear all the simple blessings that people never before realized *were* blessings—being able to urinate, to sleep on your side, to be able to swallow, to scratch an itch, etc. Could *exercises* in deprivation educate us faster about all our blessings? (p. 108)

IS AGGRESSION LEARNED SOCIAL BEHAVIOR?

The theories of aggression based on instinct and frustration assume that the aggressive urge erupts from inner emotions, and that under certain conditions it is natural (unlearned). In contrast to this assumption that aggression is "pushed" from within, social psychologists contend that, through learning, aggression is also "pulled" out of us.

Learning the Rewards of Aggression

By experience and by observing others we learn that *aggression often pays*. Animal-training experiments reveal that animals can be transformed from docile creatures into ferocious fighters through a series of successful bouts. Severe defeats, on the other hand, create submissiveness (Ginsburg & Allee, 1942; Kahn, 1951; Scott & Marston, 1953).

People, too, can learn the rewards of aggression. A child whose aggressive acts successfully intimidate other children will likely become increasingly aggressive (Patterson et al., 1967). Aggressive hockey players—the ones sent most often to the penalty box for rough play—score more goals than nonaggressive players (McCarthy & Kelly, 1978a, 1978b). In both these cases, aggression seems to be instrumental in achieving certain rewards.

Collective violence also sometimes pays. After the 1980 riot in Miami's Liberty City neighborhood, President Carter came to the neighborhood to assure residents personally of his concern and of forthcoming federal aid. After the 1967 Detroit riot, the Ford Motor Company accelerated its efforts to hire minority workers, prompting comedian Dick Gregory to joke, "Last summer the fire got too close to the Ford plant. Don't scorch the Mustangs, baby." After the 1985 riots in South Africa became severe, the government repealed laws forbidding mixed marriages, offered to restore Black "citizenship rights" (not including the right to vote, gather, or live freely), and eliminated the hated pass laws controlling the movement of Blacks. The point is not that riots are consciously planned for their instrumental value, but that aggression sometimes has payoffs. If nothing more, it gets attention.

The same is true of terrorist acts, which enable people who lack power to garner widespread attention. "Kill one, frighten ten thousand," asserts an ancient Chinese proverb. In this age of global communications, killing only a few can frighten tens of millions—as happened when the terrorist-caused deaths of 25 Americans during 1985 struck more fear into the hearts of travelers than the car-accident deaths of 46,000. Deprived of what Margaret Thatcher calls "the oxygen of publicity," terrorism would surely diminish, concludes Jeffrey Rubin (1986). It's like the 1970s incidents of naked spectators "streaking" onto football fields for a few seconds of television exposure, which ended once the networks decided to ignore the incidents.

Observational Learning

Albert Bandura, the leading proponent of the ***social learning theory*** of aggression, believes that we learn aggression not only by experiencing its payoffs, but also by

Social learning theory:
The theory that we learn social behavior by observing and imitating, and by being rewarded and punished.

observing others. Like many social behaviors, aggression can be acquired by watching others act and noting the resultant consequences.

Picture this scene from one of Bandura's experiments (Bandura et al., 1961). A Stanford Nursery School child is put to work on an interesting art activity. An adult is in another part of the room, where there are Tinker Toys, a mallet, and a big, inflated doll. After a minute of working with the Tinker Toys, the adult gets up and for almost ten minutes attacks the inflated doll—pounding it with the mallet, kicking it, and throwing it, all the while yelling such remarks as "Sock him in the nose. . . . Hit him down. . . . Kick him."

After observing this outburst, the child is then taken to a different building and placed in a room that has many very attractive toys. But after two minutes the experimenter interrupts, stating that these are her best toys and she has decided to "save them for the other children." The frustrated child now goes into an adjacent room containing a variety of toys for aggressive and nonaggressive play, two of which are a Bobo doll and a mallet.

Seldom did children not exposed to the aggressive adult model display any aggressive play or talk. Frustrated though they may have been over being deprived of the attractive toys, they nevertheless played calmly. However, those who previously had observed the aggressive adult were many times more likely to pick up the mallet and lash out at the doll. Watching the adult's aggressive behavior apparently lowered their inhibitions. But the children's observations did more than disinhibit them, for not just any aggressive behavior arose. Rather, the children often reproduced the very acts and said the very words they had previously observed in the adult models. In short, observing aggressive behavior can both lower inhibitions and teach ways to be aggressive.

Bandura (1979) believes that in everyday life aggressive models are found most often in (1) one's family, (2) one's subculture, and (3) the mass media. Children of parents who discipline with physical aggression tend to use similar tactics when relating to others. For example, the parents of violent teenage boys and of abused children have often had parents who disciplined them with lots of physical punishment (Bandura & Walters, 1959; Silver, Dublin, & Lourie, 1969; Strauss & Gelles, 1980). Although the findings may have a genetic basis as well, the phenomenon remains: Within families, violence breeds violence.

Outside the home, one's social environment can be a source of aggressive models. In communities where "macho" images not only abound but are admired, aggression is readily transmitted to new generations (Cartwright, 1975; Short, 1969; Wolfgang & Ferracuti, 1967). The violent subculture of teenage gangs, for instance, provides its junior members with numerous aggressive models.

Although one's family or subculture may at times demonstrate brutal aggression, additional opportunities to observe a wide range of violent actions are now provided by television. As we will note later in this chapter, research indicates that viewing televised violence tends to (1) increase aggressiveness, (2) desensitize viewers to violence, and (3) shape their assumptions about social reality.

To say that aggressive responses are learned both by experience and by observing aggressive models does not predict when such responses will actually occur. Bandura (1979) contends (see Figure 12-6) that aggressive acts are motivated by a variety of aversive experiences—frustration, pain, insults. Such experiences arouse us emotionally. But whether we act aggressively or instead react in some other way depends upon what consequences we anticipate. Aggression is most likely when we are aroused *and* it seems safe and rewarding to aggress.

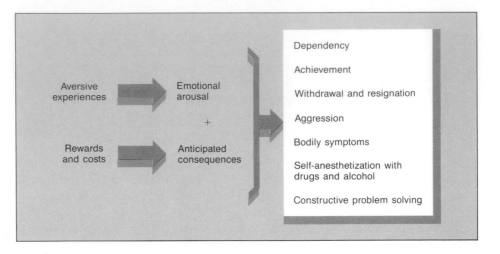

FIGURE 12-6
The social-learning view of aggression. Aggression is motivated by the emotional arousal stemming from an aversive experience. Whether aggression or some other response actually occurs depends on what consequences we have learned to expect. (Based on Bandura, 1979.)

The social-learning theory of how aggressive behavior is acquired and provoked offers a perspective from which we can view some specific influences upon aggression. In more depth, let us look now at a few of these influences.

INFLUENCES UPON AGGRESSION

To a greater or lesser extent, all of us have learned aggressive responses. We are each a potential aggressor. So, what conditions provoke our acts of aggression?

AVERSIVE INCIDENTS

Pain

Researcher Nathan Azrin wanted to know if switching off foot shocks could be used to reinforce two rats' positive interactions with each other. Azrin planned to turn on the shock and then, once the rats began to approach each other, cut off the pain. To his great surprise, the experiment proved impossible. No sooner did the rats feel pain than they attacked each other, even before the experimenter could switch off the shock. Azrin then dropped his initial research plans, and with colleagues Ronald Hutchinson (1983), Roger Ulrich, and Don Hake undertook a series of studies on this pain-attack reaction.

First, they found that the greater the shock, the more violent the aggression. They also noted that the rats did not adapt to the shock. Even when given up to several thousand shocks a day, the effect did not wear off. What is more, rats reared in isolation reacted much the same way, suggesting an innate pain-attack reaction much like the natural frustration-aggression reaction that had been theorized by John Dollard decades earlier.

Do rats alone react this way? The researchers wanted to know. So next they found that with a wide variety of species, the cruelty the animals imposed upon each other matched zap for zap the cruelty imposed upon them. As Azrin (1967) explained, the pain-attack response occurred

Today's ethical guidelines for use of animals in research restrain investigators' use of painful stimuli.

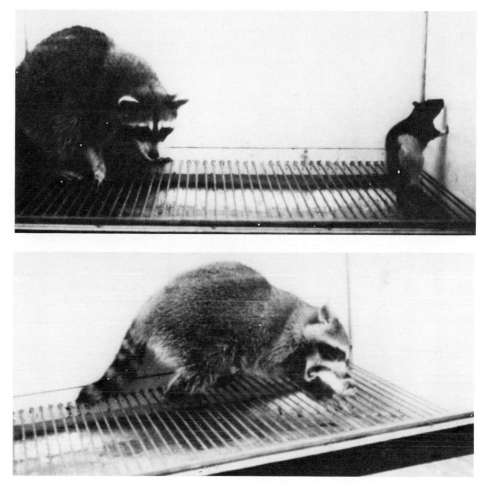

The pain-attack reaction: Upon receiving a shock or other painful effect, many animals will automatically attack whatever animal is within reach.

in many different strains of rats. Then we found that shock produced attack when pairs of the following species were caged together: some kinds of mice, hamsters, opossums, raccoons, marmosets, foxes, nutria, cats, snapping turtles, squirrel monkeys, ferrets, red squirrels, bantam roosters, alligators, crayfish, amphiuma (an amphibian), and several species of snakes including the boa constrictor, rattlesnake, brown rat-snake, cottonmouth, copperhead, and black snake. The shock-attack reaction was clearly present in many very different kinds of creatures. In all the species in which shock produced attack it was fast and consistent, in the same "push-button" manner as with the rats.

The animals were not choosey about their targets. Not only would they attack animals of their own species but also those of a different species, or stuffed dolls, or even tennis balls. Lastly, the researchers varied the source of pain. It was found that not only shocks induce attack, but also intense heat and "psychological pain"—for example, suddenly not rewarding hungry pigeons that have been trained to expect a grain reward after pecking at a disk. Such "psychological pain" is, of course, what we call frustration.

Consistent with the formulation of social learning shown in Figure 12-5, these experiments demonstrated that in many (though not all) animal species, aversive stimulation can fuel aggression. Further consistent with Figure 12-5, aversive stimulation also increases the likelihood of certain other behaviors, especially escape. Given a choice, many animals prefer to flee rather than fight. Azrin and his colleagues prevented such alternative responses by restricting the animals to a small enclosure. Escape was impossible. So, the animals did the next best thing—attack. In retrospect we can see how pain-provoked fight and flight could both have survival value. Both responses can terminate aversive stimulation.

Pain heightens aggressiveness in humans, also. Many of us can recall such a reaction after stubbing a toe or suffering a headache. Leonard Berkowitz and his associates demonstrated this by having University of Wisconsin students hold one hand in either lukewarm water or painfully cold water. Those whose hands were submerged in the cold water reported feeling more irritable and more annoyed, and they were more willing to blast another person with unpleasant noise. In view of such results, Berkowitz (1983, 1988) now believes that aversive stimulation rather than frustration is the more basic trigger of hostile aggression. Frustration is certainly one important type of unpleasantness. But, says Berkowitz, any decidedly aversive event, whether a dashed expectation, a personal insult, or a physical pain, can incite an emotional outburst. Even the torment of a depressed state can increase the likelihood of hostile aggressive behavior.

Heat

People have theorized for centuries about the effect of climate on human action. Hippocrates, comparing the civilized Greece of his day to the savagery (for example, human sacrifice) in what we now know as Germany and Switzerland, believed the cause to be northern Europe's harsher climate. Later, the British attributed their "superior" culture to *England's* ideal climate. French thinkers proclaimed the same for France. Since climate remains steady while cultural traits change, the climate theory of culture obviously has limited validity.

However, temporary climate variations can affect one's behavior. Offensive odors, cigarette smoke, and air pollution have all been linked with aggressive behaviors (Rotton & Frey, 1985). But the most-studied environmental irritant is heat. For example, William Griffitt (1970; Griffitt & Veitch, 1971) found that, compared to students who answered questionnaires in a room with a normal temperature, those who did so in an uncomfortably hot room (over 90°F) reported feeling more tired and aggressive and expressed more hostility toward a stranger they were asked to rate. Follow-up experiments by Paul Bell (1980) at Colorado State University and Brendan Gail Rule and others (1987) at the University of Alberta show that heat also triggers aggressive thoughts and retaliative actions.

Does uncomfortable heat increase aggression in the real world as well as in the laboratory? Consider:

• Merrill Carlsmith and Craig Anderson (1979) report that the riots occurring in seventy-nine U.S. cities between 1967 and 1971 were more likely on hot than cool days (see Figure 12-7).
• When the weather is hot in Houston, Texas, violent crimes are more likely (see Figure 12-8). The same is true in Des Moines, Iowa (Cotton, 1981); Dayton, Ohio (Rotton & Frey, 1985); Indianapolis, Indiana (Cotton, 1986); and Dallas, Texas (Harries & Stadler, 1988).

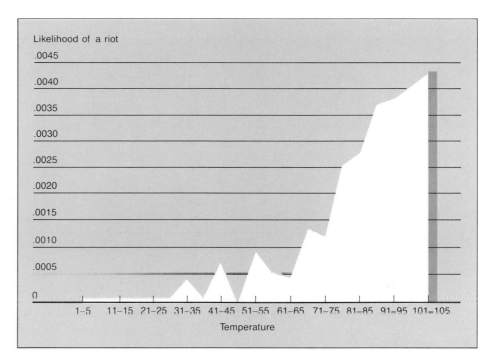

FIGURE 12-7
Between 1967 and 1971 the likelihood of a riot increased with temperature. (This does not mean that most riots occurred at temperatures above 90°F. Rather, on any given day above 90°F a riot was more likely than on any other given day of lower temperature.) (Data from Carlsmith & Anderson, 1979.)

- Not only do hotter days have more violent crimes, so also do hotter seasons of the year and hotter summers (Anderson, 1989).
- In heat-stricken Phoenix, Arizona, drivers without air conditioning are more likely to honk at a stalled car (Kenrick & MacFarlane, 1986).
- During the 1986 major league baseball season, the number of batters hit by a pitch per game was double for games played in the 90s than for games played at cooler temperatures (Reifman et al., 1988).

Does all this indicate that the discomfort of hot days fuels aggressiveness? While this conclusion appears plausible, we had best not hastily assume it. Figures 12-6 and 12-7 present simple *correlations* between temperature and riots. People certainly could be more irritable when suffering through hot sticky weather. However, there may be other contributing factors. Maybe hot summer evenings lead people into the streets. There, other group influence factors may well take over. Judging from laboratory experiments on aversive stimulation and from those on collective aggression (see the discussion below), my hunch is that such behavior is stimulated by both the heat and the group.

Attacks

Being attacked by another is especially conducive to aggression. Experiments at Kent State University by Stuart Taylor (Taylor & Pisano, 1971), at Washington State University by Harold Dengerink (Dengerink & Myers, 1977), and at Osaka University by Kennichi Ohbuchi and Toshihiro Kambara (1985) confirm that attacks breed retaliatory attacks, especially when the victim perceives the attack as intentional. In most of these experiments one person competes with another in a reaction-time contest. After each test trial, the winner gets to choose how much shock to give the loser. Actually, each

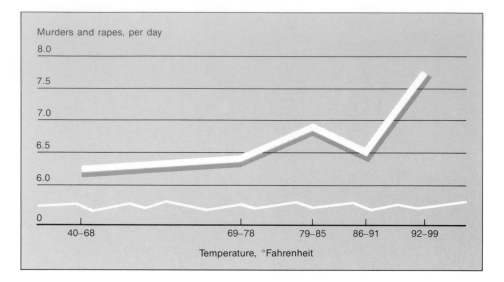

FIGURE 12-8
Aversive heat and violent crime. On days between 1980 and 1982, the number of rapes and murders in Houston, Texas, was greater when the temperature reached the mid-90s. (From Anderson & Anderson, 1984.)

"If someone hits you, you hit him back."
Defense Secretary Caspar Weinberger, justifying the U.S. bombing of Libya (quoted by Rowe, 1986)

subject is playing a programmed opponent, one who steadily escalates the amount of shock. Do the real subjects respond charitably, "turning the other cheek"? Hardly. Extracting "an eye for an eye" is the more likely response. When attacked, subjects usually retaliate in kind.

Crowding

Crowding—the subjective feeling of not having enough space—can be stressful. Crammed in the back of a bus, trapped in slow-moving freeway traffic, or living three to a room in a college dorm can diminish one's sense of control (Baron et al., 1976; McNeel, 1980). Might such experiences also heighten aggression?

The stress experienced by animals allowed to overpopulate a confined environment does produce heightened aggressiveness, along with abnormal sexual behavior and even an inflated death rate (Calhoun, 1962; Christian et al., 1960). But of course, it is a rather large leap from rats in an enclosure or deer on an island to human beings in a city (R. M. Baron & Needel, 1980; Freedman, 1979). Nevertheless, it's true that dense urban areas do suffer higher rates of crime and emotional distress (Fleming et al., 1987; Kirmeyer, 1978). Even when they *don't* suffer higher crime rates, residents of crowded cities may *feel* more fearful. People from Hong Kong, which is four times more densely populated than Toronto, report feeling more fearful on their city's streets than do people from Toronto—which actually has a crime rate four times higher (Gifford & Peacock, 1979).

Crowding:
A subjective feeling of not enough space per person.

AROUSAL

So far we have seen that various aversive stimulations can arouse people's anger. Do other types of arousal, such as those that accompany exercise or sexual excitement, have a similar effect? Imagine that Wanda, having just finished a stimulating short run, comes home to discover that her date for the evening has called and left word that he has made other plans. Will Wanda more likely explode in fury after her run than if she discovered the same message just after awakening from a nap? Or, having just exercised, will her aggressive tendencies have been exorcised? To look for an answer, let's examine some intriguing research on how we interpret and label our bodily states.

In a now famous experiment, Stanley Schachter and Jerome Singer (1962) found that an aroused bodily state can be experienced in different ways. A group of men from the University of Minnesota were aroused by an injection of adrenaline, producing feelings of body flushing, heart palpitation, and more rapid breathing. When they were forewarned that the drug would produce these effects, they felt little emotion, even when with either a hostile or a euphoric person. Of course—they could readily attribute their bodily sensations to the drug. Another group of men were led to believe the drug produced no such side effects. Then they, too, were placed in the company of a person either hostile or euphoric. How did they feel and act? Angrily when with the hostile person. Amused when with the person who was euphoric.

Although other experiments indicate that arousal is not as emotionally undifferentiated as Schachter believed, being physically stirred up does seem to intensify just about any emotion (Reisenzein, 1983). For example, Dolf Zillmann, Jennings Bryant, and their collaborators (see Zillmann, 1988) found that when aroused people—people who have just pumped an exercise bike or watched a film of a Beatles rock concert—are provoked, they often find it easy to misattribute their arousal to the provocation. They then retaliate with heightened aggression. While common sense might assume that Wanda's run would have drained her aggressive tensions, enabling her to accept the insulting news calmly, these studies suggest that being aroused can actually feed emotions.

If you understand this principle—that a given state of bodily arousal can be steered into an experience of one emotion or another, depending on how the person interprets and labels the arousal—then you will be able to predict the outcome of the following experiment. Russell Geen and his coresearchers (1972) had a confederate subject administer electric shocks to some University of Missouri men while they were reading a sexually stimulating story. Either the shocks or the story would have been sufficient to arouse the men. But, while wired to physiological instruments, some were shown dials indicating they were experiencing strong "shock arousal" but little "sexual arousal." Others were shown dials that led them to believe their arousal came from the story. Question: When their turn came to do the shocking, which group of men delivered the most shock?

Geen predicted, and found, that those led to believe they were aroused by the shocks labeled their arousal as anger (see Figure 12-9). So they reciprocated by giving the confederate what they believed were more and stronger shocks.

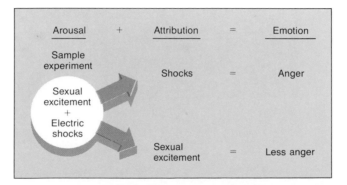

FIGURE 12-9

What emotion we experience depends on how we interpret and label our bodily states. For example, if we attribute arousal to aggressive stimuli, we will likely experience anger.

What is more, sexual arousal and other forms of arousal, such as anger, can amplify one another (Zillmann, in press). Love is never so passionate as after a fight or a scare. In the laboratory, people who have just been frightened are more strongly aroused by erotic stimuli. The excitation transfers from one realm to another.

Pornography

So, might sexual arousal similarly amplify aggressive responses to insults and aggravations? If so, what might be the social consequences of pornography? A 1986 Surgeon General's conference of twenty-one leading social scientists focused on depictions of sexual violence. A typical episode finds a rapist forcing himself upon a female victim. She at first resists, tries to fight off her attacker. But gradually she becomes sexually aroused and as she does, her resistance melts. By the end she is in ecstasy, pleading for more. We have all viewed or read nonpornographic versions of this sequence: Dashing man grabs and forcibly kisses protesting woman. Within moments, the arms that were pushing him away are clutching him tight, her resistance overwhelmed by her unleashed passion.

The social scientists concurred that viewing such fictional scenes of a man overpowering and arousing a woman can (1) distort one's perceptions of how women actually respond to sexual coercion and (2) increase men's aggression against women, at least in laboratory settings.

Distorted Perceptions of Sexual Reality

Does viewing sexual violence reinforce the myth that some women would welcome sexual assault—that " 'no' doesn't really mean no"? To find out, Neil Malamuth and James Check (1981) compared University of Manitoba men who were shown either two

Viewing sexual aggression can encourage aggressive behavior against women.

nonsexual movies or two movies depicting a man sexually overpowering a woman. A week later, when surveyed by a different experimenter, those who had seen the films with mild sexual violence were more accepting of violence against women. Note that the films' sexual message was subtle: It was unlikely to elicit counterarguing. (Recall from Chapter 8 that persuasion can occur more readily when a disagreeable message is slipped in without provoking people to counterargue.)

Viewing slasher movies can also produce a trivialization of rape. Men who recently have been viewing films such as "The Texas Chainsaw Massacre" become desensitized to brutality and more likely to view rape victims unsympathetically (Linz et al., 1988, 1989). In fact, say researchers Edward Donnerstein, Daniel Linz, and Steven Penrod (1987), one could hardly imagine a better way for an evil character to enable people to react calmly to the torture and mutilation of women than to show a gradually escalating series of such films.

Aggression Against Women

Evidence is also accumulating that pornography may contribute to men's aggression toward women. Some recent correlational studies suggest this possibility. John Court (1984) notes that across the world, as pornography became more widely available during the 1960s and 1970s, the rate of reported rapes sharply increased—except in countries and areas where pornography has been controlled. (The examples that counter this trend—such as Japan, where violent pornography is available but the rape rate is low—reminds us that other factors, such as how people are socialized, are also important.) In Hawaii, the number of reported rapes rose ninefold between 1960 and 1974, then dropped when restraints on pornography were temporarily imposed, then rose again when the restraints were lifted.

In another correlational study, Larry Baron and Murray Straus (1984, 1986) discovered that the sales rates of "soft-core" sexually explicit magazines (such as *Hustler* and *Playboy*) in each of the fifty states was correlated with state rape rates. Even when other factors were controlled, such as the percentage of young males in each state, a positive relationship remained. Alaska ranked first in sex magazine sales and first in rape, followed by Nevada, which was second on both measures.

Of course, this *correlation* cannot prove that sexually explicit depictions are a contributing *cause* of rape. For example, W. L. Marshall (1988) recently found that Ontario rapists and child molesters use pornography much more than do men who are not sexual offenders. But maybe the offenders' use of pornography is merely a symptom and not a cause of their basic deviance.

Although limited to the sorts of behaviors that can be studied in the laboratory, controlled experiments indicate that viewing sexual violence does cause an increase in some men's aggression toward women. Edward Donnerstein (1980) showed 120 University of Wisconsin men either a neutral, an erotic, or an aggressive-erotic (rape) film. Then, the men, supposedly as part of another experiment, "taught" a male or female confederate some nonsense syllables by choosing how much shock to administer for incorrect answers. The men who had watched the rape film administered markedly stronger shocks—but only toward female victims (see Figure 12-10). In subsequent experiments, Donnerstein and Leonard Berkowitz (1981) found the same result, and it did not matter whether the rape film depicted the woman as suffering or enjoying herself. Evidently, just as children's inhibitions against aggression are lowered after observing an aggressive model, so too are men's, especially when the men are angered and when their potential victim is like (for example, the same sex as) the filmed victim.

If you are troubled by the ethics of conducting experiments such as these, rest

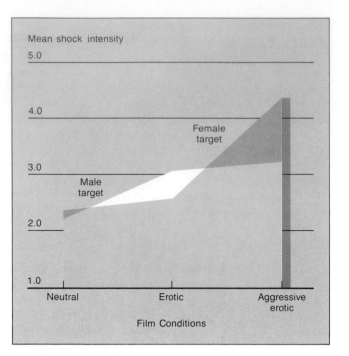

FIGURE 12-10
After viewing an aggressive-erotic film, college men delivered stronger shocks than before, especially to a woman. (Data from Donnerstein, 1980.)

assured that these researchers appreciate the controversial and powerful experience they are giving their participants. Thus the participants are forewarned about what they might be shown. Only after giving their knowing consent do they participate. Moreover, after the experiment any rape myths that the film may have communicated are discredited. One hopes that such debriefing sufficiently offsets the vivid image of a supposedly ecstatic rape victim. Judging from studies with University of Manitoba and Winnipeg students by Check and Malamuth (1984; Malamuth & Check, 1984), it does. Those who read erotic rape stories and were then debriefed became less accepting of the "women-enjoy-rape" myth than were students who had not seen the film. Similarly, Donnerstein and Berkowitz (1981) found that Wisconsin students who viewed pornography *and* were then thoroughly debriefed were later *less* likely than other students to agree that "Being roughed up is sexually stimulating to many women."

Justification for this experimentation is not only scientific, but also humanitarian. In 1987, some 91,000 U.S. females—one every 6 minutes—were known to have suffered the horror of forcible rape, more than twice the number reported annually during the mid-1960s (FBI *Uniform Crime Reports*, 1971 to 1988). Surveys suggest that unreported rapes may outnumber those reported by a 10 to 1 ratio (Russell, 1984; Koss et al., 1988), and that most unreported rapes are committed by acquaintances, often on dates (DiVasto et al., 1984; Rapaport & Burkhart, 1984). Many more women—half in one recent survey of college women (Sandberg et al., 1985)—report having suffered some form of sexual assault while on a date, and even more have experienced verbal sexual harassment.

In eight different surveys, college males have been asked whether there was any chance they would rape a woman "if you could be assured that no one would know and that you could in no way be punished" (Stille et al., 1987). A disturbing proportion—

BEHIND THE SCENES

We began our study of violence against women by examining pornography and soon realized that various depictions of women, including those in R-rated slasher films, could lead to negative attitudes and behavior toward women. It has been interesting to see how TV and newspaper reporters have tended to "read into" our reports what they expected or wanted us to say. While one individual will state that pornography leads to aggression, another will write that it does not.

Ed Donnerstein, University of California, Santa Barbara, and Neil Malamuth, University of California, Los Angeles

"In laboratory studies measuring short-term effects, exposure to violent pornography increases punitive behavior toward women."
Social science consensus at Surgeon General's Workshop on Pornography and Public Health (Koop, 1987)

"What we're trying to do is raise the level of awareness of violence against women and pornography to at least the level of awareness of racist and Ku Klux Klan literature."
Gloria Steinem (1988)

about one-third—admit to at least a slim possibility of their doing so. Are these admissions of attraction to sexual aggression believable? Researcher Malamuth (1984, 1989) believes they are. Compared to men who indicate no possibility of their raping, those who do are more like convicted rapists in their beliefs in rape myths and in their being sexually aroused even by rape depictions that portray a resistant, unaroused victim. Moreover, those who indicate most likelihood of raping behave more aggressively toward women in both laboratory and dating situations, especially if they have formed the sort of rape-supportive attitudes that pornography cultivates. Specifically, men who behave in sexually coercive, aggressive ways typically desire dominance, exhibit hostility toward women, and are sexually experienced (Malamuth, 1986).

Malamuth, Donnerstein, and Zillmann are among those alarmed by the increasing vulnerability of women to rape. They caution against oversimplifying the complex causes of rape—which is no more attributable to any one cause than is cancer. Yet they conclude that viewing violence, especially sexual violence, can have antisocial effects. Commenting on some of these results, Susan Brownmiller (1980, 1984), author of *Against Our Will: Women and Rape*, challenges our tolerance of aggressive pornography, which she views as "propaganda against women." Liberals would not tolerate pornographic depictions of Jewish victims being abused by Gentiles or of Blacks being abused by Whites but have condoned such when women are the victims of men. Brownmiller calls for an end to this double standard.

Rather than advocate censorship, many psychologists favor "media awareness training." Recall that pornography researchers have successfully resensitized and educated their participants to women's actual responses to sexual violence. Might educators similarly promote critical viewing skills in the general public? By sensitizing people to the view of women that predominates in pornography and to issues of sexual harassment and violence, it should be possible to counter the myth that women enjoy being coerced. "Our utopian and perhaps naive hope," say Edward Donnerstein, Daniel Linz, and Steven Penrod (1987, p. 196), "is that in the end the truth revealed through good science will prevail and the public will be convinced that these images not only demean those portrayed but also those who view them."

Television

We have seen that children's observations of an aggressive model can unleash their aggressive urges and teach them new ways to aggress. And we have seen that, after viewing sexual violence against a woman, college men tend to act more violently toward a woman who has angered them. Such findings prompt many people to be concerned about television's effect on the behavior and thinking of its viewers.

Consider these few facts about watching television. In 1945, the Gallup poll asked Americans, "Do you know what television is?" (Gallup, 1972, p. 551). Today, 98 percent of American households have a TV set, more than have bathtubs or telephones. In the average home, the set is on some seven hours a day and is watched by an average member of the household for about four of those hours. Women watch more than men, non-Whites more than Whites, preschoolers and retired people more than those in school or working, and the less educated more than the highly educated. For the most part, these facts about Americans' viewing habits have also characterized Europeans, Australians, and Japanese (Murray & Kippax, 1979).

During all those hours, what social behaviors are being modeled? Since 1967, George Gerbner, Larry Gross, and their fellow TV watchers (1980, 1986) at the University of Pennsylvania have been sampling network prime-time and Saturday morning entertainment programs in the United States. Their findings? Eight of ten programs contained violence. Prime-time programs have averaged five violent acts per hour; Saturday morning children's programs, about twenty per hour. Since the late 1960s

Televised violence:
A physically compelling action that threatens to hurt or kill, or actual hurting or killing.

Children often imitate the violence they see on television.

the yearly rates of televised cruelty have varied by no more than 10 percent from the average for the whole period.

So, given these two facts—(1) an enormous amount of television watching—more than 1000 hours a year per person, and (2) a heavy dose of aggression in the typical television diet—it is difficult to resist being concerned about the cumulative effects of such viewing. Does prime-time crime stimulate the behavior it depicts? Or, as viewers vicariously participate in aggressive acts, do the shows drain off aggressive energy?

Catharsis:
Emotional release. The catharsis view of aggression is that aggressive drive is reduced when one "releases" aggressive energy, either by acting aggressively or by fantasizing aggression.

The latter idea, a variation on the *catharsis* hypothesis, postulates that experiencing an emotion is a way to release it. Generalized to viewing aggression, the catharsis hypothesis would maintain that violent drama enables people to release their pent-up hostilities. Defenders of the media cite this theory frequently, and remind us that violence predates television. In an imaginary debate with one of television's critics, the medium's defender might argue, "The genocides of Jews and American Indians were certainly not provoked by television. Television mostly just reflects and caters to our tastes." "Agreed," responds the critic, "but it's also true that during America's TV age violent crime has increased several times faster than the population rate." The defender objects: "That national trend is the result of many complex factors. In fact, TV may even reduce aggression by keeping people off the streets and by offering them a harmless opportunity to vent their aggression."

"One of television's great contributions is that it brought murder back into the home where it belongs. Seeing a murder on television can be good therapy. It can help work off one's antagonisms."
Alfred Hitchcock

And so the debate goes on, with more than a thousand new articles on the effects of the media appearing in psychological journals in just the last decade (Eron & Huesmann, 1985). Studies of television viewing and aggression (which are but a fraction of the literature on television and behavior—Freedman, 1984) are generally aimed at identifying effects more subtle and pervasive than the occasional "copy-cat" murders and other crimes that capture the public's attention. In particular, two issues are addressed: (1) how television affects viewers' *behavior*—for example, are people more or less aggressive after viewing aggressive behavior?—and (2) how television affects viewers' *thinking*—for example, does viewing heavy doses of violence desensitize people to violence?

Effects on Behavior

Do viewers tend to imitate the behavior of violent models? Examples abound of people reenacting television crimes. In one informal survey of 208 prison convicts, 9 out of 10 admitted that by watching crime programs they learned new criminal tricks. And 4 out of 10 said they had attempted specific crimes they had seen on television (*TV Guide*, 1977).

Correlation of TV viewing and behavior. But such is not scientific evidence. Nor does it tell us how television affects the aggressiveness of those who have never committed violent crimes. Researchers therefore have used both correlational and experimental studies to examine the effects of viewing violence. One technique, commonly used with schoolchildren, is simply to see whether individuals' TV watching predicts their aggressiveness. Results indicate that the more violent the content of the child's TV viewing, the more aggressive the child (Eron, 1987; Turner et al., 1986). The relationship is modest, but consistently found in the United States, Europe, and Australia.

So, may we conclude that a violent TV diet contributes to aggression? Perhaps you are already thinking that this is a correlational research, so the cause-effect relation could also work in the opposite direction. Maybe aggressive children prefer aggressive programs. Or maybe some underlying third factor, such as lower intelligence, predisposes some children both to prefer aggressive programs and to act aggressively.

Researchers have developed two ways to test these alternative explanations. The "hidden-third-factor" explanation can be tested by statistically pulling out the influence of some of these possible factors. For example, British researcher William Belson (1978; Muson, 1978) studied 1565 London boys and found that, compared to those who watched little violence, those who watched a great deal (especially realistic rather than cartoon violence) admitted to 50 percent more violent acts during the preceding six months (for example, "I busted the telephone in a telephone box"). Belson also examined twenty-two likely "third factors," such as family size. The heavy and light viewers still differed after equating them with respect to potential third factors, so Belson surmised that the heavy viewers were indeed more violent *because* of their TV exposure.

Similarly, Leonard Eron and Rowell Huesmann (1980, 1985) found that the viewing of violence among 875 eight-year-olds correlated with aggressiveness even after statistically pulling out several obvious possible third factors. Moreover, when they restudied these individuals as nineteen-year-olds they discovered that the viewing of violence at age eight modestly predicted aggressiveness at age nineteen, but that aggressiveness at age eight did *not* predict the viewing of violence at age nineteen. Thus aggression followed violence viewing, not the reverse. These findings have been confirmed in newer studies of 758 Chicago-area and 220 Finnish youngsters (Huesmann et al., 1984). What is more, when Eron and Huesmann (1984) examined the later criminal conviction records of their initial sample of eight-year-olds, they found that at age 30 those men who as children had watched a great deal of violent television were more likely to have been convicted of a serious crime (see Figure 12-11). The researchers therefore surmised that viewing violence does indeed make at least a small contribution to later violent behavior.

Notice that these studies illustrate how researchers are now using correlational findings to *suggest* cause and effect. Yet, an infinite number of possible "third factors"

"I rarely turn down an invitation to speak to a PTA meeting or other civic groups in order to warn parents and other caretakers that they must control their children's viewing habits."
Leonard Eron (1985)

FIGURE 12-11
Children's television viewing and later criminal activity. Eight-year-olds who watched a great deal of television were more likely to have been convicted of a serious criminal offense by age 30. (Data from Eron & Huesmann, 1984.)

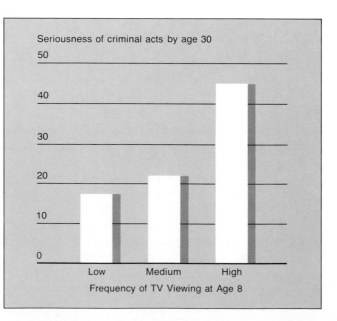

could be creating a merely coincidental relation between viewing violence and aggression. To identify and extract all these is impossible. Fortunately, however, the experimental method can control all these extraneous factors. If some children are randomly assigned to watch a violent film, and others a nonviolent film, any subsequent aggression difference between the two groups will be due to the only factor that distinguishes them: what they watched. (Recall that random assignment otherwise equalizes the two groups.)

TV viewing experiments.   The pioneering experiments were conducted by Albert Bandura and Richard Walters (1963), who sometimes had young children view the adult pounding the inflated doll on film instead of observing it live—with much the same effect—and by Leonard Berkowitz and Russell Geen (1966), who found that angered college students who viewed a violent film acted more aggressively than did similarly angered students who viewed nonaggressive films. These laboratory experiments, coupled with the American public's growing concern, were sufficient to prompt the U.S. Surgeon General to commission fifty new research studies during the early 1970s. By and large, these studies confirmed that viewing violence amplifies aggression.

In a later series of experiments, a team of researchers led by Ross Parke (1977) in the United States and Jacques Leyens (1975) in Belgium showed institutionalized American and Belgian delinquent boys a series of either aggressive or nonaggressive commercial films. Their consistent finding: "Exposure to movie violence . . . led to an increase in viewer aggression." For example, compared to the week preceding the film series, physical attacks increased sharply in cottages where boys were viewing violent films.

Likewise, when David P. Phillips (1983) analyzed day-by-day homicide rates in the United States from 1973 to 1978, he found a significant homicide increase in the week following heavyweight championship prizefights. When Tannis MacBeth Williams (1986) and colleagues observed children in a rural Canadian town, they found that playground aggression doubled after the introduction of television. And after Nicola Schutte and her coresearchers (1988) had 5- to 7-year-old children play a violent (karate) videogame, they, too, found that physical aggression doubled during a subsequent free play period.

Conclusions   Television research has involved a variety of methods and participants. One ambitious researcher, Susan Hearold (1986), assembled results from 230 correlational and experimental studies involving more than 100,000 people. Her conclusion: Viewing antisocial portrayals is indeed associated with antisocial behavior. Its effect is not overwhelming and is, in fact, at times not evident [even seldom evident, say some critics (Freedman, 1988; McGuire, 1986)]. Moreover, the aggression provoked by most of this viewing is not assault and battery; it is more on the scale of a shove in the lunch line, a cruel comment, a threatening gesture.

Nevertheless, the convergence of evidence from this variety of studies is striking. Experimental studies point most clearly to cause and effect, but they are sometimes remote from real life (for example, pushing a hurt button). Moreover, the experiments can but hint at the cumulative effects of witnessing more than 100,000 violent episodes and some 25,000 deaths, as does the average person by the time of high school graduation. On the other hand, while the correlational studies are complicated by the inclusion of an unidentifiable number of other influences, they do tap the cumulative effects.

"Then shall we simply allow our children to listen to any story anyone happens to make up, and so receive into their minds ideas often the very opposite of those we shall think they ought to have when they are grown up?"
Plato, The Republic

"The consensus among most of the research community is that violence on television does lead to aggressive behavior by children and teenagers who watch the programs."
National Institute of Mental Health (1982)

Why does TV viewing affect behavior?   The conclusion drawn by the Surgeon General and by these researchers is *not* that television is a primary cause of social violence, any more than cyclamates are a primary cause of cancer. However, it is *a* cause. And even if it is just one among many contributors, it is one that, like cyclamates, is potentially controllable. Given this convergence of correlational and experimental evidence, researchers have turned some of their attention to exploring *why* viewing violence has this effect. Perhaps from earlier sections of this chapter you can anticipate their explanations.

Three possibilities have been suggested (Geen & Thomas, 1986). One is that it's not the violent content per se that causes social violence, but the *arousal* produced by the exciting action (Zillmann, in press; Mueller et al., 1983). As we noted earlier, arousal tends to spill over: one type of arousal can energize other behaviors.

Other research indicates that viewing violence can also produce *disinhibition.* As in situations of deindividuation (see Chapter 9), viewing others performing an antisocial act can diminish one's own restraints about doing so. In Bandura's experiment, the adult's punching the Bobo doll seemed to legitimate such outbursts; thus the children's own inhibitions were lowered. Similarly, Berkowitz (1964) found that after college men view someone getting a well-deserved beating, they are less inhibited about shocking someone who is similar to (even merely having the same name as) the film's victim. Berkowitz (1984) and others (Carver et al., 1983; Josephson, 1987) also believe that violence viewing primes the viewer for aggressive behavior by activating violence-related thoughts.

That media portrayals also evoke *imitation* was made apparent when the children in Bandura's experiments reenacted the specific behaviors they had witnessed. The commercial television industry is hard-pressed to dispute that television prompts viewers to imitate what has been seen. Its advertising income is supported by this conclusion. Thus, advertisers employ models, believing that observing them affects viewers' behavior. Television's critics agree—and are troubled that on TV programs acts of assault outnumber affectionate acts 4 to 1 and that, in other ways as well, television models an unreal world (see Table 12-1). TV cops fire their guns in almost every episode, while actual Chicago police officers fire their guns an average of once every 27 years (Radecki, 1989).

If the ways of relating and problem solving modeled on television do tend to produce imitation, especially among young viewers, then modeling **prosocial behavior** should be socially beneficial. Chapter 14 contains good news: Television's subtle influence can indeed teach children positive lessons in behavior.

Effects on Thinking

Other researchers are examining the cognitive effects of viewing violence: Does prolonged viewing desensitize us to cruelty? Does it distort our perceptions of reality?

Take some emotion-arousing stimulus, say an obscene word, and repeat it over and over. What happens? If you have studied introductory psychology, you may recall that the emotional response is likely to "extinguish." After witnessing thousands of cruelties, there is good reason to expect a similar emotional numbing. Perhaps the most common response might well become, "Doesn't bother me at all." Such a response is precisely what Victor Cline and his colleagues (1973) observed when they measured the physiological arousal of 121 Utah boys viewing a brutal boxing match. Compared to boys who watched little television, those who watched a great deal were minimally aroused; their responses to the beating resembled more of a shrug than a concern.

Prosocial behavior:
Positive, constructive, helpful social behavior; the opposite of antisocial behavior.

"All television is educational. The question is, what is it teaching?"
Nicholas Johnson, Former Commissioner, Federal Communications Commission (1978)

TABLE 12-1
America's Television World versus the Real World
How closely does prime time network television drama mirror the world around us?
Compare the percentage of people and behaviors on TV dramas with those in
the real world.

Item Viewed	Seen on Television (%)	In the Real World (%)
Female	25	51
Blue collar	25	67
Characters involved in violence	> 50/week	< 1/year
Sexual intercourse: Partners not married	85	Unknown, but < 50%
Beverages consumed: percent alcoholic	45	16

From an analysis of more than 25,000 television characters since 1969 by George Gerbner & others (1986). TV sex data from Fernandez-Collado & others (1978). Alcohol data from NCTV (1988). Percent of sex that occurs among not married partners is unknown, but is surely a fraction of that depicted on TV, given that most adults are married and frequency of intercourse is higher among the married than among singles.

A Louis Harris and Associates (1988) study for Planned Parenthood found that, per hour, American network programs (not including cable television or rock videos) depicted 10 sexual innuendos, 9 kisses, 5 embraces, 1.8 references to intercourse, and 1.7 references to deviant sexual practices. During the study year—1987–88—the average person therefore viewed 14,000 sexual events, triple the number of a decade earlier.

Of course these boys might differ in ways other than their television viewing. Recall, though, that in experiments on the effects of viewing sexual violence, similar desensitization occurs among young men who view slasher films. Moreover, Ronald Drabman and Margaret Thomas (1974, 1975, 1976; Rule & Ferguson, 1986) confirmed that viewing breeds indifference—a more blasé reaction when later viewing the film of a brawl or when actually observing two children fighting.

Does viewing television's fictional world also mold our conceptions of the real world? George Gerbner and his University of Pennsylvania associates (1979; 1986) suspect this is television's most potent effect. Their surveys of both adolescents and adults show that heavy viewers (four hours a day or more) are more likely than light viewers (two hours or less) to exaggerate the frequency of violence in the world around them and to fear being personally assaulted. Similarly, a national survey of American seven- to eleven-year-old children gave evidence that heavy viewers were more likely than light viewers to admit fears "that somebody bad might get into your house," or that "when you go outside, somebody might hurt you" (Peterson & Zill, 1981). And when Jerome and Dorothy Singer and Wanda Rapaczynski (1984) closely studied 63 children over several years they found that those whose viewing was unrestricted saw the world, including their neighborhood, as scarier than did those who watched less television. Adults seem better able to dissociate television crime from the goings on in their own neighborhood. Those who often watch crime dramas are more likely than those who don't to see New York as a dangerous place and even to believe that their own city could be dangerous, but they are not more fearful of their own neighborhood (Heath & Petraitis, 1987; Tyler & Cook, 1984).

"Those of us who have been active over more than 15 years in studying [television] cannot fail to be impressed with the significance of this medium for the emerging consciousness of the developing child."
Jerome Singer and Dorothy Singer (1988)

Researchers are also investigating other positive and negative effects of television. My own hunch is that television's most influential effect occurs indirectly, as it each year replaces in people's lives a thousand or more hours of other activities they would otherwise be engaged in.

GROUP AGGRESSION

In this chapter we have considered the circumstances that induce *individuals* to aggress. The same circumstances that provoke individuals to aggress can provoke groups to do likewise. If frustrations, insults, and aggressive models heighten the aggressive tendencies of isolated people, then such factors will likely prompt the same reaction in those gathered together. For example, at a riot's beginning, acts of aggression often spread rapidly after being "triggered" by the aggressive example of one antagonistic person. Normally law-abiding bystanders, after observing looters freely helping themselves to TV sets or steaks, often drop their ethical inhibitions and imitate.

Laboratory experiments reveal two ways—the diffusion of responsibility and group polarization—in which a group situation can actually amplify aggressive reactions of individuals. Consider decisions made in wartime. Decisions to attack typically are made by strategists remote from the front lines. The strategists have a buffer between themselves and the actual violence: They give orders. Others carry them out. Does such distancing make it easier to recommend aggression?

Jacquelin Gaebelein and Anthony Mander (1978) created a laboratory version of this situation. They asked their University of North Carolina at Greensboro students either to shock someone or to advise another person how much shock to administer. When the subjects who were asked to do the shocking were provoked by the recipient, they and the advisers independently favored approximately the same amount of shock. But when the recipient was relatively innocent of any provocation, as are most victims of mass aggression, the front-line person was inclined to give lower shock levels than those recommended by the advisers. The researchers surmised that the advisers' inhibitions against aggression were diminished by their not being directly responsible for the hurting.

Responsibility diffusion increases not only with distance but with numbers. When Brian Mullen (1986a) analyzed information from sixty lynchings that occurred between

"The worst barbarity of war is that it forces men collectively to commit acts against which individually they would revolt with their whole being."
Ellen Key, War, Peace, and the Future, *1916*

FIGURE 12-12
When individuals chose how much shock to administer as punishment for wrong answers, they escalated the shock level as the experiment proceeded. Group decision making further polarized this tendency. (Data from Jaffe et al., 1981.)

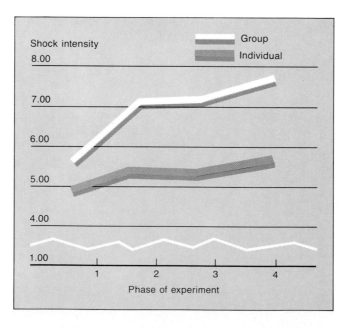

1899 and 1946 he made an interesting discovery: the greater the number of people in a lynch mob, the more vicious their murdering and mutilation.

Such situations also involve group interaction. Might groups magnify aggressive tendencies, much as they polarize other tendencies? The possibility is illustrated by what Scandinavians call "mobbing"—schoolchildren repeatedly harassing or attacking an insecure, weak schoolmate. Mobbing occurs as a group activity. One bully alone is less likely to taunt or attack the victim than when several of them gang up (Lagerspetz et al., 1982).

Experiments by Israeli social psychologists Yoram Jaffe and Yoel Yinon (1983) confirm that groups can polarize aggressive tendencies. In one, university men who were angered by a supposed fellow subject retaliated with decisions to give much stronger shocks when in groups than when alone. In another experiment (Jaffe et al., 1981), unskilled workers decided, either alone or in groups, how much punishing shock to give someone for incorrect answers on an ESP task. As Figure 12-12 indicates, individuals administered progressively more of the assumed shock as the experiment proceeded, and group decision making magnified this individual tendency. These experiments suggest that when circumstances provoke an individual's aggressive reaction, the addition of group interaction will often amplify it.

REDUCING AGGRESSION

We have examined three prominent theories about the causes of aggression (instinct, frustration-aggression, and social learning), and we have scrutinized several influences upon aggression. Obviously, the forces producing aggression cannot be eliminated. How, then, might aggression be minimized? Do theory and research suggest ways to control aggression?

CATHARSIS

"Youngsters should be taught to vent their anger." So advised Ann Landers (1969). If a person "bottles up his rage, we have to find an outlet. We have to give him an opportunity of letting off steam." So asserted the prominent psychiatrist Fritz Perls (1973). Both statements assume what has been called the hydraulic model—that one's accumulated aggressive energy, be it from the building of instinctual impulses or from frustrations, needs a release.

The concept of catharsis usually is credited to Aristotle. Although Aristotle actually said nothing about aggression, he did argue that one can purge emotions by experiencing them, and that viewing the classic tragedies therefore enabled a catharsis ("purgation") of pity and fear. To have an emotion excited, he believed, is subsequently to have that emotion released (Butcher, 1951). The catharsis hypothesis has been extended to include the emotional release supposedly obtained not only by the observations of drama, but also through the recall and reliving of past events, through the expression of emotions, and through various actions. In such ways, one can supposedly "blow off a little steam."

Assuming that aggressive action or fantasy drains pent-up aggression, thus reducing the aggressive urge, some therapists and group leaders have encouraged people to ventilate their suppressed aggression by acting it out—by whopping one another with foam bats, or beating a bed with a tennis racket while screaming. Parents have been similarly advised to encourage their children's release of emotional tension in various kinds of aggressive play. Most Americans are persuaded, as reflected in their 2-to-1 agreement with the statement that "Sexual materials provide an outlet for bottled-up impulses" (Smith, 1987). But then the same national survey revealed that most Americans also agree that "Sexual materials lead people to commit rape." So, is the catharsis approach valid or not? Does it work?

The idea indeed does have a long and distinguished history. Yet, a distinguished history does not validate a truth. Contrary to the suppositions of Freud, Lorenz, and their followers, the near consensus among social psychologists is that the catharsis view of aggression has not been confirmed (Geen and Quanty, 1977). For example, Robert Arms and his associates report that Canadian and American spectators of football, wrestling, and hockey exhibit *more* hostility after viewing the event than before (Arms et al., 1979; Goldstein & Arms, 1971; Russell, 1981, 1983). Not even a war seems to purge a people's aggressive feelings. In fact, after a war, a nation's murder rate tends to jump (Archer & Gartner, 1976).

In more direct laboratory tests of the catharsis hypothesis, Jack Hokanson and his colleagues (1961, 1962a, 1962b, 1966) found that when Florida State University students were allowed to counterattack someone who had provoked them, their arousal (as measured by their blood pressures) did more quickly return to normal. This calming effect of retaliation occurs only in specific circumstances—when the target is one's actual tormentor, not a substitute, and when the retaliation is justifiable and the target nonintimidating, so that one does not afterward feel guilty or anxious.

However, a key question is: Does such aggressing reduce subsequent aggression? We need here to distinguish between consequences in the short run and the long-run. Experiments dealing with aggression's short-run consequences give mixed results. Sometimes people who have aggressed do become less aggressive. But this result could have occurred because the procedures in these experiments produced *inhibition* rather than catharsis. The aggressor may have been inhibited by thinking, "If I overdo it, I could get into trouble" or "The poor guy has suffered enough."

In other experiments, aggressing has actually led to heightened aggression. Ebbe Ebbesen and his coresearchers (1975) interviewed 100 engineers and technicians shortly after they were angered by layoff notices. Some were asked questions that gave them the opportunity to express their hostility against their employer or supervisor—for example, "What instances can you think of where the company has not been fair with you?" Afterwards, a secretary administered a questionnaire assessing their attitudes toward the company and the supervisor. Did the previous opportunity to "vent" or "drain off" their hostility reduce it? To the contrary, their hostility substantially increased. Expressing hostility bred more hostility.

"He who gives way to violent gestures will increase his rage." *Charles Darwin*, The Expression of Emotion in Man and Animals, *1872*

Sound familiar? Recall from the Chapter 2 discussion of actions and attitudes that cruel acts beget cruel attitudes. Furthermore, as we noted in analyzing Stanley Milgram's obedience experiments, little aggressive acts can breed their own justification, thus facilitating further aggressive acts. Even if retaliation may sometimes (in the short run) reduce tension, in the long-run it may also reduce one's inhibitions. We can speculate that this will be true especially when, as often happens, the force of one's aggressive outburst is an overreaction to the provocation. Moreover, when people discover that retaliation is tension-reducing, this reinforcement may increase the likelihood of future retaliation. So, in the long-run, aggression more likely breeds aggression than reduces it.

Should we therefore bottle up our anger and aggressive urges? Silent sulking is hardly more effective, because it allows us to continue reciting our grievances as we conduct conversations in our head. Fortunately, there are other, nonaggressive ways to express our feelings and to inform others how their behavior affects us. Perhaps stating "I'm angry" or "When you talk like that I feel irritated" might communicate our feelings in a way that leads the other to make amends rather than further escalate the aggression. Remember: one can be assertive without being aggressive.

A SOCIAL LEARNING APPROACH

If aggressive behavior is learned rather than instinctive, then there is more hope for its control. However, such control will not be achieved by any simple formula. Unlike the simplicity of our instinctive kneejerk, aggression is very complex; it is influenced by a host of factors. Let us briefly review some and speculate how to counteract them.

"It was in the middle of rising expectations and the increased, though inadequate, social spending of the great society that the U.S. riots of 1967 and 1968 took place."
Jesse Jackson (1981)

We have seen that aversive experiences such as frustrated expectations and personal attacks arouse people, creating in them a readiness to aggress. Thus, it is wise to refrain from planting false, unreachable expectations in people's minds, as some believe President Lyndon Johnson did with his vision of the "Great Society"—a vision ironically followed by the 1960s riots. And in order not to provoke retaliation, we might teach people nonattacking ways to communicate their feelings.

We have seen that instrumental aggression is controlled by anticipated rewards and costs. This suggests that we should devote increased attention to how we might reward cooperative, nonaggressive behavior. Experiments have found that children become less aggressive when their aggressive behavior is ignored instead of being rewarded with attention, and when their nonaggressive behavior is reinforced (Hamblin et al., 1969). Punishing the aggressor is less consistently effective. Under ideal conditions—when the punishment is strong, prompt, and sure, when it is combined with reward for the desired behavior, and when the potential aggressor is not angry— the threat of punishment can deter aggression (R. A. Baron, 1977). Such was evident in 1969 when the Montreal police force went on a sixteen-hour strike. Widespread looting and destruction erupted—until the police returned. But the side effects of punishment, particularly physical punishment, can make it backfire. Punishment is aversive stimulation. It often models the very behavior it seeks to prevent. And it is coercive (recall that actions which are coerced with strong external justifications are not likely to be internalized). Perhaps these are some reasons why violent teenagers and child-abusing parents tend to come from homes where discipline took the form of harsh physical punishment (Bandura & Walters, 1959; Lefkowitz et al., 1976; Strauss & Gelles, 1980).

We have seen that observing aggressive models can lower one's inhibitions against aggression and elicit imitation. This suggests new steps to reduce brutal, dehumanizing portrayals on television, steps comparable to those already taken to reduce racist and sexist portrayals. It also suggests inoculating children against the effects of media violence. Despairing that the TV networks would ever "face the facts and change their programming," Eron and Huesmann (1984) taught 170 Oak Park, Illinois, children that television portrays the world unrealistically, that aggression is less common and effective than TV suggests, and that aggressive behavior is undesirable. (Drawing upon attitude research, Eron and Huesmann encouraged children to draw these inferences themselves and to attribute their expressed criticisms of television to their own convictions.) When restudied two years later, these children were less influenced by the violence they had viewed than were untrained children.

We have seen that aggression is also learned by direct experience and is elicited by aggressive stimuli. This suggests reducing the availability of weapons such as handguns. Jamaica in 1974 implemented a sweeping anticrime program that included strict gun control and censorship of gun scenes from television and movies (Diener & Crandall, 1979). In the following year, robberies dropped 25 percent, nonfatal shootings 37 percent. In Sweden, the toy industry has discontinued the sale of war toys. According to the Swedish Information Service (1980), Sweden decided that "Playing at war means learning to settle disputes by violent means."

Because arousal can be "steered" into hostility or other emotions, depending on the context, one can try to redirect a person's anger. This often works with children, whose anger can sometimes be converted to intense laughter. Once laughter occurs it is likely to breed a happier emotion. Similarly, mild sexual arousal and empathy are incompatible with anger.

All such incompatible responses tend to diminish aggression. Robert A. Baron (1976) illustrated this at an intersection near Purdue University. He instructed a driver to hesitate fifteen seconds in front of another car after the light changed to green. In response to this mild frustration, 90 percent of the drivers did what we might expect: They honked (a mildly aggressive act). If, while the light was red, a female pedestrian crossed between two cars, disappearing by the time the light changed to green, the honking rate was still close to 90 percent. However, when this procedure was repeated with the pedestrian on crutches (evoking empathy), or dressed in a revealing outfit (evoking mild sexual arousal), or wearing an outlandish clown mask (evoking humor), the honking rate dropped to about 50 percent.

Experiments by Norma Feshbach and Seymour Feshbach (1981) confirm that empathy is indeed incompatible with aggression. They put some Los Angeles elementary school children through a ten-week program that trained them to recognize others' feelings, to assume the perspective of other people, and to share their emotions. Compared to other children in control groups, those who received this empathy training became significantly less aggressive in their school behavior.

Suggestions such as these can help us minimize aggression (for more suggestions, see Goldstein et al., 1981). But given the complexity of aggression's causes and the difficulty of controlling them, who can feel the optimism expressed by Andrew Carnegie when, in 1900, he forecast that in the twentieth century, "To kill a man will be considered as disgusting as we in this day consider it disgusting to eat one." Since Carnegie uttered those cheery words, some 200 million human beings have been killed. It is a sad irony that although we, today, understand human aggression better than ever before, humanity's inhumanity is hardly diminished.

SUMMING UP

WHAT IS AGGRESSION?

Aggression manifests itself in two forms: *hostile aggression* springing from emotions such as anger and intending to injure, and *instrumental aggression*, which while also aiming to hurt, is a means to some other end.

THE NATURE OF AGGRESSION

There are three broad theories of aggression. The *instinct* view is most commonly associated with Sigmund Freud and Konrad Lorenz. It contends that, if not discharged, aggressive energy will accumulate from within, like water accumulating behind a dam. Although the available evidence tends not to support the instinct view, aggression is biologically influenced by heredity, blood chemistry, and the brain.

According to the second view, *frustration* creates anger, and when aggressive cues are present this anger may be released as aggression. Frustration stems not from deprivation per se, but from the gap between one's expectations and one's achievements. Since expectations are driven higher by past achievements and by comparing oneself with others, affluent people often feel as frustrated as those who have less.

The third view, that of *social learning*, presents aggression as a learned behavior. By experience and by observing others' success we learn that aggression sometimes pays. Thus when we are aroused by an aversive experience and when it seems both safe and rewarding to aggress, we will likely do so.

INFLUENCES UPON AGGRESSION

Aversive experiences include not only frustrations, but also discomfort, pain, and personal attacks, both physical and verbal. In fact, arousal from almost any source, even physical exercise or sexual stimulation, can be steered by the environment into anger.

American television portrays considerable violence. Laboratory studies have found that viewing violent models increases aggressive behavior. So it is no wonder that researchers are now studying the impact of television. Correlational and experimental studies converge on the conclusion that viewing violence (a) breeds a modest increase in aggressive behavior and (b) desensitizes viewers to aggression and alters their perceptions of reality. These two findings are paralleled by the results of new research on the effects of viewing pornography. However, television's greatest effect may be indirect as it preempts other activities.

Much aggression is committed by groups. Circumstances that provoke individuals may also provoke groups. In fact, the group situation seems to amplify aggressive reactions.

REDUCING AGGRESSION

Can aggression be minimized? Contrary to the catharsis hypothesis, aggression seems more often to breed than to reduce further aggression. The social learning approach suggests controlling aggression by counteracting the factors that provoke it—for example, by teaching people how to minimize aversive stimulation, by rewarding and modeling nonaggression, and by eliciting reactions incompatible with aggression.

FOR FURTHER READING

Archer, D., & Gartner, R. (1984). *Violence and crime in cross-national perspective.* New Haven: Yale University Press. Examines homicide tendencies worldwide, asking how murder rates are influenced by urbanization, the death penalty, and wars.

Groebel, J., & Hinde, R. (Eds.). (1988). *Aggression and war: Their biological and social bases.* New York: Cambridge University Press. Prominent aggression researchers summarize current understandings of the biological, psychological, and cultural sources of aggression.

Oskamp, S. (Ed.). (1988). *Television as a social issue.* Newbury Park, CA: Sage. Scholars and media insiders debate the role of television in society—how TV shapes our attitudes and actions and our assumptions about reality.

CHAPTER

13

ATTRACTION:
LIKING AND LOVING OTHERS

———

In the beginning there was attraction—the attraction between a particular man and a particular woman to which we each owe our existence. Throughout our lives our dependence on one another puts our relationships at the core of our existence. Asked, "What is it that makes your life meaningful?" or "What is necessary for your happiness?" most people mention—before anything else—satisfying close relationships with friends, family, or romantic partners (Berscheid, 1985; Berscheid & Peplau, 1983).

What predisposes one person to like, or to love, another? Few questions about human nature arouse greater interest. The ways that people's affections flourish and fade form the stuff and fluff of soap operas, popular music, novels, and much of our everyday conversation. Long before I knew there was such a field as social psychology, I had memorized Dale Carnegie's recipe for *How to Win Friends and Influence People*. In fact, so much has been written about liking and loving that almost every conceivable explanation—and its opposite—has been already proposed. Does absence make the heart grow fonder? Or is someone who is out of sight also out of mind? Is it likes that attract? Or opposites?

While scientific observation gave us an almost exact estimate of the earth's circumference more than 2000 years ago, it was not until our lifetime that liking and loving became the objects of vigorous scientific scrutiny. And then when they did, the very idea of scientifically analyzing such "subjective" phenomena was greeted with some scorn. When the National Science Foundation awarded an $84,000 grant for research on love, Wisconsin Senator William Proxmire was irate:

> I object to this not only because no one—not even the National Science Foundation—can argue that falling in love is a science; not only because I'm sure that even if they spend $84 million or $84 billion they wouldn't get an answer that anyone would believe. I'm also against it because I don't want the answer.
>
> I believe that 200 million other Americans want to leave some things in life a mystery, and right at the top of things we don't want to know is why a man falls in love with a woman and vice versa. . . .
>
> So National Science Foundation—get out of the love racket. Leave that to Elizabeth Barrett Browning and Irving Berlin! (T. G. Harris, 1978)

The press loved it. They had a field day with Proxmire's comments. Some columnists echoed his derision, others rebutted it. In the *New York Times*, James Reston (1975) acknowledged that love has unfathomable depths of mystery, yet argued, "If the sociologists and psychologists can get even a suggestion of the answer to our pattern of romantic love, marriage, disillusion, divorce—and the children left behind—it could be the best investment of federal money since Jefferson made the Louisiana Purchase."

Levels of explanation:
See Chapter One.

Social-psychological analyses of friendship and intimate love are not meant to compete with Elizabeth Barrett Browning and Irving Berlin. The social psychologist and the poet deal with love at quite different "levels." The social psychologist examines who attracts whom. The poet describes love as a sometimes sublime experience. Though social psychologists and poets might glean insights from one another, the study of who attracts whom does not preempt poetic description of the experience of love, nor does poetry decisively answer the questions posed in psychological research.

A SIMPLE THEORY OF ATTRACTION

Asked why they are friends with one person and not another, or why they were attracted to their fiancé or spouse, most people can readily answer. "I like Carol because she's warm, witty, and well-read." What such explanations leave out—and what social psychologists believe most important—is ourselves. Attraction involves the one who is attracted as well as the attractor. Thus a more psychologically accurate answer might be, "I like Carol because of how I feel when I'm with her." We are attracted to those whom *we* find it satisfying and gratifying to be with. Attraction is in the eye (and brain) of the beholder.

The point can be expressed as a simple psychological principle: Those who reward us, or who are associated with rewards, we like. This ***reward*** principle is elaborated in two allied theories. First, there is the ***minimax*** principle of motivation: Minimize costs, maximize rewards. This implies that if a relationship rewards more than it costs us, we will like it and will therefore wish to continue. Such will be especially true if the relationship is more profitable than alternative relationships (Burgess & Huston, 1979; Kelley, 1979; Rusbult, 1980). Minimax: Minimize boredom, conflicts, expenses; maximize self-esteem, pleasure, security. Some 300 years ago La Rochefoucauld (1665) conjectured similarly: "Friendship is a scheme for the mutual exchange of personal advantages and favors whereby self-esteem may profit."

If in a friendship, both partners pursue their personal desires willynilly, the friendship is not likely to survive long. Therefore, our society teaches us to exchange rewards by a rule that Elaine Hatfield, William Walster, and Ellen Berscheid (1978) call ***equity:*** What you and your friend get out of a relationship should be proportional to what you each put into it. If two people receive equal outcomes, then their contributions should be equal; otherwise the relationship is likely to be perceived as unfair. If both feel that the outcomes correspond to the assets and efforts each contributes to their relationship, then both will perceive equity.

Strangers and casual acquaintances maintain equity by directly exchanging benefits: You lend me your class notes, later I'll lend you mine; I invite you to my party, you invite me to yours. Those in love (or those who have roomed together for some time—Berg, 1984) feel not so bound to trade benefits "in kind": notes for notes, parties for parties. They feel freer to maintain equity by exchanging a variety of benefits ("When you drop by to lend me your notes, why don't you stay for dinner?") and eventually to stop keeping track of who owes whom.

That friendship and love are rooted in an equitable exchange of rewards may seem crass. Do we not sometimes give in response to a loved one's need, without expecting a reciprocal benefit? Indeed, those involved in an equitable *long-term* relationship are less concerned with *short-term* equity. Margaret Clark and Judson Mills (1979; Clark, 1984, 1986; Mills & Clark, 1982) argue that people even take pains to *avoid* calculating any exchange of benefits. When we help a good friend, we do not want instant repayment. If someone has us for dinner, we wait before reciprocating, lest the return invitation be attributed merely to paying off a social obligation. True friends tune into one another's needs even when reciprocation is impossible (Clark et al., 1986, 1989). Indeed, one clue that an acquaintance is becoming such a friend is the person's sharing when sharing is unexpected (Miller et al., 1989).

In experiments with University of Maryland students, Clark and Mills confirmed that not being calculating is a mark of friendship. Tit-for-tat exchanges boosted people's liking for one another when their relationship was relatively formal but *diminished*

Reward theory of attraction: The theory that we like those whose behavior is rewarding to us, or who have been associated with rewarding events.

Minimax: Minimize costs, maximize rewards.

Equity: A condition in which what people receive from a relationship is proportional to what they contribute to it. *Note:* Equitable outcomes needn't always be equal outcomes.

"Love is the most subtle kind of self-interest."
Holbrook Johnson

YOU KNOW, IRA, WHEN I WAS SICK, YOU WERE THERE - WHEN I FRACTURED MY RIB, YOU WERE THERE - WHEN I WAS BROKE, YOU WERE RIGHT THERE!

YOU WERE ALWAYS THERE WHEN I NEEDED HELP.

SO WHY AREN'T YOU NICER TO ME?

BECAUSE I IDENTIFY YOU WITH EVERY ROTTEN THING THAT EVER HAPPENED TO ME ...

Our liking and disliking of people is influenced by the events with which they are associated.

liking when the two sought friendship. Thus Clark and Mills surmise that marriage contracts in which each partner specifies what is expected from the other are more likely to undermine than enhance the couple's love. Only when the other's positive behavior is voluntary can it be attributed to love.

We not only like people who are rewarding to be with; we also, according to the second version of the reward principle, like those we *associate* with good feelings. According to theorists Donn Byrne and Gerald Clore (1970), and to Albert Lott and Bernice Lott (1974), social conditioning creates positive feelings toward those who have been linked to rewarding events. When, after a strenuous week, we relax in front of a fire, enjoying good food, drink, and music, we will likely feel a special warmth toward those around us, even if in their own right they are not especially rewarding. We are less likely to take a liking to someone we meet while suffering a splitting headache.

Experiments by William Griffitt (1970) and others confirm this phenomenon of liking—and disliking—by association. In one, college students who evaluated strangers in a pleasant room liked them better than did those in an uncomfortably hot room. Another experiment asked people to evaluate photographs of other people, while in either an elegant, sumptuously furnished, softly lit room or a shabby, dirty, stark room (Maslow & Mintz, 1956). Again, the warm feelings evoked by the elegant surroundings were transferred to the people being rated. It has even been found that a stranger who merely happens on the scene is liked better by someone who has just heard a radio broadcast of good rather than bad news (Veitch & Griffitt, 1976). Elaine Hatfield and William Walster (1978) find a practical tip in these research studies: "Romantic dinners, trips to the theatre, evenings at home together, and vacations never stop being important. . . . If your relationship is to survive, it's important that you *both* continue to associate your relationship with good things."

This simple theory of attraction—we like those who reward us and those associated with rewards—is helpful, but as with most sweeping generalizations it leaves many questions unanswered. What, precisely, *is* rewarding? Of course, the answer will vary from person to person and situation to situation. But, in general, is it more rewarding to be with someone who differs from us or one who is similar to us? To be lavishly flattered or constructively criticized? A theory is no better than the precision of its predictions.

With so many possibilities, we had better examine specifics that contribute to attraction. For most people most of the time, what factors are conducive to liking and loving? We will start with those factors that help initiate a friendship and then consider those that help sustain and deepen a relationship. First, however, you might pause to identify the factors that, in your experience, seem to have been instrumental in developing your close friendships. Having done so, you can compare your list with the factors that social psychologists have found conducive to liking and loving.

FIGURE 13-1
Diagram of a married-student apartment building at MIT. Had you desired to make friends after moving into one of these buildings, which apartments should you have preferred? Experimenters found that residents of apartments 1 and 5, who were functionally close to several of the upper apartments as well as to the lower apartments, had the best opportunities to form friendships.

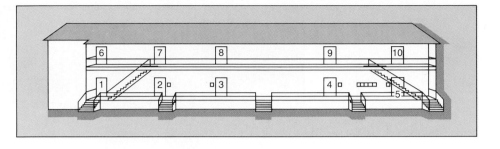

LIKING: WHO LIKES WHOM?

Initially we are powerfully attracted to other people by what seem to be, yet are not, trivial factors: mere geographical proximity, or superficial physical attributes—factors to which few of us likely attribute our friendships.

PROXIMITY

Proximity:

Geographical nearness. Proximity (or, more precisely, "functional distance") is a powerful predictor of liking.

One of the most powerful predictors of whether any two people are friends is their sheer ***proximity*** to one another. Proximity can also breed hostility; most assaults and murders involve people living in close proximity, often within the same walls. But fortunately far more often, proximity kindles liking. Though it may seem trivial to those pondering the mysterious origins of romantic love, sociologists have found that most people marry someone who lives in the same neighborhood, or works at the same job, or sits in the same class (Bossard, 1932; Burr, 1973; Clarke, 1952; Katz & Hill, 1958). Look around. If you choose to marry, it will likely be to someone who has lived or worked or studied within walking distance.

Leon Festinger, Stanley Schachter, and Kurt Back (1950) discovered that proximity leads to liking when they observed the formation of friendships in the married students' apartments at the Massachusetts Institute of Technology (Figure 13-1). Because people were assigned apartments essentially at random, without any prior friendships, the researchers could assess the importance of proximity—and important was what it turned out to be. When wives were asked to name their three closest friends within the entire complex of buildings, some two-thirds of those named lived in the same building, and two-thirds of these lived on the same floor. The person most frequently chosen? One who lived next door.

Interaction

Actually, geographical distance per se is not what is critical, but rather the "functional distance"—how often people's paths cross. People frequently become friends with those who use the same entrances, parking lots, and recreation areas. One study of workers at a California naval training center found that they most enjoyed talking to those co-workers whom they most often ran into (Monge & Kirste, 1980). At the college where I teach, the men and women students once lived on opposite sides of the campus. They understandably bemoaned the dearth of cross-sex friendships. They now occupy different areas of the same dormitories, sharing common sidewalks, lounges, and laundry facilities, and cross-sex friendships are far more frequent. So, if you're new in town

Proximity leads to liking.

and want to make friends, try to get an apartment near the complex's mailboxes, an office desk near the coffee pot, a parking spot near the main buildings. Such is the architecture of friendship.

Further evidence that what's crucial in forming friendships is not just geographical distance, but the opportunity for interaction, comes from a clever study with University of North Carolina students by Chester Insko and Midge Wilson (1977). They sat three students in a triangle facing one another and then had persons A and B converse about themselves while C observed, and B and C converse while A observed. Thus, for example, B and C were equally near A and observed the same behavior from A. But who most liked A? Usually person B, with whom person A had talked. Interacting with another generally stimulates one's liking for that person. It does so because it enables the two conversants to explore their similarities, to sense one another's liking, and to perceive themselves as a social unit (Arkin & Burger, 1980). Likewise, randomly assigned college roommates, who of course can hardly avoid frequent interaction, are far more likely to become good friends than enemies (Newcomb, 1961).

But why does proximity breed liking? One factor is the availability of people nearby; obviously, there are fewer opportunities to get to know someone who attends a different school or lives in another town. But there is more to it than that, else why do people tend to like their roommates, or those one door away, better than those two doors away? After all, those just a few doors away, or even a floor below, hardly live at an inconvenient distance. Moreover, those close by are potential enemies as well as friends. So why does proximity encourage affection more often than animosity?

"When I'm not near the one I love, I love the one I'm near."
E. Y. Harburg, Finian's Rainbow,
London: Chappell Music, 1947

Anticipation of Interaction

Already we have noted one answer: Proximity, especially functional proximity, enables people through interaction to discover commonalities and exchange rewards. What is more, merely *anticipating* interaction can boost liking. John Darley and Ellen Berscheid (1976) demonstrated this when they gave some women students at the University of Minnesota ambiguous information about two other women, one of whom the students expected to have a rather intimate conversation with. Asked how much they liked each, the women were more attracted to the person they expected to meet.

Does this occur because the anticipation of interacting with someone creates a feeling that the two of you are a group? (Recall from Chapter 11 the "ingroup bias.") Or is it because we are stimulated to perceive the other person as pleasant and compatible, thus maximizing the chance of a rewarding relationship (Knight & Vallacher, 1981; Miller & Marks, 1982; Tyler & Sears, 1977)? Likely, it is both, because people tend to feel a kinship with those in their group. Regardless, this much seems clear: The phenomenon is adaptive. Our lives are filled with relationships with people whom we may not have chosen but with whom we anticipate continuing interactions—dormmates, grandparents, teachers, classmates, coworkers. Liking such people is surely conducive to better relationships with them.

Mere Exposure

There is yet another reason why proximity leads to liking. A host of studies by Robert Zajonc and others have found, quite contrary to the old proverb about familiarity breeding contempt, that familiarity breeds fondness. Mere repeated exposure to all sorts of novel stimuli—nonsense syllables, Chinese characters, musical selections, faces—boosts people's ratings of such stimuli. Do the supposed Turkish words *nansoma*, *saricik*, and *afworbu* mean something better or something worse than the words *iktitaf*, *biwojni*, and *kadirga*? University of Michigan students tested by Zajonc (1968; 1970) preferred whichever of these words they had seen most frequently. The more times they had seen a meaningless word or Chinese ideograph, the more likely they were to say it meant something good. Among the letters of the alphabet, Europeans prefer the letters appearing in their own name and those that frequently appear in their own language (Nuttin, 1987). French students rate capital W, the least frequent letter in French, as their least favorite letter.

Mere-exposure effect:
The tendency for novel stimuli to be liked more or rated more positively after the rater has been repeatedly exposed to them.

In 1969, residents of Grand Rapids, Michigan, were presented with their new downtown landmark, a huge metal sculpture created by the artist Alexander Calder. Their reaction? "An abomination," "an embarrassment," "a waste of money," scorned some letter writers and commentators. Other people were neutral; few citizens seemed enthusiastic. But within a decade, the sculpture became an object of civic pride, its critics silent, its picture adorning bank checks, city posters, and tourist literature. Similarly, when completed in 1889, the Eiffel Tower in Paris was mocked as grotesque. Today this giant is the friendly, beloved symbol of Paris (Harrison, 1977). Such changes make one wonder about people's initial reactions to art. Do visitors to the Louvre in Paris really adore the *Mona Lisa*, or are they simply delighted to find a familiar face? It might be both: To know her is to like her.

Perhaps you are objecting, feeling that one really has to know some people in order to *dis*like them, or that some stimuli lose appeal when *over*exposed. A new musical piece that grows on you can, after the hundredth hearing, become wearisome. To be sure, the "exposure-breeds-liking" principle must be qualified. First, continuing

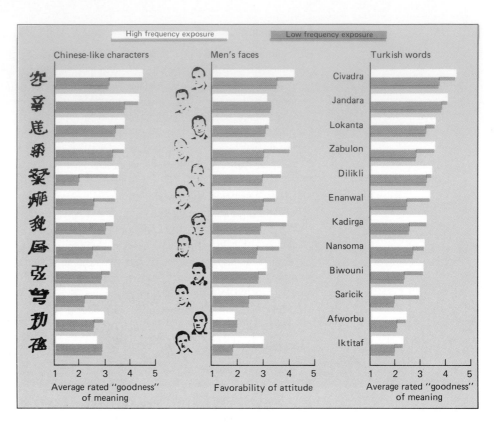

FIGURE 13-2
The mere-exposure effect. Stimuli are rated more positively after being shown repeatedly. (From Zajonc, 1968).

repetitions not only have a diminishing positive effect but can, sometimes, eventually have a negative effect (Suedfeld et al., 1975). This negative effect seems especially likely when people's initial reactions to the stimulus are already negative, rather than

The more often we see something—even if we don't like it at first—the more likely we are to grow to like it.

neutral or positive (Grush, 1976). Second, positive responses are lessened when repetitions are incessant rather than distributed among other experiences (Harrison, 1977). Third, the exposure effect, like many other influences upon us, is modest; being but one of many influences, it won't by itself overcome strong feelings from other sources.

Still, as a generalization, the principle seems indisputable. Moreover, Zajonc and his co-workers, William Kunst-Wilson and Richard Moreland, have found that exposure can lead to liking even when people are unaware of what they have been exposed to (Wilson, 1979; Kunst-Wilson & Zajonc, 1980; Moreland & Zajonc, 1977). In one experiment, women students listened in one ear over headphones to a prose passage, repeated the words out loud, and compared them to a written version, checking for errors. Meanwhile, brief and novel melodies were played into their other ear. This procedure focused their attention upon the verbal material and away from the tunes. Later, when they heard these same tunes interspersed among similar ones not previously played, they did not recognize them. Nevertheless, the tunes they *liked best* were the ones they had previously heard. In another experiment, people were shown a series of geometric figures, one at a time, each for a millisecond—just long enough to perceive but a flash of light. Although later they were unable to recognize the figures they had been shown, they nevertheless liked them best.

" *'Tis strange—but true; for truth is always strange— Stranger than fiction.*"
Lord Byron, Don Juan

Note that in both experiments people's conscious judgments about the stimuli were a far less reliable clue to what they had heard or seen than were their instant feelings. Though not consciously reasoned out, their preferences were nevertheless real. Perhaps you, too, can recall immediately liking or disliking something or someone without consciously knowing why. Only later were you able to verbalize why you felt that way. Zajonc (1980) argues that our emotions are often more instantaneous, more primitive than our thinking. For example, fearful or prejudicial feelings aren't always bred by stereotyped beliefs; sometimes the beliefs arise later as justifications for one's intuitive feelings.

What causes the familiarity-liking relationship? Although the phenomenon is indeed well-established, its explanation remains uncertain (Grush, 1979). Some believe it stems from a natural "neophobia," an adaptive tendency to be wary of unfamiliar things until one accumulates evidence that they are not dangerous. Animals, too, tend to prefer familiar over unfamiliar stimuli (Hill, 1978).

Whatever the explanation, the phenomenon colors our evaluations of people. Familiar people we like more (Swap, 1977). We even like ourselves better when we are the way we're used to seeing ourselves. In a delightful experiment, Theodore Mita, Marshall Dermer, and Jeffrey Knight (1977) photographed women students at the University of Wisconsin–Milwaukee and later showed each one her actual picture along with a mirror image of it. Asked which picture they liked better, most preferred their mirror image, which is of course the image they were used to seeing. (No wonder our photographs never look quite right.) However, when close friends of the subjects were shown the same two pictures, they preferred the true picture, the image to which *they* were accustomed.

Advertisers and politicians have learned that mere exposure works to their advantage. It is hard to separate the many factors that lead to purchases and to winning elections. But when people don't have strong feelings about a product or a candidate, mere repetition seems to boost sales or votes (McCullough & Ostrom, 1974; Winter, 1973). If the candidates are relatively unknown, as often happens in congressional and presidential primaries and in local elections, those who gain the most media exposure usually win (Patterson, 1980; Schaffner et al., 1981). Joseph Grush and his colleagues

(1978) exhaustively analyzed the 1972 U.S. congressional primaries and found that overwhelmingly, the winners were either incumbents or big spenders—a phenomenon repeated in the 1988 Congressional elections in which 98 percent of House incumbents won re-election bids. Even in presidential debates, it seems that, other things being equal, the lesser-known challenger has more to gain than does the already familiar incumbent. As one political campaign handbook put it, "Repetition breeds familiarity and familiarity breeds trust" (Meyer, 1966).

PHYSICAL ATTRACTIVENESS

"We should look to the mind, and not to the outward appearance."
Aesop, Fables

"Personal beauty is a greater recommendation than any letter of introduction."
Aristotle, Diogenes Laertius

What do (or did) you look for in a potential date? Sincerity? Good looks? Character? Conversational ability? Sophisticated, intelligent people are not greatly concerned with such superficial qualities as good looks; they know that "beauty is only skin deep" and that "you can't judge a book by its cover." At least they know that's how they *ought* to feel. As Cicero counseled, "The final good and the supreme duty of the wise man is to resist appearance."

The belief that looks matter little may be another instance of our denying real influences upon us (Chapter 4), for there is now a file drawer full of research studies indicating that appearance is a powerful determinant of initial attraction. The consistency and pervasiveness of this effect is startling, even disconcerting. Good looks are a great asset.

Dating

Like it or not, the fact is that a young woman's physical attractiveness is a moderately good predictor of how frequently she dates. A young man's attractiveness is slightly less a predictor of how frequently he dates (Berscheid et al., 1971; Krebs & Adinolfi, 1975; Reis et al., 1980, 1982; Walster et al., 1966). Does this imply, as many have surmised, that women are better at following Cicero's advice to "resist appearance"? Or does it merely reflect the fact that men more often do the inviting? If women were to indicate their preferences among various men, would looks be as important to them as to men? Philosopher Bertrand Russell (1930, p. 139) thought not: "On the whole women tend to love men for their character while men tend to love women for their appearance."

To ascertain whether indeed men are more influenced by superficial looks, researchers have provided men and women students with various pieces of information about someone of the other sex, including a picture of the person, or briefly introduced a man and a woman, and later asked how interested they would be in dating one another. In these experiments, women were virtually as much influenced by a man's looks as men were by a woman's (S. M. Andersen & S. L. Bem, 1981; Crouse & Mehrabian, 1977; Nida & Williams, 1977; Stretch & Figley, 1980). Similar effects of attractiveness—whether self-described or pictured on videotape—have been found in people's responses to commercial dating services, such as the lonely hearts ads in a singles magazine (Lynn & Shurgot, 1984; Riggio & Woll, 1984; Woll, 1986).

In one ambitious study, Elaine Hatfield and her co-workers (1966) matched 752 University of Minnesota freshmen for a "Welcome Week" computer dance. For each person, the researchers secured a variety of personality and aptitude test scores, but then actually matched the couples randomly. On the night of the dance, the couples danced and talked for two and one-half hours and then took a brief intermission to evaluate their dates. How well did the personality and aptitude tests predict attraction?

Was someone who was high in self-esteem, or low in anxiety, or different from the partner in outgoingness liked better? The researchers examined a long list of possibilities, but so far as they could determine only one thing mattered: how physically attractive the person was. The more attractive a woman was, as rated by the experimenters and, especially, as rated by her date, the more he liked her and wanted to date her again. Similarly, the more attractive the man was, the more she liked him and wanted to date him again. Pretty pleases.

After a brief date, physically attractive people are liked best. But not everyone can end up paired with someone stunningly attractive. So how do people pair off?

The Matching Phenomenon

Judging from research by Bernard Murstein (1986) and others, they pair off with people who are about as attractive as they are. For example, several studies have found a strong correspondence between the attractiveness of husbands and wives, of dating partners, and even of those within particular fraternities (Feingold, 1988). People tend to select as friends and especially to marry those who are a "good match" not only to their level of intelligence, but also to their level of attractiveness. So, while people might prefer someone maximally attractive, they usually choose and marry someone not "out of their league." This ***matching phenomenon*** has also been verified in experiments. When choosing whom to approach, knowing the other is free to say yes or no, people tend to seek equity by approaching someone whose attractiveness roughly matches their own (Berscheid et al., 1971; Huston, 1973; Stroebe et al., 1971).

Good physical matches may also be conducive to good relationships. When Gregory White (1980) studied UCLA dating couples, he found that those who were most similar in physical attractiveness were most likely, nine months later, to have fallen more deeply in love. Based on this finding, whom might we expect to be most closely matched for attractiveness—married couples or couples casually dating? White found, as have other researchers (Cavior & Boblett, 1972), the answer to be married couples.

Perhaps this research has prompted you to think of happy couples dissimilar in attractiveness. In such cases, the less attractive person often has compensating qual-

Matching phenomenon:
The tendency for men and women to choose as partners those who are a "good match" in attractiveness and other traits.

People tend to marry those who make for a good match to their level of attractiveness.

Exceptionally physically attractive people often marry someone of a higher social status.

"Love is often nothing but a favorable exchange between two people who get the most of what they can expect, considering their value on the personality market."
Erich Fromm,
The Sane Society, 1955

ities. Each partner brings assets to the social marketplace, and the value of their respective assets creates an equitable match. Personal dating advertisements exhibit this exchange of assets (Koestner & Wheeler, 1988). Men typically offer status and seek attractiveness; women more often do the reverse: "Attractive, bright woman, 38, slender, seeks warm, professional male." The social exchange process helps explain why beautiful young women often marry men whose social status exceeds their own (Elder, 1969). Prince Charles may not have been much for Lady Diana to look at, but he was extremely rich, powerful, and prestigious.

Some scholars fear that, by *describing* the romantic marketplace, researchers may *foster* a calculating, self-serving approach to relationships: If your mate gains weight or becomes wrinkled, or if you achieve notable fame and fortune, then why not dump the mate for one of better value? "It should be no surprise if a marketplace orientation to dating and mating had a hand in driving divorce rates up," state Michael and Lise Wallach (1983, p. 25). "Such an orientation would make it only natural, after all, to stay on the lookout for some better deal . . . a chance to trade upward."

The Physical-Attractiveness Stereotype

Do the benefits of being good-looking spring entirely from one's being sexually attractive? Clearly not. Young children are favorably biased toward attractive children much as adults are biased toward attractive adults (Dion, 1973; Dion & Berscheid, 1974; Langlois & Stephan, 1981). To judge from how long they gaze at someone, even babies prefer attractive over unattractive faces (Langlois et al., 1987). When adults judge children they are similarly biased. Margaret Clifford and Elaine Hatfield (Clifford & Walster, 1973) showed Missouri fifth-grade teachers identical information about a boy or girl, but with the photograph of an attractive or unattractive child attached. The teachers who judged an attractive child saw the child as more intelligent and more likely to do well in school. Or think of yourself as a playground supervisor having to discipline an unruly child. Might you, like the University of Minnesota women studied by Karen Dion (1972), be tempted to give more benefit of the doubt if the child is attractive?

What is more, beautiful people, even if of the same sex, are assumed also to possess certain desirable traits. Other things being equal, they are guessed to be happier, more intelligent, more sociable, more successful, and less socially deviant (Hatfield & Sprecher, 1986). An attractive face makes a smile seem more self-confident and makes a person seem higher in status (Forgas, 1987; Kalick, 1988).

Added together, the findings point to a ***physical-attractiveness stereotype:*** What is beautiful is good. Children are taught the stereotype quite early. Snow White and Cinderella are beautiful—and kind; the witch and the stepsisters are ugly—and wicked. As one kindergarten girl put it when asked what it means to be pretty, "It's like to be a princess. Everybody loves you" (Dion, 1979).

If physical attractiveness is this important, then permanently changing people's attractiveness should change the way others react to them. But would it be ethical to alter someone's looks? In the United States, such manipulation is performed more than a million times a year—by plastic surgeons and orthodontists (Berscheid, 1981). To examine the effect of such alterations, Michael Kalick (1977) had Harvard students indicate their impressions of eight women, judging from profile photographs taken either before or after cosmetic surgery. Not only were the women judged as more physically attractive after the surgery, but also as kinder, more sensitive, more sexually warm and responsive, more likable, and so on. Likewise, Karen Korabik (1981) found that University of Guelph (Ontario) students rated girls as more intelligent, better-adjusted, and so forth after they had completed orthodontic treatment. Amazingly, ratings were based on before and after pictures taken with mouths closed and teeth not showing. Orthodontic treatment affects facial structure as well as teeth, and the raters were apparently responding to these subtle facial changes. Ellen Berscheid (1981) notes that although such cosmetic improvements tend to boost one's self-image, they can also be temporarily disturbing:

> Most of us—at least those of us who have *not* experienced swift alterations of our physical appearance—can continue to believe that our physical attractiveness level plays a minor role in how we are treated by others. It is harder, however, for those who have actually experienced swift changes in appearance to continue to deny and to minimize the influence of physical attractiveness in their own lives—and the fact of it may be disturbing, even when the changes are for the better.

To say that attractiveness is important, other things being equal, is not to say that physical appearance is always more important than other qualities. Attractiveness probably most affects first impressions; one's appearance is vivid, it draws immediate attention. As a relationship develops, appearance *may* diminish in importance. [One study disputed this by finding attractiveness *increased* in importance with subsequent dates (Mathes, 1975).] Nevertheless, first impressions are important—and may be becoming more so as society becomes increasingly mobile and urbanized and contacts with people become more fleeting (Berscheid, 1981). Moreover, attractiveness affects first impressions in job interviews (Cash & Janda, 1984; Marvelle & Green, 1980). This helps explain why attractive people have more prestigious jobs, make more money, and describe themselves as happier (Umberson & Hughes, 1987).

Physical-attractiveness stereotype:
The presumption that physically attractive people possess other socially desirable traits as well: What is beautiful is good.

"Even virtue is fairer in a fair body."
Virgil, Aeneid

Is the Physical-Attractiveness Stereotype Accurate?

But do beautiful people indeed have desirable traits? Or was Leo Tolstoy correct when he wrote that it's "a strange illusion . . . to suppose that beauty is goodness"? There well might be a trace of truth to the stereotype. Children and young adults who are attractive tend to have slightly higher self-esteem and to be less prone to psychological disorders (Hatfield & Sprecher, 1986; Maruyama & Miller, 1981). They are more assertive, although they are also believed to be more egotistical (Jackson & Huston, 1975). They are neither more nor less academically capable (contrary to the negative stereotype that "beauty times brains equals a constant") (Sparacino & Hansell, 1979). However, they are somewhat more socially polished. William Goldman and Philip Lewis (1977) demonstrated this by having sixty University of Georgia men call and talk for five minutes with each of three women students. When, afterward, the men and women rated their unseen telephone partners, those partners who happened to be most attractive were rated as somewhat more socially skillful and likable.

Surely these small average differences between attractive and unattractive people are the result of self-fulfilling prophecies. Attractive people are valued and favored, and so may develop more social self-confidence. (You may recall from Chapter 4 an experiment in which unseen women who were *thought* to be attractive were treated in a way that led them to respond more warmly.) By this analysis, what's crucial to your social skill is not how you look but how you are treated and how you feel about yourself—whether you accept yourself, like yourself, feel comfortable with yourself. Sara Kiesler and Roberta Baral (1970) led several dozen Yale men to feel either good about themselves—by leading them to think they were scoring high on a test of intelligence and creativity—or bad about themselves. During a break in the testing the experimenter and subject went for coffee and sat down next to a supposed female acquaintance of the experimenter's. The woman, actually a confederate, was groomed either as her very attractive self or very sloppily and with her hair tied back severely and grotesque eye glasses. When the experimenter excused himself to make a phone

I vividly remember the afternoon I began to appreciate the far-reaching implications of physical attractiveness. Graduate student Karen Dion (now a professor at the University of Toronto) learned that some researchers at our Institute of Child Development had collected popularity ratings from nursery school children and taken a photo of each child. Although teachers and caregivers of children had persuaded us that "all children are beautiful" and no physical-attractiveness discriminations could be made, Dion suggested we instruct some people to rate each child's looks and correlate these with popularity. After doing so, we realized our long shot had hit home: attractive children were popular children. Indeed, the effect was far more potent than we and others had assumed, with a host of implications that investigators are still tracing.

Ellen Berscheid,
University of Minnesota

call, the confederate observed how warm and romantic the man was. Did he talk to her? Compliment her? Buy her coffee? Ask her out? Men who were feeling good about themselves behaved most romantically toward the attractive confederate. Those whose self-esteem had been lowered exhibited more interest in the plain woman.

Despite all the advantages of being beautiful, attraction researchers Elaine Hatfield and Susan Sprecher (1986) report that there is also an ugly truth about beauty. Exceptionally attractive people may suffer unwelcome sexual advances from those of the other sex and resentment by those of their own sex. They may be unsure whether others are responding to their inner qualities or just to their looks, which in time are destined to fade. They often are regarded by others as more vain and sexually unfaithful. Moreover, if they can coast on their looks, they may be less motivated to develop themselves in other ways. Ellen Berscheid wonders whether we might still be lighting our houses with candles if Charles Steinmetz, the homely and exceptionally short genius of electricity, had instead been subjected to the social enticements experienced by a Mel Gibson or Rob Lowe.

Who Is Attractive?

I have described attractiveness as if it were an objective quality like height, something some people have more of, some less. Strictly speaking, attractiveness is whatever the people of any given place and time find attractive. This, of course, varies. The western standards of beauty by which Miss "Universe" is judged are hardly even true of the whole world. And even in a given place and time, there is (fortunately) some disagreement about who's attractive and who's not (Morse & Gruzen, 1976).

But there is also some agreement. Generally, "attractive" facial and bodily features do not deviate too drastically from the average (Symons, 1981; Beck et al., 1976; Graziano et al., 1978). Noses, legs, or statures that are not unusually large or small tend to be perceived as relatively attractive. There are also sex-related differences in what makes for an attractive face. Consistent with men's historically having greater social power (see Chapter 6), women tend to be judged as more attractive if they have immature features, such as large eyes, that suggest nondominance (Cunningham, 1986;

While standards of beauty differ from culture to culture, some people are considered attractive throughout most of the world. Paulina Porizkova (from Poland), one of the highest paid models in the late 1980s, and Mel Gibson (from Australia), an actor whose good looks played a large role in his box office success, are two clear examples.

Keating, 1985). Men are judged as more attractive when their faces—and their behaviors—suggest maturity and dominance (Sadalla et al., 1987).

The Sociobiological View

Psychologists working from a sociobiological perspective explain these gender differences in terms of reproductive strategy (Buss, 1988; Kenrick & Trost, 1988). They content that evolution predisposes men to favor female features that imply youth and health—and therefore good reproductive potential—and women to favor male traits that signify an ability to provide resources for a female and her offspring. David Buss (1987) invites us to consider a world where this was not so, a world where "males expressed no preference for physical appearance cues that correlate with female reproductive capability." These males would sometimes mate with women who are no longer fertile and so "would become no one's ancestors." Thus, if a preference for women who appear young and fertile has even a slight genetic basis, then over time such preferences "would necessarily evolve." And that, Buss (1989) believes, explains why the males he studied in 37 cultures—from Australia to Zambia—do indeed prefer female characteristics that signify reproductive capacity. Culture and social learning further reinforce our preferences for the physically attractive (Dion, 1986). What evolution initiates, culture accentuates.

By the same evolutionary mechanisms women are said to prefer men whose traits and resources suggest a maximum potential contribution to their offspring. Thus status, ambition, and dominance cues are more important to women than to men, which explains why physically attractive females tend to marry high-status males and why men compete with such determination to achieve fame and fortune. Or so the sociobiological theory contends.

Attractiveness Is Relative

What's attractive to you also depends on what you have adapted to. Douglas Kenrick and Sara Gutierres (1980) had male confederates interrupt Montana State University men in their dormitory rooms, explaining, "We have a friend coming to town this week and we want to fix him up with a date, but we can't decide whether to fix him up with her or not, so we decided to conduct a survey. . . . We want you to give us your vote on how attractive you think she is . . . on a scale of 1 to 7." When shown a picture of an average young woman, those who had just been watching three beautiful women on television's *Charlie's Angels* rated her less attractive than those who hadn't. Laboratory experiments confirm this "contrast effect." To men who have recently been gazing at centerfolds, average women—or even their own wives—seem less attractive (Kenrick et al., 1988). Viewing pornographic films of strangers who meet and instantly engage in various passionate sexual behaviors tends to increase sexual discontent and dissatisfaction with one's own partner (Zilmann & Bryant, 1988). Being sexually aroused may temporarily make a member of the other sex seem more attractive. But the residual effect of exposure to perfect "10s," or to unrealistic sexual depictions, is to make one's own partner seem less appealing—more like a "5" than an "8".

We can conclude our discussion of attractiveness on a heartwarming note. Not only do we perceive attractive people as likable, but we also perceive likable people as physically attractive. Perhaps you can recall individuals who, as you grew to like them, became more attractive, their physical imperfections no longer so noticeable. For example, Alan Gross and Christine Crofton (1977) had University of Missouri–St. Louis students view someone's photograph after reading a favorable or unfavorable description of the person's personality. Those portrayed as warm, helpful, and considerate were perceived as more attractive (see also Owens & Ford, 1978; Felson & Bohrnstedt, 1979). Other researchers have found that as we discover someone's similarities to us, the person begins to seem more attractive (Beaman & Klentz, 1983; Klentz et al., 1987). Moreover, the more in love a woman is with a man, the more physically attractive she finds him (Price et al., 1974). To paraphrase Benjamin Franklin, if Jill's in love, she's no judge of Jack's handsomeness.

"Do I love you because you are beautiful, or are you beautiful because I love you?"
Prince Charming, in Rogers & Hammerstein's Cinderella

SIMILARITY VERSUS COMPLEMENTARITY

From our discussion so far, one might surmise that Leo Tolstoy was entirely correct: "Love depends . . . on frequent meetings, and on the style in which the hair is done up, and on the color and cut of the dress." Proximity and physical attractiveness do indeed help initiate a relationship. However, as people get to know one another other influences enter to help each decide whether their acquaintance is to develop into a friendship.

Do Birds of a Feather Flock Together?

Of this much we may be sure: Birds who flock together are of a feather. Friends, engaged couples, and spouses are far more likely than people randomly paired to share common attitudes, beliefs, and values. Furthermore, among married couples, the greater the similarity between husband and wife, the more likely they are to be happily married and the less likely they are to divorce (Byrne, 1971). Such findings are intriguing. But, being correlational, their cause and effect remain an enigma. Does similarity lead to liking? Does liking lead to similarity? Or do attitude similarity and liking both spring from some third factor, such as common cultural background?

Likeness Begets Liking

To discern cause and effect we experiment. Imagine that at a campus party Laurie gets involved in a long discussion of politics, religion, and personal likes and dislikes with Les and Larry. She and Les discover they agree on most everything, she and Larry on few things. Afterwards, she reflects, "Les is really intelligent, and he's so likable. I hope we meet again." In numerous controlled experiments, Donn Byrne (1971) and his colleagues captured the essence of Laurie's experience. Over and again they found that if you are simply told about someone's attitudes on various issues, the more similar the attitudes are to your own, the more likable you will find the person. This "likeness-leads-to-liking" relationship holds true not only for college students, but for children and the elderly, for people of various occupations, and those in various nations. What matters is not only the number of similar attitudes expressed by the other person (Kaplan & Anderson, 1973) but the proportion: One who shares your opinions on four out of six topics is liked better than one who agrees on eight out of sixteen (Byrne & Nelson, 1965).

This "agreement" effect has also been tested in real-life situations by observing over time who comes to like whom (Lapidus et al., 1985; Neimeyer & Mitchell, 1988). At the University of Michigan, Theodore Newcomb (1961) studied two groups of seventeen unacquainted male transfer students. After thirteen weeks of living together in a boardinghouse, those whose agreement was initially highest were most likely to have formed close friendships. One group of friends was composed of five liberal arts students, each a political liberal with strong intellectual interests. Another was made up of three conservative veterans who were all enrolled in the engineering college. Similarity breeds content.

Because the men living in the boardinghouse spent much of their time out of the house, it took a while for likes to attract. William Griffitt and Russell Veitch (1974)

"And they are friends who have come to regard the same things as good and the same things as evil, they who are friends of the same people, and they who are the enemies of the same people. . . . We like those who resemble us, and are engaged in the same pursuits."
Aristotle, Rhetoric

Without doubt, the most appealing people are those who are like us.

"What'll it be, handsome?"

compressed the getting-to-know-you process by confining thirteen unacquainted men in a fallout shelter. (The men were paid volunteers.) The researchers found that, given information about the men's opinions on various issues, they could predict with better-than-chance accuracy whom each man would most like and most dislike during the stay underground. As in the boardinghouse, the men liked best those most similar to themselves.

Like all generalizations, the similarity-attraction principle needs to be qualified. First, if we are made to feel like a faceless member of a homogeneous crowd, we will be more open to associating with people who enable us to feel a bit distinctive and unique (Snyder & Fromkin, 1980). Second, similarity sometimes divides people—when they are competing for scarce payoffs, such as A grades in a curve-graded class. Third, the *type* of similarity makes the difference. Similarity matters more on important issues than on trivial ones; we like people who exhibit our ideals (Wetzel & Insko, 1982). And while we *like* best those who share our preferred activities, we *respect* most those who share our attitudes (Lydon et al., 1988). Finally, similarity is relative: Being merely from the same country is enough to breed mutual warmth when one is a foreign student or tourist. In the Scottish town where I resided while writing this, Americans who have little in common in the United States often greet one another like old friends.

Nevertheless, the generalization is a powerful one. Studies with a variety of methods and people consistently verify that similar attitudes are a potent source of attraction. Birds of a feather do indeed flock together—a phenomenon you may have noticed upon forming a close relationship with a special someone who shares your ideas, values, and desires, a soulmate who likes the same music, the same activities, even the same foods you do.

Liking Begets Perceived Likeness

As we noted earlier, it works the other way around as well: Those who flock together perceive themselves to be of a feather. Voters overestimate the extent to which their favored candidates share their views (Judd et al., 1983). Men who feel romantically inclined toward a woman overestimate the similarity of her ideas and interests to their own (Gold et al., 1984). Even the attraction that arises from mere exposure to photographs of certain faces is enough to trigger the perception that those likable people are similar to oneself (Moreland & Zajonc, 1982). As Figure 13-3 suggests, such perceptions may then reinforce one's liking for a person. For example, strangers who are made to think they are similar (whether they are or not) will con-

FIGURE 13-3

The interplay among familiarity, similiarity, attraction, and perceived familiarity and similarity. Experiments indicate that (1) familiarity and similarity lead to liking and that (2) liking leads to perceived familiarity and similarity, which in turn (3) reinforces liking.

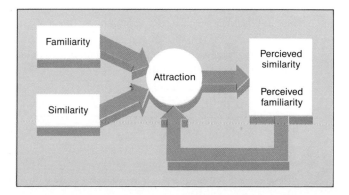

verse as intimately as friends, which may in turn cultivate their actually becoming friends (Piner & Berg, 1988).

Dissimilarity Breeds Disliking

We have a bias—the "false consensus bias" (p. 87)—to assume that others do share our attitudes. When we discover that someone's attitudes are dissimilar to our own we may dislike the person. Iowa Democrats surveyed in one study were not so much fond of other Democrats as they were disdainful of Republicans (Rosenbaum, 1986). The extent to which people of another race are perceived as similar or dissimilar therefore helps determine our racial attitudes.

In fact, except for intimate relationships, such as dating, the perception of like minds seems more important for attraction than like skins. Most Whites express more liking for, and willingness to work with, a similarly minded Black than a dissimilarly minded White (Rokeach, 1968; Insko et al., 1983). Yet "cultural racism" persists, argues James Jones (1988), because cultural differences are a fact of life. Black culture is present-oriented, expressive, spiritual, and emotionally driven; White culture tends to be more future-oriented, individualistic, materialistic, and achievement-driven, and to judge people accordingly. Rather than try to eliminate such differences, says Jones, we might better appreciate what they "contribute to the cultural fabric of a multicultural society." There are situations in which expressiveness is advantageous and situations in which future-orientation is advantageous. Thus each has much to learn from the other.

Do Opposites Attract?

But are we not also attracted to people who are in some ways *different* from ourselves, different in ways that complement our own characteristics? Researchers have explored this question by comparing friends and spouses not only in attitudes and beliefs, but also in age, religion, race, smoking behavior, economic level, education, height, intelligence, and (as we saw earlier) appearance. In all these ways and more, similarity still prevails (Buss, 1985; Kandel, 1978). Smart birds flock together. So do rich birds, Protestant birds, tall birds, pretty birds.

Still we resist: Are we not attracted to people whose needs and personalities complement our own? Would a gratifying relationship develop from the acquaintance of a sadist and a masochist? Even the *Reader's Digest* tells us that "opposites attract. . . . Socializers pair with loners, novelty-lovers with those who dislike change, free spenders with scrimpers, risk-takers with the very cautious" (Jacoby, 1986). Sociologist Robert Winch (1958) reasoned that the needs of someone who is outgoing and domineering would naturally complement those of someone who is shy and submissive. The logic seems compelling, and most of us can think of couples who view their differences as complementary: "My husband and I are perfect for each other. I'm Aquarius—a decisive person. He's Libra—can't make decisions; but he's always happy to go along with arrangements I make."

Given how persuasive the idea is, the inability of researchers to confirm it is astonishing. For example, most people feel attracted to expressive, outgoing people (Friedman et al., 1988). Would this be especially so when one is down in the dumps? Do depressed people seek out those whose gaiety will cheer them up? To the contrary, it is *non*depressed people who most prefer to be around similarly nondepressed others (Rosenblatt & Greenberg, 1988). When you're feeling blue, someone's bubbly personality is not particularly appealing.

Complementarity:
The tendency, in a relationship between two people, for each to supply what is missing in the other. The complementarity hypothesis proposes that people are attracted to those whose needs are different, in ways that complement their own.

Although some "complementarity" may evolve as a relationship progresses (even a relationship between two identical twins), people seem, if anything, slightly more prone to marry those whose needs and personalities are similar (Berscheid & Walster, 1978; Buss, 1984; Nias, 1979; D. Fishbein & Thelen, 1981a, 1981b). Perhaps we shall yet discover some ways (other than heterosexuality) in which differences commonly breed liking. But researcher David Buss (1985) doubts it: "The tendency of opposites to marry, or mate . . . has never been reliably demonstrated, with the single exception of sex." So it seems that the "opposites-attract" rule, if it's ever true, is of minuscule importance compared to the powerful tendency of likes to attract.

LIKING THOSE WHO LIKE US

With hindsight, we can use the reward principle to explain the conclusions noted so far.

- *Proximity* is rewarding because when someone lives or works close by it costs less time and effort to receive the friendship's benefits.
- We like *attractive* people because they satisfy our aesthetic taste, because we perceive that they offer other desirable traits, and because we benefit by associating with them.
- If others have *similar* opinions we feel rewarded because we presume that they like us in return (Condon & Crano, 1988). Moreover, those who share our views help validate them. Thus we especially like people if we have successfully converted them to our way of thinking (Lombardo et al., 1972; Riordan, 1980; Sigall, 1970).

If, indeed, we especially like those whose behavior is rewarding, then surely we ought to adore those who like and admire us. The best friendships should be mutual admiration societies. Do we in fact like those who like us? Let's examine the evidence.

It's true that we like those who we think like us (Sternberg, 1986). And it is also true that we presume that those we like also like us (Curry & Emerson, 1970). Yet maybe they don't; maybe we only assume that those we adore feel the same way about us. In the University of Minnesota Welcome Week dating experiment, how much a man liked his date was unrelated to how much she liked him.

With such a disconcerting finding—Do we wrongly imagine that our friends like us?—David Kenny and William Nasby (1980) wondered whether there needed to be a refining of the research method. Would doing so reveal that liking does after all tend to be reciprocated? To answer this question, they analyzed various dyads to see how person A felt about person B, *relative* to how other people felt about B and *relative* to how A felt about other people. Sure enough, one person's relative liking for another predicted the other's relative liking in return. Liking was mutual.

But does one person's liking another *cause* the other to return the appreciation? Experiments thus far indicate the answer, "Yes, indeed." Those told that certain others liked them or evaluated them highly felt immediately a reciprocal affection (Berscheid & Walster, 1978). Ellen Berscheid and her colleagues (1969) even found that University of Minnesota students liked a fellow student who said eight positive things about them better than one who said seven positive things and one negative thing. Evidently we are very sensitive to the slightest hint of criticism. Writer Larry L. King speaks for many in noting that "I have discovered over the years that good reviews strangely fail to make the author feel as good as bad reviews make him feel bad."

Just *believing* that another likes or dislikes you can be self-fulfilling. Rebecca Curtis and Kim Miller (1986) discovered this when they led some Adelphi University students to believe that someone they had briefly met either liked or disliked them. When subsequently conversing with this person, those who felt liked disclosed more about themselves, disagreed less, and exhibited a warmer attitude and tone of voice—and therefore elicited more warmth in return from the naive conversational partner.

This general principle—that we like and treat warmly those whom we perceive as liking us— was recognized long before it was confirmed by social psychologists. Observers from the ancient philosopher Hecato ("If you wish to be loved, love") to Ralph Waldo Emerson ("The only way to have a friend is to be one") to Dale Carnegie ("Dole out praise lavishly") anticipated the findings. However, what they seem not to have anticipated are the more precise conditions under which the principle is most often true.

Attribution

As we've seen, flattery *will* get you somewhere. But not everywhere. If someone's praise clearly violates what we know is true—if someone says "Your hair looks great" when we haven't washed it in days and it feels like a greasy mop—we may lose respect for the flatterer or wonder whether the compliment springs from ulterior motives (Shrauger, 1975). For such reasons, criticism is often taken as more sincere than praise (Coleman et al., 1987). Laboratory experiments reveal something we've noted in previous chapters: Our reactions depend on our attributions. Do we attribute the other's flattery to some ***ingratiating*** selfish motive? Is the person trying to con us—to get us to buy something, to acquiesce sexually, to do a favor? If so, both the flatterer and the comments lose appeal (E. E. Jones, 1964; Lowe & Goldstein, 1970). But if there is no apparent ulterior motive, then both flattery and flatterer are warmly received.

What we attribute our own actions to is similarly important. Clive Seligman, Russell Fazio, and Mark Zanna (1980) paid undergraduate dating couples to indicate "why you go out with your girl friend/boy friend." Some were asked to rank seven intrinsic reasons, such as "I go with———because we always have a good time together" and "because we share the same interests and concerns." Others ranked possible extrinsic reasons: "because my friends think more highly of me since I began seeing her/him," "because she/he knows a lot of important people." Asked later to respond to a "love scale," those whose attention had been drawn to possible extrinsic reasons for their relationship expressed less love for their partner and even saw marriage as a less likely possibility than did those made aware of possible intrinsic reasons. (Sensitive to ethical concerns, the researchers debriefed all the participants afterward and later confirmed that the experiment had no long-term effects on the participants' relationships.)

Self-Esteem and Attraction

The reward principle also implies that another's approval should be especially rewarding after one has been deprived of approval, much as eating is most powerfully rewarding when we are extremely hungry. To test this idea, Elaine Hatfield (Walster, 1965) gave some Stanford University women either very favorable or very unfavorable analyses of their personalities, thus offering an affirming boost to some while temporarily wounding the self-esteem of others. Then they were asked to evaluate several

Ingratiation:
Strategies, such as flattery, by which people seek to gain another's favor.

After this experiment Dr. Hatfield spent almost an hour explaining the experiment and talking with each woman. She reports that in the end, none remained disturbed by the temporary ego blow or the broken date.

people, including an attractive male confederate who just before the experiment had struck up a warm conversation with each subject and had asked each for a date. (Not one turned him down.) After the affirmation or criticism, which women most liked the man? It was those whose self-esteem had been temporarily shattered, and who were presumably hungry for social approval. This helps explain why people sometimes fall quickly in love on the rebound, after suffering an ego-bruising rejection.

Gaining Another's Esteem

If approval after disapproval is powerfully rewarding, then would we most like (1) someone who liked us after initially disliking us or (2) someone who liked us from the start? Dick is in a small discussion class with his roommate's cousin, Jan. After the first week of classes, Dick learns via his "pipeline" that Jan thinks him rather dull, shallow, and socially awkward. However, as the semester progresses, he learns that Jan's opinion of him is steadily rising; gradually she comes to view him as bright, thoughtful, and charming. Will Dick now like Jan as much as he would had she thought well of him from the beginning? If Dick is simply counting the number of approving comments he receives, then the answer will be no; he would like Jan better had she consistently offered affirmative comments. But if after her initial disapproval, Jan's rewards become more potent, Dick then might like her just as much as if she had been consistently affirming.

To see which is most often true, Elliot Aronson and Darwyn Linder (1965) captured the essence of Dick's experience in a controlled experiment. Eighty University of Minnesota women were allowed to overhear a sequence of evaluations of themselves by another woman. Some women heard consistently positive things about themselves, some consistently negative. Still others heard evaluations that changed either from negative to positive (like Jan's evaluations of Dick), or from positive to negative. In experiments such as this, the target person usually is liked as much or even more when the subject experiences a *gain* in the other's esteem, especially when the gain is both gradual and reverses the earlier criticism (Aronson & Mettee, 1974; Core et al., 1975). Perhaps Jan's nice words have more credibility coming after her not-so-nice words. Or perhaps after being withheld they are especially potent.

"Hatred which is entirely conquered by love passes into love, and love on that account is greater than if it had not been preceded by hatred."
Benedict Spinoza, Ethics

Aronson even speculates that constantly approving a loved one can lose value. When the complimentary husband says for the 500th time, "Gee, honey, you look great," the words carry far less impact than were he now to say, "Gee, honey, you don't look good in that dress." A loved one you've doted upon is hard to powerfully reward, but easy to powerfully hurt. This suggests that an open, honest relationship—one where people enjoy one another's esteem and acceptance, yet are candid about their negative feelings—is more likely to offer continuing rewards than one dulled by the suppression of unpleasant emotions, one in which people try only, as Dale Carnegie advised, to "lavish praise." Aronson (1988) put it this way:

> As a relationship ripens toward greater intimacy, what becomes increasingly important is authenticity—our ability to give up trying to make a good impression and begin to reveal things about ourselves that are honest even if unsavory. In addition, we must be willing to communicate a wide range of feelings to our friends under appropriate circumstances and in ways that reflect our caring. Thus . . . if two people are genuinely fond of each other, they will have a more satisfying and exciting relationship over a longer period of time if they are able to express both positive and negative feelings than if they are completely "nice" to each other at all times. (p. 323)

LOVING

In research on attraction most investigators have studied what is most easily studied—responses during brief encounters between strangers rather than during ongoing relationships. Such responses are not trivial, for first impressions often endure. Even in the face of disconfirming evidence, initial ideas often persevere. What is more, that which initially influences our liking of another—proximity, attractiveness, similarity, being liked—also influences the development of our long-term close relationships. The impressions that dating couples and college roommates quickly form of each other tend therefore to predict their long-term future (Berg, 1984, 1986). Indeed, if romances in the United States flourished *randomly*, without regard to proximity and similarity, then most Catholics (being a minority) would marry Protestants, most Blacks would marry Whites, and college graduates would be as apt to marry high school dropouts as fellow graduates.

So, first impressions are important and predictive. Nevertheless, recognizing that loving is not merely an intensification of initial liking, social psychologists are shifting

Even children can experience passion.

their attention from the mild attraction experienced during first encounters to the study of enduring, close relationships.

What is this thing called love? Loving is more complex than liking, and thus more difficult to measure, more perplexing to study. People yearn for it, live for it, die for it. Yet only in the last few years has loving—despite Senator Proxmire's scorn—become a serious topic in social psychology. Let's take a look at what has so far been concluded.

One line of investigation has been to compare the nature of love in various close relationships—same-sex friendships, parent-child relationships, and spouses or lovers (Davis, 1985; Maxwell, 1985; Sternberg & Grajek, 1984). These investigations reveal some elements of love that are common to all loving relationships: mutual understanding, giving and receiving support, valuing and enjoying being with the loved one. Although such ingredients of love apply equally to love between best friends or between husband and wife, they are spiced differently depending on the relationship. Passionate love, especially in its initial phase, is distinguished by physical affection, an expectation of exclusiveness, and an intense fascination with the loved one. Lest we think that passionate love occurs only between romantic lovers, Phillip Shaver and his coworkers (1988) note that year-old infants typically display a passionate attachment to their parents. Much like young adult lovers, they welcome physical affection, are distressed when separated, express intense affection when reunited, and take great pleasure in parental attention and approval. John Carlson and Elaine Hatfield (1989) report that 5 year olds, too, often display passionate love, by acknowledging that there is a child of the other sex whom they can't stop thinking about, whom they want to be near, and whom they like to touch and be touched by. However, it is not on these rudimentary passions that the love researchers have focused their attention but on adolescent and adult romantic loving.

PASSIONATE LOVE

The first step in scientifically studying romantic love, as in studying any variable, is to decide how to define and measure it. We have ways to measure aggression, altruism, prejudice, and liking, but how do we measure love? Elizabeth Barrett Browning asked a similar question: "How do I love thee? Let me count the ways." Social scientists have counted various ways. Psychologist Robert Sternberg (1988) views love as a triangle, whose three sides (of varying lengths) are passion, intimacy, and commitment (see Figure 13-4). Drawing from ancient philosophy and literature, sociologist John Alan Lee (1988) and psychologists Clyde Hendrick and Susan Hendrick (1986, 1988) identify three primary love styles—eros (passion), ludus (game-playing), and storge (friendship)—which, like the primary colors, combine to form secondary love styles, such as mania (a compound of eros and ludus). Pioneering love researcher Zick Rubin (1970, 1973) discerned somewhat different love factors. To tap each, he wrote questionnaire items:

1. *Attachment* (for example, "If I were lonely, my first thought would be to seek _____ out.")
2. *Caring* (for example, "If _____ were feeling bad, my first duty would be to cheer him [her] up.")
3. *Intimacy* (for example, "I feel that I can confide in _____ about virtually everything.")

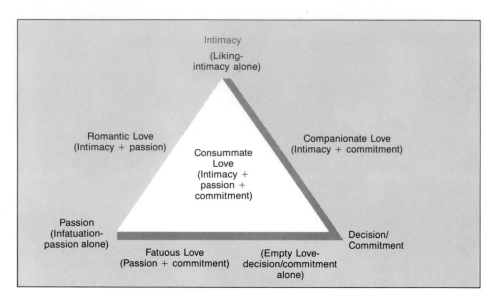

FIGURE 13-4
Robert Sternberg's (1988) conception of kinds of loving as combinations of three basic components of love.

Passionate love:
A state of intense longing for union with another. Passionate lovers are absorbed in one another, feel ecstatic at attaining their partner's love, and are disconsolate on losing it.

Rubin administered his Love Scale to hundreds of dating couples at the University of Michigan. He later invited to the laboratory some of the couples whose scores suggested their relationship was either weak or strong and loving. While each couple awaited the session, observers behind a one-way mirror clocked the time they maintained eye contact. The "weak-love" couples looked at one another less than the "strong-love" couples who gave themselves away by gazing into one another's eyes.

Passionate love is emotional, exciting, intense. Hatfield (1988) defines it as "*a state of intense longing for union with another*" (p. 193). If reciprocated, one feels fulfilled and joyous; if not, one feels empty or despairing. Like other forms of emotional excitement, passionate love involves a mix of elation and gloom, tingling exhilaration and dejected misery.

As this definition implies, people can feel passionate love toward someone who evokes pain, anxiety, and jealousy. Why? Romantic love sometimes seems not to follow the sensible principle that we like those who reward us and dislike those who cause us pain. Douglas Kenrick and Robert Cialdini (1977) argue one possible answer: While the loved one may cause pain and anxiety, the loved one also alleviates those emotions. The lover triggers jealousy when with someone else, yet also offers ecstatic relief upon returning. Loving those associated with the termination of negative feelings actually illustrates the reward principle. Perhaps you can recall a "lover's quarrel" that was almost justified by the intense pleasure of making up.

A Theory of Passionate Love

Hatfield has a quite different explanation of passionate love, one that applies a theory of emotion we considered in Chapter 12. There, we saw that a given state of arousal can be steered into any of several emotions, depending upon how one attributes the arousal. An emotion involves both body and mind, both arousal and how we interpret and label the arousal. Imagine yourself with pounding heart, trembling hands: Are you experiencing fear, anxiety, joy? Physiologically, one emotion is quite similar to another. You thus likely experience the arousal as joy if you are in a euphoric situation, anger

Two-factor theory of emotion: Arousal × label = emotion.

if your environment is hostile, and (Hatfield contends) passionate love if the situation is romantic.

If indeed passion is a revved-up state that's labeled love, then one's experience of "love" should be intensified by whatever revs one up. In several experiments, college men aroused sexually by reading or viewing erotic materials had a heightened response to a woman (for example, by scoring much higher on Rubin's Love Scale when describing their girlfriend) (Carducci et al., 1978; Dermer & Pyszczynski, 1978; Stephan et al., 1971). Proponents of the **two-factor theory of emotion** argue that when the revved-up men responded to a woman, they easily misattributed some of their arousal to her.

According to this theory, being aroused by *any* source should intensify one's passionate feelings—providing one's mind is free to attribute some of the arousal to a romantic stimulus. Donald Dutton and Arthur Aron (1974) invited University of British Columbia men to participate in a learning experiment. After meeting their attractive female partner, some were frightened with the news that they would be suffering some "quite painful" electric shocks. Before the experiment was to begin, the researcher gave a brief questionnaire, "to get some information on your present feelings and reactions, since these often influence performance on the learning task." Asked how much they would like to date and kiss their female partner, the aroused (frightened) men expressed more intense attraction toward the woman than did men who had not been aroused. Likewise, Gregory White and his coresearchers (1981; White & Kight, 1984) found that when college men were aroused—whether by running in place, by listening to a Steve Martin comedy routine, or by hearing a grisly tape of human mutilation—they then responded more intensely to a confederate female; they expressed greater liking for an attractive woman and disliking for an unattractive woman.

Does this phenomenon occur outside the laboratory? Dutton and Aron (1974) had an attractive young woman individually approach young men as they crossed a narrow, wobbly 450-foot-long suspension walkway hanging 230 feet above British Columbia's rocky Capilano River. She asked each man to help her fill out a class questionnaire. When he had finished, she scribbled out her name and phone number and invited him to call if he wanted to hear more about the project. Of those who had helped, most accepted the phone number, and half who did so called. By contrast, men approached by the woman on a low, solid bridge, and men approached on the high bridge by a *male* interviewer, rarely called. So, once again, physical arousal seemed to accentuate the men's romantic responses. Adrenaline made the heart grow fonder.

"The 'adrenaline' associated with a wide variety of highs can spill over and make passion more passionate. (Sort of a 'Better loving through chemistry' phemomenon.)"
Elaine Hatfield and Richard Rapson (1987)

But does it usually? Social psychologists debate this (Kenrick et al., 1979; Furst et al., 1980). The two-factor theory of romantic love predicts that arousal will most intensify love when its source is ambiguous, leaving us free to misattribute the arousal to passion. My hunch is that sometimes the source of our arousal is *un*ambiguous; we know all too well why we're feeling anxious, irritated, or frightened. Ruminating on the problem can leave us *less* open to experiencing romantic love. Other times, as when we are elated or stirred by a happening that doesn't gnaw at our minds, our arousal is more open to being steered into passion. One reason this occurs is that our actual arousal after some experience—say, the elevated heart rate that lingers several minutes after exercising—outlasts our *feeling* aroused (Cacioppo et al., 1987). This lingering but unperceived arousal means that we need less stimulation to raise our responses back up to the threshold for feeling aroused. Thus the lingering arousal spills over into the new emotion. Even when we know that something like exercise has previously aroused us, the arousal adds fuel to any other fire that is currently burning (Allen et al., 1989).

BEHIND THE SCENES

I've found it most exciting to spend my time investigating critically important, but difficult, perplexing, sometimes overlooked topics, topics that scientists once dismissed as impossibly difficult, taboo, or "trivial"—but which common sense said were critically important: physical attractiveness, love, sex, and emotion.

Elaine Hatfield,
University of Hawaii

Variations in Love

Variations over Time and Culture

There is always a temptation (the false consensus effect) to assume that our own feelings and ideas are shared by others. For example, we take it as a given that love is a precondition for marriage. This assumption is not shared in cultures that practice arranged marriages. Moreover, until recently in North America, marital choices, especially those by women, were strongly influenced by considerations of economic security, family background, and professional status. But today, as Figure 13-5 indicates, almost 9 in 10 young adults surveyed indicate that love is essential for marriage. Thus cultures (even our own) vary in the importance placed upon romantic love. In ours today, love generally precedes marriage; in some others, it more often follows marriage.

FIGURE 13-5

Passionate love: now, but not always, an essential precondition for marriage in North America. In recent decades, as college women have become freer of economic dependence on men, they have also become more likely to regard love as a prerequisite for marriage. (From Simpson et al., 1986).

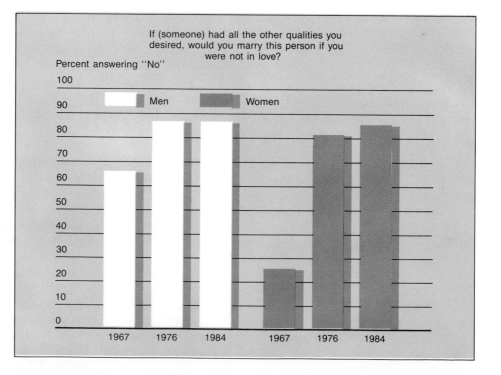

Variations by Personality

Within any given place and time, individuals also vary in their approach to heterosexual relationships. Some seek a succession of short involvements, others value the intimacy of an exclusive and enduring relationship. In a series of studies, Mark Snyder and his colleagues (1985, 1988; Snyder & Simpson, 1985) identified a personality difference that is linked with these two approaches to romance. In Chapter 2 we noted that some people—those high in "self-monitoring"—skillfully monitor their own behavior so that it creates the desired effect in any given situation. Others—those low in self-monitoring—are more internally guided, more likely to report that they act the same way regardless of the situation. Which type of person—someone high or low in self-monitoring—would you guess to be more affected by a prospect's physical appearance? to be more willing to end a relationship in favor of a new partner and therefore to date more people for shorter periods of time? to be more sexually promiscuous? Snyder and Simpson report that in each case the answer is the person high in self-monitoring. Such people are skilled in managing first impressions, but tend to be less committed to deep and enduring relationships. Low self-monitors, being less externally focused, are more loyally committed and display more concern with people's inner qualities. Thus, when perusing folders to examine potential dates or employees, they place a higher premium on personal attributes than on appearance. And given a choice between someone who shares their attitudes or their preferred activities, low self-monitors (unlike high self-monitors) feel drawn to those with kindred attitudes (Jamieson et al., 1987).

Variation by Gender

Males and females often differ in how they experience passionate love. Studies of men and women falling in and out of love have revealed some surprises. Most people, including the writer of the following letter to a newspaper advice columnist, suppose that women fall in love more readily:

> Dear Dr. Brothers:
> Do you think it's effeminate for a 19-year-old guy to fall in love so hard it's like the whole world's turned around? I think I'm really crazy because this has happened several times now and love just seems to hit me on the head from nowhere. . . . My father says this is the way girls fall in love and that it doesn't happen this way with guys—at least it's not supposed to. I can't change how I am in this way but it kind of worries me.—P.T. (quoted by Dion & Dion, 1985)

P.T. would be reassured by the repeated finding that it is actually men who tend to fall more readily in love (Dion & Dion, 1985; Peplau & Gordon, 1985). Men also seem to fall out of love more slowly and are less likely than women to initiate the breakup of a premarital romance. However, women in love are typically as emotionally involved as their partners, or more so—they are if anything more likely to report feeling euphoric and "giddy and carefree," as if they were "floating on a cloud." Women are also somewhat more likely than men to focus on the intimacy of the friendship and their concern for their partner, while men are more likely than women to think about the playful and physical aspects of the relationship.

COMPANIONATE LOVE

Although passionate love burns hot, it inevitably simmers down. Much as we develop tolerance for drug-induced highs, so also the passionate high we feel for a romantic

Unlike the wild emotions of passionate love, companionate love is a deep, affectionate attachment.

Companionate love:
The affection we feel for those with whom our lives are deeply intertwined.

"When two people are under the influence of the most violent, most insane, most delusive, and most transient of passions, they are required to swear that they will remain in that excited, abnormal, and exhausting condition continuously until death do them part."
George Bernard Shaw

partner is fated to become more lukewarm. The longer a relationship endures, the fewer are its emotional ups and downs (Berscheid et al., 1989). The high of romance may be sustained for a few months, even a couple of years. But as we noted in Chapter 12's discussion of adaptation level, no high lasts forever. Thus, if a close relationship is to endure, it settles to a steadier but still warm afterglow that Hatfield calls ***companionate love.***

Unlike the wild emotions of passionate love, companionate love is lower-key; it's a deep, affectionate attachment. And it is just as real. Even if one has developed tolerance for a drug, withdrawal from the loss of it can be painful. So with close relationships. Mutually dependent couples who no longer feel the flame of passionate love will often, upon divorce or death, discover that they have lost more than they expected. Having focused on what was not working, they failed to notice all the things that did work, including their hundreds of interdependent activities (Carlson & Hatfield, 1989).

The cooling of passionate love over time and the growing importance of other factors, such as shared values, can be seen in the feelings of those who enter arranged versus love-based marriages in India. When Usha Gupta and Pushpa Singh (1982) asked fifty couples in Jaipur, India, to complete Zick Rubin's love scale, they found that those who married out of love reported less intense feelings of love if they had been married more than five years. By contrast, those in arranged marriages reported *more* love if they were not newlyweds (Figure 13-6). Apparently, the romantic love that enabled a marriage's initial success did not necessarily make for a successful relationship in the long run.

The cooling of intense romantic love often triggers a period of disillusionment, especially among those who regard such love as essential both for the establishment of a marriage (recall Figure 13-4) and for its continuation. Thus Jeffry Simpson, Bruce Campbell, and Ellen Berscheid (1986) suspect that "the sharp rise in the divorce rate in the past two decades is linked, at least in part, to the growing importance of intense

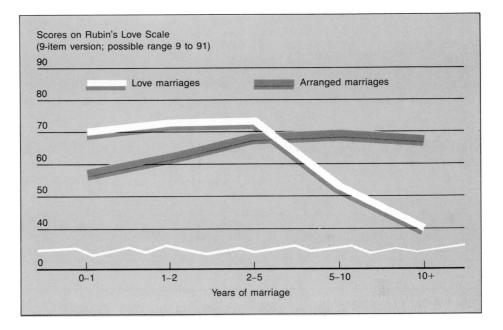

FIGURE 13-6
Romantic love between partners in arranged or love marriages in Jaipur, India. (Data from Gupta & Singh, 1982).

positive emotional experiences (e.g., romantic love) in people's lives, experiences that may be particularly difficult to sustain over time." Compared to North Americans, Asians tend to be less focused on personal feelings such as passion and more concerned with the practical aspects of social attachments (Dion & Dion, 1988). Thus, they may be less vulnerable to disillusionment.

The decline in intense mutual fascination may, for our species' survival, be natural and adaptive. The result of passionate love is frequently children, whose survival is aided by the parents' waning obsession with one another (Kenrick & Trost, 1986). Nevertheless, for those married more than twenty years some of the lost romantic feeling is often renewed as the family nest empties and the parents are once again free to focus their attention on one another (Hatfield & Sprecher, 1986). If the relationship

ENDLESS LOVE? EMOTIONS WERE BOTTLED UP

SEATTLE, WASH. (UPI)—Ten years ago a man wrote a love poem to his wife, slipped it into a bottle with an envelope and dropped it into the Pacific Ocean halfway between Seattle and Hawaii.

Chris Willie, an employee of the National Wildlife Federation, found the bottle recently while jogging on a beach in Guam. After replacing the envelope—the 10-cent stamp was a bit behind the times—he dutifully mailed the letter to Seattle.

When it was returned with "no longer at this address," Willie sent it to the *Seattle Times*.

The printed note was unabashed, old-fashioned romanticism.

"If, by the time this letter reaches you, I am old and gray, I know that our love will be as fresh as it is today.

"It may take a week or it may take years for this note to find you. Whatever the case may be, it shall have traveled by a strange and unpredictable messenger—the sea.

"If this should never reach you, it will still be written in my heart that I will go to extreme means to prove my love for you. Your husband, Bob."

The woman to whom the letter was addressed was reached by phone and the note was read to her. She burst out laughing—and the more she heard the harder she laughed.

"We're divorced," she said, slamming down the phone.

Note: Milwaukee Journal, August 27, 1981, p. 1.

has been intimate and mutually rewarding, companionate love is likely also to be thriving. But what is "intimacy"? And what is "mutually rewarding"?

Self-Disclosure

Deep, companionate relationships are intimate. They enable us to be known as we truly are and feel accepted. This delicious experience we enjoy in a good marriage or a close friendship—a relationship where trust displaces anxiety and where we are therefore free to be open without fear of losing the other's affection (Holmes & Rempel, 1989). Such relationships are characterized by what the late Sidney Jourard called ***self-disclosure***, or what Dalmas Taylor (1979) and Irwin Altman (Altman & Taylor, 1973) have called "social penetration." As such a relationship grows, those involved reveal more and more of themselves to one another; their knowledge of one another penetrates to deeper and deeper levels, until it reaches an appropriate level. Lacking such opportunities for intimacy, one may experience the pain of loneliness (Berg & Peplau, 1982; Solano et al., 1982).

Experiments have probed both the *causes* and the *effects* of self-disclosure. Researchers have wondered: When are people most willing to disclose intimate information concerning "what you like and don't like about yourself" or "what you're most ashamed and most proud of"? And what effects do such revelations have upon those who reveal and receive them?

The most reliable finding is the ***disclosure reciprocity*** effect: Disclosure begets disclosure (Berg, 1987; Reis & Shaver, 1988). Thus we reveal more to those who have been open with us. But intimacy is seldom instant. Far more often it progresses like a dance: I reveal a little, you reveal a little—but not too much; you then reveal more, as do I.

In other ways, too, some people are especially skilled "openers"—people who readily elicit intimate disclosures from others, even from those who normally don't reveal very much of themselves (Miller et al., 1983). Such people tend to be very good listeners. During conversation they maintain attentive facial expressions and appear to be comfortable and enjoying themselves (Purvis et al., 1984). They may also express interest by uttering supportive phrases while their conversational partner is speaking. They are what psychologist Carl Rogers (1980) called "growth-promoting" listeners— people who are *genuine* in revealing their own feelings; who are *accepting* of others feelings; and who are *empathic*, sensitive, reflective listeners.

The partner's disposition matters, too. Some people are naturally more intimate in their close relationships (Prager, 1986). And nearly everyone reveals more when in a good mood (M. Cunningham, 1988). When in a bad mood, we tend to clam up.

What are the effects of such self-disclosure? Jourard (1964) argued that dropping our masks, letting ourselves be known as we are, nurtures love. He presumed that it is gratifying to open up to another and then to receive the trust another implies by being open with us. For example, having an intimate friend with whom we can discuss threats to our self-image seems to help us comfortably survive such stresses (Swann & Predmore, 1985). A true friendship is a special relationship that helps us to cope with our other relationships.

While it is surely true that intimacy can also be rewarding, the results of many experiments caution us not to presume that self-disclosure will automatically kindle love. It's just not that simple. While it seems true that we like best those to whom we've disclosed ourselves (R. L. Archer et al., 1980), we are not always fond of those who most intimately reveal themselves to us (Archer & Burleson, 1980; Archer et al., 1980). Someone who early in an acquaintanceship rushes to tell us intimate details may

Self-disclosure:
Revealing intimate aspects of oneself to others.

Disclosure reciprocity:
The tendency for one person's intimacy of self-disclosure to match that of a conversational partner.

"What is a Friend? I will tell you. It is a person with whom you dare to be yourself."
Frank Crane,
A Definition of Friendship

come across as indiscreet, immature, even unstable (Dion & Dion, 1978; Miell et al., 1979). Often, though, people prefer an open, self-disclosing person to one who holds back. This is especially so when the disclosure is responsive to the conversation, as when someone who is normally reserved says that "something" about the partner "made me feel like opening up" and sharing confidential information (Archer & Cook, 1986; D. Taylor et al., 1981). Apparently, it is gratifying to be singled out for another's disclosure.

Even if it does not automatically trigger attraction, intimate self-disclosure does seem to be one of the delights of companionate love. Dating and married couples who most reveal themselves to one another tend to express most satisfaction with their relationship, and are more likely to endure in it (Berg & McQuinn, 1986; Hendrick et al., 1988; Sprecher, 1987). Researchers have also found that women are often more willing to disclose their fears and weaknesses than are men (J. Cunningham, 1981). As Kate Millett (1975) put it, "Women express, men repress." Nevertheless, men today, particularly men with egalitarian gender-role attitudes, seem increasingly willing to reveal their intimate feelings, and to enjoy the satisfactions that accompany a relationship of mutual trust and self-disclosure.

Equity

Earlier, we noted an equity rule at work in the matching phenomenon: People usually bring equal assets to their romantic relationships. Often they are matched for attractiveness, status, and so forth. And if mismatched in one area (for example, in attractiveness), they tend to be compensatingly mismatched in some other area (for example, status); thus in total assets they are an equitable match. No one says, and likely few even think, "I'll trade you my good looks for your big income." But especially in relationships that last, equity is the rule.

For one thing, those in a relationship that is equitable are more content (Fletcher et al., 1987; Gray-Little & Burks, 1983; Hatfield et al., 1985). Those who perceive their relationship as inequitable frequently feel discomfort; the one who has the better deal may feel guilty, and the one who senses a raw deal may feel strong irritation. (Given the self-serving bias, the person who is "over-benefited" may be less sensitive to the inequity.) Robert Schafer and Patricia Keith (1980) surveyed several hundred married couples of all ages, noting those who felt their marriage was somewhat unfair because one spouse contributed too little to the cooking, housekeeping, and tasks of providing, or to the roles of companion and parent. Inequity took its toll: those who perceived some inequity also tended to feel more distressed and depressed.

Ending a Close Relationship

What do people do when they perceive a relationship is inequitable? Some will exit the relationship. Among dating couples, the closer and longer the relationship and the fewer the available alternatives, the more painful is the breakup (Simpson, 1987). Among married couples, breakup has additional costs: shocked parents and friends, restricted parental rights, guilt over broken vows. Still, annually millions of couples are willing to pay such costs in order to extricate themselves from what they perceive as the greater costs of continuing a painful, unrewarding relationship.

Caryl Rusbult and her colleagues (1986, 1987) have explored three other ways of coping with a failing relationship. Some people exhibit *loyalty*—passively but optimistically waiting for conditions to improve. The problems are too painful to speak of, and the risks of separation too great, so the loyal partner grits teeth and perseveres, hoping the good old days will return. Others (especially men) display *neglect*, by passively

BEHIND THE SCENES

My interest in self-disclosure grew as I observed pairs of sailors getting acquainted during experiments in social isolation. In the early 1960s assignments to the new Polaris submarine and assignments to Antarctica, where men wintered in for long periods, brought about behavior problems that the Navy wanted to understand and alleviate. In our la- boratories at Bethesda Naval Hospital, we simulated such confinement by having pairs of men live and work in sound-proofed rooms for up to twenty-one days. During this isolation, self-disclosure occurred rapidly. So we developed ways to measure self-disclosure and then studied factors that stimulate it.

Dalmas Taylor,
Wayne State University

allowing the relationship to deteriorate. When the painful dissatisfactions are ignored, an insidious emotional uncoupling ensues, as the partners begin redefining their lives without each other. Still others, however, will *voice* their concerns and take active steps to improve the relationship. Researcher Robert Sternberg (1988) believes this approach is the only way to sustain a close relationship:

> "Living happily every after" need not be a myth, but if it is to be a reality, the happiness must be based upon different configurations of mutual feelings at various times in a rela- tionship. Couples who expect their passion to last forever, or their intimacy to remain un- challenged, are in for disappointment. . . . We must constantly work at understanding, build- ing, and rebuilding our loving relationships. Relationships are constructions, and they decay over time if they are not maintained and improved. We cannot expect a relationship simply to take care of itself, any more than we can expect that of a building. Rather, we must take responsibility for making our relationships the best they can be.

SUMMING UP

A Simple Theory of Attraction

Who likes whom, and why? Few of social psychology's questions have been of more perennial interest. Several influences upon our attraction to one another can be ex- plained with the aid of a simple principle: We like people whose behavior is rewarding to us or who have been associated with rewarding events.

Liking: Who Likes Whom

This chapter examined four powerful influences upon liking. The best predictor of whether any two people are friends is their sheer *proximity* to one another. Proximity is conducive to interaction, which enables people to discover their similarities and to feel one another's liking. Liking also receives a boost from the mere anticipation of interacting with someone. Finally, proximity exposes one to others, and mere repeated exposure tends to trigger liking.

A second determinant of one's initial attraction to another is the person's *physical attractiveness*. Both in laboratory studies and in field experiments involving blind dates, college students tend to like best someone who's attractive. In everyday life, however, people tend actually to choose and marry someone whose attractiveness roughly matches their own (or someone who, if less attractive, has other compensating qualities). Positive attributions about attractive people are so wide-ranging that many researchers believe there exists a strong physical-attractiveness stereotype—an assumption that what is beautiful is good. But then again, attractiveness is relative—not only relative to our culture's definition of attractiveness, but also relative to whom we're comparing a person to, and relative to how much we like the person.

As an acquaintance progresses, two other factors further help determine whether the acquaintance becomes a friendship. One's liking for another is greatly aided by *similarity* of attitudes, beliefs, and values. A wide variety of laboratory and field experiments have consistently found that likeness leads to liking. Researchers so far have been able to discover needs and traits for which people seek out those different from themselves. Apparently, opposites rarely attract.

We are also likely to develop friendships with people who *like us*. The tendency to be fond of those who like and admire us is especially strong when (1) we do not attribute the other's flattery to ingratiating motives, (2) we have recently been deprived of approval, and (3) the other's praise reverses earlier criticism.

Loving

Occasionally, an acquaintance develops not just into friendship, but into *passionate love*. Such love is often a bewildering confusion of ecstasy and anxiety, elation and pain. Advocates of the reward principle argue that we can love someone who causes us pain because the loved one also alleviates the pain. Advocates of the two-factor theory of emotion argue that when one is in a romantic context, arousal from any source, even painful experiences, can be steered into passion.

In the best of relationships, the initial romantic high settles to a steadier, more affectionate relationship called *companionate love*. One delight of companionate love is intimate self-disclosure, a state achieved gradually as each partner reveals more and more. Companionate love is most likely to endure when both partners feel it to be equitable, in that both receive from the relationship in proportion to what they contribute to it.

FOR FURTHER READING

Brehm, S. S. (1985). *Intimate relationships*. New York: Random House. Integrates research from social, developmental, and clinical psychology in describing the lifecycle of close relationships. Discusses ways to improve intimate relationships.

Duck, S. (1983). *Friends for life*. New York: St. Martins Press. A short, readable exploration of how friendships develop among children and adults.

Hatfield, E., & Sprecher, S. (1986). *Mirror, mirror: The importance of looks in everyday life*. Albany, NY: SUNY Press. A readable and definitive review of the ramifications of physical attractiveness for people of all ages.

Marsh, P. (Ed.). (1988). *Eye to eye: How people interact*. Salem House Publishers: Topsfield, MA. A popular, lavishly illustrated book, authored by a team of predominantly British psychologists. Its 31 chapters explore nonverbal communication, family relations, love, jealousy, marriage, and breaking up.

Perlman, D. S., & Duck, S. (Eds.). (1986). *Intimate relationships: Development, dynamics, and deterioration*. Beverly Hills, CA: Sage. Prominent researchers explore all phases of close relationships, from initiation to breakup and the aftermath.

Sternberg, R. J., & Barnes, M. L. (Eds.). (1988). *The psychology of love*. New Haven, CT: Yale University Press. Love researchers present their new theories of love with supporting biological, cognitive, and cultural evidence.

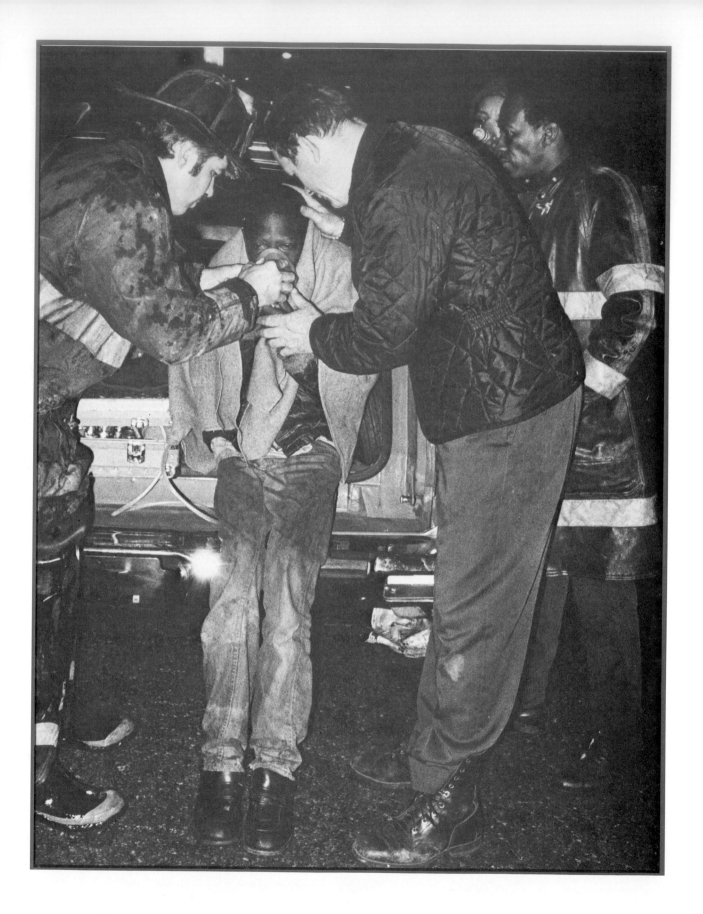

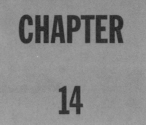

CHAPTER

14

ALTRUISM:
HELPING OTHERS

The half-starved, brutalized body of sixteen-year-old Sylvia Likens was discovered on October 26, 1965, in Indianapolis, Indiana. Since that July, she had boarded with Gertrude Braniszewski, who, aided by her three teenage children and two neighborhood boys, had beaten, burned, and branded the youngster. Sylvia had not accepted her degradation passively. She had fought back. Many neighbors heard Sylvia's screams. Her biographer, Kate Millett (1979), records:

> They heard it for weeks on end. Judy Duke observed Sylvia's beatings and even described them to her mother once in the kitchen over the dinner dishes; the verdict was that the child deserved punishment. Mrs. Vermillion, living next door, her house a mere fourteen feet from Sylvia's basement window, must have heard the child's suffering almost to madness week after week, before another sound, the sound of a coal shovel scraping the floor, made her trouble herself with the notion of calling the police. And stopped short of doing it. Just as Sylvia stopped short, the shovel no longer moving, signaling, crying out finally for help. . . .
>
> And so Mrs. Vermillion put down the phone, grumbled one more time to her husband . . . and slumped back into moral lassitude again. (pp. 22–23)

Why had Sylvia's neighbors not come to her aid? Were they callous, indifferent, apathetic? Were they, as Millett surmises, "vegetable minds"? If so, there are many such minds. Consider the following:

> Kitty Genovese is set upon by a knife-wielding stalker as she returns to her apartment house at 3:00 a.m. Thirty-eight of her neighbors are aroused by her screams of terror and pleas for help: "Oh my God, he stabbed me! Please help me! Please help me!" Many of them come to their windows and watch while, for 35 minutes, she struggles to escape her attacker. Not until her attacker departs does anyone so much as call the police. Soon after, she dies.
>
> Andrew Mormille is knifed in the stomach as he rides the subway home. After his attackers leave the car, eleven other riders watch the young man bleed to death.
>
> An 18-year-old switchboard operator, working alone, is sexually assaulted. She momentarily escapes and runs naked and bleeding to the street, screaming for help. Forty pedestrians watch as the rapist tries to drag her back inside. Fortunately, two police officers happen by and arrest the assailant.
>
> Eleanor Bradley trips and breaks her leg while shopping. Dazed and in pain, she pleads for help. For 40 minutes the stream of shoppers simply parts and flows around her. Finally, a cab driver helps her to a doctor (Darley & Latané, 1968).

What is shocking is not that in these cases some people failed to help, but that in each of these groups (groups of thirty-eight, eleven, forty, and hundreds) almost 100 percent of those involved failed to respond. Why? Placed in the same or similar situations, would you, would I, react as they did?

Of course, there are also anecdotes of great heroism:

> Hearing the rumble of an approaching subway train, Everett Sanderson leapt down onto the tracks and raced toward the approaching headlights to rescue Michelle De Jesus, a four-year-old who had fallen from the platform. Three seconds before the train would have run her over, Sanderson flung Michelle into the crowd above. As the trained roared in, he himself failed in his first effort to jump back to the platform. At the last instant, bystanders pulled him to safety (Young, 1977).

It was two o'clock on a mid-summer's afternoon in 1983 when Joe Delaney, a football player with the Kansas City Chiefs, saw people standing around a huge hole that had filled with water. Three boys had waded in, unaware that a short way out the bottom dropped off. Suddenly they were in over their heads and thrashing and screaming for help. As Joe alone dashed for the pond a little boy asked, "Can you swim?" "I can't swim good," Joe answered, "but I've got to save those kids. If I don't come up, get somebody." One boy struggled back to safety. The other two—and Joe Delaney—were hauled out by rescuers a short while later, dead (Deford, 1983).

On a hillside in Jerusalem, 800 trees form a simple line, The Avenue of the Righteous. Beneath each tree is a plaque with the name of a European Christian who, during the Nazi holocaust, gave refuge to one or more Jews. These "Righteous Gentiles" knew that if the refugees were discovered, Nazi policy dictated that both host and refugee would suffer a common fate. Many did (Hellman, 1980; Wiesel, 1985).

Less dramatic acts of comforting, caring, and helping abound: Without asking anything in return, people offer directions, donate money, give blood. Why and when will people perform such acts? And what can be done to lessen indifference and increase altruism? These are this chapter's primary questions.

Altruism is selfishness in reverse. An altruistic person is concerned and helpful even when no benefits are offered or expected in return. The classic illustration of altruism is Jesus's parable of the Good Samaritan:

> There was once a man who was going down from Jerusalem to Jericho when robbers attacked him, stripped him, and beat him up, leaving him half dead. It so happened that a priest was going down that road; but when he saw the man, he walked on by on the other side. In the same way a Levite also came there, went over and looked at the man, and then walked on by on the other side. But a Samaritan who was traveling that way came upon the man, and when he saw him, his heart was filled with pity. He went over to him, poured oil and wine on his wounds and bandaged them; then he put the man on his own animal and took him to an inn, where he took care of him. The next day he took out two silver coins and gave them to the innkeeper. "Take care of him," he told the innkeeper, "and when I come back this way I will pay you whatever else you spend on him." (Luke 10:30–35)

The Samaritan illustrates altruism in a pure form. Filled with compassion, he voluntarily gives time, energy, and money to a total stranger, expecting neither repayment nor appreciation.

To study altruistic acts, social psychologists have examined the conditions under which people will perform such deeds. Before looking at what these experiments reveal, let us first set a foundation by considering three theories of altruism.

WHY DO WE HELP ONE ANOTHER?

SOCIAL EXCHANGE: THE BENEFITS AND COSTS OF HELPING

One explanation for altruism comes from **social-exchange theory**: Human interactions are guided by a "social economics." We exchange not only material goods and money, but also *social* goods—love, services, information, status (Foa & Foa, 1975). In doing so, we are said to use the "minimax" strategy—minimize costs, maximize rewards. Social-exchange theory does not contend that we consciously keep track of costs and

Altruism:
Concern and help for others that asks nothing in return; devotion to others without conscious regard for one's self-interests.

Social-exchange theory:
The theory that human interactions are transactions that aim to maximize one's rewards and minimize one's costs.

rewards, but only that such considerations can be used to predict our behavior. Thus if we walk by an empty car with its lights on, we may briefly pause to try the driver's door, but if it is locked, we are unlikely to make the more costly effort of searching for the owner. We are more likely to give telephone change to a classmate (someone who can later reciprocate our help or whose esteem we covet) than to a stranger.

How might this cost-benefit theory explain a person's decision whether or not to donate blood? Suppose that your campus is having a blood drive and someone solicits your participation. Might you not weigh the *costs* of donating (pain, time, fatigue) versus those of not donating (guilt, disapproval)? Might you not also weigh the *benefits* of donating (feeling good about helping someone, free refreshments) versus those of not donating (saving the time, discomfort, and anxiety)? According to social exchange theory—and to studies of Wisconsin blood donors by Jane Allyn Piliavin, Dorcas Evans, and Peter Callero (1982)—such are the subtle calculations that precede decisions to help or not.

"Men do not value a good deed unless it brings a reward."
Ovid, Epistulae ex Ponto

Altruism as Disguised Self-interest

Rewards that motivate helping may be either external or internal. When businesses donate money to improve their corporate images, or when someone offers a ride to another hoping to receive appreciation or friendship, the desired reward is external. We give to get. Thus we are most eager to help someone attractive to us, someone whose approval we desire (Krebs, 1970; Unger, 1979b).

The benefits of helping also include internal self-rewards, such as calming one's own anxiety. When near someone in distress, people typically respond with empathy. A woman's scream outside your window arouses and distresses you. If you cannot reduce your arousal by interpreting the scream as a playful shriek, then you may investigate or give aid, thereby reducing your distress (Piliavin & Piliavin, 1973). Indeed, Dennis Krebs (1975) found that Harvard University men whose physiological responses and self-reports revealed the most distress in response to another's distress also gave the most help to the person. As Everett Sanderson remarked after saving the child who fell from the subway platform, "If I hadn't tried to save that little girl, if I had just stood there like the others, I would have died inside. I would have been no good to myself from then on." Altruistic acts also increase our sense of self-worth. For example, nearly all blood donors in Jane Piliavin's research agreed that giving blood "makes you feel good about yourself" and "gives you a feeling of self-satisfaction."

Some readers may object that the cost-benefit business is demeaning, because it takes the selflessness out of altruism. Perhaps. In defense of the theory, however, is it not a credit to humanity that we can derive pleasure from helping others, that much of our behavior is not antisocial but "prosocial," that we can even find fulfillment in the giving of love? How much worse if we gained pleasure only by serving ourselves?

"True," the reader may reply, "Still, doesn't social-exchange theory imply that a helpful act is never truly altruistic, that we merely *call* it altruistic when its rewards are inconspicuous? If we help the screaming woman so that we might gain social approval, relieve our distress, or boost our self image, is it really altruistic?" This is reminiscent of B. F. Skinner's (1971) analysis of altruism. We credit people for their good deeds, said Skinner, only when we don't know why they do them. (In the language of attribution theory, we attribute their behavior to their inner dispositions only when we lack external explanations.) When the external causes are conspicuous, we credit them, not the person.

Empathizing with the physical stress experienced by these runners, volunteers hand out water during the New York Marathon for altruistic, rather than self-beneficial, reasons.

There is, however, a weakness in social-exchange theory. It easily degenerates into explaining-by-naming. If someone volunteers for the Big Sister tutor program, it is tempting to "explain" her compassionate action in terms of the satisfaction it brings her. But such after-the-fact naming of rewards creates a circular explanation: "Why did she volunteer?" "Because of the inner rewards." "How do you know there are inner rewards?" "Why else would she have volunteered?" Because of such circularity, the philosophical doctrine of "psychological egoism"—the idea that all behavior must be motivated by self-interest—has fallen into disrepute.

To escape the circularity, we must define the rewards and costs independently of the behavior that is being explained. If social approval is presumed to motivate helping, then in experiments we should find that when approval is tied to helping, helping increases. And it does (Staub, 1978). Moreover, the cost-benefit analysis says something else. It suggests that the passive bystanders who observed the switchboard operator being dragged by the rapist may not have been apathetic. They might actually have been greatly distressed, yet paralyzed by their awareness of the potential costs of intervening.

Empathy as a Source of Genuine Altruism

Are life-saving heroes, everyday blood donors, and "sacrificial" Peace Corps volunteers *ever*, to any extent, motivated by genuine altruism, by an ultimate goal of selfless concern for another? Or is their ultimate goal always some form of self-benefit, even if a laudatory one such as the relief of one's own distress or the avoidance of later guilt?

This philosophical issue is illustrated in a conversation that Abraham Lincoln once had with a fellow passenger in a horse-drawn coach. After Lincoln had argued that all

"Are you all right, Mister? Is there anything I can do?"

"Young man, you're the only one who bothered to stop! I'm a millionaire and I'm going to give you five thousand dollars!"

We never know what benefits may come from helping someone in distress.

good deeds are prompted by selfishness, he noticed a sow making a terrible noise because her piglets had gotten into a pond and were in danger of drowning. Lincoln called the coach to a halt, jumped out, ran back, and lifted the little pigs to safety. Upon his return, his companion remarked, "Now, Abe, where does selfishness come in on this little episode?" "Why, bless your soul, Ed, that was the very essence of selfishness. I should have had no peace of mind all day had I gone and left that suffering old sow worrying over those pigs. I did it to get peace of mind, don't you see?" (F. C. Sharp, cited by Batson et al., 1986). Until recently, psychologists would have sided with Lincoln, denying the possibility of genuine altruism.

Psychologist Daniel Batson (1987), however, theorizes that our willingness to help is influenced by both self-serving *and* selfless considerations (see Figure 14-1). Feeling

FIGURE 14-1
Egoistic and altruistic routes to helping. Viewing another's distress can evoke a mixture of self-focused distress and other-focused empathy. Researchers agree that distress triggers egoistic motives but are debating whether empathy can trigger a pure altruistic motive. (Adapted from Batson, Fultz, & Schoenrade, 1987.)

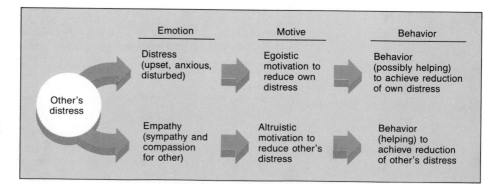

distress over someone's suffering can motivate us to relieve our troubled state, either by escaping the distressing situation (as did the priest and Levite) or to help (as did the Samaritan). But especially when we feel attached to someone, report Batson and his colleagues, we also feel *empathy*. Loving parents internally weep when their children suffer and rejoice over their children's joys—an empathy lacking in child abusers and other perpetrators of cruelty (Miller & Eisenberg, 1988). When feeling empathy we focus not so much on our own distress as on the sufferer. Such genuine sympathy and compassion motivates us to help the person for his or her own sake.

Often distress and empathy together motivate responses to a crisis. In 1983, people watched on television as an Australian bushfire wiped out hundreds of homes near Melbourne. Afterwards, Paul Amato (1986) studied people's donations of money and goods. He found that those who felt angry or indifferent gave less than those who felt either distressed (shocked and sickened) or empathic (sympathetic and worried for the victims). To separate egoistic distress reduction from altruistic empathy, Batson's research group conducted seven studies that aroused people's feelings of empathy and then observed whether they would reduce their own distress by escaping the situation or whether they would go out of their way to aid the person. The results were consistent: If their empathy was aroused, they usually helped; seldom did they "walk by on the other side."

In one of these experiments, Batson and his associates (1981) had University of Kansas women observe a young woman suffering while she supposedly received electric shocks. During a pause in the experiment, the obviously upset victim explained to the experimenter that a childhood fall against an electric fence left her acutely sensitive to shocks. In sympathy, the experimenter suggested that perhaps the observer (the actual subject in this experiment) might be willing to trade places and take the remaining shocks for her. Previously, half of these actual subjects had been led to believe the suffering person was a kindred spirit on matters of values and interests (thus arousing their empathy). Some also were led to believe that their part in the experiment was completed, so that in any case they were done observing the woman's suffering. Nevertheless, their empathy aroused, virtually all these student observers willingly offered to substitute for the victim, taking on her suffering.

But is this pure altruism? Mark Schaller and Robert Cialdini (1988) doubt it. Feeling empathy for a sufferer makes one sad, they note. In one of their experiments they led people to believe that their sadness was going to be relieved by a different sort of mood-boosting experience—listening to a comedy tape. Under such conditions, people who felt empathy were not especially helpful. Schaller and Cialdini concluded that if we feel empathy but know that something else will make us feel better, we aren't so likely to help.

Other findings suggest that genuine altruism may, however, exist. For example, empathy produces helping only when people believe the other will really be helped (Dovidio et al., 1988). Moreover, people whose empathy is aroused will help even when they believe no one will know about their helping, and their concern remains until someone *has* helped (Fultz et al., 1986). And people will sometimes persist in wanting to help a suffering person even when they believe their distressed mood has been temporarily frozen by a "mood-fixing" drug (Schroeder et al., 1988).

SOCIAL NORMS

Often we help others not because we have consciously calculated that such behavior is in our self-interest, but simply because something tells us we *ought* to. We ought to

BEHIND THE SCENES

Attempting to answer the question of altruism versus egoism—of whether we humans are capable of genuine caring for each other or only of caring for ourselves—has been like coming home for me. It's the kind of question about human nature that I often asked, first in college studying philosophy and later in seminary studying theology. When Jay Coke and I began studying people's emotional reactions to witnessing others in need, I realized that we were approaching a longstanding philosophical and theological puzzle. I was excited to think that if we could ascertain whether people's concerned reactions were genuine, and not simply a subtle form of selfishness, then we could shed new light on a basic issue regarding human nature.

C. Daniel Batson,
University of Kansas

help a new neighbor move in. We ought to turn off a vacant car's lights. We ought to return the wallet we found. Norms (as you may recall from Chapter 6) are social expectations. They *prescribe* proper behavior, the *oughts* of our lives. Researchers studying helping behavior have identified two social norms that seem to motivate altruism.

The Reciprocity Norm

Reciprocity norm:
An expectation that people will help, not hurt, those who have helped them.

Sociologist Alvin Gouldner (1960) contended that a universal moral code is a **norm of reciprocity:** We should return help, not harm, to those who have helped us. Gouldner believes that this norm is as universal as the incest taboo. We "invest" in others and expect dividends. Politicians know that the one who gives a favor can later expect a favor in return. The reciprocity norm even applies with marriage; sometimes one may give more than one receives. But in the long run, one expects the exchange to balance out. In all such interactions, to receive without giving in return violates the reciprocity norm. Those who do so can expect rejection.

The norm may well be universal; yet the extent of one's obligation to reciprocate varies according to circumstance. We feel deeply indebted when someone freely makes a big sacrifice on our behalf, but less so when the sacrifice is small and expected (Tesser et al., 1968; Wilke & Lanzetta, 1970). Consider, for example, the White South African high school students who took part in an experiment by Stanley Morse and his colleagues (1977). Each student won a hit record, aided by hints from a quizmaster. Later, when the quizmaster asked for help on a project, those who had not expected any hints volunteered nearly twice as much of their time as those who had been led to expect help. So the norm seems to be: Return favors, especially big, unexpected favors. People who most strongly assume this norm of reciprocity often behave generously, preferring to have people in their debt rather than to feel indebted (Eisenberger et al., 1987).

"There is no duty more indispensable than that of returning a kindness."
Cicero

The reciprocity norm applies most strongly to our interactions with our equals. Those who do not see themselves as inferior or as dependent will more strongly feel the need to reciprocate. Thus if help cannot be reciprocated, such people are likely to feel threatened and demeaned by accepting aid and so are more reluctant to seek help than are low self-esteem people (Fisher et al., 1983; Nadler et al., 1985). With people who clearly are dependent and unable to reciprocate—children, the severely impoverished and handicapped, and others perceived as unable to return as much as they receive—we are goaded to help by another widespread social norm:

The Social-Responsibility Norm

The reciprocity norm governs social exchange: it reminds us to balance giving and receiving in our social relations. However, if only a reciprocity norm existed, the Samaritan would not have been the Good Samaritan. In the parable, Jesus obviously had something more humanitarian in mind, something explicit in his other teachings: "If you love those who love you [the reciprocity norm], what right have you to claim any credit? . . . I say to you, Love your enemies" (Matthew 5:46, 44).

Social-responsibility norm: An expectation that people will help those dependent upon them.

The belief that people should help those who need help, without regard to future exchanges, has been labeled the ***norm of social responsibility*** (Berkowitz, 1972b; Schwartz, 1975). The norm ranges from someone's retrieving a dropped book for a person on crutches to parents caring for their children (R. D. Clark, 1975).

Experiments show that people are frequently willing to help needy people—even when the helpers remain anonymous and have no expectation of receiving any social reward (Shotland & Stebbins, 1983). In practice, however, people usually apply the social-responsibility norm selectively—to those whose need seems not due to their own negligence. The norm seems to be: Give people what they deserve. If they are victims of circumstance, say of natural disaster, then by all means be generous. If, however, they seem to have created their own problem, by laziness or lack of foresight, then they should get what they deserve. People's responses are thus closely tied to their *attributions*. If we attribute the need to an uncontrollable predicament, we help. If we attribute another's need to the person's choices, fairness does not require us to help; after all, it's the person's own fault (Weiner, 1980).

To make this point concrete, imagine yourself as one of the University of Wisconsin students in a study by Richard Barnes, William Ickes, and Robert Kidd (1979). You receive a call from a "Tony Freeman" who explains that he is in your introductory

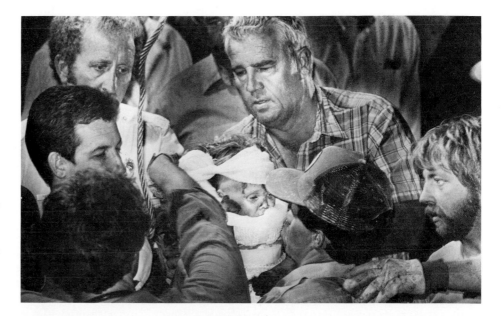

In 1988, when 18-month-old Jessica McClure fell 22 feet into an abandoned mine shaft, it took 2½ days for the people of Midland, Texas to free her. With only the incentive of social responsibility, these people worked around the clock to save Baby Jessica.

psychology class. He says he needs help for the upcoming exam, and that he has gotten your name from the class roster. "I don't know. I just don't seem to take good notes in there," Tony explains. "I know I can, but sometimes I just don't feel like it, so most of the notes I have aren't very good to study with." How sympathetic would you feel toward Tony? How much of a sacrifice would you make to lend him your notes? If you are like the students in this experiment, you would probably be much less inclined to help than if Tony had just explained that his troubles were beyond his control. Other experiments have produced similar results (Gruder et al., 1978; Meyer & Mulherin, 1980): When people need our help, we are often willing to help them—if we do not blame them for their problem.

SOCIOBIOLOGY

The third explanation of altruism is rooted in evolutionary theory. Chapters 6 and 13 briefly explained how sociobiologists study and theorize about the evolution of social behavior. Sociobiology contends that the essence of life is gene survival. Our genes drive us in ways that maximize their chance of survival. When we die, they usually live on.

As suggested by the title of one popular book, *The Selfish Gene* (Dawkins, 1976), sociobiology offers a humbling human image—one that psychologist Donald Campbell (1975a,b) has called a biological reaffirmation of a deep, self-serving "original sin." Sociobiologist David Barash (1979) put it bluntly: "Real, honest-to-God altruism simply doesn't occur in nature" (p. 135). Genes that would predispose people to selflessly promote the welfare of strangers would not survive in the evolutionary competition. Nevertheless, consider how genetic selfishness actually could predispose two specific types of selfless or even self-sacrificial behavior.

"Fallen heroes do not have children. If self-sacrifice results in fewer descendants, the genes that allow heroes to be created can be expected to disappear gradually from the population."
E. O. Wilson (1978, pp. 152–153)

Kin Protection: Genes Care for Relatives in Whom They Reside

One form of self-sacrifice that *would* contribute to the survival of our genes is devotion to our children. Parents who put their children's welfare ahead of their own will be more likely to have their genes passed on to posterity than parents who ignore their children's welfare. One could say then that evolution *has* selected altruism toward one's children. (Children have less at stake in the survival of their parents' genes. This may explain why parents are generally more devoted to their children than their children are to them.)

Other relatives share genes in proportion to their biological closeness. You share one-half your genes with your brothers and sisters, one-eighth with your cousins. That "genes help themselves by being nice to themselves, even if they are enclosed in different bodies" (Barash, 1979, p. 153), led the evolutionary biologist, J. B. S. Haldane to jest that while he would not give up his life for his brother, he would sacrifice himself for *three* brothers—or for nine cousins. Haldane would not be surprised that, compared to fraternal twins, genetically identical twins are noticeably more mutually supportive (Segal, 1984).

The point is not that we calculate genetic relatedness before helping, but that the social world operates in such a way that close kin are usually favored. The Carnegie Medal for bravery is never awarded for saving the life of a relative. That is expected. What is unexpected (and therefore honored) is the altruism of those who, like our subway hero Everett Sanderson, risk themselves to save a nonrelative.

We also share common genes with many others. Genes for blue eyes are shared with other blue-eyed people. But how do we detect the people in which copies of our genes will be found most abundantly? As the blue-eyes example suggests, one clue lies in physical similarities (Rushton et al., 1984). Also, in evolutionary history one's genes were more likely found in neighbors than in foreigners. Are we therefore biologically biased to act more altruistically toward those similar to us and those who live near us? In the aftermath of natural disasters, the order of who gets helped would not surprise a sociobiologist: family members first, friends and neighbors second, strangers last (Form & Nosow, 1985).

Kin selection:
The idea that evolution has selected altruism toward one's close relatives to enhance the survival of mutually shared genes.

Although biased altruism may no longer be conducive to human survival, some sociobiologists believe our evolutionary past has endowed us with such tendencies. If so, sociobiologist E. O. Wilson (1978) concludes, ***kin selection***—sociobiologists' term for favoritism toward those who share our genes—is a mixed blessing. For "altruism based on kin selection is the enemy of civilization. If human beings are to a large extent guided . . . to favor their own relatives and tribe, only a limited amount of global harmony is possible" (p. 167).

Reciprocity

The theory that genetic self-interest underlies altruism toward others who carry one's genes also predicts reciprocity. An organism helps another, biologist Robert Trivers argues, because it expects help in return (the giver expects later to be the getter) and because failure to reciprocate is punished and thus not favored by natural selection (Binham, 1980). The cheat, the turncoat, the traitor are universally despised.

Reciprocity works best in small, isolated groups, groups in which one will again interact with the people for whom one does favors. Thus reciprocity is stronger in the remote Cook Islands of the South Pacific than in New York City (Barash, 1979, p. 160). Small towns, small schools, small churches, small work teams, small dorms are all conducive to a community spirit in which people are more likely to care for each other and enjoy being cared for in return. Perhaps this is why researchers have observed that, compared to people in nonurban environments, those in big cities are less willing to relay a phone message, less likely to mail "lost" letters, less cooperative with survey interviewers, less helpful to a lost child, and less willing to do small favors (Steblay, 1987).

If individual self-interest inevitably wins in genetic competition, then why does nonreciprocal altruism toward strangers occur? What causes an Everett Sanderson to act as he does? A Mother Teresa to act as she does?

Donald Campbell's (1975a; 1975b) answer is that human societies have evolved ethical and religious rules that serve as brakes on the biological bias toward self-interest. Commandments such as "Love your neighbor" admonish us to balance self-concern with concern for the group, and so contribute to the survival of the group. Sociobiologist Richard Dawkins (1976) reaches a similar conclusion: "Let us try to *teach* generosity and altruism, because we are born selfish. Let us understand what our selfish genes are up to, because we may then at least have the chance to upset their designs, something no other species has ever aspired to" (p. 3).

Batson (1983) believes that religious images of "brotherly and sisterly" love toward all our fellow "children of God" in the human "family" extend the reach of kin-linked altruism beyond our biological relatives. Although it is unclear how religious devotion relates to the spur-of-the-moment help offered to strangers, it does seem linked with long-term altruism, and not only in the occasional Mother Teresas. Among Americans

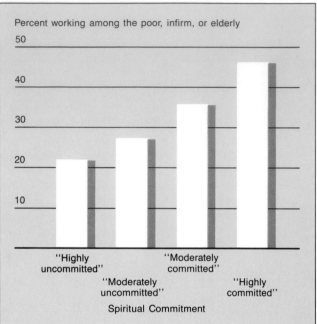

FIGURE 14-2

Religion and long-term altruism. Those whom George Gallup (1984) classifies as "highly spiritually committed" are more likely to report working among the needy.

whom George Gallup (1984) classified as "highly spiritually committed," 46 percent said they were presently working among the poor, the infirm, or the elderly—many more than among those less committed (see Figure 14-2).

COMPARING AND EVALUATING THEORIES OF ALTRUISM

By now you have perhaps noticed similarities among the social exchange, social norm, and sociobiological views of altruism. The parallels are indeed striking. As Table 14-1 indicates, each proposes two types of prosocial behavior: a tit-for-tat reciprocal exchange and a more unconditional helpfulness. In fact, we might think of these theories as three complementary levels of explanation. Indeed, if the sociobiological view of altruism is correct, then our genetic predispositions should manifest themselves in psychological and sociological phenomena. Thus theorists from any of the three camps have ready explanations for, say, reciprocal altruism.

Each theory appeals to logic. Yet each is vulnerable to charges of being speculative and after-the-fact. When one starts with a known effect (the give and take of everyday life) and explains it by conjecturing a social exchange process, a "reciprocity norm," or an evolutionary origin, one might be merely explaining-by-naming. For example, the argument that a behavior occurs because of its survival function is hard to disprove. With hindsight, it's easy to think that it had to be that way for survival. If *any* conceivable behavior can be explained after the fact as the result of a social exchange, a norm, or natural selection, then the theories cannot be falsified. Each theory's task is therefore to generate predictions that enable us to test it.

An effective theory also provides a coherent scheme for summarizing diverse observations. On this criterion, the three theories of altruism get higher marks. Each offers us a broad perspective from which we can understand both enduring commit-

TABLE 14-1
Comparing Theories of Altruism

| Theory | Level of Explanation | How Is Altruism Explained? | |
		Mutual "Altruism"	Intrinsic Altruism
Social norms	Sociological	Reciprocity norm	Social responsibility norm
Social exchange	Psychological	External rewards for helping	Distress → inner rewards for helping
Sociobiology	Biological	Reciprocity	Kin selection

ments of time or monies and the sorts of spontaneous help studied in the experiments described below.

WHEN WILL WE HELP?

Social psychologists were curious and concerned about bystanders' lack of involvement during such events as the Kitty Genovese murder. So they undertook experiments to identify when people will help in an emergency. More recently, the question has been broadened to also ask: When will people help in nonemergencies—by such deeds as giving money, donating blood, or contributing time? Let's examine these experiments, looking first at the *circumstances* that enhance helpfulness and then at the characteristics of the *people* who help.

When it comes to giving, some people stop at nothing.

SITUATIONAL INFLUENCES: WHEN ARE WE LIKELY TO BE GOOD SAMARITANS?

Number of Bystanders

The passivity of bystanders during emergencies prompted social commentators to lament our culture's alienation, apathy, indifference, and unconscious sadistic impulses. Note that all these explanations attribute the nonintervention to the bystanders' dispositions. This allows us to reassure ourselves that we are not the type of people who would fail to help. If we feel appalled when reading about these incidents, we can tell ourselves we are not similarly indifferent. Why then were those bystanders such dehumanized characters?

Two social psychologists, Bibb Latané and John Darley (1970), were not convinced that the bystanders were dehumanized. So Latané and Darley staged a number of ingenious emergencies and found that a single situational factor—the presence of other bystanders—greatly decreased intervention. By 1980 some four dozen comparisons had been accumulated of help given by bystanders who perceived themselves to be either alone or with others. In about 90 percent of these comparisons, involving nearly 6000 people, lone bystanders were more likely to help (Latané & Nida, 1981). Sometimes, the victim was actually less likely to get help if many people could help. For example, when Latané, James Dabbs (1975) and 145 collaborators "accidentally" dropped coins or pencils during 1497 elevator rides they were helped 40 percent of the time when one other person was on the elevator and less than 20 percent of the time when there

BEHIND THE SCENES

S hocked by the Kitty Genovese murder, Bibb Latané and I met over dinner and began to analyze the bystanders' reactions. Being social psychologists, we thought not about the personality flaws of the "apathetic" individuals, but rather about how anyone in that situation might react as did these people. By the time we finished our dinner, we had formulated several factors that together could lead to the surprising result: no one helping. Then we set about conducting experiments that isolated each factor and demonstrated its importance in an emergency situation.

John M. Darley, Princeton University

were six passengers. Why? Latané and Darley surmised that as the number of bystanders increases, any given bystander is less likely to *notice* the incident, less likely to *interpret* the incident as an emergency, and less likely to *assume responsibility* for taking action. Taking these one at a time, let us examine why.

Noticing

Twenty minutes after Eleanor Bradley has fallen and broken her leg on a crowded city sidewalk, you come along. Your eyes are focused on the backs of the pedestrians in front of you (it is bad manners to stare at those you pass) and your private thoughts are focused on the events of the day. Would you therefore be less likely to notice the injured woman than if the sidewalk were virtually deserted?

To check this conjecture, Latané and Darley (1968) had Columbia University men fill out a questionnaire in a room, either by themselves or with two strangers. While working (and being observed through a one-way mirror) there was a staged emergency: Smoke poured into the room through a wall vent. *Solitary* students, who often glanced idly about the room while working, noticed the smoke almost immediately—usually in less than five seconds. Those in *groups* kept their eyes on their work. It typically took them about twenty seconds to notice the smoke.

Interpreting

Once an ambiguous event is noticed, it calls for an interpretation. Put yourself in the room filling with smoke. Though a bit worried, you don't want to embarrass yourself by getting flustered. You glance at the others. They look calm, indifferent. Assuming everything must be okay, you shrug it off and go back to work. Then one of the others notices the smoke and, noting your apparent unconcern, reacts similarly. This is yet another example of informational influence (Chapter 7), each person using others' behavior as clues to reality.

And so it happened in the actual experiment. When those working alone noticed the smoke, they usually hesitated a moment, then got up, walked over to the vent, felt, sniffed, and waved at the smoke, hesitated again, and then went to report it. In dramatic contrast, those in groups of three did not move. Among the twenty-four men in eight groups, only one person reported the smoke within the first four minutes (Figure 12-2). By the end of the six-minute experiment, the smoke was so thick that

Is this an emergency? Or is the man drunk or asleep? Other people's reactions to him can influence our interpretation of the situation.

the men's vision was becoming obscured and they were rubbing their eyes and coughing. Still, in only three of the eight groups did even a single person leave to report the problem.

Equally interesting, subsequent interviews revealed that the group's passivity had

FIGURE 14-3

The smoke filled room experiment. Smoke pouring into the testing room was much more likely to be reported by individuals working alone than by three-person groups. (Data from Latané & Darley, 1968).

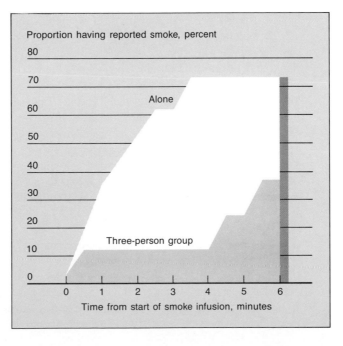

affected members' interpretations. What caused the smoke? "A leak in the air conditioning," "Chemistry labs in the building," "Steam pipes," "Truth gas." They offered many explanations. Not one said "fire." The group members, in serving as nonresponsive models, had influenced each other's interpretation of the situation as not being an emergency.

This experimental dilemma parallels dilemmas each of us have faced. Are the shrieks outside merely playful antics, or the desperate screams of someone being assaulted? Is the boys' scuffling a friendly tussle, or a vicious fight? Is the woman slumped in the doorway sleeping, or is she seriously ill, perhaps in a diabetic coma?

Unlike the smoke-filled-room experiment, however, each of these everyday situations involves danger to another person rather than to oneself. To see if the same **bystander effect** could occur in such situations Latané and Judith Rodin (1969) staged an experiment around a woman in distress. In this experiment, a female researcher set Columbia University men to work on a questionnaire and then left through a curtained doorway to work in her adjacent office. Four minutes later she could be heard (from a high-fidelity tape recorder) climbing up on a chair to reach some papers. This was followed by a scream and a loud crash as the chair collapsed and she fell to the floor. "Oh, my God, my foot . . . I . . . I . . . can't move it," she sobbed. "Oh . . . my ankle . . . I . . . can't get this . . . thing . . . off me." Only after two minutes of moaning did she manage to make it out her office door.

Seventy percent of those who were alone when the "accident" was overheard came into the room or called out to offer help. But in only 40 percent of the pairs of strangers confronting the emergency did either person offer help. This again demonstrates the bystander effect: As the number of people known to be aware of an emergency increases, any given person becomes *less* likely to help. For the victim there was therefore no safety in numbers. Those who did nothing apparently interpreted the situation as a nonemergency. "A mild sprain," said some. "I didn't want to embarrass her," explained others.

People's interpretations also affect their reactions to street crimes. In staging physical fights between a man and a woman, Lance Shotland and Margaret Straw (1976) found that bystanders intervened 65 percent of the time when the woman shouted "Get away from me, I don't know you," and 19 percent of the time when she shouted "Get away from me, I don't know why I ever married you." In the second situation, people perceived the woman as less threatened and themselves as more threatened were they to intervene. Harold Takooshian and Herzel Bodinger (1982) suspected that interpretations could also affect bystanders' reactions to burglaries. When they staged hundreds of car burglaries in eighteen cities (using a coat hanger to gain access to a valuable object such as a TV set or fur coat), they were astonished that fewer than one out of ten passersby so much as questioned their activity. Many of the pedestrians noticed, and even stopped to stare, snicker, or offer help. Some apparently interpreted the "burglar" as the car's owner.

Assuming Responsibility

But misinterpretation was not the only factor. Even when a shabby 14-year-old was the "burglar," when someone simultaneously broke into two adjacent cars, or when onlookers observed a different person breaking into the car than had just gotten out of it, Takooshian and Bodinger report there still was virtually no intervention by New Yorkers. And what about those times when it is obvious that an emergency is occurring? Those who watched Kitty Genovese being attacked and heard her pleas for help

Bystander effect:
The finding that a person is less likely to provide help when there are other bystanders.

FIGURE 14-4
Latané and Darley's decision tree. Only one path up the tree leads to helping. At each fork of the path, the presence of other bystanders may divert a person down a branch toward not helping. (Adapted from Darley & Latané, 1968).

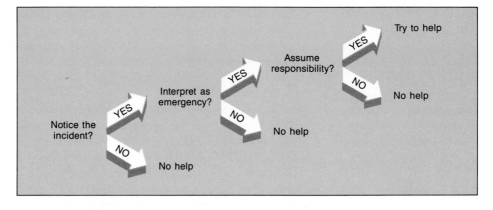

correctly interpreted what was happening. But the lights and silhouetted figures in neighboring windows told them that others were also watching. This diffused the responsibility for action.

Few of us have observed a murder. But all of us have at times been slower to react to a need when others were present. To explore further why bystanders can inhibit our acting, Darley and Latané (1968) simulated the Genovese drama. They placed people in separate rooms from which the subjects would hear a victim crying for help. To create this situation, Darley and Latané asked some New York University students to discuss over a laboratory intercom their problems with university life. The students were told that to guarantee their anonymity they would not see each other, nor would the experimenter eavesdrop. During the ensuing discussion, the participants heard one person, when the experimenter turned his microphone on, lapse into an epileptic seizure; with increasing intensity and speech difficulty, he pled for someone to help.

Of those led to believe they were the only listener, 85 percent sought help. Of those who believed four others also overheard the victim, only 31 percent went for help. Were those who did not respond apathetic and indifferent? When the experimenter entered the room to terminate the experiment, she did not find them so. In fact, most of these subjects immediately expressed concern; many had trembling hands and sweating palms. They believed an emergency had occurred, but were undecided about whether they should act.

After the smoke-filled-room, the lady-in-distress, and the seizure experiments, Latané and Darley asked the participants whether the others' presence had influenced them. Obviously, the other bystanders had actually had a dramatic effect. Yet, the participants almost invariably denied that they had been influenced. The typical reply? "I was aware of the others, but I would have reacted just the same if they weren't there." This response once again demonstrates a point stressed in Chapter 4: We often do not know why we do what we do. And that, of course, is why experiments such as these are revealing. A survey of uninvolved bystanders following a real emergency likely would have left the bystander effect hidden.

Further experiments, however, have revealed some situations in which the presence of others sometimes does *not* inhibit people from offering help. Irving Piliavin and his colleagues (1969) staged an emergency in a laboratory on wheels, the unwitting subjects being 4450 riders of New York's subway. On each of 103 occasions, a confederate entered a subway car and stood in the center next to a pole. After the train pulled out of the station, he staggered, then collapsed. When the victim carried a cane, one or more bystanders almost always promptly offered help. Even when the victim carried a bottle and smelled of liquor, he was often promptly offered aid—aid that was especially prompt when several male bystanders were close by. Why? Did the presence of other passengers provide a sense of security to those who helped? Was it because the situation was unambiguous? (The passengers couldn't help but notice and realize what was happening).

To test this latter possiblity, Linda Solomon, Henry Solomon, and Ronald Stone (1978) conducted a series of experiments in which New Yorkers either saw and heard someone's distress, as in the subway experiment, or only heard it, as in the lady-in-distress experiment (leaving the situation more open to interpretation). When the emergencies were unambiguous, those in groups were only slightly less likely to be helpful than were those alone. However, when the emergencies were somewhat ambiguous, the subjects who were in groups were far less likely to help than were solitary bystanders.

In the subway experiment, another significant factor may have been that the passengers sat face to face, allowing them to see the alarm on one another's faces. To explore this idea, Darley, Allan Teger, and Lawrence Lewis (1973) created a situation in which people were working either face to face or back to back when they heard a crash in the adjacent room as several metal screens fell on a workman. Unlike those who were working alone, who almost always offered help, pairs working back to back seldom offered help. However, a person working face to face with a partner was able to notice that the other was startled and knew that the other had observed likewise. Apparently this led both to interpret the situation as an emergency and to feel some responsibility to act, for these pairs were virtually as likely to give aid as were those working alone. Being designated the leader of a group has much the same effect, for leaders are as likely to aid someone in distress as are those working alone (Baumeister et al., 1988). The same is true of those of who feel especially competent to give aid, such as registered nurses who observe an accident (Cramer et al., 1988).

Finally, all the experiments we have considered involved groups of strangers. Imagine yourself facing any of these emergencies with a group of friends. Would your acquaintance with your fellow bystanders make a difference? Experiments conducted in two Israeli cities and at the University of Illinois at Chicago suggest that the answer is yes (Rutkowski et al., 1983; Yinon et al., 1982). Cohesive groups are *less* inhibited about helping than are solitary individuals. To summarize: The presence of other bystanders inhibits helping *if* the emergency is *ambiguous* and the other bystanders are *strangers* who *cannot easily read one another's reactions.*

This seems a good point to raise again the issue of research ethics. Is it right to force hundreds of subway riders to witness someone's apparent collapse? Were the researchers in the seizure experiment ethical when they forced people to decide whether to abort the discussion to report the problem? Would you object to being in such a study? Note that it would have been impossible to obtain your "informed consent"; doing so would have destroyed the cover for the experiment.

Two things can be said in defense of the researchers. First, they were always careful to debrief their laboratory participants, explaining both the experiment and its purposes. After explaining the seizure experiment, probably the most stressful, the experimenter gave the participants a questionnaire. One hundred percent said the deception was justified and that they would be willing to take part in similar experiments in the future. None of the participants reported feeling angry at the experimenter. Other researchers similarly report that the overwhelming majority of subjects in such experiments say afterwards that their participation was both instructive and ethically justified (Schwartz & Gottlieb, 1981). In the field experiments, an accomplice assisted the victim if no one else did, thus eventually reassuring bystanders that the problem was dealt with.

Second, remember that the social psychologist has a twofold ethical obligation: to protect the participants and to enhance human welfare by discovering influences upon human behavior. Such discoveries can alert us to unwanted influences and clue us, as we will see, to how we might exert positive influences. The ethical principle thus seems to be: If the welfare of participants is protected, as it apparently was in this research, social psychologists fulfill their responsibility to society by doing such research.

Models: Helping When Someone Else Does

If observing a model of aggression can heighten aggression (Chapter 12), and if models who are unresponsive can heighten nonresponding, then might not models of helpfulness promote helping? Imagine hearing a crash followed by sobs and moans. If another bystander's reaction implied, "Uh oh. This is an emergency! I've got to do something," would this not also help stimulate others to help?

The evidence is clear: Prosocial models do indeed promote altruism in others. James Bryan and Mary Ann Test (1967) found that Los Angeles drivers were more likely to offer help to a female driver with a flat tire if a quarter mile earlier they had seen someone helping another woman change a tire. In another experiment, Bryan and Test observed that New Jersey Christmas shoppers were more likely to drop money in a Salvation Army kettle if they had just observed someone else do the same. And in a study with British adults, Philippe Rushton and Anne Campbell (1977) found people usually unwilling to donate blood, unless they were approached after observing a confederate consent to donating.

Sometimes models contradict in practice what they preach. Parents may advise their children to "Do as I say, not as I do." Experiments indicate that children learn moral judgments from both what they hear preached and what they see practiced (Rice & Grusec, 1975; Rushton, 1975). When exposed to hypocrites, they tend to model the model: They do what the model does and say what the model says.

However, models are not always emulated. The example set by a *disliked* model can boomerang. Imagine being one of the several hundred Madison, Wisconsin, residents who found an addressed envelope with several personal documents showing. Wrapped around the documents was a note from someone who had found the envelope but dropped it. In the note, this first finder identified himself as a South African who was "very disappointed with how self-centered and childish Americans are," adding, "You have much to learn from the honest way we keep our Negroes down," and "I must say, it has been annoying to have to get involved with whole problem of returning these things" (Schwartz & Ames, 1977). Under these conditions—having a repulsive model who disliked helping—fully three-fourths of the second finders mailed the envelopes. It seemed that the typical subject felt, "If he's against helping, I'm for it." When the model was disliked, yet expressed *enjoyment* of helping, only about half the second finders mailed the envelope. "I'm not sure I want to go along with what a jerk like that does."

"We are, in truth, more than half what we are by imitation. The great point is, to choose good models and to study them with care."
Lord Chesterfield,
Letters *January 18, 1750*
Old Scottish proverb

Children learn by imitating, their parents' behaviors.

People in a Hurry

Darley and Batson (1973), discerned another determinant of helping in the Good Samaritan parable. The priest and the Levite were both busy, important people, probably hurrying to their duties. The lowly Samaritan surely was less pressed for time. To see whether people in a hurry would behave as the priest and Levite did, Darley and Batson cleverly staged the situation described in the parable.

After being asked to collect their thoughts prior to recording a brief extemporaneous talk (which, for half the participants, was on the Good Samaritan parable), Princeton Theological Seminary students were directed to a recording studio in an adjacent building. En route, they passed a man sitting slumped in a doorway, head down, coughing and groaning. Some of the students had been sent off nonchalantly: "It will be a few minutes before they're ready for you, but you might as well head on over." Of these, almost two-thirds stopped to offer help. Others were told, "Oh, you're late. They were expecting you a few minutes ago . . . so you'd better hurry." Of these, only 10 percent offered help.

Reflecting on these findings, Darley and Batson remarked that

A person not in a hurry may stop and offer help to a person in distress. A person in a hurry is likely to keep going. Ironically, he is likely to keep going even if he is hurrying to speak on the parable of the Good Samaritan, thus inadvertently confirming the point of the parable.

(Indeed, on several occasions, a seminary student going to give his talk on the parable of the Good Samaritan literally stepped over the victim as he hurried on his way!)

This is one of the most ironically humorous scenes ever noted in a social psychology experiment: A contemporary "priest" passing by a slumped, groaning victim while pondering the parable of the Good Samaritan.

Yet, perhaps we are being unfair to the seminary students, who were, after all, hurrying to *help* the experimenter. Perhaps they keenly felt the social responsibility norm, but found it pulling them two ways—toward the experimenter and toward the victim. In another enactment of the Good Samaritan situation, Batson and his associates (1978) directed forty University of Kansas students to an experiment in another building. Half were told they were late; half knew they had plenty of time. Half thought their participation was vitally important to the experimenter; half thought it was unessential. The results: Those who, like the White Rabbit in *Alice's Adventures in Wonderland*, were late for a very important date, seldom stopped to help. They had a pressing social obligation elsewhere. Those on their way to an unimportant appointment usually stopped to help.

Can we conclude that those who were rushed were callous? Did the seminarians notice the victim's distress and then consciously choose to ignore it? No. In their hurry, they never fully grasped the situation. Harried, preoccupied, rushing to meet a deadline, they simply did not take time to tune into the person in need.

Whom Do We Help?

When we discussed the social-responsibility norm, we noted the tendency to help those most in need, those most deserving. In the subway experiment, the "victim" was helped far more promptly when carrying a cane than when carrying a liquor bottle. Grocery store shoppers have been found to be more willing to give change to a woman who, they are led to believe, wants to buy milk than to one who wants to buy cookie dough (Bickman & Kamzan, 1973).

Gender

If, indeed, one's perception of another's need strongly determines one's willingness to help, will women, if perceived as less competent and more dependent, receive more help than men? In the United States, such indeed is the case. Alice Eagly and Maureen Crowley (1986) located thirty-five studies that compared help received by male or female victims. (Virtually all of the studies involved short-term encounters with strangers in need—the very sorts of situations in which males are expected to be chivalrous, note Eagly and Crowley.) When the potential helpers were males, female victims were more likely to receive aid than male victims in four out of five studies. When the potential helpers were females, female and male victims were equally likely to receive aid. Several experiments have found that women with disabled cars (for example, with a flat tire) get many more offers of help than do men (Penner et al., 1973; Pomazal & Clore, 1973; West et al., 1975). Similarly, solo female hitchhikers receive far more offers of help than do solo males or couples (Pomazal & Clore, 1973; M. Snyder et al., 1974).

Of course, men's chivalry toward lone women may be motivated by something other than altruism. Some of the helpful men may reason that the cost of helping is minimal (at least in terms of risk to one's safety), but the potential benefits maximal. So it won't come as a great surprise to learn that men more frequently help attractive than less attractive women (Mims et al., 1975; Stroufe et al., 1977; West & Brown, 1975).

Similarity

Perhaps because similarity is conducive to liking (see Chapter 13) and liking is conducive to helping, we are also biased toward those *similar* to us. The similarity bias applies to both dress and beliefs. Tim Emswiller and his fellow researchers (1971) had confederates, dressed either conservatively or in counterculture garb, approach "straight" and "hip" Purdue University students seeking a dime for a phone call. Fewer than half the students did the favor for those dressed differently from themselves, but two-thirds did so for those dressed similarly. Similarly, on election day, 1972, Stuart Karabenick, Richard Lerner, and Michael Beecher (1973) had Nixon and McGovern workers "accidentally" drop campaign leaflets near voting polls. The workers were helped by fewer than half the passersby who preferred the other candidate, but by more than two-thirds of those whose preference was the same.

Does the similarity bias extend to race? During the 1970s, researchers explored this question with confusing results: Some studies found a same-race bias (Benson et al., 1976; R. D. Clark, 1974; Franklin, 1974; Gaertner, 1973; Gaertner & Bickman, 1971; Sissions, 1981). Others found no bias (Gaertner, 1975; R. M. Lerner & Frank, 1974; D. W. Wilson & Donnerstein, 1979; Wispe & Freshley, 1971). And still others— especially those involving face-to-face situations—found a bias toward helping those of a different race (Dutton, 1971, 1973; Dutton & Lake, 1973; I. Katz et al., 1975). Is there a general rule that can resolve these seemingly contradictory finding?

One possibility is that people tend to favor their own race, but keep this bias secret in order to preserve a positive image. Few want to appear prejudiced. If this explanation is correct, the same-race bias should appear when, and only when, one's failure to help someone of another race can be attributed to factors other than race. And so it happened in experiments by Samuel Gaertner and John Dovidio (1977, 1986). For example, White University of Delaware women were less willing to help a Black than a White "lady in distress" *if* their responsibility could be diffused among the bystanders ("I didn't help the Black woman because there were others who could"); when there were no other bystanders the women were equally helpful to the Black and the White women. The rule seems to be: When norms for appropriate behavior are well-defined, Whites don't discriminate; when norms are ambiguous or conflicting, racial similarity may bias responses.

PERSONAL INFLUENCES: WHO ARE THE GOOD SAMARITANS?

We have considered several influences upon one's decision to help—number of bystanders, modeling, hurrying, and characteristics of the person in need. We also need to consider internal factors, factors having to do with the state or the characteristics of the helper.

Guilt

Throughout recorded history, guilt has been a painful emotion, so painful, in fact, that cultures have institutionalized a variety of ways to relieve it: sacrifices both animal and human, offerings of grain and money, penitent behavior, confession, denial. In ancient Israel, the sins of the people were periodically laid on a "scapegoat" animal

Many people alleviate guilt by confessing, either to someone of authority or to friends.

that was then led into the wilderness, thus carrying away the people's guilt (de Vaux, 1965).

To examine the consequences of guilt, social psychologists have induced people to either accidentally or intentionally transgress: to lie, to deliver shock, to knock over a table loaded with alphabetized cards, to break a machine, to cheat. Afterward, the guilt-laden participants have been subtly offered a convenient way to relieve their guilt, such as by confessing, by disparaging the one harmed, or by doing a benevolent deed to offset the malevolent one. The results are remarkably consistent: People will do whatever can be done to expunge the guilt and restore their self-image.

Picture yourself as a participant in one such experiment conducted by David McMillen and James Austin (1971) with Mississippi State University students. You and another student, each seeking to earn credit toward a course requirement, arrive for the experiment. Soon after, an accomplice of the experimenter enters, portraying himself as a previous subject looking for a book he had lost. He strikes up a conversation in which he mentions that the experiment involves taking a multiple-choice test, for which most of the correct answers are "B". After the accomplice departs, the experimenter arrives, explains the experiment, then asks, "Has either of you been in this experiment before or heard anything about it?"

Would you lie? The behavior of those who have gone before you in this experiment—100 percent of whom told the little lie—suggests that you would. After you have taken the test (without receiving any feedback on it), the experimenter mentions, "You are free to leave. However, if you have some spare time, I could use your help in scoring some questionnaires." Assuming you have told the lie, do you think you would now be more willing to volunteer some time? Judging from the results, the answer again is yes. On the average, those who had not been induced to lie volunteered only two minutes of time. But those who had lied were apparently eager to redeem their self-image; on the average they offered a whopping sixty-three minutes. One moral of this experiment was well expressed by a seven-year-old girl, who, in one of our own experiments, wrote, "Don't Lie or youl Live with gilt." And if you suffer guilt, you will feel a need to relieve it.

Our eagerness to do good after doing bad reflects both our need to reduce *private* guilt and restore our shaken self-image, and our desire to reclaim a positive *public* image. In an upstate New York shopping center, Dennis Regan and his associates (1972) demonstrated the effect of private guilt by leading women to think they had broken a camera. A few moments later a confederate, carrying a shopping bag with candy spilling out, crossed paths with each woman. Compared to other women who were not put on the guilt trip—only 15 percent of whom bothered to alert the confederate to the spillage—nearly four times as many of the guilt-laden women did so. The guilt-laden women had no need to redeem themselves in the eyes of the confederate. So their helpfulness is best explained as a way of relieving their private guilt feelings. If those feelings can be relieved in other ways—as by confession—then subsequent helping is similarly reduced (Carlsmith et al., 1968).

Closely connected with our private feelings of guilt is our concern for our public image. We are therefore even more likely to redeem ourselves with altruistic behavior when other people know about our misdeeds (Carlsmith & Gross, 1969).

Mood

If guilt increases helping, do other negative feelings, such as sadness, likewise increase helping? If, just after being depressed by a bad grade, you saw someone in front of you spill some papers on the sidewalk, would you be more likely than usual to help? Or less likely?

At first glance, the results are confusing. Putting people in a negative mood (for example, by having them read or think about something sad) sometimes increases altruism, sometimes decreases it. Such an apparent contradiction excites the scientist's detective spirit. Looking more closely, we find clues to an order amidst the confusion. First, the studies in which negative mood decreases helping generally have involved children (Isen et al., 1973; Kenrick et al., 1979; Moore et al., 1973); those that find increased helping usually have studied adults (Aderman & Bekowitz, 1970; Apsler, 1975; Cialdini et al., 1973; Cialdini & Kenrick, 1976). Why, do you suppose, are children and adults affected differently?

Robert Cialdini, Douglas Kenrick, and Donald Baumann (1981; Baumann et al., 1981) surmise that for adults, altruism is self-gratifying. It carries its own inner rewards. Blood donors feel better about themselves for having donated. Thus, when an adult is in a guilty, sad, or otherwise negative mood, a helpful deed (or any other mood-improving experience) can help neutralize the bad feelings. This implies (and experiments confirm) that if someone in a negative mood is first given some other mood boost (for example, finding money, listening to a humorous tape) and then given an opportunity to be helpful, helping will be unaffected by the original negative mood (Cialdini et al., 1973; Cunningham et al., 1980; Kidd & Berkowitz, 1976). Likewise, if people are led to think their mood state has been temporarily fixed by a drug and cannot be changed, then being in a negative mood does not affect their willingness to help (Manucia et al., 1984). To repeat: When being helpful is a way to improve one's mood, a sad adult is helpful.

But why doesn't this work with children? Cialdini, Kenrick, and Baumann argue that altruism is not similarly rewarding for children. When reading stories, early elementary children view unhelpful characters as happier than helpful ones; as children grow older, their views reverse (Perry et al., 1986). Although young children are not without empathy, they do not take much pleasure in being helpful; such behavior is a product of *socialization*, or so Cialdini and his colleagues believe. To test their belief, they had children in early elementary school, late elementary school, and high school reminisce about sad or neutral experiences prior to being given a chance to donate prize coupons privately to other children (Cialdini & Kenrick, 1976). When sad, the youngest children donated slightly less, the middle groups donated slightly more, and the teenage group donated significantly more. Only the teenagers seemed to find generosity a self-gratifying technique for cheering themselves up. As the researchers note, these results are consistent with Donald Campbell's sociobiological view: We are born selfish; thus, altruism must be socially indoctrinated. Such results are, however, also consistent with the view that, like height, altruism naturally grows with age as the child develops the capacity to see things from another person's point of view (Bar-Tal, 1982; Rushton, 1976; Underwood & Moore, 1982). Perhaps some combination of these ideas ("altruism as socialized," "altruism as natural") is even closer to the truth.

Can we conclude that among well-socialized adults the "feel-bad, do-good" phenomenon is always to be expected? No. In the previous chapter, we saw that one negative mood, anger, produces anything but compassion. Another likely exception to the phenomenon is depression, which, more than guilt, deactivates people with a brooding self-concern unaccompanied by social concern (Carlson & Miller, 1987). Yet another exception is profound grief. People who have suffered the loss of a spouse or a child, whether through death or separation, often undergo a period of intense self-preoccupation, a state that makes it difficult to be self-giving (Aderman & Berkowitz, 1983; Gibbons & Wicklund, 1982).

In a powerfully involving laboratory simulation of self-focused grief, William Thompson, Claudia Cowan, and David Rosenhan (1980) had Stanford University students privately listen to a taped description of a person (whom they were to imagine was their best friend of the other sex) dying of cancer. For some, the experiment focused their attention on their own worry and grief:

> He (she) could die and you would lose him, never be able to talk to him again. Or worse, he could die slowly. You would know every minute could be your last time together. For months you would have to be cheerful for him while you were sad. You would have to watch him die in pieces, until the last piece finally went, and you would be alone.

For others, it focused their attention on the friend:

> He spends his time lying in bed, waiting those interminable hours, just waiting and hoping for something to happen. Anything. He tells you that it's not knowing that is the hardest.

The researchers report that, regardless of which tape was heard, the participants were profoundly moved and sobered by the experience, yet not the least regretful of having participated (although some of the participants in a control condition who listened to a boring tape were regretful). Did their mood affect their helpfulness? When immediately thereafter they were given a chance to anonymously help a graduate student with her research, 25 percent of those whose attention had been self-focused did so, while of those whose attention was other-focused, 83 percent helped. The two groups were equally touched. But only the other-focused participants found helping someone especially rewarding. In short, the "feel-bad, do-good" effect seems to occur with people whose attention is focused on others, people for whom altruism is therefore rewarding (Barnett et al., 1980; McMillen et al., 1977). Unless self-preoccupied, sad people are sensitive, helpful people.

So, are happy people unhelpful? Quite the contrary. There are few more consistent findings in the entire literature of psychology: Happy people are helpful people. This effect occurs with both children and adults, regardless of whether the good mood is produced by an ego-boosting success, by pondering happy thoughts, or by any of several other positive experiences. One woman recalled her experience after falling in love:

> At the office, I could hardly keep from shouting out how deliriously happy I felt. The work was easy; things that had annoyed me on previous occasions were taken in stride. And I had strong impulses to help others; I wanted to share my joy. When Mary's typewriter broke down, I virtually sprang to my feet to assist. Mary! My former "enemy"! (Tennov, 1979, p. 22)

In experiments the one helped usually is someone encountered "after" the experiment—someone seeking a donation, an experimenter seeking help with paperwork, a woman who drops papers. Alice Isen, Margaret Clark, and Mark Schwartz (1976) had a confederate who had supposedly spent her last dime on a wrong number call people who, from zero to twenty minutes earlier, had been given a free sample of stationery. As Figure 14-5 indicates, their willingness to relay the phone message rose slightly during the first four or five minutes afterward, perhaps as the gift "sank in" or as they become less distracted. But as the good mood wore off, helpfulness dropped.

If sad people are, at least under some conditions, extra helpful, how can it be that happy people are also helpful? Experiments suggest that several factors are at work (Carlson et al., 1988). Much as negative mood can often be alleviated by positive

FIGURE 14-5
Percentage of those willing to relay a phone message 0 to 20 minutes after receiving a free sample. Of control subjects who did not receive a gift, only 10 percent helped. (Data from Isen et al., 1976.)

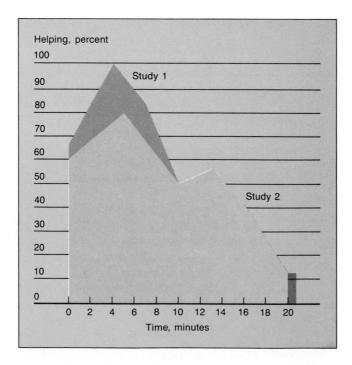

Recall from Chapter 5 the effect of depressed versus happy moods on cognition.

behavior, a positive mood is sustained by positive behavior. A positive mood also is conducive to positive thoughts and positive self-esteem, which help predispose positive behavior (Berkowitz, 1987; Isen et al., 1978). People who are in a good mood, say after being given a gift or while feeling the warm glow of success, are more likely to have positive thoughts and to have positive associations with being helpful. Positive thinkers, it seems, are likely to be positive actors.

Personality Traits

We have thus far seen that the mood and guilt of a person dramatically affect altruism. Are there similar dramatic effects of a person's enduring personality traits? Surely there must be some traits which distinguish the other-focused Albert Schweitzers and Mother Teresas from those blinded by their own self-centeredness.

"There are . . . reasons why personality should be rather unimportant in determining people's reactions to the emergency. For one thing, the situational forces affecting a person's decision are so strong. . . . "
Bibb Latané and John Darley (1970, p. 115)

Surely. But for many years social psychologists were unable to discover a single personality trait that predicted altruistic behavior with anything close to the predictive power of the situational, guilt, and mood factors. Some modest relationships were found between helping and certain personality variables, such as need for social approval. But by and large, the personality tests were unable to identify the helpers.

So, the prevailing conclusion in 1980 was that the situation could powerfully affect one's willingness to help, and that personality made little difference. If that has a familiar ring, it could be from a similar conclusion by conformity researchers (Chapter 7): Conformity, too, seemed influenced greatly by the situation, but essentially unpredictable from personality tests. Perhaps, though, you also recall that who we are does affect what we do. In Chapter 2 we noted that while attitude and trait measures seldom predict a *specific* act (which is what most experiments on altruism measure, in contrast to the lifelong altruism of an Albert Schweitzer), they better predict a person's general behavior across many situations.

Sure enough, personality researchers have responded to the challenge, first by demonstrating that there are individual differences in helpfulness and that these differences persist over time and may be noticed by one's peers (Hampson, 1984; Rushton et al., 1981). Second, researchers are gathering clues to the network of traits that predispose one to helpfulness. Preliminary indications are that those who are high in empathy and self-efficacy are most likely to be helpful (Batson, 1987; Tice & Baumeister, 1985).

Third, personality influences how people react to particular situations (Romer et al., 1986; Wilson & Petruska, 1984). High self-monitoring people, being highly attuned to people's expectations, are especially helpful *if* they are led to think that helpfulness is socially rewarded (White & Gerstein, 1987). People low in self-monitoring, being more internally guided, are less affected by others' opinions of helping.

This interaction of person and situation can also be clearly seen in the 172 studies that have compared the helpfulness of their nearly 50,000 male and female subjects. Digesting the results from all these investigations, Alice Eagly and Maureen Crowley (1986) report that when faced with potentially dangerous situations in which strangers need help (such as with a flat tire or after falling in a subway), men are more likely to help. (Eagly and Crowley also report that among 6767 individuals who have received the Carnegie medal for heroism in saving human life, 90 percent have been men.) But in safer situations, such as volunteering to help with an experiment or spend time with retarded children, women seem slightly more likely to help. Thus the gender difference interacts with (depends upon) the situation. And Eagly and Crowley suspect that if researchers were to study caring behavior in long-term, close relationships rather than in short-term encounters with strangers, they would discover that women are significantly more helpful.

People's long-term altruism is influenced by their personal values. For example, Peter Benson and his colleagues (1980) found that during the preceding year religiously committed Earlham College students recalled volunteering more hours as tutors, relief workers, campaigners for social justice, and so forth than did those who were less religiously committed (see also, Batson & Gray, 1981; Batson & Ventis, 1982.) Future research will no doubt reveal other influences upon people's long-term as well as short-term helpfulness.

HOW CAN HELPING BE INCREASED?

As social scientists, our goal is to understand human behavior, thus also suggesting ways to improve it. Social psychologists therefore wonder how the insights emerging from research on altruism can be used to increase altruism.

UNDOING THE RESTRAINTS ON HELPING

One way to promote altruism is to reverse those factors that inhibit altruism. Given that hurried, preoccupied people are less likely to help, can we think of ways to encourage them to slow down and turn their attention outward? If the presence of others diminishes each bystander's sense of responsibility, how can we enhance a bystander's sense of responsibility?

Reduce Ambiguity, Increase Responsibility

If Latané and Darley's decision tree (Figure 14-3) describes accurately the dilemmas bystanders face, then assisting people to correctly interpret an incident and to assume responsibility should increase their involvement. Leonard Bickman and his colleagues (1975; 1977; 1979) tested this presumption in a series of experiments on crime reporting. In each experiment, supermarket or bookstore shoppers witnessed a shoplifting. Some witnesses had seen signs that attempted both to sensitize them to shoplifting and to inform them how to report it. But the signs had little effect. Other witnesses heard a bystander interpret the incident: "Say, look at her. She's shoplifting. She put that into her purse." (The bystander then left to look for a lost child.) Still others heard this person add, "We saw it. We should report it. It's our responsibility." Both of these face-to-face comments substantially boosted reporting of the crime.

The potency of direct personal influence has been apparent in other research as well. Robert Foss (1978) surveyed several hundred blood donors and found that neophyte donors, unlike veterans, were usually there because someone had personally asked them. Leonard Jason and his collaborators (1984) confirm that personal appeals for blood donation are much more effective than posters and media announcements—if the personal appeals come from friends. Nonverbal appeals also can be effective, when personalized. Mark Snyder and his co-workers (1974) found that hitchhikers doubled the number of rides they were offered by looking drivers straight in the eye. Being personally approached seems to make one feel less anonymous, more responsible.

A similar effect of reduced anonymity was observed in experiments by Henry Solomon and Linda Solomon (1978; Solomon et al., 1981). They found that bystanders

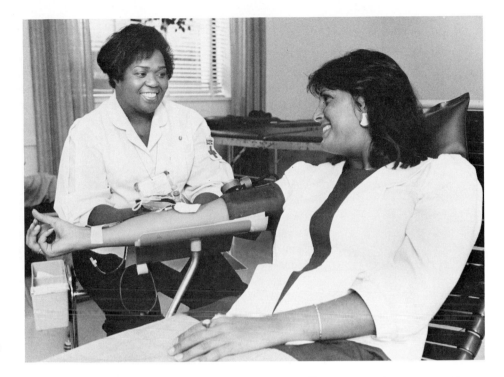

What made this woman agree to give blood?

who had identified themselves to one another by name, age, and so forth were more likely to offer aid to a sick person than were those who remained anonymous. Similarly, when a female experimenter caught the eye of a fellow shopper and gave her a warm smile prior to stepping on an elevator, that shopper was far more likely than other shoppers to offer help when the experimenter later said, "Damn. I've left my glasses. Can anyone tell me what floor the umbrellas are on?" Even a trivial momentary conversation—"Excuse me, aren't you Suzie Spear's sister?" "No, I'm not."—dramatically increased the subsequent helpfulness of the person addressed.

Altruism also increases when one expects later to meet and talk with a victim and other witnesses. Using a laboratory intercom system, Jody Gottlieb and Charles Carver (1980) led University of Miami students to believe they were discussing problems of college living with other students. (Actually, the other discussants were tape-recorded.) When one of the supposed fellow discussants had a choking fit and cried out for help, she was helped most quickly by subjects who believed they would soon be meeting their fellow discussants face to face. In short, anything that personalizes bystanders—a personal request, eye contact, stating one's name, anticipation of interaction—also increases their willingness to act.

Bystanders' feeling that they are being treated personally probably makes them more self-aware and therefore more attuned to their own altruistic ideals. Recall (from Chapters 2 and 9) that people made self-aware (for example, by acting in front of a mirror or TV camera) usually exhibit increased consistency between their attitudes and their actions. By contrast, people who are "deindividuated" tend to be less responsible. This implies that circumstances that increase self-awareness—name tags, being watched and evaluated, undistracted quiet—will also increase altruism. Shelley Duval, Virginia Duval, and Robert Neely (1979) confirmed this supposition by showing

University of Southern California women their own image on a TV screen or having them complete a biographical questionnaire just before giving them a chance to contribute time and money to people in need. Those made self-aware contributed more. Similarly, pedestrians who have just had their picture taken by someone become more likely to help another pedestrian pick up dropped envelopes (Hoover et al., 1983). To be self-aware, yet not self-preoccupied, makes people more likely to enact their ideals.

Guilt and Concern for Self-Image

Earlier we noted that people who have transgressed are eager to reduce their private feelings of guilt and to reestablish their self-worth. Can heightening people's awareness of their transgressions therefore increase their desire to help? A Reed College research team led by Richard Katzev (1978) wondered. So when visitors to the Portland Art Museum disobeyed a "Please do not touch" sign, experimenters reprimanded some of them: "Please don't touch the objects. If everyone touches them, they will deteriorate." Likewise, when visitors to the Portland zoo fed unauthorized food to the bears, some of them were admonished with, "Hey don't feed unauthorized food to the animals. Don't you know it could hurt them?" In both cases, 58 percent of the now guilt-laden subjects shortly thereafter offered help to another experimenter who had "accidentally" dropped something. Of those not so reprimanded, only about one-third helped.

People are also concerned about their public images. This, too, can be used as a means to get them to help others. When Robert Cialdini and his colleagues (1975) asked some of their Arizona State University students to chaperone delinquent children on a zoo trip, only 32 percent agreed to do so. With other students the questioner first made a very large request—that the students commit two years as volunteer counselors to delinquent children. After getting the ***door-in-the-face*** in response to this request (all refused), the questioner then counteroffered with the chaperoning request, saying, in effect, "OK, if you won't do that, would you do just this much?" With this technique, nearly twice as many—56 percent—agreed to help.

Morton Goldman (1986) elicited more frequent agreement to a request for help when he combined the door-in-the-face procedure with the foot-in-the-door procedure (p. 44). When he called a sample of Kansas City residents on behalf of the local zoo and asked their help in stuffing and addressing 75 envelopes, only 22 percent said yes. With others, he first made a hard request—"Would you call 150 people . . . and conduct a survey about the zoo?" After receiving a door-in-the-face, Goldman followed with the 75 envelope request; now, 42 percent salvaged their self-image by saying yes. With yet another group, Goldman followed the door-in-the-face request with an easy foot-in-the-door request for an interview, following which 57 percent agreed to help with the 75 envelopes.

Concern for self-image was also apparent in another experiment, in which Cialdini and David Schroeder (1976) had a solicitor approach suburbanites and say, "I'm collecting money for the American Cancer Society;" 29 percent contributed, averaging $1.44 each. When the solicitor added "Even a penny will help," 50 percent contributed, averaging $1.54 each. When James Weyant (1984) repeated this experiment he found almost identical results: The "even a penny will help" line boosted the number contributing from 39 to 57 percent. And when 6000 people were solicited by mail for the American Cancer Society, those who were asked for small amounts were more likely to give—and gave no less on average—than those asked for larger amounts (Weyant & Smith, 1987). Apparently, it's hard to turn down a request for a paltry contribution and still maintain one's altruistic self-image.

Door-in-the-face technique:
A strategy for gaining a concession in which, after someone is first given opportunity to turn down a large request (the door in the face), the same requester counteroffers with a more reasonable request.

SOCIALIZING ALTRUISM

If altruism is indeed not inborn, but learned, then how can it be taught? Here are three possibilities.

Modeling Altruism

Earlier we learned that when we see our fellow bystanders not respond, we are not likely to help, whereas if we see someone being helpful, we are more likely to offer assistance. A similar modeling effect has been observed within families. Studies of European Christians who risked their lives to rescue Jews, and of the civil rights activists of the late 1950s, revealed that in both cases these exceptional altruists had close relationships with at least one parent who was, similarly, a strong "moralist" or committed to humanitarian causes (London, 1979; Oliner & Oliner, 1988; Rosenhan, 1970). Their family—and often their friends and church—had taught them the norm of helping and caring for others.

Do the effects of positive models extend to television, much as its aggressive portrayals promote aggression? The research indicates that television's prosocial models have actually had even greater effects than its antisocial models. Susan Hearold (1979; also Rushton, 1979) statistically combined 108 comparisons of prosocial versus either neutral programs or no program and found that, on the average, "If the viewer watched prosocial programs instead of neutral programs, he would [at least temporarily] be elevated from the 50th to the 74th percentile in prosocial behavior—typically altruism."

In one such study, researchers Lynette Friedrich and Aletha Stein (1973; Stein & Friedrich, 1972) showed preschool children *Mister Rogers' Neighborhood* episodes each day for four weeks as part of their nursery school program. (*Mister Rogers* is an educational program designed to enhance young children's social and emotional development.) During this viewing period, children from less educated homes became more cooperative, helpful, and likely to state their feelings. In a subsequent study, kindergarteners who viewed four *Mister Rogers* programs were able to state its prosocial content, both on a test and in puppet play (Friedrich & Stein, 1975; also Coates et al., 1976).

Attributing One's Helpful Behavior to Altruistic Motives

Another clue to socializing altruism comes from research on the "overjustification effect": When the justification for an act is overly sufficient, the person may attribute the act to the extrinsic justification rather than to an inner motive. Thus, rewarding people for doing what they would do anyway can undermine their intrinsic motivation. This principle can be stated positively: By providing people with just enough justification to prompt a good deed (weaning them from bribes and threats when possible), we may help maximize their pleasure in doing such deeds on their own.

The overjustification phenomenon has been illustrated by Daniel Batson and his associates (1978; 1979). In several experiments they found that University of Kansas students felt most altruistic after they had agreed to help someone without payment or implied social pressure. When pay had been offered or social pressures were present, people felt less altruistic after helping. In another experiment, students who were drawn into helping someone were led to attribute their doing so either to compliance ("I guess we really don't have a choice") or to compassion ("The guy really needs help . . ."). Subsequently, when the students were asked to volunteer their time to a

"Children can learn to be altruistic, friendly and self-controlled by looking at television programs depicting such behavior patterns."
National Institute of Mental Health, Television and Behavior *1982*

Overjustification effect:
See Chapter 2.

local service agency, 25 percent of those who had been led to perceive their previous helpfulness as mere compliance now volunteered; of those led to see themselves as compassionate, 60 percent volunteered. The moral? Simple: When people wonder, "Why am I helping?" it's best if the circumstances enable them to answer, "Because help was needed and I am a caring, giving, helpful person." Anything beyond that may undermine one's altruistic feeling, as Batson and his coworkers (1987) discovered. They asked people to describe a "situation in which you voluntarily helped someone at considerable cost to yourself" and then to reflect on "why you helped" by writing out the pertinent reasons. Compared to those who did not analyze their reasons for helping, those who did so ended up feeling less selflessly altruistic.

As you may recall from Chapter 2, rewards undermine intrinsic motivation when they function as controlling bribes. An unanticipated compliment, however, can boost intrinsic motivation, by making people feel competent and worthy. When Joe is coerced with "If you quit being chicken and give blood, we'll win the fraternity prize for most donations," he'll likely not attribute his donation to altruism. When Jocelyn is rewarded with "That's terrific that you'd choose to take an hour out of such a busy week to give blood," she's more likely to walk away with an altruistic self-image—and thus to contribute again (J. A. Piliavin et al., 1982; G. C. Thomas & Batson, 1981; Thomas et al., 1981).

Indeed, many people begin giving blood because of the incentives and social pressures for doing so, but then with repeated donations become more and more self-motivated (Callero & Piliavin, 1983). Goodness, like evil, often evolves in small steps. The Gentiles who saved Jews often began with but a small commitment—to hide someone for but a day or two. Having taken that step, they began to see themselves differently, as ones who help, and then to become more intensely involved (Goleman, 1985).

The importance of one's self-image is also apparent in research on the effect of labeling people. After they had made a charitable contribution, Robert Kraut (1973) told some New Haven, Connecticut, women, "You are a generous person." Two weeks later, these women were more willing than those not labeled to contribute to a different charity. Likewise, Angelo Strenta and William DeJong (1981) told some students that their personality test revealed that "You are a kind, thoughtful person." These students were later more likely than other students to be kindly and thoughtful toward a confederate who dropped a stack of computer cards.

Learning about Altruism

Researchers have found another way to boost altruism, one that provides a happy conclusion to our chapter. Some social psychologists have been concerned that as people become more aware of social psychology's findings, their behavior may change, thus invalidating the findings (Gergen, 1973). Will having learned about the factors that inhibit altruism make people less influenced by these factors? Sometimes, such "enlightenment" is not our problem but one of our goals, a goal that leads to more compassionate behavior.

Experiments with University of Montana students by Arthur Beaman and his colleagues (1978) reveal that once people understand why the presence of bystanders inhibits helping, they become more likely to help in group situations. The researchers used a lecture to inform some students how bystanders' refusal to help can affect both one's interpretation of an emergency and one's feelings of responsibility. Other students heard either a different lecture, or no lecture at all. Two weeks later, as part of a different experiment in a different location, the participants found themselves walking (with an unresponsive confederate) past someone slumped over, or past a person sprawled beneath a bicycle. Of those who had not heard the helping lecture, about a fourth paused to offer help; of those "enlightened," twice as many did so.

Coincidentally, shortly before I wrote the last paragraph, a former student, now living in Washington, D.C., stopped by. She mentioned that she recently found herself part of a stream of pedestrians striding past a man lying unconscious on the sidewalk. "It took my mind back to our social psych class and the accounts of why people fail to help in such situations. Then I thought, well, if I just walk by, too, who's going to help him?" So she made a call to an emergency help number and waited with the victim—and other bystanders who now joined her—until help arrived.

SUMMING UP

WHY DO WE HELP ONE ANOTHER?

Three prominent theories attempt to explain altruistic behavior. The *social-exchange theory* assumes that helping, like other social behaviors, is motivated by people's desire to minimize their costs and maximize their rewards—rewards either external (for example, social approval) or internal (for example, reducing distress, increasing self-satisfaction). Other psychologists believe that helping can also be motivated purely by a genuine altruistic concern for another's welfare.

Our willingness to help is also motivated by *social norms*. The *reciprocity norm* stimulates us to return help, not harm, to those who have helped us. The *social-responsibility norm* leads us to feel we should help needy, deserving people, even if they cannot reciprocate.

Sociobiology assumes two types of altruism that are favored by natural selection: devotion to one's kin and reciprocity. However, most sociobiologists believe that the genes of selfish individuals are more likely to survive than the genes of self-sacrificing individuals, and that society must therefore teach altruism.

These three theories complement one another. Each uses psychological, sociological, or biological concepts to account for two types of altruism: (1) an "altruism" of reciprocal exchange—when you scratch my back, I'm more likely to scratch yours—and (2) an unconditional altruism. Yet each theory is vulnerable to charges both of being speculative and of inventing explanations, explanations that more clearly describe than predict altruism.

WHEN WILL WE HELP?

Several situational influences work either to inhibit or to encourage altruism. As the number of bystanders at an emergency increases, any given bystander is (1) less likely to notice the incident, (2) less likely to interpret it as an emergency, and (3) less likely to assume responsibility. This is especially true when the situation is ambiguous, or when the bystanders cannot easily detect one another's alarm.

When are people most likely to help? (1) After observing someone else helping and (2) when not hurried. And *who* are those most likely to elicit our help? (1) Those judged to both need and deserve it and (2) those similar to us.

Helping is further affected by such personal influences as people's moods. After transgressing, one often becomes more willing to offer help, apparently hoping to relieve guilt or to restore one's self-image. People who are sad also tend to be helpful, especially when such behavior is a way to eliminate the mood. However, this "feel-bad, do-good" effect is generally not found in young children, suggesting that the inner rewards of helping are a product of later socialization. Finally, it has consistently been found that happy people are helpful people.

In contrast to altruism's potent situational and mood determinants, personality test scores have served only modestly as predictors of helping. However, new evidence indicates that some people are consistently more helpful than others and that the effect of one's personality or gender may depend on the situation.

HOW CAN HELPING BE INCREASED?

Research suggests that we can enhance helpfulness in two ways. First, reverse those factors that inhibit helping. We can take steps to reduce the ambiguity of an emergency situation, or to increase people's feelings of responsibility (for example, by reducing feelings of anonymity or increasing self-awareness). And we can even use reprimands or the door-in-the face technique to evoke guilt feelings or a concern for people's self-images.

Second, we can teach altruism. For example, research into television's portrayals of prosocial models clearly indicates the medium's power to teach positive behavior. Children who view helpful behavior tend to act similarly. However, if we attempt to coax altruistic behavior from people, we had best also remember the overjustification effect: When either excessive rewards or threats are used to coerce good deeds, people's intrinsic love of the activity often diminishes. If people are provided with enough justification for them to decide to do good, but not much more, they are likely to attribute their behavior to their own altruistic motivation and henceforth be more willing to help.

FOR FURTHER READING

Gilkey, L. (1966). *Shantung Compound.* New York: Harper & Row. A first person account of human nature laid bare among 1800 Westerners crowded into a Japanese internment camp during World War II. Self-centeredness prevailed but was interspersed by incidents of selfless altruism.

Oliner, S. P., & Oliner, P. M. (1988). *The altruistic personality: Rescuers of Jews in Nazi Europe.* New York: The Free Press. From interviews with over 400 European rescuers and nonrescuers, the Oliners explore the moral and social roots of heroic behavior.

Piliavin, J. A., Dovidio, J. F., Gaertner, S. L., & Clark, R. D., III (1981). *Emergency intervention.* New York: Academic Press. Examines factors that influence bystanders' helping in crisis situations.

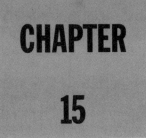

CHAPTER

15

APPLICATION: CONFLICT AND PEACEMAKING

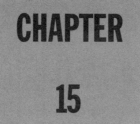

CHAPTER

15

APPLICATION: CONFLICT AND PEACEMAKING

ometimes a destructive drain on human potential; sometimes a constructive stimulus for growth: Such is conflict—conflict between individuals, between groups, between nations. Consider the following instances of each.

Between individuals: George and his roommate are hardly speaking to one another. Apart from a few snide allusions to "the lousy socks on the floor" and "that loud, distracting music," they have each settled into a quiet smolder. The longer silence prevails, the more George assumes his roommate feels hostile, and the more hostile George feels in return. Where will it lead? Will they split? Or will they somehow reach a new understanding that restores the friendship they once enjoyed?

Between groups: Workers at the Acme Manufacturing Company are out on strike. Disgruntled over low pay and minimal benefits, they insist they'll not return without a significant boost in their compensation. The company's reply: "Given your high absenteeism and low productivity, we simply can't afford to meet your demands." Where will it end? Will the strike force the company into bankruptcy and the workers out of their jobs? Or might it be possible to recast the current employer-employee relationship, making possible both higher productivity and profits for the company and higher wages for the workers?

Between nations: There is a speech that has been spoken in many languages, by the leaders of many countries. It goes like this: "The intentions of our country are entirely peaceful. Yet, we are also aware of the world's unrest, and of the threat that other nations, with their new weapons, pose to us. Thus we would be remiss not to take adequate steps to increase our ability to defend against attack. By so doing, we shall protect our way of life and preserve the peace" (L. F. Richardson, 1969). Almost every nation claims concern only for peace but, mistrusting other nations, arms itself in self-defense. The end result: a world in which there are 5 soldiers for every doctor, a world in which every nine hours humanity spends as much on arms as it does annually on the United Nations (Sivard, 1987).

As suggested in these examples, conflict varies. It is at times minimal, at times immense; at times hidden, at times open; at times destructive, at times constructive. Despite such variation, this much can be said for sure: Any time people, or groups, are so bound together that their actions affect one another, conflict is natural and inevitable. Granted, it may be suppressed. But unless the two parties have identical needs and desires, their wishes will sometimes clash. A relationship or an organization without conflict is likely an apathetic one. So conflict is not inherently evil. Rather, it signifies people's involvement, commitment, and caring; if understood, if recognized, it can stimulate renewed and improved human relations. Without conflict, problems seldom are faced and resolved.

Let's clarify our terms. ***Conflict*** is a perceived incompatibility of actions or goals. Whether their perceptions are accurate or inaccurate, people in conflict sense that one side's gain is the other's loss. "I'd like the music off." "I'd like it on." "We want more pay." "We can't give it to you." "We want peace and security." "So do we, but you threaten us."

Peace, in its most positive sense, is more than the suppression of open conflict, more than a tense, fragile, surface calmness. Peace is the outcome of a creatively managed conflict, one in which the parties reconcile their perceived differences and reach genuine accord. "We got our increased pay. You got your increased profit. Now we're helping each other achieve our aspirations."

But what kindles conflict? And what steps can be taken to help transform closed fists into open arms? Social-psychological studies have identified several ingredients of conflict. What's striking (and what simplifies our task considerably) is that these social-

"We . . . are not the creators of tension. We merely bring to the surface the hidden tension that is already alive. We bring it out in the open, where it can be seen and dealt with."
Martin Luther King, Jr.

Conflict:
A perceived incompatibility of actions or goals.

psychological ingredients are common to all levels of social conflict, whether interpersonal conflicts or more complex intergroup or international conflicts.

CONFLICT

As we examine the ingredients of conflict, bear in mind that social psychology provides but one perspective on significant social conflicts. For example, international conflicts also spring from differing histories, ideologies, and economics—all of which are carefully studied by political scientists. Having identified some important elements of conflict, we can then ponder ways to promote peace.

SOCIAL DILEMMAS

Several of the problems that most threaten our human future—the nuclear arms race, the greenhouse effect, pollution, overpopulation, the depletion of natural resources— arise as various parties rationally pursue or protect their self-interest, but do so, ironically, to their collective detriment. Anyone can reason: "It would cost me lots of money to buy expensive pollution controls. And, besides, by itself my pollution is trivial." Many others reason similarly, resulting in befouled air and water. Likewise, in some societies individuals benefit by having lots of children who, it is assumed, can assist with the family tasks and provide security for their parents' old age. But when nearly everyone has lots of children, the end result can be the collective devastation of overpopulation. Therefore, we have an urgent dilemma: How can the well-being of individual parties—their rights to freely pursue their personal interests—be reconciled with the well-being of the community?

Laboratory Dilemmas

To isolate this dilemma, social psychologists have used laboratory games that expose the heart of many real social conflicts. By showing us how well-meaning people become trapped in mutually destructive behavior, they illuminate some fascinating, yet troubling paradoxes of human existence. Consider two examples: the Prisoner's Dilemma and the Commons Dilemma.

The Prisoner's Dilemma

The first and the most widely researched game was derived from an anecdote concerning two suspects who are questioned separately by the district attorney (Rapoport, 1960). They are indeed guilty; however, the DA presently has only enough evidence to convict them of a lesser offense. So the DA offers each a chance to confess privately, explaining that if one confesses and the other doesn't, the confessor will be granted immunity and the confession will be used to convict the other of a maximum offense. If both confess, each will receive a moderate sentence for the lesser offense. If neither confesses, each will receive a light sentence. The dilemma faced by each prisoner can be summarized in the form of a matrix (see Figure 15-1). Faced with such a dilemma, would you confess?

Many would, despite the fact that mutual confession would elicit more severe sentences than would mutual nonconfession. Note from the matrix that no matter what the other prisoner decides, each is better off confessing. If the other confesses, one

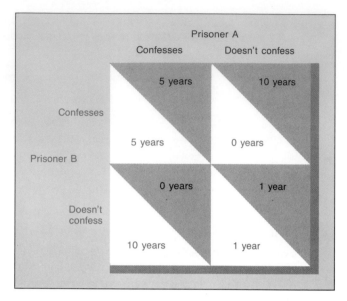

FIGURE 15-1
The Prisoner's Dilemma. In each box, the number above the diagonal is prisoner A's outcome. Thus, if both prisoners confess, both get five years. If neither confesses, each gets a year. If one confesses, that prisoner is set free in exchange for evidence used to convict the other of a crime bringing a ten-year sentence. If you were one of the prisoners, would you confess?

then gets a moderate sentence instead of a severe one. If the other does not confess, one goes free. Of course, each prisoner reasons the same. Hence, the social trap.

In hundreds of experiments, university students have been faced with variations on the Prisoner's Dilemma with the outcomes being not prison terms, but chips, money, or course points. As Figure 15-2 illustrates, on any given decision a person is better off not cooperating (because such behavior either exploits the other's cooperation or protects against exploitation by the other). However—and here's the rub—by mutually not cooperating both parties end up far worse off than if they trusted each other and

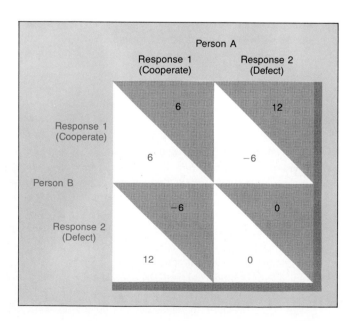

FIGURE 15-2
Laboratory version of the Prisoner's Dilemma. The numbers represent some reward, such as money. In each box, the number above the diagonal line is the outcome for person A.

cooperated. This dilemma often traps each in a maddening predicament, a predicament in which both realize they *could* mutually profit but, mistrusting one another, become "locked in" to not cooperating.

In such dilemmas, the unbridled pursuit of self-interest can be detrimental to all. So it is between the United States and the Soviet Union. A disinterested observer from another planet would likely note that the military policy of "Mutually Assured Destruction" is, as its acronym implies, MAD. As Dwight D. Eisenhower lamented,

> Every gun that is made, every warship launched, every rocket fired signifies, in the final sense, a theft from those who hunger and are not fed, those who are cold and are not clothed. This world in arms is not spending money alone. It is spending the sweat of its laborers, the genius of its scientists, the hopes of its children. . . This is not a way of life, at all, in any true sense. Under the cloud of threatening war, it is humanity hanging from a cross of iron.

It may occasionally be true that maintaining a balance of terror helps prevent a combat that might occur if one nation believed it could easily exploit another's weaknesses. But neither the historical record (Lebow & Stein, 1987) nor the psychological evidence we will consider supports the idea that threatening an enemy with big sticks, such as nuclear weapons, deters wars. More wars were fought during the heavily armed 1980s than in any previous decade in history (Sivard, 1987). Moreover, the people of both nations would surely be more secure if there were no weapons threat, and if their billion-dollar-per-day military spending were made available for productive rather than destructive purposes.

Granted, such a solution is easily said. The dilemma faced by national leaders— and by college students faced with laboratory simulations of the arms-race dilemma— is that one-sided disarmament makes one vulnerable to exploitation. [Indeed, in the

"When multiplied by 2, a national policy of Peace Through Strength leads inevitably to an arms race."
George Levinger (1987)

Mutually destructive conflict. When Iran and Iraq laid down their arms in 1988 after suffering more than a million civilian and military casualties and bankrupting their economies, their borders ended up exactly where they started when their war began eight years earlier.

laboratory, those who adopt an unconditionally cooperative strategy often are exploited (Oskamp, 1971; Reychler, 1979; Shure et al., 1965).] So, alas, the arms race continues.

Unlike the U.S.-U.S.S.R. arms race, many of our other pressing social dilemmas involve numerous participants. The looming greenhouse effect stems mostly from widespread deforestation and from the carbon dioxide emissions of countless cars, oil burners, and coal-fired power plants. Similarly, each of those who pollute and exploit limited natural resources contributes an infinitesimal part of the world's pollution, and the harm each does is diffused over many people. To model such social predicaments, researchers have developed laboratory dilemmas that involve several people.

The Commons Dilemma

A powerful metaphor for the insidious nature of social dilemmas is what ecologist Garrett Hardin (1968) has called the "tragedy of the commons." He derived the name from the pasture often centrally located in old English towns. However, the "commons" can be air, water, whales, cookies, or any jointly used finite resource. If all use the resource in moderation, it may replenish itself as rapidly as it's harvested. The grass will grow, the whales will reproduce, the cookie jar will get restocked.

But imagine 100 farmers surrounding a commons capable of sustaining 100 cows. When each grazes one cow; the common feeding ground is fully used, without being overtaxed. But then one may reason: "If I put a second cow in the pasture, I'll double my output, minus the mere one percent increase in the overcrowding of the meadow." So this farmer adds a second cow. Then so does each of the other farmers. The inevitable result? The tragedy of the commons—an overgrazed mudfield.

Many real-life predicaments parallel this story. Environmental pollution is the sum of many minor pollutions, each of which benefits the individual polluters much more than they could benefit themselves (and the environment) if they stopped only their small "contribution" to pollution. We litter public places—dorm lounges, parks, zoos— but keep our personal spaces clean. And we deplete our natural resources, because the immediate personal benefits of, say, taking a long, hot shower outweigh the costs; the costs appear inconsequential for they are diffused among all. Whalers knew that others would exploit the whales if they didn't and that their taking a few whales would not perceptibly diminish the whale count—and therein lay the tragedy. Everybody's business is nobody's business.

The elements essential to the Commons Dilemma have been isolated in such laboratory games as the following. Put yourself in the place of Arizona State University students playing Julian Edney's Nuts Game (1979a; 1979b). You and several others are sitting around a shallow bowl that initially contains ten metal nuts. The experimenter explains that your goal is to accumulate as many nuts as possible, that each of you at any time may take as many as you want, and that every ten seconds the number of nuts remaining in the bowl will be doubled. Would you leave the nuts in the bowl to regenerate, thus producing a greater harvest for all?

Likely not. Unless they were given time to devise and agree upon a strategy for conservation, 65 percent of Edney's groups never reached the first ten-second replenishment. In fact, often the people knocked the bowl on the floor grabbing for their share. Is such individualism uniquely American? Kaori Sato (1987) gave students in a more communal culture, Japan, opportunities to harvest—for actual money—trees from a simulated forest. When the students shared equally the costs of planting the forest, more than half of the trees were harvested before they had grown to the most profitable size—a result much like that obtained in Western cultures.

Edney's nut bowl and Sato's forest remind me of the cookie jar in our home. What we *should* do is conserve cookies during the interval between weekly restockings, so that each day we can each enjoy two or three. But, lacking regulation and believing that the resource will soon be depleted, what we actually do is maximize our individual cookie consumption by downing one after the other. The result: Within twenty-four hours the cookie glut ends, the jar sits empty, and we are forced to await its replenishment.

The Prisoner's Dilemma and Commons Dilemma games have several similar features. In both, people are tempted to explain their own behavior situationally ("I had to protect myself against exploitation by my opponent") and to explain their partners' behavior dispositionally ("she was greedy," "he was untrustworthy"). Most never realize that their counterparts are viewing them with the same fundamental attribution error.

Second, during the course of entrapment, motives often change. At first, people are eager to make some easy money, then to minimize their losses, and finally to save face and avoid defeat (Brockner et al., 1982; Teger, 1980). These shifting motives are strikingly similar to President Johnson's apparently shifting motives during the buildup of the Vietnam war. At first, his speeches included many positive references to America's concern for democracy, freedom, and justice. As the conflict escalated, his expressed concern became increasingly to protect America's honor and to avoid the national humiliation of losing a war.

Non-zero-sum-games:
Games in which one side's winning need not be balanced by the other's losing; that is, outcomes need not sum to zero. With cooperation, both can win; with competition, both can lose.

Finally, like many real-life conflicts, the Prisoner's Dilemma and Commons Dilemma are **non-zero-sum games:** The two sides' profits and losses need not add up to zero; both can win, both can lose. Each game pits the immediate interests of individuals against the well-being of the group. Each is a diabolical social trap that shows how, even when individuals behave "rationally," harm can result. No malicious person planned for Los Angeles to be smothered in smog, nor for the horrendous destruction of the Vietnam conflict, nor for the earth's atmosphere to be warmed by a blanket of carbon dioxide.

However, we must take care not to overstate the point. Not all self-serving behavior leads to collective doom. In a plentiful commons—as in the world of the eighteenth-century capitalist economist Adam Smith—individuals who seek to maximize their own profit may also give the community what it needs: "It is not from the benevolence of the butcher, the brewer, or the baker, that we expect our dinner, but from their regard to their own interest" (Smith, 1776, p. 18).

But in those situations that are indeed social traps, how can we induce people to cooperate for their mutual betterment?

Resolving Social Dilemmas

Research with the laboratory dilemmas has revealed several methods for promoting cooperation.

Regulation

Reflecting on the Commons Dilemma, Garrett Hardin (1968) observed, "Ruin is the destination to which all men rush, each pursuing his own best interest in a society that believes in the freedom of the commons. Freedom in a commons brings ruin to all." Consider: if taxes were entirely voluntary, how many would pay their full share?

Surely, many would not, which is why modern societies do not depend on voluntary charity to meet their needs for social and military security. We also develop other laws and regulations for our common good. An International Whaling Commission sets an agreed-upon "harvest" that will enable whales to regenerate. The United States and the Soviet Union mutually commit themselves to the Atmospheric Test Ban Treaty that reduces radiation in our common air. When enforced, environmental regulations equalize the burden for all; no steel company need fear that other companies will gain a competitive advantage by disregarding their environmental responsibilities.

Similarly, participants in laboratory games often seek ways to regulate their behavior for what they know to be their common good. For example, players of the Nuts Game may agree to take but one or two nuts every ten seconds, leaving the rest to regenerate, or they may elect a leader to decide each person's share (Messick et al., 1983; Samuelson et al., 1984).

We can see then that regulating behavior is one solution to social dilemmas. But in everyday life, regulation has costs—costs of administering and enforcing the regulations, costs of diminished personal freedom. A volatile political question thus arises: At what point does a regulation's cost exceed its benefits?

Small Is Beautiful

Given the costs of regulation, other ways of resolving social dilemmas are also needed. One suggestion: Keep the group small. In laboratory dilemma games, people who interact with but a few others cooperate more than do those in larger groups (Dawes, 1980). The smaller the commons, the more responsibility each person feels for it, the more effective a contribution each person feels capable of making, and the more identified each person feels with the group's success (Kerr, 1989). Although group identification occurs more readily in small groups, anything that gives people a "we feeling"—even just a few minutes of discussion or just believing that one shares similarities with others in the group—will promote cooperation (Brewer, 1987; Orbell et al., 1988).

"For that which is common to the greatest number has the least care bestowed upon it."
Aristotle

On the Puget Sound island where I grew up, our small neighborhood shared a communal water supply. On hot summer days when the reservoir ran low, a light came on, signaling our fifteen families to conserve. Recognizing our responsibility to one another, each of us conserved. Never did the reservoir run dry. In a much larger commons—say a large city—such voluntary conservation is generally far less successful. The harm one does is diffused across many others. Thus one can rationalize away personal accountability. Some political theorists and social psychologists have therefore argued that, where feasible, the commons should be divided into smaller territories (Edney, 1980). In his 1902 *Mutual Aid*, the Russian revolutionary Pyotr Kropotkin set forth a vision of small communities making decisions for the benefit of all by consensus, thereby reducing the need for central government (Gould, 1988). U.S. Senator Mark Hatfield (1972, 1975) has similarly envisioned neighborhood governments that would take over certain responsibilities for sanitation, beautification, and policing.

Communication

To escape a social trap, people must communicate with one another. In the laboratory, groups able to communicate sometimes degenerate into threats and name calling (Deutsch & Krauss, 1960). But often, communication enables groups to cooperate more—much more (Bornstein & Rapoport, 1988; Jorgenson & Papciak, 1981). Discussing the dilemma not only forges group identity, it also enables people to commit themselves to cooperation, thereby often doubling the actual cooperation.

Open, clear, forthright communication can reduce people's mistrust of one another. Without communication, those who expect others not to cooperate usually refuse to

"My own belief is that Russian and Chinese behavior is as much influenced by suspicion of our intentions as ours is by suspicion of theirs. This would mean that we have great influence on their behavior—that, by treating them as hostile, we assure their hostility."
U.S. Senator J. William Fulbright (1971)

cooperate themselves (Messé & Sivacek, 1979; Pruitt & Kimmel, 1977). One who mistrusts almost has to be uncooperative (to protect against exploitation), and noncooperation is rationalized by further mistrust ("What else could I do? It's a dog-eat-dog world"). In experiments, communication seems to reduce mistrust greatly, enabling people to reach agreements that lead to their common betterment. In times of serious everyday conflict, how can we structure communication in order to produce similar results? To this question, we shall later return.

Changing the Payoffs

Experimenters have repeatedly found that cooperation rises when the pay-off matrix is changed to make cooperation more rewarding, exploitation less rewarding (Pruitt & Rubin, 1986; Komorita & Barth, 1985).

Changing payoffs might likewise help resolve actual dilemmas. In some cities, freeways clog and skies smog because people prefer the convenience of driving themselves directly to work. Each knows that one more car does not add noticeably to the congestion and pollution. To alter the personal cost-benefit calculations, many of these cities now give incentives to carpoolers—faster freeway lanes are designated for their use, while single-occupant cars bide their time in the crowded lanes.

Appeals to Altruistic Norms

In Chapter 14, we noted a social responsibility norm, and saw how increasing people's feelings of responsibility for others can boost altruism. In light of this finding, can we assume that appeals to altruistic motives will therefore prompt people to leash their selfish desires and to act instead for the common good?

The evidence is mixed. On the one hand, it seems that just *knowing* about the dire consequences of noncooperation has little effect. In laboratory dilemma games, people realize that their self-serving choices are mutually destructive, yet they continue to make such choices (Cass & Edney, 1978; Edney & Harper, 1978). Outside the laboratory, warnings of doom and appeals to conserve have triggered little response. Knowing the good does not necessarily lead to doing the good.

Still, most people do have a sense of social responsibility. The problem is how to tap such feelings. When participants in laboratory games are permitted to communicate, frequently they appeal emphatically to the social-responsibility norm: "If you defect on the rest of us, you're going to have to live with it for the rest of your life" (Dawes et al., 1977). Noting this, researcher Robyn Dawes (1980) and his associates gave people a short sermon about group benefits, exploitation, and ethics. Then the people played a dilemma game. The appeal worked. People were convinced to forgo immediate personal gain for the common good.

Could such appeals ever work in large-scale dilemmas? Michael Lynn and Andrew Oldenquist (1986) believe yes. When cooperation obviously serves the public good, one can usefully appeal to the social-responsibility norm. Basketball players will pass up a good shot to offer a teammate a better shot. Struggling for civil rights, many marchers willingly agreed, for the sake of their larger group, to suffer harassment, beatings, and jailings. In wartime, people can be persuaded to make great personal sacrifices for the good of their group. As Winston Churchill said of the Battle of Britain, the actions of the Royal Air Force pilots certainly looked like altruism for the common good: A great many people owed very much to the actions of the relative few who flew into battle knowing the high probability that they would not return.

To summarize, destructive entrapment in social dilemmas can be minimized by establishing rules that regulate self-serving behavior, by keeping groups small, by

"Never in the field of human conflict was so much owed by so many to so few."
Sir Winston Churchill, House of Commons, August 20, 1940

enabling people to communicate, by changing payoffs to make cooperation more rewarding than exploitation, and by invoking altruistic norms.

COMPETITION

In Chapter 11 we noted that racial hostilities arise most often when groups must compete for jobs and housing. When interests clash, conflict erupts. This was powerfully evident in the Shantung Compound, a World War II internment camp into which the Japanese military herded foreigners residing in China. According to one of those interned, theologian Langdon Gilkey (1966), the need to distribute the barely adequate food and floor space provoked frequent conflicts involving people of various types— doctors, missionaries, lawyers, professors, business people, junkies, prostitutes. The potential effects of such competition for space, jobs, and political power has also been tragically evident in Northern Ireland, where since 1969, hostilities between the ruling Protestant majority and the Catholic minority have claimed nearly 3,000 lives. (A comparable proportion of the North American population would number close to 400,000 in the United States and 40,000 in Canada.)

But is it competition itself that provokes such hostile conflicts? Real-life situations are so complex that it is hard to be sure. If competition is indeed responsible, then it should be possible to provoke conflict in an experiment. We would want to randomly divide people into two groups, then have the groups compete for a scarce resource and note what happens. Such is precisely what Muzafer Sherif (1966) and his colleagues did in a dramatic series of experiments with typical eleven- and twelve-year-old boys. After ascertaining what seemed the conditions necessary to provoke hostility between the groups, Sherif introduced these apparent essentials into several three-week summer camping experiences.

In one such study, twenty-two unacquainted Oklahoma City boys were divided into two groups, taken to a Boy Scout camp in separate buses, settled in bunkhouses about a half mile apart, and for most of the first week kept unaware of the other group's existence. By cooperating in various activities—preparing meals, camping out, fixing up a swimming hole, building a rope bridge—each group soon became close-knit. They even gave themselves names: "Rattlers" and "Eagles." Typifying the good feeling, a sign was put up in one cabin: "Home Sweet Home."

Group identity thus established, the stage was set for the conflict. Toward the end of the first week, the Rattlers "discovered the Eagles on 'our' baseball field." Antagonisms soon surfaced. So when the camp staff proposed a tournament of competitive activities between the two groups (baseball games, tugs-of-war, cabin inspections, treasure hunts, and so forth), both groups responded enthusiastically. This was win-lose competition. The spoils (medals, knives) would all go to the tournament victor.

The result? Within several days the camp degenerated into open warfare. It was like a scene from William Golding's novel *Lord of the Flies*, which depicted the social disintegration of some boys of similar age marooned on an island. In Sherif's study, the conflict began with each side calling the other derogatory names during the competitive activities, and soon escalated to "garbage wars" in the dining hall, flag burnings, cabin ransackings, and even fistfights that had to be broken up by the camp staff. Asked to describe the other group, the boys invariably said "they" were "sneaky," "smart alecks," "stinkers," while referring to their own group as "brave," "tough," "friendly."

This win-lose competition had produced intense conflict, negative images of the

Competition kindles conflict. Here, in Sherif's experiment, one group of boys raids the bunkhouse of another.

out-group, and strong in-group cohesiveness and pride. Note that all this occurred without any cultural, physical, or economic differences between the two groups, and with boys who were the "cream of the crop" of their communities. Sherif commented that had you or I visited the camp at this point we likely would have concluded that these "were wicked, disturbed, and vicious bunches of youngsters" (1966, p 85). In fact, their evil behavior was triggered by an evil situation.

Fortunately, Sherif not only made strangers into enemies; he then made the enemies into friends. How? The secret of his peacemaking will be explained shortly.

PERCEIVED INJUSTICE

"That's unfair!" "What a ripoff!" "We deserve better!" Such comments typify conflicts bred by perceived injustice. But what is "justice"? According to some social-psychological theorists, people perceive justice as equity—the distribution of rewards in proportion to individuals' contributions (Walster [Hatfield], et al., 1978). If you and I have a relationship (employer-employee, teacher-student, husband-wife, colleague-colleague), it is equitable if:

$$\frac{\text{My outcomes}}{\text{My inputs}} = \frac{\text{Your outcomes}}{\text{Your inputs}}$$

"Do unto others 20% better than you would expect them to do unto you, to correct for subjective error."
Linus Pauling (1962)

If you contribute more and benefit less than I do, you likely will feel exploited and irritated; I may feel exploitative and guilty. Chances are, though, that you more than I will be sensitive to the inequity and eager to remedy it (Messick & Sentis, 1979; Greenberg, 1986).

While we may agree with the equity principle's definition of justice, we may, however, strongly disagree on whether our relationship is equitable. If two people are colleagues, what will each consider a relevant input? The one who is older may favor basing pay on seniority, the other on current productivity.

Given such a disagreement, whose definition is likely to prevail? More often than not, researchers have found that those with the most social power more successfully convince themselves and others that they deserve what they're getting (Mikula, 1984). Karl Marx anticipated this finding: "The ideas of the *ruling* class are in every epoch the ruling ideas: i.e., the class, which is the ruling material force of society, is at the same time its ruling intellectual force" (Walster et al., 1978, p. 220). This has been called a "golden" rule: Whoever has the gold makes the rules.

As this suggests, the exploiter can relieve guilt by valuing or devaluing inputs so as to justify the existing outcomes. Some men may perceive the lower pay of women as equitable, given women's "less important" inputs. As we noted in Chapter 11, those who inflict harm may even blame the victim, and thus maintain their belief in a just world.

And those exploited? How do they react? Elaine Hatfield, William Walster, and Ellen Berscheid (1978) detect three possibilities. They can accept and justify their inferior position ("We're poor; it's what we deserve, but we're happy"). They can demand compensation, perhaps by harassing, embarrassing, even cheating their exploiter. Or, if all else fails, they may attempt to restore equity by retaliating, perhaps vindictively.

An interesting implication of equity theory—an implication that has been confirmed experimentally—is that the more competent and worthy people feel (the more they value their inputs), the more likely they are to feel that a given outcome is insufficient and thus to retaliate (M. Ross et al., 1971). Intense social protests generally come from those who believe themselves worthy of more than they are receiving. Since 1970, professional opportunities for women have significantly increased (see page 191). Ironically, though understandably to an equity theorist, so have women's feelings that their status is inequitable and that more needs to be done to improve it (Roper, 1985). So long as women compared their opportunities and earnings with other women, they felt generally satisfied. Now that women are more likely to see themselves as men's equals, their sense of relative deprivation has grown (Major, 1987; Major & Testa, 1988).

"Awards should be 'according to merit'; for all men agree that what is just in distribution must be according to merit in some sense, though they do not all specify the same sort of merit."
Aristotle

Critics argue that equity is not the only conceivable definition of justice. (Pause a moment: can you anticipate any other basis for defining justice?) Edward Sampson (1975) says that equity theorists wrongly assume that the economic principles that guide western, capitalist nations are universal. Some noncapitalist cultures define justice not as equity (deservingness) but as equality, or even fulfillment of need: "From each according to his abilities, to each according to his needs." Indeed, when rewards are to be distributed to those within one's group, people socialized under the influence of communally oriented cultures, such as China and India, are more likely to favor need or equality and less likely to favor equity than are their more individualistic American counterparts (Leung & Bond, 1984; Murphy-Berman et al., 1984). And conflict theorist Morton Deutsch (1985) reminds us that, even within individualistic cultures, criteria other than equity sometimes define justice. In a family or an altruistic helping institution, the criterion may be need. In a friendship, it may be equality. In a competitive relationship, the winner may take all the reward.

Indeed, people's criteria for justice do vary. When the appropriate criteria is unclear, men tend to favor making rewards proportional to input, whereas women lean more toward equality; when asked to split rewards between themselves and a partner whose performance has been inferior, men tend to divide them equitably, women to divide them 50-50 (Major & Adams, 1983). When social harmony is stressed, an equality norm often prevails; roommates tend to overlook merit and distribute rewards equally (Austin, 1980). When productivity is stressed, or when people's attention is drawn to their responsibility for the outcomes, equity is favored (Greenberg, 1979, 1980).

Different reward systems have varying effects. Imagine that bonus money was made available to your work group for its efforts on some task. Under which payment system would you work hardest? *Winner-takes-all* (whoever performs best gets the entire bonus)? *Equity* (each paid according to contribution)? *Equality* (all paid the same)? Or *need*? In a series of experiments, Morton Deutsch (1985) found no evidence that people work more productively when their individual earnings are tied to their performance. The Columbia University students who participated in these experiments seemed more motivated by their own needs to excel than by the greater pay they could potentially earn in the winner-takes-all and equity conditions. (Given many other experiments which indicate that behavior is strengthened by positive reinforcement, and given the phenomenon of social loafing by those willing to free ride on others' efforts, one wonders whether Deutsch's finding is applicable in everyday work situations.) Deutsch also reports that compared to competitive payment systems, cooperative systems of distributing rewards have more favorable effects on group morale, friendly feelings, and self-esteem. Moreover, those who care most about such things are more likely to prefer equal or need-based rewards. This helps explain why women are more likely than men to prefer equality or need, for women tend to be less competitive than men and more concerned with others' feelings and harmonious relations (Kahn & Gaeddert, 1985).

How universal, then, is the tendency to define justice as equity? And on what basis *should* rewards be distributed? Need? Equality? Merit? Some combination of these? Such questions are being debated still. However, one thing is clear: One source of human conflict is our varying perceptions of what is fair and what is unjust.

MISPERCEPTION

Recall that conflict is a *perceived* incompatibility of actions or goals. It is important to realize that conflicts often contain but a small core of truly incompatible goals. The bigger problem is their being surrounded by many misperceptions of the other's motives and goals. The Eagles and the Rattlers did indeed have some genuinely incompatible aims. But their hateful perceptions of each other soon subjectively magnified their differences.

In earlier chapters we considered several seeds of such misperception. The *self-serving bias* leads individuals and groups to accept credit for their good deeds and shuck responsibility for bad deeds, without according others the same benefit of the doubt. A tendency to *self-justify* further inclines people to deny the wrong of evil acts that cannot be shucked off. One filters the information and interprets it to fit one's *preconceptions*. Groups frequently *polarize* these self-serving, self-justifying, biasing tendencies. One symptom of *groupthink* is the tendency to perceive one's own group as moral and strong, the opposition as evil and weak. Terrorist acts that are despicable brutality to most people are "holy war" to some Middle Eastern sects. Indeed, the mere fact of being in a group can trigger an *ingroup bias*. And negative *stereotypes*, once formed, are often resilient to contradictory evidence.

Given these seeds of social misperception, it should not surprise us, though it should sober us, to discover that people in conflict frequently form distorted, diabolical images of one another. Yet the types of misperception are intriguingly predictable.

Mirror-Image Perceptions

To a striking degree, the misperceptions of those in conflict are mutual. They tend to attribute the same virtues to themselves and vices to the other. When American psy-

"Solutions to the distribution problem are nontrivial. Children fight, colleagues complain, group members resign, tempers flare, and nations battle over issues of fairness. As parents, employers, teachers, and presidents know, the most frequent response to an allocation decision is 'not fair.' "
Arnold Kahn & William Gaeddert (1985)

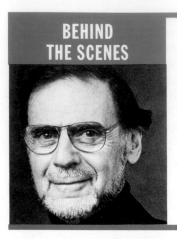

BEHIND THE SCENES

I am brash enough to believe that laboratory studies of conflict can illumine our understanding of the dynamics of war, peace, and social justice. From small groups to nations, the social processes appear similar. Thus social psychologists who study conflict are in much the same position as the astronomers. We cannot conduct true experiments with large-scale social events. But we can identify the conceptual similarities between the large scale and the small, as the astronomers have between the planets and Newton's apple. By experimenting with small-scale social situations, we may thus be able to understand, predict, and influence large-scale social processes. That is why the games people play as subjects in our laboratory may advance our understanding of war, peace, and social justice.

Morton Deutsch,
Columbia University

"The present tensions with their threat of national annihilation are kept alive by two great illusions. The one, a complete belief on the part of the Soviet world that the capitalist countries are preparing to attack it; that sooner or later we intend to strike. And the other, a complete belief on the part of the capitalist countries that the Soviets are preparing to attack us; that, sooner or later, they intend to strike."
General Douglas MacArthur (1966)

chologist Urie Bronfenbrenner (1961) visited Russia in 1960 and conversed with many ordinary citizens in the Russian tongue, he was astonished to hear most Russians saying the same things about America that Americans were saying about Russia. The Soviets said that the U.S. government was militarily aggressive; that it exploited and deluded the American people; that in diplomacy it was not to be trusted. "Slowly and painfully, it forced itself upon one that the Russians' distorted picture of us was curiously similar to our view of them—a mirror image."

More recent analysis of American and Soviet perceptions by psychologists (such as Ralph White, 1984) and political scientists (such as Robert Jervis, 1985) indicate that mirror-image perceptions persist. The American government viewed the Soviet involvement in Afghanistan much as the Soviet government viewed American involvement in Vietnam. As the Soviets viewed American "warmongering" in support of guerrillas trying to overthrow the Nicaraguan government, so Americans viewed the communist "evil empire's" support of guerrillas trying to overthrow the El Salvadoran government. Such mirror-image perceptions fuel a potentially catastrophic arms race. Studies of politicians and political statements reveal that people in both nations (*a*) prefer mutual disarmament to all other outcomes, (*b*) want above all to avoid disarming while the other side arms, but (*c*) perceive the other side as preferring to achieve

FIGURE 15-3
Most conflicts contain a core of truly incompatible goals surrounded by a larger exterior of misperceptions.

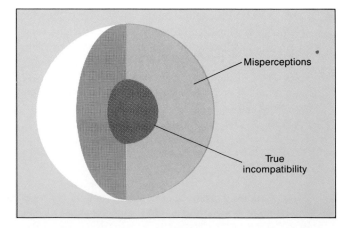

Misperceptions

True incompatibility

TABLE 15-1
Mirror-Image Perceptions: As We See Them, So They See Us

Assumption	Sample Statement by President Reagan	Sample Statement by the Soviet General Secretary
1: "We prefer mutual disarmament."	"We want more than anything else to join with them in reducing the number of weapons." (*New York Times*, 6/15/84)	"We do not strive . . . for military superiority over them; we want termination, not continuation of the arms race." (*New York Times*, 3/12/85)
2: "We must avoid disarming while the other side arms."	"We refuse to become weaker while potential adversaries remain committed to their imperialist adventures." (*New York Times*, 6/18/82)	"Our country does not seek [nuclear] superiority, but it also will not allow superiority to be gained over it." (*Pravda* 4/9/84)
3: "Unlike us, the other side aims for military superiority."	"For the Soviet leaders peace is not the real issue; rather, the issue is the attempt to spread their dominance using military power." (*New York Times*, 6/28/84)	"The main obstacle—and the entire course of the Geneva talks is persuasive evidence of this—is the attempts by the U.S. and its allies to achieve military superiority." (*Pravda*, 1/13/84)

Adapted from Plous, 1985.

military superiority (Plous, 1985—see Table 15-1). Thus though both nations claim to prefer disarmament, both feel compelled to arm themselves to counter the other's weapons buildup.

In times of tension—as prevails during international crisis—rational thinking becomes more difficult (Janis, 1988). Views of the enemy become more rigid and stereotyped, and premature seat-of-the-pants judgments become more likely. Social psychologist Philip Tetlock (1988) observed this phenomenon when analyzing the complexity of Soviet and American rhetoric since 1945. During the Berlin blockade, the Korean War, and the Soviet invasion of Afghanistan, political statements became simplified into stark, good-versus-bad terms. At other times—most notably since Mikhail Gorbachev became General Secretary of the Soviet Union (see Figure 15-4)—political statements have more often acknowledged that each country's motives are complex. Such shifts away from simplistic we-are-good-they-are-bad rhetoric have typically preceded new U.S.-Soviet agreements, reports Tetlock. Tetlock's optimism was confirmed when President Reagan in 1988 traveled to Moscow to sign the American-Soviet intermediate-range nuclear force (INF) treaty, and then Gorbachev visited New York and told the United Nations that he would remove 500,000 Soviet troops from Eastern Europe and suggested that

> We should jointly seek the way leading to the supremacy of the universal human idea over the endless multitude of centrifugal forces. . . I would like to believe that our hopes will be matched by our joint effort to put an end to an era of wars, confrontation and regional

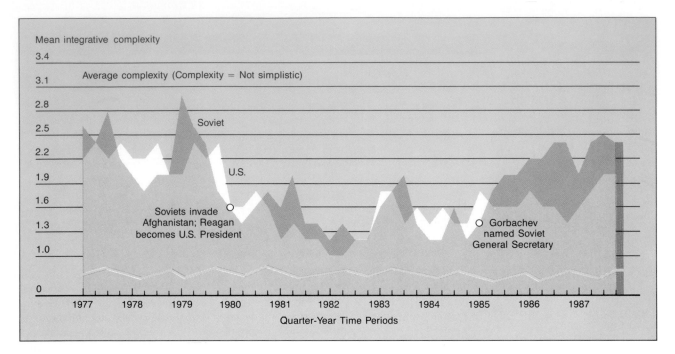

Mean integrative complexity

Average complexity (Complexity = Not simplistic)

Soviet

U.S.

Soviets invade
Afghanistan; Reagan
becomes U.S. President

Gorbachev
named Soviet
General Secretary

Quarter-Year Time Periods

FIGURE 15-4
Complexity of official U.S. and
Soviet policy statements,
1977–1986. (From Tetlock,
1988.)

conflicts, to aggressions against nature, to the terror of hunger and poverty as well as to political terrorism. This is our common goal and we can only reach it together.

When, however, two sides see things discordantly, at least one of the two is misperceiving the other. And when such misperceptions exist, noted Bronfenbrenner, "It is a psychological phenomenon without parallel in the gravity of its consequences . . . for *it is characteristic of such images that they are self-confirming.*" As we have seen before, if A expects B to be hostile, A may treat B in such a way that B fulfills A's expectations, thus beginning a vicious circle. Morton Deutsch (1986) explains: "You hear the false rumor that a friend is saying nasty things about you; you snub him; he then badmouths you, confirming your expectation. Similarly, if the policy-makers of East and West believe that war is likely and either attempts to increase its military security vis-a-vis the other, the other's response will justify the initial move."

Mirror-image perception:
Reciprocal views of one another often held by parties in conflict; for example, each may view itself as moral and peace-loving and the other as evil and aggressive.

Some observers of the Arab-Israeli conflict have similarly concluded that negative ***mirror-image perceptions*** are a chief obstacle to peace. Both sides insist that "we" are motivated by our need to protect our security and our territory, while "they" want to obliterate us and gobble up our land (R. K. White, 1977; Heradstveit, 1979). Both sides have difficulty appreciating how their own actions sustain the other's fear and anger. Given such intense mistrust, negotiation is next to impossible.

Destructive mirror-image perceptions also operate in conflicts between small groups and even between individuals. As we saw in the dilemma games, both parties may say, "We want to cooperate. But their refusal to cooperate forces us to react defensively." In a study of executives, Kenneth Thomas and Louis Pondy (1977) uncovered similar self-serving attributions. Asked to describe their behavior during a significant recent conflict, 74 percent perceived themselves as cooperative, 21 percent as competitive. Only 12 percent felt the other party was similarly cooperative; 73

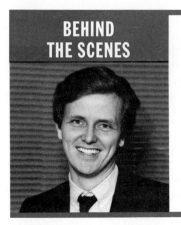

BEHIND THE SCENES

For ten years we have been studying policymakers' styles of reasoning when explaining and justifying their views. Using methods developed in social psychological experiments, we code their statements along dimensions such as simplicity (all considerations point to one conclusion; alternate ways of looking at issues are not weighed) versus complexity (competing considerations are weighed against each other). In examining the speeches and policy statements of European leaders prior to World War I, Japanese leaders prior to World War II, British parliamentarians, Soviet leaders since World War II, and American presidents and senators, we discovered that their reasoning styles provide clues to their momentous future decisions.

Philip Tetlock,
University of California, Berkeley

percent judged the other party as competitive. The executives explained that they had "suggested," "informed" and "recommended," while their antagonist had "demanded," "disagreed with everything I said," and "refused."

The Blacktop Illusion

Blacktop illusion:
The belief that the real enemy is the other group's leaders, who intimidate and mislead their innocent people.

International conflicts are also fueled and prolonged by what Ralph White (1969) has called the *blacktop illusion:* The enemy's top leaders are perceived as evil and coercive; their people, though controlled and manipulated, are seen as much more pro-us. Such beliefs have characterized Americans' and Russians' views of each other. Likewise, the United States entered the Vietnam war believing that in areas dominated by the communist Vietcong "terrorists," many of the people were our allies-in-waiting. As suppressed information later revealed, these beliefs were mere wishful thinking. White wondered:

> Suppose our policy-makers had known that most of the emotionally involved [Vietnamese] people were against us, and had known it clearly, at the time they were making those fateful commitments and staking American prestige on the outcome. . . . Would we now have all the tragedy of the Vietnam War? . . . I doubt it. (p. 37)

The blacktop illusion serves several psychological functions. It reinforces one's own "good intentions." It provides a convenient devil—the leaders—on whom to focus hostility. And it provides hope that the other group's people, if no longer intimidated, would gladly overthrow those who are controlling them and rally to the correct side, one's own.

Shifting Perceptions

If misperceptions accompany conflict, then they should appear and disappear as conflicts wax and wane. And so they do, with startling ease. The same processes that create the enemy's image can reverse that image when the enemy becomes an ally. Thus the "bloodthirsty, cruel, treacherous, buck-toothed little Japs" of World War II became soon after—in American minds (Gallup, 1972) and in the American media—our "intelligent, hardworking, self-disciplined, resourceful allies." Our World War II allies, the Russians, now became the "warlike, treacherous" ones. The Germans, whom Americans after two world wars hated, then admired, and then again hated, were once again admired—apparently no longer plagued by what earlier was presumed to be cruelty in their national character. And within the memory of many of us, the supposedly despicable Chinese "Reds" whom Americans fought in North Korea have become the more gracious, industrious people of the enchanting Republic of China. Clearly, our images of those with whom we are in conflict not only justify our actions, but also are adjusted with amazing ease.

The exent of misperceptions during conflict provides a chilling reminder that people need not be insane or abnormally evil to form distorted, diabolical images of their antagonists. When in conflict with another nation, another group, or simply a roommate or parent, we readily develop a host of misperceptions that allow us to perceive our own motives and actions as wholly good, the other's as evil. And our antagonists most likely form a mirror-image perception of us. So the conflict continues until something enables us both to peel away our misperceptions and work at reconciling our actual differences.

PEACEMAKING

We have seen how conflicts are ignited: by social traps, perceived injustices, competition, and social misperceptions. The picture indeed appears grim. But the reality is not hopeless. Sometimes hostilities are transformed into friendships, conflicts into harmony. Social psychologists have focused their research upon four possible strategies for helping enemies become comrades. These might be called the four C's of peacemaking: contact, cooperation, communication, conciliation.

CONTACT

Might putting two conflicting individuals or groups into close contact enable them better to know and like each other? We have previously noted some reasons why it might. In Chapter 13, we saw that proximity—and the accompanying interaction, anticipation of interaction, and mere exposure—boosts liking. In Chapter 2, we noted that the recent downturn in blatant racial prejudice in the U.S. followed closely on the heels of desegregation, seemingly illustrating the principle that "attitudes follow behavior." [If this social-psychological principle now seems obvious, remember, that's how things usually seem—once you know them. To the U.S. Supreme Court in 1896 (Plessy v. Ferguson) the idea that desegregated behavior might influence racial attitudes was anything but obvious. What seemed obvious at the time was that "Legislation is powerless to eradicate racial instincts."]

During the last thirty years in the United States, segregation and prejudice have diminished together. But was interracial contact the *cause* of these improved attitudes? Were those who actually experienced desegregation affected by it?

Does Desegregation Improve Racial Attitudes?

School desegregation has produced measureable benefits, such as small improvements in Black reading achievement at no costs in White achievement and leading more Blacks to attend and succeed in college (Stephan, 1988). Does desegregation of neighborhoods,

Does desegregation encourage
unbiased racial attitudes?

workplaces, and schools also produce favorable social consequences? The evidence is mixed. On the one hand, many studies conducted during and shortly after the desegregation following World War II found Whites' attitudes toward Blacks improving markedly. Whether the people were department store clerks and customers, merchant marines, government workers, police officers, neighbors, or students, racial contact led to diminished prejudice (Amir, 1969; T. F. Pettigrew, 1969). For example, near the end of World War II, the Army partially desegregated some of its rifle companies (Stouffer et al., 1949). When asked their opinions of such desegregation, 11 percent of the White soldiers in segregated companies, and 60 percent of those in desegregated companies, approved.

When Morton Deutsch and Mary Collins (1951) took advantage of a made-to-order natural experiment, they observed similar results. In accordance with state law, two New York City public housing units were desegregated; families were assigned apartments at random, without regard to race. In a similar development in nearby Newark, Blacks and Whites were assigned to separate buildings. When a survey was conducted with White women in the two developments, those in the desegregated development were far more likely to favor interracial housing and to say that their attitudes toward Blacks had improved. Exaggerated stereotypes had wilted in the face of reality. As one woman, put it, "I've really come to like it. I see they're just as human as we are."

These encouraging findings influenced the Supreme Court's 1954 decision to desegregate U.S. schools and helped fuel the civil rights movement of the 1960s (Pettigrew, 1986). Yet studies of the effects of school desegregation have been less encouraging. Social psychologist Walter Stephan (1986) reviewed all such studies and concluded that racial attitudes have not been much affected by desegregation. Sometimes desegregation has been followed by increased prejudice (especially by Whites toward Blacks) and sometimes it has been followed by decreased prejudice (especially by Blacks toward Whites). But on balance the effects seem minimal for both Black and White students. For Blacks the more noticeable consequence of desegregated schooling is a long-term one—an increased likelihood of enrolling in integrated (or predominantly White) colleges, of living in integrated neighborhoods, and of working in integrated settings.

Some readers may be bewildered by such conflicting evidence; sometimes desegregation improves racial attitudes, sometimes it doesn't. But as we have seen before, such disagreements excite the scientist's detective spirit. When one set of research findings points to one conclusion and another to a differing one, an important factor is probably at work. So far, we've been lumping all desegregation together. Actual desegregation occurs in many ways, and under vastly different conditions. So it is surely an oversimplification to say that desegregation, per se, has either this effect or that.

When Does Desegregation Improve Racial Attitudes?

To discern the crucial differences between our two sets of studies we can compare the two in detail. But there is a simpler method. Drawing upon theories developed from laboratory research, we can speculate what factors might make a difference, and then see whether these factors are indeed present in one set of studies but not the other.

Let us go back to where we began: Is the amount of interracial *contact* a factor? Indeed it seems to be. Researchers have gone into dozens of desegregated schools and observed with whom children of a given race eat, loiter, and talk. Though less decisive than sex, race is nevertheless a potent factor. Whites disproportionately associate with Whites, Blacks with Blacks (Schofield, 1982, 1986). And academic tracking programs often amplify such resegregation by separating academically advantaged White students into predominantly White classes. Researchers Andrew Sagar and Janet Ward Schofield (1980a) conclude that "simply throwing alienated groups together in the same school offers little hope of . . . dispelling the misunderstandings, biases, and fears which continue to divide the American people."

In contrast, the more encouraging older studies of store clerks, soldiers, and housing project neighbors involved considerable interracial contact. More recent studies involving prolonged, personal contact—between Black and White prison inmates, and between Black and White girls in an interracial summer camp—have shown similar benefits of contact (Clore et al., 1978; Foley, 1976).

Note that the social psychologists who advocated desegregation never claimed that contact of *any* sort would improve attitudes. They expected less than favorable results from contacts that were competitive, unsupported by authorities, and unequal (Pettigrew, 1988; Stephan, 1987). Prior to 1954, many prejudiced Whites had ample contact with Blacks—with the latter in subordinate roles as slaves, shoe-shine boys, and domestic workers. But as we saw in Chapter 11, contacts on such an unequal basis breed attitudes that merely justify the continuation of such relations. So it's important that people in contact have **equal status**. Such were the contacts between the store clerks, the soldiers, the neighbors, the prisoners, the summer campers.

Equal-status contact:
Just as a relationship between people of unequal status breeds attitudes consistent with their relationship, so do relationships between those of equal status. Thus, to reduce prejudice, interracial contact should be between persons equal in status.

This kind of contact has been lacking in desegregated schools: Researchers report that White students are generally more active, more influential, more successful (E. G. Cohen, 1980a; Riordan & Ruggiero, 1980). When an eighth-grade Black girl from an academically inferior school is dropped suddenly into a predominantly White middle-class junior high school with White middle-class teachers who expect less of her, chances are she will be perceived both by her classmates and herself as having lower academic status.

COOPERATION

Though equal-status contact can help, it is sometimes not enough. It didn't help when Sherif terminated the Eagles versus Rattlers competition and brought the groups together for noncompetitive activities such as watching movies, shooting off fireworks, and eating. By this time, their hostility was so strong that mere contact provided the opportunity for taunts and attacks. When an Eagle was bumped by a Rattler his fellow Eagles urged him to "brush off the dirt." Obviously, desegregating the two groups had hardly promoted their social integration.

Given such preexisting hostilities, it may seem that bringing about peace is hopeless. What can a peacemaker do? Think back to some of the successful and unsuccessful desegregation efforts. The Army's racial mixing of rifle companies not only brought Blacks and Whites into equal-status contact, but also made them interdependent. Together, they were fighting against a common enemy, striving toward a shared goal.

Contrast this interdependence with the competitive situation found in the typical school classroom, desegregated or not. There, students compete for good grades, teacher approval, and various honors and privileges. Is the following scene familiar (Aronson, 1980)? The teacher asks a question. Several students' hands shoot up; other students sit, eyes downcast, trying to look invisible. When the teacher calls on one of the eager faces, the others hope for a wrong answer, giving them a chance to display their knowledge. Those who fail to answer correctly, and those with the downcast looks who already feel like losers in this academic sport, often resent those who succeed. The situation abounds with both competition and painfully obvious status inequalities; it could hardly be better designed to create divisions among the children.

Does this suggest a second factor that predicts whether the effect of desegregation will be favorable? Does competitive contact divide and cooperative contact unite? Let's examine what happens to people who together face a common predicament or work together toward a shared goal.

Common External Threats

Together with others, have you ever been victimized by the weather; harrassed as part of your initiation into a group; punished by a teacher; or persecuted and ridiculed because of your social, racial, or religious identity? If so, you may recall sharing feelings of closeness with those who faced the predicament with you. Perhaps previous social barriers were dropped as you helped one another dig out of the snow or struggled to cope with your common enemy.

Such friendliness is what research on experiencing a shared threat leads us to expect. John Lanzetta (1955) observed such a phenomenon thirty years ago when he put four-man groups of Naval ROTC cadets to work on several problem-solving tasks, and then began informing them over a loudspeaker that their answers were wrong, their productivity inexcusably low, their thinking stupid. Other groups did not receive this harassment. Lanzetta observed that the group members under duress became friendlier to one another, more cooperative, less argumentative, less competitive. They were in it together. And the result was a cohesive spirit.

The unifying effect of having a common enemy was also evident within the groups of competing boys in Sherif's camping experiments, and in many subsequent experiments (K. L. Dion, 1979). America's conflicts with Germany and Japan during World War II, and with Iran during 1980, aroused Americans' feelings of patriotism and heightened their sense of unity. Our enemy's enemy becomes our friend (Aronson & Cope, 1968). Times of interracial strife may therefore be times of heightened group pride. Just being reminded of an outgroup (say, a rival school) heightens people's responsiveness to their own group (Wilder & Shapiro, 1984). When keenly conscious of who "they" are, we also know who "we" are.

Leaders have even been known to create a threatening external enemy as a technique for building group cohesiveness. George Orwell's novel *Nineteen Eighty-Four* illustrates the tactic: The leader of the protagonist nation uses border conflicts with the other two major powers to lessen internal strife. From time to time the enemy shifts, but there is always an enemy. Indeed, the nation seems to *need* an enemy. For the world, for a nation, for a group, having a common enemy is powerfully unifying. Soviet Foreign Ministry spokesperson Gennady Gerasimov (1988) seemed to recognize this during the Reagan-Gorbachev Moscow summit. "We are going to do something awful to you," he explained to a U.S. television audience. "We are going to deprive you of an enemy."

"I couldn't help but say to [Mr. Gorbachev], just think how easy his task and mine might be in these meetings that we held if suddenly there was a threat to this world from some other species from another planet. [We'd] find out once and for all that we really are all human beings here on this earth together."
Ronald Reagan, December 4, 1985, speech

Superordinate Goals

Superordinate goal:
A shared goal that necessitates cooperative effort; a goal that overrides people's differences from one another.

Closely related to the unifying power of an external threat is the unifying power of *superordinate goals*, goals compelling for all in a group and requiring cooperative effort. To promote harmony among his warring campers, Sherif introduced such goals. He created a problem with the camp water supply, necessitating their cooperation to restore the water. Later, when given an opportunity to rent a movie, one expensive enough to require the joint resources of both groups, they again cooperated. When a truck "broke down" on a camping trip, a staff member casually left the tug-of-war rope nearby, prompting one boy to suggest that they all pull the truck to get it started. When it did, a backslapping celebration ensued over their victorious "tug-of-war against the truck."

After working together to achieve such superordinate goals, the boys began eating together and enjoyed themselves around a campfire. Friendships sprouted across group lines. Hostilities plummeted (see Figure 15-5). And, on the last day, the boys agreed they wanted to travel home together on one bus. During the trip they no longer sat by groups. As the bus approached Oklahoma City and home, they as one spontaneously sang "Oklahoma" and then bade their friends farewell. With isolation and competition, Sherif had made strangers into bitter enemies. With superordinate goals, he had made enemies into friends.

Are Sherif's experiments mere child's play? Or can pulling together to achieve superordinate goals be similarly beneficial with conflicting groups of adults? Robert Blake and Jane Mouton (1979) wondered. So in a series of two-week experiments involving more than 1000 executives in 150 different groups, they recreated the essential features of the situation experienced by the Rattlers and Eagles. Each group first engaged in activities by itself, then competed with another group, and then co-

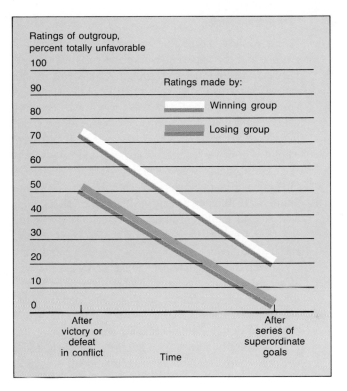

FIGURE 15-5

After competition, the Eagles and Rattlers rated each other unfavorably. After working cooperatively to achieve superordinate goals, hostility dropped sharply. (Data from Sherif, 1966, p. 84.)

operated with the other group in working toward superordinate goals decided upon by both. Their results were indeed similar to Sherif's, providing, in the words of the researchers, "Unequivocal evidence that adult reactions parallel those of Sherif's younger subjects."

Extending these findings, Samuel Gaertner and his collaborators (1988, 1989) report that working cooperatively has especially favorable effects under conditions that lead people to define a new, inclusive group that dissolves their former subgroups. If, for example, the members of two groups are seated alternately around a table (rather than on opposite sides), give their new group a single name, and then work together, their old feelings of bias against the former outsiders will diminish. During World War II, the United States and the U.S.S.R. along with other nations formed one united group, named "the Allies," to combat Nazi Germany. So long as the superordinate goal of defeating their common enemy lasted, U.S. attitudes toward the Soviets greatly improved.

Now, however, recall that all the cooperative efforts by Rattlers and Eagles ended in success. Would the same harmony have emerged if the water had remained off, the movie unaffordable, the truck still stalled? Likely not. In experiments with University of Virginia students, Stephen Worchel and his associates (1977, 1978, 1980) confirmed that *successful* cooperation between two groups boosts their attraction for one another. However, if previously conflicting groups *fail* in a cooperative effort, *and* if conditions allow them to attribute their failure to each other, their conflict may actually be worsened. Sherif's groups were already feeling hostile to one another, so we can speculate that failure to raise sufficient funds for the movie might have been attributed to the "stinginess" and "selfishness" of the other group, and thus might have exacerbated rather than alleviated their conflict.

Cooperative Learning

So far we have noted the apparently meager social benefits of typical school desegregation, and the apparently dramatic social benefits of successful, cooperative contacts between members of rival groups. Could putting these two findings together suggest a constructive alternative to traditional desegregation practices? Several independent research teams speculated "yes." Each wondered whether, without hurting academic achievement, one might promote interracial friendships by replacing competitive learning situations with cooperative ones. Given the diversity of their methods, their consistently positive results are striking and very heartening.

Are students who participate in already existing cooperative activities, such as interracial athletic teams and class projects, less prejudiced? Robert Slavin and Nancy Madden (1979) analyzed survey data from 2400 students in seventy-one American high schools and found encouraging results. Those of different races who play and work together are more likely to report having friends of another race and to express positive racial attitudes.

From this correlational finding can we conclude that cooperative interracial activity at school improves racial attitudes? One way to find out is to experiment. Randomly designate some students to work together in racially mixed groups. For example, Slavin (1985) and his colleagues divided dozens of classes into interracial "teams," each composed of four or five students from all achievement levels. The team members sit together, study a variety of subjects together, and at the end of each week compete with the other teams in a class tournament. All team members can contribute to their team's score by doing well, sometimes by competing with other students whose recent achievements are similar to their own, sometimes by competing with their own previous scores. Therefore everyone stands a chance to succeed, and the team's members are motivated to help one another prepare for the weekly tournament—perhaps by drilling each other on fractions, or spelling, or historical events—whatever is the next event. Competition is thus used not to isolate students from one another but to bring them into closer contact and to draw out their mutual support.

Another research team, led by Elliot Aronson (1978, 1979, Aronson & Gonzalez, 1988), elicited similar group cooperation with a "jigsaw" technique. In experiments in elementary schools in Texas and California, children were assigned to racially and academically diverse six-member groups. The material to be learned was then divided into six parts, with each student becoming the expert on his or her part. For example, in a unit on Chile, one student might be the expert on Chile's history, another on its geography, another on its culture, and so on. First, the various "historians," "geographers," and so forth got together to master their material. Then they each returned to their home group to teach it to their classmates. Each group member held, so to speak, a•piece of the jigsaw. Note that the self-confident students had therefore to draw out and listen to the normally more reticent students, who in turn could soon realize that they had something important to offer their peers.

Other research teams—led by David Johnson and Roger Johnson (1987, 1989) at the University of Minnesota, Elizabeth Cohen (1980b) at Stanford University, Shlomo Sharan and Yael Sharan (1976) at Tel Aviv University, and Stuart Cook (1985) at the University of Colorado—have devised additional methods for cooperative learning. From all this research, what can we conclude? The investigators speak for themselves. Slavin (1980) observes that cooperative learning is an "effective means of increasing positive race relations and achievement in desegregated schools." Aronson reports that "children in the interdependent, jigsaw classrooms grow to like each other better, develop a greater liking for school, and develop greater self-esteem than children in traditional classrooms" (1980, p. 232). Researchers also note that cross-racial friendships begin to blossom, that the exam scores of minority students improve (perhaps because academic achievement is now peer-supported), and that many teachers continue using cooperative learning after the experiments are over (D. W. Johnson et al., 1981). "It is clear," wrote race-relations expert John McConahay (1981), that cooperative learning "is the most effective practice for improving race relations in desegregated schools that we know of to date." So encouraging are the results that more than 25,000 teachers have already utilized interracial cooperative learning in their classrooms (Kohn, 1987).

Should we have "known it all along"? At the time of the 1954 Supreme Court decision, Gordon Allport spoke for many social psychologists in predicting that "Prejudice . . . may be reduced by equal status contact between majority and minority groups in the pursuit of common goals" (1954, p. 281). Unfortunately, school desegregation did not usually meet these conditions. Rather, it was carried out under conditions already known to minimize its effectiveness, and did little if anything to improve student achievement, self-esteem, and race relations (Cook, 1985). The experiments that designed and then tested the results of a more constructive method of desegregation have confirmed Allport's insight. Robert Slavin (1985) is therefore optimistic: "Thirty years after Allport laid out the basic principles operationalized in cooperative

As the Pennsylvania Amish experience when they meet to help a neighbor build a barn, successful cooperation builds cohesiveness.

learning methods, we finally have practical, proven methods for implementing contract theory in the desegregated classroom."

So, because cooperative, equal-status contacts exert a positive influence upon boy campers, industrial executives, college students, and schoolchildren, can we assume that the principle extends to all levels of human relations? Are families unified by pulling together to farm the land, restore an old house, or sail a sloop? Are communal identities forged by barn raisings, group singing, or cheering on the football team? Is international understanding bred by international collaboration in science and space, by joint efforts to feed the world and conserve resources, by friendly personal contacts between people of different nations? Indications are that the answer to all these questions is yes (Brewer & Miller, 1988; Deutsch, 1985). Thus an important challenge facing our divided world is to identify and agree on our superordinate goals, and to structure cooperative efforts to achieve them.

COMMUNICATION

Conflicting parties have several other means by which they can try to resolve their differences. When husband and wife, or labor and management, or nation X and nation Y disagree, they can **bargain** with one another directly; they can ask a third party to **mediate** by making suggestions and facilitating their negotiations; or they can **arbitrate** by submitting their disagreement to someone who will study the issues and impose a settlement.

Bargaining

When conflicts are neither intense nor at an impasse, people usually prefer to bargain on their own (J. Z. Rubin, 1980). If you or I want to buy or sell a new car or house, are we better off adopting a tough bargaining stance—opening with an extreme offer so that splitting the difference will yield a favorable result? Or are we better off beginning with a sincere "good-faith" offer?

Experiments suggest no simple answer. On the one hand, those who demand more will often get more (Deutsch, 1980). This finding, obtained in many laboratory studies, was confirmed by Robert Cialdini, Leonard Bickman, and John Cacioppo (1979) in an actual car sale. In a control condition, they approached various Chevrolet dealers and asked the price of a new Monte Carlo sports coupe with designated options. In an experimental condition, they approached other dealers and first struck a tougher bargaining stance, asking for and rejecting a price on a *different* car ("I need a lower price than that . . . That's a lot"). When they then asked the price of the Monte Carlo, exactly as in the control condition, they received offers that averaged some $200 lower.

Tough bargaining may lower the other party's expectations, making the other side willing to settle for less (Yukl, 1974). But being tough can sometimes backfire. Many a conflict is not over a pie of fixed size, but over a pie that may shrink if the conflict continues. When a strike is prolonged, both labor and management are the losers. Being tough can also diminish the chances of actually reaching an agreement. If the other party responds with an equally extreme position, both may be locked into positions from which neither can back down without losing face.

Mediation

In such situations, a third-party mediator may be able to offer suggestions that enable the conflicting parties to make concessions and still save face (Pruitt, 1981b). If my

"The greenhouse effect, the depletion of the ozone layer and the global ecological crisis [is] the most serious issue facing this country and the world. . . . We know how to solve the problem. It will be unimaginably difficult. The cooperation required will be unprecedented. But we know what to do."
U.S. Senator Albert Gore (1989)

Bargaining:
Seeking an agreement through direct negotiation between parties to a conflict.

Mediation:
Attempts by a neutral third party to help resolve a conflict by facilitating communication and offering suggestions.

Arbitration:
Resolution of a conflict by a neutral third party who studies both sides and imposes a settlement.

concession can be attributed to a mediator, who is gaining an equal concession from my antagonist, then neither of us will be viewed as caving in to the other's demands.

Turning Win-Lose into Win-Win

Mediators can also help resolve conflicts by facilitating constructive communication. Their first task is to help the parties rethink the conflict. By prodding them to set aside their conflicting demands and opening offers and to think instead about their underlying needs, interests, and goals, the mediator aims to replace a competitive "win-lose" orientation with a cooperative "win-win" orientation that aims at a mutually beneficial resolution.

A favorite story of conflict researchers concerns the two sisters who quarreled over an orange (Fisher & Ury, 1981). Finally they compromised and split the orange in half, whereupon one sister squeezed her half for juice while the other used the peel in making a cake. In experiments at the State University of New York at Buffalo, Dean Pruitt and his associates induced bargainers to search for ***integrative agreements***. If the quarrelsome sisters had agreed to split the orange, giving one sister all the juice and the other all the peel, they would have hit on such an agreement, one that integrates both parties' interests (Pruitt & Lewis, 1975, 1977; Kimmel et al., 1980). Compared to compromises, in which each party sacrifices something important, integrative agreements are more enduring and, because they are mutually rewarding, lead to better ongoing relationships (Pruitt, 1986).

Unraveling Misperceptions with Controlled Communications

Communication often helps by reducing self-fulfilling misperceptions. Perhaps you can recall experiences similar to that of the following college student:

> Often, after a prolonged period of little communication, I perceive Martha's silence as an indication of her dislike for me. She, in turn, thinks that my quietness is a result of my being mad at her. My silence induces her silence, which makes me even more silent . . . until this snowballing effect is broken by some occurrence that makes it necessary for us to interact. And the communication then unravels all the misinterpretations we had made about one another.

The outcome of such conflicts often depends on *how* people communicate their feelings to one another. Roger Knudson and his colleagues (1980) invited married couples to come to the University of Illinois psychology laboratory and relive, through role playing, one of their past conflicts. Before, during, and after their conversation (which often generated as much emotion as their actual previous conflict) the couples were closely observed and questioned. These observations revealed that those who evaded the issue—by failing to make their positions clear or failing to acknowledge their spouse's position—tended to be left with the illusion that they were more in harmony and agreement than they really were. Often, they afterward believed they now agreed more when actually they agreed less. In contrast, those who engaged the issue—by making their positions clear and by taking one another's views into account—achieved more actual agreement and gained more accurate information about one another's perceptions. That helps explain why happily married couples tend to be those in which both wife and husband communicate their concerns directly and openly (Grush & Glidden, 1987).

Conflict researchers believe that a key factor is *trust*. If you believe the other is well-intentioned, not out to exploit you, you will then more likely divulge your needs and concerns. If, however, you lack such trust, you probably will be cautious, fearing that being open will give the other party information that might be used against you.

Integrative agreements: Win-win agreements that reconcile both parties' interests to their mutual benefit.

"In the research on the effects of mediation one finding stands out: The worse the state of the parties' relationship is with one another, the dimmer the prospects that mediation will be successful."
Kenneth Kressel & Dean Pruitt (1985)

When the two parties mistrust each other and communicate unproductively, a third-party mediator—be it a marriage counselor, a labor mediator, a diplomat—can sometimes help. After coaxing the conflicting parties to rethink their perceived win-lose conflict, the mediator often then has each party identify and rank its goals. If the actual incompatibility of their goals is not great, the ranking procedure may make it easier for each to concede on less important goals so that both may be able to achieve their chief goals (Erickson et al., 1974; Schulz & Pruitt, 1978). For example, once labor and management both believe that management's goal of higher productivity and profit is not necessarily incompatible with labor's goal of better wages and working conditions, they can begin to work for an integrative win-win solution.

When the parties are then convened to communicate directly, they are usually *not* set loose in the hope that, because they are meeting eyeball to eyeball, the conflict will resolve itself. In the midst of a threatening, stressful conflict, people's emotions often disrupt their ability to understand the other party's point of view. Thus communication may become most difficult just when it is most needed (Tetlock, 1985). So the mediator will often structure the encounter in hopes of assuring that each party will both understand and feel understood by the other.

For example, in order to build mutual understanding the conflicting parties may be encouraged to restrict their own arguments to statements of fact, including statements of how they feel and how they respond when the other acts in a given way: "I enjoy having music on. But when it's loud, I find it difficult to concentrate. That makes me crabby." Also, they may be asked to reverse roles and argue one another's position or to restate one another's positions before replying with their own: "My turning up the stereo seems to bug you." Such communication may cut away many of the accumulated misperceptions, as each party is flooded with information that contradicts its misperceptions. This differs from everyday life, in which we receive contradictory information bit by bit, making it easier to rationalize or dismiss each contradictory bit (Jervis, 1973).

These peacemaking principles, based partly on laboratory experiments, partly on practical experience, have been successful in mediating both international and industrial conflicts (Blake & Mouton, 1962, 1979; Burton, 1969; Wehr, 1979). One small team of Arab and Jewish Americans, led by social psychologists Herbert Kelman and Stephen Cohen (1979, 1986), have conducted several workshops bringing together influential Arabs and Israelis, and Pakistanis and Indians. By using methods such as those we've considered, Kelman and Cohen sought to eliminate misperceptions and to have the participants creatively seek solutions for their common good. Isolated, the participants are free to speak directly to their adversaries without fearing their constituents' reactions to what they are saying. The result? Participants from both sides typically come to understand better the other country's perspective and how its people respond to their own country's actions.

When direct communication is impossible, a third party can meet with one party, then the other. Henry Kissinger's "shuttle diplomacy" in the two years after the Arab-Israeli war of 1973 produced three disengagement agreements between Israel and its Arab neighbors. Kissinger's mediating strategy gave him considerable control over the communications and enabled both sides to concede to him without appearing to capitulate to one another (Pruitt, 1981a).

The complex process of internation negotiation can sometimes receive an added boost from smaller mediating efforts. In 1976, Kelman drove an Egyptian social scientist, Boutros Ghali, to the Boston airport. En route, they formulated plans for an

Egyptian conference on misperceptions in Arab-Israeli relations. The conference later took place, and Kelman conveyed its promising results to influential Israelis. A year later, Ghali became Egypt's acting foreign minister, and Egyptian President Anwar Sadat made his historic trip to Israel, beginning a road to peace. Afterward, Ghali said happily to Kelman, "You see the process that we started at the Boston airport last year" (Armstrong, 1981). A year later, mediator Jimmy Carter secluded Sadat and Israeli Prime Minister Begin at Camp David. Rather than begin by having each side state their demands, Carter had them identify their underlying interests and goals—security for Israel, authority over its historic territory for Egypt. Thirteen days later, the trio emerged with "A Framework for Peace in the Middle East" granting each what they desired—security in exchange for territory (Rubin, 1989). Six months later, after further mediation by President Carter during visits to both countries, Begin and Sadat signed a treaty ending the state of war that had existed since 1948.

Arbitration

Some conflicts are so intractable, the underlying interests so divergent, that a mutually satisfactory resolution is unattainable. Those who believe and those who don't believe that a fetus is a person with inalienable human rights are unlikely to reach an integrative agreement regarding abortion policies. Arabs and Palestinians cannot both have jurisdiction over the same homelands. In a divorce dispute over custody of a child, both parents cannot enjoy full custody. In these and many other cases (involving disputes over tenants' repair bills, athletes' wages, and national territories), a third party mediator may—or may not—help resolve the conflict.

If not, the parties may turn to *arbitration* by having the mediator or another third party *impose* a settlement. Disputants generally prefer to settle their differences without arbitration, thereby retaining control over the outcome. Neil McGillicuddy and others (1987) observed this preference in an experiment involving disputants coming to the Dispute Settlement Center in Buffalo, New York. When the people knew they would face an arbitrated settlement if mediation failed, they tried harder to resolve the problem, exhibited less hostility, and thus were more likely to reach agreement.

However, in cases where the differences are perceived as large and irreconcilable, the prospect of arbitration may have an opposite effect (Pruitt, 1986). The disputants may freeze their positions, hoping to gain an advantage when the arbitrator decides on a compromise. To combat this tendency, some disputes, such as those involving salaries of major league baseball players, are settled with "final-offer arbitration," in which the third party chooses one of the two final offers. Final-offer arbitration motivates each party to make a reasonable-sounding proposal.

Typically, however, the final offer is not so reasonable as it would be if each party, free of self-serving bias, saw its own proposal through others' eyes. Negotiation researchers report that most disputants are made stubborn by overconfidence. Successful mediation is hindered when, as often happens, both parties believe they have a two-thirds chance of winning a final-offer arbitration (Bazerman, 1986).

CONCILIATION

So, direct communication often helps. But sometimes the tension and suspicion run so high that communication, much less resolution, becomes all but impossible. In such times, each party may threaten, coerce, or retaliate against the other. Unfortunately,

People perceive that *they* respond more favorably to conciliation, but that *others* might be responsive to coercion.

"Don't worry, dear -- it's just a <u>peace</u> offensive."

such acts tend to be reciprocated, thus escalating the conflict. So, would an opposite strategy—appeasing the other party by being unconditionally cooperative—likely produce a satisfying result? Often not. In laboratory games, those who are 100 percent cooperative are frequently exploited. Politically, a one-sided pacifism is generally out of the question anyway; neither the Soviets nor the Americans are about to disarm without the assurance that the other is doing likewise.

Is there a third alternative—one conciliatory rather than retaliatory, yet strong enough to discourage exploitation? Charles Osgood (1962, 1980), a University of Illinois social psychologist, has for twenty-five years advocated one such alternative. Osgood calls it *G*raduated and *R*eciprocated *I*nitiatives in *T*ension-reduction, nicknamed **GRIT**, a name that delightfully and insightfully suggests the kind of determination it requires. GRIT aims to reverse the arms race, by triggering reciprocal deescalating acts. To do so, it draws upon social-psychological concepts, such as the norm of reciprocity and research on attribution of motives.

GRIT:
Graduated and reciprocated initiatives in tension reduction—a strategy designed to deescalate international tensions.

GRIT requires one side to initiate a few small deescalatory actions, undertaken in ways that encourage the adversary's reciprocation. The first steps in the strategy *announce one's conciliatory intent*. The initiator states its desire to reduce tension, declares each conciliatory act prior to making it, and invites the adversary to reciprocate. Such announcements create a framework that helps the adversary interpret correctly what otherwise might be seen as weak or tricky actions, and they elicit public pressure on the adversary to adhere to the reciprocity norm.

Next, the initiator establishes credibility and genuineness by carrying out, exactly as announced, several verifiable *conciliatory acts*. This intensifies pressure to reciprocate. Making the conciliatory acts diverse—perhaps offering medical information, closing a military base, and lifting a trade ban—keeps the initiator from making a significant sacrifice in any one area and leaves the adversary freer to choose its own means of reciprocation. If the adversary reciprocates voluntarily, its own conciliatory behavior may also soften its hostile attitudes.

GRIT *is* conciliatory. But it is not "surrender on the installment plan." The remaining aspects of the plan protect one's self-interest by *maintaining retaliatory capability*. The initial conciliatory steps entail some small risk, but do not jeopardize one's security; rather they simply are calculated to begin edging both sides down the tension ladder. If one side takes an aggressive action, it is reciprocated in kind, making it clear that no exploitation will be tolerated. Yet, this reciprocal act is not to be an overresponse which would likely reescalate the conflict. If the adversary offers its own conciliatory acts, these too are matched, or even slightly exceeded.

Does it really work? In laboratory dilemma games the most successful strategy has proven to be simple "tit-for-tat," which begins with a cooperative opening play and thereafter matches the other party's last response (Axelrod & Dion, 1988; Smith, 1987). Thus tit-for-tat tries to cooperate and is forgiving, yet does not tolerate exploitation. In a lengthy series of experiments at Ohio University, Svenn Lindskold and his associates (1976 to 1988) have directly tested other aspects of the GRIT strategy. Lindskold (1978) concludes that his own and others' studies provide "strong support for the various steps in the GRIT proposal." In laboratory games, announcing one's cooperative intent does boost cooperation. Repeated conciliatory acts do breed greater trust (although self-serving biases often make one's own acts seem more conciliatory and less hostile than those of one's adversary). Maintaining an equality of power does protect one against being exploited.

Lindskold is not contending that the world of the laboratory experiment mirrors the more complex world of everyday life. Rather, as we noted way back in Chapter 1, experiments enable us to formulate and to verify powerful theoretical principles such as the reciprocity norm, the self-serving bias, and the principles that predict whether one will attribute cooperative or deceitful motives to another. And, notes Lindskold (1981), "It is the theories, not the individual experiments that are used to interpret the world."

GRIT-like strategies have occasionally been tried outside the laboratory, and with promising results. During the Berlin Crisis of the early 1960s, U.S. and Soviet tanks faced one another barrel-to-barrel. The crisis was defused when the Americans pulled back their tanks step-by-step. The Russians reciprocated each step. More recently, small concessions by Israel and Egypt (for example, Israel allowing Egypt to open up the Suez Canal, Egypt allowing ships bound for Israel to pass through) helped reduce tension to a point where the negotiations between the two nations became possible (J. Z. Rubin, 1981).

To many, the most significant attempt at GRIT was the so-called "Kennedy experiment" (Etzioni, 1967). On June 10, 1963, President Kennedy gave a major speech, "A Strategy for Peace." In it he noted that "our problems are man-made . . . and can be solved by man," and then announced his first conciliatory act: The U.S. was stopping all atmospheric nuclear tests and would not resume them unless another country did. In the Soviet Union, Kennedy's speech was published in full. Five days later Premier Krushchev reciprocated, announcing he had halted production of strategic bombers. There soon followed further reciprocal gestures: The U.S. agreed to sell wheat to Russia, the Soviets agreed to a "hot line" between the two countries, and the two countries soon achieved a test-ban treaty. These conciliatory initiatives did, for a time, warm relations between the two countries.

"Perhaps the best policy in the nuclear age is to speak softly and carry a small- to medium-sized stick."
Richard Ned Lebow (1987)

"I am not suggesting that principles of individual behavior can be applied to the behavior of nations in any direct, simpleminded fashion. What I am trying to suggest is that such principles may provide us with hunches about internation behavior that can be tested against experience in the larger arena."
Charles E. Osgood (1966)

Despite these occasional conciliatory successes, belief in the power of coercion remains strong. Such beliefs led Nazi Germany to think that bombing British cities would move the British toward surrender, led the allies later to believe that bombing raids over Germany would diminish the Germans' "will to resist," led the Japanese to assume that a devastating attack on Pearl Harbor might dissuade the United States from waging war in the western Pacific, and led the United States to assume that sustained bombing of North Vietnam would decrease their "will to wage war" and bring them to the negotiating table. In each case, the attempted coercion instead strengthened the resolve to resist. Myron Rothbart and William Hallmark (1988) experimentally explored this belief in the power of coercion. After assuming the role of defense minister of a hypothetical nation, subjects perceived that *they* would be more responsive to a conciliatory than to a coercive gesture from another country, but that the *other* country would be relatively more responsive to coercion. To perceive more clearly the likely effect of an action on another party, suggest Rothbart and Hallmark, ask what effect that action would have if directed against oneself. "If they treated me the way I'm going to treat them, how would I feel?"

Our discussion of conciliation has focused on reversing the arms race and reducing international tensions. Might conciliatory efforts also help reduce tension between groups, or between individuals? The theoretical principles that underlie the strategy are derived from research with individuals and small groups, so its applicability to the tensions of our daily existence seems promising. When a relationship is strained and communication nonexistent, it sometimes takes only a conciliatory gesture—a soft answer, a warm smile, a gentle touch—for both parties to begin easing down the tension ladder, to a rung where communication can be reestablished and the conflict creatively resolved.

SUMMING UP

CONFLICT

Whenever two people, two groups, or two nations interact, their perceived needs and goals may conflict. In this chapter, we identified some common ingredients of conflicts, and we considered ways to resolve them constructively and peacefully.

Social dilemmas Many social problems arise as people pursue their individual self-interests, to their common detriment. Two laboratory games, the Prisoner's Dilemma and the Commons Dilemma, capture this clash of individual versus communal well-being. In each game, the participants choose whether to pursue their immediate interests or to cooperate for their common betterment. Ironically and tragically, each game often taps well-meaning participants into decisions that shrink their common pie. In real life, as in laboratory experiments, such traps can be avoided by establishing rules that regulate self-serving behavior; by keeping social groups small so that people feel responsibility for one another; by enabling people to communicate, thus reducing mistrust; by changing payoffs to make exploitation less and cooperation more rewarding; and by invoking altruistic norms.

Competition When people compete for scarce resources, human relations can sink into prejudice and hostility. In a famous series of experiments, Muzafer Sherif found that win-lose competition quickly made strangers into enemies, triggering outright warfare even among normally upstanding boys.

Perceived injustice   Conflicts are also kindled when people feel unjustly treated. According to equity theory, people define justice as equity—the distribution of rewards in proportion to people's contributions. Conflicts occur when people disagree on the extent of their contributions and thus on the equity of their outcomes. Other theorists argue that people sometimes define justice not as equity, but as equality, or even in terms of people's needs.

Misperception   Conflicts frequently contain a small core of truly incompatible goals, surrounded by a thick layer of misperceptions of the adversary's motives and goals. Often, conflicting parties have *mirror-image perceptions*—each attributing the same virtues to themselves and vices to the other. When both sides believe "We are peace-loving, they are hostile," each may treat the other in ways that provoke confirmation of their expectations. International conflicts are also fed by a *blacktop illusion:* The enemy's leaders are perceived as evil and coercive, its own people as more innocent or even as sympathetic to one's own point of view. Such perceptions of our antagonists easily adjust themselves as conflicts wax and wane.

PEACEMAKING

Conflicts are readily kindled and fueled by these ingredients, but fortunately some equally powerful forces can transform hostility into harmony.

Contact   Might putting people into close contact reduce their hostilities? There are good reasons to think so. Yet, despite some encouraging early studies of desegregation, more recent studies in the U.S. show that mere desegregation of schools has little effect upon racial attitudes. However, in most schools, interracial contact is seldom prolonged or intimate. When it is, and when it is structured to convey *equal status*, hostilities often lessen.

Cooperation   Contacts are especially beneficial when people work together to overcome a common threat or to achieve a superordinate goal. In his boys' camp experiments, Sherif used the unifying effect of a common enemy to create cohesive groups. Then he used the unifying power of cooperative effort to reconcile the warring groups. Taking their cue from experiments on cooperative contact, several research teams have replaced competitive classroom learning situations with opportunities for cooperative learning. Their heartening results suggest how desegregation might be more constructively implemented, and strengthen our confidence that cooperative activities can benefit human relations at all levels.

Communication   Conflicting parties can also seek to resolve their differences by bargaining either directly with one another or through a third-party mediator. When a pie of fixed size is to be divided, adopting a tough negotiating stance tends to gain one a larger piece (for example, a better price). When the pie can vary in size, as in the dilemma situations, toughness more often backfires. Third-party mediators can help by prodding the antagonists to replace their competitive win-lose view of their conflict with a more cooperative win-win orientation. Mediators can also structure communications that will peel away misperceptions and increase mutual understanding and trust. When a negotiated settlement is not reached, the conflicting parties may defer the outcome to an arbitrator, who either dictates a settlement or selects one of the two final offers.

Conciliation Sometimes tensions run so high that genuine communication is impossible. In such times, small conciliatory gestures by one party may elicit reciprocal conciliatory acts by the other party. Thus tension may be reduced to a level where communication can occur. One such conciliatory strategy, Graduated and Reciprocated Initiatives in Tension-reduction, aims to alleviate tense international situations.

Those who mediate tense labor-management and international conflicts sometimes use one other peacemaking strategy. They instruct the participants, as this chapter instructed you, in the dynamics of conflict and peacemaking. The hope is that understanding—understanding how conflicts are fed by social traps, perceived injustice, competition, and misperceptions, and understanding how conflicts can be resolved through equal-status contact, cooperation, communication, and conciliation—can help us as we seek to establish and enjoy peaceful, rewarding relationships.

FOR FURTHER READING

Johnson, D. W., & Johnson, R. T. (1987). *Learning together and alone: Cooperative, competitive and individualistic learning* (2nd ed.). Englewood Cliffs, NJ: Prentice-Hall. Offers teachers strategies for implementing various goals, including steps for creating interdependent learning activities.

Katz, P. A., & Taylor, D. A. (Eds.). (1988). *Eliminating racism: Profiles in controversy.* New York: Plenum. Prominent researchers explore modern racism and evaluate various efforts to reduce it.

Pruitt, D. G., & Rubin, J. Z. (1986). *Social conflict: Escalation, stalemate, and settlement.* New York: Random House. Two prominent social psychologists draw on both research and anecdote to explain how conflicts arise, escalate, and are resolved.

Rubin, J. Z., & Rubin, C. (1989). *When families fight: How to manage conflict with those you love.* New York: Arbor House/William Morrow. Identifies the reasons families fight and how they can manage conflict more constructively.

Wagner, R. V., de Rivera, J., & Watkins, M. (Ed.). (1988). Special issue. *Psychology and the promotion of peace. Journal of Social Issues, 44*(2). A state-of-the art summary of the dynamics of international conflict and likely routes to peace.

White, R. K. (1986). *Psychology and the prevention of nuclear war.* New York: New York University Press. A helpful collection of thirty-five classic and contemporary essays on the psychological roots of war and peace.

Wollman, N. (Ed.). (1985). *Working for peace: A handbook of practical psychology and other tools.* San Luis Obispo, CA: Impact Publishers. Three dozen experts offer suggestions for organizing peace workers, reducing conflict, and changing attitudes.

GLOSSARY

Acceptance Both acting and believing in accord with social pressure.

Adaptation-level phenomenon The tendency to adapt to a given level of stimulation and thus to notice and react to *changes* from that level.

Aggression Physical or verbal behavior intended to hurt someone. In laboratory experiments, aggression might mean delivering electric shocks or saying something likely to hurt another's feelings. Note that one can be socially assertive without being aggressive.

Altruism Concern and help for others that asks nothing in return; devotion to others without conscious regard for one's self-interests.

Androgyny (andros, *man*, + gyne, *woman*) Possession of both "masculine" and "feminine" psychological traits. The androgynous person is said to be high in both traditionally masculine qualities (for example, independence, assertiveness, competitiveness) and traditionally feminine qualities (for example, warmth, tenderness, compassion).

Arbitration Resolution of a conflict by a neutral third party who studies both sides and imposes a settlement

Attitude A favorable or unfavorable evaluative reaction toward something or someone, exhibited in one's beliefs, feelings, or intended behavior.

Attractiveness Having qualities which appeal to an audience. An appealing communicator (often someone similar to the audience) is most persuasive on matters of subjective preference.

Attribution theory The theory of how people explain others' behavior—for example, by attributing it either to internal *dispositions* (enduring traits, motives, and attitudes) or to external *situations*.

Autokinetic phenomenon Self (auto) motion (kinetic). The apparent movement of a stationary point of light in the dark.

Availability heuristic An efficient but fallible rule of thumb that judges the likelihood of things in terms of their availability in memory. If instances of something come readily to mind, we presume it to be commonplace.

Bargaining Seeking an agreement through direct negotiation between parties to a conflict

Base-rate fallacy The tendency to ignore or underuse base-rate information (information that describes most people) and instead to be influenced by distinctive features of the case being judged.

Behavioral confirmation A type of self-fulfilling prophecy whereby people's social expectations lead them to act in ways that cause others to confirm their expectations.

Behavioral medicine An interdisciplinary field that integrates and applies behavioral and medical knowledge regarding health and disease.

Belief perseverance Clinging to one's initial conceptions, as when the foundation for one's belief is discredited but an explanation of why the belief might be true survives.

Blacktop illusion The belief that the real enemy is the other group's leaders, who intimidate and mislead their innocent people.

Bogus pipeline A procedure for detecting people's true attitudes. Participants are first convinced that a new machine can use their psychological responses to measure their private attitudes. Then they are asked to predict the machine's reading, thus revealing their attitudes.

Burnout Hostility, apathy, or loss of idealism resulting from prolonged stress or from conflict between those in antagonistic roles.

Bystander effect The finding that a person is less likely to provide help when there are other bystanders.

Catharsis Emotional release. The catharsis view of aggression is that aggressive drive is reduced when one "releases" aggressive energy, either by acting aggressively or by fantasizing aggression.

Channel of communication How a message is delivered—whether face to face, in writing, on film, or in some other way.

Clinical psychology The study, assessment, and treatment of people with psychological difficulties.

Coactors A group of people working simultaneously and individually on a noncompetitive task.

Cognitive dissonance Feelings of tension that arise when one is simultaneously aware of two inconsistent cognitions. For example, dissonance may occur when we make a decision favoring one alternative despite reasons favoring another or when we realize that we have, with little justification, acted contrary to our attitudes.

Cohesiveness A "we feeling"—the extent to which members of a group are bound together, such as by attraction for one another.

Companionate love The affection we feel for those with whom our lives are deeply intertwined.

Complementarity The supposed tendency, in a relationship between two people, for each to supply what is missing in the other. The complementarity hypothesis proposes that people are attracted to those whose needs are different, in ways that complement their own.

Compliance Publicly acting in accord with social pressure while privately disagreeing.

Confederate An accomplice of the experimenter

Confirmation bias A tendency to search for information that confirms one's preconceptions.

Conflict A perceived incompatibility of actions or goals.

Conflict between person and role Tension between one's personality or attitudes and the expectations of one's role.

Conformity A change in behavior or belief as a result of real or imagined group pressure.

Correlational research The study of the naturally occurring relationships among variables.

Credibility Believability. A credible communicator is perceived as both expert and trustworthy.

Crowding A subjective feeling of not enough space per person.

Cult A group typically characterized by (1) the distinctive ritual of its devotion to a god or a person, (2) isolation from the surrounding "evil" culture, and (3) a living charismatic leader.

Deindividuation Loss of self-awareness and evaluation apprehension; deindividuation occurs in group situations that foster anonymity and draw attention away from the individual.

Demand characteristics Cues in an experiment that tell the participant what behavior is expected.

Depressive realism The tendency of mildly depressed people to make accurate rather than self-serving judgments, attributions, and predictions.

Disclosure reciprocity The tendency for one person's intimacy of self-disclosure

to match that of a conversational partner.

Discrimination Unjustifiable negative behavior toward a group and its members.

Displacement Redirecting aggression to a target other than the source of the frustration. Generally, the new target is a safer target, one that is less likely to retaliate or against whom aggression is more socially accepted.

Door-in-the-face technique A strategy for gaining a concession in which, after someone is first given opportunity to turn down a large request (the door in the face), the same requester counteroffers with a more reasonable request.

Dyad A group of two. In social psychology, two people interacting one to one.

Empathy The vicarious experience of another's feelings; putting oneself in another's shoes.

Equal-status contact Relationships between people who have equal status. Just as a relationship between people of unequal status breeds attitudes consistent with their relationship, so do relationships between those of equal status. Thus, to reduce prejudice, interracial contact should be between persons equal in status.

Equity A condition in which people receive from a relationship in proportion to what they contribute to it. *Note*: Equitable outcomes needn't be equal outcomes.

Ethnocentrism A belief in the superiority of one's own ethnic and cultural group, and a corresponding disdain for all other groups.

Evaluation apprehension Concern for how others are evaluating oneself.

Experimental realism Degree to which an experiment absorbs and involves its participants.

Experimental research Studies that seek clues to cause-effect relationships by manipulating one or more factors while controlling others (holding them constant).

False consensus effect The tendency to *over*estimate the commonality of one's opinions and one's undesirable or unsuccessful behaviors.

False uniqueness effect The tendency to

*under*estimate the commonality of one's abilities and one's desirable or successful behaviors.

Field research Research done in natural, real-life settings outside the laboratory.

Foot-in-the-door phenomenon The tendency for people who have first agreed to a small request to comply later with a larger request.

Free riders People who benefit from the group but give little in return.

Frustration The blocking of goal-directed behavior.

Fundamental attribution error The tendency for observers to underestimate situational influences and overestimate dispositional influences upon others' behavior. (Also called "correspondence bias"—the assumption that people's dispositions correspond to their behavior.)

Gender role A set of behavior expectations (norms) for males or females.

GRIT *G*raduated and *r*eciprocated *i*nitiatives in *t*ension-reduction—a strategy designed to deescalate international tensions.

Group Two or more people who, for longer than a few moments, interact with and influence one another and perceive one another as "us."

Group polarization Group-produced enhancement of members' preexisting tendencies. Refers to a strengthening of the members' average tendency, *not* to a split within the group.

Groupthink The mode of thinking that persons engage in when *concurrence-seeking* becomes so dominant in a cohesive ingroup that it tends to override realistic appraisal of alternative courses of action.

Health psychology A subfield of psychology that provides psychology's contribution to behavioral medicine.

Hindsight bias The tendency to exaggerate one's ability to have foreseen how something turned out *after* learning the outcome. Also known as the "I-knew-it-all-along phenomenon."

Hostile aggression Aggression driven by anger and performed as an end in itself.

Hypothesis A testable proposition that describes a relationship that may exist between events.

I - knew - it - all - along phenomenon See "hindsight bias."

Illusion of control Perception of uncontrollable events as subject to one's control or as more controllable than they are.

Illusory correlation Perception of a relationship where none exists, or perception of a stronger relationship than actually exists. For example, a false impression that two variables, say gender and intelligence, are associated.

Informational influence Conformity that results from accepting evidence about reality provided by other people.

Informed consent An ethical principal requiring that research participants be told enough to enable them to choose whether they wish to participate.

Ingratiation Strategies, such as flattery, by which people seek to gain another's favor.

Ingroup A group of people who share a sense of belonging, a feeling of common identity.

Ingroup bias The tendency to favor one's own group.

Inoculation Exposing people to weak attacks upon their attitudes, so that when stronger attacks come they will have refutations available.

Instinctive behavior An innate, unlearned behavior pattern exhibited by all members of a species.

Instrumental aggression Aggression that is a means to some other end.

Insufficient justification effect Reduction of dissonance by internally justifying one's behavior, especially when external inducements are "insufficient" to fully justify it.

Integrative agreements Win-win agreements that reconcile both parties' interests to their mutual benefit.

Interaction The effect of one factor (such as biology) depends on another factor (such as environment).

Interrole conflict Tension between the requirements of two different roles that must be played at once.

Intrarole conflict Tension created by contradictory expectations about how a given role should be played.

Just-world phenomenon The tendency of people to believe that the world is just and that people therefore get what they deserve and deserve what they get.

Kin selection The idea that evolution has selected altruism toward one's close relatives to enhance the survival of mutually shared genes.

Leadership The process by which certain group members motivate and guide the group.

Low-ball technique A technique for getting people to agree to do something. People who have agreed to (but have not yet performed) an initial request are more likely to comply when the requester makes the request more costly than are people who are approached only with the costly request.

Matching phenomenon The tendency for men and women to choose as partners those who are a "good match" in attractiveness and other traits.

Mediation Attempts by neutral third party to help resolve a conflict by facilitating communication and offering suggestions.

Mere-exposure effect The tendency for novel stimuli to be liked more or rated more positively after one has been repeatedly exposed to them.

Minimax Minimize costs, maximize rewards.

Mirror-image perception Reciprocal views of one another often held by parties in conflict; for example, each party may view itself as moral and peace-loving and the other as evil and aggressive.

Mundane realism Degree to which an experiment is superficially similar to everyday situations.

Naturalistic fallacy Defining what is good in terms of what is observable. For example: What's typical is normal; what's normal is good.

Non-zero-sum games Games in which one side's winning need not be balanced by the other's losing; that is, outcomes need not sum to zero. With cooperation, both can win; with competition, both can lose.

Normative influence Conformity based on a person's desire to be accepted by the group.

Norms Rules for accepted and expected behavior. Norms prescribed "proper" behavior.

Outgroup A group that is perceived as distinctively different from or apart from the ingroup.

Overconfidence phenomenon The tendency to be more confident than correct—to overestimate the accuracy of one's beliefs.

Overjustification effect The consequence of bribing people to do what they already like doing, which leads them to see their action as externally controlled rather than intrinsically appealing.

Passionate love A state of intense longing for union with another. Passionate lovers are absorbed in one another, feel ecstatic at attaining their partner's love, and are disconsolate on losing it.

Personal space The buffer zone we like to maintain around our bodies. Its size depends upon our familiarity with whomever is near us.

Physical-attractiveness stereotype The presumption that physically attractive people possess other socially desirable traits as well: What is beautiful is good.

Pluralistic ignorance People's lack of awareness of how other people are thinking, feeling, or responding.

Prejudice An unjustifiable negative attitude toward a group and its individual members.

Primacy effect Other things being equal, information presented first usually has the most influence.

Priming The activation of particular associations in memory.

Prosocial behavior Positive, constructive, helpful social behavior; the opposite of antisocial behavior.

Proximity Geographical nearness. Proximity (or, more precisely, "functional distance") is a powerful predictor of liking.

Racism (1) Prejudicial attitudes and discriminatory behavior toward people of a given race, or (2) institutional practices (even if not motivated by prejudice) that subordinate people of a given race.

Random assignment Assigning participants to the conditions of an experiment such that all participants have the same chance of being in a given condition. This equalizes the conditions at the beginning of the experiment. Thus if participants in the different conditions later behave differently, it will rarely be due to preexisting differences among them. (Note the distinction between random *assignment* in experiments and random *sampling* in surveys.)

Random sample Survey procedure in which every person in the population studied has an equal chance of being selected.

Reactance A motive to protect or restore one's sense of freedom. Reactance is aroused when freedom of action is threatened.

Recency effect When information presented last has the most influence. Recency effects are less common than primacy effects.

Reciprocity norm An expectation that people will help, not hurt, those who have helped them.

Regression toward the average The statistical tendency for extreme scores or extreme behavior to return toward one's average.

Relative deprivation The perception that one is less well off than others to whom one compares oneself.

Reward theory of attraction The theory that we like those whose behavior is rewarding to us, or who have been associated with rewarding events.

Role A set of norms that defines how people in a given social position ought to behave.

Self-awareness A self-conscious state in which attention is focused on oneself. Makes people more sensitive to their own attitudes and dispositions.

Self-disclosure Revealing intimate aspects of oneself to others.

Self-efficacy A sense that one is competent and effective. Distinguished from self-esteem, a sense of one's self-worth. A bombardier might feel high self-efficacy and low self-esteem.

Self-fulfilling prophecy The tendency for one's expectations to evoke behavior that confirms the expectation.

Self-handicapping Protecting one's self-image by creating a handy excuse for failure.

Self-monitoring Being attuned to the way one presents oneself in social situations and adjusting one's performance to create the desired impression.

Self-perception theory The theory that when we are unsure of our attitudes we infer them much as would someone observing us—by looking at our behavior and the circumstances under which it occurs.

Self-presentation Expressing oneself and behaving in ways designed to create either a favorable impression or an impression that corresponds to one's ideals. (Also called "impression management.")

Self-reference effect The tendency to process efficiently and remember well information related to oneself.

Self-serving bias The tendency to perceive oneself favorably.

Sexism (1) Prejudicial attitudes and discriminatory behavior toward people of a given sex, or (2) institutional practices (even if not motivated by prejudice) that subordinate people of a given sex.

Sleeper effect A delayed impact of a message; occurs when the message is remembered but a reason for discounting it is forgotten.

Social comparison Evaluating one's opinions and abilities by comparing oneself to others.

Social-exchange theory The theory that human interactions are transactions that aim to maximize one's rewards and minimize one's costs.

Social facilitation (1) Original meaning—the tendency of people to perform simple or well-learned tasks better when others are present. (2) Current meaning—the strengthening of dominant (prevalent, likely) responses due to the presence of others.

Social learning theory The theory that we learn social behavior by observing and imitating and by being rewarded and punished.

Social loafing The tendency for people to exert less effort when they pool their efforts toward a common goal than when they are individually accountable.

Social psychology The scientific study of how people think about, influence, and relate to one another.

Social representations Socially shared beliefs. Widely held ideas and values, including our assumptions and cultural ideologies. Our social representations help us make sense of our world.

Social-responsibility norm An expectation that people will help those dependent upon them.

Sociobiology The study of the emergence of social behavior using the principle of evolutionary biology.

Stereotype A generalization about a group of people that distinguishes those people from others. Stereotypes can be overgeneralized, inaccurate, and resistant to new information.

Superordinate goal A shared goal that necessitates cooperative effort; a goal that overrides people's differences from one another.

Televised violence Depiction of physically compelling action that threatens hurt or killing, or of actual hurting or killing.

Theory An integrated set of principles that explain and predict observed events.

Two-factor theory of emotion Arousal × label = emotion.

Two-step flow of communication Media influence that occurs through opinion leaders, who in turn influence others.

Ultimate attribution error Granting the benefit of the doubt to members of one's own group but not to members of other groups. Thus negative behavior by outgroup members is attributed to their dispositions, positive behavior explained away. (Also called "group-serving bias.")

BIBLIOGRAPHY

Abbey, A. (1987). Misperceptions of friendly behavior as sexual interest: A survey of naturally occurring incidents. *Psychology of Women Quarterly*, 11, 173–194.

Abelson, R. (1972). Are attitudes necessary? In B. T. King & E. McGinnies (Eds.), *Attitudes, conflict and social change*. New York: Academic Press.

Abelson, R. P., Kinder, D. R., Peters, M. D., & Fiske, S. T. (1982). Affective and semantic components in political person perception. *Journal of Personality and Social Psychology*, 42, 619–630.

Abramson, L. Y. (Ed.). (1988). *Social cognition and clinical psychology: A synthesis*. New York: Guilford.

Abramson, L. Y., Alloy, L. B., & Rosoff, R. (1981). Depression and the generation of complex hypotheses in the judgment of contingency. *Behavior Research and Theory*, 19, 34–45.

Abramson, L. Y., Metalsky, G. I., & Alloy, L. B. (1989). Hopelessness depression: A theory-based subtype. *Psychological Review*, 96, 358–372.

Acorn, D. A., Hamilton, D. L., & Sherman, S. J. (1988). Generalization of biased perceptions of groups based on illusory correlations. *Social Cognition*, 6, 345–372.

Adair, J. G., Dushenko, T. W., & Lindsay, R. C. L. (1985). Ethical regulations and their impact on research practice. *American Psychologist*, 40, 59–72.

Adams, D., & 19 others (1987). Statement on violence. *Medicine and War*, 3, 191–193.

Aderman, D., & Berkowitz, L. (1970). Observational set, empathy, and helping. *Journal of Personality and Social Psychology*, 14, 141–148.

Aderman, D., & Berkowitz, L. (1983). Self-concern and the unwillingness to be helpful. *Social Psychology Quarterly*, 46, 293–301.

Adler, R. P., Lesser, G. S., Meringoff, L. K., Robertson, T. S., & Ward, S. (1980). *The effects of television advertising on children*. Lexington, Mass.: Lexington Books.

Adorno, T., Frenkel-Brunswik, E., Levinson, D., & Sanford, R. N. (1950). *The authoritarian personality*, New York: Harper.

Agres, S. J. (1987). Rational, emotional and mixed appeals in advertising: Impact on recall and persuasion. Paper presented at the American Psychological Association convention. (Available from Lowe Marochalk, Inc., 1345 Avenue of the Americas, New York, N.Y., 10105.)

Ajzen, I. (1982). On behaving in accordance with one's attitudes. In M. P. Zanna, E. T. Higgins, & C. P. Herman (Eds.). *Consistency in Social Behavior: The Ontario Symposium*, vol. 2. Hillside, N.J.: Erlbaum.

Ajzen, I., & Fishbein, M. (1977). Attitude-behavior relations: A theoretical analysis and review of empirical research. *Psychological Bulletin*, 84, 888–918.

Ajzen, I., & Timko, C. (1986). Correspondence between health attitudes and behavior. *Basic and Applied Social Psychology*, 7, 259–276.

Albee, G. (1979, June 19). Politics, power, prevention, and social change. Keynote address to Vermont Conference on Primary Prevention of Psychopathology.

Allee, W. C., & Masure, R. M. (1936). A comparison of maze behavior in paired and isolated shell-parakeets *(Melopsittacus undulatus Shaw)* in a two-alley problem box. *Journal of Comparative Psychology*, 22, 131–155.

Allen, J. B., Kenrick, D. T., Linder, D. E., & McCall, M. A. (1989). Arousal and attraction: A response facilitation alternative to misattribution and negative reinforcement models. *Journal of Personality and Social Psychology*, in press.

Allen, V. L., & Levine, J. M. (1969). Consensus and conformity. *Journal of Experimental Social Psychology*, 5, 389–399.

Allen, V. L., & Wilder, D. A. (1979). Group categorization and attribution of belief similarity. *Small Group Behavior*, 10, 73–80.

Allen, V. L., & Wilder, D. A. (1980). Impact of group consensus and social support on stimulus meaning: Mediation of conformity by cognitive restructuring. *Journal of Personality and Social Psychology*, 39, 1116–1124.

Allgeier, A. R., Byrne, D., Brooks, B., & Revnes, D. (1979). The waffle phenomenon: Negative evaluations of those who shift attitudinally. *Journal of Applied Social Psychology*, 9, 170–182.

Allison, S. T., & Messick, D. M. (1985). The group attribution error. *Journal of Experimental Social Psychology* 21, 563–579.

Allison, S. T., & Messick, D. M. (1987). From individual inputs to group outputs, and back again: Group processes and inferences about members. In C. Hendrick (Ed.), *Group processes: Review of personality and social psychology*, Vol. 8. Newbury Park, Ca.: Sage.

Alloy, L. B., & Abramson, L. Y. (1979). Judgment of contingency in depressed and nondepressed students: Sadder but wiser? *Journal of Experimental Psychology: General*, 108, 441–485.

Alloy, L. B., & Abramson, L. Y. (1980). The cognitive component of human helplessness and depression: A critical analysis. In J. Garber & M. E. P. Seligman (Eds.), *Human helplessness: Theory and applications*. New York: Academic Press.

Alloy, L. B., & Abramson, L. Y. (1982). Learned helplessness, depression, and the illusion of control. *Journal of Personality and Social Psychology*, 42, 1114–1126.

Alloy, L. B., & Abramson, L. Y. (1988). Depressive realism: Four theoretical perspectives. In L. B. Alloy (Ed.), *Cognitive processes in depression*. New York: Guilford.

Alloy, L. B., Abramson, L. Y., & Viscusi, Z. (1981). Induced mood and the illusion of control. *Journal of Personality and Social Psychology*, 41, 1129–1140.

Allport, F. M. (1920). The influence of the group upon association and thought. *Journal of Experimental Psychology*, 3, 159–182.

Allport, G. (1954). *The nature of prejudice*. Cambridge, Mass.: Addison-Wesley.

Allport, G. W. (1978). *Waiting for the Lord: 33 Meditations on God and Man* (Edited by P. A. Bertocci). New York: Macmillan.

Allport, G. W., & Postman, L. (1958). *The psychology of rumor*. New York: Henry Holt and Co., 1975. (Originally published, 1947). Also in E. E. Maccoby, T. M. Newcomb, & E. L. Hartley (Eds.), *Readings in social psychology*. New York: Holt, Rinehart and Winston.

Allport, G. W., & Ross, J. M. (1967). Personal religious orientation and prejudice. *Journal of Personality and Social Psychology*. 5, 432–443.

Altemeyer, B. (1988). *Enemies of freedom: Understanding right-wing authoritarianism*. San Francisco: Jossey-Bass.

Altman, I., & Taylor, D. (1973). *Social penetion: The development of interpersonal relations*. New York: Holt, Rinehart and Winston.

Altman, I., & Vinsel, A. M. (1978). Personal space: An analysis of E. T. Hall's proxemics framework. In I. Altman & J. Wohlwill (Eds.), *Human behavior and the environment*. New York: Plenum Press.

Alwin, D. F. (1989). Historical changes in parental orientations to children. In N. Mandell (Ed.), *Sociological studies of child development*, Vol. 3. Greenwich, Ct.: JAI Press, in press.

Amabile, T. M., & Glazebrook, A. H. (1982). A negativity bias in interpersonal evaluation. *Journal of Experimental Social Psychology*, 18, 1–22.

Amato, P. R. (1979). Juror-defendant similarity and the assessment of guilt in politically motivated crimes. *Australian Journal of Psychology*, 31, 79–88.

Amato, P. R. (1983). Helping behavior in urban and rural environments: Field studies based on a taxonomic organization of helping episodes. *Journal of Personality and Social Psychology*, 45, 571–586.

Amato, P. R. (1986). Emotional arousal and helping behavior in a real-life emergency. *Journal of Applied Social Psychology*, 16, 633–641.

American Psychological Association (1981). Ethical principles of psychologists. *American Psychologist*, 36, 633–638.

Amir, Y. (1969). Contact hypothesis in ethnic relations. *Psychological Bulletin*, 71, 319–342.

Anderson, C. A. (1982). Inoculation and counterexplanation: Debiasing techniques in the perseverance of social theories. *Social Cognition*, 1, 126–139.

Anderson, C. A., & Anderson, D. C. (1984). Ambient temperature and violent crime: Tests of the linear and curvilinear hypotheses. *Journal of Personality and Social Psychology*, 46, 91–97.

Anderson, C. A. (1988). Attributions as decisions: A two-stage information processing model. Paper presented to the Third Attribution Conference, California School of Professional Psychology, Los Angeles.

Anderson, C. A. (1989). Temperature and aggression: The ubiquitous effects of heat on the occurrence of human violence. *Psychological Bulletin*, in press.

Anderson, C. A., & Harvey, R. J. (1988). Discriminating between problems in living: An examination of measures of depression, loneliness, shyness, and social anxiety. *Journal of Social and Clinical Psychology*, 6, 482–491.

Anderson, C. A., Horowitz, L. M., & French, R. D. (1983). Attributional style of lonely and depressed people. *Journal of Personality and Social Psychology*, 45, 127–136.

Anderson, C. A., Jennings, D. L., & Arnoult, L. H. (1988). Validity and utility of the attributional style construct at a moderate level of specificity. *Journal of Personality and Social Psychology*, 55, 979–990.

Anderson, C. A., Lepper, M. R., & Ross, L. (1980). Perseverance of social theories: The role of explanation in the persistence of discredited information. *Journal of Personality and Social Psychology*, 39, 1037–1049.

Anderson, C. A., & Sechler, E. S. (1986). Effects of explanation and counterexplanation on the development and use of social theories. *Journal of Personality and Social Psychology*, 50, 24–34.

Anderson, N. H. (1968). A simple model of information integration. In R. B. Abelson, E. Aronson, W. J. McGuire, T. M. Newcomb, M. J. Rosenberg, & P. H. Tannenbaum (Eds.), *Theories of cognitive consistency: A sourcebook*. Chicago: Rand McNally.

Anderson, N. H. (1974). Cognitive algebra: Integration theory applied to social attribution. In L. Berkowitz (Ed.), *Advances in Experimental Social Psychology*, Vol. 7. New York: Academic Press.

Anderson, S. M., & Bem, S. L. (1981). Sex typing and androgyny in dyadic interaction: Individual differences in responsiveness to physical attractiveness. *Journal of Personality and Social Psychology*, 41, 74–86.

Andrews, K. H., & Kandel, D. B. (1979). Attitude and behavior: A specification of the contingent consistency hypothesis. *American Sociological Review*, 44, 298–310.

Antill, J. K. (1983). Sex role complementarity versus similarity in married couples. *Journal of Personality and Social Psychology*, 45, 145–155.

Apsler, R. (1975). Effects of embarrassment on behavior toward others. *Journal of Personality and Social Psychology*, 32, 145–153.

Archea, J. (1980). The architectural basis for analyzing certain aspects of spatial behavior. Paper presented at the American Psychological Association convention.

Archer, D., & Gartner, R. (1976). Violent acts and violent times: A comparative approach to postwar homicide rates. *American Sociological Review*, 41, 937–963.

Archer, D., & Gartner, R. (1984). Violence and crime in cross-national perspective. New Haven, CT: Yale University Press.

Archer, D., Iritani, B., Kimes, D. B., & Barrios, M. (1983). Face-ism: Five studies of sex differences in facial prominence. *Journal of Personality and Social Psychology*, 45, 725–735.

Archer, R. L., Berg, J. M., & Burleson, J. A. (1980). Self-disclosure and attraction: A self-perception analysis. Unpublished manuscript, University of Texas at Austin.

Archer, R. L., Berg, J. M., & Runge, T. E. (1980). Active and passive observers' attraction to a self-disclosing other. *Journal of Experimental Social Psychology*, 16, 130–145.

Archer, R. L., & Burleson, J. A. (1980). The effects of timing of self-disclosure on attraction and reciprocity. *Journal of Personality and Social Psychology*, 38, 120–130.

Archer, R. L., & Cook, C. E. (1986). Personalistic self-disclosure and attraction: Basis for relationship or scarce resource. *Social Psychology Quarterly*, 49, 268–272.

Archer, R. L., Foushees, H. C., Davis, M. H., & Aderman, D. (1979). Emotional empathy in a courtroom simulation: A person-situation interaction. *Journal of Applied Social Psychology*, 9, 275–291.

Arendt, H. (1963). *Eichmann in Jerusalem: A report on the banality of evil*. New York: Viking Press.

Arendt, H. (1971). Organized guilt and universal responsibility. In R. W. Smith (Ed.), *Guilt: Man and society*. Garden City, N.Y.: Doubleday Anchor Books. Reprinted from *Jewish Frontier*, 1945, 12.

Argyle, M. (1988). A social psychologist visits Japan. *The Psychologist*, 1, 361–363.

Argyle, M., & Dean, J. (1965). Eye-contact, distance and affiliation. *Sociometry*, 28, 289–304.

Argyle, M., & Henderson, M. (1985). *The anatomy of relationships*. London: Heinemann.

Argyle, M., Shimoda, K., & Little, B. (1978). Variance due to persons and situations in England and Japan. *British Journal of Social and Clinical Psychology*, 17, 335–337.

Aristotle, *Poetics*, Book Six.

Arkes, H. R., Faust, D., Guilmette, T. J., & Hart, K. (1988). Eliminating the hindsight bias. *Journal of Applied Psychology*, 73, 305–307.

Arkes, H. R., & Rothbart, M. (1985). Memory, retrieval, and contingency judgments. *Journal of Personality and Social Psychology*, 49, 598–606.

Arkin, R. M., Appelman, A., & Burger, J. M. (1980). Social anxiety, self-presentation, and the self-serving bias in causal attribution. *Journal of Personality and Social Psychology*, 38, 23–35.

Arkin, R. M. & Baumgardner, A. H. (1985). Self-handicapping. In J. H. Harvey & C. Weary (Eds.), *Attribution: Basic issues and applications*. New York: Academic Press.

Arkin, R. M. & Burger, J. M. (1980). Effects of unit relation tendencies on interpersonal attraction. *Social Psychology Quarterly*, 43, 380–391.

Arkin, R. M., Cooper, H., & Kolditz, T. (1980). A statistical review of the literature concerning the self-serving attribution bias in interpersonal influence situations. *Journal of Personality*, 48, 435–448.

Arkin, R. M., Lake, E. A., & Baumgardner, A. H. (1986). Shyness and self-presentation. In W. H. Jones, J. M. Cheek, & S. R. Briggs (Eds.), *Shyness: Perspectives on research and treatment*. New York: Plenum.

Arkin, R. M., & Maruyama, G. M. (1979). Attribution, affect, and college exam performance. *Journal of Educational Psychology*, 71, 85–93.

Arms, R. L., Russell, G. W., & Sandilands, M. L. (1979). Effects on the hostility of spectators of viewing aggressive sports. *Social Psychology Quarterly*, 42, 275–279.

Armstrong, B. (1981). An interview with Herbert Kelman. *APA Monitor*, January, pp. 4–5, 55.

Aronson, E. (1988). *The social animal*. New York: Freeman.

Aronson, E., Blaney, N., Stephan, C., Sikes, J., & Snapp, M. (1978). *The jigsaw classroom*. Beverly Hills, Calif.: Sage Publications.

Aronson, E., Brewer, M., & Carlsmith, J. M. (1985). Experimentation in social psychology. In G. Lindzey & E. Aronson (Eds.), *Handbook of Social Psychology*, vol. 1. Hillsdale, N.J.: Erlbaum.

Aronson, E., & Bridgeman, D. (1979). Jigsaw groups and the desegregated classroom: In pursuit of common goals. *Personality and Social Psychology Bulletin*, 5, 438–446.

Aronson, E., & Carlsmith, J. M. (1969). Experimentation in social psychology. In G. Lindzey & E. Aronson (Eds.), *Handbook of Social Psychology* (2d ed.), Vol. 2. Reading, Mass.: Addison-Wesley.

Aronson, E., & Cope, V. (1968). My enemy's enemy is my friend. *Journal of Personality and Social Psychology*, 8, 8–12.

Aronson, E., & Gonzalez, A. (1988). Desegregation, jigsaw, and the Mexican-American experience. In P. A. Katz & D. Taylor (Eds.), *Towards the elimination of racism: Profiles in controversy*. New York: Plenum.

Aronson, E., & Linder, D. (1965). Gain and loss of esteem as determinants of interpersonal attractiveness. *Journal of Experimental Social Psychology*, 1, 156–171.

Aronson, E., & Mettee, D. R. (1974). Affective reactions to appraisal from others. *Foundations of Interpersonal Attraction*. New York: Academic Press.

Aronson, E., & Mills, J. (1959). The effect of severity of initiation on liking for a group. *Journal of Abnormal and Social Psychology*, 59, 177–181.

Aronson, E., Turner, J. A., & Carlsmith, J. M. (1963). Communicator credibility and communicator discrepancy as determinants of opinion change. *Journal of Abnormal and Social Psychology*, 67, 31–36.

Asch, S.E. (1946). Forming impressions of personality. *Journal of Abnormal and Social Psychology*, 41, 258–290.

Asch, S. E. (1955, November). Opinions and social pressure. *Scientific American*, pp. 31–35.

Asch, S. E. (1956). Studies of independence and conformity: A minority of one against a unanimous majority. *Psychological Monographs*, 70, (9, Whole No. 416).

Asendorpf, J. B. (1987). Videotape reconstruction of emotions and cognitions related to shyness. *Journal of Personality and Social Psychology*, 53, 542–549.

Asher, J. (1987, April). Born to be shy? *Psychology Today*, pp. 56–64.

Associated Press (1988, July 10). Rain in Iowa. *Grand Rapids Press*, p. A6.

Astin, A. W. (1972). *Four critical years*. San Francisco: Jossey-Bass.

Astin, A. W., Green, K. C., & Korn, W. S. (1987). *The American freshman: Twenty year trends*. Los Angeles: Higher Education Research Institute, UCLA. (a)

Astin, A. W., Green, K. C., Korn, W. S., & Schalit, M. (1987). *The American freshman: National norms for Fall 1987*. Los Angeles: Higher Education Research Institute, UCLA. (b)

Austin, W. (1980). Friendship and fairness: Effects of type of relationship and task performance on choice of distribution rules. *Personality and Social Psychology Bulletin*, 6, 402–408.

Averill, J. R. (1983). Studies on anger and aggression: Implications for theories of emotion. *American Psychologist*, 38, 1145–1160.

Aviello, J. R., Thompson, D. E., & Brodzinsky, D. M. (1983). How funny is crowding anyway? Effects of room size, group size, and the introduction of humor. *Basic and Applied Social Psychology*, 4, 193–207.

Axelrod, R., & Dion, D. (1988). The further evolution of cooperation. *Science*, 242, 1385–1390.

Axsom, D., Yates, S., & Chaiken, S. (1987). Audience response as a heuristic cue in persuasion. *Journal of Personality and Social Psychology*, 53, 30–40.

Azrin, N. H. (1967, May). Pain and aggression. *Psychology Today*, pp. 27–33.

Azrin, N. H., Hutchinson, R. R., & Hake, D. F. (1966). Extinction-induced aggression. *Journal of the Experimental Analysis of Behavior*, 9, 191–204.

Babad, E. (1987). Wishful thinking and objectivity among sports fans. *Social Behaviour*, 2, 231–240.

Bachman, J. G., Johnston, L. D., O'Malley, P. M., & Humphrey, R. N. (1988). Explaining the recent decline in marijuana use: Differentiating the effects of perceived risks, disapproval, and general lifestyle factors. *Journal of Health and Social Behavior*, 29, 92–112.

Baer, R., Hinkle, S., Smith, K., & Fenton, M. (1980). Reactance as a function of actual versus projected autonomy. *Journal of Personality and Social Psychology*, 38, 416–422.

Bales, R. F. (1958). Task roles and social roles in problem-solving groups. In E. E. Maccoby, T. M. Newcomb, & E. L. Hartley (Eds.), *Readings in Social Psychology*, (3d ed.). New York: Holt, Rinehart and Winston.

Bandura, A. (1979). The social learning perspective: Mechanisms of aggression. In H. Toch (Ed.), *Psychology of crime and criminal justice*. New York: Holt, Rinehart & Winston.

Bandura, A. (1982). Self-efficacy: Mechanism in human agency. *American Psychologist*, 37, 122–147.

Bandura, A. (1986). *Social foundations of thought and action: A social cognitive theory*. Englewood Cliffs, N.J.: Prentice-Hall.

Bandura, A., Ross, D., & Ross, S. A. (1961). Transmission of aggression through imitation of aggressive models. *Journal of Abnormal and Social Psychology*, 63, 575–582.

Bandura, A., & Walters, R. H. (1959). *Adolescent aggression*. New York: Ronald Press.

Bandura, A., & Walters, R. H. (1963). *Social learning and personality development*. New York: Holt, Rinehart and Winston.

Barash, D. (1979). *The whisperings within*. New York: Harper & Row.

Bargh, J. A. (1989). Conditional automaticity: Varieties of automatic influence in social perception and cognition. In J. S. Uleman & J. A. Bargh (Eds.), *Unintended thought: Causes and consequences for judgment, emotion, and behavior*. New York: Guilford.

Bar-Hillel, M., & Fischoff, B. (1981). When do base rates affect prediction? *Journal of Personality and Social Psychology*, 41, 671–680.

Barker, R. G., and associates. (1978). *Habitats, environments, and human behavior*. San Francisco: Jossey-Bass.

Barnes, R. D., Ickes, W., & Kidd, R. F. (1979). Effects of the perceived intentionality and stability of another's dependency on helping behavior. *Personality and Social Psychology Bulletin*, 5, 367–372.

Barnett, M. A., King, L. M., Howard, J. A., & Melton, E. M. (1980). Experiencing negative affect about self or other: Effects on helping behavior in children and adults. Paper presented at the Midwestern Psychological Association convention.

Barnett, P. A., & Gotlib, I. H. (1988). Psychosocial functioning and depression: Distinguishing among antecedents, concomitants, and consequences. *Psychological Bulletin*, 104, 97–126.

Baron, J., & Hershey, J. C. (1988). Outcome bias in decision evaluation. *Journal of Personality and Social Psychology*, 54, 569–579.

Baron, L., & Straus, M. A. (1984). Sexual stratification, pornography, and rape in the United States. In N. M. Malamuth & E. Donnerstein (Eds.), *Pornography and sexual aggression*. New York: Academic Press.

Baron, R. A. (1976). The reduction of human aggression: A field study of the influence of incompatible reactions. *Journal of Applied Social Psychology*, 6, 260–274.

Baron, R. M., Mandel, D. R., Adams, C. A., & Griffen, L. M. (1976). Effects of social density in university residential environments. *Journal of Personality and Social Psychology*, 34, 434–446.

Baron, R. M., & Needel, S. P. (1980). Toward an understanding of the differences in the responses of humans and other animals to density. *Psychological Review*, 87, 320–326.

Baron, R. S. (1986). Distraction-conflict theory: Progress and problems. In L. Berkowitz (Ed.), *Advances in Experimental Social Psychology*, Orlando, Fla.: Academic Press.

Baron, R. S., Moore, D., & Sanders, G. S. (1978). Distraction as a source of drive in social facilitation research. *Journal of Personality and Social Psychology*, 36, 816–824.

Bar-Tal, D. (1982). Sequential development of helping behavior: A cognitive-learning approach. *Developmental Review*, 2, (2), 101–124.

Baruch, G. K., Barnett, R. (1986). Role quality, multiple role involvement, and psychological well-being in midlife women. *Journal of Personality and Social Psychology*, 51, 578–585.

Barzun, J. (1975). *Simple and direct*. New York: Harper & Row, pp. 173–174.

Batson, C. D. (1975). Rational processing or rationalization? The effect of disconfirming information on a stated religious belief. *Journal of Personality and Social Psychology*, 32, 176–184.

Batson, C. D. (1983). Sociobiology and the role of religion in promoting prosocial behavior: An alternative view. *Journal of Personality and Social Psychology*, 45, 1380–1385.

Batson, C. D. (1987). Prosocial motivation: Is it ever truly altruistic? In L. Berkowitz (Ed.), *Advances in experimental social psychology*, Vol. 20. Orlando, Fl.: Academic Press.

Batson, C. D., Bolen, M. H., Cross, J. A., & Neuringer-Benefiel, H. E. (1986). Where is the altruism in the altruistic personality? *Journal of Personality and Social Psychology*, 50, 212–220.

Batson, C. D., Cochran, P. J., Biederman, M. F., Blosser, J. L., Ryan, M. J., & Vogt, B. (1978). Failure to help when in a hurry: Callousness or conflict? *Personality and Social Psychology Bulletin*, 4, 97–101.

Batson, C. D., Coke, J. S., Jasnoski, M. L., & Hanson, M. (1978). Buying kindness: Effect of an extrinsic incentive for helping on perceived altruism. *Personality and Social Psychology Bulletin*, 4, 86–91.

Batson, C. D., Duncan, B. D., Ackerman, P., Buckley, T., & Birch, K. (1981). Is empathic emotion a source of altruistic motivation? *Journal of Personality and Social Psychology*, 40, 290–302.

Batson, C. D., Flink, C. H., Schoenrade, P. A., Fultz, J., & Pych, V. (1986). Religious orientation and overt versus covert racial prejudice. *Journal of Personality and Social Psychology*, 50, 175–181.

Batson, C. D., Fultz, J., & Schoenrade, P. A. (1987). Distress and empathy: Two qualitatively distinct vicarious emotions with different motivational consequences. *Journal of Personality*, 55, 19–40.

Batson, C. D., Fultz, J., Schoenrade, P. A., & Paduano, A. (1987). Critical self-reflection and self-perceived altruism: When self-reward fails. *Journal of Personality and Social Psychology*, 53, 594–602.

Batson, C. D., & Gray, R. A. (1981). Religious orientation and helping behavior: Responding to one's own or to the victim's needs? *Journal of Personality and Social Psychology*, 40, 511–520.

Batson, C. D., Harris, A. C., McCaul, K. D., Davis, M., & Schmidt, T. (1979). Compassion or compliance: Alternative dispositional attributions for one's helping behavior. *Social Psychology Quarterly*, 42, 405–409.

Batson, C. D., Schoenrade, P. A., & Pych, V. (1985). Brotherly love or self-concern? Behavioural consequences of religion. In L. B. Brown (Ed.), *Advances in the psychology of religion*. Oxford: Pergamon Press.

Batson, C. D., & Ventis, W. L. (1982). *The religious experience: A social psychological perspective*. New York: Oxford University Press.

Baum, A., Aiello, J. R., & Calesnick, L. E. (1978). Crowding and personal control: Social density and the development of learned helplessness. *Journal of Personality and Social Psychology*, 36, 1000–1011.

Baum, A., & Davis, G. E. (1980). Reducing the stress of high-density living: An architectural intervention. *Journal of Personality and Social Psychology*, 38, 471–481.

Baum, A., & Gatchel, R. J. (1981). Cognitive determinants of reaction to uncontrollable events: Development of reactance and learned helplessness. *Journal of Personality and Social Psychology*, 40, 1078–1089.

Baum, A., Harpin, R. E., & Valins, S. (1975). The role of group phenomena in the experience of crowding. *Environmental and Behavior*, 7, 185–198.

Baum, A., & Valins, S. (1977). *Architectural and social behavior*. Hillsdale, N.J.: Lawrence Erlbaum.

Baumann, D. J., Cialdini, R. B., & Kenrick, D. T. (1981). Altruism as hedonism: Helping and self-gratification as equivalent responses. *Journal of Personality and Social Psychology*, 40, 1039–1046.

Baumeister, R. F. (1982). A self-presentational view of social phenomena. *Psychological Bulletin*, 91, 3–26.

Baumeister, R. F. (1985). Four selves and two motives: Outline of self-presentation theory.

Paper presented to the Midwestern Psychological Association convention.

Baumeister, R. F., & Darley, J. M. (1982). Reducing the biasing effect of perpetrator attractiveness in jury simulation. *Personality and Social Psychology Bulletin*, 8, 286–292.

Baumeister, R. F., Chesner, S. P., Senders, P. S., & Tice, D. M. (1988). Who's in charge here? Group leaders do lend help in emergencies. *Personality and Social Psychology Bulletin*, 14, 17–22.

Baumeister, R. F., Hutton, D. B., & Tice, D. M. (1989). Cognitive processes during deliberate self-presentation: How self-presenters alter and misinterpret the behavior of their interaction partners. *Journal of Experimental Social Psychology*, 25, 59–78.

Baumeister, R. F., & Scher, S. J. (1988). Self-defeating behavior patterns among normal individuals: Review and analysis of common self-destructive tendencies. *Psychological Bulletin*, 104, 3–22.

Baumeister, R. F., & Steinhilber, A. (1984). Paradoxical effects of supportive audiences on performance under pressure: The home field disadvantage in sports championships. *Journal of Personality and Social Psychology*, 47, 85–93.

Baumeister, R. F., & Tice, D. M. (1984). Role of self-presentation and choice in cognitive dissonance under forced compliance: Necessary or sufficient causes? *Journal of Personality and Social Psychology*, 46, 5–13.

Baumgardner, A. H., & Brownlee, E. A. (1987). Strategic failure in social interaction: Evidence for expectancy disconfirmation process. *Journal of Personality and Social Psychology*, 52, 525–535.

Baumhart, R. (1968). *An honest profit*. New York: Holt, Rinehart & Winston.

Baxter, T. L., & Goldberg, L. R. (1987). Perceived behavioral consistency underlying trait attributions to oneself and another: An extension of the actor-observer effect. *Personality and Social Psychology Bulletin*, 13, 437–447.

Bayer, E. (1929). Beitrage zur zeikomponenten theorie des hungers. *Zeitschrift fur Psychologie*, 112, 1–54.

Bazerman, M. H. (1986, June). Why negotiations go wrong. *Psychology Today*, pp. 54–58.

Beaman, A. L., Barnes, P. J., Klentz, B., & McQuirk, B. (1978). Increasing helping rates through information dissemination: Teaching pays. *Personality and Social Psychology Bulletin*, 4, 406–411.

Beaman, A. L., Cole, C. M., Preston, M., Klentz, B., & Steblay, N. M. (1983). Fifteen years of foot-in-the-door research: A meta-analysis. *Personality and Social Psychology Bulletin*, 9, 181–196.

Beaman, A. L., & Klentz, B. (1983). The supposed physical attractiveness bias against supporters of the women's movement: A meta-analysis. *Personality and Social Psychology Bulletin*, 9, 544–550.

Beaman, A. L., Klentz, B., Diener, E., & Svanum, S. (1979). Self-awareness and transgression in children: Two field studies. *Journal of Personality and Social Psychology*, 37, 1835–1846.

Beauvois, J. L., & Dubois, N. (1988). The norm of internality in the explanation of psychological events. *European Journal of Social Psychology*, 18, 299–316.

Beck, A. T. (1982). *Depression: Clinical, experimental, and theoretical aspects*. New York: Harper & Row.

Beck, A. T., & Young, J. E. (1978, September). College blues. *Psychology Today*, pp. 80–92.

Beck, S. B., Ward-Hull, C. I., & McLear, P. M. (1976). Variables related to women's somatic preferences of the male and female body. *Journal of Personality and Social Psychology*, 34, 1200–1210.

Becker, B. J. (1986). Influence again: Another look at studies of gender differences in social influence. In J. S. Hyde & M. Linn (Eds.), *The psychology of gender: Advances through meta-analysis*. Baltimore: Johns Hopkins University Press.

Becker, F. D., Sommer, R., Bee, J., & Oxley, B. (1973). College classroom ecology. *Sociometry*, 36, 514–525.

Becker, L. J. (1978). Joint effect of feedback and goal setting on performance: A field study of residential energy conservation. *Journal of Applied Psychology*, 63, 428–433.

Becker, L. J., & Seligman, C. (1978). Reducing air conditioning waste by signaling it is cool outside. *Personality and Social Psychology Bulletin*, 4, 412–415.

Becker, L. J., Seligman, C., & Darley, J. M. (1979). Psychological strategies to reduce energy consumption: Project summary report. Princeton, N.J.: Center for Energy and Environmental Studies, Princeton University.

Becker, L. J., Seligman, C., Fazio, R. H., & Darley, J. M. (1981). Relating attitudes to residential energy use. *Environment and Behavior*, 13, 590–609.

Bell, P. A. (1980). Effects of heat, noise, and provocation on retaliatory evaluative behavior. *Journal of Social Psychology*, 110, 97–100.

Bell, B. E., & Loftus, E. F. (1988). Degree of detail of eyewitness testimony and mock juror judgments. *Journal of Applied Social Psychology*, 18, 1171–1192.

Bell, R. Q., & Chapman, M. (1986). Child effects in studies using experimental or brief longitudinal approaches to socialization. *Developmental Psychology*, 22, 595–603.

Belson, W. A. (1978). *Television violence and the adolescent boy*. Westmead, England: Saxon House, Teakfield Ltd.

Bem, D. J. (1972). Self-perception theory. In L. Berkowitz (Ed.), *Advances in experimental social psychology*. Vol. 6. New York: Academic Press.

Bem, D. J., & McConnell, H. K. (1970). Testing the self-perception explanation of dissonance phenomena: On the salience of premanipulation attitudes. *Journal of Personality and Social Psychology*, 14, 23–31.

Bem, S. L. (1987). Masculinity and femininity exist only in the mind of the perceiver. In J. M. Reinisch, L. A. Rosenblum, & S. A. Sanders (Eds.), *Masculinity/femininity: Basic perspectives*. New York: Oxford University Press

Bennis, W. (1984). Transformative power and leadership. In T. J. Sergiovani & J. E. Corbally (Eds.), *Leadership and organizational culture*. Urbana: University of Illinois Press.

Ben-Shakhar, G., Bar-Hillel, M., Bilu, Y., Ben-Abba, E., & Flug, A. (1986). Can graphology predict occupational success? Two empirical studies and some methodological ruminations. *Journal of Applied Psychology*, 71, 645–653.

Benson, P. L., Dehority, J., Garman, L., Hanson, E., Hochschwender, M., Lebold, C., Rohr, R., & Sullivan, J. (1980). Intrapersonal correlates of nonspontaneous helping behavior. *Journal of Social Psychology*, 110, 87–95.

Bentler, P. M., & Speckart, G. (1981). Attitudes "cause" behaviors: A structural equation analysis. *Journal of Personality and Social Psychology*, 40, 226–238.

Benware, C., & Deci, E. (1975). Attitude change as a function of the inducement for exposing a proattitudinal communication. *Journal of Experimental Social Psychology*, 11, 271–278.

Berg, J. H. (1984). Development of friendship between roommates. *Journal of Personality and Social Psychology*, 46, 346–356.

Berg, J. H. (1987). Responsiveness and self-disclosure. In V. J. Derlega & J. H. Berg (Eds.), *Self-disclosure: Theory, research, and therapy*. New York: Plenum.

Berg, J. H., & McQuinn, R. D. (1986). Attraction and exchange in continuing and noncontinuing dating relationships. *Journal of Personality and Social Psychology*, 50, 942–952.

Berg, J. H., & McQuinn, R. D. (1988). Loneliness and aspects of social support networks. Unpublished manuscript, University of Mississippi.

Berg, J. H., & Peplau, L. A. (1982). Loneliness: The relationship of self-disclosure and androgyny. *Personality and Social Psychology Bulletin*, 8, 624–630.

Berg, J. H., & Wright-Buckley, C. (in press). Effects of racial similarity and interviewer intimacy in a peer counseling analog. *Journal of Counseling.*

Berger, P. (1963). *Invitation to sociology: A humanistic perspective.* Garden City, N.Y.: Doubleday Anchor Books.

Berglas, S., & Jones, E. E. (1978). Drug choice as a self-handicapping strategy in response to noncontingent success. *Journal of Personality and Social Psychology*, 36, 405–417.

Berkowitz, L. (1954). Group standards, cohesiveness, and productivity. *Human Relations*, 7, 509–519.

Berkowitz, L. (1964, February). The effects of observing violence. *Scientific American*, pp. 35–41.

Berkowitz, L. (1968, September). Impulse, aggression and the gun. *Psychology Today*, pp. 18–22.

Berkowitz, L. (1972). Frustrations, comparisons, and other sources of emotional arousal as contributors to social unrest. *Journal of Social Issues*, 28, 77–91. (a)

Berkowitz, L. (1972). Social norms, feelings, and other factors affecting helping and altruism. In L. Berkowitz (Ed.), *Advances in experimental social psychology* (Vol. 6). New York: Academic Press. (b)

Berkowitz, L. (1978). Whatever happened to the frustration-aggression hypothesis? *American Behavioral Scientists*, 21, 691–708.

Berkowitz, L. (1981, June). How guns control us. *Psychology Today*, pp. 11–12. (b)

Berkowitz, L. (1983). Aversively stimulated aggression: Some parallels and differences in research with animals and humans. *American Psychologist*, 38, 1135–1144.

Berkowitz, L. (1984). Some effects of thoughts on anti- and prosocial influences of media events: A cognitive-neoassociation analysis. *Psychological Bulletin*, 95, 140–427.

Berkowitz, L. (1987). Mood, self-awareness, and willingness to help. *Journal of Personality and Social Psychology*, 52, 721–729.

Berkowitz, L. (1988). Frustrations, appraisals, and aversively stimulated aggression. *Aggressive Behavior*, 14, 3–11.

Berkowitz, L., & Geen, R. G. (1966). Film violence and the cue properties of available targets. *Journal of Personality and Social Psychology*, 3, 525–530.

Berkowitz, L., & LePage, A. (1967). Weapons as aggression-eliciting stimuli. *Journal of Personality and Social Psychology*, 7, 202–207.

Berman, J. J., Murphy-Berman, & Pachauri, A. (1988). Sex differences in friendship patterns in India and in the United States. *Basic and Applied Social Psychology*, 9, 61–71.

Bernstein, W. M., Stephan, W. G., & Davis, M. H. (1979). Explaining attributions for achievement: A path analytic approach. *Journal of Personality and Social Psychology*, 37, 1810–1821.

Berry, D. S., & Zebrowitz-McArthur, L. (1988). What's in a face: Facial maturity and the attribution of legal responsibility. *Personality and Social Psychology Bulletin*, 14, 23–33.

Berscheid, E. (1981). An overview of the psychological effects of physical attractiveness and some comments upon the psychological effects of knowledge of the effects of physical attractiveness. In W. Lucker, K. Ribbens, & J. A. McNamera (Eds.), *Logical aspects of facial form (craniofacial growth series).* Ann Arbor: University of Michigan Press.

Berscheid, E. (1985). Interpersonal attraction. In G. Lindzey & E. Aronson (Eds.), *The Handbook of Social Psychology.* New York: Random House.

Berscheid, E. (in press). The importance of physical attractiveness. In C. P. Herman (Ed.), *The Ontario Symposium*, vol. III. Beverly Hills, Ca.: Erlbaum.

Berscheid, E., Boye, D., & Walster (Hatfield), E. (1968). Retaliation as a means of restoring equity. *Journal of Personality and Social Psychology*, 10, 370–376.

Berscheid, E., Dion, K., Walster (Hatfield), E., & Walster, G. W. (1971). Physical attractiveness and dating choice: A test of the matching hypothesis. *Journal of Experimental Social Psychology*, 7, 173–189.

Berscheid, E., & Peplau, L. A. (1983). The emerging science of relationships. In H. H. Kelley, E. Berscheid, A. Christensen, J. H. Harvey, T. L. Huston, G. Levinger, E. McClintock, L. A. Peplau, & D. R. Peterson (Eds.), *Close relationships.* New York: Freeman.

Berscheid, E., Snyder, M., & Omoto, A. M. (1989). Issues in studying close relationships: Conceptualizing and measuring closeness. In C. Hendrick (Ed.), *Review of personality and social psychology*, Vol. 10. Newbury Park, Ca.: Sage.

Berscheid, E., & Walster (Hatfield), E. (1978). *Interpersonal attraction.* Reading, Mass.: Addison-Wesley.

Berscheid, E., Walster, G. W., & Walster (Hatfield), E. (1978). Effects of accuracy and positivity of evaluation on liking for the evaluator. Unpublished manuscript, 1969. Summarized by E. Berscheid and E. Walster (Hatfield) in *Interpersonal attraction.* Reading, Mass.: Addison-Wesley.

Bersoff, D. N. (1987). Social science data and the Supreme Court: Lockhart as a case in point. *American Psychologist*, 42, 52–58.

Bettelheim, B. (1966). Violence: A neglected mode of behavior. *Annals of American Academy of Political Social Science*, 364, 50–59. Cited by K. Menninger, in *The crime of punishment.* New York: Viking, 1968, p. 173.

Bickman, L. (1975). Bystander intervention in a crime: The effect of a mass-media campaign. *Journal of Applied Social Psychology*, 5, 296–302.

Bickman, L. (1979). Interpersonal influence and the reporting of a crime. *Personality and Social Psychology Bulletin*, 5, 32–35.

Bickman, L., & Green, S. K. (1977). Situational cues and crime reporting: Do signs make a difference? *Journal of Applied Social Psychology*, 7, 1–18.

Bickman, L., & Kamzan, M. (1973). The effect of race and need on helping behavior. *Journal of Social Psychology*, 89, 73–77.

Bickman, L., & Rosenbaum, D. P. (1977). Crime reporting as a function of bystander encouragement, surveillance, and credibility. *Journal of Personality and Social Psychology*, 35, 577–586.

Bickman, L., Teger, A., Gabriele, T., McLaughlin, C., Berger, M., & Sunaday, E. (1973). Dormitory density and helping behavior. *Environment and Behavior*, 5, 465–490.

Bierbrauer, G. (1979). Why did he do it? Attribution of obedience and the phenomenon of dispositional bias. *European Journal of Social Psychology*, 9, 67–84.

Bierly, M. M. (1985). Prejudice toward contemporary outgroups as a generalized attitude. *Journal of Applied Social Psychology*, 15, 189–199.

Bigam, R. G. (1981). Voir dire: The attorney's job. *Trial 13*, March 1977, p. 3. Cited by G. Bermant & J. Shepard in "The voir dire examination, juror challenges, and adversary advocacy." In B. D. Sales (Ed.), *Perspectives in law and psychology (Vol. II): The trial process.* New York: Plenum Press.

Billig, M. (1988). Social representation, objectification and anchoring: A rhetorical analysis. *Social Behaviour*, 3, 1–16.

Billig, M., & Tajfel, H. (1973). Social categorization and similarity in intergroup behaviour.

European Journal of Social Psychology, 3, 27–52.

Binham, R. (1980, March–April). Trivers in Jamaica. *Science 80,* pp. 57–67.

Bishop, G. D. (1987). Lay conceptions of physical symptoms. *Journal of Applied Social Psychology,* 17, 127–146.

Blackburn, R. T., Pellino, G. R., Boberg, A., & O'Connell, C. (1980). Are instructional improvement programs off target? *Current Issues in Higher Education,* 1, 32–48.

Blackstone, W. (1980). *Commentaries on the laws of England of public wrongs.* Boston: Beacon Press, 1972. (Originally published 1769). Cited by M. F. Kaplan and C. Scherschling in "Reducing juror bias: An experimental approach." In P. D. Lipsitt & B. D. Sales (Eds.), *New directions in psychological research.* New York: Van Nostrand Reinhold.

Blake, R. R., & Mouton, J. S. (1962). The intergroup dynamics of win-lose conflict and problem-solving collaboration in union-management relations. In M. Sherif (Ed.), *Intergroup relations and leadership.* New York: Wiley.

Blake, R. R., & Mouton, J. S. (1979). Intergroup problem solving in organizations: From theory to practice. In W. G. Austin and S. Worchel (Eds.), *The social psychology of intergroup relations.* Monterey, Calif.: Brooks/Cole.

Blanchard, F. A., & Cook, S. W. (1976). Effects of helping a less competent member of a co-operating interracial group on the development of interpersonal attraction. *Journal of Personality and Social Psychology,* 34, 1245–1255.

Blank, P. D., Rosenthal, R., & Cordell, L. H. (1985). The appearance of justice: Judges' verbal and nonverbal behavior in criminal jury trials. *Stanford Law Review,* 38, 89–164.

Block, J., & Funder, D. C. (1986). Social roles and social perception: Individual differences in attribution and error. *Journal of Personality and Social Psychology,* 51, 1200–1207.

Bodenhausen, G. V. (1988). Stereotypic biases in social decision making and memory: Testing process models of stereotype use. *Journal of Personality and Social Psychology,* 55, 726–737.

Boggiano, A. K., Barrett, M., Weiher, A. W., McClelland, G. H., & Lusk, C. M. (1987). *Journal of Personality and Social Psychology,* 53, 866–879.

Boggiano, A. K., Harackiewicz, J. M., Bessette, J. M., & Main, D. S. (1985). Increasing children's interest through performance-contingent reward. *Social Cognition,* 3, 400–411.

Boggiano, A. K., & Ruble, D. N. (1985). Chil-dren's responses to evaluative feedback. In R. Schwarzer (Ed.), *Self-related cognitions in anxiety and motivation.* Hillsdale, N.J.: Erlbaum.

Bohner, G., Bless, H., Schwarz, N., & Strack, F. (1988). What triggers causal attributions? The impact of valence and subjective probability. *European Journal of Social Psychology,* 18, 335–345.

Bond, C. F., Jr., & Anderson, E. L. (1987). The reluctance to transmit bad news: Private discomfort or public display? *Journal of Experimental Social Psychology,* 23, 176–187.

Bond, C. F., Jr., & Titus, L. J. (1983). Social facilitation: A meta-analysis of 241 studies. *Psychological Bulletin,* 94, 265–292.

Bond, M. H. (1979). Winning either way: The effect of anticipating a competitive interaction on person perception. *Personality and Social Psychology Bulletin,* 5, 316–319.

Bond, M. H. (1988). *The cross-cultural challenge to social psychology.* Newbury Park, Ca.: Sage.

Bond, M. H. (1989). Finding universal dimensions of individual variation in multi-cultural studies of values: The Rokeach and Chinese Value Surveys. *Journal of Personality and Social Psychology,* in press.

Borchard, E. M. (1932). *Convicting the innocent: Errors of criminal justice.* New Haven: Yale University Press. Cited by E. R. Hilgard & E. F. Loftus (1979) "Effective interrogation of the eyewitness." *International Journal of Clinical and Experimental Hypnosis,* 27, 342–359.

Borgida, E. (1981). Legal reform of rape laws. In L. Bickman (Ed.), *Applied Social Psychology Annual.* Vol. 2. Beverly Hills, Calif.: Sage Publications, pp. 211–241.

Borgida, E., & Brekke, N. (1985). Psycholegal research on rape trials. In A. W. Burgess (Ed.), *Rape and sexual assault: A research handbook.* New York: Garland.

Borgida, E., & Campbell, B. (1982). Belief relevance and attitude-behavior consistency: The moderating role of personal experience. *Journal of Personality and Social Psychology,* 42, 239–247.

Borgida, E., Locksley, A., & Brekke, N. (1981). Social stereotypes and social judgment. In N. Cantor & J. Kihlstrom (Eds.), *Cognition, social interaction, and personality.* Hillsdale, N.J.: Lawrence Erlbaum.

Borgida, E., & White, P. (1980). Judgmental bias and legal reform. Unpublished manuscript, University of Minnesota.

Bornstein, G., & Rapoport, A. (1988). Intergroup competition for the provision of step-level public goods: Effects of preplay commu-nication. *European Journal of Social Psychology* 18, 125–142.

Bossard, J. H. S. (1932). Residential propinquity as a factor in marriage selection. *American Journal of Sociology,* 38, 219–224.

Bothwell, R. K., Brigham, J. C., & Malpass, R. S. (1989). Cross-racial identification. *Personality and Social Psychology Bulletin,* 15, 19–25.

Bothwell, R. K., Deffenbacher, K. A., & Brigham, J. C. (1987). Correlation of eyewitness accuracy and confidence: Optimality hypothesis revised. *Journal of Applied Psychology,* 72, 691–695.

Bowen, E. (1988, April 4). What ever became of Honest Abe? *Time,* p. 68.

Bower, G. H. (1981, June). Mood and memory. *Psychology Today,* pp. 60–69.

Bower, G. H. (1986). Prime time in cognitive psychology. In P. Eelen (Ed.), *Cognitive research and behavior therapy: Beyond the conditioning paradigm.* Amsterdam: North Holland Publishers.

Bower, G. H. (1987). Commentary on mood and memory. *Behavioral Research and Therapy,* 25, 443–455.

Boyd, B. (1988, December 17). Women in the board room. *Detroit News,* p. C1.

Bower, G. H., & Masling, M. (1979). Causal explanations as mediators for remembering correlations. Unpublished manuscript, Stanford University.

Bradley, W., & Mannell, R. C. (1984). Sensitivity of intrinsic motivation to reward procedure instructions. *Personality and Social Psychology Bulletin,* 10, 426–431.

Brandon, R., & Davies, C. (1973). *Wrongful imprisonment: Mistaken convictions and their consequences.* Hamden, Conn.: Archon Books.

Bray, R. M., & Kerr, N. L. (1982). Methodological considerations in the study of the psychology of the courtroom. In N. L. Kerr & R. M. Bray (Eds.), *The psychology of the courtroom.* Orlando, Fla.: Academic Press.

Bray, R. M., & Noble, A. M. (1978). Authoritarianism and decisions of mock juries: Evidence of jury bias and group polarization. *Journal of Personality and Social Psychology,* 36, 1424–1430.

Bray, R. M., & Sugarman, R. (1980). Social facilitation among interacting groups: Evidence for the evaluation apprehension hypothesis. *Personality and Social Psychology Bulletin,* 6, 137–142.

Breckler, S. J. (1984). Empirical validation of affect, behavior, and cognition as distinct components of attitude. *Journal of Personality and Social Psychology,* 47, 1191–1205.

Bregman, N. J., & McAllister, H. A. (1982).

Eyewitness testimony: The role of commitment in increasing reliability. *Social Psychology Quarterly, 45,* 181–184.

Brehm, J. W. (1956). Post-decision changes in desirability of alternatives. *Journal of Abnormal Social Psychology, 52,* 384–389.

Brehm, S., & Brehm, J. W. (1981). *Psychological reactance: A theory of freedom and control.* New York: Academic Press.

Brehm, S. S., & Smith, T. W. (1986). Social psychological approaches to psychotherapy and behavior change. In S. L. Garfield & A. E. Bergin (Eds.), *Handbook of psychotherapy and behavior change,* 3rd ed. New York: Wiley.

Brenner, S. N., & Molander, E. A. (1977). Is the ethics of business changing? *Harvard Business Review,* January–February, pp. 57–71.

Bretl, D. J., & Cantor, J. (1988). The portrayal of men and women in U.S. television commercials: A recent content analysis and trends over 15 years. *Sex Roles, 18,* 595–609.

Brewer, M. B. (1979). In-group bias in the minimal intergroup situation: A cognitive-motivational analysis. *Psychological Bulletin, 86,* 307–324.

Brewer, M. B. (1987). Collective decisions. *Social Science, 72,* 140–143.

Brewer, M. B. (1988). A dual process model of impression formation. In T. Srull & R. Wyer (Eds.), *Advances in Social Cognition,* Vol. 1. Hillsdale, N.J.: Erlbaum.

Brewer, M. B., & Lui, L. (1984). Categorization of the elderly by the elderly: Effects of perceiver's category membership. *Personality and Social Psychology Bulletin, 10,* 585–595.

Brewer, M. B., & Miller, N. (1988). Contact and cooperation: When do they work? In P. A. Katz & D. Taylor (Eds.), *Towards the elimination of racism: Profiles in controversy.* New York: Plenum.

Brewer, M. B., & Silver, M. (1978). In-group bias as a function of task characteristics. *European Journal of Social Psychology, 8,* 393–400.

Brickman, P. (1978). Is it real? In J. Harvey, W. Ickes, & R. Kidd (Eds.), *New directions in attribution research.* Vol. 2. Hillsdale, N.J.: Erlbaum.

Brickman, P., & Campbell, D. T. (1971). Hedonic relativism and planning the good society. In M. H. Appley (Ed.), *Adaptation-level theory.* New York: Academic Press.

Brickman, P., Coates, D., & Janoff-Bulman, R. J. (1978). Lottery winners and accident victims: Is happiness relative? *Journal of Personality and Social Psychology, 36,* 917–927.

Brickman, P., Rabinowitz, V. C., Karuza, J.,

Jr., Coates, D., Cohn, E., & Kidder, L. (1982). Models of helping and coping. *American Psychologist, 37,* 368–384.

Brickner, M. A., Harkins, S. G., & Ostrom, T. M. (1986). Effects of personal involvement: Thought-provoking implications for social loafing. *Journal of Personality and Social Psychology, 51,* 763–769.

Brigham, J. C., & Cairns, D. L. (1988). The effect of mugshot inspections on eyewitness identification accuracy. *Journal of Applied Social Psychology, 18,* 1394–1410.

Brigham, J. C., & Malpass, R. S. (1985). The role of experience and contact in the recognition of faces of own- and other-race persons. *Journal of Social Issues, 41,* 139–155.

Brigham, J. C., & Richardson, C. B. (1979). Race, sex, and helping in the marketplace. *Journal of Applied Social Psychology, 9,* 314–322.

Brigham, J. C., & Williamson, N. L. (1979). Cross-racial recognition and age: When you're over 60, do they still all look alike? *Personality and Social Psychology Bulletin, 5,* 218–222.

Brock, T. C. (1965). Communicator-recipient similarity and decision change. *Journal of Personality and Social Psychology, 1,* 650–654.

Brockner, J., & Hulton, A. J. B. (1978). How to reverse the vicious cycle of low self-esteem: The importance of attentional focus. *Journal of Experimental Social Psychology, 14,* 564–578.

Brockner, J., Rubin, J. Z., Fine, J., Hamilton, T. P., Thomas, B., & Turetsky, B. (1982). Factors affecting entrapment in escalating conflicts: The importance of timing. *Journal of Research in Personality, 16,* 247–266.

Brodt, S. E., & Zimbardo, P. G. (1981). Modifying shyness-related social behavior through symptom misattribution. *Journal of Personality and Social Psychology, 41,* 437–449.

Bronfenbrenner, U. (1961). The mirror image in Soviet-American relations. *Journal of Social Issues, 17*(3), 45–56.

Brook, P. (1969). Filming a masterpiece. *Observer Weekend Review,* July 26, 1964. Cited by L. Tiger in *Men in groups.* New York: Random House, p. 163.

Brooks, W. N., & Doob, A. N. (1975). Justice and the jury. *Journal of Social Issues, 31,* 171–182.

Brown, D. (1971). *Bury my heart at Wounded Knee.* New York: Holt, Rinehart, & Winston.

Brown, J. D. (1986). Evaluations of self and others: Self-enhancement biases in social judgments. *Social Cognition, 4,* 353–376.

Brown, J. D., Collins, R. L., & Schmidt, G. W. (1988). Self-esteem and direct versus indirect

forms of self-enhancement. *Journal of Personality and Social Psychology, 55,* 445–453.

Brown, J. D., & Siegel, J. M. (1988). Attributions for negative life events and depression: The role of perceived control. *Journal of Personality and Social Psychology, 54,* 316–322.

Brown, J. D., & Taylor, S. E. (1986). Affect and the processing of personal information: Evidence for mood-activated self-schemata. *Journal of Experimental Social Psychology, 22,* 436–452.

Brown, R. (1965). *Social psychology.* New York: Free Press.

Brown, R. (1974). Further comment on the risky shift. *American Psychologist, 29,* 468–470.

Brownmiller, S. (1980). Comments on the "pornography and aggression" symposium at the American Psychological Association convention.

Brownmiller, S. (1984, November). Comments in debate on "The place of pornography," *Harper's,* pp. 31–45.

Bruck, C. (1976, April). Zimbardo: Solving the maze. *Human Behavior,* pp. 25–31.

Bryan, J. H., & Test, M. A. (1967). Models and helping: Naturalistic studies in aiding behavior. *Journal of Personality and Social Psychology, 6,* 400–407.

Bryant, J., & Zillmann, D. (1979). Effect of intensification of annoyance through unrelated residual excitation on substantially delayed hostile behavior. *Journal of Experimental Social Psychology, 15,* 470–480.

Buckhout, R. (1974, December). Eyewitness testimony. *Scientific American,* pp. 23–31.

Bulletin of the Atomic Scientists (1988, April). Nuclear pursuits. p. 60.

Bundy, T. (1989, January 25). Interview with James Dobson. *Detroit Free Press,* pp. 1A, 5A.

Burchill, S. A. L., & Stiles, W. B. (1988). Interactions of depressed college students with their roommates: Not necessarily negative. *Journal of Personality and Social Psychology, 55,* 410–419.

Burger, J. M. (1986). Temporal effects on attributions: Actor and observer differences. *Social Cognition, 4,* 377–387.

Burger, J. M. (1987). Increased performance with increased personal control: A self-presentation interpretation. *Journal of Experimental Social Psychology, 23,* 350–360.

Burger, J. M., & Burns, L. (1988). The illusion of unique invulnerability and the use of effective contraception. *Personality and Social Psychology Bulletin, 14,* 264–270.

Burger, J. M., & Petty, R. E. (1981). The lowball compliance technique: Task or person commitment? *Journal of Personality and Social Psychology, 40*, 492–500.

Burgess, R. L., & Huston, T. L. (Eds.) (1979). *Social exchange in developing relationships.* New York: Academic Press.

Burns, D. D. (1980). *Feeling good: The new mood therapy.* New York: Signet.

Burnstein, E., & Kitayama, S. (1989). Persuasion in groups. In T. C. Brock & S. Shavitt (Eds.), *The psychology of persuasion.* San Francisco: Freeman.

Burnstein, E., & Vinokur, A. (1977). Persuasive argumentation and social comparison as determinants of attitude polarization. *Journal of Experimental Social Psychology, 13*, 315–332.

Burnstein, E., & Worchel, P. (1962). Arbitrariness of frustration and its consequences for aggression in a social situation. *Journal of Personality, 30*, 528–540.

Burr, W. R. (1973). *Theory construction and the sociology of the family.* New York: Wiley.

Burros, M. (1988, February 24). Women: Out of the house but not out of the kitchen. *New York Times.*

Burton, J. W. (1969). *Conflict and communication.* New York: Free Press.

Buss, A. H. (1971). Aggression pays. In J. L. Singer (Ed.), *The control of aggression and violence: Cognitive and physiological factors.* New York: Academic Press.

Buss, D. M. (1984). Toward a psychology of person-environment (PE) correlation: The role of spouse selection. *Journal of Personality and Social Psychology, 47*, 361–377.

Buss, D. M. (1985). Human mate selection. *American Scientist, 73*, 47–51.

Buss, D. M. (1987). Sex differences in human mate selection criteria: An evolutionary perspective. In C. Crawford, M. Smith, & D. Krebs (Eds.), *Sociobiology and psychology: Issues, ideas, and findings.* Hillsdale, N.J.: Erlbaum.

Buss, D. M. (1988). The evolution of human intrasexual competition: Tactics of mate attraction. *Journal of Personality and Social Psychology, 54*, 616–628.

Buss, D. M. (1989). Sex differences in human mate preferences: Evolutionary hypotheses tested in 37 cultures. *Behavioral and Brain Sciences, 12*, 1–49.

Butcher, S. H. (1951). *Aristotle's theory of poetry and fine art.* New York: Dover Publications.

Byrne, D. (1971). *The attraction paradigm.* New York: Academic Press.

Byrne, D., & Clore, G. L. (1970). A reinforcement model of evaluative responses. *Personality: An International Journal, 1*, 103–128.

Byrne, D., & Nelson, D. (1965). Attraction as a linear function of proportion of positive reinforcements. *Journal of Personality and Social Psychology, 1*, 659–663.

Byrne, D., & Wong, T. J. (1962). Racial prejudice, interpersonal attraction, and assumed dissimilarity of attitudes. *Journal of Abnormal and Social Psychology, 65*, 246–253.

Bytwerk, R. L. (1976). Julius Streicher and the impact of *Der Stürmer. Wiener Library Bulletin, 29*, 41–46.

Bytwerk, R. L., & Brooks, R. D. (1980). Julius Streicher and the rhetorical foundations of the holocaust. Paper presented to the Central States Speech Association convention.

Cacioppo, J. T., Martzke, J. S., Petty, R. E., & Tassinary, L. G. (1988). Specific forms of facial EMG response index emotions during an interview: From Darwin to the continuous flow hypothesis of affect-laden information processing. *Journal of Personality and Social Psychology, 54*, 592–604.

Cacioppo, J. T., & Petty, R. E. (1986). Social processes. In M. G. H. Coles, E. Donchin, & S. W. Porges (Eds.), *Psychophysiology.* New York: Guilford Press.

Cacioppo, J. T., Petty, R. E., Kao, C. F., & Rodriguez, R. (1986). Central and peripheral routes to persuasion: An individual difference perspective. *Journal of Personality and Social Psychology, 51*, 1032–1043.

Cacioppo, J. T., Petty, R. E., & Morris, K. J. (1983). Effects of need for cognition on message evaluation, recall, and persuasion. *Journal of Personality and Social Psychology, 45*, 805–818.

Cacioppo, J. T., Tassinary, L. G., Stonebraker, T. B., & Petty, R. E. (1987). Self-report and cardiovascular measures of arousal fractionation during residual arousal. *Biological Psychology, 25*, 1–17.

Calhoun, J. B. (1962, February). Population density and social pathology. *Scientific American*, pp. 139–148.

Callero, P. L., & Piliavin, J. A. (1983). Developing a commitment to blood donation: The impact of one's first experience. *Journal of Applied Social Psychology, 13*, 1–16.

Cameron, P. (1977). *The life cycle: Perspectives and commentary.* Oceanside, N.Y.: Dabor.

Campbell, D.T. (1975). The conflict between social and biological evolution and the concept of original sin. *Zygon, 10*, 234–249. (*a*)

Campbell, D. T. (1975). On the conflicts between biological and social evolution and between psychology and moral tradition. *American Psychologist, 30*, 1103–1126. (*b*)

Campbell, E. Q., & Pettigrew, T.F. (1959). Ra-

cial and moral crisis: The role of Little Rock ministers. *American Journal of Sociology, 64*, 509–516.

Cann, A., Calhoun, L. G., & Selby, J. W. (1979). Attributing responsibility to the victim of rape: Influence of information regarding past sexual experience. *Human Relations, 32*, 57–67.

Cantril, H., & Bumstead, C. H. (1960). *Reflections on the human venture.* New York: New York University Press.

Caplan, N. (1970). The new ghetto man: A review of recent empirical studies. *Journal of Social Issues, 26*(1), 59–73.

Caproni, V., Levine, D., O'Neal, E., McDonald, P., & Garwood, G. (1977). Seating position, instructor's eye contact availability, and student participation in a small seminar. *Journal of Social Psychology, 103*, 315–316.

Carducci, B. J., Cosby, P. C., & Ward, C. D. (1978). Sexual arousal and interpersonal evaluations. *Journal of Experimental Social Psychology, 14*, 449–457.

Carlsmith, J. M., & Anderson, C. A. (1979). Ambient temperature and the occurrence of collective violence: A new analysis. *Journal of Personality and Social Psychology, 37*, 337–344.

Carlsmith, J. M., & Gross, A. E. (1968). Some effects of guilt on compliance. *Journal of Personality and Social Psychology. 11*, 232–239.

Carlsmith, J. M., Ellsworth, P., & Whiteside, J. (1978). Guilt, confession and compliance. Unpublished manuscript, Stanford University, 1968. Cited by J. L. Freeman, D. O. Sears, & J. M. Carlsmith in *Social psychology.* Englewood Cliffs, N.J.: Prentice-Hall, pp. 275–276.

Carlson, J. G., & Hatfield, E. (1989). *Psychology of emotion.* Belmont, Ca.: Wadsworth.

Carlson, M., Charlin, V., & Miller, N. (1988). Positive mood and helping behavior: A test of six hypotheses. *Journal of Personality and Social Psychology, 55*, 211–229.

Carlson, M., & Miller, N. (1987). Explanation of the relation between negative mood and helping. *Psychological Bulletin, 102*, 91–108.

Carlson, S. (1985). A double-blind test of astrology. *Nature, 318*, 419–425.

Carlston, D. E., & Shovar, N. (1983). Effects of performance attributions on others' perceptions of the attributor. *Journal of Personality and Social Psychology, 44*, 515–525.

Carretta, T. R., & Moreland, R. L. (1982). Nixon and Watergate: A field demonstration of belief perseverance. *Personality and Social Psychology Bulletin, 8*, 446–453.

Carroll, E. I. (1971). *The face of emotion.* New York: Appleton.

Carter, B. D., & McCloskey, L. A. (1983–1984). Peers and the maintenance of sex-typed behavior: The development of children's conceptions of cross-gender behavior in their peers. *Social Cognition*, 2, 294–314.

Cartwright, D. S. (1975). The nature of gangs. In D. S. Cartwright, B. Tomson, & H. Schwartz (Eds.), *Gang delinquency*. Monterey, Calif.: Brooks/Cole.

Carver, C. S., Ganellen, R. J., Froming, W. J., & Chambers, W. (1983). Modeling: An analysis in terms of category accessibility. *Journal of Experimental Social Psychology*, 19, 403–421.

Carver, C. S., & Scheier, M. F. (1978). Self-focusing effects of dispositional self-consciousness, mirror presence, and audience presence. *Journal of Personality and Social Psychology*, 36, 324–332.

Carver, C. S., & Scheier, M. F. (1981). *Attention and self-regulation*. New York: Springer-Verlag.

Carver, C. S., & Scheier, M. F. (1986). Analyzing shyness: A specific application of broader self-regulatory principles. In W. H. Jones, J. M. Cheek, & S. R. Briggs (Eds.), *Shyness: Perspectives on research and treatment*. New York: Plenum.

Cash, T. F. (1981). Physical attractiveness: An annotated bibliography of theory and research in the behavioral sciences (Ms. 2370). *Catalog of Selected Documents in Psychology*, 11, 83.

Cash, T. F., & Janda, L. H. (1984, December). The eye of the beholder. *Psychology Today*, pp. 46–52.

Cass, R. C., & Edney, J. J. (1978). The commons dilemma: A simulation testing the effects of resource visibility and territorial division. *Human Ecology*, 6, 371–386.

CBS News/New York Times (1979, January-February). Poll on sex-role norms, October 1977. Reported in *Public Opinion*, p. 37.

Ceci, S. J., & Peters, D. (1984). Letters of reference: A naturalistic study of the effects of confidentiality. *American Psychologist*, 39, 29–31.

Ceci, S. J., Toglia, M. P., & Ross, D. F. (1987). *Children's eyewitness memory*. New York: Springer-Verlag.

Chagnon, N. A. (1988). Life histories, blood revenge, and warfare in a tribal population. *Science*, 239, 985–991.

Chaiken, S. (1979). Communicator physical attractiveness and persuasion. *Journal of Personality and Social Psychology*, 37, 1387–1397.

Chaiken, S. (1980). Heuristic versus systematic information processing and the use of source versus message cues in persuasion. *Journal of Personality and Social Psychology*, 39, 752–766.

Chaiken, S. (1987). The heuristic model of persuasion. In M. P. Zanna, J. M. Olson, & C. P. Herman (Eds.), *Social influence: The Ontario symposium*, Vol. 5. Hillsdale, N.J.: Erlbaum.

Chaiken, S., & Eagly, A. H. (1978). Communication modality as a determinant of message persuasiveness and message comprehensibility. *Journal of Personality and Social Psychology*, 34, 605–614.

Chaiken, S., & Eagly, A. H. (1983). Communication modality as a determinant of persuasion: The role of communicator salience. *Journal of Personality and Social Psychology*, 45, 241–256.

Chance, J. E. (1985). Faces, folklore, and research hypotheses. Presidential address to the Midwestern Psychological Association convention.

Chance, J. E., & Goldstein, A. G. (1981). Depth of processing in response to own- and other-race faces. *Personality and Social Psychology Bulletin*, 7, 475–480.

Chapman, L. J., & Chapman, J. P. (1969). Genesis of popular but erroneous psychodiagnostic observations. *Journal of Abnormal Psychology*, 74, 272–280.

Chapman, L. J., & Chapman J. P. (1971, November). Test results are what you think they are. *Psychology Today*, pp. 18–22, 106–107.

Charny, I. W. (1982). *How can we commit the unthinkable? Genocide: The human cancer*. Boulder, Co.: Westview Press.

Check, J., & Malamuth, N. (1984). Can there be positive effects of participation in pornography experiments? *Journal of Sex Research*, 20, 14–31.

Chen, S. C. (1937). Social modification of the activity of ants in nest-building. *Physiological Zoology*, 10, 420–436.

Chickering, A. W., & McCormick, J. (1973). Personality development and the college experience. *Research in Higher Education*, No. 1, 62–64.

Christensen, L. (1988). Deception in psychological research: When is its use justified? *Personality and Social Psychology Bulletin*, 14, 664–675.

Christian, J. J., Flyger, V., & Davis, D. E. (1960). Factors in the mass mortality of a herd of sika deer, *Cervus Nippon*. *Chesapeake Science*, 1, 79–95.

Church, G. J. (1986, January 6). China. *Time*, pp. 6–19.

Cialdini, R. B. (1988). *Influence: Science and practice*. Glenview, Il.: Scott, Foresman/Little, Brown.

Cialdini, R. B., Bickman, L., & Caccioppo, J. T. (1979). An example of consumeristic social psychology: Bargaining tough in the new car showroom. *Journal of Applied Social Psychology*, 9, 115–126.

Cialdini, R. B., Borden, R. J., Thorne, A., Walker, M. R., Freeman, S., & Sloan, L. R. (1976). Basking in reflected glory: Three (football) field studies. *Journal of Personality and Social Psychology*, 39, 406–415.

Cialdini, R. B., Cacioppo, J. T., Bassett, R., & Miller, J. A. (1978). Lowball procedure for producing compliance: Commitment then cost. *Journal of Personality and Social Psychology*, 36, 463–476.

Cialdini, R. B., Darby, B. L., & Vincent, J. E. (1973). Transgression and altruism: A case for hedonism. *Journal of Experimental Social Psychology*, 9, 502–516.

Cialdini, R. B., & Kenrick, D. T. (1976). Altruism as hedonism: A social development perspective on the relationship of negative mood state and helping. *Journal of Personality and Social Psychology*, 34, 907–914.

Cialdini, R. B., Kenrick, D. T., & Baumann, D. J. (1981). Effects of mood on prosocial behavior in children and adults. In N. Eisenberg-Berg (Ed.), *The development of prosocial behavior*. New York: Academic Press.

Cialdini, R. B., & Richardson, K. D. (1980). Two indirect tactics of image management: Basking and blasting. *Journal of Personality and Social Psychology*, 39, 406–415.

Cialdini, R. B., & Schroeder, D. A. (1976). Increasing compliance by legitimizing paltry contributions: When even a penny helps. *Journal of Personality and Social Psychology*, 34, 599–604.

Cialdini, R. B., Vincent, J. E., Lewis, S. K., Catalan, J., Wheeler, D., & Danby, B. L. (1975). Reciprocal concessions procedure for inducing compliance: The door-in-the-face technique. *Journal of Personality and Social Psychology*, 31, 206–215.

Cicero. *De Finibus*. Book iii, chap. 9, sec. 31.

Clark, K., & Clark, M. (1947). Racial identification and preference in Negro children. In T. M. Newcomb & E. L. Hartley (Eds.), *Readings in social psychology*. New York: Holt.

Clark, M. S. (1984). Record keeping in two types of relationships. *Journal of Personality and Social Psychology*, 47, 549–557.

Clark, M. S. (1986). Evidence for the effectiveness of manipulations of desire for communal versus exchange relationships. *Personality and Social Psychology Bulletin*, 12, 414–425.

Clark, M. S., & Mills, J. (1979). Interpersonal attraction in exchange and communal relationships. *Journal of Personality and Social Psychology*, **37**, 12–24.

Clark, M. S., Mills, J., & Corcoran, D. (1989). Keeping track of needs and inputs of friends and strangers. *Personality and Social Psychology Bulletin*, in press.

Clark, M. S., Mills, J., & Powell, M. C. (1986). Keeping track of needs in communal and exchange relationships. *Journal of Personality and Social Psychology*, **51**, 333–338.

Clark, R. D., III (1974). Effects of sex and race on helping behavior in a nonreactive setting. *Representative Research in Social Psychology*, **5**, 1–6.

Clark, R. D., III (1975). The effects of reinforcement, punishment and dependency on helping behavior. *Personality and Social Psychology Bulletin*, **1**, 596–599.

Clark, R. D., III, & Maas, A. (1988). Social categorization in minority influence: The case of homosexuality. *European Journal of Social Psychology*, **18**, 347–364.

Clark, R. D., III, & Maas, A. (1989). The role of social categorization and perceived source credibility in minority influence. *European Journal of Social Psychology*, **19**, in press.

Clarke, A. C. (1952). An examination of the operation of residual propinquity as a factor in mate selection. *American Sociological Review*, **27**, 17–22.

Cleghorn, R. (1980, October 31). ABC News, meet the Literary Digest. *Detroit Free Press*.

Clifford, M. M., & Walster, E. H. (1973). The effect of physical attractiveness on teacher expectation. *Sociology of Education*, **46**, 248–258.

Cline, V. B., Croft, R. G., & Courrier, S. (1973). Desensitization of children to television violence. *Journal of Personality and Social Psychology*, **27**, 360–365.

Clore, G. L., Bray, R. M., Itkin, S. M., & Murphy, P. (1978). Interracial attitudes and behavior at a summer camp. *Journal of Personality and Social Psychology*, **36**, 107–116.

Clore, G. L., Wiggins, N. H., & Itkin, G. (1975). Gain and loss in attraction: Attributions from nonverbal behavior. *Journal of Personality and Social Psychology*, **31**, 706–712.

Coates, B., Pusser, H. E., & Goodman, I. (1976). The influence of "Sesame Street" and "Mister Rogers' Neighborhood" on children's social behavior in the preschool. *Child Development*, **47**, 138–144.

Cocozza, J. J., & Steadman, H. J. (1978). Prediction in psychiatry: An example of misplaced confidence in experts. *Social Problems*, **25**, 265–276.

Codol, J.-P. (1976). On the so-called superior conformity of the self behavior: Twenty experimental investigations. *European Journal of Social Psychology*, **5**, 457–501.

Cohen, D. (1980, March). Familiar faces at the British psychology society meeting. *APA Monitor*, p. 13.

Cohen, E. G. (1980). Design and redesign of the desegregated school: Problems of status, power and conflict. In W. G. Stephan & J. R. Feagin (Eds.), *School desegregation: Past, present, and future*. New York: Plenum Press. (*a*)

Cohen, E. G. (1980). A multi-ability approach to the integrated classroom. Paper presented at the American Psychological Association convention. (*b*)

Cohen, S. (1980). Training to understand TV advertising: Effects and some policy implications. Paper presented at the American Psychological Association convention.

Coherty, W. J., & Baldwin, C. (1985). Shifts and stability in locus of control during the 1970s: Divergence of the sexes. *Journal of Personality and Social Psychology*, **48**, 1048–1053.

Cole, D. L. (1982). Psychology as a liberating art. *Teaching of Psychology*, **9**, 23–26.

Coleman, J. S. (1957). *Community conflict*. New York: Free Press.

Coleman, L. M., Jussim, L., & Abraham, J. (1987). Students' reactions to teachers' evaluations: The unique impact of negative feedback. *Journal of Applied Social Psychology*, **17**, 1051–1070.

Collins, B. E., & Hoyt, M. F. (1972). Personal responsibility-for-consequences: An integration and extension of the forced compliance literature. *Journal of Experimental Social Psychology*, **8**, 558–593.

Condon, J. W., & Crano, W. D. (1988). Inferred evaluation and the relation between attitude similarity and interpersonal attraction. *Journal of Personality and Social Psychology*, **54**, 789–797.

Condran, J. G. (1979). Changes in white attitudes toward blacks: 1963–1977. *Public Opinion Quarterly*, **43**, 463–476.

Condry, J., & Condry, S. (1976). Sex differences: A study in the eye of the beholder. *Child Development*, **47**, 812–819.

Converse, P. E., & Traugott, M. W. (1986). Assessing the accuracy of polls and surveys. *Science*, **234**, 1094–1098.

Conway, F., & Siegelman, J. (1979). *Snapping: America's epidemic of sudden personality change*. New York: Delta Books.

Conway, M., & Ross, M. (1984). Getting what you want by revising what you had. *Journal of Personality and Social Psychology*, **47**, 738–748.

Conway, M., & Ross, M. (1985). Remembering one's own past: The construction of personal histories. In R. Sorrentino & E. T. Higgins (Eds.), *Handbook of motivation and cognition*. New York: Guilford.

Cook, S. W. (1978). Interpersonal and attitudinal outcomes in cooperating interracial groups. *Journal of Research and Development in Education*, **12**, 97–113.

Cook, S. W. (1985). Experimenting on social issues: The case of school desegregation. *American Psychologist*, **40**, 452–460.

Cook, T. D., & Curtin, T. R. (1987). The mainstream and the underclass: Why are the differences so salient and the similarities so unobtrusive? In J. C. Masters & W. P. Smith (Eds.), *Social comparison, social justice, and relative deprivation: Theoretical, empirical, and policy perspectives*. Hillsdale, N.J.: Erlbaum.

Cook, T. D., & Flay, B. R. (1978). The persistance of experimentally induced attitude change. In L. Berkowitz (Ed.), *Advances in experimental social psychology*. Vol. 11. New York: Academic Press.

Cooper, H. (1983). Teacher expectation effects. In L. Bickman (Ed.), *Applied social psychology annual*, Vol. 4. Beverly Hills, Ca.: Sage.

Cooper, H. M. (1979). Statistically combining independent studies: A metaanalysis of sex differences in conformity research. *Journal of Personality and Social Psychology*. **37**, 131–146.

Cooper, J., & Fazio, R. H. (1984). A new look at dissonance theory. In L. Berkowitz (Ed.), *Advances in Experimental Social Psychology*, Vol. 17. New York: Academic Press.

Cooper, J., Zanna, M. P., & Taves, P. A. (1978). Arousal as a necessary condition for attitude change following induced compliance. *Journal of Personality and Social Psychology*, **36**, 1101–1106.

Cota, A. A., & Dion, K. L. (1986). Salience of gender and ad hoc group sex composition: An experimental test of distinctiveness theory. *Journal of Personality and Social Psychology*, in press.

Cotton, J. L. (1981). Ambient temperature and violent crime. Paper presented at the Midwestern Psychological Association convention.

Cotton, J. L. (1986). Ambient temperature and violent crime. *Journal of Applied Social Psychology*, **16**, 786–801.

Cottrell, N. B., Wack, D. L., Sekerak, G. J., & Rittle, R. M. (1968). Social facilitation of dominant responses by the presence of an audience and the mere presence of others. *Jour-*

nal of Personality and Social Psychology, **9**, 245–250.

Court, J. H. (1985). Sex and violence: A ripple effect. In N. M. Malamuth & E. Donnerstein (Eds.), *Pornography and sexual aggression*. New York: Academic Press.

Cousins, N. (1978, September 16). The taxpayers revolt: Act two. *Saturday Review*, p. 56.

Cousins, S. D. (1989). Culture and self-perception in Japan and the United States. *Journal of Personality and Social Psychology*, **56**, 124–131.

Cramer, R. E., McMaster, M. R., Bartell, P. A., & Dragna, M. (1988). Subject competence and minimization of the bystander effect. *Journal of Applied Social Psychology*, **18**, 1133–1148.

Crandall, C. S. (1988). Social contagion of binge eating. *Journal of Personality and Social Psychology*, **55**, 588–598.

Crano, W. D., & Mellon, P. M. (1978). Causal influence of teachers' expectations on children's academic performance: A cross-legged panel analysis. *Journal of Educational Psychology*, **70**, 39–49.

Crawford, T. J. (1974). Sermons on racial tolerance and the parish neighborhood context. *Journal of Applied Social Psychology*, **4**, 1–23.

Crocker, J. (1981). Judgment of covariation by social perceivors. *Psychological Bulletin*, **90**, 272–292.

Crocker, J., & Gallo, L. (1985). The self-enhancing effect of downward comparison. Paper presented at the American Psychological Association convention.

Crocker, J., Hannah, D. B., & Weber, R. (1983). Personal memory and causal attributions. *Journal of Personality and Social Psychology*, **44**, 55–56.

Crocker, J., & McGraw, K. M. (1984). What's good for the goose is not good for the gander: Solo status as an obstacle to occupational achievement for males and females. *American Behavioral Scientist*, **27**, 357–370.

Crocker, J., & Park, B. (1985). The consequences of social stereotypes. Unpublished manuscript, Northwestern University.

Crocker, J., Thompson, L. L., McGraw, K. M., & Ingerman, C. (1987). Downward comparison, prejudice, and evaluations of others: Effects of self-esteem and threat. *Journal of Personality and Social Psychology*, **52**, 907–916.

Crosby, F. (1982). *Relative deprivation and working women*. New York: Oxford University Press.

Crosby, F., Bromley, S., & Saxe, L. (1980). Recent unobtrusive studies of black and white

discrimination and prejudice: A literature review. *Psychological Bulletin*, **87**, 546–563.

Crosby, F., Pufall, A., Snyder, R. C., O'Connell, M., & Whalen, P. (1989). The denial of personal disadvantage among you, me, and all the other ostriches. In M. Crawford & M. Gentry (Eds.), *Gender and thought*. New York: Springer-Verlag, in press.

Cross, P. (1977). Not *can* but *will* college teaching be improved? *New directions for Higher Education*, Spring, No. 17, pp. 1–15.

Crouse, B. B., & Mehrabian, A. (1977). Affiliation of opposite-sexed strangers. *Journal of Research in Personality*, **11**, 38–47.

Croxton, J. S., Eddy, T., & Morrow, N. (1984). Memory biases in the reconstruction of interpersonal encounters. *Journal of Social and Clinical Psychology*, **2**, 348–354.

Croxton, J. S., & Miller, A. G. (1987). Behavioral disconfirmation and the observer bias. *Journal of Social Behavior and Personality*, **2**, 145–152.

Croxton, J. S., & Morrow, N. (1984). What does it take to reduce observer bias? *Psychological Reports*, **55**, 135–138.

Croyle, R. T., & Cooper, J. (1983). Dissonance arousal: Physiological evidence. *Journal of Personality and Social Psychology*, **45**, 782–791.

Crutchfield, R. A. (1955). Conformity and character. *American Psychologist*, **10**, 191–198.

Cunningham, J. D. (1981). Self-disclosure intimacy: Sex, sex-of-target, cross-national, and generational differences. *Personality and Social Psychology Bulletin*, **7**, 314–319.

Cunningham, M. R. (1986). Levites and brother's keepers: A sociobiological perspective on prosocial behavior. *Humboldt Journal of Social Relations*, **12**, 35–67.

Cunningham, M. R. (1986). Measuring the physical in physical attractiveness: Quasi-experiments on the sociobiology of female facial beauty. *Journal of Personality and Social Psychology*, **50**, 925–935.

Cunningham, M. R. (1988). Does happiness mean friendliness? Induced mood and heterosexual self-disclosure. *Personality and Social Psychology Bulletin*, **14**, 283–297. (a)

Cunningham, M. R. (1988). What do you do when you're happy or blue? Mood, expectancies and behavioral interest. *Motivation and Emotion*, in press. (b)

Cunningham, S. (1983, November). Not such a long way, baby: Women and cigarette ads. *APA Monitor*, p. 15.

Curry, T. J., & Emerson, R. M. (1970). Balance theory: A theory of interpersonal attraction? *Sociometry*, **33**, 216–238.

Curtis, R. C., & Miller, K. (1986). Believing an-

other likes or dislikes you: Behaviors making the beliefs come true. *Journal of Personality and Social Psychology*, **51**, 284–290.

Cutler, B. L., & Penrod, S. D. (1988). Context reinstatement and eyewitness identification. In G. M. Davies & D. M. Thomson (Eds.), *Context reinstatement and eyewitness identification*. New York: Wiley. (a)

Cutler, B. L., & Penrod, S. D. (1988). Improving the reliability of eyewitness identification: Lineup construction and presentation. *Journal of Applied Psychology*, **73**, in press. (b)

Cutler, B. L., Penrod, S. D., & Dexter, H. R. (1988). The eyewitness, the expert psychologist and the jury. *Law and Human Behavior*, in press.

Cutler, B. L., Penrod, S. D., & Martens, T. K. (1987). The reliability of eyewitness identification: The role of system and estimator variables. *Law and Human Behavior*, **11**, 233–258.

Cutler, B. L., Penrod, S. D., & Stuve, T. E. (1988). Juror decision making in eyewitness identification cases. *Law and Human Behavior*, **12**, 41–55.

Dabbs, J. M., & Janis, I. L. (1965). Why does eating while reading facilitate opinion change? An experimental inquiry. *Journal of Experimental Social Psychology*, **1**, 133–144.

Dabbs, Jr., J. M., Ruback, R. B., Frady, R. L., Hopper, C. H., & Sgoutas, D. S. (1988). Saliva testosterone and criminal violence among women. *Personality and Individual Differences*, **7**, 269–275.

Dallas, M. E. W., & Baron, R. S. (1985). Do psychotherapists use a confirmatory strategy during interviewing? *Journal of Social and Clinical Psychology*, **3**, 106–122.

Daniels, R. (1975). *The decision to relocate the Japanese Americans*. New York: Lippincott.

Darley, J. M., & Batson, C. D. (1973). From Jerusalem to Jericho: A study of situational and dispositional variables in helping behavior. *Journal of Personality and Social Psychology*, **27**, 100–108.

Darley, J. M., & Berscheid, E. (1967). Increased liking as a result of the anticipation of personal contact. *Human Relations*, **20**, 29–40.

Darley, J. M., Fleming, J. H., Hilton, J. L., & Swann, W. B., Jr. (1988). Dispelling negative expectancies: The impact of interaction goals and target characteristics on the expectancy confirmation process. *Journal of Experimental Social Psychology*, **24**, 19–36.

Darley, J. M., & Gross, P. H. (1983). A hypothesis-conforming bias in labelling effects. *Jour-*

nal of Personality and Social Psychology, 44, 20–33.

Darley, J. M., & Latané, B. (1968). Bystander intervention in emergencies: Diffusion of responsibility. Journal of Personality and Social Psychology, 8, 377–383.

Darley, J. M., & Latane, B. (1968, December). When will people help in a crisis? Psychology Today, pp. 54–57, 70–71.

Darley, J. M., Seligman, C., & Becker, L. J. (1979, April). The lesson of twin rivers: Feedback works. Psychology Today, pp. 16, 23–24.

Darley, J. M., Teger, A. I., & Lewis, L. D. (1973). Do groups always inhibit individuals' response to potential emergencies? Journal of Personality and Social Psychology, 26, 395–399.

Darley, S., & Cooper, J. (1972). Cognitive consequences of forced noncompliance. Journal of Personality and Social Psychology, 24, 321–326.

Darrow, C, (1933), cited by E. H. Sutherland & D. R. Cressy, Principles of criminology. Philadelphia: Lippincott, 1966, p. 442.

Dashiell, J. F. (1930). An experimental analysis of some group effects. Journal of Abnormal and Social Psychology, 25, 190–199.

Davis, J. H., Holt, R. W., Spitzer, C. E., & Stasser, G. (1981). The effects of consensus requirements and multiple decisions on mock juror verdict preferences. Journal of Experimental Social Psychology, 17, 1–15.

Davis, J. H., Kerr, N. L., Atkin, R. S., Holt, R., & Meek, D. (1975). The decision processes of 6- and 12-person mock juries assigned unanimous and two-thirds majority rules. Journal of Personality and Social Psychology, 32, 1–14.

Davis, J. H., Kerr, N. L., Strasser, G., Meek, D., & Holt, R. (1977). Victim consequences, sentence severity, and decision process in mock juries. Organizational Behavior and Human Performance, 18, 346-365.

Davis, K. E. (1985, February). Near and dear: Friendship and love compared. Psychology Today, pp. 22–30.

Davis, K. E., & Jones, E. E. (1960). Changes in interpersonal perception as a means of reducing cognitive dissonance. Journal of Abnormal and Social Psychology, 61, 402–410.

Davis, L., Laykasek, L., & Pratt, R. (1984). Teamwork and friendship: Answers to social loafing. Paper presented at the Southwestern Psychological Association, New Orleans.

Davis, M. H. (1979). The case for attributional egotism. Paper presented at the American Psychological Association convention.

Davis, M. H., & Franzoi, S. L. (1986). Adolescent loneliness, self-disclosure, and private self-consciousness: A longitudinal investigation. Journal of Personality and Social Psychology, 51, 595–608.

Davis, M. H., & Stephan, W. G. (1980). Attributions for exam performance. Journal of Applied Social Psychology, 10, 235–248.

Dawes, R. M. (1976). Shallow psychology. In J. S. Carroll & J. W. Payne (Eds.), Cognition and social behavior. Hillsdale, N.J.: Lawrence Erlbaum.

Dawes, R. M. (1980). Social dilemmas. Annual Review of Psychology, 31, 169–193.

Dawes, R. M. (1980). You can't systematize human judgment: Dyslexia. In R. A. Shweder (Ed.), New directions for methodology of social and behavioral science: Fallible judgment in behavioral research. San Francisco: Jossey-Bass.

Dawes, R. M. (1989, January). Resignation letter to the American Psychological Association. APS Observer, pp. 14–15.

Dawes, R. M., McTavish, J., & Shaklee, H. (1977). Behavior, communication, and assumptions about other people's behavior in a commons dilemma situation. Journal of Personality and Social Psychology, 35, 1–11.

Dawkins, R. (1976). The selfish gene. New York: Oxford University Press.

Deaux, K. (1984). From individual differences to social categories: Analysis of a decade's research on gender. American Psychologist, 39, 105–116.

Deaux, K., & Emswiller, T. (1974). Explanations of successful performance on sex-linked tasks: What is skill for the male is luck for the female. Journal of Personality and Social Psychology, 29, 80–85.

Deaver, M. (1985, October 9). Quoted in L. H. Gelb, Reagan: A master of political compromise and ideological purity. International Herald Tribune, p. 10.

Deci, E. L., Nezlek, J., & Sheinman, L. (1981). Characteristics of the rewarder and intrinsics of motivation of the rewardee. Journal of Personality and Social Psychology, 40, 1–10.

Deci, E. L., & Ryan, R. M. (1985). Intrinsic motivation and self-determination in human behavior. New York: Plenum.

Deci, E. L., & Ryan, R. M. (1987). The support of autonomy and the control of behavior. Journal of Personality and Social Psychology, 53, 1024–1037.

Deford, F. (1983, November 7). Sometimes the good die young. Sports Illustrated, pp. 44–50.

DeJong, W. (1979). An examination of self-perception mediation of the foot-in-the-door effect. Journal of Personality and Social Psychology, 37, 2221–2239.

DeJong-Gierveld, J. (1987). Developing and testing a model of loneliness. Journal of Personality and Social Psychology, 53, 119–128.

Delgado, J. (1973). In M. Pines, The brain changers. New York: Harcourt Brace Jovanovich.

Dembroski, T. M., & Costa, P. T., Jr. (1987). Coronary prone behavior: Components of the Type A pattern and hostility. Jounal of Personality, 55, 211–236.

Dembroski, T. M., Lasater, T. M., & Ramirez, A. (1978). Communicator similarity, fear arousing communications, and compliance with health care recommendations. Journal of Applied Social Psychology, 8, 254–269.

Dengerink, H. A., & Myers, J. D. (1977). Three effects of failure and depression on subsequent aggression. Journal of Personality and Social Psychology, 35, 88–96.

DePaulo, B. M., Kenny, D. A., Hoover, C. W., Webb, W., & Oliver, P. V. (1987). Journal of Personality and Social Psychology, 52, 303–315.

Derlega, V., Winstead, B. A., Wong, P. T. P., & Hunter, S. (1985). Gender effects in an initial encounter: A case where men exceed women in disclosure. Journal of Social and Personal Relationships, 2, 25–44.

Dermer, M., Cohen, S. J., Jacobsen, E., & Anderson, E. A. (1979). Evaluative judgments of aspects of life as a function of vicarious exposure to hedonic extremes. Journal of Personality and Social Psychology, 37, 247–260.

Dermer, M., & Pyszczynski, T. A. (1978). Effects of erotica upon men's loving and liking responses for women they love. Journal of Personality and Social Psychology, 36, 1302–1309.

Dermer, M., & Thiel, D. L. (1975). When beauty may fail. Journal of Personality and Social Psychology, 31, 1168–1176.

Desmond, E. W. (1987, November 30). Out in the open. Time, pp. 80–90.

Desor, J. A. (1972). Toward a psychological theory of crowding. Journal of Personality and Social Psychology, 21, 79–83.

Deutsch, M. (1985). Distributive justice: A social psychological perspective. New Haven: Yale University Press.

Deutsch, M. (1986). Folie à deux: A psychological perspective on Soviet-American relations. In M. P. Kearns (Ed.), Persistent patterns and emergent structures in a waving century. New York: Praeger.

Deutsch, M., & Collins, M. E. (1951). Interracial housing: A psychological evaluation of a social experiment. Minneapolis: University of Minnesota Press.

Deutsch, M., & Gerard, H. B. (1955). A study of normative and informational social influence upon individual judgment. *Journal of Abnormal and Social Psychology,* **51,** 629–636.

Deutsch, M., & Krauss, R. M. (1960). The effect of threat upon interpersonal bargaining. *Journal of Abnormal and Social Psychology,* **61,** 181–189.

deVaux, R. (1965). *Ancient Israel (Vol. 2): Religious institutions.* New York: McGraw-Hill.

Devine, P. G. (1989). Stereotypes and prejudice: Their automatic and controlled components. *Journal of Personality and Social Psychology,* **56,** 5–18.

Devine, P. G., & Malpass, R. S. (1985). Orienting strategies in differential face recognition. *Personality and Social Psychology Bulletin,* **11,** 33–40.

De Vries, N. K., & van Knippenberg, A. (1987). Biased and unbiased self-evaluations of ability: The effects of further testing. *British Journal of Social Psychology,* **26,** 9–15.

Dickson, D. H., & Kelly, I. W. (1985). The "Barnum effect" in personality assessment: A review of the literature. *Psychological Reports,* **57,** 367–382.

Diener, E. (1976). Effects of prior destructive behavior, anonymity, and group presence on deindividuation and aggression. *Journal of Personality and Social Psychology,* **33,** 497–507.

Diener, E. (1979). Deindividuation, self-awareness, and disinhibition. *Journal of Personality and Social Psychology,* **37,** 1160–1171.

Diener, E. (1980). Deindividuation: The absence of self-awareness and self-regulation in group members. In P. Paulus (Ed.), *The psychology of group influence.* Hillsdale, N.J.: Erlbaum.

Dierner, E., & Crandall, R. (1979). An evaluation of the Jamaican anticrime program. *Journal of Applied Social Psychology,* **9,** 135–146.

Diener, E., Fraser, S. C., Beaman, A. L., & Kelem, R. T. (1976). Effects of deindividuation variables on stealing among Halloween trick-or-treaters. *Journal of Personality and Social Psychology,* **33,** 178–183.

Diener, R., & Wallbom, M. (1976). Effects of self-awareness on antinormative behavior. *Journal of Research in Personality,* **10,** 107–111.

Dillard, J. P., Hunter, J. E., & Burgoon, M. (1984). Sequential-request persuasive strategies: Metaanalysis of foot-in-the-door and door-in-the-face. *Human Communication Research,* **10,** 461–488.

Dillehay, R. C., & Nietzel, M. T. (1980). Constructing a science of jury behavior. In L. Wheeler (Ed.), *Review of personality and social psychology* (Vol. 1). Beverly Hills, Calif.: Sage Publications.

Dion, K. K. (1972). Physical attractiveness and

evaluations of children's transgressions. *Journal of Personality and Social Psychology,* **24,** 207–213.

Dion, K. K. (1973). Young children's stereotyping of facial attractiveness. *Developmental Psychology,* **9,** 183–188.

Dion, K. K. (1979). Physical attractiveness and interpersonal attraction. In M. Cook & G. Wilson (Eds.), *Love and attraction.* New York: Pergamon Press.

Dion, K. K., & Berscheid, E. (1974). Physical attractiveness and peer perception among children. *Sociometry,* **37,** 1–12.

Dion, K. K., & Dion, K. L. (1978). Defensiveness, intimacy, and heterosexual attraction. *Journal of Research in Personality,* **12,** 479–487.

Dion, K. K., & Dion, K. L. (1985). Personality, gender, and the phenomenology of romantic love. In P. R. Shaver (Ed.), *Review of personality and social psychology,* vol. 6. Beverly Hills, Ca.: Sage.

Dion, K. K., & Stein, S. (1978). Physical attractiveness and interpersonal influence. *Journal of Experimental Social Psychology,* **14,** 97–109.

Dion, K. L. (1979). Intergroup conflict and intragroup cohesiveness. In W. G. Austin, & S. Worchel (Eds.), *The social psychology of intergroup relations.* Monterey, Calif.: Brooks/Cole.

Dion, K. L. (1986). Responses to perceived discrimination and relative deprivation. In J. M. Olson, C. P. Herman, & M. P. Zanna (Eds.), *Relative deprivation and social comparison: The Ontario symposium,* vol. 4. Hillsdale, N.J.: Erlbaum.

Dion, K. L. (1987). What's in a title? The Ms. stereotype and images of women's titles of address. *Psychology of Women Quarterly,* **11,** 21–36.

Dion, K. L., & Dion, K. K. (1988). Romantic love: Individual and cultural perspectives. In R. J. Sternberg & M. L. Barnes (Eds.), *The psychology of love.* New Haven, Conn.: Yale University Press.

DiVasto, P. V., Kaufman, A., Rosner, L., Jackson, R., Christy, J., Pearson, S., & Burgett, T. (1984). The prevalence of sexually stressful events among females in the general population. *Archives of Sexual Behavior,* **13,** 59–67.

Dixon, B. (1986, April). Dangerous thoughts: How we think and feel can make us sick. *Science 86,* pp. 63–66.

Doise, W. (1986). *Levels of explanation in social psychology.* Cambridge: Cambridge University Press.

Dollard, J., Doob, L., Miller, N., Mowrer,

O. H., & Sears, R. R. (1939). *Frustration and aggression.* New Haven, Conn.: Yale University Press.

Doms, M., & Van Avarmaet, E. (1980). Majority influence, minority influence and conversion behavior: A replication. *Journal of Experimental Social Psychology,* **16,** 283–292.

Donnerstein, E. (1980). Aggressive erotica and violence against women. *Journal of Personality and Social Psychology,* **39,** 269–277.

Donnerstein, E., & Berkowitz, L. (1981). Victim reactions in aggressive erotic films as a factor in violence against women. *Journal of Personality and Social Psychology,* **41,** 710–724.

Donnerstein, E., Linz, D., & Penrod, S. (1987). *The question of pornography.* London: Free Press.

Doob, A. N., & Kirshenbaum, H. M. (1973). Bias in police lineups—partial remembering. *Journal of Police Science and Administration,* **1,** 287–293.

Doob, A. N., & Roberts, J. (1988). Public attitudes toward sentencing in Canada. In N. Walker & M. Hough (Eds.), *Sentencing and the public.* London: Gower.

Douglass, F. (1845/1960). *Narrative of the life of Frederick Douglass, an American slave: Written by himself.* (B. Quarles, Ed.). Cambridge, Mass.: Harvard University Press.

Dovidio, J. F., Brown, C. E., Heltman, K., Ellyson, S. L., & Keating, C. F. (1988). Power displays between women and men in discussions of gender-linked tasks: A multichannel study. *Journal of Personality and Social Psychology,* **55,** 580–587.

Dovidio, J. F., Ellyson, S. L., Keating, C. F., Heltman, K., & Brown, C. E. (1988). The relationship of social power to visual displays of dominance between men and women. *Journal of Personality and Social Psychology,* **54,** 233–242.

Dovidio, J. F., & Gaertner, S. L. (1988). Changes in the expression and assessment of racial prejudice. Conference on "Opening Doors: An Appraisal of Race Relations in America," University of Alabama.

Dovidio, J. F., Mann, J., & Gaertner, S. L. (1989). Resistance to affirmative action: The implications of aversive racism. In F. Blanchard & F. Crosby (Eds.), *Affirmative action in perspective.* New York: Springer-Verlag.

Dovidio, J. F., Schroeder, D. A., Allen, J., Johnston, K., & Sibicky, M. (1988). Relieving another person's distress: Egoistic or altruistic motivation? Paper presented at the Eastern Psychological Association convention.

Drabman, R. S., & Thomas, M. H. (1974). Does media violence increase children's toleration of real-life aggression? *Developmental Psychology*, 10, 418–421.

Drabman, R. S., & Thomas, M. H. (1975). Does TV violence breed indifference? *Journal of Communications*, 25(4), 86–89.

Drabman, R. S., & Thomas, M. H. (1976). Does watching violence on television cause apathy? *Pediatrics*, 57, 329–331.

Duncan, B. L. (1976). Differential social perception and attribution of intergroup violence: Testing the lower limits of stereotyping of blacks. *Journal of Personality and Social Psychology*, 34, 590–598.

Dunning, D., Milojkovic, J. H., & Ross, L. (1989). The overconfidence effect in social prediction. *Journal of Personality and Social Psychology*, in press.

Dunning, D., Meyerowitz, J. A., & Holzberg, A. D. (1989). Ambiguity and self-evaluation. *Journal of Personality and Social Psychology*, in press.

Dunning, D., & Ross, L. (1988). Overconfidence in individual and group prediction: Is the collective any wiser? Unpublished manuscript, Cornell University.

Dutton, D. G. (1971). Reactions of restaurateurs to blacks and whites violating restaurant dress regulations. *Canadian Journal of Behavioural Science*, 3, 298–302.

Dutton, D. G. (1973). Reverse discrimination: The relationship of amount of perceived discrimination toward a minority group on the behavior of majority group members. *Canadian Journal of Behavioural Science*, 5, 34–45.

Dutton, D. G., & Aron, A. P. (1974). Some evidence for heightened sexual attraction under conditions of high anxiety. *Journal of Personality and Social Psychology*, 30, 510–517.

Dutton, D. G., & Lake, R. A. (1973). Threat of own prejudice and reverse discrimination in interracial situations. *Journal of Personality and Social Psychology*, 28, 94–100.

Duval, S. (1976). Conformity on a visual task as a function of personal novelty on attitudinal dimensions and being reminded of the object status of self. *Journal of Experimental Social Psychology*, 12, 87–98.

Duval, S., Duval, V. H., & Neely, R. (1979). Self-focus, felt responsibility, and helping behavior. *Journal of Personality and Social Psychology*, 37, 1769–1778.

Duval, S., & Wicklund, R. A. (1972). *A theory of objective self-awareness*. New York: Academic Press.

Eagly, A. H. (1987). Sex differences in social behavior: A social-role interpretation. Hillsdale, N.J.: Erlbaum.

Eagly, A. H., & Carli, L. L. (1981). Sex of researcher and sex-typed communications as determinants of sex differences in influenceability: A meta-analysis of social influence studies. *Psychological Bulletin*, 90, 1–20.

Eagly, A. H., & Crowley, M. (1986). Gender and helping behavior: A meta-analytic review of the social psychological literature. *Psychological Bulletin*, 100, 309–330.

Eagly, A. H., & Johnson, B. T. (1988). Gender and leadership style: meta-analysis. Unpublished manuscript, Purdue University.

Eagly, A. H., & Steffen, V. J. (1986). Gender and aggressive behavior: A meta-analytic review of the social psychological literature. *Psychological Bulletin*, 100, 309–330.

Eagly, A. H., & Wood, W. (1982). Inferred sex differences in status as a determinant of gender stereotypes about social influence. *Journal of Personality and Social Psychology*, 43, 915–928.

Eagly, A. H., & Wood, W. (1985). Gender and influenceability: Stereotype versus behavior. In V. E. O'Leary, R. K. Unger, & B. S. Wallston (Eds.), *Women, gender, and social psychology*. Hillsdale, N.J.: Erlbaum.

Eagly, A. H., & Wood, W. (1988). Explaining sex differences in social behavior: A meta-analytic perspective. Paper presented to the American Psychological Association convention.

Eagly, A. H., Wood, W., & Chaiken, S. (1978). Casual inferences about communicators and their effect on opinion change. *Journal of Personality and Social Psychology*, 36, 424–435.

Eagly, A. H., Wood, W., & Fishbaugh, L. (1981). Sex differences in conformity: Surveillance by the group as a determinant of male conformity. *Journal of Personality and Social Psychology*, 40, 384–394.

Eaton, W. O., & Enns, L. R. (1986). Sex differences in human motor activity level. *Psychological Bulletin*, 100, 19–28.

Ebbesen, E. B., Duncan, B., & Konecni, V. J. (1975). Effects of content of verbal agression on future verbal aggression: A field experiment. *Journal of Experimental Social Psychology*, 11, 192–204.

Edney, J. J. (1979, August). Free riders en route to disaster. *Psychology Today*, pp. 80–87, 102. (a)

Edney, J. J. (1979). The nuts game: A concise commons dilemma analog. *Environmental Psychology and Nonverbal Behavior*, 3, 252–254. (b)

Edney, J. J. (1980). The commons problem: Alternative perspectives. *American Psychologist*, 35, 131–150.

Edney, J. J., & Harper, C. S. (1978). The commons dilemma: A review of contributions from

psychology. *Environmental Management*, 2, 491–507.

Efran, M. G. (1974). The effect of physical appearance on the judgment of guilt, interpersonal attraction, and severity of recommended punishment in a simulated jury task. *Journal of Research in Personality*, 8, 45–54.

Ehrhardt, A. A. (1987). A transactional perspective on the development of gender differences. In J. M. Reinisch, L. A. Rosenblum, & S. A. Sanders (Eds.), *Masculinity/femininity: Basic perspectives*. New York: Oxford University Press.

Eisenberg, N., Cialdini, R. B., McCreath, H., & Shell, R. (1987). Consistency-based compliance: When and why do children become vulnerable? *Journal of Personality and Social Psychology*, 52, 1174–1181.

Eisenberg, N., & Lennon, R. (1983). Sex differences in empathy and related capacities. *Psychological Bulletin*, 94, 100–131.

Eisenberger, R., Cotterell, N., & Marvel, J. (1987). Reciprocation ideology. *Journal of Personality and Social Psychology*, 50, 743–750.

Eisinger, R., & Mills, J. (1968). Perception of the sincerity and competence of a communicator as a function of the extremity of his position. *Journal of Experimental Social Psychology*, 4, 224–232.

Elashoff, J. R., & Snow, R. E. (1971). *Pygmalion reconsidered*. Worthington, Ohio: Charles A. Jones.

Elder, G. H., Jr. (1969). Appearance and education in marriage mobility. *American Sociological Review*, 34, 519–533.

Eldersveld, S. J., & Dodge, R. W. (1954). Personal contact or mail propaganda? An experiment in voting turnout and attitude change. In D. Katz, D. Cartwright, S. Eldersveld, & A. M. Lee (Eds.), *Public opinion and propaganda*. New York: Dryden Press.

Eliot, T. S. (1958). "The Hollow Men." In *The Complete Poems and Plays, 1909–1950*. New York: Harcourt Brace and Company.

Elkin, I. (1986). Outcome findings and therapist performance. Paper presented at the American Psychological Association convention.

Elliott, G. C. (1986). Self-esteem and self-consistency: A theoretical and empirical link between two primary motivations. *Social Psychological Quarterly*, 49, 207–218.

Ellis, H. D. (1981). Theoretical aspects of face recognition. In G. H. Davies, H. D. Ellis, & J. Shepherd (Eds.), *Perceiving and remembering faces*. London: Academic Press.

Ellsworth, P. (1985, July). Juries on trial. *Psychology Today*, pp. 44–46.

Ellyson, S. L., & Dovidio, J. F. (1985). *Power,*

dominance, and nonverbal behavior. New York: Springer-Verlag.

Elwork, A., Sales, B. D., & Alfini, J. J. (1982). *Making jury instructions understandable.* Charlottesville, Va.: The Michie Co.

Emswiller, T., Deaux, K., & Willits, J. E. (1971). Similarity, sex, and requests for small favors. *Journal of Applied Social Psychology,* 1, 284–291.

Epstein, J. F., O'Neal, E. C., & Jones, K. J. (1980). Prior experience with firearms can mitigate the weapons effect. Paper presented at the American Psychological Association convention.

Epstein, S. (1980). The stability of behavior: II. Implications for psychological research. *American Psychologist,* 35, 790–806.

Epstein, S., & Feist, G. J. (1988). Relation between self- and other-acceptance and its moderation by identification. *Journal of Personality and Social Psychology,* 54, 309–315.

Erickson, B., Holmes, J. G., Frey, R., Walker, L., & Thibaut, J. (1974). Functions of a third party in the resolution of conflict: The role of a judge in pretrial conferences. *Journal of Personality and Social Psychology,* 30, 296–306.

Erickson, B., Lind, E. A., Johnson, B. C., & O'Barr, W. M. (1978). Speech style and impression formation in a court setting: The effects of powerful and powerless speech. *Journal of Experimental Social Psychology,* 14, 266–279.

Eron, L. D. (1981). Parent-child interaction, television violence, and aggression of children. *American Psychologist,* 37, 197–211.

Eron, L. D. (1985). The social responsibility of the researchers. In J. H. Goldstein (Ed.), *Reporting science: The case of aggression.* Hillsdale, N.J.: Erlbaum.

Eron, L. D. (1987). The development of aggressive behavior from the perspective of a developing behaviorism. *American Psychologist,* 42, 425–442.

Eron, L. D., & Huesmann, L. R. (1980). Adolescent aggression and television. *Annals of the New York Academy of Sciences,* 347, 319–331.

Eron, L. D., & Huesmann, L. R. (1984). The control of aggressive behavior by changes in attitudes, values, and the conditions of learning. In R. J. Blanchard & C. Blanchard (Eds.), *Advances in the study of aggression,* vol. 1. Orlando, Fla.: Academic Press.

Eron, L. D., & Huesmann, L. R. (1985). The role of television in the development of prosocial and antisocial behavior. In D. Olweus, M. Radke-Yarrow, and J. Block (Eds.), *De-*

velopment of antisocial and prosocial behavior. Orlando, Fla.: Academic Press.

Esses, V. M., & Webster, C. D. (1988). Physical attractiveness, dangerousness, and the Canadian criminal code. *Journal of Applied Social Psychology,* 18, 1017–1031.

Etzioni, A. (1967). The Kennedy experiment. *The Western Political Quarterly,* 20, 361–380.

Etzioni, A. (1972, June 3). Human beings are not very easy to change after all. *Saturday Review,* 45–47.

European Economic Community Commission (1980). Survey, October-November, 1977. Reported in *Public Opinion,* February-March, p. 37.

Evans, G. W. (1979). Behavioral and physiological consequences of crowding in humans. *Journal of Applied Social Psychology,* 9, 27–46.

Evans, R. I., Smith, C. K., & Raines, B. E. (1984). Deterring cigarette smoking in adolescents: A psycho-social-behavioral analysis of an intervention strategy. In A. Baum, J. Singer, & S. Taylor (Eds.), *Handbook of psychology and health: Social psychological aspects of health,* vol. 4, Hillsdale, N.J.: Erlbaum.

Faranda, J. A., Kaminski, J. A., & Giza, B. K. (1979). An assessment of attitudes toward women with the bogus pipeline. Paper presented at the American Psychological Association convention.

Farquhar, J. W., Maccoby, N., Wood, P. D., Alexander, J. K., Breitrose, H., Brown, B. W., Jr., Haskell, W. L., McAlister, A. L., Meyer, A. J., Nash, J. D., & Stern, M. P. (1977, June 4). Community education for cardiovascular health. *Lancet,* 1192–1195.

Faust, D., & Ziskin, J. (1988). The expert witness in psychology and psychiatry. *Science,* 241, 31–35.

Fazio, R. (1987). Self-perception theory: A current perspective. In M. P. Zanna, J. M. Olson, & C. P. Herman (Eds.), *Social influence: The Ontario symposium,* vol. 5. Hillsdale, N.J.: Erlbaum.

Fazio, R. H. (1981). On the self-perception explanation of the overjustification effect: the role of the salience of initial attitude. *Journal of Experimental Social Psychology,* 17, 417–426.

Fazio, R. H. (1986). How do attitudes guide behavior? In R. M. Sorrentino & E. T. Higgins (Eds.), *The handbook of motivation and cognition: Foundations of social behavior.* New York: Guilford Press.

Fazio, R. H., Effrein, E. A., & Falender, V. J. (1981). Self-perceptions following social inter-

action. *Journal of Personality and Social Psychology,* 41, 232–242.

Fazio, R. H., & Zanna, M. P. (1981). Direct experience and attitude-behavior consistency. In L. Berkowitz (Ed.), *Advances in experimental social psychology,* Vol. 14. New York: Academic Press.

Fazio, R. H., Zanna, M. P., & Cooper, J. (1977). Dissonance versus self-perception: An integrative view of each theory's proper domain of application. *Journal of Experimental Social Psychology,* 13, 464–479.

Fazio, R. H., Zanna, M. P., & Cooper, J. (1979). On the relationship of data to theory: A reply to Ronis and Greenwald. *Journal of Experimental Social Psychology,* 15, 70–76.

Feather, N. T. (1983). Causal attributions and beliefs about work and unemployment among adolescents in state and independent secondary schools. *Australian Journal of Psychology,* 35, 211–232. (*a*)

Feather, N. T. (1983). Causal attributions for good and bad outcomes in achievement and affiliation situations. *Australian Journal of Psychology,* 35, 37–48. (*b*)

Feierabend, I., & Feierabend, R. (1968, May). Conflict, crisis, and collision: A study of international stability. *Psychology Today,* pp. 26–32, 69–70.

Feierabend, I., & Feierabend, R. (1972). Systemic conditions of political aggression: An application of frustration-aggression theory. In I. K. Feierabend, R. L. Feierabend, & T. R. Gurr (Eds.), *Anger, violence, and politics: Theories and research.* Englewood Cliffs, N.J.: Prentice Hall.

Feingold, A. (1988). Matching for attractiveness in romantic partners and same-sex friends: A meta-analysis and theoretical critique. *Psycholgical Bulletin,* 104, 226–235.

Feldman, K. A., & Newcomb, T. M. (1969). *The impact of college on students.* San Francisco: Jossey-Bass.

Feldman, R. S., & Prohaska, T. (1979). The student as Pygmalion: Effect of student expectation on the teacher. *Journal of Educational Psychology,* 71, 485–493.

Feldman, R. S., & Theiss, A. J. (1982). The teacher and student as Pygamalions: Joint effects of teacher and student expectations. *Journal of Educational Psychology,* 74, 217–223.

Feldman-Summers, S., & Kiesler, S. B. (1974). Those who are number two try harder: The effect of sex on attributions of causality. *Journal of Personality and Social Psychology,* 30, 846–855.

Feller, W. (1980). *An introduction to probability theory and its applications* (Vol. 1). New

York: Wiley, 1968. Cited by B. Fischhoff in, For those condemned to study the past: Reflections on historical judgment. In R. A. Shweder (Ed.), *New directions for methodology of social and behavior science.* San Francisco: Jossey-Bass.

Felson, R. B. (1984). The effect of self-appraisals on ability on academic performance. *Journal of Personality and Social Psychology, 47,* 944–952.

Felson, R. B., & Bohrnstedt, G. W. (1979). Are the good beautiful or the beautiful good? The relationship between children's perceptions of ability and perceptions of physical attractiveness. *Social Psychology Quarterly, 42,* 385–392.

Fenigstein, A. (1984). Self-consciousness and the overperception of self as a target. *Journal of Personality and Social Psychology, 47,* 860–870.

Fenigstein, A., & Carver, C. S. (1978). Self-focusing effects of heartbeat feedback. *Journal of Personality and Social Psychology, 36,* 1241–1250.

Fernandez-Collado, C., & Greenberg, B. S., with Korzenny, F., & Atkin, C. K. (1978). Sexual intimacy and drug use in TV series, *Journal of Communication, 28*(3), 30–37.

Feshbach, N. D. (1980). The child as "psychologist" and "economist": Two curricula. Paper presented at the American Psychological Association convention.

Feshbach, N. D. & Feshbach, S. (1981). Empathy training and the regulation of aggression: Potentialities and limitations. Paper presented at the Western Psychological Association convention.

Feshbach, S. (1970). Aggression. In P.H. Mussen (Ed.), *Carmichael's manual of child psychology* (Vol. 3). New York: Wiley.

Feshbach, S. (1980). Television advertising and children: Policy issues and alternatives. Paper presented at the American Psychological Association convention.

Festinger, L. (1954). A theory of social comparison processes. *Human Relations, 7,* 117–140.

Festinger, L. (1957). *A theory of cognitive dissonance.* Stanford: Stanford University Press.

Festinger, L. (1964). Behavioral support for opinion change. *Public Opinion Quarterly, 28,* 404–417.

Festinger, L., & Carlsmith, J. M. (1959). Cognitive consequences of forced compliance. *Journal of Abnormal and Social Psychology, 58,* 203–210.

Festinger, L., & Maccoby, N. (1964). On resistance to persuasive communications. *Journal of Abnormal and Social Psychology, 68,* 359–366.

Festinger, L., Pepitone, A., & Newcomb, T. (1952). Some consequences of deindividuation in a group. *Journal of Abnormal and Social Psychology, 47,* 382–389.

Festinger, L., Schachter, S., & Back, K. (1950). *Social Pressures in informal groups: A study of human factors in housing.* New York: Harper & Bros.

Feynman, R. (1967). *The character of physical law.* Cambridge, Mass.: MIT Press.

Fichter, J. (1968). *America's forgotten priests: What are they saying?* New York: Harper.

Fiedler, F. E. (1987, September). When to lead, when to stand back. *Psychology Today,* pp. 26–27.

Fiedler, F. W. (1981). Leadership effectiveness. *American Behavioral Scientist, 24,* 619–632.

Fields, J. M., & Schuman, H. (1976). Public beliefs about the beliefs of the public. *Public Opinion Quarterly, 40,* 427–448.

Finch, J. F., & Cialdini, R. B. (1989). Another indirect tactic of (self-) image management: Boosting. *Personality and Social Psychology Bulletin,* in press.

Fincham, F. D., Beach, S. R., & Baucom, D. H. (1987). Attribution processes in distressed and nondistressed couples: 4. Self-partner attribution differences. *Journal of Personality and Social Psychology, 52,* 739–748.

Fincham, F. D., & Jaspars, J. M. (1980). Attribution of responsibility: From man the scientist to man as lawyer. In L. Berkowitz (Ed.), *Advances in Experimental Social Psychology* (Vol. 13). New York: Academic Press.

Findley, M. J., & Cooper, H. M. (1983). Locus of control and academic achievement: A literature review. *Journal of Personality and Social Psychology, 33,* 419–427.

Fine, M., & Bowers, C. (1984). Racial self-identification: The effects of social history and gender. *Journal of Applied Social Psychology, 14,* 136–146.

Fischer, K., Schoeneman, T. J., & Rubanowitz, D. E. (1987). Attributions in the advice columns: II. The dimensionality of actors' and observers' explanations for interpersonal problems. *Personality and Social Psychology Bulletin, 13,* 458–466.

Fischhoff, B., & Bar-Hillel, M. (1984). Diagnosticity and the base rate effect. *Memory and Cognition, 12,* 402–410.

Fischhoff, B., & Beyth, R. (1975). "I knew it would happen": Remembered probabilities of once-future things. *Organizational Behavior and Human Performance, 13,* 1–16.

Fischhoff, B., Slovic, P., & Lichtenstein, S. (1977). Knowing with certainty: The appropriateness of extreme confidence. *Journal of*

Experimental Psychology: Human Perception and Performance, 3, 552–564.

Fishbein, D., & Thelen, M. H. (1981). Husband-wife similarity and marital satisfaction: A different approach. Paper presented at the Midwestern Psychological Association convention. (a)

Fishbein, D., & Thelen, M. H. (1981). Psychological factors in mate selection and marital satisfaction: A review (Ms. 2374). *Catalog of Selected Documents in Psychology, 11,* 84. (b)

Fishbein, M., & Ajzen, I. (1974). Attitudes toward objects as predictive of single and multiple behavioral criteria. *Psychological Review, 81,* 59–74.

Fisher, G. H. (1968). Ambiguity of form: Old and new. *Perception and Psychophysics, 4,* 189–192.

Fisher, J. D., Nadler, A., & DePaulo, B. M. (1983). *New directions in helping. Vol. 1: Recipient reactions to aid.* Orlando, Fla.: Academic Press.

Fisher, R., & Ury, W. L. (1981). *Getting to YES. Negotiating agreement without giving in.* Boston: Houghton Mifflin.

Fisher, R. P., Geiselman, R. E., & Amador, M. (1989). Field test of the cognitive interview: Enhancing the recollection of actual victims and witnesses of crime. *Journal of Applied Psychology,* in press.

Fisher, R. P., Geiselman, R. E., & Raymond, D. S. (1987). Critical analysis of police interview techniques. *Journal of Police Science and Administration, 15,* 177–185.

Fiske, S. T. (1987). People's reactions to nuclear war: Implications for psychologists. *American Psychologist, 42,* 207–217.

Fiske, S. T., & Pavelchak, M. A. (1986). Category-based versus piecemeal-based affective responses: Developments in schema-triggered affect. In B. M. Sorrentino & E. T. Higgins (Eds.), *The handbook of motivation and cognition: Foundations of social behavior.* New York: Guilford Press.

Fiske, S. T., & Taylor, S. E. (1984). *Social Cognition.* Reading, Mass.: Addison-Wesley.

Fitzpatrick, A. R., & Eagly, A. H. (1981). Anticipatory belief polarization as a function of the expertise of a discussion partner. *Personality and Social Psychology Bulletin, 1,* 636–642.

Flay, B. R., Ryan, K. B., Best, J. A., Brown, K. S., Kersell, M. W., d'Avernas, J. R., & Zanna, M. P. (1985). Are social-psychological smoking prevention programs effective? The Waterloo study. *Journal of Behavioral Medicine, 8,* 37–59.

Fleischer, R. A., & Chertkoff, J. M. (1986). Effects of dominance and sex on leader selection in dyadic work groups. *Journal of Personality and Social Psychology, 50,* 94–99.

Fleming, I., Baum, A., & Weiss, L. (1987). Social density and perceived control as mediators of crowding stress in high-density residential neighborhoods. *Journal of Personality and Social Psychology, 52,* 899–906.

Fletcher, G. J. O., Danilovics, P., Fernandez, G., Peterson, D., & Reeder, G. D. (1986). Attributional complexity: An individual differences measure. *Journal of Personality and Social Psychology, 51,* 875–884.

Fletcher, G. J. O., Fincham, F. D., Cramer, L., & Heron, N. (1987). The role of attributions in the development of dating relationships. *Journal of Personality and Social Psychology, 53,* 481–489.

Fletcher, G. J. O., & Ward, C. (1989). Attribution theory and processes: A cross-cultural perspective. In M. H. Bond (Ed.), *The cross-cultural challenge to social psychology.* Newbury Park, Ca.: Sage.

Foa, U. G., & Foa, E. B. (1975). *Resource theory of social exchange.* Morristown, N.J.: General Learning Press.

Foley, L. A. (1976). Personality and situational influences on changes in prejudice: A replication of Cook's railroad game in a prison setting. *Journal of Personality and Social Psychology, 34,* 846–856.

Fonberg, E. (1979). Physiological mechanisms of emotional and instrumental aggression. In S. Feshbach & A. Fraczek (Eds.), *Aggression and behavior change.* New York: Praeger.

Forer, B. R. (1949). The fallacy of personal validation: A classroom demonstration of gullibility. *Journal of Abnormal and Social Psychology, 44,* 118–123.

Forgas, J. P. (1987). The role of physical attractiveness in the interpretation of facial expression cues. *Personality and Social Psychology Bulletin, 13,* 478–489.

Forgas, J. P., Bower, G. H., & Krantz, S. E. (1984). The influence of mood on perceptions of social interactions. *Journal of Experimental Social Psychology, 20,* 497–513.

Forgas, J. P., & Moylan, S. (1987). After the movies: Transient mood and social judgments. *Personality and Social Psychology Bulletin, 13,* 467–477.

Form, W. H., & Nosow, S. (1958). *Community in disaster.* New York: Harper.

Försterling, F. (1986). Attributional conceptions in clinical psychology. *American Psychologist, 41,* 275–285.

Forsyth, D. R., Berger, R. E., & Mitchell, T. (1981). The effects of self-serving vs. other-serving claims of responsibility on attraction and attribution in groups. *Social Psychology Quarterly, 44,* 59–64.

Forward, J. R., & Williams, J. R. (1970). Internal-external control and black militancy. *Journal of Social Issues, 26*(1), 75–92.

Foss, R. D. (1978). The role of social influence in blood donation. Paper presented at the American Psychological Association convention.

Foss, R. D. (1981). Structural effects in simulated jury decision making. *Journal of Personality and Social Psychology, 40,* 1053–1062.

Foulke, E., & Sticht, T. G. (1969). Review of research on the intelligibility and comprehension of accelerated speech. *Psychological Bulletin, 72,* 50–62.

Fox, D. L., & Schofield, J. W. (1989). Issue salience, perceived efficacy and perceived risk: An experimental study of the origins of antinuclear war activity. *Journal of Applied Social Psychology,* in press.

Frank, J. D. (1984). Open letter on behalf of Council for a Livable World.

Frank, M. G., & Gilovich, T. (1988). The dark side of self and social perception: Black uniforms and aggression in professional sports. *Journal of Personality and Social Psychology, 54,* 74–85.

Frankel, A., & Snyder, M. L. (1987). Egotism among the depressed: When self-protection becomes self-handicapping. Paper presented at the American Psychological Association convention.

Franklin, B. J. (1974). Victim characteristics and helping behavior in a rural southern setting. *Journal of Social Psychology, 93,* 93–100.

Franzoi, S. L., Davis, M. H. & Young, R. D. (1985). the effects of private self-consciousness and perspective taking on satisfaction in close relationships. *Journal of Personality and Social Psychology, 48,* 1584–1594.

Freedman, J. L. (1979). Reconciling apparent differences between the responses of humans and other animals to crowding. *Psychological Review, 86,* 80–85.

Freedman, J. L. (1984). Effect of television violence on aggressiveness. *Psychological Bulletin, 96,* 227–246.

Freedman, J. L. (1988). Television violence and aggression: What the evidence shows. In S. Oskamp (Ed.), *Television as a social issue. Applied Social Psychology Annual,* Vol. 8. Newbury Park, Ca.: Sage.

Freedman, J. L., Birsky, J., & Cavoukian, A. (1980). Environmental determinants of behavioral contagion: Density and number. *Basic and Applied Social Psychology, 1,* 155–161.

Freedman, J. L., & Fraser, S. C. (1966). Compliance without pressure: The foot-in-the-door technique. *Journal of Personality and Social Psychology, 4,* 195–202.

Freedman, J. L., & Perlick, D. (1979). Crowding, contagion, and laughter. *Journal of Experimental Social Psychology, 15,* 295–303.

Freedman, J. L., & Sears, D. O. (1965). Warning, distraction, and resistance to influence. *Journal of Personality and Social Psychology, 1,* 262–266.

Freedman, J. S. (1965). Long-term behavioral effects of cognitive dissonance. *Journal of Experimental Social Psychology, 1,* 145–155.

French, J. R. P. (1968). The conceptualization and the measurement of mental health in terms of self-identity theory. In S. B. Sells (Ed.), *The definition and measurement of mental health.* Washington, D. C.: Department of Health, Education, and Welfare. (Cited by M. Rosenberg, 1979, *Conceiving the self.* New York: Basic Books.)

Friedman, H. S., Riggio, R. E., & Casella, D. F. (1988). Nonverbal skill, personal charisma, and initial attraction. *Personality and Social Psychology Bulletin, 14,* 203–211.

Friedrich, L. K., & Stein, A. H. (1973). Aggressive and prosocial television programs and the natural behavior of preschool children. *Monographs of the Society for Research in Child Development, 38* (4, Serial No. 151).

Friedrich, L. K., & Stein, A. H. (1975). Prosocial television and young children: The effects of verbal labeling and role playing on learning and behavior. *Child Development, 46,* 27–38.

Froming, W. J., Walker, G. R., & Lopyan, K. J. (1982). Public and private self-awareness: when personal attitudes conflict with societal expectations. *Journal of Experimental Social Psychology, 18,* 476–487.

Fulbright, J. W. (1972). United Press International, April 5, 1971. Cited by A. C. Elms, *Social psychology and social reliance.* Boston: Little, Brown.

Fuld, K., & Nevin, J. A. (1988). Why doesn't everyone work to prevent nuclear war? A decision theory analysis. *Journal of Applied Social Psychology, 18,* 59–65.

Fultz, J., Batson, C. D., Fortenbach, V. A., McCarthy, P. M., & Varney, L. L. (1986). Social evaluation and the empathy-altruism hypothesis. *Journal of Personality and Social Psychology, 50,* 761–769.

Funder, D. C. (1980). On seeing ourselves as others see us: Self-other agreement and discrepancy in personality ratings. *Journal of Personality, 48,* 473–493.

Funder, D. C. (1987). Errors and mistakes:

Evaluating the accuracy of social judgment. *Psychological Bulletin*, 101, 75–90.

Furnham, A. (1982). Explanations for unemployment in Britain. *European Journal of Social Psychology*, 12, 335–352.

Furnham, A., & Gunter, B. (1984). Just world beliefs and attitudes towards the poor. *British Journal of Social Psychology*, 23, 265–269.

Furst, C. J., Burnam, M. A., & Kocel, K. M. (1980). Life stressors and romantic affiliation. Paper presented at the Western Psychological Association convention.

Gabrenya, W. K., Jr., Wang, Y.-E., & Latané, B. (1985). Cross-cultural differences in social loafing on an optimizing task: Chinese and Americans. *Journal of Cross-Cultural Psychology*, 16, 223–242.

Gaebelein, J. W., & Mander, A. (1978). Consequences for targets of aggression as a function of aggressor and instigator roles: Three experiments. *Personality and Social Psychology Bulletin*, 4, 465–468.

Gaertner, S. L. (1973). Helping behavior and racial discrimination among liberals and conservatives. *Journal of Personality and Social Psychology*, 25, 335–341.

Gaertner, S. L. (1975). The role of racial attitudes in helping behavior. *Journal of Social Psychology*, 97, 95–101.

Gaertner, S. L., & Bickman, L. (1971). Effects of race on the elicitation of helping behavior. *Journal of Personality and Social Psychology*, 20, 218–222.

Gaertner, S. L., & Dovidio, J. F. (1977). The subtlety of white racism, arousal, and helping behavior. *Journal of Personality and Social Psychology*, 35, 691–707.

Gaertner, S. L., & Dovidio, J. F. (1986). The aversive form of racism. In J. F. Dovidio & S. L. Gaertner (Eds.), *Prejudice, discrimination, and racism*. Orlando, Fl.: Academic Press.

Gaertner, S. L., Dovidio, J. F. & Johnson, G. (1982). Race of victim, nonresponsive bystanders, and helping behavior. *Journal of Social Psychology*, 117, 69–77.

Gaertner, S. L., Mann, J., Murrell, A., & Dovidio, J. F. (1989). Reducing intergroup bias: The benefits of recategorization. *Journal of Personality and Social Psychology*, in press.

Gaertner, S. L., Mann, J., Murrell, A., Pomare, M., & Dovidio, J. F. (1988). How does cooperation reduce intergroup bias? Paper presented to the Eastern Psychological Association convention.

Galizio, M., & Hendrick, C. (1972). Effect of musical accompaniment on attitude: The guitar as a prop for persuasion. *Journal of Applied Social Psychology*, 2, 350–359.

Gallup Opinion Index (1980). December, No. 183, p. 75.

Gallup Organization (1986, June). Cigarette smoking audit. *Gallup Report* No. 263, pp. 20–21.

Gallup poll (1981). December 5–8, 1980. Reported in *Public Opinion*, April-May, p. 38.

Gallup poll (1981). Equal rights amendment. Reported by NBC *Today Show*, December 4.

Gallup poll (1981). February 14–23, 1981. Reported in *Newsweek*, March 9.

Gallup, G., Jr. (1984, March). Religion in America. *The Gallup Report*, Report No. 222.

Gallup, G. H. (1972). *The Gallup poll: Public opinion 1935–1971.* (Vol. 3). New York: Random House, pp. 551, 1716.

Gallup Report (1983, September). Prejudice in politics, pp. 9–14 in Report No. 216.

Gamson, W. A., Fireman, B., & Rytina, S. (1982). *Encounters with unjust authority.* Homewood, Ill.: Dorsey Press.

Ganellen, R. J., & Carver, C. S. (1985). Why does self-reference promote incidental encoding? *Journal of Experimental Social Psychology*, 21, 284–300.

Garbarino, J., & Bronfenbrenner, U. (1976). The socialization of moral judgment and behavior in cross-cultural perspective. In T. Lickona (Ed.), *Moral development and behavior: Theory, research, and social issues*. New York: Holt, Rinehart and Winston.

Gaskie, M. F. (1980, mid-August). Toward workability of the workplace. *Architectural Record*, pp. 70–75.

Gastorf, J. W., Suls, J., & Sanders, G. S. (1980). Type A coronary-prone behavior pattern and social facilitation. *Journal of Personality and Social Psychology*, 8, 773–780.

Gates, M. F., & Allee, W. C. (1933). Conditioned behavior of isolated and grouped cockroaches on a simple maze. *Journal of Comparative Psychology*, 15, 331–358.

Gavanski, I., & Hoffman, C. (1987). *Journal of Personality and Social Psychology*, 52, 453–463.

Gazzaniga, M. (1972). The split brain in man. In R. Held & W. Richard (Eds.), *Perception: Mechanisms and models*. San Francisco: W. H. Freeman.

Gazzaniga, M. (1985). *The social brain: Discovering the networks of the mind.* New York: Basic Books.

Geen, R. G. (1981). Evaluation apprehension and social facilitation: A reply to Sanders. *Journal of Experimental Social Psychology*, 17, 252–256.

Geen, R. G., & Gange, J. J. (1983). Social facilitation: Drive theory and beyond. In H. H. Blumberg, A. P. Hare, V. Kent, & M. Davies (Eds.), *Small groups and social interaction*, Vol. 1. London: Wiley.

Geen, R. G., & Quanty, M. B. (1977). The catharsis of aggression: An evaluation of a hypothesis. In L. Berkowitz (Ed.), *Advances in experimental social psychology* (Vol. 10). New York: Academic Press.

Geen, R. G., Rakosky, J. J., & Pigg, R. (1972). Awareness of arousal and its relation to aggression. *British Journal of Social and Clinical Psychology*, 11, 115–121.

Geen, R. G., & Thomas, S. L. (1986). The immediate effects of media violence on behavior. *Journal of Social Issues*, 42(3), 7–28.

Geis, F. L., Brown, V., Jennings (Walstedt), J., & Porter, N. (1984). TV commercials as achievement scripts for women. *Sex Roles*, 10, 513–525.

Gerard, H. B., & Mathewson, G. C. (1966). The effects of severity of initiation on liking for a group: A replication. *Journal of Experimental Social Psychology*, 2, 278–287.

Gerard, H. B., Wilhelmy, R. A., & Conolley, E. S. (1968). Conformity and group size. *Journal of Personality and Social Psychology*, 8, 79–82.

Gerasimov, G. (1988). Quoted in *Parade*, July 10, 1988, p. 2.

Gerbasi, K. C., Zuckerman, M., & Reis, H. T. (1977). Justice needs a new blindfold: A review of mock jury research. *Psychological Bulletin*, 84, 323–345.

Gerbner, G., Gross, L., Morgan, M., & Signorielli, N. (1986). Living with television: The dynamics of the cultivation process. In J. Bryant & D. Zillman (Eds.), *Perspectives on media effects*. Hillsdale, N.J.: Erlbaum.

Gerbner, G., Gross, L., Signorielli, N., & Morgan, M. (1980). Television violence, victimization, and power. *American Behavioral Scientist*, 23, 705–716.

Gerbner, G., Gross, L., Signorielli, N., Morgan, M., & Jackson-Beeck, M. (1979). The demonstration of power: Violence profile No. 10. *Journal of Communication*, 29(3), 177–196.

Gergen, K. J., Gergen, M. M., & Barton, W. N. (1973, October). Deviance in the dark. *Psychology Today*, pp. 129–130.

Gibbons, F. X. (1978). Sexual standards and reactions to pornography: Enhancing behavioral consistency through self-focused attention. *Journal of Personality and Social Psychology*, 36, 976–987.

Gibbons, F. X. (1986). Social comparison and depression: Company's effect on misery. *Jour-*

nal of Personality and Social Psychology, 51, 140–148.

Gibbons, F. X., & Wicklund, R. A. (1982). Self-focused attention and helping behavior. *Journal of Personality and Social Psychology*, 43, 462–474.

Gifford, R., & Peacock, J. (1979). Crowding: More fearsome than crime-provoking? Comparison of an Asian city and a North American city. *Psychologia*, 22, 79–83.

Gilbert, D. T., & Jones, E. E. (1986). Perceiver-induced constraint: Interpretations of self-generated reality. *Journal of Personality and Social Psychology*, 50, 269–280.

Gilbert, D. T., Pelham, B. W., & Krull, D. S. (1988). On cognitive busyness: When person perceivers meet persons perceived. *Journal of Personality and Social Psychology*, 54, 733–740.

Gilkey, L. (1966). *Shantung compound*. New York: Harper & Row.

Gilligan, C. (1982). *In a different voice: Psychological theory and women's development*. Cambridge, Mass.: Harvard University Press.

Gillis, J. S., & Avis, W. E. (1980). The male-taller norm in mate selection. *Personality and Social Psychology Bulletin*, 6, 396–401.

Gilmor, T. M., & Reid, D. W. (1979). Locus of control and causal attribution for positive and negative outcomes on university examinations. *Journal of Research in Personality*, 13, 154–160.

Gilovich, T. (1981). Seeing the past in the present: The effect of associations to familiar events on judgments and decisions. *Journal of Personality and Social Psychology*, 40, 797–808.

Gilovich, T. (1983). Biased evaluation and persistence in gambling. *Journal of Personality and Social Psychology*, 44, 1110–1126.

Gilovich, T. (1987). Secondhand information and social judgment. *Journal of Experimental Social Psychology*, 23, 59–74.

Gilovich, T. (1988). How we know what isn't so: The foundations of questionable and erroneous beliefs. Unpublished manuscript, Cornell University.

Gilovich, T. (1989). Judgmental biases in the world of sports. In W. F. Straub & J. M. Williams (Eds.), *Cognitive sports psychology*. New York: Sports Science Associates, in press.

Gilovich, T., & Douglas, C. (1986). Biased evaluations of randomly determined gambling outcomes. *Journal of Experimental Social Psychology*, 22, 228–241.

Ginossar, Z., & Trope, Y. (1987). Problem solving in judgment under uncertainty. *Journal of Personality and Social Psychology*, 52, 464–474.

Ginsburg, B., & Allee, W. C. (1942). Some effects of conditioning on social dominance and subordination in inbred strains of mice. *Physiological Zoology*, 15, 485–506.

Glass, D. C. (1964). Changes in liking as a means of reducing cognitive discrepancies between self-esteem and aggression. *Journal of Personality*, 32, 591–549.

Gleason, J. M., & Harris, V. A. (1979). Group discussion and defendant's socio-economic status as determinants of judgments by simulated jurors. *Journal of Applied Social Psychology*, 6, 186–191.

Glenn, N. D. (1980). Aging and attitudinal stability. In O. G. Brim, Jr., & J. Kagan (Eds.), *Constancy and change in human development*. Cambridge, Mass.: Harvard University Press.

Glenn, N. D. (1981). Personal communication.

Goethals, G. R., & Nelson, E. R. (1973). Similarity in the influence process: The belief-value distinction. *Journal of Personality and Social Psychology*, 25, 117–122.

Goethals, G. R., & Zanna, M. P. (1979). The role of social comparison in choice shifts. *Journal of Personality and Social Psychology*, 37, 1469–1476.

Goffman, E. (1967). *Interaction ritual*. Garden City, N.Y.: Doubleday Anchor.

Goggin, W. C., & Range, L. M. (1985). The disadvantages of hindsight in the perception of suicide. *Journal of Social and Clinical Psychology*, 3, 232–237.

Gold, J. A., Ryckman, R. M., & Mosley, N. R. (1984). Romantic mood induction and attraction to a dissimilar other: Is love blind? *Personality and Social Psychology Bulletin*, 10, 358–368.

Goldberg, L. R. (1968). Simple models or simple processes? Some research on clinical judgments. *American Psychologist*, 23, 483–496.

Goldberg, P. (1968, April). Are women prejudiced against women? *Transaction*, pp. 28–30.

Golding, W. (1962). *Lord of the flies*. New York: Coward-McCann.

Goldman, C. (1980). An examination of social facilitation. Unpublished manuscript, University of Michigan, 1967. Cited by R. B. Zajonc in, Compresence, in P. B. Paulus (Ed.), *Psychology of group influence*. Hillsdale, N.J.: Lawrence Erlbaum.

Goldman, M. (1986). Compliance employing a combined foot-in-the-door and door-in-the-face procedure. *Journal of Social Psychology*, 126, 111–116.

Goldman, W., & Lewis, P. (1977). Beautiful is good: Evidence that the physically attractive are more socially skillful. *Journal of Experimental Social Psychology*, 13, 125–130.

Goldstein, A. G., Chance, J. E., & Schneller, G. R. (1989). Frequency of eyewitness identification in criminal cases: A survey of prosecuters. *Bulletin of the Psychonomic Society*, in press.

Goldstein, A. P., Garr, E. G., Davidson, W. S., II, & Wehr, P. *In response to aggression: Methods of control and prosocial alternatives*. Elmsford, N.Y.: Pergamon Press.

Goldstein, J. H., & Arms, R. L. (1971). Effects of observing athletic contests on hostility. *Sociometry*, 34, 83–90.

Goleman, D. (1985, March 5). Great altruists: Science ponders soul of goodness. *New York Times*, pp. C1, C2.

Gonzales, M. H., Aronson, E., & Costanzo, M. A. (1988). Using social cognition and persuasion to promote energy conservation: A quasi-experiment. *Journal of Applied Social Psychology*, 18, 1049–1066.

Goodhart, D. E. (1986). The effects of positive and negative thinking on performance in an achievement situation. *Journal of Personality and Social Psychology*, 51, 117–124.

Gormly, J. (1983). Predicting behavior from personality trait scores. *Personality and Social Psychology Bulletin*, 9, 267–270.

Gorsuch, R. L. (1976). Religion as a significant predictor of important human behavior. In W. J. Donaldson, Jr. (Ed.), *Research in Mental Health and Religious Behavior*, Psychological Studies Institute.

Gorsuch, R. L. (1988). Psychology of religion. *Annual Review of Psychology*, 39, 201–222.

Gorsuch, R. L., & Aleshire, D. (1974). Christian faith and ethnic prejudice: A review and interpretation of research. *Journal for the Scientific Study of Religion*, 13, 281–307.

Gottlieb, J., & Carver, C. S. (1980). Anticipation of future interaction and the bystander effect. *Journal of Experimental Social Psychology*, 16, 253–260.

Gould, R., Brounstein, P. J., & Sigall, H. (1977). Attributing ability to an opponent: Public aggrandizement and private denigration. *Sociometry*, 40, 254–261.

Gould, S. J. (1988, July). Kropotkin was no crackpot. *Natural History*, pp. 12–21.

Gouldner, A. W. (1960). The norm of reciprocity: A preliminary statement. *American Sociological Review*, 25, 161–178.

Gray-Little, B., & Burks, N. (1983). Power and satisfaction in marriage: A review and critique. *Psychological Bulletin*, 93, 513–538.

Graziano, W., Brothen, T., & Berscheid, E. (1978). Height and attraction: Do men and women see eye-to-eye? *Journal of Personality*, 46, 128–145.

Greeley, A. M. (1976). Pop psychology and the Gospel. *Theology Today*, 23, 224–231.

Greeley, A. M., & Sheatsley, P. B. (1971). Attitudes toward racial integration. *Scientific American*, 225(6), 13–19. (*b*)

Greenberg, J. (1979). Group vs. individual equity judgments: Is there a polarization effect? *Journal of Experimental Social Psychology*, 15, 504–512.

Greenberg, J. (1980). Attentional focus and locus of performance causality as determinants of equity behavior. *Journal of Personality and Social Psychology*, 38, 579–585.

Greenberg, J. (1986). Differential intolerance for inequity from organizational and individual agents. *Journal of Applied Social Psychology*, 16, 191–196.

Greenwald, A. G. (1968). Cognitive learning, cognitive response to persuasion, and attitude change. In A. G. Greenwald, T. C. Brock, & T. M. Ostrom (Eds.), *Psychological foundations of attitudes*. New York: Academic Press.

Greenwald, A. G. (1975). On the inconclusiveness of crucial cognitive tests of dissonance versus self-perception theories. *Journal of Experimental Social Psychology*, 11, 490–499.

Greenwald, A. G. (1980). The totalitarian ego: Fabrication and revision of personal history. *American Psychologist*, 35, 603–618.

Greenwald, A. G., & Breckler, S. J. (1985). To whom is the self presented? In B. R. Schlenker (Ed.), *The self and social life*. New York: McGraw-Hill.

Greenwald, A. G., Carnot, C. G., Beach, R., & Young, B. (1987). Increasing voting behavior by asking people if they expect to vote. *Journal of Applied Psychology*, 72, 315–318.

Greenwald, J. (1986, January 13). Is there cause for fear of flying? *Time*, pp. 39–40.

Griffin, B. Q., Combs, A. L., Land, M. L., & Combs, N. N. (1983). Attribution of success and failure in college performance. *Journal of Psychology*, 114, 259–266.

Griffitt, W. (1970). Environmental effects on interpersonal affective behavior. Ambient effective temperature and attraction. *Journal of Personality and Social Psychology*, 15, 240–244.

Griffitt, W., & Veitch, R. (1971). Hot and crowded: Influences of population density and temperature on interpersonal affective behavior. *Journal of Personality and Social Psychology*, 17, 92–98.

Griffitt, W., & Veitch, R. (1974). Preacquaintance attitude similarity and attraction revisited: Ten days in a fallout shelter. *Sociometry*, 37, 163–173.

Grofman, B. (1980). The slippery slope: Jury size and jury verdict requirements—legal and social science approaches. In B. H. Raven (Ed.), *Policy studies review annual* (Vol. 4). Beverly Hills, Calif.: Sage Publications.

Gross, A. E., & Crofton, C. (1977). What is good is beautiful. *Sociometry*, 40, 85–90.

Gross, A. E., & Fleming, I. (1982). Twenty years of deception in social psychology. *Personality and Social Psychology Bulletin*, 8, 402–408.

Grube, J. W., Kleinhesselink, R. R., & Kearney, K. A. (1982). Male self-acceptance and attraction toward women. *Personality and Social Psychology Bulletin*, 8, 107–112.

Gruder, C. L. (1977). Choice of comparison persons in evaluating oneself. In J. M. Suls & R. L. Miller (Eds.), *Social comparison processes*. Washington: Hemisphere Publishing.

Gruder, C. L., Cook, T. D., Hennigan, K. M., Flay, B., Alessis, C., & Kalamaj, J. (1978). Empirical tests of the absolute sleeper effect predicted from the discounting cue hypothesis. *Journal of Personality and Social Psychology*, 36, 1061–1074.

Gruder, C. L., Romer, D., & Korth, B. (1978). Dependency and fault as determinants of helping. *Journal of Experimental Social Psychology*, 14, 227–335.

Gruman, J. C., Sloan, R. P. (1983). Disease as justice: Perceptions of the victims of physical illness. *Basic and Applied Social Psychology*, 4, 39–46.

Grunberger, R. (1971). *The 12-year-Reich: A social history of Nazi Germany 1933–1945*. New York: Holt, Rinehart & Winston.

Grush, J. E. (1976). Attitude formation and mere exposure phenomena: A nonartifactual explanation of empirical findings. *Journal of Personality and Social Psychology*, 33, 281–290.

Grush, J. E. (1979). A summary review of mediating explanations of exposure phenomena. *Personality and Social Psychology Bulletin*, 5, 154–159.

Grush, J. E. (1980). Impact of candidate expenditures, regionality, and prior outcomes on the 1976 Democratic presidential primaries. *Journal of Personality and Social Psychology*, 38, 337–347.

Grush, J. E., & Glidden, M. V. (1987). Power and satisfaction among distressed and nondistressed couples. Paper presented at the Midwestern Psychological Association convention.

Grush, J. E., McKeough, K. L., & Ahlering, R. F. (1978). Extrapolating laboratory exposure research to actual political elections. *Journal of Personality and Social Psychology*, 36, 257–270.

Gudykunst, W. B. (1989). Culture and intergroup processes. In M. H. Bond (Ed.), *The cross-cultural challenge to social psychology*. Newbury Park, Ca.: Sage.

Guerin, B. (1986). Mere presence effects in humans: A review. *Journal of Personality and Social Psychology*, 22, 38–77.

Guerin, B., & Innes, J. M. (1982). Social facilitation and social monitoring: A new look at Zajonc's mere presence hypothesis. *British Journal of Social Psychology*, 21, 7–18.

Gunter, B., Furnham, A., & Leese, J. (1986). Memory for information from a party political broadcast as a function of the channel of communication. *Social Behaviour*, 1, 135–142.

Gupta, U., & Singh, P. (1982). Exploratory study of love and liking and type of marriages. *Indian Journal of Applied Psychology*, 19, 92–97.

Gurr, T. R. (1972). The calculus of civil conflict. *Journal of Social Issues*, 28(1), 27–47.

Haan, N. (1978). Two moralities of action contexts: Relationships to thought, ego regulation, and development. *Journal of Personality and Social Psychology*, 36, 286–305.

Hacker, H. M. (1951). Women as a minority group. *Social Forces*, 30, 60–69.

Hackman, J. R. (1986). The design of work teams. In J. Lorsch (Ed.), *Handbook of organizational behavior*. Englewood Cliffs, N.J.: Prentice-Hall.

Hadden, J. K. (1969). *The gathering storm in the churches*. Garden City, N.Y.: Doubleday.

Haemmerlie, F. M. (1983). Heterosexual anxiety in college females: A biased interaction treatment. *Behavior Modification*, 7, 611–623.

Haemmerlie, F. M. (1987). Creating adaptive illusions in counseling and therapy using a self-perception theory perspective. Paper presented at the Midwestern Psychological Association, Chicago.

Haemmerlie, F. M., & Montgomery, R. L. (1982). Self-perception theory and unobtrusively biased interactions: A treatment for heterosocial anxiety. *Journal of Counseling Psychology*, 29, 362–370.

Haemmerlie, F. M., & Montgomery, R. L. (1984). Purposefully biased interventions: Reducing heterosocial anxiety through self-perception theory. *Journal of Personality and Social Psychology*, 47, 900–908.

Haemmerlie, F. M., & Montgomery, R. L. (1986). Self-perception theory and the treatment of shyness. In W. H. Jones, J. M. Cheek, & S. R. Briggs (Eds.), *A sourcebook on shyness: Research and treatment*. New York: Plenum.

Hagiwara, S. (1983). Role of self-based and sample-based consensus estimates as mediators of responsibility judgments for automobile accidents. *Japanese Psychological Research*, **25**, 16–28.

Halberstadt, A. G., & Saitta, M. B. (1987). Gender, nonverbal behavior, and perceived dominance: A test of the theory. *Journal of Personality and Social Psychology*, **53**, 257–272.

Hall, C. S. (1978). The incredible Freud. *Contemporary Psychology*, **23**, 38–39.

Hall, J. A. (1984). *Nonverbal sex differences: Communication accuracy and expressive style*. Baltimore: Johns Hopkins University Press.

Hall, J. A. (1987). On explaining gender differences: The case of nonverbal communication. In P. Shaver & C. Hendrick (Eds.), *Sex and gender: review of personality and social psychology*, Vol. 7. Beverly Hills: Sage.

Hall, T. (1985, June 25). The unconverted: Smoking of cigarettes seems to be becoming a lower-class habit. *Wall Street Journal*, pp. 1, 25.

Hamblin, R. L., Buckholdt, D., Bushell, D., Ellis, D., & Ferritor, D. (1969). Changing the game from get the teacher to learn. *Transaction*, January, pp. 20–25, 28–31.

Hamill, R., Wilson, T. D., & Nisbett, R. E. (1980). Insensitivity to sample bias: Generalizing from atypical cases. *Journal of Personality and Social Psychology*, **39**, 578–589.

Hamilton, D. L. (1981). Illusory correlation as a basis for stereotyping. In D. L. Hamilton (Ed.), *Cognitive processes in stereotyping and intergroup behavior*. Hillsdale, N.J.: Erlbaum.

Hamilton, D. L., & Bishop, G. D. (1976). Attitudinal and behavioral effects of initial integration of white suburban neighborhoods. *Journal of Social Issues*, **32**(2), 47–67.

Hamilton, D. L., Carpenter, S., & Bishop, G. D. (1984). Desegregation of suburban neighborhoods. In N. Miller & M. B. Brewer (Eds.), *Groups in contact: The psychology of desegregation*. Orlando, Fla.: Academic Press.

Hamilton, D. L., & Gifford, R. K. (1976). Illusory correlation in interpersonal perception: A cognitive basis of stereotypic judgments. *Journal of Experimental Social Psychology*, **12**, 392–407.

Hamilton, D. L., & Rose, T. L. (1980). Illusory correlation and the maintenance of stereotypic beliefs. *Journal of Personality and Social Psychology*, **39**, 832–845.

Hamilton, D. L., & Sherman, S. J. (1989). Illusory correlations: Implications for stereotype theory and research, In D. Bar-Tal, C. F. Graumann, A. W. Kruglanski, & W. Stroebe (Eds.), *Stereotypes and prejudice:*

Changing conceptions. New York: Springer-Verlag, in press.

Hamilton, D. L., & Zanna, M. P. (1972). Differential weighting of favorable and unfavorable attributes in impressions of personality. *Journal of Experimental Research in Personality*, **6**, 204–212.

Hampson, R. B. (1984). Adolescent prosocial behavior: Peer-group and situational factors associated with helping. *Journal of Personality and Social Psychology*, **46**, 153–162.

Hans, V. P. (1981). Evaluating the jury: A case study of the uses of research in policy formation. In R. Roesch & R. Corrado (Eds.), *Evaluation and criminal justice policy*. Beverly Hills, Calif.: Sage Publications.

Hans, V. P., & Vidmar, N. (1981). Jury selection. In N. L. Kerr & R. M. Bray (Eds.), *The psychology of the courtroom*. New York: Academic Press.

Hansen, C. H. (1989). Priming sex-role stereotypic event schemas with rock music videos: Effects on impression favorability, trait inferences, a recall of a subsequent male-female interaction. *Basic and Applied Social Psychology*, in press.

Hansen, C. H., & Hansen, R. D. (1988). Priming stereotypic appraisal of social interactions: How rock music videos can change what's seen when boy meets girl. *Sex Roles*, **19**, 287–316.

Hardin, G. (1968). The tragedy of the commons. *Science*, **162**, 1243–1248.

Hardy, C., & Latané, B. (1986). Social loafing on a cheering task. *Social Science*, **71**, 165–172.

Haritos-Fatouros, M. (1988). The official torturer: A learning model for obedience to the authority of violence. *Journal of Applied Social Psychology*, **18**, 1107–1120.

Harkins, S. G. (1981). Effects of task difficulty and task responsibility on social loafing. Presentation to the First International Conference on Social Processes in Small Groups, Kill Devil Hills, North Carolina.

Harkins, S. G., & Jackson, J. M. (1985). The role of evaluation in eliminating social loafing. *Personality and Social Psychology Bulletin*, **11**, 457–465.

Harkins, S. G., & Latané, B. (1980). Population and political participation. Paper presented at the American Psychological Association convention.

Harkins, S. G., Latané, B., & Williams, K. (1980). Social loafing; Allocating effort or taking it easy? *Journal of Experimental Social Psychology*, **16**, 457–465.

Harkins, S. G., & Petty, R. E. (1982). Effects of task difficulty and task uniqueness on social

loafing. *Journal of Personality and Social Psychology*, **43**, 1214–1229.

Harkins, S. G., & Petty, R. E. (1987). Information utility and the multiple source effect. *Journal of Personality and Social Psychology*, **52**, 260–268.

Harkins, S. G., & Szymanski, K. (1987). Social loafing and social facilitation: New wine in old bottles. In C. Hendrick (Ed.), *Group processes and intergroup relations: Review of personality and social psychology*, Vol. 9. Newbury Park, Ca.: Sage.

Harkins, S. G., & Szymanski, K. (1988). Social loafing and self-evaluation with an objective standard. *Journal of Experimental Social Psychology*, **24**, 354–365.

Harries, K. D., & Stadler, S. J. (1988). Heat and violence: New findings from Dallas field data, 1980–1981. *Journal of Applied Social Psychology*, **18**, 129–138.

Harris, L. & Associates (1988, January 26). Sexual material on American network television during the 1987–88 season. Conducted for Planned Parenthood Federation of America, New York.

Harris, M. J. & Rosenthal, R. (1985). Mediation of interpersonal expectancy effects: 31 meta-analyses. *Psychological Bulletin*, **97**, 363–386.

Harris, T. G. (1978). Introduction to E. H. Walster and G. W. Walster, *A new look at love*. Reading, Mass.: Addison-Wesley.

Harrison, A. A. (1977). Mere exposure. In L. Berkowitz (Ed.), *Advances in experimental social psychology* (Vol. 10). New York: Academic Press, pp. 39–83.

Harvey, J. H. (1987). Attribution in close relationships: Research and theory developments. *Journal of Social and Clinical Psychology*, **5**, 420–434.

Harvey, J. H., Town, J. P., & Yarkin, K. L. (1981). How fundamental is the fundamental attribution error? *Journal of Personality and Social Psychology*, **40**, 346–349.

Hassan, I. N. (1980). Role and status of women in Pakistan: An empirical research review. *Pakistan Journal of Psychology*, **13**, 36–56.

Hastie, R., Penrod, S. D., & Pennington, N. (1983). *Inside the jury*. Cambridge, Mass.: Harvard University Press.

Hastorf, A., & Cantril, H. (1954). They saw a game: A case study. *Journal of Abnormal and Social Psychology*, **49**, 129–134.

Hatfield, E. See also E. Walster (Hatfield).

Hatfield, E. (1988). Passionate and compassionate love. In R. J. Sternberg & M. L. Barnes (Eds.), *The psychology of love*. New Haven, Conn.: Yale University Press.

Hatfield, E., & Rapson, R. L. (1987). Passionate love: New directions in research. In W. H.

Jones & D. Perlman (Eds.), *Advances in personal relationships*, Vol. 1. Greenwich, Ct.: JAI Press.

Hatfield, E., & Sprecher, S. (1985). Measuring passionate love in intimate relations. Unpublished manuscript, University of Hawaii at Manoa.

Hatfield, E. & Sprecher, S. (1986). *Mirror, mirror: The importance of looks in everyday life:* Albany, N.Y.: SUNY Press.

Hatfield, E., Traupmann, J., Sprecher, S., Utne, M., & Hay, J. (1985). Equity and intimate relations: Recent research. In W. Ickes (Ed.), *Compatible and incompatible relationships*. New York: Springer-Verlag.

Hatfield, E., Walster, G. W., & Traupmann, J. (1979). Equity and premarital sex. In M. Cook and G. Wilson (Eds.), *Love and attraction*. New York: Pergamon Press.

Hatfield, M. O. (1972). On neighborhood government. Statement to the Platform Committee, Republican National Convention.

Hatfield, M. O. (1975, October 1). Neighborhood government act of 1975. *Congressional Record*, **121**, No. 146, p. 30.

Hatvany, N., & Strack, F. (1980). The impact of a discredited key witness. *Journal of Applied Social Psychology*, **10**, 490–509.

Haugtvedt, C., Petty, R. E., Cacioppo, J. T., & Steidley, T. (1988). Personality and ad effectiveness. *Advances in Consumer Research*, **15**, in press.

Hayduck, L. A. (1983). Personal space: Where we now stand. *Psychological Bulletin*, **94**, 293–335.

Hays, R. B. (1985). A longitudinal study of friendship development. *Journal of Personality and Social Psychology*, **48**, 909–924.

Hearold, S. (1986). A synthesis of 1043 effects of television on social behavior. In G. Comstock (Ed.), *Public communication and behavior*, Vol. 1. Orlando, Fl.: Academic Press.

Heath, L., & Petraitis, J. (1987). Television viewing and fear of crime: Where is the mean world? *Basic and Applied Social Psychology*, **8**, 97–123.

Hebb, D. O. (1980). *Essay on mind*. Hillsdale, N.J.: Erlbaum.

Heesacker, M. (1986). Extrapolating from the elaboration likelihood model of attitude change to counseling. In F. J. Dorn (Ed.), *The social influence process in counseling and psychotherapy*. Springfield, Il.: Charles C. Thomas. (a)

Heesacker, M. (1986). Counseling pretreatment and the elaboration likelihood model of attitude change. *Journal of Counseling Psychology*, **33**, 107–114. (b)

Heider, F. (1958). *The psychology of interpersonal relations*. New York: Wiley.

Heilman, M. E. (1976). Oppositional behavior as a function of influence attempt intensity and retaliation threat. *Journal of Personality and Social Psychology*, **33**, 574–578.

Hellman, P. (1980). *Avenue of the righteous of nations*. New York: Atheneum.

Hemsley, G. D., & Doob, A. N. (1978). The effect of looking behavior on perceptions of a communicator's credibility. *Journal of Applied Social Psychology*, **8**, 136–144.

Hendrick, C. (1988). Roles and gender in relationships. In S. Duck (Ed.), *Handbook of personal relationships*. Chichester, England: Wiley.

Hendrick, C., & Hendrick, S. S. (1986). A theory and method of love. *Journal of Personality and Social Psychology*, **50**, 392–402.

Hendrick, C., & Hendrick, S. S. (1988). Lovers wear rose colored glasses. *Journal of Social and Personal Relationships*, **5**, 161–183.

Hendrick, S. S., Hendrick, C., & Adler, N. L. (1988). Romantic relationships: Love, satisfaction, and staying together. *Journal of Personality and Social Psychology*, **54**, 980–988.

Hendrick, S. S., Hendrick, C., Slapion-Foote, J., & Foote, F. H. (1985). Gender differences in sexual attitudes. *Journal of Personality and Social Psychology*, **48**, 1630–1642.

Hendrick, S. S. (1981). Self disclosure and marital satisfaction. *Journal of Personality and Social Psychology*, **40**, 1150–1159.

Henley, N. (1977). *Body politics: Power, sex, and nonverbal communication*. Englewood Cliffs, N.J.: Prentice-Hall.

Hennigan, K. M., Del Rosario, M. L., Heath, L., Cook, T. D., Wharton, J. D., & Calder, B. J. (1982). Impact of the introduction of television on crime in the United States: Empirical findings and theoretical implications. *Journal of Personality and Social Psychology*, **42**, 461–477.

Henslin, M. (1967). Craps and magic. *American Journal of Sociology*, **73**, 316–330.

Hepworth, J. T., & West, S. G. (1988). Lynchings and the economy: A time-series reanalysis of Hovland and Sears (1940). *Journal of Personality and Social Psychology*, **55**, 239–247.

Heradstveit, D. (1980). *The Arab-Israeli conflict: Psychological obstacles to peace* (Vol. 28). Oslo, Norway: Universitetsforlaget, 1979. Distributed by Columbia University Press. Reviewed by R. K. White, *Contemporary Psychology*, **25**, 11–12.

Herek, G. M. (1986). The instrumentality of attitudes: Toward a neofunctional theory. *Journal of Social Issues*, **42**(2), 99–114.

Herek, G. M. (1987). Can functions be measured? A new perspective on the functional approach to attitudes. *Social Psychology Quarterly*, **50**, 285–303.

Herek, G. M. (1987). Religious orientation and prejudice: A comparison of racial and sexual attitudes. *Personality and Social Psychology Bulletin*, **13**, 34–44. (b)

Hewstone, M. (1988). Causal attribution: From cognitive processes to collective beliefs. *The Psychologist*, **8**, 323–327.

Hewstone, M., Jaspars, J., & Lalljee, M. (1982). Social representations, social attribution and social identity: The intergroup images of "public" and "comprehensive" schoolboys. *European Journal of Social Psychology*, **12**, 241–269.

Hewstone, M., & Ward, C. (1985). Ethnocentrism and causal attribution in southeast Asia. *Journal of Personality and Social Psychology*, **48**, 614–623.

Higbee, K. L., Millard, R. J., & Folkman, J. R. (1982). Social psychology research during the 1970s: Predominance of experimentation and college students. *Personality and Social Psychology Bulletin*, **8**, 180–183.

Higgins, E. T., Bargh, J. A. (1987). Social cognition and social perception. *Annual Review of Psychology*, **38**, 369–425.

Higgins, E. T., & McCann, C. D. (1984). Social encoding and subsequent attitudes, impressions and memory: "Context-driven" and motivational aspects of processing. *Journal of Personality and Social Psychology*, **47**, 26–39.

Higgins, E. T., & Rholes, W. S. (1978). Saying is believing: Effects of message modification on memory and liking for the person described. *Journal of Experimental Social Psychology*, **14**, 363–378.

Hilgard, E. R., & Loftus, E. F. (1979). Effective interrogation of the eyewitness. *International Journal of Clinical and Experimental Hypnosis*, **27**, 342–357.

Hill, G. W. (1982). Group versus individual performance: Are N + 1 heads better than one? *Psychological Bulletin*, **91**, 517–539.

Hill, W. F. (1978). Effects of mere exposure on preferences in nonhuman animals. *Psychological Bulletin*, **85**, 1177–1198.

Hinde, R. A. (1984). Why do the sexes behave differently in close relationships? *Journal of Social and Personal Relationships*, **1**, 471–501.

Hirt, E. R., & Kimble, C. E. (1981). The home-field advantage in sports: Differences and correlates. Paper presented at the Midwestern Psychological Association convention.

Hodges, B. H. (1974). Effect of valence on relative weighting in impression formation. *Journal of Personality and Social Psychology*, 30, 378–381.

Hoffman, M. L. (1981). Is altruism part of human nature? *Journal of Personality and Social Psychology*, 40, 121–137.

Hofling, C. K., Brotzman, E., Dalrymple, S., Graves, N., & Pierce, C. M. (1966). An experimental study in nurse-physician relationships. *Journal of Nervous and Mental Disease*, 143, 171–180.

Hokanson, J. E., & Burgess, M. (1962). The effects of frustration and anxiety on overt aggression. *Journal of Abnormal and Social Psychology*, 65, 232–237. (a)

Hokanson, J. E., & Burgess, M. (1962). The effects of three types of aggression on vascular processes. *Journal of Abnormal and Social Psychology*, 64, 446–449. (b)

Hokanson, J. E., Burgess, M., & Cohen, M. F. (1963). Effects of displaced aggression on systolic blood pressure. *Journal of Abnormal and Social Psychology*, 67, 214–218.

Hokanson, J. E., & Edelman, R. (1966). Effects of three social responses on vascular processes. *Journal of Personality and Social Psychology*, 3, 442–447.

Hokanson, J. E., & Shetler, S. (1961). The effect of overt aggression on physiological arousal. *Journal of Abnormal and Social Psychology*, 63, 446–448.

Hollander, E. P. (1958). Conformity, status, and idiosyncrasy credit. *Psychological Review*, 65, 117–127.

Hollander, E. P. (1985). Leadership and power. In G. Lindzey & E. Aronson (Eds.), *The Handbook of Social Psychology*, 3rd ed. New York: Random House.

Holmes, J. G., & Rempel, J. K. (1989). Trust in close relationships. In C. Hendrick (Ed.), *Review of personality and social psychology*, Vol. 10. Newbury Park, Ca.: Sage.

Holmes, O. W. (1975). Law in science and science in law. *Harvard Law Review*, 1889, 12, 443. Cited by W. N. Brooks and A. N. Doob. Justice and the jury. *Journal of Social Issues*, 31, 171–182.

Holtzworth-Munroe, A., & Jacobson, N. S. (1985). Causal attributions of married couples: When do they search for causes? What do they conclude when they do? *Journal of Personality and Social Psychology*, 48, 1398–1412.

Hoover, C. W., Wood, E. E., & Knowles, E. S. (1983). Forms of social awareness and helping. *Journal of Experimental Social Psychology*, 19, 577–590.

Hormuth, S. E. (1986). Lack of effort as a result of self-focused attention: An attributional am-biguity analysis. *European Journal of Social Psychology*, 16, 181–192.

Hornstein, H. (1976). *Cruelty and kindness*. Englewood Cliffs, N.J.: Prentice-Hall.

Houlden, P., LaTour, S., Walker, L., & Thibaut, J. (1978). Preference for modes of dispute resolution as a function of process and decision control. *Journal of Experimental Social Psychology*, 14, 13–30.

House, R. (1977). A 1976 theory of charismatic leadership. In J. G. Hunt, & L. Larson (Eds.), *Leadership: The cutting edge*. Carbondale, Ill.: Southern Illinois Press.

House, R. J., & Singh, J. V. (1987). Organizational behavior: Some new directions for I/O psychology. *Annual Review of Psychology*, 38, 669–718.

Hovland, C. I., Lumsdaine, A. A., & Sheffield, F. D. (1949). *Experiments on mass communication. Studies in social psychology in World War II* (Vol. III). Princeton, N.J.: Princeton University Press.

Hovland, C. I., & Sears, R. (1940). Minor studies of aggression: Correlation of lynchings with economic indices. *Journal of Psychology*, 9, 301–310.

Howard, A., Pion, G. M., Gottfredson, G. D., Flattau, P. E., Oskamp, S., Pfafflin, S. M., Bray, D. W., & Burstein, A. G. (1986). The changing face of American psychology: A report from the committee on employment and human resources. *American Psychologist*, 41, 1311–1327.

Howes, M. J., Hokanson, J. E., & Loewenstein, D. A. (1985). Induction of depressive affect after prolonged exposure to a mildly depressed individual. *Journal of Personality and Social Psychology*, 49, 1110–1113.

Huesmann, L. R., Lagerspetz, K., & Eron, L. D. (1984). Intervening variables in the TV violence-aggression relation: Evidence from two countries. *Developmental Psychology*, 20, 746–775.

Hull, J. G., & Bond, Jr., C. F. (1986). Social and behavioral consequences of alcohol consumption and expectancy: A meta-analysis. *Psychological Bulletin*, 99, 347–360.

Hull, J. G., Levenson, R. W., Young, R. D., & Sher, K. J. (1983). Self-awareness-reducing effects of alcohol consumption. *Journal of Personality and Social Psychology*, 44, 461–473.

Hull, J. G., & Young, R. D. (1983). The self-awareness-reducing effects of alcohol consumption: Evidence and implications. In J. Suls & A. G. Greenwald (Eds.), *Psychological perspectives on the self*, Vol. 2. Hillsdale, N.J.: Erlbaum.

Hunt, P. J., & Hillery, J. M. (1973). Social facilitation in a location setting: An examination of the effects over learning trials. *Journal of Experimental Social Psychology*, 9, 563–571.

Huston, T. L. (1973). Ambiguity of acceptance, social desirability, and dating choice. *Journal of Experimental Social Psychology*, 9, 32–42.

Hutchinson, R. R. (1983). The pain-aggression relationship and its expression in naturalistic settings. *Aggressive Behavior*, 9, 229–242.

Hyde, J. S. Gender differences in aggression. In J. S. Hyde & M. C. Linn (Eds.), *The psychology of gender: Advances through meta-analysis*. Baltimore: Johns Hopkins University Press.

Hyman, H. H., & Sheatsley, P. B. (1956 & 1964). Attitudes toward desegregation. *Scientific American*, 195(6), 35–39, and 211(1), 16–23.

Hyman, R. (1981). Cold reading: How to convince strangers that you know all about them. In K. Frazier (Ed.), *Paranormal borderlands of science*. Buffalo, N.Y.: Prometheus Books.

Ickes, B. (1980). On disconfirming our perceptions of others. Paper presented at the American Psychological Association convention.

Ickes, W. (1981). Sex role influences in dyadic interaction: A theoretical model. In C. Mayo & N. Henley (Eds.), *Gender and nonverbal behavior*. New York: Springer-Verlag.

Ickes, W. (1985). Sex-role influences on compatibility in relationships. In W. Ickes (Ed.), *Compatible and incompatible relationships*. New York: Springer-Verlag.

Ickes, W., & Barnes, R. D. (1978). Boys and girls together—and alienated: On enacting stereotyped sex roles in mixed-sex dyads. *Journal of Personality and Social Psychology*, 36, 669–683.

Ickes, W., & Layden, M. A. (1978). Attributional styles. In J. H. Harvey, W. Ickes, & R. F. Kidd (Eds.), *New directions in attribution research* (Vol. 2). Hillsdale, N.J.: Lawrence Erlbaum.

Ickes, W., Layden, M. A., & Barnes, R. D. (1978). Objective self-awareness and individuation: An empirical link. *Journal of Personality*, 46, 146–161.

Ickes, W., Patterson, M. L., Rajecki, D. W., & Tanford, S. (1982). Behavioral and cognitive consequences of reciprocal versus compensatory responses to preinteraction expectancies. *Social Cognition*, 1, 160–190.

Ingham, A. G., Levinger, G., Graves, J., & Peckham, V. (1974). The Ringelmann effect: Studies of group size and group performance. *Journal of Experimental Social Psychology*, 10, 371–384.

Inglehart, R., & Rabier, J. R. (1986). Aspirations adapt to situations—but why are the Belgians so much happier than the French? A cross-cultural analysis of the subjective quality of life. In F. M. Andrews (Ed.), *Research on the quality of life.* Ann Arbor, Mi.: Survey Research Center, Institute of Social Research, University of Michigan.

Insko, C. A., Nacoste, R. W., & Moe, J. L. (1983). Belief congruence and racial discrimination: Review of the evidence and critical evaluation. *European Journal of Social Psychology, 13,* 153–174.

Insko, C. A., Smith, R. H., Alicke, M. D., Wade, J., & Taylor, S. (1985). Conformity and group size: The concern with being right and the concern with being liked. *Personality and Social Psychology Bulletin, 11,* 41–50.

Insko, C. A., & Wilson, M. (1977). Interpersonal attraction as a function of social interaction. *Journal of Personality and Social Psychology, 35,* 903–911.

Instone, D., Major, B., & Bunker, B. B. (1983). Gender, self confidence, and social influence strategies: An organizational simulation. *Journal of Personality and Social Psychology, 44,* 322–333.

Isen, A. M., Clark, M., & Schwartz, M. F. (1976). Duration of the effect of good mood on helping: Footprints on the sands of time. *Journal of Personality and Social Psychology, 34,* 385–393.

Isen, A. M., & Means, B. (1983). The influence of positive affect on decision-making strategy. *Social Cognition, 2,* 28–31.

Isen, A. M., Shalker, T. E., Clark, M., & Karp, L. (1978). Affect, accessibility of material in memory, and behavior: A cognitive loop. *Journal of Personality and Social Psychology, 36,* 1–12.

Isozaki, M. (1984). The effect of discussion on polarization of judgments. *Japanese Psychological Research, 26,* 187–193.

ISR Newsletter (1975). Institute for Social Research, University of Michigan, 3(4), 4–7.

Jackman, M. R., & Senter, M. S. (1981). Beliefs about race, gender, and social class different, therefore unequal: Beliefs about trait differences between groups of unequal status. In D. J. Treiman & R. V. Robinson (Eds.), *Research in stratification and mobility* (Vol. 2). Greenwich, Conn.: JAI Press.

Jackson, D. J., & Huston, T. L. (1975). Physical attractiveness and assertiveness. *Journal of Social Psychology, 96,* 79–84.

Jackson, J. (1981, July 19). Syndicated newspaper column.

Jackson, J., & Williams, K. D. (1985). Social loafing on difficult tasks: Working collectively can improve performance. *Journal of Personality and Social Psychology, 49,* 937–942.

Jackson, J. M., & Harkins, S. G. (1985). Equity in effort: An explanation of the social loafing effect. *Journal of Personality and Social Psychology, 49,* 1199–1206.

Jackson, J. M., & Latané, B. (1981). All alone in front of all those people: Stage fright as a function of number and type of co-performers and audience. *Journal of Personality and Social Psychology, 40,* 73–85.

Jackson, J. M., & Williams, K. D. (1988). Social loafing: A review and theoretical analysis. Unpublished manuscript, Fordham University.

Jacobs, R. C., & Campbell, D. T. (1961). The perpetuation of an arbitrary tradition through several generations of a laboratory microculture. *Journal of Abnormal and Social Psychology, 62,* 649–658.

Jacoby, S. (1986, December). When opposites attract. *Reader's Digest,* pp. 95–98.

Jaffe, Y., Shapir, N., & Yinon, Y. (1981). Aggression and its escalation. *Journal of Cross-Cultural Psychology, 12,* 21–36.

Jaffe, Y., & Yinon, Y. (1983). Collective aggression: The group-individual paradigm in the study of collective antisocial behavior. In H. H. Blumberg, A. P. Hare, V. Kent, & M. Davies (Eds.), *Small groups and social interaction,* Vol. 1. Cambridge: Wiley.

James, W. (1958). *The varieties of religious experience.* New York: Mentor Books. (Originally published 1902.)

James, W. (1976). *Talks to teachers on psychology: And to students on some of life's ideals.* New York: Holt, 1922, p. 33. (Originally published, 1899). Cited by W. J. McKeachie, Psychology in America's bicentennial year. *American Psychologist, 31,* 819–833.

Jamieson, D. W., Lydon, J. E., Stewart, G., & Zanna, M. P. (1987). Pygmalion revisited: New evidence for student expectancy effects in the classroom. *Journal of Educational Psychology, 79,* 461–466.

Jamieson, D. W., Lydon, J. E., & Zanna, M. P. (1987). Attitude and activity preference similarity: Differential bases of interpersonal attraction for low and high self-monitors. *Journal of Personality and Social Psychology, 53,* 1052–1060.

Jamieson, D. W., & Zanna, M. P. (1983). The lie detector expectation procedure: Ensuring veracious self-reports of attitude. Paper presented to the Canadian Psychological Association, Winnipeg.

Jamieson, D. W., & Zanna, M. P. (1989). Need for structure in attitude formation and expression. In A. R. Pratkanis, S. J. Breckler, & A. G. Greenwald (Eds.), *Attitude structure and function.* Hillsdale, N.J.: Erlbaum.

Janis, I. (1989). Crucial decisions: Leadership in policymaking and crisis management. New York: Free Press.

Janis, I. L. (1982). *Groupthink,* 2nd ed. Boston: Houghton Mifflin.

Janis, I. L. (1971, November). Groupthink. *Psychology Today,* pp. 43–46.

Janis, I. L. (1982). Counteracting the adverse effects of concurrence-seeking in policy-planning groups: Theory and research perspectives. In H. Brandstatter, J. H. Davis, & G. Stocker-Kreichgauer (Eds.), *Group decision making.* New York: Academic Press. (a)

Janis, I. L. (1985). Sources of error in strategic decision making. In J. M. Pennings (Ed.), *Organizational strategy and change.* San Francisco: Jossey-Bass.

Janis, I. L., Kaye, D., & Kirschner, P. (1965). Facilitating effects of eating while reading on responsiveness to persuasive communications. *Journal of Personality and Social Psychology, 1,* 181–186.

Janis, I. L., & Mann, L. (1965). Effectiveness of emotional role-playing in modifying smoking habits and attitudes. *Journal of Experimental Research in Personality, 1,* 84–90.

Janis, I. L., & Mann, L. (1977). *Decision-making: A psychological analysis of conflict, choice and commitment.* New York: Free Press.

Janoff-Bulman, R., Timko, C., & Carli, L. L. (1985). Cognitive biases in blaming the victim. *Journal of Experimental Social Psychology, 21,* 161–177.

Jason, L. A., Rose, T., Ferrari, J. R., & Barone, R. (1984). Personal versus impersonal methods for recruiting blood donations. *Journal of Social Psychology, 123,* 139–140.

Jeffery, R. (1964). The psychologist as an expert witness on the issue of insanity. *American Psychologist, 19,* 838–843.

Jelalian, E., & Miller, A. G. (1984). The perseverance of beliefs: Conceptual perspectives and research developments. *Journal of Social and Clinical Psychology, 2,* 25–56.

Jellison, J. M., & Green, J. (1981). A self-presentation approach to the fundamental attribution error: The norm of internality. *Journal of Personality and Social Psychology, 40,* 643–649.

Jemmott, J. B., III., & Locke, S. E. (1984). Psychosocial factors, immunologic mediation, and human susceptibility to infectious diseases: How much do we know? *Psychological Bulletin, 95,* 78–108.

Jennings, D. L., Amabile, T. M., & Ross, L. (1982). Informal covariation assessment: Data-based vs theory-based judgments. In D. Kahneman, P. Slovic, & A. Tversky (Eds.), *Judgment under uncertainty: Heuristics and biases.* New York: Cambridge University Press.

Jennings, D. L., Lepper, M. R., & Ross, L. (1981). Persistence of impressions of personal persuasiveness: Perseverance of erroneous self-assessments outside the debriefing paradigm. *Personality and Social Psychology Bulletin,* 7, 257–262.

Jennings (Walstedt), J., Geis, F. L., & Brown, V. (1980). Influence of television commercials on women's self-confidence and independent judgment. *Journal of Personality and Social Psychology,* 38, 203–210.

Jervis, R. (1973). Hypotheses on misperception. In M. Halperin & A. Kanter (Eds.), *Readings in American foreign policy.* Boston: Little, Brown.

Jervis, R. (1985). Perceiving and coping with threat: Psychological perspectives. In R. Jervis, R. N. Lebow, & J. Stein (Eds.), *Psychology and deterrence.* Baltimore: Johns Hopkins University Press.

Jervis, R. (1985, April 2). Quoted by D. Coleman, Political forces come under new scrutiny of psychology. *New York Times,* pp. C1, C4.

Johnson, B. T., & Eagly, A. H. (1989). The effects of involvement on persuasion: A meta-analysis. *Psychological Bulletin,* in press.

Johnson, D. W., & Johnson, R. T. (1987). *Learning together and alone: Cooperative, competitive, and individualistic learning,* 2nd ed. Englewood Cliffs, N.J.: Prentice-Hall.

Johnson, D. W., & Johnson, R. T. (1989). *A meta-analysis of cooperative, competitive, and individualistic goal structures.* Hillsdale, N.J.: Erlbaum.

Johnson, M. H., & Magaro, P. A. (1987). Effects of mood and severity on memory processes in depression and mania. *Psychological Bulletin,* 101, 28–40.

Johnson, D. W., Maruyama, G., Johnson, R., Nelson, D., & Skon, L. (1981). Effects of cooperative, competitive, and individualistic goal structures on achievement: A meta-analysis. *Psychological Bulletin,* 89, 47–62.

Johnson, E. J., & Tversky, A. (1983). Affect, generalization, and the perception of risk. *Journal of Personality and Social Psychology,* 45, 20–31.

Johnson, J. T., Gain, L. M., Falke, T. L., Hayman, J., & Perillo, E. (1985). The "Barnum Effect" revisited: Cognitive and motivational factors in the acceptance of personality descriptions. *Journal of Personality and Social Psychology,* 49, 1378–1391.

Johnson, J. T., Jemmott, III, J. B., & Petti-grew, T. F. (1984). Causal attribution and dispositional inference: Evidence of inconsistent judgments. *Journal of Experimental Social Psychology,* 20, 567–585.

Johnson, N., Horton, R. W., & Santogrossi, D. A. (1978). Mitigating the impact of televised violence. Paper presented at the American Psychological Association convention.

Johnson, N. R., Stemler, J. G., & Hunter, D. (1977). Crowd behavior as risky shift: A laboratory experiment. *Sociometry,* 40, 183–187.

Johnson, R. D., & Downing, L. J. (1979). Deindividuation and valence of cues: Effects of prosocial and antisocial behavior. *Journal of Personality and Social Psychology,* 37, 1532–1538.

Johnson, R. N. (1972). *Aggression in man and animals.* Philadelphia: W. B. Saunders.

Johnston, L. D. (1988, January 13). Summary of 1987 drug study results. Media statement delivered in the Offices of the Secretary of Health and Human Services.

Johnson, P. (1988, November 25–27). Hearst seeks pardon. *USA Today,* p. 3A.

Jones, E. E. (1964). *Ingratiation.* New York: Appleton-Century-Crofts.

Jones, E. E. (1976). How do people perceive the causes of behavior? *American Scientist,* 64, 300–305.

Jones, E. E. (1979). The rocky road from acts to dispositions. *American Psychologist,* 34, 107–117.

Jones, E. E., & Berglas, S. (1978). Control of attributions about the self through self-handicapping strategies: The appeal of alcohol and the role of underachievement. *Personality and Social Psychology,* 4, 200–206.

Jones, E. E., & Davis, K. E., (1965). From acts to dispositions: The attribution process in person perception. In L. Berkowitz (Ed.), *Advances in experimental social psychology* (Vol. 2). New York: Academic Press.

Jones, E. E., & Harris, V. A. (1967). The attribution of attitudes. *Journal of Experimental Social Psychology,* 3, 2–24.

Jones, E. E., & Nisbett, R. E. (1971). *The actor and the observer: Divergent perceptions of the causes of behavior.* Morristown, N.J.: General Learning Press.

Jones, E. E., Rhodewalt, F., Berglas, S., & Skelton, J. A. (1981). Effects of strategic self-presentation on subsequent self-esteem. *Journal of Personality and Social Psychology,* 41, 407–421.

Jones, E. E., Rock, L., Shaver, K. G., Goethals, G. R., & Ward, L. M. (1968). Pattern of performance and ability attribution: An unexpected primacy effect. *Journal of Personality and Social Psychology,* 10, 317–340.

Jones, E. E., & Sigall, H. (1971). The bogus pipeline: A new paradigm for measuring affect and attitude. *Psychological Bulletin,* 76, 349–364.

Jones, J. M. (1983). The concept of race in social psychology: From color to culture. In L. Wheeler & P. Shaver (Eds.), *Review of personality and social psychology,* Vol. 4. Beverly Hills, Ca.: Sage.

Jones, J. M. (1988). Piercing the veil: Bi-cultural strategies for coping with prejudice and racism. Invited address at the national conference, "Opening Doors: An Appraisal of Race Relations in America," University of Alabama, June 11.

Jones, R. A., & Brehm, J. W. (1970). Persuasiveness of one- and two-sided communications as a function of awareness there are two sides. *Journal of Experimental Social Psychology,* 6, 47–56.

Jones, W. H., Freemon, J. E., & Goswick, R. A. (1981). The persistence of loneliness: Self and other determinants. *Journal of Personality,* 49, 27–48.

Jones, W. H., Hobbs, S. A., & Hockenbury, D. (1982). Loneliness and social skill deficits. *Journal of Personality and Social Psychology,* 42, 682–689.

Jones, W. H., Sansone, C., & Helm, B. (1983). Loneliness and interpersonal judgments. *Personality and Social Psychology Bulletin,* 9, 437–441.

Jorgenson, D. O., & Papciak, A. S. (1981). The effects of communication, resource feedback, and identifiability on behavior in a simulated commons. *Journal of Experimental Social Psychology,* 17, 373–385.

Josephson, W. L. (1987). Television violence and children's aggression: Testing the priming, social script, and disinhibition predictions. *Journal of Personality and Social Psychology,* 53, 882–890.

Jourard, S. M. (1964). *The transparent self.* Princeton, N.J.: Van Nostrand.

Judd, C. M., Kenny, D. A., & Krosnick, J. A. (1983). Judging the positions of political candidates: Models of assimilation and contrast. *Journal of Personality and Social Psychology,* 44, 952–963.

Judd, C. M., & Park, B. (1988). Out-group homogeneity: Judgments of variability at the individual and group levels. *Journal of Personality and Social Psychology,* 54, 778–788.

Jussim, L. (1986). Self-fulfilling prophecies: A theoretical and integrative review. *Psychological Review,* 93, 429–445.

Kagan, J., Reznick, J. S., & Snidman, N. (1988). Biological bases of childhood shyness. *Science,* 240, 167–171.

Kagehiro, D. K., & Stanton, W. C. (1985). Legal vs. quantified definitions of standards of proof. *Law and Human Behavior*, **9**, 159–178.

Kahle, L. R. (1983). *Attitudes, attributes and adaptation*. London: Pergamon Press.

Kahle, L. R., & Beatty, S. E. (1987). Cognitive consequences of legislating postpurchase behavior: Growing up with the bottle bill. *Journal of Applied Social Psychology*, **17**, 828–843.

Kahle, L. R., & Berman, J. (1979). Attitudes cause behaviors: A cross-lagged panel analysis. *Journal of Personality and Social Psychology*, **37**, 315–321.

Kahn, A. S., Gaeddert, W. P. (1985). From theories of equity to theories of justice. In V. W. O'Leary, R. K. Unger, & B. S. Wallston (Eds.), *Women, gender, and social psychology*. Hillsdale, N.J.: Erlbaum.

Kahn, M. W. (1951). The effect of severe defeat at various age levels on the aggressive behavior of mice. *Journal of Genetic Psychology*, **79**, 117–130.

Kahneman, D., Slovic, P., & Tversky, A. (Eds.) (1982). *Judgment under uncertainty: Heuristics and biases*. N.Y.: Cambridge University Press.

Kahneman, D., & Tversky, A. (1972). Subjective probability: A judgment of representativeness. *Cognitive Psychology*, **3**, 430–454.

Kahneman, D., & Tversky, A. (1973). On the psychology of prediction. *Psychological Review*, **80**, 237–251.

Kahneman, D., & Tversky, A. (1979). Intuitive prediction: Biases and corrective procedures. *Management Science*, **12**, 313–327.

Kalick, S. M. (1981). *Plastic surgery, physical appearance, and person perception*. Unpublished doctoral dissertation, Harvard University, 1977. Cited by E. Berscheid in, An overview of the psychological effects of physical attractiveness and some comments upon the psychological effects of knowledge of the effects of physical attractiveness. In W. Lucker, K. Ribbens, & J. A. McNamera (Eds.), *Logical aspects of facial form* (craniofacial growth series). Ann Arbor: University of Michigan Press.

Kalick, S. M. (1988). Physical attractiveness as a status cue. *Journal of Experimental Social Psychology*, **24**, 469–489.

Kallgren, C. A., & Wood, W. (1986). Access to attitude-relevant information in memory as a determinant of attitude-behavior consistency. *Journal of Experimental Social Psychology*, **22**, 328–338.

Kalven, H., Jr., & Zeisel, H. (1966). *The American jury*. Chicago: University of Chicago Press.

Kamen, L. P., Seligman, M. E. P., Dwyer, J., & Rodin, J. (1988). Pessimism and cell-mediated immunity. Unpublished manuscript, University of Pennsylvania.

Kammer, D. (1982). Differences in trait ascriptions to self and friend: Unconfounding intensity from variability. *Psychological Reports*, **51**, 99–102.

Kandel, D. B. (1978). Similarity in real-life adolescent friendship pairs. *Journal of Personality and Social Psychology*, **36**, 306–312.

Kanekar, S., & Nazareth, A. (1988). Attributed rape victim's fault as a function of her attractiveness, physical hurt, and emotional disturbance. *Social Behaviour*, **3**, 37–40.

Kaplan, M. F., & Anderson, N. H. (1973). Information integration theory and reinforcement theory as approaches to interpersonal attraction. *Journal of Personality and Social Psychology*, **28**, 301–312.

Kaplan, M. F., & Miller, C. E. (1987). Group decision making and normative versus informational influence: Effects of type of issue and assigned decision rule. *Journal of Personality and Social Psychology*, **53**, 306–313.

Kaplan, M. F., & Schersching, C. (1980). Reducing juror bias: An experimental approach. In P. D. Lipsitt & B. D. Sales (Eds.), *New directions in psycholegal research*. New York: Van Nostrand Reinhold, pp. 149–170.

Karabenick, S. A., Lerner, R. M., & Beecher, M. D. (1973). Relation of political affiliation to helping behavior on election day, November 7, 1972. *Journal of Social Psychology*, **91**, 223–227.

Karlins, M., Coffman, T. L., & Walters, G. (1969). On the fading of social stereotypes: Studies in three generations of college students. *Journal of Personality and Social Psychology*, **13**, 1–17.

Kassin, S. M. (1979). Consensus information, prediction, and causal attribution: A review of the literature and issues. *Journal of Personality and Social Psychology*, **37**, 1966–1981.

Kassin, S. M., & Wrightsman, L. S. (1979). On the requirements of proof: The timing of judicial instruction and mock juror verdicts. *Journal of Personality and Social Psychology*, **37**, 1877–1887.

Katz, A. M., & Hill, R. (1958). Residential propinquity and marital selection: A review of theory, method, and fact. *Marriage and Family Living*, **20**, 237–335.

Katz, E. (1957). The two-step flow of communication: An up-to-date report on a hypothesis. *Public Opinion Quarterly*, **21**, 61–78.

Katz, I., Cohen, S., & Glass, D. (1975). Some determinants of cross-racial helping behavior.

Journal of Personality and Social Psychology, **32**, 964–970.

Katz, L. S., & Reid, J. F. (1977). Expert testimony on the fallibility of eyewitness identification. *Criminal Justice Journal*, **1**, 177–206.

Katzev, R., Edelsack, L., Steinmetz, G., & Walker, T. (1978). The effect of reprimanding transgressions on subsequent helping behavior: Two field experiments. *Personality and Social Psychology Bulletin*, **4**, 126–129.

Keating, C. F. (1985). Gender and the physiognomy of dominance and attractiveness. *Social Psychology Quarterly*, **48**, 61–70.

Keating, J. P., & Brock, T. C. (1974). Acceptance of persuasion and the inhibition of counterargumentation under various distraction tasks. *Journal of Experimental Social Psychology*, **10**, 301–309.

Kelley, H. H. (1972). Attribution in social interaction. In E. E. Jones, D. E. Kanouse, H. H. Kelley, R. E. Nisbett, S. Valins, & B. Weiner (Eds.), *Attribution: Perceiving the causes of behavior*. Morristown, N.J.: General Learning Press.

Kelley, H. H. (1973). The process of causal attribution. *American Psychologist*, **28**, 107–128.

Kelley, H. H. (1979). *Personal relationships: Their structures and processes*. Hillsdale, N.J.: Lawrence Erlbaum.

Kelley, H. H., & Stahelski, A. J. (1970). The social interaction basis of cooperators' and competitors' beliefs about others. *Journal of Personality and Social Psychology*, **16**, 66–91.

Kelman, H. C., & Cohen, S. P. (1979). Reduction of international conflict: An interactional approach. In W. G. Austin and S. Worchel, *The social psychology of intergroup relations*. Monterey, Calif.: Brooks/Cole.

Kelman, H. C., & Cohen, S. P. (1986). Resolution of international conflict: An interactional approach. In S. Worchel & W. G. Austin (Eds.), *Psychology of intergroup relations*. Chicago: Nelson-Hall.

Kennedy, J. F. (1956). *Profiles in courage*. New York: Harper.

Kenny, D. A., & Albright, L. (1987). Accuracy in interpersonal perception: A social relations analysis. *Psychological Bulletin*, **102**, 390–402.

Kenny, D. A., & Nasby, W. (1980). Splitting the reciprocity correlation. *Journal of Personality and Social Psychology*, **38**, 249–256.

Kenrick, D. T. (1987). Gender, genes, and the social environment: A biosocial interactionist perspective. In P. Shaver & C. Hendrick (Eds.), *Sex and gender: Review of personality and social psychology*, vol. 7. Beverly Hills, Ca.: Sage.

Kenrick, D. T., Baumann, D. J., & Cialdini, R. B. (1979). A step in the socialization of altruism as hedonism: Effects of negative mood on children's generosity under public and private conditions. *Journal of Personality and Social Psychology, 37,* 747–755.

Kenrick, D. T., & Cialdini, R. B. (1977). Romantic attraction: Misattribution versus reinforcement explanations. *Journal of Personality and Social Psychology, 35,* 381–391.

Kenrick, D. T., Cialdini, R. B., & Linder, D. E. (1979). Misattribution under fear-producing circumstances: Four failures to replicate. *Personality and Social Psychology Bulletin, 5,* 329–334.

Kenrick, D. T., & Gutierres, S. E. (1980). Contrast effects and judgments of physical attractiveness: When beauty becomes a social problem. *Journal of Personality and Social Psychology, 38,* 131–140.

Kenrick, D. T., Gutierres, S. E., & Goldberg, L. L. (1989). Influence of popular erotica on judgments of strangers and mates. *Journal of Experimental Social Psychology, 25,* 159–167.

Kenrick, D. T., & MacFarlane, S. W. (1986). Ambient temperature and horn-honking: A field study of the heat/aggression relationship. *Environment and Behavior, 18,* 179–191.

Kenrick, D. T., & Trost, M. R. (1987). A biosocial theory of heterosexual relationships. In K. Kelly (Eds.), *Females, males, and sexuality.* Albany: State University of New York Press.

Kenrick, D. T., & Trost, M. R. (1989). Reproductive exchange model of heterosexual relationships: Putting proximate economics in ultimate perspective. In C. Hendrick (Ed.), *Review of personality and social psychology,* Vol. 10. Newbury Park, Ca.: Sage.

Kerr, N. L. (1978). Beautiful and blameless: Effects of victim attractiveness and responsibility on mock jurors' verdicts. *Journal of Personality and Social Psychology Bulletin, 4,* 479–482. (a)

Kerr, N. L. (1978). Severity of prescribed penalty and mock jurors' verdicts. *Journal of Personality and Social Psychology, 36,* 1431–1442. (b)

Kerr, N. L. (1981). Effects of prior juror experience on juror behavior. *Basic and Applied Social Psychology, 2,* 175–193.

Kerr, N. L. (1983). Motivation losses in small groups: A social dilemma analysis. *Journal of Personality and Social Psychology, 45,* 819–828.

Kerr, N. L. (1989). Illusions of efficacy: The effects of group size on perceived efficacy in social traps. *Journal of Experimental Social Psychology,* in press.

Kerr, N. L., Atkin, R. S., Stasser, G., Meek, D., Holt, R. W., & Davis, J. H. (1976). Guilt beyond a reasonable doubt: Effects of concept definition and assigned decision rule on the judgments of mock jurors. *Journal of Personality and Social Psychology, 34,* 282–294.

Kerr, N. L., & Bruun, S. E. (1981). Ringelmann revisited: Alternative explanations for the social loafing effect. *Personality and Social Psychology Bulletin, 7,* 224–231.

Kerr, N. L., & Bruun, S. E. (1983). Dispensibility of member effort and group motivation losses: Free-rider effects. *Journal of Personality and Social Psychology, 44,* 78–94.

Kerr, N. L., Harmon, D. L., & Graves, J. K. (1982). Independence of multiple verdicts by jurors and juries. *Journal of Applied Social Psychology, 12,* 12–29.

Kerr, N. L., & MacCoun, R. J. (1985). The effects of jury size and polling method on the process and product of jury deliberation. *Journal of Personality and Social Psychology, 48,* 349–363.

Khrushchev, N. (1980). Quoted in *Time,* June 23, p. 65.

Kidd, J. B., & Morgan, J. R. (1969). A predictive informations system for management. *Operational Research Quarterly, 20,* 149–170.

Kidd, R. F., & Berkowitz, L. (1976). Effect of disonance arousal on helpfulness. *Journal of Personality and Social Psychology, 33,* 613–622.

Kiesler, C. A., & Kiesler, S. B. (1969). *Conformity.* Reading, Mass.: Addison-Wesley.

Kiesler, C. A., & Pallak, M. S. (1975). Minority influence: The effect of majority reactionaries and defectors, and minority and majority compromisers, upon majority opinion and attraction. *European Journal of Social Psychology, 5,* 237–256.

Kiesler, S. B., & Baral, R. L. (1970). The search for a romantic partner: The effects of self-esteem and physical attractiveness on romantic behavior. In K. Gergen & D. Marlowe (Eds.), *Personality and Social Behavior.* Reading, Mass.: Addison Wesley.

Kihlstrom, J. F., Cantor, N., Albright, J. S., Chew, B. R., Klein, S. B., & Niedenthal, P. M. (1988). Information processing and the study of the self. In L. Berkowitz (Ed.), *Advances in experimental social psychology.* Orlando, Fl.: Academic Press.

Kimble, C. E., Fitz, D., & Onorad, J. R. (1977). Effectiveness of counteraggression strategies in reducing interactive aggression by males. *Journal of Personality and Social Psychology, 35,* 272–278.

Kimmel, M. J., Pruitt, D. G., Magenau, J. M., Konar-Goldband, E., & Carnevale, P. J. D. (1980). Effects of trust, aspiration, and gender on negotiation tactics. *Journal of Personality and Social Psychology, 38,* 9–22.

Kimura, D. (1985, November). Male brain, female brain—The hidden difference. *Psychology Today,* pp. 50–58.

Kinder, D. R. (1986). The continuing American dilemma: White resistance to racial change 40 years after Myrdal. *Journal of Social Issues, 42,* 151–171.

Kinder, D. R., & Sears, D. O. (1981). Prejudice and politics: Symbolic racism versus racial threats to the good life. *Journal of Personality and Social Psychology, 40,* 414–431.

Kinder, D. R., & Sears, D. O. (1985). Public opinion and political action. In G. Lindzey & E. Aronson (Eds.), *The handbook of social psychology,* 3rd ed. New York: Random House.

Kirkpatrick, J. (1981). Speech to National Conservative Political Action Conference, March 21.

Kirmeyer, S. L. (1978). Urban density and pathology: A review of research. *Environment and Behavior, 10,* 257–269.

Kitson, G. C., & Sussman, M. B. (1982). Marital complaints, demographic characteristics, and symptoms of mental distress in divorce. *Journal of Marriage and the Family, 44,* 87–101.

Klaas, E. T. (1978). Psychological effects of immoral actions: The experimental evidence. *Psychological Bulletin, 85,* 756–771.

Klayman, J., & Ha, Y-W. (1987). Confirmation, disconfirmation, and information in hypothesis testing. *Psychological Review, 94,* 211–228.

Kleck, R. E., & Strenta, A. (1980). Perceptions of the impact of negatively valued physical characteristics on social interaction. *Journal of Personality and Social Psychology, 5,* 861–873.

Kleinke, C. L. (1977). Compliance to requests made by gazing and touching experimenters in field settings. *Journal of Experimental Social Psychology, 13,* 218–223.

Klentz, B., Beaman, A. L., Mapelli, S. D., & Ullrich, J. R. (1987). Perceived physical attractiveness of supporters and nonsupporters of the women's movement: An attitude-similarity-mediated error (AS-ME). *Personality and Social Psychology Bulletin, 13,* 513–523.

Klopfer, P. M. (1958). Influence of social interaction on learning rates in birds. *Science, 128,* 903–904.

Knight, G. P., & Dubro, A. F. (1984). Cooperative, competitive, and individualistic social values: An individualized regression and clustering approach. *Journal of Personality and Social Psychology,* **46,** 98–105.

Knight, J. A., & Vallacher, R. R. (1981). Interpersonal engagement in social perception: The consequences of getting into the action. *Journal of Personality and Social Psychology,* **40,** 990–999.

Knight, P. A., & Weiss, H. M. (1980). Benefits of suffering: Communicator suffering, benefiting, and influence. Paper presented at the American Psychological Association convention.

Knowles, E. S. (1983). Social physics and the effects of others: Tests of the effects of audience size and distance on social judgment and behavior. *Journal of Personality and Social Psychology,* **45,** 1263–1279.

Knox, R. E., & Inkster, J. A. (1968). Postdecision dissonance at post-time. *Journal of Personality and Social Psychology,* **8,** 319–323.

Knudson, R. M., Sommers, A. A., & Golding, S. L. (1980). Interpersonal perception and mode of resolution in marital conflict. *Journal of Personality and Social Psychology,* **38,** 751–763.

Koestner, R., & Wheeler, L. (1988). Self-presentation in personal advertisements: The influence of implicit notions of attraction and role expectations. *Journal of Social and Personal Relationships,* **5,** 149–160.

Kohlberg, L. (1981). The philosophy of moral development: Essays in moral development (Vol. I). New York: Harper & Row.

Kohlberg, L. (1984). *The psychology of moral development: Essays on moral development,* (Vol. II). San Francisco: Harper & Row.

Kohn, A. (1987, October). It's hard to get left out of a pair. *Psychology Today,* pp. 53–57.

Komorita, S. S., & Barth, J. M. (1985). Components of reward in social dilemmas. *Journal of Personality and Social Psychology,* **48,** 364–373.

Koocher, G. P. (1977). Bathroom behavior and human dignity. *Journal of Personality and Social Psychology,* **35,** 120–121.

Koop, C. E. (1987). Report of the Surgeon General's workshop on pornography and public health. *American Psychologist,* **42,** 944–945.

Korabik, K. (1981). Changes in physical attractiveness and interpersonal attraction. *Basic and Applied Social Psychology,* **2,** 59–66.

Koriat, A., Lichtenstein, S., & Fischhoff, B. (1980). Reasons for confidence. *Journal of Experimental Psychology: Human Learning and Memory,* **6,** 107–118.

Korte, C. (1980). Urban-nonurban differences in social behavior and social psychological models of urban impact. *Journal of Social Issues,* **36,** 29–51.

Koss, M. P., Dinero, T. E., Seibel, C. A., & Cox, S. L. (1988). Stranger and acquaintance rape. *Psychology of Women,* **12,** 1–24.

Kraut, R. E. (1973). Effects of social labeling on giving to charity. *Journal of Experimental Social Psychology,* **9,** 551–562.

Kraut, R. E., & Poe, D. (1980). Behavioral roots of person perception: The deception judgments of customs inspectors and laymen. *Journal of Personality and Social Psychology,* **39,** 784–798.

Kravitz, D. A., & Martin, B. (1986). Ringelmann rediscovered: The original article. *Journal of Personality and Social Psychology,* **50,** 936–941.

Krebs, D. (1970). Altruism—An examination of the concept and a review of the literature. *Psychological Bulletin,* **73,** 258–302.

Krebs, D. (1975). Empathy and altruism. *Journal of Personality and Social Psychology,* **32,** 1134–1146.

Krebs, D., & Adinolfi, A. A. (1975). Physical attractiveness, social relations, and personality style. *Journal of Personality and Social Psychology,* **31,** 245–253.

Krech, D., Crutchfield, R. A., & Ballachey, E. I. (1962). *Individual in society.* New York: McGraw-Hill.

Kressel, K., & Pruitt, D. G. (1985). Themes in the mediation of social conflict. *Journal of Social Issues,* **41**(2), 179–198.

Kristiansen, C. M., & Harding, C. M. (1988). A comparison of the coverage of health issues by Britain's quality and popular press. *Social Behaviour,* **3,** 25–32.

Krosnick, J. A., & Schuman, H. (1988). Attitude intensity, importance, and certainty and susceptibility to response effects. *Journal of Personality and Social Psychology,* **54,** 940–952.

Krueger, J., & Rothbart, M. (1988). Use of categorical and individuating information in making inferences about personality. *Journal of Personality and Social Psychology,* **55,** 187–195.

Kruglanski, A. W., & Ajzen, I. (1983). Bias and error in human judgment. *European Journal of Social Psychology,* **13,** 1–44.

Kruglanski, A. W., & Freund, T. (1983). The freezing and unfreezing of lay-inferences. Effects of impressional primacy, ethnic stereotyping, and numerical anchoring. *Journal of Experimental Social Psychology,* **19,** 448–468.

Kuiper, N. A. (1978). Depression and causal attributions for success and failure. *Journal of Personality and Social Psychology,* **36,** 236–246.

Kuiper, N. A., & Higgins, E. T. (1985). Social cognition and depression: A general integrative perspective. *Social Cognition,* **3,** 1–15.

Kunda, Z. (1987). Motivated inference: Self-serving generation and evaluation of causal theories. *Journal of Personality and Social Psychology,* **53,** 636–647.

Kunst-Wilson, W. R., & Zajonc, R. B. (1980). Affective discrimination of stimuli that cannot be recognized. *Science,* **207,** 557–558.

Kurdek, L. A., & Schmitt, J. P. (1986). Interaction of sex role self-concept with relationship quality and relationship beliefs in married, heterosexual cohabiting, gay, and lesbian couples. *Journal of Personality and Social Psychology,* **51,** 365–370.

LaFrance, M. (1985). Does your smile reveal your status? *Social Science News Letter,* **70** (Spring), 15–18.

Lagerspetz, K. (1979). Modification of aggressiveness in mice. In S. Feshbach & A. Fraczek (Eds.), *Aggression and behavior change.* New York: Praeger.

Lagerspetz, K. M. J., Bjorkqvist, K., Berts, M., & King, E. (1982). Group aggression among school children in three schools. *Scandinavian Journal of Psychology,* **23,** 45–52.

Laird, J. D. (1974). Self-attribution of emotion: The effects of expressive behavior on the quality of emotional experience. *Journal of Personality and Social Psychology,* **29,** 475–486.

Laird, J. D. (1984). The real role of facial response in the experience of emotion: A reply to Tourangeau and Ellsworth, and others. *Journal of Personality and Social Psychology,* **47,** 909–917.

Lalljee, M., Lamb, R., Furnham, A., & Jaspars, J. (1984). Explanations and information search: Inductive and hypothesis-testing approaches to arriving at an explanation. *British Journal of Social Psychology,* **23,** 201–212.

Lamal, P. A. (1979). College student common beliefs about psychology. *Teaching of Psychology,* **6,** 155–158.

Landers, A. (1973). Syndicated newspaper column. April 8, 1969. Cited by L. Berkowitz in, The case for bottling up rage. *Psychology Today,* September, pp. 24–31.

Landers, A. (1985, August). Is affection more important than sex? *Reader's Digest,* pp. 44–46.

Landers, S. (1988, July). Sex, drugs 'n' rock: Relation not causal. *APA Monitor,* p. 40.

Langer, E. J. (1977). The psychology of chance. *Journal for the Theory of Social Behavior,* **7,** 185–208.

Langer, E. J., & Imber, L. (1980). The role of mindlessness in the perception of deviance.

Journal of Personality and Social Psychology, 39, 360–367.

Langer, E. J., Janis, I. L., & Wofer, J. A. (1975). Reduction of psychological stress in surgical patients. *Journal of Experimental Social Psychology*, 11, 155–165.

Langer, E. J., & Rodin, J. (1976). The effects of choice and enhanced personal responsibility for the aged: A field experiment in an institutional setting. *Journal of Personality and Social Psychology*, 334, 191–198.

Langer, E. J., & Roth, J. (1975). Heads I win, tails it's chance: The illusion of control as a function of the sequence of outcomes in a purely chance task. *Journal of Personality and Social Psychology*, 32, 951–955.

Langlois, J. H., Roggman, L. A., Casey, R. J., Ritter, J. M., Rieser-Danner, L. A., & Jenkins, V. Y. (1987). Infant preferences for attractive faces: Rudiments of a stereotype? *Developmental Psychology*, 23, 363–369.

Langlois, J. H., & Stephan, C. W. (1981). Beauty and the beast: The role of physical attractiveness in the development of peer relations and social behavior. In S. S. Brehm, S. M. Kassin, & F. X. Gibbons (Eds.), *Developmental social psychology*. New York: Oxford University Press.

Lansing, J. B., Marans, R. W., & Zehner, R. G. (1970). *Planned residential environments*. Ann Arbor, Mich.: Institute for Social Research, University of Michigan.

Lanzetta, J. T. (1955). Group behavior under stress. *Human Relations*, 8, 29–53.

Lapidus, J., Green, S. K., & Baruh, E. (1985). Factors related to roommate compatibility in the residence hall—a review. *Journal of College Student Personnel*, 26, 420–434.

La Rochefoucauld (1965). *Maxims*, 1665. Translated by J. Heard, 1917. Boston: International Pocket Library.

Larsen, K. (1974). Conformity in the Asch experiment. *Journal of Social Psychology*, 94, 303–304.

Larsen, R. J., & Diener, E. (1987). Affect intensity as an individual difference characteristic: A review. *Journal of Research in Personality*, 21, 1–39.

Larson, R. J., Csikszentmihalyi, N., & Graef, R. (1982). Time alone in daily experience: Loneliness or renewal? In L. A. Peplau & D. Perlman (Eds.), *Loneliness: A sourcebook of current theory, research and therapy*. New York: Wiley.

Larwood, L. (1978). Swine flu: A field study of self-serving biases. *Journal of Applied Social Psychology*, 18, 283–289.

Larwood, L., & Whittaker, W. (1977). Managerial myopia: Self-serving biases in organizational planning. *Journal of Applied Psychology*, 62, 194–198.

Lassiter, G. D., & Irvine, A. A. (1986). Videotaped confessions: The impact of camera point of view on judgments of coercion. *Journal of Applied Social Psychology*, 16, 268–276.

Latané, B. (1981). The psychology of social impact. *American Psychologist*, 36, 343–356.

Latané, B., & Dabbs, J. M., Jr. (1975). Sex, group size and helping in three cities. *Sociometry*, 38, 180–194.

Latané, B., & Darley, J. M. (1968). Group inhibition of bystander intervention in emergencies. *Journal of Personality and Social Psychology*, 10, 215–221.

Latané, B., & Darley, J. M. (1970). *The unresponsive bystander: Why doesn't he help?* New York: Appleton-Century-Crofts.

Latané, B., & Nida, S. (1981). Ten years of research on group size and helping. *Psychological Bulletin*, 89, 308–324.

Latané, B., & Rodin, J. (1969). A lady in distress: Inhibiting effects of friends and strangers on bystander intervention. *Journal of Experimental Social Psychology*, 5, 189–202.

Latané, B., Williams, K., & Harkins, S. (1979). Many hands make light the work: The causes and consequences of social loafing. *Journal of Personality and Social Psychology*, 37, 822–832.

Laughlin, P. R. (1980). Social combination processes of cooperative problem-solving groups in verbal intellective tasks. In M. Fishbein (Ed.), *Progress in social psychology*. Hillsdale, N.J.: Erlbaum.

Laughlin, P. R., & Adamopoulos, J. (1980). Social combination processes and individual learning for six-person cooperative groups on an intellective task. *Journal of Personality and Social Psychology*, 38, 941–947.

Layden, M. A. (1982). Attributional therapy. In C. Antaki & C. Brewin (Eds.), *Attributions and psychological change: Applications of attributional theories to clinical and educational practice*. London: Academic Press.

Leary, M. R. (1982). Hindsight distortion and the 1980 presidential election. *Personality and Social Psychology Bulletin*, 8, 257–263.

Leary, M. R. (1984). *Understanding social anxiety*. Beverly Hills, Ca.: Sage.

Leary, M. R. (1986). The impact of interactional impediments on social anxiety and self-presentation. *Journal of Experimental Social Psychology*, 22, 122–135.

Leary, M. R., & Kowalski, R. M. (1989). Impression management: A literature review and two-component model. *Psychological Bulletin*, in press.

Leary M. R., & Maddux, J. E. (1987). Progress toward a viable interface between social and clinical-counseling psychology. *American Psychologist*, 42, 904–911.

Lebow, R. N., & Stein, J. G. (1987). Beyond deterrence. *Journal of Social Issues*, 43(4), 5–71.

Lee, J. A. (1988). Love-styles. In R. J. Sternberg & M. L. Barnes (Eds.), *The psychology of love*. New Haven: Yale University Press.

Lee, M. T. & Ofshe, R. (1981). The impact of behavioral style and status characteristics on social influence: A test of two competing theories. *Social Psychology Quarterly*, 44, 73–82.

Lefcourt, H. M. (1982). *Locus of control: Current trends in theory and research*. Hillsdale, N.J.: Erlbaum.

Lefebvre, L. M. (1979). Causal attributions for basketball outcomes by players and coaches. *Psychological Belgica*, 19, 109–115.

Leffler, A., Gillespie, D. L., & Conaty, J. C. (1982). The effects of status differentiation on nonverbal behavior. *Social Psychology Quarterly*, 45, 153–161.

Lefkowitz, M. M., Eron, L. D., Walder, L. O., & Huesmann, L. R. (1976). *Growing up to be violent*. New York: Pergamon.

Lehman, D. R., Lempert, R. O., & Nisbett, R. E. (1988). The effects of graduate training on reasoning: Formal discipline and thinking about everyday-life events. *American Psychologist*, 43, 431–442.

Lehman, D. R., & Nisbett, R. E. (1985). Effects of higher education on inductive reasoning. Unpublished manuscript, University of Michigan.

Lehman, D. R., & Reifman, A. (1987). Spectator influence on basketball officiating. *Journal of Social Psychology*, 127, 673–675.

Leippe, M. R. (1985). The influence of eyewitness nonidentification on mock-jurors. *Journal of Applied Social Psychology*, 15, 656–672.

Leippe, M. R., Brigham, J. C., Cousins, C., & Romanczyk, A. (1988). The opinions and practices of criminal attorneys regarding child eyewitnesses: A survey. In S. J. Ceci, D. F. Ross, & M. P. Toglia (Eds.), *Perspectives on children's testimony*. New York: Springer-Verlag.

Leippe, M. R., & Elkin, R. A. (1987). When motives clash: Issue involvement and response involvement as determinants of persuasion. *Journal of Personality and Social Psychology*, 52, 269–278.

Leippe, M. R., & Elkin, R. A. (1987). Dissonance reduction strategies and accountability to self and others: Ruminations and some initial research. Presentation to the Fifth International Conference on Affect, Motivation, and Cognition, Nags Head Conference Center.

Leippe, M. R., & Romanczyk, A. (1989). Reactions to child (versus adult) eyewitnesses: The influence of jurors' preconceptions and witness behavior. *Law and Human Behavior, 13,* 103–132.

Leymyre, L., & Smith, P. M. (1985). Intergroup discrimination and self-esteem in the minimal group paradigm. *Journal of Personality and Social Psychology, 49,* 660–670.

Lenihan, K. J. (1965). Perceived climates as a barrier to housing desegregation. Unpublished manuscript, Bureau of Applied Social Research, Columbia University.

Leon, D. (1979). *The Kibbutz: A new way of life.* London: Pergamon Press, 1969. Cited by B. Latané, K. Williams, & S. Harkins in, Many hands make light the work: The causes and consequences of social loafing. *Journal of Personality and Social Psychology, 37,* 822–832.

Lepper, M. R., & Greene, D. (Eds.) (1979). *The hidden costs of reward.* Hillsdale, N.J.: Erlbaum.

Lepper, M. R., Ross, L., & Lau, R. R. (1986). Persistence of inaccurate beliefs about the self: Perseverance effects in the classroom. *Journal of Personality and Social Psychology, 50,* 482–491.

Lerner, M. J. (1980). *The belief in a just world: A fundamental delusion.* New York: Plenum.

Lerner, M. J., & Miller, D. T. (1978). Just world research and the attribution process: Looking back and ahead. *Psychological Bulletin, 85,* 1030–1051.

Lerner, M. J., & Simmons, C. H. (1966). Observer's reaction to the "innocent victim": Compassion or rejection? *Journal of Personality and Social Psychology, 4,* 203–210.

Lerner, R. M., & Frank, P. (1974). Relation of race and sex to supermarket helping behavior. *Journal of Social Psychology, 94,* 201–203.

Leung, K., & Bond, M. H. (1984). The impact of cultural collectivism on reward allocation. *Journal of Personality and Social Psychology, 47,* 793–804.

Leventhal, G. S. (1976). The distribution of rewards and resources in groups and organizations. In L. Berkowitz & E. Walster (Hatfield) (Eds.), *Advances in experimental social psychology* (Vol. 9). New York: Academic Press.

Leventhal, H. (1970). Findings and theory in the study of fear communications. In L. Berkowitz (Ed.), *Advances in experimental social psychology* (Vol. 5). New York: Academic Press.

Levin, I. P. (1987). Associative effects of information framing. *Bulletin of the Psychonomic Society, 25,* 85–86.

Levin, I. P., Schnittjer, S. K., & Thee, S. L. (1988). Information framing effects in social and personal decisions. *Journal of Experimental Social Psychology, 24,* 520–529.

Levine, D. W., O'Neal, E. C., Garwood, S. G., & McDonald, P. J. (1980). Classroom ecology: The effects of seating position on grades and participation. *Personality and Social Psychology Bulletin, 6,* 409–412.

Levine, J. M. (1980). Reaction to opinion deviance in small groups. In P. B. Paulus, *Psychology of group influence.* Hillsdale, N.J.: Erlbaum.

Levine, J. M. (1989). Reaction to opinion deviance in small groups. In P. Paulus (Ed.), *Psychology of group influence: New perspectives.* Hillsdale, N.J.: Erlbaum.

Levine, J. M., & Moreland, R. L. (1985). Innovation and socialization in small groups. In S. Moscovici, G. Mugny, & E. Van Avermaet (Eds.), *Perspectives on minority influence.* Cambridge: Cambridge University Press.

Levine, J. M., & Moreland, R. L. (1987). Social comparison and outcome evaluation in group contexts. In J. C. Masters & W. P. Smith (Eds.), *Social comparison, social justice, and relative deprivation: Theoretical, empirical, and policy perspectives.* Hillsdale, N.J.: Erlbaum.

Levine, J. M., & Russo, E. M. (1987). Majority and minority influence. In C. Hendrick (Ed.), *Group processes: Review of personality and social psychology,* Vol. 8. Newbury Park, Ca.: Sage.

Levine, R., & Uleman, J. S. (1979). Perceived locus of control, chronic self-esteem, and attributions to success and failure. *Journal of Personality and Social Psychology, 5,* 69–72.

Levinger, G. (1987). The limits of deterrence: An introduction. *Journal of Social Issues, 43*(4), 1–4.

Levy, S., Seligman, M. E. P., Morrow, L., Bagley, C., & Lippman, M. (1988). Survival hazards analysis in first recurrent breast cancer patients: Seven-year follow-up. *Psychosomatic Medicine,* in press.

Levy-Leboyer, C. (1988). Success and failure in applying psychology. *American Psychologist, 43,* 779–785.

Lewicki, P. (1983). Self-image bias in person perception. *Journal of Personality and Social Psychology, 45,* 384–393.

Lewicki, P. (1985). Nonconscious biasing effects of single instances on subsequent judgments. *Journal of Personality and Social Psychology, 48,* 563–574.

Lewin, K. (1936). *A dynamic theory of personality.* New York: McGraw-Hill.

Lewinsohn, P. M., Hoberman, H., Teri, L., & Hautziner, M. (1985). An integrative theory of depression. In S. Reiss & R. Bootzin (Eds.), *Theoretical issues in behavior therapy.* New York: Academic Press.

Lewinsohn, P. M., Mischel, W., Chapline, W., & Barton, R. (1980). Social competence and depression: The role of illusionary self-perceptions. *Journal of Abnormal Psychology, 89,* 203–212.

Lewinsohn, P. M., & Rosenbaum, M. (1987). Recall of parental behavior by acute depressives, remitted depressives, and nondepressives. *Journal of Personality and Social Psychology, 52,* 611–619.

Lewis, C. S. (1960). *Mere Christianity.* New York: Macmillan.

Lewis, C. S. (1974). *The horse and his boy.* New York: Collier Books.

Lewis, H. W. (1985, September 2). Proven probabilities should help us assess risks. *International Herald Tribune,* p. 4.

Leyens, J. P., Camino, L., Parke, R. D., & Berkowitz, L. (1975). Effects of movie violence on aggression in a field setting as a function of group dominance and cohesion. *Journal of Personality and Social Psychology, 32,* 346–360.

Lichtenstein, S., & Fischhoff, B. (1980). Training for calibration. *Organizational Behavior and Human Performance, 26,* 149–171.

Lieberman, S. (1956). The effects of changes in roles on the attitudes of role occupants. *Human Relations. 9,* 385–402.

Liebert, R. M., & Baron, R. A. (1972). Some immediate effects of televised violence on children's behavior. *Developmental Psychology, 6,* 469–475.

Liebrand, W. B. G., Messick, D. M., & Wolters, F. J. M. (1986). Why we are fairer than others: A cross-cultural replication and extension. *Journal of Experimental Social Psychology, 22,* 590–604.

Life (1988, Spring). What we believe. Pp. 69–70.

Lindsay, R. C. L., & Wells, G. L. (1985). Improving eyewitness identifications from line-ups: Simultaneous versus sequential lineup presentation. *Journal of Applied Psychology, 70,* 556–564.

Lindsay, R. C. L., Wells, G. L., & Rumpel, C. H. (1981). Can people detect eyewitness-identification accuracy within and across situations? *Journal of Applied Psychology, 66,* 79–89.

Lindskold, S. (1978). Trust development, the GRIT proposal, and the effects of conciliatory acts on conflict and cooperation. *Psychological Bulletin, 85,* 772–793.

Lindskold, S. (1979). Conciliation with simultaneous or sequential interaction: Variations in trustworthiness and vulnerability in the prisoner's dilemma. *Journal of Conflict Resolution*, 23, 704–714.

Lindskold, S. (1983). Cooperators, competitors, and response to GRIT. *Journal of Conflict Resolution*, 27, 521–532.

Lindskold, S. (1979). Managing conflict through announced conciliatory initiatives backed with retaliatory capability. In W. G. Austin and S. Worchel (Eds.), *The social psychology of intergroup relations*. Monterey, Calif.: Brooks/Cole. (a)

Lindskold, S. (1981). The laboratory evaluation of GRIT: Trust, cooperation, aversion to using conciliation. Paper presented at the American Association for the Advancement of Science convention. (b)

Lindskold, S., & Aronoff, J. R. (1980). Conciliatory strategies and relative power. *Journal of Experimental Social Psychology*, 16, 187–198.

Lindskold, S., Bennett, R., & Wayner, M. (1976). Retaliation level as a foundation for subsequent conciliation. *Behavioral Science*, 21, 13–18.

Lindskold, S., Betz, B., & Walters, P. S. (1986). Transforming competitive or cooperative climate. *Journal of Conflict Resolution*, 30, 99–114.

Lindskold, S., & Collins, M. G. (1978). Inducing cooperation by groups and individuals. *Journal of Conflict Resolution*, 22, 679–690.

Lindskold, S., & Finch, M. L. (1981). Styles of announcing conciliation. *Journal of Conflict Resolution*, 25, 145–155.

Lindskold, S., & Han, G. (1988). GRIT as a foundation for integrative bargaining. *Personality and Social Psychology Bulletin*, 14, 335–345.

Lindskold, S., Han, G., & Betz, B. (1986). The essential elements of communication in the GRIT strategy. *Personality and Social Psychology Bulletin*, 12, 179–186. (a)

Lindskold, S., Han, G., & Betz, B. (1986). Repeated persuasion in interpersonal conflict. *Journal of Personality and Social Psychology*, 51, 1183–1188. (b)

Lindskold, S., Walters, P. S., Koutsourais, H., & Shayo, R. (1981). Cooperators, competitors, and response to GRIT. Unpublished manuscript, Ohio University.

Linville, P. W. (1987). Self-complexity as a cognitive buffer against stress-related illness and depression. *Journal of Personality and Social Psychology*, 52, 663–676.

Linz, D. G., Donnerstein, E., & Adams, S. M. (1989). Physiological desensitization and judgments about female victims of violence. *Human Communication Research*, 15, in press.

Linz, D. G., Donnerstein, E., & Penrod, S. (1988). Effects of long term exposure to violent and sexually degrading depictions of women. *Journal of Personality and Social Psychology*, 55, 758–768.

Lipset, S. M. (1966). University students and politics in underdeveloped countries. *Comparative Education Review*, 10, 132–162.

Locksley, A., Borgida, E., Brekke, N., & Hepburn, C. (1980). Sex stereotypes and social judgment. *Journal of Personality and Social Psychology*, 39, 821–831.

Locksley, A., Hepburn, C., & Ortiz, V. (1982). Social stereotypes and judgments of individuals: An instance of the base-rate fallacy. *Journal of Experimental Social Psychology*, 18, 23–42.

Locksley, A., Ortiz, V., & Hepburn, C. (1980). Social categorization and discriminatory behavior: Extinguishing the minimal intergroup discrimination effect. *Journal of Personality and Social Psychology*, 39, 773–783.

Locksley, A., & Stangor, C. (1984). Why versus how often: Causal reasoning and the incidence of judgmental bias. *Journal of Experimental Social Psychology*, 20, 470–483.

Lofland, J., & Stark, R. (1965). Becoming a worldsaver: A theory of conversion to a deviant pespective. *American Sociological Review*, 30, 862–864.

Loftus, E. F. (1974, December). Reconstructing memory: The incredible eyewitness. *Psychology Today*, pp. 117–119.

Loftus, E. F. (1979). *Eyewitness testimony*. Cambridge, Mass.: Harvard University Press. (a)

Loftus, E. F. (1979). The malleability of human memory. *American Scientist*, 67, 312–320. (b)

Loftus, E. F. (1980). Impact of expert psychological testimony on the unreliability of eyewitness identification. *Journal of Applied Psychology*, 65, 9–15. (a)

Loftus, E. F. (1980). *Memories are made of this: New insights into the workings of human memory*. Reading, Mass.: Addison-Wesley. (b)

Loftus, E. F., & Loftus, G. R. (1980). On the permanence of stored information in the human being. *American Psychologist*, 35, 409–420.

Loftus, E. F., & Miller, D. G., & Burns, H. J. (1978). Semantic integration of verbal information into a visual memory. *Journal of Experimental Psychology: Human Learning and Memory*, 4, 19–31.

Loftus, E. F., & Palmer, J. C. (1973). Reconstruction of automobile destruction: An example of the interaction between language and memory. *Journal of Verbal Learning and Verbal Behavior*, 13, 585–589.

Loftus, E. F., & Zanni, G. (1975). Eyewitness testimony: The influence of the wording in a question. *Bulletin of the Psychonomic Society*, 5, 86–88.

Lombardo, J. P., Weiss, R. F., & Buchanan, W. (1972). Reinforcing and attracting functions of yielding. *Journal of Personality and Social Psychology*, 21, 359–368.

London, P. (1970). The rescuers: Motivational hypotheses about Christians who saved Jews from the Nazis. In J. Macaulay & L. Berkowitz (Eds.), *Altruism and helping behavior*. New York: Academic Press.

Lonner, W. J. (1989). The introductory psychology text and cross-cultural psychology: Beyond Ekman, Whorf, and biased I.Q. tests. In D. Keats, D. R. Munro & L. Mann (Eds.), *Heterogeneity in cross-cultural psychology*. Lisse, Netherlands: Swets & Zeitlinger.

Lord, C. G., Lepper, M. R., & Preston, E. (1984). Considering the opposite: A corrective strategy for social judgment. *Journal of Personality and Social Psychology*, 47, 1231–1243.

Lord, C. G., Ross, L., & Lepper, M. (1979). Biased assimilation and attitude polarization: The effects of prior theories on subsequently considered evidence. *Journal of Personality and Social Psychology*, 37, 2098–2109.

Lord, C. G. & Saenz, D. S. (1985). Memory deficits and memory surfeits: Differential cognitive consequences of tokenism for tokens and observers. *Journal of Personality and Social Psychology*, 49, 918–926.

Lorenz, K. (1976). *On aggression*. New York: Bantam Books.

Lott, A. J., & Lott, B. E. (1961). Group cohesiveness, communication level, and conformity. *Journal of Abnormal and Social Psychology*, 62, 408–412.

Lott, A. J., & Lott, B. E. (1974). The role of reward in the formation of positive interpersonal attitudes. In T. Huston (Ed.), *Foundations of interpersonal attraction*. New York: Academic Press.

Louis Harris & Associates (with analysis by Simon, W., & Miller, P.) (1979). *The Playboy report on American men*. Chicago: Playboy.

Louw-Potgieter, J. (1988). The authoritarian personality: An inadequate explanation for intergroup conflict in South Africa. *Journal of Social Psychology*, 128, 75–87.

Lowe, C. A., & Goldstein, J. W. (1970). Reciprocal liking and attributions of ability: Mediating effects of perceived intent and personal involvement. *Journal of Personality and Social Psychology*, 16, 291–297.

Lowry, D. T., Love, G., & Kirby, M. (1981). Sex on the soap operas: Patterns of intimacy. *Journal of Communication*, 31(3), 90–96.

Loy, J. W. & Andrews, D. S. (1981). They also saw a game: A replication of a case study. *Replications in Social Psychology*, **1**(2), 45–59.

Lumsdaine, A. A., & Janis, I. L. (1953). Resistance to "counter-propaganda" produced by one-sided and two-sided "propaganda" presentations. *Public Opinion Quarterly*, **17**, 311–318.

Lumsden, A., Zanna, M. P., & Darley, J. M. (1980). When a newscaster presents counter-attitudinal information: Education or propaganda? Paper presented to the Canadian Psychological Association annual convention.

Lydon, J. E., Jamieson, D. W., & Zanna, M. P. (1988). Interpersonal similarity and the social and intellectual dimensions of first impressions. *Social Cognition*, **6**, 269–286.

Lynn, M., & Oldenquist, A. (1986). Egoistic and nonegoistic motives in social dilemmas. *American Psychologist*, **41**, 529–534.

Lynn, M., & Shurgot, B. A. (1984). Responses to lonely hearts advertisements: Effects of reported physical attractiveness, physique, and coloration. *Personality and Social Psychology*, **10**, 349–357.

Maass, A., Brigham, J. C., & West, S. G. (1985). Testifying on eyewitness reliability: Expert advice is not always persuasive. *Journal of Applied Social Psychology*, **15**, 207–229.

Maass, A., & Clark, R. D., III (1984). Hidden impact of minorities: Fifteen years of minority influence research. *Psychological Bulletin*, **95**, 428–450.

Maass, A., & Clark, R. D., III. (1986). Conversion theory and simultaneous majority/minority influence: Can reactance offer an alternative explanation? *European Journal of Social Psychology*, **16**, 305–309.

Maass, A., West, S. G., & Cialdini, R. B. (1987). Minority influence and conversion. In C. Hendrick (Ed.), *Group processes: Review of personality and social psychology*, Vol 8. Newbury Park, CA.: Sage.

MacArthur, D. (1973). Quoted in J. D. Frank's statement on psychological aspects of international relations before a hearing of the Committee on Foreign Relations, United States Senate, May 25, 1966. Reprinted in D. E. Linder (Ed.), *Psychological dimensions of social interaction: Readings and perspectives*. Reading, Mass.: Addison-Wesley.

Maccoby, E. E. (1980). *Social development*. New York: Harcout Brace Jovanovich.

Maccoby, E. E., & Jacklin, C. N. (1974). *The psychology of sex differences*. Stanford, Calif.: Stanford University Press.

Maccoby, N. (1980). Promoting positive health behaviors in adults. In L. A. Bond & J. C. Rosen (Eds.), *Competence and coping during adulthood*. Hanover, N. H.: University Press of New England.

Maccoby, N., & Alexander, J. (1980). Use of media in lifestyle programs. In P. O. Davidson & S. M. Davidson (Eds.). *Behavioral medicine: Changing health lifestyles*. New York: Brunner/Mazel.

MacCoun, R. J., & Kerr, N. L. (1988). Asymmetric influence in mock jury deliberation: Jurors' bias for leniency. *Journal of Personality and Social Psychology*, **54**, 21–33.

MacKay, J. L. (1980). Selfhood: Comment on Brewster Smith. *American Psychologist*, **35**, 106–107.

Mackie, D. M. (1987). Systemic and nonsystematic processing of majority and minority persuasive communications. *Journal of Personality and Social Psychology*, **53**, 41–52.

Mackie, D. M., & Allison, S. T. (1987). Group attribution errors and the illusion of group attitude change. *Journal of Experimental Social Psychology*, **23**, 460–480.

Mackie, D. M., & Worth, L. T. (1988). Cognitive deficits and the mediation of positive affect in persuasion. Unpublished manuscript, University of California, Santa Barbara.

MacLachlan, J. (1979, November). What people really think of fast talkers. *Psychology Today*, pp. 113–117.

MacLachlan, J., & Siegel, M. H. (1980). Reducing the costs of TV commercials by use of time compressions. *Journal of Marketing Research*, **17**, 52–57.

Maddux, J. E. (1986). Self-efficacy theory in contemporary psychology: An overview. *Journal of Social and Clinical Psychology*, **4**, 249–255.

Maddux, J. E., Norton, L. W., & Leary, M. R. (1988). Cognitive components of social anxiety: An investigation of the integration of self-presentation theory and self-efficacy theory. *Journal of Social and Clinical Psychology*, **6**, 180–190.

Maddux, J. E., & Rogers, R. W. (1980). Effects of source expertness, physical attractiveness, and supporting arguments on persuasion: A case of brains over beauty. *Journal of Personality and Social Psychology*, **39**, 235–244.

Maddux, J. E., & Rogers, R. W. (1983). Protection motivation and self-efficacy: A revised theory of fear appeals and attitude change. *Journal of Experimental Social Psychology*, **19**, 469–479.

Magnuson, E. (1986, March 10). "A serious deficiency": The Rogers Commission faults NASA's "flawed" decision-making process. *Time*, pp. 40–42, international ed.

Magnusson, S. (1981). *The flying Scotsman*. London: Quartet Books.

Major, B. (1987). Gender, justice, and the psychology of entitlement. In P. Shaver & C. Hendrick (Eds.), *Sex and gender: Review of personality and social psychology*, Vol. 7. Beverly Hills: Sage.

Major, B., & Adams, J. B. (1983). Role of gender, interpersonal orientation, and self-presentation in distributive-justice behavior. *Journal of Personality and Social Psychology*, **45**, 598–608.

Major, B., & Testa, M. (1989). Social comparison processes and judgments of entitlement and satisfaction. *Journal of Experimental Social Psychology*, **25**, 101–120.

Malamuth, N. M. (1984). Aggression against women: Cultural and individual causes. In N. M. Malamuth & E. Donnerstein (Eds.), *Pornography and sexual aggression*. Orlando, Fla.: Academic Press.

Malamuth, N. M. (1986). Predictors of naturalistic sexual aggression. *Journal of Personality and Social Psychology*, **50**, 953–962.

Malamuth, N. M. (1989). The attraction to sexual aggression scale: Part one. *Journal of Sex Research*, **25**, in press.

Malamuth, N. M., & Check, J. V. P. (1981). The effects of media exposure on acceptance of violence against women: A field experiment. *Journal of Research in Personality*, **15**, 436–446.

Malamuth, N. M., & Check, J. V. P. (1984). Debriefing effectiveness following exposure to pornographic rape depictions. *Journal of Sex Research*, **20**, 1–13.

Malkiel, B. G. (1985). *A random walk down Wall Street*, 4th ed. New York: W. W. Norton.

Malpaas, R. S., & Devine, P. G. (1984). Research on suggestion in lineups and photospreads. In G. L. Wells & E. F. Loftus (Eds.), *Eyewitness identification: Psychological perspectives*. New York: Cambridge University Press.

Manis, M. (1977). Cognitive social psychology. *Personality and Social Psychology Bulletin*, **3**, 550–566.

Manis, M., Avis, N. E., & Cardoze, S. (1981). Reply to Bar-Hillel and Fischoff. *Journal of Personality and Social Psychology*, **41**, 681–683.

Manis, M. Cornell, S. D., & Moore, J. C. (1974). Transmission of attitude-relevant information through a communication chain. *Journal of Personality and Social Psychology*, **30**, 81–94.

Manis, M., Dovalina, I., Avis, N. E., & Cardoze, S. (1980). Base-rates *can* affect individual predictions. *Journal of Personality and Social Psychology, 38,* 231–248.

Manis, M., Nelson, T. E., & Shedler, J. (1988). Stereotypes and social judgment: Extremity, assimilation, and contrast. *Journal of Personality and Social Psychology, 55,* 28–36.

Mann, L. (1981). The baiting crowd in episodes of threatened suicide. *Journal of Personality and Social Psychology, 41,* 703–709.

Mann, L., & Janis, I. L. (1968). A follow-up study on the long-term effects of emotional role playing. *Journal of Personality and Social Psychology, 8,* 339–342.

Mantell, D. M. (1971). The potential for violence in Germany. *Journal of Social Issues, 27*(4), 101–112.

Manz, C. C., & Sims, H. P., Jr. (1982). The potential for "groupthink" in autonomous work groups. *Human Relations, 35,* 773–784.

Marcus, S. (1974). Review of *Obedience to authority. New York Times Book Review,* January 13, pp. 1–2.

Marks, G. (1984). Thinking one's abilities are unique and one's opinions are common. *Personality and Social Psychology Bulletin, 10,* 203–208.

Marks, G., & Miller, N. (1987). Ten years of research on the false-consensus effect: An empirical and theoretical review. *Psychological Bulletin, 102,* 72–90.

Marks, G., Miller, N., & Maruyama, G. (1981). Effect of targets' physical attractiveness on assumptions of similarity. *Journal of Personality and Social Psychology, 41,* 198–206.

Marks, G., Miller, N., & Maruyama, G. (1981). The effect of physical attractiveness on assumptions of similarity. *Journal of Personality and Social Psychology, 41,* 198–206.

Markus, H., & Sentis, K. (1982). The self in information processing. In J. Suls (Ed.), *Psychological perspectives on the self,* Vol. 1. Hillsdale, N.J.: Erlbaum.

Markus, H., & Wurf, E. (1987). The dynamic self-concept: A social psychological perspective. *Annual Review of Psychology, 38,* 299–337.

Marler, P. (1974). Aggression and its control in animal society. Presentation to the American Psychological Association convention.

Marshall, W. L. (1988). The use of sexually explicit stimuli by rapists, child molesters, and nonoffenders. *The Journal of Sex Research, 25,* 267–288.

Martin, C. L. (1987). A ratio measure of sex stereotyping. *Journal of Personality and Social Psychology, 52,* 489–499.

Martin, J. (1980). Relative deprivation: A theory of distributive injustice for an era of shrinking

resources. In *Research in organizational behavior* (Vol. 3). Greenwich, Conn.: JAI Press.

Marty, M. E. (1982). Watch your language. *Context,* April 15, p. 6.

Maruyama, G., & Miller, N. (1981). Physical attractiveness and personality. In B. A. Maher & W. B. Maher (Eds.), *Progress in Experimental Personality Research.* New York: Academic Press.

Maruyama, G., Rubin, R. A., & Kingbury, G. (1981). Self-esteem and educational achievement: Independent constructs with a common cause? *Journal of Personality and Social Psychology, 40,* 962–975.

Marvelle, K., & Green, S. (1980). Physical attractiveness and sex bias in hiring decisions for two types of jobs. *Journal of the National Association of Women Deans, Administrators, and Counselors, 44*(1), 3–6.

Maslach, C. (1978). The client role in staff burnout. *Journal of Social Issues, 34*(4), 111–124.

Maslach, C. (1982). *Burnout: The cost of caring.* Englewood Cliffs, N.J.: Prentice-Hall.

Maslach, C., & Jackson, S. E. (1979, May). Burned-out cops and their families. *Psychology Today,* pp. 59–62.

Maslow, A. H., & Mintz, N. L. (1956). Effects of esthetic surroundings: I. Initial effects of three esthetic conditions upon perceiving "energy" and "well-being" in faces. *Journal of Psychology, 41,* 247–254.

Maslow, B. G. (Ed.) (1972). *Abraham H. Maslow: A memorial volume.* Monterey, Calif.: Brooks/Cole.

Mathes, E. (1975). The effects of physical attractiveness and anxiety on heterosexual attraction over a series of five encounters. *Journal of Marriage and the Family, 37,* 769–774.

Maxwell, G. M. (1985). Behaviour of lovers: Measuring the closeness of relationships. *Journal of Social and Personal Relationships, 2,* 215–238.

Mayer, F. S., Duval, S., & Duval, V. H. (1980). An attributional analysis of commitment. *Journal of Personality and Social Psychology, 39,* 1072–1080.

Mayer, J. D., & Salovey, P. (1987). Personality moderates the interaction of mood and cognition. In K. Fiedler & J. Forgas (Eds.), *Affect, cognition, and social behavior.* Toronto: Hogrefe.

McAlister, A., Perry, C., Killen, J., Slinkard, L. A., & Maccoby, N. (1980). Pilot study of smoking, alcohol and drug abuse prevention. *American Journal of Public Health, 70,* 719–721.

McAlister, A. L., Perry, C., & Maccoby, N. (1979). Adolescent smoking: Onset and prevention. *Pediatrics, 63,* 650–658.

McAndrew, F. T. (1981). Pattern of performance and attributions of ability and gender. *Personality and Social Psychology Bulletin, 7,* 583–587.

McArthur, L. A. (1972). The how and what of why: Some determinants and consequences of causal attribution. *Journal of Personality and Social Psychology, 22,* 171–193.

McArthur, L. Z., & Friedman, S. A. (1980). Illusory correlation in impression formation: Variations in the shared distinctiveness effect as a function of the distinctive person's age, race, and sex. *Journal of Personality and Social Psychology, 39,* 615–624.

McCain, G., Cox, C., & Paulus, P. B. (1981). The relationship between crowding and manifestations of illness in prison settings. In D. J. Osborne et al. (Eds.), *Research in psychology and medicine* (Vol. II). New York: Academic Press.

McCann, C. D., & Hancock, R. D. (1983). Self-monitoring in communicative interactions: Social cognitive consequences of goal-directed message modification. *Journal of Experimental Social Psychology, 19,* 109–121.

McCanne, T. R., & Anderson, J. A. (1987). Emotional responding following experimental manipulation of facial electromyographic activity. *Journal of Personality and Social Psychology, 52,* 759–768.

McCarrey, M., Edwards, H. P., & Rozario, W. (1982). Ego-relevant feedback, affect, and self-serving attributional bias. *Personality and Social Psychology Bulletin, 8,* 189–194.

McCarthy, D. P., & Saegert, S. (1979). Residential density, social overload, and social withdrawal. In J. R. Aiello & A. Baum (Eds.), *Residential crowding and design.* New York: Plenum Press.

McCarthy, J. D., & Hoge, D. R. (1984). The dynamics of self-esteem and delinquency. *American Journal of Sociology, 90,* 396–410.

McCarthy, J. F., & Kelly, B. R. (1978). Aggression, performance variables, and anger self-report in ice hockey players. *Journal of Psychology, 99,* 97–101. (*b*)

McCarthy, J. F., & Kelly, B. R. (1978). Aggressive behavior and its effect on performance over time in ice hockey athletes: An archival study. *International Journal of Sport Psychology, 9,* 90–96. (*a*)

McCaul, K. D., Hinsz, V. B., & McCaul, H. S. (1987). The effects of commitment to performance goals on effort. *Journal of Applied Social Psychology, 17,* 437–452.

McCaul, K. D., & Maki, R. H. (1984). Self-reference versus desirability ratings and memory for traits. *Journal of Personality and Social Psychology, 47,* 953–955.

McCauley, C. R., & Segal, M. E. (1987). Social psychology of terrorist groups. In C. Hendrick (Ed.), *Group processes and intergroup relations: Review of personality and social psychology*, Vol. 9. Newbury Park, Ca.: Sage.

McClelland, L., & Cook, S. W. (1979–1980). Energy conservation effects of continuous in-home feedback in all-electric homes. *Journal of Environmental Systems*, 9, 169–173. (*a*)

McClelland, L., & Cook, S. W. (1980). Promoting energy conservation in mastered-metered apartments through group financial incentives. *Journal of Applied Social Psychology*, 10, 20–31. (*b*)

McConahay, J. B. (1981). Reducing racial prejudice in desegregated schools. In W. D. Hawley (Ed.), *Effective school desegregation*. Beverly Hills, Calif.: Sage.

McConahay, J. B. (1982). Self-interest versus racial attitudes as correlates of anti-busing attitudes in Louisville: Is it the buses or the blacks? *Journal of Politics*, 44, 692–720.

McConahay, J. B. (1983). It is still the blacks and *not* the buses: Self-interest vs. racial attitudes as correlates of opposition to busing in Louisville, a replication. Unpublished manuscript, Institute of Policy Sciences and Public Affairs, Duke University.

McConahay, J. B., Hardee, B. B., & Batts, V. (1981). Has racism declined in America: It depends upon who is asking and what is asked. *Journal of Conflict Resolution*, 25(4), 563–579.

McCullough, J. L., & Ostrom, T. M. (1974). Repetition of highly similar messages and attitude change. *Journal of Applied Psychology*, 59, 395–397.

McFarland, C., & Ross, M. (1985). The relation between current impressions and memories of self and dating partners. Unpublished manuscript, University of Waterloo.

McGillicuddy, N. B., Welton, G. L., & Pruitt, D. G. (1987). Third-party intervention: A field experiment comparing three different models. *Journal of Personality and Social Psychology*, 53, 104–112.

McGillis, D. (1979). Biases and jury decision making. In I. H. Frieze, D. Bar-Tal, & J. S. Carroll, *New approaches to social problems*. San Francisco: Jossey-Bass.

McGrath, J. E. (1984). *Groups: Interaction and performance*. Englewood Cliffs, N.J.: Prentice-Hall.

McGuinness, D., & Pribram, K. (1978). The origins of sensory bias in the development of gender differences in perception and cognition. In M. Bortner (Ed.), *Cognitive growth and development: Essays in honor of Herbert G. Birch*. New York: Brunner/Mazel, 1978.

Cited by D. Goleman in Special abilities of the sexes: Do they begin in the brain? *Psychology Today*, November, pp. 48–59, 120.

McGuire, W. J. (1964). Inducing resistance to persuasion: Some contemporary approaches. In L. Berkowitz (Ed.), *Advances in experimental social psychology* (Vol. 1). New York: Academic Press.

McGuire, W. J. (1968). Personality and susceptibility to social influence. In E. F. Borgatta & W. W. Lambert (Eds.), *Handbook of personality theory and research*. Chicago: Rand-McNally.

McGuire, W. J. (1978). An information-processing model of advertising effectiveness. In H. L. Davis & A. J. Silk (Eds.), *Behavioral and management sciences in marketing*. New York: Ronald Press.

McGuire, W. J. (1986). The myth of massive media impact: Savagings and salvagings. In G. Comstock (Ed.), *Public communication and behavior*, Vol. 1. Orlando, Fl.: Academic Press

McGuire, W. J., & McGuire, C. V. (1986). Differences in conceptualizing self versus conceptualizing other people as manifested in contrasting verb types used in natural speech. *Journal of Personality and Social Psychology*, 51, 1135–1143.

McGuire, W. J., McGuire, C. V., Child P., & Fujioka, T. (1978). Salience of ethnicity in the spontaneous self-concept as a function of one's ethnic distinctiveness in the social environment. *Journal of Personality and Social Psychology*, 36, 511–520.

McGuire, W. J., McGuire, C. V., & Winton, W. (1979). Effects of household sex composition on the salience of one's gender in the spontaneous self-concept. *Journal of Experimental Social Psychology*, 15, 77–90.

McGuire, W. J., & Padawer-Singer, A. (1978). Trait salience in the spontaneous self-concept. *Journal of Personality and Social Psychology*, 33, 743–754.

McMillen, D. L., & Austin, J. B. (1971). Effect of positive feedback on compliance following transgression. *Psychonomic Science*, 24, 59–61.

McMillen, D. L., Sanders, D. Y., & Solomon, G. S. (1977). Self-esteem, attentiveness, and helping behavior. *Personality and Social Psychology Bulletin*, 3, 257–261.

McNeel, S. P. (1980). Tripling up: Perceptions and effects of dormitory crowding. Paper presented at the American Psychological Association convention.

Medalia, N. Z., & Larsen, O. N. (1958). Diffusion and belief in a collective delusion: The Seattle windshield pitting epidemic. *American Sociological Review*, 23, 180–186.

Meehl, P. E. (1954). *Clinical vs. statistical prediction: A theoretical analysis and a review of evidence*. Minneapolis: University of Minnesota Press.

Meehl, P. E. (1986). Causes and effects of my disturbing little book. *Journal of Personality Assessment*, 50, 370–375.

Meeus, W. H. J., & Raaijmakers, Q. A. W. (1986). Administrative obedience: Carrying out orders to use psychological-administrative violence. *European Journal of Social Psychology*, 16, 311–324.

Mehrabian, A., & Diamond, S. G. (1971). Effects of furniture arrangement, props, and personality on social interaction. *Journal of Personality and Social Psychology*, 20, 18–30.

Meindl, J. R., & Lerner, M. J. (1984). Exacerbation of extreme responses to an out-group. *Journal of Personality and Social Psychology*, 47, 71–84.

Melton, G. B., Monahan, J., & Saks, M. J. (1987). Psychologists as law professors. *American Psychologist*, 42, 502–509.

Mendonca, P. J., & Brehm, S. S. (1983). Effects of choice on behavioral treatment of overweight children. *Journal of Social and Clinical Psychology*, 1, 343–358.

Menninger, K. (1968, September 7). The crime of punishment. *Saturday Review*, pp. 21–24.

Mento, A. J., Steel, R. P., & Karren, R. J. (1987). A meta-analytic study of the effects of goal setting on task performance: 1966–1984. *Organizational Behavior and Human Decision Processes*, 39, 52–83.

Merton, R. K., & Kitt, A. S. (1950). Contributions to the theory of reference group behavior. In R. K. Merton & P. F. Lazarsfeld (Eds.), *Continuities in social research: Studies in the scope and method of the American soldier*. Glencoe, Ill.: Free Press.

Messe, L. A., & Sivacek, J. M. (1979). Predictions of others' responses in a mixed-motive game: Self-justification or false consensus? *Journal of Personality and Social Psychology*, 37, 602–607.

Messick, D. M., Bloom, S., Boldizar, J. P., & Samuelson, C. D. (1985). Why we are fairer than others. *Journal of Experimental Social Psychology*, 21, 480–500.

Messick, D. M., & Sentis, K. P. (1979). Fairness and preference. *Journal of Experimental Social Psychology*, 15, 418–434.

Messick, D. M., Wilke, H., Brewer, M. B., Kramer, R. M., Zemke, P. E., & Lui, L. (1983). Individual adaptations and structural change as solutions to social dilemmas. *Journal of Personality and Social Psychology*, 44, 294–309.

Meyer, D. S. (1975). *The winning candidate:*

How to defeat your political candidate. New York: Heinemann, 1966. Cited by P. Suedfeld, D. Rank, and R. Borre in Frequency of exposure and evaluation of candidates and campaign speeches. *Journal of Applied Social Psychology, 15,* 118–126.

Meyer, J. P., & Mulherin, A. (1980). From attribution to helping: An analysis of the mediating effects of affect and expectancy. *Journal of Personality and Social Psychology, 39,* 201–210.

Michaels, J. W., Blommel, J. M., Brocato, R. M., Linkous, R. A., & Rowe, J. S. (1982). Social facilitation and inhibition in a natural setting. *Replications in Social Psychology, 2,* 21–24.

Middlemist, R. D., Knowles, E. S., & Matter, C. F. (1976). Personal space invasions in the lavatory: Suggestive evidence for arousal. *Journal of Personality and Social Psychology, 33,* 541–546.

Middlemist, R. D., Knowles, E. S., & Matter, C. F. (1977). What to do and what to report: A reply to Koocher. *Journal of Personality and Social Psychology, 35,* 122–124.

Miell, D., Duck, S., & La Gaipa, J. (1979). Interactive effects of sex and timing in self disclosure. *British Journal of Social and Clinical Psychology, 18,* 355–362.

Mikula, G. (1984). Justice and fairness in interpersonal relations: Thoughts and suggestions. In H. Tajfel (Ed.), *The social dimension: European developments in social psychology,* Vol. 1, Cambridge: Cambridge University Press.

Milgram, S. (1961, December). Nationality and conformity. *Scientific American,* December, pp. 45–51.

Milgram, S. (1965). Some conditions of obedience and disobedience to authority. *Human Relations, 18,* 57–76.

Milgram, S. (1974). *Obedience to authority.* New York: Harper and Row.

Milgram, S. (1984). Cyranoids. Paper presented at the American Psychological Association convention.

Milgram, S., Bickman, L., & Berkowitz, L. (1969). Note on the drawing power of crowds of different size. *Journal of Personality and Social Psychology, 13,* 79–82.

Milgram, S., & Sabini, J. (1983). On maintaining social norms: A field experiment in the subway. In H. H. Blumberg, A. P. Hare, V. Kent, and M. Davies (Eds.), *Small groups and social interaction,* Vol. 1. London: Wiley.

Millar, M. G., & Tesser, A. (1985). Effects of affective and cognitive focus on the attitude-behavior relationship. Unpublished manuscript, Institute for Behavioral Research, University of Georgia.

Millar, M. G., & Tesser, A. (1986). Thought-induced attitude change: The effects of schema structure and commitment. *Journal of Personality and Social Psychology, 51,* 259–269.

Millar, M. G., & Tesser, A. (1989). The effects of affective-cognitive consistency and thought on the attitude-behavior relation. *Journal of Experimental Social Psychology, 25,* 189–202.

Miller, A. G. (1986). *The obedience experiments: A case study of controversy in social science.* New York: Praeger.

Miller, A. G., Gillen, B., Schenker, C., & Radlove, S. (1973). Perception of obedience to authority. *Proceedings of the 81st annual convention of the American Psychological Association, 8,* 127–128.

Miller, C. E., & Anderson, P. D. (1979). Group decision rules and the rejection of deviates. *Social Psychology Quarterly, 42,* 354–363.

Miller, D. T. (1977). Altruism and threat to a belief in a just world. *Journal of Experimental Social Psychology, 13,* 113–124.

Miller, D. T., & McFarland, C. (1987). Pluralistic ignorance: When similarity is interpreted as dissimilarity. *Journal of Personality and Social Psychology, 53,* 298–305.

Miller, D. T., & Turnbull, W. (1986). Expectancies and interpersonal processes. In M. R. Rosenzweig & L. W. Porter (Eds.), *Annual Review of Psychology,* Vol. 37. Palo Alto: Annual Reviews.

Miller, F. D., Smith, E. R., & Uleman, J. (1981). Measurement and interpretation of situational and dispositional attributions. *Journal of Experimental Social Psychology, 17,* 80–95.

Miller, G. R., & Fontes, N. E. (1979). *Videotape on trial: A view from the jury box.* Beverly Hills, Calif.: Sage Publications.

Miller, J. G. (1984). Culture and the development of everyday social explanation. *Journal of Personality and Social Psychology, 46,* 961–978.

Miller, K. I., & Monge, P. R. (1986). Participation, satisfaction, and productivity: A meta-analytic review. *Academy of Management Journal, 29,* 727–753.

Miller, L. C., Berg, J. H., & Archer, R. L. (1983). Openers: Individuals who elicit intimate self-disclosure. *Journal of Personality and Social Psychology, 44,* 1234–1244.

Miller, L. C., Berg, J. H., & Rugs, D. (1989). Selectivity and sharing: Needs and norms in developing friendships. Unpublished manuscript, Scripps College.

Miller, L. E., & Grush, J. E. (1986). Individual differences in attitudinal versus normative determination of behavior. *Journal of Experimental Social Psychology, 22,* 190–202.

Miller, N., & Campbell, D. T. (1959). Recency and primacy in persuasion as a function of the timing of speeches and measurements. *Journal of Abnormal and Social Psychology, 59,* 1–9.

Miller, N., & Marks, G. (1982). Assumed similarity between self and other: Effect of expectation of future interaction with that other. *Social Psychology Quarterly, 45,* 100–105.

Miller, N., Maruyama, G., Beaber, R. J., & Valone, K. (1976). Speed of speech and persuasion. *Journal of Personality and Social Psychology, 34,* 615–624.

Miller, N. E. (1941). The frustration-aggression hypothesis. *Psychological Review, 48,* 337–342.

Miller, N. E., & Bugelski, R. (1948). Minor studies of aggression: II. The influence of frustrations imposed by the in-group on attitudes expressed toward out-groups. *Journal of Psychology, 25,* 437–442.

Miller, P. A., & Eisenberg, N. (1988). The relation of empathy to aggressive and externalizing/antisocial behavior. *Psychological Bulletin, 103,* 324–344.

Miller, P. C., Lefcourt, H. M., Holmes, J. G., Ware, E. E., & Saley, W. E. (1986). Marital locus of control and marital problem solving. *Journal of Personality and Social Psychology, 51,* 161–169.

Miller, R. S., & Schlenker, B. R. (1985). Egotism in group members: Public and private attributions of responsibility for group performance. *Social Psychology Quarterly, 48,* 85–89.

Millett, K. (1975). The shame is over. *Ms.,* January, pp. 26–29.

Millett, K. (1979). *The basement: Meditations on human sacrifice.* New York: Simon & Schuster.

Mills, J., & Clark, M. S. (1982). Exchange and communal relationships. In L. Wheeler (Ed.), *Review of personality and social psychology* (Vol. III). Beverly Hills, Calif.: Sage.

Mims, P. R., Hartnett, J. J., & Nay, W. R. (1975). Interpersonal attraction and help volunteering as a function of physical attractiveness. *Journal of Psychology, 89,* 125–131.

Minard, R. D. (1952). Race relationships in the Pocohontas coal field. *Journal of Social Issues, 8*(1), 29–44.

Mirels, H. L., & McPeek, R. W. (1977). Self-advocacy and self-esteem. *Journal of Consulting and Clinical Psychology 45,* 1132–1138.

Mischel, W. (1968). *Personality and assessment.* New York: Wiley.

Mita, T. H., Dermer, M., & Knight, J. (1977). Reversed facial images and the mere-exposure hypothesis. *Journal of Personality and Social Psychology*, 35, 597–601.

Moghaddam, F, M. (1987). Psychology in the three worlds: As reflected by the crisis in social psychology and the move toward indigenous third-world psychology. *American Psychologist*, 42, 912–920.

Monaco, C. (1988, Spring/Summer). The difficult birth of the typewriter. *Invention and Technology*, pp. 11–21.

Money, J. (1987). Sin, sickness, or status? Homosexual gender identity and psychoneuroendocrinology. *American Psychologist*, 42, 384–399.

Monge, P. T., & Kirste, K. K. (1980). Measuring proximity in human organization. *Social Psychology Quarterly*, 43, 110–115.

Monson, T. C., Hesley, J. W., & Chernick, L. (1982). Specifying when personality traits can and cannot predict behavior: An alternative to abandoning the attempt to predict single-act criteria. *Journal of Personality and Social Psychology*, 43, 385–399.

Monson, T. C., & Snyder, M. (1977). Actors, observers, and the attribution process: Toward a reconceptualization. *Journal of Experimental Social Psychology*, 13, 89–111.

Moody, K. (1980). *Growing up on television: The TV effect*. New York: Times Books.

Moore, D. L., & Baron, R. S. (1983). Social facilitation: A physiological analysis. In J. T. Cacioppo & R. Petty (Eds.), *Social psychophysiology*. New York: Guilford Press.

Moran, G., & Comfort, J. C. (1982). Scientific juror selection: Sex as a moderator of demographic and personality predictors of impaneled felony juror behavior. *Journal of Personality and Social Psychology*, 43, 1052–1063.

Moreland, R. L., & Zajonc, R. B. (1977). Is stimulus recognition a necessary condition for the occurrence of exposure effects? *Journal of Personality and Social Psychology*, 35, 191–199.

Moreland, R. L., & Zajonc, R. B. (1982). Exposure effects in person perception: Familiarity, similarity and attraction. *Journal of Experimental Social Psychology*, 18, 395–415.

Morgan, R. (1980). Theory and practice: Pornography and rape. In L. Lederer (Ed.), *Take back the night: Women on pornography*. New York: Morrow.

Morris, W. N., & Miller, R. S. (1975). The effects of consensus-breaking and consensus-preempting partners on reduction of conformity. *Journal of Experimental Social Psychology*, 11, 215–223.

Morrow, L. (1983, August 1). All the hazards and threats of success. *Time*, pp. 20–25.

Morse, S. J., Gergen, K. J., Peele, S., & van Ryneveld, J. (1977). Reactions to receiving expected and unexpected help from a person who violates or does not violate a norm. *Journal of Experimental Social Psychology*, 13, 397–402.

Morse, S. J., & Gruzen, J. (1976). The eye of the beholder: A neglected variable in the study of physical attractiveness. *Journal of Psychology*, 44, 209–225.

Moscovici, s. (1985). Social influence and conformity. In G. Lindzey & E. Aronson (Eds.), *The Handbook of Social Psychology*, 3rd ed. Hillsdale, N.J.: Erlbaum.

Moscovici, S. (1988). Notes towards a description of social representations. *European Journal of Social Psychology*, 18, 211–250.

Moscovici, S., Lage, S., & Naffrechoux, M. (1969). Influence on a consistent minority on the responses of a majority in a color perception task. *Sociometry*, 32, 365–380.

Moscovici, S., & Personnaz, B, (1980). Studies in social influence: V. Minority influence and conversion behavior in a perceptual task. *Journal of Experimental Social Psychology*, 16, 270–282.

Moscovici, S., & Zavalloni, M. (1969). The group as a polarizer of attitudes. *Journal of Personality and Social Psychology*, 12, 124–135.

Moyer, K. E. (1976). *The psychobiology of aggression*. New York: Harper & Row.

Moyer, K. E. (1983). The physiology of motivation: Aggression as a model. In C. J. Scheier & A. M. Rogers (Eds.), *G. Stanley Hall Lecture Series, Vol. 3*. Washington, D.C.: American Psychological Association.

Moynihan, D. P. (1979). Social science and the courts. *Public Interest*, 54, 12–31.

Muehlenhard, C. L. (1988). Misinterpreted dating behaviors and the risk of date rape. *Journal of Social and Clinical Psychology*, 6, 20–37.

Mueller, C. W., Donnerstein, E., & Hallam, J. (1983). Violent films and prosocial behavior. *Personality and Social Psychology Bulletin*, 9, 83–89.

Mullen, B. (1985). Strength and immediacy of sources: A meta-analytic evaluation of the forgotten elements of social impact theory. *Journal of Personality and Social Psychology*, 48, 1458–1466.

Mullen, B. (1986). Atrocity as a function of lynch mob composition: A self-attention perspective. *Personality and Social Psychology Bulletin*, 12, 187–197. (a)

Mullen, B. (1986). Stuttering, audience size, and the other-total ratio: A self-attention perspective. *Journal of Applied Social Psychology*, 16, 139–149. (b)

Mullen, B., Atkins, J. L., Champion, D. S., Edwards, C., Hardy, D., Story, J. E., & Vanderklok, M. (1985). The false consensus effect: A meta-analysis of 115 hypothesis tests. *Journal of Experimental Social Psychology*, 21, 262–283.

Mullen, B., & Baumeister, R. F. (1987). Group effects on self-attention and performance: Social loafing, social facilitation, and social impairment. In C. Hendrick (Ed.), *Group processes and intergroup relations: Review of personality and Social Psychology*, Vol. 9. Newbury Park, Ca.: Sage.

Mullen, B., Cooper, C., Driskell, J. E. (1988). Jaywalking as a function of model behavior. Unpublished manuscript, Syracuse University.

Mullen, B., Goethals, G. R., Worth, L. T., & Chapman, J. G. (1988). The causes and consequences of social projection. Unpublished manuscript, Syracuse University.

Mullen, B., & Hu, L. T. (1989). Perceptions of ingroup and outgroup variability: A meta-analytic integration. *Basic and Applied Social Psychology*, in press. (a)

Mullen, B., & Hu, L. T. (1988). Social projection as a function of cognitive mechanisms: Two meta-analytic integrations. *British Journal of Social Psychology*, 27, 333–356. (b)

Mullen, B., & Johnson, C. (1988). Distinctiveness-based illusory correlations and stereotyping: A meta-analytic integration. Unpublished manuscript, Syracuse University.

Mullen, B., & Riordan, C. A. (1988). Self-serving attributions for performance in naturalistic settings: A meta-analytic review. *Journal of Applied Social Psychology*, 18, 3–22.

Mumford, M. D. (1986). Leadership in the organizational context: A conceptual approach and its applications. *Journal of Applied Social Psychology*, 16, 508–531.

Murdock, G. P. (1945). The common denominator of cultures. In R. Linton (Ed.), *The science of man and the world crisis*. New York: Columbia University Press.

Murphy-Berman, V., Berman, J. J., Singh, P., Pachauri, A., & Kumar, P. (1984). Factors affecting allocation to needy and meritorious recipients: A cross-cultural comparison. *Journal of Personality and Social Psychology*, 46, 1267–1272.

Murphy-Berman, V., & Sharma, R. (1986). Testing the assumptions of attribution theory in India. *Journal of Social Psychology*, 126, 607–616.

Murstein, B. L. (1986). *Paths to marriage*. Newbury Park, Ca.: Sage.

Muson, G. (1978). Teenage violence and the telly. *Psychology Today*, March, pp. 50–54.

Myers, D. G. (1967). Enhancement of initial risk tendencies in social situations. Unpublished doctoral dissertation, University of Iowa. (University Microfilms No. 68–958).

Myers, D. G. (1978). Polarizing effects of social comparison. *Journal of Experimental Social Psychology*, 14, 554–563.

Myers, D. G. (1986). *Psychology*. New York: Worth.

Myers, D. G., & Bach, P. J. (1976). Group discussion effects on conflict behavior and self-justification. *Psychological Reports*, 38, 135–140.

Myers, D. G., & Bishop, G. D. (1970). Discussion effects on racial attitudes. *Science*, 169, 778–789.

Nadler, A., Goldberg, M., & Jaffe, Y. (1982). Effect of self-differentiation and anonymity in group on deindividuation, *Journal of Personality and Social Psychology*, 42, 1127–1136.

Nadler, A., Mayseless, O., Peri, N., & Chemerinski, A. (1985). Effects of opportunity to reciprocate and self-esteem on help-seeking behavior. *Journal of Personality*, 53, 23–35.

Nagar, D., & Pandey, J. (1987). Affect and performance on cognitive task as a function of crowding and noise. *Journal of Applied Social Psychology*, 17, 147–157.

Napolitan, D. A., & Goethals, G. R. (1979). The attribution of friendliness. *Journal of Experimental Social Psychology*, 15, 105–113.

National Commission on the Causes and Prevention of Violence (1969). *To establish justice, insure domestic tranquility*. Washington, D.C.: U.S. Government Printing Offices.

National Institute of Mental Health (1982). *Television and Behavior: Ten Years of Scientific Progress and Implications for the Eighties.*

National Opinion Research Center (1980). *General social surveys, 1972–1980: Cumulative codebook*. Storrs, Conn.: Roper Public Opinion Research Center, University of Connecticut.

NBC News Poll (1979). November 29–30, 1977. Cited by *Public Opinion*, January–February, p. 36. (*b*)

NCTV (1988). TV and film alcohol research. *NCTV News*, 9,(3–4), 4.

Neimeyer, R. A., & Mitchell, K. A. (1988). Similarity and attraction: A longitudinal study. *Journal of Social and Personal Relationships*, 5, 131–148.

Nemeth, C. (1977). Interactions between jurors as a function of majority vs. unanimity decision rules. *Journal of Applied Social Psychology*, 7, 38–56.

Nemeth, C. (1979). The role of an active minority in intergroup relations. In W. G. Austin and S. Worchel (Eds.), *The social psychology of intergroup relations*. Monterey, Calif.: Brooks/Cole.

Nemeth, C. (1984). *Group process and trial by jury: The U.S. and France*. In S. Moscovici (Ed.), Manuel de psychologie sociale. Paris: Presses Universitaires de France.

Nemeth, C. (1986). Differential contributions of majority and minority influence. *Psychological Review*, 93, 23–32.

Nemeth, C. (1986). Intergroup relations between majority and minority. In S. Worchel and W. G. Austin (Eds.), *Psychology of intergroup relations*. Chicago: Nelson-Hall.

Nemeth, C., & Chiles, C. (1988). Modelling courage: The role of dissent in fostering independence. *European Journal of Social Psychology*, 18, 275–280.

Nemeth, C., & Wachtler, J. (1974). Creating the perceptions of consistency and confidence: A necessary condition for minority influence. *Sociometry*, 37, 529–540.

Neuberg, S. L. (1989). The goal of forming accurate impressions during social interactions: Attenuating the impact of negative expectancies. *Journal of Personality and Social Psychology*, 56, 374–386.

Newcomb, T. M. (1961). *The acquaintance process*. New York: Holt, Rinehart and Winston.

Newman, H. M., & Langer, E. J. (1981). Post-divorce adaptation and the attribution of responsibility. *Sex Roles*, 7, 223–231.

Newman, O. (1972). *Defensible space*. New York: Macmillan.

Newman, O. (1973). *Architectural design for crime prevention*. Government Printing Office: U.S. Department of Justice.

Newsweek. (1981). March 2, 1981, p. 38; March 9, 1981, p. 28.

Nias, D. K. B. (1979). Marital choice: Matching or complementation? In M. Cook and G. Wilson (Eds.), *Love and attraction*. Oxford: Pergamon.

Nicholson, N., Cole, S. G., & Rocklin, T. (1985). Conformity in the Asch situation: A comparison between contemporary British and U. S. university students. *British Journal of Social Psychology*, 24, 59–63.

Nida, S. A., & Williams J. E. (1977). Sex-stereotyped traits, physical attractiveness, and interpersonal attraction. *Psychological Reports*, 41, 1311–1322.

Nigro, G. N., Hill, D. E., Gelbein, M. E., & Clark, C. L. (1988). Changes in the facial prominence of women and men over the last decade. *Psychology of Women Quarterly*, 12, 225–235.

Nisbett, R. (1988, Fall). The Vincennes incident: Congress hears psychologists. *Science Agenda* (American Psychological Association), p. 4.

Nisbett, R. E., & Bellows, N. (1977). Verbal reports about causal influences on social judgments: Private access versus public theories. *Journal of Personality and Social Psychology*, 35, 613–624.

Nisbett, R. E., Borgida, E., Crandall, R., & Reed, H. (1976). Popular induction: Information is not necessarily informative. In J. S. Carroll and J. W. Payne (Eds.), *Cognition and social behavior*. Hillsdale, N.J.: Erlbaum.

Nisbett, R. E., Fong, G. T., Lehman, D. R., & Cheng, P. W. (1987). Teaching reasoning. *Science*, 238, 625–631.

Nisbett, R. E., & Ross, L. (1980). *Human inference: Strategies and shortcomings of social judgment*. Englewood Cliffs, N. J.: Prentice-Hall.

Nisbett, R. E., & Schachter, S. (1966). Cognitive Manipulation of pain. *Journal of Experimental Social Psychology*, 2, 227–236.

Nisbett, R. E., & Wilson, T. D. (1977). Telling more than we can know: Verbal reports on mental process. *Psychological Review*, 84, 231–259.

Nisbett, R. E., Zukier, H., & Lemley, R. E. (1981). The dilution effect: Nondiagnostic information weakens the implications of diagnostic information. *Cognitive Psychology*, 13, 248–277.

Noel, J. G., Forsyth, D. R., & Kelley, K. N. (1987). Improving the performance of failing students by overcoming their self-serving attributional biases. *Basic and Applied Social Psychology*, 8, 151–162.

Nolen-Hoeksema, S., Girgus, J. S., & Seligman, M. E. P. (1986). Learned helplessness in children: A longitudinal study of depression, achievement, and explanatory style. *Journal of Personality and Social Psychology*, 51, 435–442.

Noon, E., & Hollin, C. R. (1987). Lay knowledge of eyewitness behaviour: A British survey. *Applied Cognitive Psychology*, 1, 143–153.

Norem, J. K., & Cantor, N. (1986). Defensive pessimism: Harnessing anxiety as motivation. *Journal of Personality and Social Psychology*, 51, 1208–1217.

Nuttin, J. M., Jr. (1987). Affective consequences of mere ownership: The name letter effect in twelve European languages. *European Journal of Social Psychology*, 17, 318–402.

O'Dea, T. F. (1968). Sects and cults. In D. L. Sills (Ed.), *International encyclopedia of the social sciences* (Vol. 14). New York: Macmillan.

O'Gorman, H. J., & Garry, S. L. (1976). Pluralistic ignorance—a replication and extension. *Public Opinion Quarterly*, 40, 449–458.

Ohbuchi, K., & Kambara. T. (1985). Attacker's intent and awareness of outcome, impression management, and retaliation. *Journal of Experimental Social Psychology*, 21, 321–330.

O'Leary, M. R., & Dengerink, H. A. (1973). Aggression as a function of the intensity and pattern of attack. *Journal of Experimental Research in Personality*, 7, 61–70.

O'Leary, V. E., & Donoghue, J. M. (1978). Latitudes of masculinity: Reactions to sex-role deviance in men. *Journal of Social Issues*, 34, 17–28.

Olguin, A., Oskamp, S., & Meredith, L. (1988). Effects of the television series *AMERIKA* on public attitudes. Paper presented at the American Psychological Association convention.

Oliner, S. P., & Oliner, P. M. (1988). *The altruistic personality: Rescuers of Jews in Nazi Europe*. New York: The Free Press.

Olsen, M. E. (1981). Consumers' attitudes toward energy conservation. *Journal of Social Issues*, 37(2), 108–131.

Olson, J. M., & Cal, A. V. (1984). Source credibility, attitudes, and the recall of past behaviours. *European Journal of Social Psychology*, 14, 203–210.

Olson, J. M., Herman, C. P., & Zanna, M. P. (1986). *Relative deprivation and social comparison: The Ontario Symposium*, Vol. 4. Hillsdale, N.J.: Erlbaum.

Olson, J. M., & Zanna, M. P. (1981). Promoting physical activity: A social psychological perspective. Report prepared for the Ministry of Culture and Recreation, Sports and Fitness Branch, 77 Bloor St. West, 8th Floor, Toronto, Ontario M7A 2R9, November.

Olweus, D. (1979). Stability of aggressive reaction patterns in mles; A review. *Psychological Bulletin*, 86, 852–875.

Orbell, J. M., van de Kragt, A. J. C., & Dawes, R. M. (1988). Explaining discussion-induced cooperation. *Journal of Personality and Social Psychology*, 54, 811–819.

Orive, R. (1984). Group similarity, public self-awareness, and opinion extremity: A social projection explanation of deindividuation effects. *Journal of Personality and Social Psychology*, 47, 727–737.

Orlofsky, J. L., & O'Heron, C. A. (1987). Stereotypic and nonstereotypic sex role trait and behavior orientations: Implications for personal adjustment. *Journal of Personality and Social Psychology*, 52, 1034–1052.

Osberg, T. M., & Shrauger, J. S. (1986). Self-prediction: Exploring the parameters of accuracy. *Journal of Personality and Social Psychology*, 51, 1044–1057.

Osgood, C. E. (1962). *An alternative to war or surrender*. Urbana, Ill.: University of Illinois Press.

Osgood, C. E. (1973). Statement on psychological aspects of international relations. Committee on Foreign Relations, United States Senate, May 25, 1966. Reprinted in D. G. Linder (Ed.), *Psychological dimensions of social interaction*. Reading, Mass.: Addison-Wesley.

Osgood, C. E. (1980). GRIT: A strategy for survival in mankind's nuclear age? Paper presented at the Pugwash Conference on New Directions in Disarmament, Racine, Wis.

Oskamp, S. (1971). Effects of programmed strategies on cooperation in the prisoner's dilemma and other mixed-motive games. *Journal of Conflict Resolution*, 15, 225–229.

Oskamp, S., King, J. C., Burn, S. M., Konrad, A. M., Pollard, J. A., & White, M. A. (1985). The media and nuclear war: Fallout from TV's "The Day After." In S. Oskamp (Ed.), *Applied social psychology annual* (Vol. 6). Beverly Hills, Calif.: Sage.

Osterhouse, R. A., & Brock, T. C. (1970). Distraction increases yielding to propaganda by inhibiting counterarguing. *Journal of Personality and Social Psychology*, 15, 344–358.

Owens, G., & Ford, J. G. (1978). Further consideration of the "what is good is beautiful" finding. *Social Psychology*, 41, 73–75.

Padgett, V. R. (1986). Predicting violence in totalitarian organizations: An application of 11 powerful principles of obedience from Milgram's experiments on obedience to authority. Unpublished manuscript, Marshall University.

Page, M. M., & Scheidt, R. J. (1971). The elusive weapons effect: Demand awareness, evaluation, apprehension, and slightly sophisticated subjects. *Journal of Personality and Social Psychology*, 20, 304–318.

Pallak, M. S., Cook, D. A., & Sullivan, J. J. (1980). Commitment and energy conservation. In L. Bickman (Ed.), *Applied social psychology annual* (Vol. 1). Beverly Hills, Calif.: Sage Publications.

Pallak, M. S., Mueller, M., Dollar, K., & Pallak, J. (1972). Effect of commitment on responsiveness to an extreme consonant communication. *Journal of Personality and Social Psychology*, 23, 429–436.

Pallak, S. R., Murroni, E., & Koch, J. (1983). Communicator attractiveness and expertise, emotional versus rational appeals, and persuasion: A heuristic versus systematic processing interpretation. *Social Cognition*, 2, 122–141.

Palmer, E. L., & Dorr, A. (Eds.) (1980). *Children and the faces of television: Teaching, violence, selling*. New York: Academic Press.

Paloutzian, R. (1979). Pro-ecology behavior: Three field experiments on litter pickup. Paper presented at the Western Psychological Association convention.

Pandey, J., Sinha, Y., Prakash, A., & Tripathi, R. C. (1982). Right-left political ideologies and attribution of the causes of poverty. *European Journal of Social Psychology*, 12, 327–331.

Park, B., & Rothbart, M. (1982). Perception of out-group homogeneity and levels of social categorization: Memory for the subordinate attributes of in-group and out-group members. *Journal of Personality and Social Psychology*, 42, 1051–1068.

Parke, R. D. (1974). Rules, roles, and resistance to deviation: Recent advances in punishment, discipline, and self-control. In A. Pick (Ed.), *Symposia of Child Psychology* (Vol. 8). Minneapolis: University of Minnesota Press.

Parke, R. D., Berkowitz, L., Leyens, J. P., West, S. G., & Sebastian, J. (1977). Some effects of violent and nonviolent movies on the behavior of juvenile delinquents. In L. Berkowitz (Ed.), *Advances in experimental social psychology* (Vol. 10). New York: Academic Press.

Patterson, G. R., Littman, R. A., & Bricker, W. (1967). Assertive behavior in children: A step toward a theory of aggression. *Monographs of the Society for Research in Child Development* (Serial No. 113), 32, 5.

Patterson, M. L. (1976). An arousal model of interpersonal crowding. *Psychological Review*, 83, 235–245.

Patterson, T. E. (1980). The role of the mass media in presidential campaigns: The lessons of the 1976 election. *Items*, 34, 25–30. Social Science Research Council, 605 Third Avenue, New York, N.Y. 10016.

Paulhus, D. (1982). Individual differences, self-presentation, and cognitive dissonance: Their concurrent operation in forced compliance. *Journal of Personality and Social Psychology*, 43, 838–852.

Pauling, L. (1962). Quoted by Etzioni, A. *The hard way to peace: A new strategy*. New York: Collier.

Penner, L. A., Dertke, M. C., & Achenbach, C. J. (1973). The "flash" system: A field study of altruism. *Journal of Applied Social Psychology*, 3, 362–370.

Penrod, S. (1981). Research summary from study of attorney and scientific jury selection models. Unpublished manuscript, University of Wisconsin.

Penrod, S., & Cutler, B. L. (1987). Assessing the competence of juries. In I. B. Weiner & A. K. Hess (Eds.), *Handbook of forensic psychology*. New York: Wiley.

Peplau, L. A., & Gordon, S. L. (1985). Women and men in love: Gender differences in close heterosexual relationships. In V. E. O'Leary, R. K. Unger, & B. S. Wallston (Eds.), *Women, gender, and social psychology*. Hillsdale, N.J.: Erlbaum.

Perloff, L. S. (1987). Social comparison and illusions of invulnerability. In C. R. Snyder & C. R. Ford (Eds.), *Coping with negative life events: Clinical and social psychological perspectives*. New York: Plenum.

Perloff, L. S., & Farbisz, R. (1985). Perceptions of uniqueness and illusions of invulnerability to divorce. Paper presented at the Midwestern Psychological Association convention.

Perloff, R. M., & Brock, T. C. (1980). " . . . And thinking makes it so": Cognitive responses to persuasion. In M. E. Roloff & G. R. Miller (Eds.), *Persuasion: New directions in theory and research*. Beverly Hills: Sage Publications.

Perls, F. S. (1973). *Ego, hunger and aggression: The beginning of Gestalt therapy*. Random House, 1969. Cited by Berkowitz in The case for bottling up rage. *Psychology Today*, July, pp. 24–30.

Perrin, S., & Spencer, C. (1980). The Asch effect—a child of its time? *Bulletin of the British Psychology Society*, 32, 405–406.

Perrin, S., & Spencer, C. (1981). Independence or conformity in the Asch experiment as a reflection of cultural or situational factors. *British Journal of Social Psychology*, 20, 205–209.

Perry, L. C., Perry, D. G., & Weiss, R. J. (1986). Age differences in children's beliefs about whether altruism makes the actor feel good. *Social Cognition*, 4, 263–269.

Pessin, J. (1933). The comparative effects of social and mechanical stimulation on memorizing. *American Journal of Psychology*, 45, 263–270.

Pessin, J., & Husband, R. W. (1933). Effects of social stimulation on human maze learning. *Journal of Abnormal and Social Psychology*, 28, 148–154.

Peterson, C., & Barrett, L. C. (1987). Explanatory style and academic performance among university freshmen. *Journal of Personality and Social Psychology*, 53, 603–607.

Peterson, C., Schwartz, S. M., & Seligman, M. E. P. (1981). Self-blame and depression symptoms. *Journal of Personality and Social Psychology*, 41, 253–259.

Peterson, C., & Seligman, M. E. P. (1984). Causal explanations as a risk factor for depres-

sion: Theory and evidence. *Psychological Review*, 91, 347–374.

Peterson, C., & Seligman, M. E. P. (1987). Explanatory style and illness. *Journal of Personality*, 55, 237–265.

Peterson, C., Seligman, M. E. P., & Vaillant, G. E. (1988). Pessimistic explanatory style is a risk factor for physical illness: A thirty-five-year longitudinal study. *Journal of Personality and Social Psychology*, 55, 23–27.

Peterson, J. L., & Zill, N. (1981). Television viewing in the United States and children's intellectual, social, and emotional development. *Television and Children*, 2(2), 21–28.

Pettigrew, T. F. (1958). Personality and sociocultural factors in intergroup attitudes: A cross-national comparison. *Journal of Conflict Resolution*, 2, 29–42.

Pettigrew, T. F. (1969). Racially separate or together? *Journal of Social Issues*, 2, 43–69.

Pettigrew, T. F. (1978). Three issues in ethnicity: Boundaries, deprivations, and perceptions. In J. M. Yinger & S. J. Cutler (Eds.), *Major social issues: A multidisciplinary view*. New York: Free Press.

Pettigrew, T. F. (1979). The ultimate attribution error: Extending Allport's cognitive analysis of prejudice. *Personality and Social Psychology Bulletin*, 5, 461–476.

Pettigrew, T. F. (1980). Prejudice. In S. Thernstrom et al. (Eds.), *Harvard encyclopedia of American ethnic groups*. Cambridge, Mass.: Harvard University Press.

Pettigrew, T. F. (1985). New patterns of racism: The different worlds of 1984 and 1964. *Rutgers Law Review*, 37, 673–706.

Pettigrew, T. F. (1986). The intergroup contact hypothesis reconsidered. In M. Hewstone & R. Brown (Eds.), *Contact and conflict in intergroup encounters*. Oxford: Basil Blackwell.

Pettigrew, T. F. (1988). Advancing racial justice: Past lessons for future use. Paper for the University of Alabama Conference: "Opening Doors: An Appraisal of Race Relations in America."

Pettingale, K. W., Morris, T., Greer, S., & Haybittle, J. L. (1985, March 30). Mental attitudes to cancer: An additional prognostic factor. *Lancet*, p. 750.

Petty, R. E., & Brock, T. C. (1979). Effects of "Barnum" personality assessments on cognitive behavior. *Journal of Consulting and Clinical Psychology*, 47, 201–203.

Petty, R. E., & Cacioppo, J. T. (1977). Forewarning cognitive responding, and resistance to persuasion. *Journal of Personality and Social Psychology*, 35, 645–655.

Petty, R. E., & Cacioppo, J. T. (1979). Effects of forewarning of persuasive intent and in-

volvement on cognitive response and persuasion. *Personality and Social Psychology Bulletin*, 5, 173–176. (a)

Petty, R. E., & Cacioppo, J. T. (1979). Issue involvement can increase or decrease persuasion by enhancing message-relevant cognitive responses. *Journal of Personality and Social Psychology*, 37, 1915–1926. (b)

Petty, R. E., & Cacioppo, J. T. (1986). The elaboration likelihood model of persuasion. In L. Berkowitz (Ed.), *Advances in experimental social psychology*, Vol. 19. New York: Academic Press.

Petty, R. E., Cacioppo, J. T., & Heesacker, M. (1984). Central and peripheral routes to persuasion: Application to counseling. In R. P. McGlynn, J. E. Maddux, C. D. Stoltenberg, & J. H. Harvey (Eds.), *Social perception in clinical and counseling psychology*. Lubbock, Texas: Texas Tech Press.

Petty, R. E., Cacioppo, J. T., & Schumann, D. (1983). Central and peripheral routes to advertising effectiveness: The moderating role of involvement. *Journal of Consumer Research*, 10, 135–146.

Petty, R. E., Ostrom, T. M., & Brock, T. C. (Eds.). (1981). *Cognitive responses in persuasion*. Hillsdale, N.J.: Erlbaum.

Petty, R. E., Wells, G. L., & Brock, T. C. (1976). Distraction can enchance or reduce yielding to propaganda: Thought disruption versus effort justification. *Journal of Personality and Social Psychology*, 34, 874–884.

Phillips, D. P. (1983). The impact of mass media violence on U.S. homicides. *American Sociological Review*, 48, 560–568.

Phillips, D. P. (1985). Natural experiments on the effects of mass media violence on fatal aggression: Strengths and weaknesses of a new approach. In L. Berkowitz (Ed.), *Advances in Experimental Social Psychology*, Vol. 19. Orlando, Fla.: Academic Press.

Piliavin, I. M., Rodin, J., & Piliavin, J. A. (1969). Good Samaritanism: An underground phenomenon. *Journal of Personality and Social Psychology*, 13, 289–299.

Piliavin, J. A., Evans, D. E., & Callero, P. (1982). Learning to "Give to unnamed strangers": The process of commitment to regular blood donation. In E. Staub, D. Bar-Tal, J. Karylowski, & J. Reykawski (Eds.), *The Development and Maintenance of Prosocial Behavior: International Perspectives*. New York: Plenum.

Piliavin, J. A., & Piliavin, I. M. (1973). The Good Samaritan: Why *does* he help? Unpublished manuscript, University of Wisconsin.

Piner, K. E., & Berg, J. H. (1988). The effects of availability on verbal interaction styles. Paper presented at the American Psychological Association convention.

Platz, S. J., & Hosch, H. M. (1988). Cross-racial/ethnic eyewitness identification: A field study. *Journal of Applied Social Psychology*, 18, 972–984.

Pleck, J. (1981). Changing patterns of work and family roles. Working paper no. 81, Wellesley College, Center for Research on Women, Wellesley, Mass. 02181.

Pliner, P., Hart, H., Kohl, J., & Saari, D. (1974). Compliance without pressure: Some further data on the foot-in-the-door technique. *Journal of Experimental Social Psychology*, 10, 17–22.

Plous, S. (1985). Perceptual illusions and military realities: A social-psychological analysis of the nuclear arms race. *Journal of Conflict Resolution*, 29, 363–389.

Polivy, J., & Herman, C. P. (1985, hardcover 1983). *Breaking the diet habit: The natural weight alternative*. New York: Basic Books.

Pomazal, R. J., & Clore, G. L. (1973). Helping on the highway: The effects of dependency and sex. *Journal of Applied Social Psychology*, 3, 150–164.

Pomerleau, O. F., & Rodin, J. (1986). Behavioral medicine and health psychology. In S. L. Garfield & A. E. Bergin (Eds.), *Handbook of psychotherapy and behavior change*, 3rd ed. New York: Wiley.

Porter, N., Geis, F. L., & Jennings (Walstedt), J. (1983). Are women invisible as leaders? *Sex Roles*, 9, 1035–1049.

Powell, J. L. (1988). A test of the knew-it-along effect in the 1984 presidential and statewide elections. *Journal of Applied Social Psychology*, 18, 760–773.

Prager, K. J. (1986). Intimacy status: Its relationship to locus of control, self-disclosure, and anxiety in adults. *Personality and Social Psychology Bulletin*, 12, 91–109.

Pratkanis, A. R., Greenwald, A. G., Leippe, M. R., & Baumgardner, M. H. (1988). In search of reliable persuasion effects: III. The sleeper effect is dead. Long live the sleeper effect. *Journal of Personality and Social Psychology*, 54, 203–218.

Prentice-Dunn, S., & Rogers, R. W. (1980). Effects of deindividuating situational cues and aggressive models on subjective deindividuation and aggression. *Journal of Personality and Social Psychology*, 39, 104–113.

Prentice-Dunn, S., & Rogers, R. W. (1989). Deindividuation and the self-regulation of behavior. In P. B. Paulus (Ed.), *Psychology of group influence*, 2nd. ed. Hillsdale, N.J.: Erlbaum.

Price, G. H., Dabbs, J. M., Jr., Clower, B. J.,

& Resin, R. P. (1979). At first glance—Or, is physical attractiveness more than skin deep? Paper presented at the Eastern Psychological Association convention, 1974. Cited by K. L. Dion & K. K. Dion. Personality and behavioral correlates of romantic love. In M. Cook & G. Wilson (Eds.), *Love and attraction*. Oxford: Pergamon.

Propst, R., Adams, J., & Propst, C. (1977). *The Senator Hatfield office innovation project*. Ann Arbor, Mich.: Herman Miller Research Corp., 3971 South Research Park Drive.

Pruitt, D. G. (1981). Kissinger as a traditional mediator with power. In J. Z. Rubin (Ed.), *Dynamics of third party intervention: Kissinger in the Middle East*. New York: Praeger. (a)

Pruitt, D. G. (1981). *Negotiation behavior*. New York: Academic Press. (b)

Pruitt, D. G. (1986). Achieving integrative agreements in negotiation. In R. K. White (Ed.), *Psychology and the prevention of nuclear war*. New York: New York University Press.

Pruitt, D. G. (1986, July) Trends in the scientific study of negotiation. *Negotiation Journal*, pp. 237–244.

Pruitt, D. G., & Lewis, S. A. (1975). Development of integrative solutions in bilateral negotiation. *Journal of Personality and Social Psychology*, 31, 621–633.

Pruitt, D. G., & Lewis, S. A. (1977). The psychology of integrative bargaining. In D. Druckman (Ed.), *Negotiations: A social-psychological analysis*. New York: Halsted.

Pruitt, D. G., & Rubin, J. Z. (1986). *Social conflict*. San Francisco: Random House.

Public Opinion (1984, August/September). Tradeoffs, p. 36.

Public Opinion (1984, August/September). Vanity fare, p. 22.

Public Opinion (1984, August/September). Need vs. greed (summary of Roper Report 84-1), p. 25.

Public Opinion (1985, February/March). Defining woman's place, p. 40.

Purvis, J. A., Dabbs, Jr., J. M., & Hopper, C. H. (1984). The "opener": Skilled user of facial expression and speech pattern. *Personality and Social Psychology Bulletin*, 10, 61–66.

Pyszczynski, T., & Greenberg, J. (1983). Determinants of reduction in intended effort as a strategy for coping with anticipated failure. *Journal of Research in Personality*, 17, 412–422.

Pyszczynski, T., & Greenberg, J. (1987). Self-regulatory perseveration and the depressive self-focusing style: A self-awareness theory of

reactive depression. *Psychological Bulletin*, 102, 122–138. (a)

Pyszczynski, T., & Greenberg, J. (1987). Toward an integration of cognitive and motivational perspectives on social inference: A biased hypothesis-testing model. In L. Berkowitz (Ed.), *Advances in experimental social psychology*, Vol. 20. San Diego, Ca.: Academic Press.

Pyszczynski, T., Greenberg, J., & Holt, K. (1985). Maintaining consistency between self-serving beliefs and available data: A bias in information evaluation. *Personality and Social Psychology Bulletin*, 11, 179–190.

Quattrone, G. A. (1982). Behavioral consequences of attributional bias. *Social Cognition*, 1, 358–378.

Quattrone, G. A. Overattribution and unit formation: When behavior engulfs the person. *Journal of Personality and Social Psychology*, 42, 593–607. (a)

Quattrone, G. A., & Jones, E. E. (1980). The perception of variability within in-groups and out-groups. Implications for the law of small numbers. *Journal of Personality and Social Psychology*, 38, 141–152.

Radecki, T. (1989, February–March). On picking good television and film entertainment. *NCTV NEWS*, 10(1–2), pp. 5–6.

Ramirez, A. (1988). Racism toward Hispanics: The culturally monolithic society. In P. A. Katz & D. A. Taylor (Eds.) *Eliminating racism: Profiles in controversy*. New York: Plenum.

Rank, S. G., & Jacobson, C. K. (1977). Hospital nurses' compliance with medication overdose orders: A failure to replicate. *Journal of Health and Social Behavior*, 18, 188–193.

Rapapart, K., & Burkhart, B. R. (1984). Personality and attitudinal characteristics of sexually coercive college males. *Journal of Abnormal Psychology*, 93, 216–221.

Rapoport, A. (1980). *Fights, games, and debates*. Ann Arbor: University of Michigan Press.

RCAgenda (1979). November-December, p. 11. 475 Riverside Drive, New York, N.Y. 10027.

Reeder, G. D., McCormick, C. B., & Esselman, E. D. (1987). Self-reference processing and recall of prose. *Journal of Educational Psychology*, 79, 243–248.

Regan, D. T., & Cheng, J. B. (1973). Distraction and attitude change: A resolution. *Journal of Experimental Social Psychology*, 9, 138–147.

Regan, D. T., & Fazio, R. (1977). On the consistency between attitudes and behavior: Look to the method of attitude formation. *Journal of Experimental Social Psychology*, **13**, 28–45.

Regan, D. T., Williams, M., & Sparling, S. (1972). Voluntary expiation of guilt: A field experiment. *Journal of Personality and Social Psychology*, **24**, 42–45.

Reichner, R. F. (1979). Differential responses to being ignored: The effects of architectural design and social density on interpersonal behavior. *Journal of Applied Social Psychology*, **9**, 13–26.

Reifman, A. S., Larrick, R., & Fein, S. (1988). The heat-aggression relationship in major-league baseball. Paper presented at the American Psychological Association convention.

Reilly, M. E. (1978). A case study of role conflict: Roman Catholic priests. *Human Relations*, **31**, 77–90.

Reis, H. T., Nezlek, J., & Wheeler, L. (1980). Physical attractiveness in social interaction. *Journal of Personality and Social Psychology*, **38**, 604–617.

Reis, H. T., Senchak, M., & Solomon, B. (1985). Sex differences in the intimacy of social interaction: Further examination of potential explanations. *Journal of Personality and Social Psychology*, **48**, 1204–1217.

Reis, H. T., & Shaver, P. (1988). Intimacy as an interpersonal process. In S. Duck (Ed.), *Handbook of personal relationships: Theory, relationships and interventions*. Chichester, England: Wiley.

Reis, H. T., Wheeler, L., Spiegel, N., Kernis, M. H., Nezlek, J., & Perri, M. (1982). Physical attractiveness in social interaction: II. Why does appearance affect social experience? *Journal of Personality and Social Psychology*, **43**, 979–996.

Reisenzein, R. (1983). The Schacter theory of emotion: Two decades later. *Psychological Bulletin*, **94**, 239–264.

Reitzes, D. C. (1953). The role of organizational structures: Union versus neighborhood in a tension situation. *Journal of Social Issues*, **9**(1), 37–44.

Remley, A. (1988, October). From obedience to independence. *Psychology Today*, pp. 56–59.

Renaud, H., & Estess, F. (1961). Life history interviews with one hundred normal American males: "Pathogenecity" of childhood. *American Journal of Orthopsychiatry*, **31**, 786–802.

Reston, J. (1975, March 14). Proxmire on love. *New York Times*.

Reychler, L. (1979). The effectiveness of a pacifist strategy in conflict resolution. *Journal of Conflict Resolution*, **23**, 228–260.

Reyes, R. M., Thompson, W. C., & Bower, G. H. (1980). Judgmental biases resulting from differing availabilities on arguments.

Journal of Personality and Social Psychology, **39**, 2–12.

Rhine, R. J., & Severance, L. J. (1970). Ego-involvement, discrepancy, source credibility, and attitude change. *Journal of Personality and Social Psychology*, **16**, 175–190.

Rhodewalt, F. (1987). Is self-handicapping an effective self-protective attributional strategy? Paper presented at the American Psychological Association convention.

Rhodewalt, F., & Agustsdottir, S. (1986). Effects of self-presentation on the phenomenal self. *Journal of Personality and Social Psychology*, **50**, 47–55.

Rhodewalt, F., Saltzman, A. T., & Wittmer J. (1984). Self-handicapping among competitive athletes: The role of practice in self-esteem protection. *Basic and Applied Social Psychology*, **5**, 197–209.

Rholes, F. H., Jr. (1981). Thermal comfort and strategies for energy conservation. *Journal of Social Issues*, **37**(2), 132–149.

Rholes, W. S., Riskind, J. H., & Neville, B. (1985). The relationship of cognitions and hopelessness to depression and anxiety. *Social Cognition*, **3**, 36–50.

Rianoshek, R. (1980). A comment on Sampson's psychology and the American ideal. *Journal of Personality and Social Psychology*, **38**, 105–107.

Rice, B. (1985, September). Performance review: The job nobody likes. *Psychology Today*, pp. 30–36.

Rice, M. E., & Grusec, J. E. (1975). Saying and doing: Effects on observer performance. *Journal of Personality and Social Psychology*, **32**, 584–593.

Richardson, J. T. (1985). Psychological and psychiatric studies of new religions. In L. B. Brown (Eds.), *Advances in the Psychology of Religion*. Oxford: Pergamon Press.

Richardson, L. F. (1960). Generalized foreign policy. *British Journal of Psychology Monographs Supplements*, 1969, **23**. Cited by A. Rapoport in *Fights, games, and debates*. Ann Arbor: University of Michigan Press, p. 15.

Riess, M., Rosenfeld, P., Melburg, V., & Tedeschi, J. T. (1981). Self-serving attributions: Biased private perceptions and distorted public descriptions. *Journal of Personality and Social Psychology*, **41**, 224–231.

Riggio, R. E., & Woll, S. B. (1984). The role of nonverbal cues and physical attractiveness in the selection of dating partners. *Journal of Social and Personal Relationships*, **1**, 347–357.

Riggs, J. M., & Cantor, N. (1984). Getting acquainted: The role of the self-concept and preconceptions. *Personality and Social Psychology Bulletin*, **10**, 432–445.

Riordan, C. A. (1980). Effects of admission of influence on attributions and attraction. Paper presented at the American Psychological Association convention.

Riordan, C. A., & Ruggiero, J. (1980). Producing equal status interracial interaction: A replication. *Social Psychology Quarterly*, **43**, 131–136.

Robberson, M. R., & Rogers, R. W. (1988). Beyond fear appeals: Negative and positive persuasive appeals to health and self-esteem. *Journal of Applied Social Psychology*, **18**, 277–287.

Robertson, I. (1987). *Sociology*. New York: Worth Publishers.

Robinson, C. L., Lockard, J. S., & Adams, R. M. (1979). Who looks at a baby in public. *Ethology and Sociobiology*, **1**, 87–91.

Robinson, J. P. (1988, December). Who's doing the housework? *American Demographics*, pp. 24–28, 63.

Rodin, J., & Langer, E. J. (1977). Long-term effects of a control-relevant intervention with the institutionalized age. *Journal of Personality and Social Psychology*, **35**, 897–902.

Rogers, C. R. (1958). Reinhold Niebuhr's *The self and the dramas of history: A criticism. Pastoral Psychology*, **9**, 15–17.

Rogers, R. W., & Mewborn, C. R. (1976). Fear appeals and attitude change: Effects of a threat's noxiousness, probability of occurrence, and the efficacy of coping responses. *Journal of Personality and Social Psychology*, **34**, 54–61.

Rogers, R. W., & Prentice-Dunn, S. (1981). Deindividuation and anger-mediated interracial aggression: Unmasking regressive racism. *Journal of Personality and Social Psychology*, **41**, 63–73.

Rohrer, J. H., Baron, S. H., Hoffman, E. L., & Swander, D. V. (1954). The stability of autokinetic judgments. *Journal of Abnormal and Social Psychology*, **49**, 595–597.

Rokeach, M. (1968). *Beliefs, attitudes, and values*. San Francisco: Jossey-Bass.

Rokeach, M., & Mezei, L. (1966). Race and shared beliefs as factors in social choice. *Science*, **151**, 167–172.

Romer, D., Gruder, C. L., & Lizzadro, T. (1986). A person-situation approach to altruistic behavior. *Journal of Personality and Social Psychology*, **51**, 1001–1012.

Rook, K. S. (1984). Promoting social bonding: Strategies for helping the lonely and socially isolated. *American Psychologist*, **39**, 1389–1407.

Root, L. (1980, November 5). Designers modify the open house to meet complaints of workers. *Wall Street Journal*, p. 29.

Roper Organization (1985). *The 1985 Virginia Slims American Women's Opinion Poll.* Storrs, Ct.: The Roper Organization.

Rosenbaum, M. E. (1986). The repulsion hypothesis: On the nondevelopment of relationships. *Journal of Personality and Social Psychology*, **51**, 1156–1166.

Rosenbaum, M. E., & Holtz, R. (1985). The minimal intergroup discrimination effect: Outgroup derogation, not in-group favorability. Paper presented at the American Psychological Association convention.

Rosenberg, L. A. (1961). Group size, prior experience and conformity. *Journal of Abnormal and Social Psychology*, **63**, 436–437.

Rosenblatt, A., & Greenberg, J. (1988). Depression and interpersonal attraction: The role of perceived similarity. *Journal of Personality and Social Psychology*, **55**, 112–119.

Rosenfeld, D. (1979). The relationship between self-esteem and egotism in males and females. Unpublished manuscript, Southern Methodist University.

Rosenfeld, D., Folger, R., & Adelman, H. F. (1980). When rewards reflect competence: A qualification of the overjustification effect. *Journal of Personality and Social Psychology*, **39**, 368–376.

Rosenhan, D. L. (1970). The natural socialization of altruistic autonomy. In J. Macaulay & L. Berkowitz (Eds.) *Altruism and helping behavior.* New York: Academic Press.

Rosenhan, D. L. (1973). On being sane in insane places. *Science*, **179**, 250–258.

Rosenkrantz, P. S., Vogel, S. R., Bee, H., Broverman, I. K., & Broverman, D. M. (1968). Sex-role stereotypes and self-concepts in college students. *Journal of Consulting and Clinical Psychology*, **32**, 287–295.

Rosenthal, R. (1985). From unconscious experimenter bias to teacher expectancy effects. In J. B. Dusek, V. C. Hall, & W. J. Meyer (Eds.), *Teacher expectancies.* Hillsdale, N. J.: Erlbaum.

Rosenthal, R. (1987, December). Pygmalion effects: Existence, magnitude, and social importance. *Educational Researcher*, pp. 37–41.

Rosenthal, R., & Jacobson, L. (1968). *Pygmalion in the classroom: Teacher expectation and pupils' intellectual development.* New York: Holt, Rinehart & Winston.

Rosenthal, R., & Rubin, D. B. (1978). Interpersonal expectancy effects: The first 345 studies. *Behavioral and Brain Science*, **2**, 377–415.

Rosenzweig, M. R. (1972). Cognitive dissonance. *American Psychologist*, **27**, 769.

Rosewicz, B. (1983, January 31). Study finds grim link between liquor, crime. *Detroit Free Press*, pp. 1A, 4A.

Ross, C. (1979, February 12). Rejected. *New West*, pp. 39–43.

Ross, L. D. (1977). The intuitive psychologist and his shortcomings: Distortions in the attribution process. In L. Berkowitz (Ed.), *Advances in experimental social psychology* (Vol. 10). New York: Academic Press.

Ross, L. D. (1981). The "intuitive scientist" formulation and its developmental implications. In J. H. Havell & L. Ross (Eds.), *Social cognitive development: Frontiers and possible futures.* Cambridge, England: Cambridge University Press.

Ross, L. D. (1988). Situationist perspectives on the obedience experiments. Review of A. G. Miller's *The obedience experiments. Contemporary Psychology*, **33**, 101–104.

Ross, L. D., Amabile, T. M., & Steinmetz, J. L. (1977). Social roles, social control, and biases in social-perception processes. *Journal of Personality and Social Psychology*, **35**, 485–494.

Ross, L. D., & Anderson, C. A. (1982). Shortcomings in the attribution process: On the origins and maintenance of erroneous social assessments. In D. Kahneman, P. Slovic, & A. Tversky (Eds.), *Judgment under uncertainty: Heuristics and biases.* New York: Cambridge University Press.

Ross, L. D., & Lepper, M. R. (1980). The perseverance of beliefs: Empirical and normative considerations. In R. A. Shweder (Ed.), *New directions for methodology of behavioral science: Fallible judgment in behavioral research.* San Francisco: Jossey-Bass.

Ross, L. D., Lepper, M. R., Strack, F., & Steinmetz, J. (1977). Social explanation and social expectation: Effects of real and hypothetical explanations on subjective likelihood. *Journal of Personality and Social Psychology*, **35**, 817–829.

Ross, L. D., Turiel, E., Josephson, J., & Lepper, M. R. (1978). Developmental perspectives on the fundamental attribution error. Unpublished manuscript, Stanford University.

Ross, M., & Fletcher, G. J. O. (1985). Attribution and social perception. In G. Lindzey & E. Aronson (Eds.), *The Handbook of Social Psychology*, 3rd ed. New York: Random House.

Ross, M., McFarland, C., & Fletcher, G. J. O. (1981). The effect of attitude on the recall of personal histories. *Journal of Personality and Social Psychology*, **40**, 627–634.

Ross, M., & Sicoly, F. (1979). Egocentric biases in availability and attribution. *Journal of Personality and Social Psychology*, **37**, 322–336.

Ross, M., Thibaut, J., & Evenbeck, S. (1971). Some determinants of the intensity of social protest. *Journal of Experimental Social Psychology*, **7**, 401–418.

Rossi, A. (1978, June). The biosocial side of parenthood. *Human Nature*, pp. 72–79.

Roth, D. L., Snyder, C. R., & Pace, L. M. (1986). Dimensions of favorable self-presentation. *Journal of Personality and Social Psychology*, **51**, 867–874.

Rothbart, M., & Birrell, P. (1977). Attitude and the perception of faces. *Journal of Research Personality*, **11**, 209–215.

Rothbart, M., Fulero, S., Jensen, C., Howard, J., & Birrell, P. (1978). From individual to group impressions: Availability heuristics in stereotype formation. *Journal of Experimental Social Psychology*, **14**, 237–255.

Rothbark, M., & Hallmark, W. (1988). Ingroup-out-group differences in the perceived efficacy of coercion and conciliation in resolving social conflict. *Journal of Personality and Social Psychology*, **55**, 248–257.

Rothbart, M., & John, O. P. (1985). Social categorization and behavioral episodes: A cognitive analysis of the effects of intergroup contact. *Journal of Social Issues*, **41**(3), 81–104.

Rothbart, M., & Lewis, S. (1988). Inferring category attributes from exemplar attributes: Geometric shapes and social categories. *Journal of Personality and Social Psychology*, **55**, 861–872.

Rothbart, M., & Park, B. (1986). On the confirmability and disconfirmability of trait concepts. *Journal of Personality and Social Psychology*, **50**, 131–142.

Rotter, J. (1973). Internal-external locus of control scale. In J. P. Robinson & R. P. Shaver (Eds.), *Measures of social psychological attitudes.* Ann Arbor: Institute for Social Research.

Rotton, J., & Frey, J. (1985). Air pollution, weather, and violent crimes: Concomitant time-series analysis of archival data. *Journal of Personality and Social Psychology*, **49**, 1207–1220.

Rowe, D. (1986). Letter. *Bulletin of the British Psychological Society*, **39**, 425–426.

Ruback, R. B., Carr, T. S., & Hoper, C. H. (1986). Perceived control in prison: Its relation to reported crowding, stress, and symptoms. *Journal of Applied Social Psychology*, **16**, 375–386.

Rubin, J. Z. (1980). Experimental research on third-party intervention in conflict: Toward some generalizations. *Psychological Bulletin*, **87**, 379–391.

Rubin, J. Z. (Ed.) (1981). *Third party interven-*

tion in conflict: Kissinger in the Middle East. New York: Praeger.

Rubin, J. Z. (1986). Can we negotiate with terrorists: Some answers from psychology. Paper presented at the American Psychological Association convention.

Rubin, J. Z. (1989). Some wise and mistaken assumptions about conflict and negotiation. *Journal of Social Issues,* in press.

Rubin, R. B. (1981). Ideal traits and terms of address for male and female college professors. *Journal of Personality and Social Psychology,* 41, 966–974.

Rubin, Z. (1970). Measurement of romantic love. *Journal of Personality and Social Psychology,* 16, 265–273.

Rubin, Z. (1973). *Liking and loving: An invitation to social psychology.* New York: Holt, Rinehart and Winston.

Ruble, D. N., Feldman, S. N., Higgins, E. T., & Karlovac, M. (1979). Locus of causality and the use of information in the development of causal attribtuions. *Journal of Personality,* 47, 595–614.

Ruble, D. N., Fleming, A. S., Hackel, L. S., & Stangor, C. (1988). Changes in the marital relationship during the transition to first-time motherhood: Effects of violated expectations concerning division of household labor. *Journal of Personality and Social Psychology,* 55, 78–87.

Ruff, C., Associates (1980, June 2). The office the 80's: Designing for people and productivity. *Fortune* (unnumbered insert).

Rule, B. G., & Ferguson, T. J. (1986). The effects of media violence on attitudes, emotions, and cognitions. *Journal of Social Issues,* 42(3), 29–50.

Rule, B. G., Taylor, B. R., & Dobbs, A. R. (1987). Priming effects of heat on aggressive thoughts. *Social Cognition,* 5, 131–143.

Rusbult, C. E., Johnson, D. J., & Morrow, G. D. (1986). Impact of couple patterns of problem solving on distress and nondistress in dating relationships. *Journal of Personality and Social Psychology,* 50, 744–753.

Rusbult, C. E. (1980). Commitment and satisfaction in romantic associations: A test of the investment model. *Journal of Experimental Social Psychology,* 16, 172–186.

Rusbult, C. E., Morrow, G. D., & Johnson, D. J. (1987). Self-esteem and problem-solving behaviour in close relationships. *British Journal of Social Psychology,* 26, 293–303.

Rushton, J. P. (1975). Generosity in children: Immediate and long-term effects of modeling, preaching, and moral judgment. *Journal of Personality and Social Psychology,* 31, 459–466.

Rushton, J. P. (1976). Socialization and the altruistic behavior of children. *Psychological Bulletin,* 83, 898–913.

Rushton, J. P. (1979). The effects of prosocial television and film material on the behavior of viewers. In L. Berkowitz (Ed.), *Advances in experimental social psychology* (Vol. 12). New York: Academic Press.

Rushton, J. P. (1980). *Altruism, socialization, and society.* Englewood Cliffs, N.J.: Prentice-Hall.

Rushton, J. P., Brainerd, C. J., & Pressley, M. (1983). Behavioral development and construct validity: The principle of aggregation. *Psychological Bulletin,* 94, 18–38.

Rushton, J. P., & Campbell, A. C. (1977). Modeling, vicarious reinforcement and extraversion on blood donating in adults: Immediate and long-term effects. *European Journal of Social Psychology,* 7, 297–306.

Rushton, J. P., Chrisjohn, R. D., & Fekken, G. C. (1981). The altruistic personality and the self-report altruism scale. *Personality and Individual Differences,* 2, 293–302.

Rushton, J. P., Fulker, D. W., Neale, M. C., Nias, D. K. B., & Eysenck, H. J. (1986). Altruism and aggression: The heritability of individual differences. *Journal of Personality and Social Psychology,* 50, 1192–1198.

Rushton, J. P., Russell, R. J. H., & Wells, P. A. (1984). Genetic similarity theory: Beyond kin selection. *Behavior Genetics,* 14, 179–193.

Russell, B. (1930/1980). *The conquest of happiness.* London: Unwin Paperbacks.

Russell, D. E. H. (1984). *Sexual exploitation: Rape, child sexual abuse, and workplace harassment.* Beverly Hills, Ca.: Sage.

Russell, G. W. (1983). Psychological issues in sports aggression. In J. H. Goldstein (Ed.), *Sports violence.* New York: Springer-Verlag.

Russell, G. W. (1985). Spectator moods at an aggressive sports event. *Journal of Sport Psychology,* 3, 217–227.

Rutkowski, G. K., Gruder, C. L., & Romer, D. (1983). Group cohesiveness, social norms, and bystander intervention. *Journal of Personality and Social Psychology,* 44, 545–552.

Ruzzene, M., & Noller. P. (1986). Feedback motivation and reactions to personality interpretations that differ in favorability and accuracy. *Journal of Personality and Social Psychology,* 51, 1293–1299.

Sabini, J., & Silver, M. (1982). *Moralities of everyday life.* New York: Oxford University Press.

Sacks, C. H., & Bugental, D. P. (1987). Attributions as moderators of affective and behav-

ioral responses to social failure. *Journal of Personality and Social Psychology,* 53, 939–947.

Sadalla, E. K., Kenrick, D. T., & Vershure, B. (1987). Dominance and heterosexual attraction. *Journal of Personality and Social Psychology,* 52, 730–738.

Sagar, H. A., & Schofield, J. W. (1980). Integrating the desegregated school: Perspectives, practices and possibilities. In M. Wax (Ed.), *Comparative studies in interracial education.* Washington, D.C.: Government Printing Office. (a)

Sagar, H. A., & Schofield, J. W. (1980). Race and gender barriers: Preadolescent peer behavior in academic classrooms. Paper presented at the American Psychological Association convention. (b)

Sagar, H. A., & Schofield, J. W. (1980). Racial and behavioral cues in black and white children's perceptions of ambiguously aggressive acts. *Journal of Personality and Social Psychology,* 39, 590–598. (c)

Saks, M. J. (1974). Ignorance of science is no excuse. *Trial,* 10(6) 18–20.

Saks, M. J. (1977). *Jury verdicts.* Lexington, Mass.: Heath.

Saks, M. J., & Hastie, R. (1978). *Social psychology in court.* New York: Van Nostrand Reinhold.

Sakurai, M. M. (1975). Small group cohesiveness and detrimental conformity. *Sociometry,* 38, 340–357.

Sales, S. M. (1972). Economic threat as a determinant of conversion rates in authoritarian and nonauthoritarian churches. *Journal of Personality and Social Psychology,* 23, 420–428.

Saltzstein, H. D., & Sandberg, L. (1979). Indirect social influence: Change in judgmental processor anticipatory conformity. *Journal of Experimental Social Psychology,* 15, 209–216.

Sampson, E. E. (1975). On justice as equality. *Journal of Social Issues,* 31(3). 45–64.

Sampson, E. E. (1977). Psychology and the American ideal. *Journal of Personality and Social Psychology,* 35, 767–782.

Samuelson, C. D., Messick, D. M., Rutte, C. G., & Wilke, H. (1984). Individual and structural solutions to resource dilemmas in two cultures. *Journal of Personality and Social Psychology,* 47, 94–104.

Sandberg, G. G., Jackson, T. L., & Petretic-Jackson, P. (1985). Sexual aggression and courtship violence in dating relationships. Paper presented at the Midwestern Psychological Association convention.

Sande, G. N., Goethals, G. R., & Radloff, C. E. (1988). Perceiving one's own traits and others': The multifaceted self. *Journal of Personality and Social Psychology*, **54**, 13–20.

Sanders, G. S. (1981). Driven by distraction: An integrative review of social facilitation and theory and research. *Journal of Experimental Social Psychology*, **17**, 227–251 (a)

Sanders, G. S. (1981). Toward a comprehensive account of social facilitation: Distraction/conflict does not mean theoretical conflict. *Journal of Experimental Social Psychology*, **17**, 262–265. (b)

Sanders, G. S., & Baron, R. S. (1975). The motivating effects of distraction on task performance. *Journal of Personality and Social Psychology*, **32**, 956–963.

Sanders, G. S., & Baron, R. S. (1977). Is social comparison irrelevant for producing choice shifts? *Journal of Experimental Social Psychology*, **13**, 303–314.

Sanders, G. S., Baron, R. S., & Moore, D. L. (1978). Distraction and social comparison as mediators of social facilitation effects. *Journal of Experimental Social Psychology*, **14**, 291–303.

Sanders, G. S., & Chiu, W. (1988). Eyewitness errors in the free recall of actions. *Journal of Applied Social Psychology*, **18**, 1241–1259.

Sansone, C. (1986). A question of competence: The effects of competence and task feedback on intrinsic interest. *Journal of Personality and Social Psychology*, **51**, 918–931.

Sapadin, L. A. (1988). Friendship and gender: Perspectives of professional men and women. *Journal of Social and Personal Relationships*, **5**, 387–403.

Sasfy, J., & Okun, M. (1974). Form of evaluation and audience expertness as joint determinants of audience effects. *Journal of Experimental Social Psychology*, **10**, 461–467.

Sato, K. (1987). Distribution of the cost of maintaining common resources. *Journal of Experimental Social Psychology*, **23**, 19–31.

Sawyer, J. (1966). Measurement *and* prediction, clinical *and* statistical. *Psychological Bulletin*, **66**, 178–200.

Schachter, S. (1951). Deviation, rejection and communication. *Journal of Abnormal and Social Psychology*, **46**, 190–207.

Schachter, S., & Singer, J. E. (1962). Cognitive, social and physiological determinants of emotional state. *Psychological Review*, **69**, 379–399.

Schafer, R. B., & Keith, P. M. (1980). Equity and depression among married couples. *Social Psychology Quarterly*, **43**, 430–435.

Schaffner, P. E. (1985). Specious learning about reward and punishment. *Journal of Personality and Social Psychology*, **48**, 1377–1386.

Schaffner, P. E., Wandersman, A., & Stang, D. (1981). Candidate name exposure and voting: Two field studies. *Basic and Applied Social Psychology*, **2**, 195–203.

Schaller, M., & Cialdini, R. B. (1988). The economics of empathic helping: Support for a mood management motive. *Journal of Experimental Social Psychology*, **24**, 163–181.

Scheier, M. F., & Carver, C. S. (1987). Dispositional optimism and physical well-being: The influence of generalized outcome expectancies on health. *Journal of Personality*, **55**, 169–210.

Scheier, M. F., & Carver, C. S. (1988). A model of behavioral self-regulation: Translating intention into action. In L. Berkowitz (Ed.), *Advances in Experimental Social Psychology*, Vol. 21. San Diego, Ca.: Academic Press.

Schein, E. H. (1956). The Chinese indoctrination program for prisoners of war: A study of attempted brainwashing. *Psychiatry*, **19**, 149–172.

Schiffenbauer, A., & Schiavo, R. S. (1976). Physical distance and attraction: An intensification effect. *Journal of Experimental Social Psychology*, **12**, 274–282.

Schlenker, B. R. (1976). Egocentric perceptions in cooperative groups: A conceptualization and research review. Final Report, Office of Naval Research Grant NR 170–797.

Schlenker, B. R. (1980). *Impression Management: The self-concept, social identity, and interpersonal relations:* Belmont, Calif.: Brooks/Cole.

Schlenker, B. R. (1985). Introduction: Foundations of the self in social life. In B. R. Schlenker (Ed.), *The self and social life*. New York: McGraw-Hill.

Schlenker, B. R. (1986). Self-identification: Toward an integration of the private and public self. In R. Baumeister (Ed.), *Public self and private self*. New York: Springer-Verlag.

Schlenker, B. R. (1987). Threats to identity: Self-identification and social stress. In C. R. Snyder & C. E. Ford (Eds.), *Coping with negative life events: Clinical and social psychological perspectives*. New York: Plenum Press.

Schlenker, B. R., & Forsyth, D. R. (1977). On the ethics of psychological research. *Journal of Experimental Social Psychology*, **13**, 369–396.

Schlenker, B. R., & Leary, M. R. (1982). Audiences' reactions to self-enhancing, self-denigrating, and accurate self-presentations. *Journal of Experimental Social Psychology*, **18**, 89–104. (a)

Schlenker, B. R., & Leary, M. R. (1982). Social anxiety and self-presentation: A conceptualization and model. *Psychological Bulletin*, **92**, 641–669. (b)

Schlenker, B. R., & Leary, M. R. (1985). Social anxiety and communication about the self. *Journal of Language and Social Psychology*, **4**, 171–192.

Schlenker, B. R., & Miller, R. S. (1977). Group cohesiveness as a determinant of egocentric perceptions in cooperative groups. *Human Relations*, **30**, 1039–1055. (a)

Schlenker, B. R., & Miller, R. S. (1977). Egocentrism in groups: Self-serving biases or logical information processing? *Journal of Personality and Social Psychology*, **35**, 755–764. (b)

Schlenker, B. R., Miller, R. S., Leary, M. R., & McGown, N. E. (1979). Group performance and interpersonal evaluations as determinants of egotistical attributions in groups. *Journal of Personality*, **47**, 575–594.

Schlesinger, A. M., Jr. (1972). *A thousand days*. Boston: Houghton Mifflin, 1965. Cited by I. L. Janis in *Victims of groupthink*. Boston: Houghton Mifflin, p. 40.

Schofield, J. (1982). *Black and white in school: Trust, tension, or tolerance?* New York: Praeger.

Schofield, J., & Pavelchak, M. (1985). The day after: The impact of a media event. *American Psychologist*, **40**, 542–548.

Schofield, J. W. (1986). Causes and consequences of the colorblind perspective. In J. F. Dovidio & S. L. Gaertner (Eds.), *Prejudice, discrimination, and racism*. Orlando, Fl.: Academic Press.

Schooler, J. W., Gerhard, D., & Loftus, E. F. (1986). Qualities of the unreal. *Journal of Experimental Psychology: Learning, Memory, and Cognition*, **12**, 171–181.

Schroeder, D. A., Dovidio, J. F., Sibicky, M. E., Matthews, L. L., & Allen, J. L. (1988). Empathic concern and helping behavior: Egoism or altruism: *Journal of Experimental Social Psychology*, **24**, 333–353.

Schulz, J. W., & Pruitt, D. G. (1978). The effects of mutual concern on joint welfare. *Journal of Experimental Social Psychology*, **14**, 480–492.

Schulz, R., & Decker, S. (1985). Long-term adjustment to physical disability: The role of social support, perceived control, and self-blame. *Journal of Personality and Social Psychology*, **48**, 1162–1172.

Schuman, H., & Kalton, G. (1985). Survey methods. In G. Lindzey & E. Aronson (Eds.), *Handbook of Social Psychology*, Vol. 1. Hillsdale, N.J.: Erlbaum.

Schuman, H., & Ludwig, J. (1983). The norm of even-handedness in surveys as in life. *American Sociological Review*, **48**, 112–120.

Schuman, H., & Scott, J. (1987). Problems in the use of survey questions to measure public opinion. *Science*, **236**, 957–959.

Schutte, N. S., Malouff, J. M., Post-Gorden, J. C., & Rodasta, A. L. (1988). Effects of playing videogames on children's aggressive and other behaviors. *Journal of Applied Social Psychology*, **18**, 454–460.

Schwarz, N., Strack, F., Kommer, D., & Wagner, D. (1987). Soccer, rooms, and the quality of your life: Mood effects on judgments of satisfaction with life in general and with specific domains. *European Journal of Social Psychology*, **17**, 69–79.

Schwartz, S. H. (1975). The justice of need and the activation of humanitarian norms. *Journal of Social Issues*, **31**(3), 111–136.

Schwartz, S. H., & Ames, R. E. (1977). Positive and negative referent others as source of influence: A case of helping. *Sociometry*, **40**, 12–21.

Schwartz, S. H., & Gottlieb, A. (1981). Participants' post-experimental reactions and the ethics of bystander research. *Journal of Experimental Social Psychology*, **17**, 396–407.

Schwarzwald, J., Bizman, A., & Raz, M. (1983). The foot-in-the-door paradigm: Effects of second request size on donation probability and donor generosity. *Personality and Social Psychology Bulletin*, **9**, 443–450.

Schwebel, A. I., & Cherlin, D. L. (1972). Physical and social distance in teacher-pupil relationships. *Journal of Educational Psychology*, **63**, 543–550.

Scott, J. P., & Marston, M. V. (1953). Nonadaptive behavior resulting from a series of defeats in fighting mice. *Journal of Abnormal and Social Psychology*, **48**, 417–428.

Sears, D. O. (1979). Life stage effects upon attitude change, especially among the elderly. Manuscript prepared for Workshop on the Elderly of the Future, Committee on Aging, National Research Council, Annapolis, Md., May 3–5.

Sears, D. O. (1986). College sophomores in the laboratory: Influences of a narrow data base on social psychology's view of human nature. *Journal of Personality and Social Psychology*, **51**, 515–530.

Sears, D. O., Hensler, C. P., & Speer, L. K. (1979). Whites' opposition to "busing": Self-interest or symbolic politics? *American Political Science Review*, **73**, 369–384.

Seaver, W. B., & Patterson, A. H. (1976). Decreasing fuel-oil consumption through feedback and social commendation. *Journal of Applied Behavior Analysis*, **9**, 147–152.

Seber, R., & Crocker, J. (1983). Cognitive processes in the revision of stereotypic beliefs.

Journal of Personality and Social Psychology, **45**, 961–977.

Segal, H. A. (1954). Initial psychiatric findings of recently repatriated prisoners of war. *American Journal of Psychiatry*, **61**, 358–363.

Segal, N. L. (1984). Cooperation, competition, and altruism within twin sets: A reappraisal. *Ethology and Sociobiology*, **5**, 163–177.

Selby, J. W., Calhoun, L. G., & Brock, T. A. (1977). Sex differences in the social perception of rape victims. *Personality and Social Psychology Bulletin*, **3**, 412–415.

Seligman, C., Fazio, R. H., Zanna, M. P. (1980). Effects of salience of extrinsic rewards on liking and loving. *Journal of Personality and Social Psychology*, **38**, 453–460.

Seligman, M. E. P. (1975). *Helplessness: On depression, development and death.* San Francisco: W. H. Freeman.

Seligman, M. E. P. (1977, May). Submissive death: Giving up on life. *Psychology Today*, pp. 80–85.

Seligman, M. E. P. (1988). Why is there so much depression today? The waxing of the individual and the waning of the commons. The G. Stanely Hall Lecture, American Psychological Association convention.

Seligman, M. E. P., & Schulman, P. (1986). Explanatory style as a predictor of productivity and quitting among life insurance sales agents. *Journal of Personality and Social Psychology*, **50**, 832–838.

Seligman, M. E. P., & Visintainer, M. A. (1985). Tumor rejection and early experience of uncontrollable shock in the rat. In F. R. Brush & J. B. Overmier (Eds.), *Affect, conditioning, and cognition: Essays on the determinants of behavior.* Hillsdale, N.J.: Erlbaum.

Seltzer, L. F. (1983). Influencing the "shape" of resistance: An experimental exploration of paradoxical directives and psychological reactance. *Basic and Applied Social Psychology*, **4**, 47–71.

Seta, J. J. (1982). The impact of comparison processes on coactors' task performance. *Journal of Personality and Social Psychology*, **42**, 281–291.

Sethi, A. S., & Bala, N. (1983). Relationship between sex-role orientation and self-esteem in Indian college of females. *Psychologia*, **23**, 124–127.

Shakespeare, W. *A midsummer night's dream.* Act II, Scene 2, 1. 115.

Ssaran, S. & Sharan, Y. (1976). *Small group teaching.* Englewood Cliffs, N.J.: Educational Technology.

Sharma, N. (1981). Some aspect of attitude and

behaviour of mothers. *Indian Psychological Review*, **20**, 35–42.

Shaver, P., Hazan, C., & Bradshaw, D. (1988). Love as attachment: The integration of three behavioral systems. In R. J. Sternberg & M. L. Barnes (Eds.), *The psychology of love.* New Haven: Yale University Press.

Shavit, H., & Shouval, R. (1980). Self-esteem and cognitive consistency effects on self-other evaluation. *Journal of Experimental Social Psychology*, **16**, 417–425.

Shaw, G. B. (1977). The quintessence of Ibsenism. In D. H. Lawrence (Ed.), *Selected nondramatic writings of Bernard Shaw.* Boston: Houghton Mifflin (undated). Cited by C. Tavris & C. Offir in *The longest war: Sex differences in perspective.* New York: Harcourt Brace Jovanovich.

Shaw, M. E. (1981). *Group dynamics: The psychology of small group behavior.* New York: McGraw-Hill.

Sheppard, B. H., & Vidmar, N. (1980). Adversary pretrial procedures and testimonial evidence: Effects of lawyer's role and machiavellianism. *Journal of Personality and Social Psychology*, **39**, 320–322.

Sherif, M. (1937). An experimental approach to the study of attitudes. *Sociometry*, **1**, 90–98.

Sherif, M. (1966). *In common predicament: Social psychology of intergroup conflict and cooperation.* Boston: Houghton Mifflin.

Sherif, M., & Sherif, C. W. (1969). *Social psychology.* New York: Harper & Row.

Sherman, S. J. (1980). On the self-erasing nature of errors of prediction. *Journal of Personality of Social Psychology*, **39**, 211–221.

Sherman, S. J., Cialdini, R. B., Schwartzman, D. F., & Reynolds, K. D. (1985). Imagining can heighten or lower the perceived likelihood of contracting a disease: The mediating effect of ease of imagery. *Personality and Social Psychology Bulletin*, **11**, 118–127.

Sherman, S. J., & Fazio, R. H. (1983). Parallels between attitudes and traits as predictors of behavior. *Journal of Personality*, **51**, 308–345.

Sherman, S. J., & Gorkin, L. (1980). Attitude bolstering when behavior is inconsistent with central attitudes. *Journal of Experimental Social Psychology*, **16**, 388–403.

Sherman, S. J., Presson, C. C., Chassin, L., Bensenberg, M., Corty, E., & Olshavsky, R. (1983). Smoking intentions in adolescents: Direct experience and predictability. *Personality and Social Psychology Bulletin*, **8**, 376–383.

Short, J. F., Jr. (Ed.) (1969). *Gang delinquency and delinquent subcultures.* New York: Harper & Row.

Shotland, R. L. (1989). A model of the causes of date rape in developing and close relationships. In C. Hendrick (Ed.), *Review of Personality and Social Psychology*, Vol. 10. Beverly Hills; Sage.

Shotland, R. L., & Craig, J. M. (1988). Can men and women differentiate between friendly and sexually interested behavior? *Social Psychology Quarterly*, **51**, 67–73.

Shotland, R. L., & Straw, M. K. (1976). Bystander response to an assault: When a man attacks a woman. *Journal of Personality Social Psychology*, **34**, 990–999.

Shotland, R. L., & Stebbins, C. A. (1983). Emergency and cost as determinants of helping behavior and the slow accumulation of social psychological knowledge. *Social Psychology Quarterly*, **46**, 36–46.

Shouval, R., Venaki, S. K., Bronfenbrenner, U., Devereus, E. C., & Kiely, E. (1975). Anomalous reactions to social pressure of Israeli and Soviet children raised in family versus collective settings. *Journal of Personality and Social Psychology*, **32**, 477–489.

Showers, C., & Ruben, C. (1987). Distinguishing pessimism from depression: Negative expectations and positive coping mechanisms. Paper presented at the American Psychological Association convention.

Shrauger, J. S. (1975). Responses to evaluation as a function of initial self-perceptions. *Psychological Bulletin*, **82**, 581–596.

Shrauger, J. S. (1983). The accuracy of self-prediction: How good are we and why? Paper presented at the Midwestern Psychological Association convention.

Shubik, M. (1971). The dollar auction game: A paradox in noncooperating behavior and escalation. *Journal of Conflict Resolution*, **15**, 109–111.

Shure, G. H., Meeker, R. J., & Hansford, E. A. (1965). The effectiveness of pacifist strategies in bargaining games. *Journal of Conflict Resolution*, **9**(1), 106–117.

Sigall, H. (1970). Effects of competence and consensual validation on a communicator's liking for the audience. *Journal of Personality and Social Psychology*, **16**, 252–258.

Sigall, H., & Page, R. (1971). Current stereotypes: A little fading, a little faking. *Journal of Personality and Social Psychology*, **18**, 247–255.

Silver, L. B., Dublin, C. C., & Lourie, R. S. (1969). Does violence breed violence? Contributions from a study of the child abuse syndrome. *American Journal of Psychiatry*, **126**, 404–407.

Silver, M., & Geller, D. (1978). On the irrelevance of evil: The organization and individual action. *Journal of Social Issues*, **34**, 125–136.

Simon, H. A. (1957). *Models of man: Social and rational*. New York: Wiley.

Simon, P. (1980). Interview in *Wittenburg Door*, June–July, p. 20.

Simpson, J. A. (1987). The dissolution of romantic relationships: Factors involved in relationship stability and emotional distress. *Journal of Personality and Social Psychology*, **53**, 683–692.

Simpson, J. A., Campbell, B., & Berscheid, E. (1986). The association between romantic love and marriage: Kephart (1967) twice revisited. *Personality and Social Psychology Bulletin*, **12**, 363–372.

Singer, J. L., & Singer, D. G. (1988). Some hazards of growing up in a television environment: Children's aggression and restlessness. In S. Oskamp (Ed.), *Television as a social issue: Applied Social Psychology Annual*, Vol. 8. Newbury Park, Ca.: Sage.

Singer, J. L., Singer, D. G., & Rapaczynski, W. S. (1984). Family patterns and television viewing as predictors of children's beliefs and aggression. *Journal of Communication*. 34(2), 73–89.

Singer, M. (1979). Cults and cult members. Address to the American Psychological Association convention. (a)

Singer, M. (1979, July–August). Interviewed by M. Freeman. Of cults and communication: A conversation with Margaret Singer. *APA Monitor*, pp. 6–7. (b)

Sissons, M. (1981). Race, sex, and helping behavior. *British Journal of Social Psychology*, **20**, 285–292.

Sivacek, J., & Crano, W. D. (1982). Vested interest as a moderator of attitude-behavior consistency. *Journal of Personality and Social Psychology*, **43**, 210–221.

Sivard, R. L. (1987). *World military and social expenditures 1987–1988*, 12th ed. Washington, D.C.: World Priorities.

Six, B., & Krahe, B. (1984). Implicit psychologists' estimates of attitude-behavior consistencies. *European Journal of Social Psychology*, **14**, 79–86.

Skinner, B. F. (1971). *Beyond freedom and dignity*. New York: Knopf.

Skov, R. B., & Sherman, S. J. (1986). Information-gathering processes: Diagnosticity, hypothesis-confirmatory strategies, and perceived hypothesis confirmation. *Journal of Experimental Social Psychology*, **22**, 93–121.

Slavin, R. E. (1980). Cooperative learning and desegregation. Paper presented at the American Psychological Association convention.

Slavin, R. E. (1985). Cooperative learning: Applying contact theory in desegregated schools. *Journal of Social Issues*, **41**(3), 45–62.

Slavin, R. E., & Madden, N. A. (1979). School practices that improve race relations. *Journal of Social Issues*, **16**, 169–180.

Sloan, J. H., Kellerman, A. L., Reay, D. T., Ferris, J. A., Koepsell, T., Rivara, F. P., Rice, C., Gray, L., & LoGerfo, J. (1988). Handgun regulations, crime, assaults, and homicide: A tale of two cities. *New England Journal of Medicine*, **319**, 1256–1261.

Slovic, P. (1972). From Shakespeare to Simon: Speculations—and some evidence—about man's ability to process information. *Oregon Research Institute Research Bulletin*. 12(2).

Slovic, P. (1985, January 30). Only new laws will spur seat-belt use. *Wall Street Journal.*

Slovic, P., & Fischhoff, B. (1977). On the psychology of experimental surprises. *Journal of Experimental Psychology: Human Perception and Performance*, **3**, 455–551.

Slusher, M. P., & Anderson, C. A. (1989). Belief perseverance and self-defeating behavior. In R. Curtis (Ed.), *Self-defeating behaviors: Experimental research and practical implications*. New York: Plenum.

Smedley, J. W., & Bayton, J. A. (1978). Evaluative race-class stereotypes by race and perceived class of subjects. *Journal of Personality and Social Psychology*, **3**, 530–535.

Smith, A. (1976). *The wealth of nations*. Book 1. Chicago: University of Chicago Press. (Originally published, 1776).

Smith, D. E., Gier, J. A., & Willis, F. N. (1982). Interpersonal touch and compliance with a marketing request. *Basic and Applied Social Psychology*, **3**, 35–38.

Smith, E. E. (1977). Methods for changing consumer attitudes: A report of three experiments. Cited by P. G. Zimbardo, E. B. Ebbesen, & C. Maslach. *Influencing attitudes and changing behavior*. Reading, Mass.: Addison-Wesley.

Smith, H. (1979) *The Russians*. New York: Ballantine Books, 1976. Cited by B. Latané, K. Williams, and S. Harkins in, Many hands make light the work. *Journal of Personality and Social Psychology*, **37**, 822–832.

Smith, H. W. (1981). Territorial spacing on a beach revisited: A cross-national exploration. *Social Psychology Quarterly*, **44**, 132–137.

Smith, M. B. (1978). Psychology and values. *Journal of Social Issues*, **34**, 181–199.

Smith, M. L., Glass, G. V., & Miller, R. L. (1980). *The benefits of psychotherapy*. Baltimore: Johns Hopkins Press.

Smith, P. B., & Tayeb, M. (1989). Organizational structure and processes. In M. Bond

(Ed.), *The cross-cultural challenge to social psychology*. Newbury Park, Ca.: Sage.

Smith, T. W. (1979). Happiness: Time trends, seasonal variations, intersurvey differences, and other mysteries. *Social Psychology Quarterly*, **42**, 18–30.

Smith, T. W. (1984). The polls: Gender and attitudes toward violence. *Public Opinion Quarterly*, **48**, 384–396.

Smith, T. W. (1987). The use of public opinion data by the Attorney General's Commission on Pornography. *Public Opinion Quarterly*, **51**, 249–267.

Smith, T. W., & Sheatsley, P. B. (1984, October/November). American attitudes toward race relations. *Public Opinion*, pp. 14–15, 50.

Smith, V. L., Ellsworth, P. C. (1987). The social psychology of eyewitness accuracy: Misleading questions and communicator expertise. *Journal of Applied Psychology*, **72**, 294–300.

Smith, V. L., Kassin, S. M., & Ellsworth, P. C. (1989). Eyewitness accuracy and confidence: Within- versus between-subjects correlations. *Journal of Applied Psychology*, **74**, 356–359.

Smith, W. P. (1987). Conflict and negotiation: Trends and emerging issues. *Journal of Applied Social Psychology*, **17**, 641–677.

Snodgrass, M. A. (1987). The relationships of differential loneliness, intimacy, and characterological attributional style to duration of loneliness. *Journal of Social Behavior and Personality*, **2**, 173–186.

Snodgrass, S. E., Higgins, J. G., & Todisco, L. (1986). The effects of walking behavior on mood. Paper presented at the American Psychological Association convention.

Snyder, C. R. (1978). The "illusion" of uniqueness. *Journal of Humanistic Psychology*, **18**, 33–41.

Snyder, C. R. (1980). The uniqueness mystique. *Psychology Today*, March, pp. 86–90.

Snyder, C. R., & Fromkin, H. L. (1980). *Uniqueness; The human pursuit of difference.* New York: Plenum.

Snyder, C. R., & Higgins, R. L. (1988). Excuses: Their effective role in the negotiation of reality. *Psychological Bulletin*, **104**, 23–35.

Snyder, C. R., & Newburg, C. L. (1981). The Barnum effect in a group setting. *Journal of Personality Assessment*, **45**, 622–729.

Snyder, C. R., & Smith. T. W. (1986). On being "shy like a fox": A self-handicapping analysis. In W. H. Jones et al. (Eds.), *Shyness: Perspectives on research and treatment.* New York: Plenum.

Snyder, M. (1981). Seek, and ye shall find: Testing hypotheses about other people. In E. T.

Higgins, C. P. Herman, & M. P. Zanna (Eds.), *Social cognition: The Ontario symposium on personality and social psychology.* Hillsdale, N.J.: Erlbaum. (*a*)

Snyder, M. (1982). When believing means doing: Creating links between attitudes and behavior. In M. Zanna, E. T. Higgins, & C. P. Herman (Eds.), *Consistency in social behavior: The Ontario symposium* (Vol. 2). Hillsdale, N.J.: Erlbaum. (*b*)

Snyder, M. (1983). The influence of individuals on situations: Implications for understanding the links between personality and social behavior. *Journal of Personality*, **51**, 497–516.

Snyder, M. (1984). When belief creates reality. In L. Berkowitz (Ed.), *Advances in Experimental Social Psychology*, Vol. 18. New York: Academic Press.

Snyder, M. (1988). Experiencing prejudice first hand: The "discrimination day" experiments. *Contemporary Psychology*, **33**, 664–665.

Snyder, M. (1987). *Public appearances/private realities: The psychology of self-monitoring.* New York: Freeman.

Snyder, M., Berscheid, E., & Glick, P. (1985). Focusing on the exterior and the interior: Two investigations of the initiation of personal relationships. *Journal of Personality and Social Psychology*, **48**, 1427–1439.

Snyder, M., Berscheid, E., & Matwychuk, A. (1988). Orientations toward personnel selection: Differential reliance on appearance and personality. *Journal of Personality and Social Psychology*, **54**, 972–979.

Snyder, M., Campbell, B., & Preston, E. (1982). Testing hypotheses about human nature: Assessing the accuracy of social stereotypes. *Social Cognition*, **1**, 256–272.

Snyder, M., & Copeland, J. (1989). Self-monitoring processes in organizational settings. In R. A. Giacalone & P. Rosenfeld (Eds.), *Impression management in the organization.* Hillsdale, N.J.: Erlbaum.

Snyder, M., & DeBono, K. G. (1987). A functional approach to attitudes and persuasion. In M. P. Zanna, J. M. Olson, & C. P. Herman (Eds.), *Social influence: The Ontario symposium*, Vol. 5. Hillsdale, N.J.: Erlbaum.

Snyder, M., & DeBono, K. G. (1989). Understanding the functions of attitudes: Lessons from personality and social behavior. In A. R. Pratkanis, S. J. Breckler, & A. G. Greenwald (Eds.), *Attitude structure and function.* Hillsdale, N.J.: Erlbaum.

Snyder, M., Grether, J., & Keller, K. (1974). Staring and compliance: A field experiment on hitch-hiking. *Journal of Applied Social Psychology*, **4**, 165–170.

Snyder, M., & Ickes, W. (1985). Personality and

social behavior. In G. Lindzey & E. Aronson (Eds.), *Handbook of social psychology* (3rd ed.). New York: Random House.

Snyder, M., & Simpson, J. (1985). Orientations toward romantic relationships. In S. Duck & D. Perlman (Eds.), *Understanding personal relationships.* Beverly Hills, Ca.: Sage.

Snyder, M., Simpson, J. A., & Gangestad, S. (1986). Personality and sexual relations. *Journal of Personality and Social Psychology*, **51**, 181–190.

Snyder, M., & Swann, W. B., Jr. (1976). When actions reflect attitudes: The politics of impression management. *Journal of Personality and Social Psychology*, **34**, 1034–1042.

Snyder, M., & Swann, W. B., Jr. (1978). Behavioral confirmation in social interaction: From social perception to social reality. *Journal of Experimental Social Psychology*, **14**, 148–162. (*a*)

Snyder, M., Tanke, E. D., & Berscheid, E. (1977). Social perception and interpersonal behavior: On the self-fulfilling nature of social stereotypes. *Journal of Personality and Social Psychology*, **35**, 656–666. (*b*)

Snyder, M., & Thomsen, C. J. (1988). Interactions between therapists and clients: Hypothesis testing and behavioral confirmation. In D. C. Turk & P. Salovey (Eds.), *Reasoning, inference, and judgment in clinical psychology.* New York: Free Press.

Sohn, D. (1980). Critique of Cooper's meta-analytic assessment of the findings on sex differences in conformity behavior. *Journal of Personality and Social Psychology*, **39**, 1215–1221.

Sokoll, G. R., & Mynatt, C. R. (1984). Arousal and free throw shooting. Paper presented at the Midwestern Psychological Association convention, Chicago.

Solano, C. H. Batten, P. G., & Parish, E. A. (1982). Loneliness and patterns of self-disclosure. *Journal of Personality and Social Psychology*, **43**, 524–531.

Solomon, H., & Solomon, L. Z. (1978). Effects of anonymity on helping in emergency situations. Paper presented at the Eastern Psychological Association convention.

Solomon, H., Solomon, L. Z., Arnone, M. M., Maur, B. J., Reda, R. M., & Rother, E. O. (1981). Anonymity and helping. *Journal of Social Psychology*, **113**, 37–43.

Solomon, L. Z., Solomon, H., & Stone, R. (1978). Helping as a function of number of bystanders and ambiguity of emergency. *Personality and Social Psychology Bulletin*, **4**, 318–321.

Sommer, R. (1967). Classroom ecology. *Journal of Applied Behavioral Science*, **3**, 489–503.

Sommer, R. (1969). *Personal space.* Englewood Cliffs, N.J.: Prentice-Hall.

Sommer, R., & Olsen, H. (1980). The soft classroom. *Environment and Behavior, 5,* 3–16.

Sommer, R., & Ross, H. (1958). Social interaction on a geriatrics ward. *International Journal of Social Psychiatry, 4,* 128–133.

Sonne, J., & Janoff, D. (1979). The effect of treatment attributions on the maintenance of weight reduction: A replication and extension. *Cognitive Therapy and Research, 3,* 389–397.

Sorrentino, R. M., Bobocel, D. R., Gitta, M. Z., Olsen, J. M., & Hewitt, E. C. (1988). Uncertainty orientation and persuasion: Individual differences in the effects of personal relevance on social judgments. *Journal of Personality and Social Psychology, 55,* 357–371.

Sorrentino, R. M., King, G., & Leo, G. (1980). The influence of the minority on perception: A note on a possible alternative explanation. *Journal of Experimental Social Psychology, 16,* 293–301.

Sparacino, J., & Hansell, S. (1979). Physical attractiveness and academic performance: Beauty is not always talent. *Journal of Personality, 47,* 449–469.

Sparrell, J. A., & Shrauger, J. S. (1984). Self-confidence and optimism in self-prediction. Paper presented at the American Psychological Association convention.

Spector, P. E. (1986). Perceived control by employees: A meta-analysis of studies concerning autonomy and participation at work. *Human Relations, 39,* 1005–1016.

Speer, A. (1971). *Inside the Third Reich: Memoirs.* (P. Winston & C. Winston. trans.). New York: Avon Books.

Spence, J. T., Deaux, K., & Helmreich, R. L. (1985). Sex roles in contemporary American society. In G. Lindzey & E. Aronson (Eds.), *Handbook of Social Psychology* (3rd ed.). Hillsdale, N.J.: Erlbaum.

Spiegel, H. W. (1971). *The growth of economic thought.* Durham, N.C.: Duke University Press.

Spitzberg, B. H., & Hurt, H. T. (1987). The relationship of interpersonal competence and skills to reported loneliness across time. *Journal of Social Behavior and Personality, 2,* 157–172.

Spivak, J. (1979, June 6). *Wall Street Journal.*

Sprecher, S. (1987). The effects of self-disclosure given and received on affection for an intimate partner and stability of the relationship. *Journal of Personality and Social Psychology, 4,* 115–127.

Standing, L., & Keays, G. (1986). Computer assessment of personality: A demonstration of gullibility. *Social Behavior and Personality, 14,* 197–202.

Stark, R., & Bainbridge, W. S. (1980). Networks of faith: Interpersonal bonds and recruitment to cults and sects. *American Journal of Sociology, 85,* 1376–1395.

Stasser, G., Kerr, N. L., & Bray, R. M. (1981). The social psychology of jury deliberations: Structure, process, and product. In N. L. Kerr & R. M. Bray (Eds.), *The psychology of the courtroom.* New York: Academic Press.

Staub, E. (1989). The psychology of torture and torturers. *Journal of Social Issues,* in press.

Steblay, N. M. (1987). Helping behavior in rural and urban environments: A meta-analysis. *Psychological Bulletin, 102,* 346–356.

Steele, C. M. (1988). The psychology of self-affirmation: Sustaining the integrity of the self. In L. Berkowitz (Ed.), *Advances in experimental social psychology,* Vol. 21. Orlando, Fl.: Academic Press.

Steele, C. M., & Southwick, L. (1985). Alcohol and social behavior I: The psychology of drunken excess. *Journal of Personality and Social Psychology, 48,* 18–34.

Steele, C. M., Southwick, L. L., & Critchlow, B. (1981). Dissonance and alcohol: Drinking your troubles away. *Journal of Personality and Social Psychology, 11,* 831–846.

Stein, A. H., & Friedrich, L. K. (1972). Television content and young children's behavior. In J. P. Murray, E. A. Rubinstein, & G. A. Comstock (Eds.), *Television and social learning.* Washington, D.C.: Government Printing Office.

Stein, D. D., Hardyck, J. A., & Smith, M. B. (1965). Race and belief: An open and shut case. *Journal of Personality and Social Psychology, 1,* 281–289.

Stein, R. T., & Heller, T. (1979). An empirical analysis of the correlations between leadership status and participation rates reported in the literature. *Journal of Personality and Social Psychology, 37,* 1993–2002.

Steinem, G. (1988). Six great ideas that television is missing. In S. Oskamp. (Ed.), *Television as a social issue: Applied Social Psychology Annual,* Vol. 8. Newbury Park, Ca.: Sage.

Steiner, I. D. (1972). *Group process and productivity.* New York: Academic Press.

Steiner, I. D. (1982). Heuristic models of groupthink. In M. Brandstatter, J. H. Davis, & G. Stocker-Kreichgauer (Eds.), *Group decision making.* New York: Academic Press, pp. 503–524.

Stephan, C. W., & Stephan, W. G. (1986). Habla Ingles? The effects of language translation on simulated juror decisions. *Journal of Applied Social Psychology, 16.* 577–589.

Stephan, W. G. (1986). The effects of school desegregation: An evaluation 30 years after *Brown.* In R. Kidd, L. Saxe, & M. Saks (Eds.), *Advances in applied social psychology.* New York: Erlbaum.

Stephan, W. G. (1987). The contact hypothesis in intergroup relations. In C. Hendrick (Ed.), *Group processes and intergroup relations.* Newbury Park, Ca.: Sage.

Stephan, W. G. (1988). School desegregation: Short-term and long-term effects. Paper presented at the national conference "Opening doors: An appraisal of race relations in America," University of Alabama.

Stephan, W. G., Bernstein, W. M., Stephan, C., & Davis, M. H. (1979). Attributions for achievement: Egotism vs. expectancy confirmation. *Social Psychology Quarterly, 42,* 5–17.

Stephan, W. G., Berscheid, E., & Walster, E. (1971). Sexual arousal and heterosexual perception. *Journal of Personality and Social Psychology, 20,* 93–101.

Stephenson, G. M., Abrams, D., Wagner, W., & Wade, G. (1986). Partners in recall. Collaborative order in the recall of a police interrogation. *British Journal of Social Psychology, 25,* 341–343. (*a*)

Stephenson, G. M., Brandstatter, H., & Wagner, W. (1983). An experimental study of social performance and delay on the testimonial validity of story recall. *European Journal of Social Psychology, 13,* 175–191.

Stephenson, G. M., Clark, N. K., & Wade, G. S. (1986). Meetings make evidence? An experimental study of collaborative and individual recall of a simulated police interrogation. *Journal of Personality and Social Psychology, 50,* 1113–1122. (*b*)

Sternberg, R. J. (1988). Triangulating love. In R. J. Sternberg & M. L. Barnes (Eds.), *The psychology of love.* New Haven: Yale University Press.

Sternberg, R. J., & Grajek, S. (1984). The nature of love. *Journal of Personality and Social Psychology, 47,* 312–329.

Stewart, J. E., II. (1980). Defendant's attractiveness as a factor in the outcome of criminal trials: An observational study. *Journal of Applied Social Psychology, 10,* 348–361.

Stewart, J. E., II. (1983). Appearance as a factor in conviction and sentencing: The attraction-leniency effect in the courtroom. Paper presented at the Midwestern Psychological Association convention.

Stille, R. G., Malamuth, N., & Schallow, J. R. (1987). Prediction of rape proclivity by rape myth attitudes and hostility toward women. Paper presented at the American Psychological Association convention.

Stires, L. (1980). Classroom seating location, student grades, and attitudes: Environment or self-selection. *Environment and Behavior*, 12, 241–254.

Stockdale, J. E. (1978). Crowding: Determinants and effects. In L. Berkowitz (Ed.), *Advances in experimental social psychology* (Vol. 11). New York: Academic Press.

Stokes, J., & Levin, I. (1986). Gender differences in predicting loneliness from social network characteristics. *Journal of Personality and Social Psychology*, 51, 1069–1074.

Stone, A. A., Hedges, S. M., Neale, J. M., & Satin, M. S. (1985). Prospective and cross-sectional mood reports offer no evidence of a "blue Monday" phenomenon. *Journal of Personality and Social Psychology*, 49, 129–134.

Stone, A. L., & Glass, C. R. (1986). Cognitive distortion of social feedback in depression. *Journal of Social and Clinical Psychology*, 4, 179–188.

Stoner, J. A. F. (1962). A comparison of individual and group decisions involving risk. Unpublished master's thesis, Massachusetts Institute of Technology, 1961. Cited by D. G. Marquis in, Individual responsibility and group decisions involving risk. *Industrial Management Review*, 3, 8–23.

Storms, M. D. (1973). Videotape and the attribution process: Reversing actors' and observers' points of view. *Journal of Personality and Social Psychology*, 27, 165–175.

Storms, M. D., & Thomas, G. C. (1977). Reactions to physical closeness. *Journal of Personality and Social Psychology*, 35, 412–418.

Stouffer, S. A., Suchman, E. A., DeVinney, L. C., Star, S. A., & Williams, R. M., Jr. (1949). *The American soldier: Adjustment during army life* (Vol. 1.). Princeton, N.J.: Princeton University Press.

Strack, F., Martin, L. L., & Stepper, S. (1988). Inhibiting and facilitating conditions of the human smile: A nonobstrusive test of the facial feedback hypothesis. *Journal of Personality and Social Psychology*, 54, 768–777.

Strack, S., & Coyne, J. C. (1983). Social confirmation of dysphoria: Shared and private reactions to depression. *Journal of Personality and Social Psychology*, 44, 798–806.

Strauss, M. A., & Gelles, R. J. (1980). *Behind closed doors: Violence in the American family*. New York: Anchor/Doubleday.

Strenta, A., & DeJong, W. (1981). The effect of a prosocial label on helping behavior. *Social Psychology Quarterly*, 44, 142–147.

Stretch, R. H., & Figley, C. R. (1980). Beauty

and the boast: Predictors of interpersonal attraction in a dating experiment. *Psychology, A Quarterly Journal of Human Behavior*, 17, 34–43.

Stroebe, W., Insko, C. A., Thompson, V. D., & Layton, B. D. (1971). Effects of physical attractiveness, attitude similarity, and sex on various aspects of interpersonal attraction. *Journal of Personality and Social Psychology*, 18, 79–91.

Strong, S. R. (1978). Social psychological approach to psychotherapy research. In S. L. Garfield & A. E. Bergin (Eds.), *Handbook of psychotherapy and behavior change*, 2nd ed. New York: Wiley.

Strumpel, B. (1976). Economic life-styles, values, and subjective welfare. In B. Strumpel (Ed.), *Economic means for human needs*. Ann Arbor, Mich.: Institute for Social Research, University of Michigan.

Sue, S., Smith, R. E., & Caldwell, C. (1973). Effects of inadmissible evidence on the decisions of simulated jurors: A moral dilemma. *Journal of Applied Social Psychology*, 3, 345–353.

Suedfeld, P., Rank, D., & Borrie, R. (1975). Frequency of exposure and evaluation of candidates and campaign speeches. *Journal of Applied Social Psychology*, 5, 118–126.

Suls, J., & Tesch, F. (1978). Students' preferences for information about their test performance: A social comparison study, *Journal of Experimental Social Psychology*, 8, 189–197.

Suls, J., & Wan, C. K. (1987). In search of the false-uniqueness phenomenon: Fear and estimates of social consensus. *Journal of Personality and Social Psychology*, 52, 211–217.

Suls, J., Wan, C. K., & Sanders, G. S. (1988). False consensus and false uniqueness in estimating the prevalence of health-protective behaviors. *Journal of Applied Social Psychology*, 18, 66–79.

Summers, G., & Feldman, N. S. (1984). Blaming the victim versus blaming the perpetrator: An attributional analysis of spouse abuse. *Journal of Social and Clinical Psychology*, 2, 339–347.

Sundstrom, E., & Sundstrom, M. G. (1983). *Workplaces: The psychology of the physical environment in organizations*. Monterey, Calif.: Brooks/Cole.

Supreme Court of the United States (1986, May 5). Lockhart, Director, Arkansas Department of Corrections v. McCree. No. 84–1865 opinion of the Court and dissenting opinions.

Surgeon General (1983). *The health consequences of smoking: Cardiovascular disease*.

Washington, D.C.: U.S. Government Printing Office.

Svenson, O. (1981). Are we all less risky and more skillful than our fellow drivers? *Acta Psychologica*, 47, 143–148.

Swann, W. B., Jr. (1984). Quest for accuracy in person perception: A matter of pragmatics. *Psychological Review*, 91, 457–475.

Swann, W. B., Jr. (1987). Identity negotiation: Where two roads meet. *Journal of Personality and Social Psychology*, 53, 1038–1051.

Swann, W. B., Jr., & Ely, R. J. (1984). A battle of wills: Self-verification versus behavioral confirmation. *Journal of Personality and Social Psychology*, 46, 1287–1302.

Swann, W. B., Jr., & Giuliano, T. (1987). Confirmatory search strategies in social interaction: How, when, why, and with what consequences. *Journal of Social and Clinical Psychology*, 5, 511–524.

Swann, W. B., Jr., Giuliano, T., & Wegner, D. M. (1982). Where leading questions can lead: The power of conjecture in social interaction. *Journal of Personality and Social Psychology*, 42, 1025–1035.

Swann, W. B., Jr., Pelham, B. W., & Chidester, T. R. (1988). Change through paradox: Using self-verification to alter beliefs. *Journal of Personality and Social Psychology*, 54, 268–273.

Swann, W. B., Jr., & Predmore, S. C. (1985). Intimates as agents of social support: Sources of consolation or despair? *Journal of Personality and Social Psychology*, 49, 1609–1617.

Swann, W. B., Jr. & Read, S. J. (1981). Acquiring self-knowledge: The search for feedback that fits. *Journal of Personality and Social Psychology*, 41, 1119–1128. (a)

Swann, W. B., Jr., & Read, S. J. (1981). Self-verification processes: How we sustain our self-conceptions. *Journal of Experimental Social Psychology*, 17, 351–372. (b)

Swap, W. C. (1977). Interpersonal attraction and repeated exposure to rewarders and punishers. *Personality and Social Psychology Bulletin*, 3, 248–251.

Swedish Information Service (1980). *Social change in Sweden*, September, No. 19, p. 5. (Published by the Swedish Consulate General, 825 Third Avenue, New York, N.Y. 10022.)

Sweeney, J. (1973). An experimental investigation of the free rider problem. *Social Science Research*, 2, 277–292.

Sweeney, P. D., Anderson, K., & Bailey, S. (1986). Attributional style in depression: A meta-analytic review. *Journal of Personality and Social Psychology*, 50, 974–991.

Swim, J., Borgida, E., Maruyama, G., & Myers, D. G. (1989). Joan McKay vs. John

McKay: Do gender stereotypes bias evaluations? *Psychological Bulletin*, in press.

Symons, D. (interviewed by S. Keen). (1981, February). Eros and alley cop. *Psychology Today*, p. 54.

Tajfel, H. (1970, November). Experiments in intergroup discrimination. *Scientific American*, pp. 96–102.

Tajfel, H. (1981). *Human groups and social categories: Studies in social psychology*. London: Cambridge University Press.

Tajfel, H. (1982). Social psychology of intergroup relations. *Annual Review of Psychology*, 33, 1–39.

Tajfel, H., & Billig, M. (1974). Familiarity and categorization in intergroup behavior. *Journal of Experimental Social Psychology*, 10, 159–170.

Takooshian, H., & Bodinger, H. (1982). Bystander indifference to street crime. In I. Savitz & N. Johnston (Eds.), *Contemporary Criminology*. New York: Wiley.

Tanke, E. D., & Tanke, T. J. (1979). Getting off a slippery slope: Social science in the judicial processes. *American Psychologist*, 34, 1130–1138.

Tapp, J. L. (1980). Psychological and policy perspectives on the law: Reflections on a decade. *Journal of Social Issues*, 36(2), 165–192.

Tavris, C. (1982). *Anger. The misunderstood emotion*. New York: Simon & Schuster.

Tavris, C., & Wade, C. (1984). *The longest war: Sex differences in perspective*. New York: Harcourt Brace Jovanovich.

Taylor, D. A. (1979). Motivational bases. In G. J. Chelune (Ed.), *Self-disclosure: Origins, patterns, and implications of openness in interpersonal relationships*. San Francisco: Jossey-Bass.

Taylor, D. A., Gould, R. J., & Brounstein, P. J. (1981). Effects of personalistic self-disclosure. *Personality and Social Psychology Bulletin*, 7, 487–492.

Taylor, D. G., Sheatsley, P. B., & Greeley, A. M. (1978). Attitudes toward racial integration. *Scientific American*, 238(6), 42–49.

Taylor, D. M., & Doria, J. R. (1981). Self-serving and group-serving bias in attribution. *Journal of Social Psychology*, 113, 201–211.

Taylor, S. E. (1979). Remarks at symposium on social psychology and medicine, American Psychological Association convention.

Taylor, S. E. (1981). A categorization approach to stereotyping. In D. L. Hamilton (Ed.), *Cognitive processes in stereotyping and intergroup behavior*. Hillsdale, N.J.: Erlbaum.

Taylor, S. E. (1983). Adjustments to threatening events: A theory of cognitive adaptation. *American Psychologist*, 38, 1161–1173.

Taylor, S. E., & Brown, J. D. (1988). Illusion and well-being: A social psychological perspective on mental health. *Psychological Bulletin*, 103, 193–210.

Taylor, S. E., Crocker J., Fiske, S. T., Sprinzen, M., & Winkler, J. D. (1979). The generalizability of salience effects. *Journal of Personality and Social Psychology*, 37, 357–368.

Taylor, S. E., & Fiske, S. T. (1978). Salience, attention, and attribution: Top of the head phenomena. In L. Berkowitz (Ed.), *Advances in experimental social psychology* (Vol. 11). New York: Academic Press.

Taylor, S. E., Fiske, S. T., Etcoff, N. L., & Ruderman, A. J. (1978). Categorical and contextual bases of person memory and stereotyping. *Journal of Personality and Social Psychology*, 36, 778–793.

Taylor, S. P., & Leonard, K. E. (1983). Alcohol and human physical aggression. *Aggression*, 2, 77–101.

Taylor, S. P., & Pisano, R. (1971). Physical aggression as a function of frustration and physical attack. *Journal of Social Psychology*, 84, 261–267.

Taynor, J., & Deaux, K. (1973). When women are more deserving than men: Equity, attribution, and perceived sex differences. *Journal of Personality and Social Psychology*, 28, 360–367.

Taynor, J., & Deaux, K. (1975). Equity and perceived sex differences: Role behavior as defined by the task, the mode, and the actor. *Journal of Personality and Social Psychology*, 32, 381–390.

Tedeschi, J. T., Nesler, M., & Taylor, E. (1987). Misattribution and the bogus pipeline: A test of dissonance and impression management theories. Paper presented at the American Psychological Association convention.

Tedeschi, J. T., Schlenker, B. R., & Bonoma, T. V. (1973). *Conflict, power, and games*. Chicago: Aldine.

Teger, A. I. (1980). *Too much invested to quit*. New York: Pergamon Press.

Teigen, K. H. (1986). Old truths or fresh insights? A study of students' evaluations of proverbs. *British Journal of Social Psychology*, 25, 43–50.

Telch, M. J., Killen, J. D., McAlister, A. L., Perry, C. L., & Maccoby, N. (1981). Long-term follow-up of a pilot project on smoking prevention with adolescents. Paper presented at the American Psychological Association convention.

Tennen, H., & Affleck, G. (1987). The costs and benefits of optimistic explanations and dispositional optimism. *Journal of Personality*, 55, 377–393.

Tennov, D. (1979). *Love and limerence: The experience of being in love*. New York: Stein and Day, p. 22.

Tesser, A. (1978). Self-generated attitude change. In L. Berkowitz (Ed.), *Advances in experimental social psychology* (Vol. 11). New York: Academic Press.

Tesser, A. (1985). Some effects of self-evaluation maintenance on cognition and action. In R. M. Sorrentino & E. T. Higgins (Eds.), *The handbook of motivation and cognition: Foundations of social behavior*. New York: Guilford.

Tesser, A. (1988). Toward a self-evaluation maintenance model of social behavior. In L. Berkowitz (Ed.), *Advances in experimental social psychology*, Vol. 21. San Diego, Ca.: Academic Press.

Tesser, A., Gatewood, R., & Driver, M. (1968). Some determinants of gratitude. *Journal of Personality and Social Psychology*, 9, 233–236.

Tesser, A., Millar, M., & Moore, J. (1988). Some affective consequences of social comparison and reflection processes: The pain and pleasure of being close. *Journal of Personality and Social Psychology*, 54, 49–61.

Tesser, A., & Paulhus, D. (1983). The definition of self: Private and public self-evaluation management strategies. *Journal of Personality and Social Psychology*, 44, 672–682.

Tesser, A., Rosen, S., & Conlee, M. C. (1972). News valence and available recipient as determinants of news transmission. *Sociometry*, 35, 619–628.

Tetlock, P. E. (1981). Personality and isolationism: Content analysis of senatorial speeches. *Journal of Personality and Social Psychology*, 41, 737–743. (*a*)

Tetlock, P. E. (1981). Pre- to post-election shifts in presidential rhetoric: Impression management or cognitive adjustment. *Journal of Personality and Social Psychology*, 41, 207–212. (*b*)

Tetlock, P. E. (1983). Accountability and complexity of thought. *Journal of Personality and Social Psychology*, 45, 74–83.

Tetlock, P. E. (1985). Integrative complexity of American and Soviet foreign policy rhetoric: A time-series analysis. *Journal of Personality and Social Psychology*, 49, 1565–1585.

Tetlock, P. E., & Manstead, A. S. R. (1985). Impression management versus intrapsychic explanations in social psychology: A useful dichotomy? *Psychological Review*, 92, 59–77.

Thomas, G. C., & Batson, C. D. (1981). Effect of helping under normative pressure on self-perceived altruism. *Social Psychology Quarterly*, 44, 127–131.

Thomas, G. C., Batson, C. D., & Coke, J. S. (1981). Do Good Samaritans discourage helpfulness? Self-perceived altruism after exposure to highly helpful others. *Journal of Personality and Social Psychology*, 40, 194–200.

Thomas, K. W., & Pondy, L. R. (1977). Toward an "intent" model of conflict management among principal parties. *Human Relations*, 30, 1089–1102.

Thomas, L. (1978). Hubris in science? *Science*, 200, 1459–1462.

Thomas, L. (1981). Quoted by J. L. Powell. Testimony before the Senate Subcommittee on Science, Technology and Space, April 22.

Thompson, L. L., & Crocker, J. (1985). Prejudice following threat to the self-concept. Effects of performance expectations and attributions. Unpublished manuscript, Northwestern University.

Thompson, W. C., Cowan, C. L., & Rosenhan, D. L. (1980). Focus of attention mediates the impact of negative affect on altruism. *Journal of Personality and Social Psychology*, 38, 291–300.

Thompson, W. C., & Schumann, E. L. (1987). Interpretation of statistical evidence in criminal trials. *Law and Human Behavior*, 11, 167–187.

Thorndike, R. L. (1968). Review of *Pygmalion in the classroom*. *American Educational Research Journal*, 5, 707–711.

Thornton, A., & Freedman, D. (1979). Changes in the sex role attitudes of women, 1962–1977: Evidence from a panel study. *American Sociological Review*, 44, 831–842.

Tice, D. M., & Baumeister, R. F. (1985). Masculinity inhibits helping in emergencies: Personality does predict the bystander effect. *Journal of Personality and Social Psychology*, 49, 420–428.

Time (1981, March 16), p. 31.

Toronto News (1977, July 26).

Towson, S. M. J., & Zanna, M. P. (1983). Retaliation against sexual assault: Self-defense or public duty? *Psychology of Women Quarterly*, 8, 89–99.

Travis, L. E. (1925). The effect of a small audience upon eye-hand coordination. *Journal of Abnormal and Social Psychology*, 20, 142–146.

Triandis, H. C. (1981). Some dimensions of intercultural variation and their implications for interpersonal behavior. Paper presented at the American Psychological Association convention.

Triandis, H. C. (1982). Incongruence between intentions and behavior: A review. Paper presented at the American Psychological Association convention.

Triandis, H. C., Bontempo, R., Villareal, M. J., Asai, M., & Lucca, N. (1988). Individualism and collectivism: Cross-cultural perspectives on self-ingroup relationships. *Journal of Personality and Social Psychology*, 54, 323–338.

Trimble, J. E. (1988). Stereotypical images, American Indians, and prejudice. In P. A. Katz & D. A. Taylor (Eds.), *Eliminating racism: Profiles in controversy*. New York: Plenum.

Triplet, R. G., Cohn, E. S., & White, S. O. (1988). The effect of residence hall judicial policies on attitudes toward rule-violating behaviors. *Journal of Applied Social Psychology*, 18, 1288–1294.

Triplett, N. (1898). The dynamogenic factors in pacemaking and competition. *American Journal of Psychology*, 9, 507–533.

Trolier, T. K., & Hamilton, D. L. (1986). Variables influencing judgments of correlational relations. *Journal of Personality and Social Psychology*, 50, 879–888.

Trope, Y., Bassok, M., & Alon, E. (1984). The questions lay interviewers ask. *Journal of Personality*, 52, 90–106.

Trost, M. R., Cialdini, R. B., & Maas, A. (1989). Effects of an international conflict simulation on perceptions of the Soviet Union: A FIREBREAKS backfire. *Journal of Social Issues*, in press.

Tschann, J. M. (1988). Self-disclosure in adult friendship: Gender and marital status differences. *Journal of Social and Personal Relationships*, 5, 65–81.

Tuan, Yi-Fu (1982). Segmented worlds and self. Minneapolis, Minn.: University of Minnesota Press.

Tubbs, M. E. (1986). Goal setting: A meta-analytic examination of the empirical evidence. *Journal of Applied Psychology*, 71, 474–483.

Tumin, M. M. (1958). Readiness and resistance to desegregation: A social portrait of the hard core. *Social Forces*, 36, 256–273.

Turner, C. W., Hesse, B. W., & Peterson-Lewis, S. (1986). Naturalistic studies of the long-term effects of television violence. *Journal of Social Issues*, 42(3), 51–74.

Turner, J. C. (1984). Social identification and psychological group formation. In H. Tajfel (Ed.), *The social dimension: European developments in social psychology*, vol. 2. London: Cambridge University Press.

Turner, J. C. (1987). *Rediscovering the social group: A self-categorization theory.* New York: Basil Blackwell.

TV Guide (1977, January 26), pp. 5–10.

Tversky, A. (1985, June). Quoted by Kevin McKean, Decisions, decisions. *Discover*, pp. 22–31.

Tversky, A., & Kahneman, D. (1973). Availability: A heuristic for judging frequency and probability. *Cognitive Psychology*, 5, 207–232.

Tverksy, A., & Kahneman, D. (1974). Judgment under uncertainty: Heuristics and biases. *Science*, 185, 1123–1131.

Tversky, A., & Kahneman, D. (1980). Causal schemas in judgments under uncertainty. In M. Fishbein (Ed.), *Progress in social psychology* (Vol. 1). Hillsdale, N.J.: Erlbaum.

Tversky, A., & Kahneman, D. (1981). The framing of decisions and the psychology of choice. *Science*, 211, 453–458.

Tyler, T. R., & Cook, F. L. (1984). The mass media and judgments of risk: Distinguishing impact on personal and societal level judgments. *Journal of Personality and Social Psychology*, 47, 693–708.

Tyler, T. R., & Sears, D. O. (1977). Coming to like obnoxious people when we must live with them. *Journal of Personality and Social Psychology*, 35, 200–211.

Ugwuegbu, C. E. (1979). Racial and evidential factors in juror attribution of legal responsibility. *Journal of Experimental Social Psychology*, 15, 133–146.

Uleman, J. S. (1989). A framework for thinking intentionally about unintended thoughts. In J. S. Uleman & J. A. Bargh (Eds.), *Unintended thought: The limits of awareness, intention, and control*. New York: Guilford, in press.

Umberson, D., & Hughes, M. (1987). The impact of physical attractiveness on achievement and psychological well-being. *Social Psychology Quarterly*, 50, 227–236.

Underwood, B., & Moore, B. (1982). Perspective-taking and altruism. *Psychological Bulletin*, 91, 143–173.

Unger, R. K. (1979). Whom does helping help? Paper presented at the Eastern Psychological Association convention, April. (a)

Unger, R. K. (1979). Toward a redefinition of sex and gender. *American Psychologist*, 34, 1085–1094.

Unger, R. K. (1983). Through the looking glass: No wonderland yet! (The reciprocal relationship between methodology and models of reality). *Psychology of Women Quarterly*, 8, 9–32.

Unger, R. K. (1985). Epistomological consistency and its scientific implications. *American Psychologist*, 40, 1413–1414.

UPI. (1970). September 23, 1967. Cited by P. G. Zimbardo, in The human choice: Individuation, reason, and order versus deindividuatioin, impulse, and chaos. In W. J. Arnold & D. Levine (Eds.), *Nebraska Symposium on Motivation, 1969.* Lincoln: University of Nebraska Press.

U.S. Commission on Obscenity and Pornography. (1970). *The report of the Commission on Obscenity and Pornography.* Washington, D.C.: Government Printing Office.

U.S. Department of Commerce News. (1981, May 3). Bureau of Economic Analysis.

U.S. Department of Justice. (1980). *Sourcebook of criminal justice statistics.* Washington, D.C.: Government Printing Office.

U.S. Department of Labor. (1981). *Employment in perspective: Working women* (Report 647). Washington, D.C.: Bureau of Labor Statistics.

U.S. Supreme Court, Plessy v. Ferguson. (1896). Quoted by L. J. Severy, J. C. Brigham, & B. R. Schlenker, *A contemporary introduction to social psychology.* New York: McGraw-Hill, p. 126.

Vallone, R. P., Ross, L., & Lepper, M. R. (1985). The hostile media phenomenon: Biased perception and perceptions of media bias in coverage of the "Beirut Massacre." *Journal of Personality and Social Psychology, 49,* 577–585.

Van der Plight, J., Eiser, J. R., & Spears, R. (1987). Comparative judgments and preferences: The influence of the number of response alternatives. *British Journal of Social Psychology, 26,* 269–280.

Vanderslice, V. J., Rice, R. W., & Julian, J. W. (1987). The effects of participation in decision-making on worker satisfaction and productivity: An organizational simulation. *Journal of Applied Social Psychology, 17,* 158–170.

Van Leeuwen, M. S. (1978). A cross-cultural examination of psychological differentiation in males and females. *International Journal of Psychology, 13,* 87–122.

Vanneman, R. D., & Pettigrew, T. (1972). Race and relative deprivation in the urban United States. *Race, 13,* 461–486.

Van Staden, F. J. (1987). White South Africans' attitudes toward the desegregation of public amenities. *Journal of Social Psychology, 127,* 163–173.

Vaughan, K. B., & Lanzetta, J. T. (1981). The effect of modification of expressive displays on vicarious emotional arousal. *Journal of Experimental Social Psychology, 17,* 16–30.

Veitch, R., DeWood, R., & Bosko, K. (1977). Radio news broadcasts: Their effect on interpersonal helping. *Sociometry, 40,* 383–386.

Veitch, R., & Griffitt, W. (1976). Good news—

bad news: Affective and interpersonal effects. *Journal of Applied Social Psychology, 6,* 69–75.

Vidmar, N. (1979). The other issues in jury simulation research. *Law and Human Behavior, 3,* 95–106.

Vidmar, N., & Laird, N. M. (1983). Adversary social roles: Their effects on witnesses' communication of evidence and the assessments of adjudicators. *Journal of Personality and Social Psychology, 44,* 888–898.

Visher, C. A. (1987). Juror decision making: The importance of evidence. *Law and Human Behavior, 11,* 1–17.

Visintainer, M. A., & Seligman, M. E. (1983, July/August). The hope factor. *American Health,* pp. 59–61.

Visintainer, M. A., & Seligman, M. E. P. (1985). Tumor rejection and early experience of uncontrollable shock in the rat. Unpublished manuscript, University of Pennsylvania. See also, M. A. Visintainer et al. (1982). Tumor rejection in rats after inescapable versus escapable shock. *Science, 216,* 437–439.

Vitelli, R. (1988). The crisis issue assessed: An empirical analysis. *Basic and Applied Social Psychology, 9,* 301–309.

Von Baeyer, C. L., Sherk, D. L., & Zanna, M. P. (1981). Impression management in the job interview: When the female applicant meets the male (chauvinist) interviewer. *Personality and Social Psychology Bulletin, 7,* 45–51.

Wachtler, J., & Counselman, E. (1981). When increasing liking for a communicator decreases opinion change: An attribution analysis of attractiveness. *Journal of Experimental Social Psychology, 17,* 386–395.

Wagstaff, G. (1982). Attitudes to rape: The "just world" strikes again? Bulletin of the *British Psychological Society, 35,* 277–279.

Wagstaff, G. F. (1983). Attitudes to poverty, the Protestant ethic, and political affiliation: A preliminary investigation. *Social Behavior and Personality, 11,* 45–47.

Walker, I., & Mann, L. (1987). Unemployment, relative deprivation, and social protest. *Personality and Social Psychology Bulletin, 13,* 275–283.

Walker, M., Harriman, S., & Costello, S. (1980). The influence of appearance on compliance with a request. *Journal of Social Psychology, 112,* 159–160.

Wallach, M. A., & Wallach, L. (1983). *Psychology's sanction for selfishness: The error of egoism in theory and therapy.* San Francisco: Freeman.

Wallbott, H. G. (1988). In and out of context:

Influences of facial expression and context information on emotion attributions. *British Journal of Social Psychology, 27,* 357–369.

Wallston, B. S. (1981). What are the questions in psychology of women? A feminist approach to research. *Psychology of Women Quarterly, 5,* 597–617.

Wallston, B. S. (1987). Social psychology of women and gender. *Journal of Applied Social Psychology, 17,* 1025–1050.

Walster (Hatfield), E. (1965). The effect of self-esteem on romantic liking. *Journal of Experimental Social Psychology, 1,* 184–197.

Walster (Hatfield), E., Aronson, V., Abrahams, D., & Rottman, L. (1966). Importance of physical attractiveness in dating behavior. *Journal of Personality and Social Psychology, 4,* 508–516.

Walster (Hatfield), E., & Festinger, L. (1962). The effectiveness of "overheard" persuasive communications. *Journal of Abnormal and Social Psychology, 65,* 395–402.

Walster (Hatfield), E., Walster, G. W., & Berscheid, E. (1978). *Equity: Theory and research.* Boston: Allyn and Bacon.

Ward, W. C., & Jenkins, H. M. (1965). The display of information and the judgment of contingency. *Canadian Journal of Psychology, 19,* 231–241.

Wason, P. C. (1960). On the failure to eliminate hypotheses in a conceptual task. *Quarterly Journal of Experimental Psychology, 12,* 129–140.

Watson, D. (1982). The actor and the observer: How are their perceptions of causality divergent? *Psychological Bulletin, 92,* 682–700.

Watson, R. I., Jr. (1973). Investigation into deindividuation using a cross-cultural survey technique. *Journal of Personality and Social Psychology, 25,* 342–345.

Watts, W. A. (1967). Relative persistence of opinion change induced by active compared to passive participation. *Journal of Personality and Social Psychology, 5,* 4–15.

Wax, S. L. (1958). A survey of restrictive advertising and discrimination by summer reports in the province of Ontario. Canadian Jewish Congress. *Information and Comment,* 1948, 7, 1–13. Cited by G. W. Allport in *The nature of prejudice.* Garden City, N.Y.: Doubleday Anchor Books, p. 5.

Weary, G., Harvey, J. H., Schwieger, P., Olson, C. T., Perloff, R., & Pritchard, S. (1982). Self-presentation and the moderation of self-serving biases. *Social Cognition, 1,* 140–159.

Wehr, P. (1979). *Conflict regulation.* Boulder, Colo.: Westview Press.

Weinberger, M., Hiner, S. L., & Tierney,

W. M. (1987). In support of hassles as a measure of stress in predicting health outcomes. *Journal of Behavioral Medicine*, 10, 19–31.

Weiner, B. (1980). A cognitive (attribution)-emotion-action model of motivated behavior: An analysis of judgments of help-giving. *Journal of Personality and Social Psychology*, 39, 186–200.

Weiner, B. (1981). The emotional consequences of causal ascriptions. Unpublished manuscript, UCLA.

Weiner, B. (1965). "Spontaneous" causal thinking. *Psychological Bulletin*, 97, 74–84.

Weinstein, N. D. (1980). Unrealistic optimism about future life events. *Journal of Personality and Social Psychology*, 39, 806–820.

Weinstein, N. D. (1982). Unrealistic optimism about susceptibility to health problems. *Journal of Behavioral Medicine*, 5, 441–460.

Weinstein, N. D., & Lachendro, E. (1982). Egocentrism and unrealistic optimism about the future. *Personality and Social Psychology Bulletin*, 8, 195–200.

Weiss, J., & Brown, P. (1976). Self-insight error in the explanation of mood. Unpublished manuscript, Harvard University.

Wells, G. L. (1984). The psychology of lineup identifications. *Journal of Applied Social Psychology*, 14, 89–103.

Wells, G. L. (1986). Expert psychological testimony. *Law and Human Behavior*, 10, 83–95.

Wells, G. L., Ferguson, T. J., & Lindsay, R. C. L. (1981). The tractability of eyewitness confidence and its implications for triers of fact. *Journal of Applied Psychology*, 66, 688–696.

Wells, G. L., & Leippe, M. R. (1981). How do triers of fact enter the accuracy of eyewitness identification? Memory for peripheral detail can be misleading. *Journal of Applied Psychology*, 66, 682–687.

Wells, G. L., Lindsay, R. C. L., & Ferguson, T. (1979). Accuracy, confidence, and juror perceptions in eyewitness identification. *Journal of Applied Psychology*, 64, 440–448.

Wells, G. L., Lindsay, R. C. L., & Tousignant, J. P. (1980). Effects of expert psychological advice on human performance in judging the validity of eyewitness testimony. *Law and Human Behavior*, 4, 275–285.

Wells, G. L., & Murray, D. M. (1983). What can psychology say about the *Neil v. Biggers* criteria for judging eyewitness accuracy? *Journal of Applied Psychology*, 68, 347–362.

Wells, G. L., & Murray, D. M. (1984). Eyewitness confidence. In G. L. Wells & E. F. Loftus (Eds.), *Eyewitness testimony: Psychological perspectives*, New York: Cambridge University Press.

Wells, G. L., & Petty, R. E. (1980). The effects of overt head movements on persuasion: Compatibility and incompatibility of responses. *Basic and Applied Social Psychology*, 1, 219–230.

Wells, G. L., & Turtle, J. W. (1986). Eyewitness identification: The importance of line-up models. *Psychological Bulletin*, 99, 320–329.

Wells, G. L., & Turtle, J. W. (1987). Eyewitness testimony research: Current knowledge and emergent controversies. *Canadian Journal of Behavioral Science*, 19, 363–388.

Wells, G. L., Wrightsman, L. S., & Miene, P. K. (1985). The timing of the defense opening statement: Don't wait until the evidence is in. *Journal of Applied Social Psychology*, 15, 758–772.

Wener, R., Frazier, W., & Farbstein, J. (1987, June). Building better jails. *Psychology Today*, pp. 40–49.

Werner, C. M., & Kagehiro, D. K., & Strube, M. J. (1982). Conviction proneness and the authoritarian juror: Inability to disregard information or attitudinal bias? *Journal of Applied Psychology*, 67, 629–636.

West, L. J., & Singer, M. T. (1980). Cults, quacks and nonprofessional psychotherapies. In H. I. Kaplan, A. M. Freedman, & B. J. Sadock (Eds.), *Comprehensive textbook of Psychiatry/III* Baltimore: Williams & Wilkins.

West, S. G., & Brown, T. J. (1975). Physical attractiveness, the severity of the emergency and helping: A field experiment and interpersonal simulation. *Journal of Experimental Social Psychology*, 11, 531–538.

West, S. G., Gunn, S. P., & Chernicky, P. (1975). Ubiquitous Watergate: An attributional analysis. *Journal of Personality and Social Psychology*, 32, 55–65.

West, S. G., Whitney, G., & Schnedler, R. (1975). Helping a motorist in distress: The effects of sex, race, and neighborhood. *Journal of Personality and Social Psychology*, 31, 691–698.

Wetzel, C. G., & Insko, C. A. (1982). The similarity-attraction relationship: Is there an ideal one? *Journal of Experimental Social Psychology*, 18, 253–276.

Weyant, J. M. (1984). Applying social psychology to induce charitable donations. *Journal of Applied Social Psychology*, 14, 441–447.

Weyant, J. M., & Smith, S. L. (1987). Getting more by asking for less: The effects of request size on donations of charity. *Journal of Applied Social Psychology*, 17, 392–400.

Wheeler, L. Koestner, R., & Driver, R. E. (1982). Related attributes in the choice of comparison others: It's there, but it isn't all there is. *Journal of Experimental Social Psychology*, 18, 489–500.

White, G. L. (1980). Physical attractiveness and courtship progress. *Journal of Personality and Social Psychology*, 39, 660–668.

White, G. L., Fishbein, S., & Rutsein, J. (1981). Passionate love and the misattribution of arousal. *Journal of Personality and Social Psychology*, 41, 56–62.

White, G. L., & Kight, T. D. (1984). Misattribution of arousal and attraction: Effects of salience of explanations for arousal. *Journal of Experimental Social Psychology*, 20, 55–64.

White, M. J., & Gerstein, L. H. (1987). Helping: The influence of anticipated social sanctions and self-monitoring. *Journal of Personality*, 55, 41–54.

White, P. A., & Younger, D. P. (1988). Differences in the ascription of transient internal states to self and other. *Journal of Experimental Social Psychology*, 24, 292–309.

White, R. (1984). *Fearful warriors: A psychological profile of U.S.-Soviet relations*. New York: Free Press.

White, R. K. (1969). Three not-so-obvious contributions of psychology to peace. *Journal of Social Issues*, 25(4), 23–39.

White, R. K. (1971, November). Selective inattention. *Psychology Today*, pp. 47–50, 78–84.

White, R. K. (1977). Misperception in the Arab-Israeli conflict. *Journal of Social Issues*, 33(1), 190–221.

White, R. K. (1988). Specifics in a positive approach to peace. *Journal of Social Issues*, 44, 191–202.

Whitehead, III, G. I., Smith, S. H., & Eichhorn, J. A. (1982). The effect of subject's race and other's race on judgments of causality for success and failure. *Journal of Personality*, 50, 193–202.

Whitley, B. E., Jr. (1985). Sex-role orientation and psychological well-being: Two meta-analyses. *Sex Roles*, 12, 207–225.

Whitley, B. E., Jr. (1987). The effects of discredited eyewitness testimony: A meta-analysis. *Journal of Social Psychology*, 127, 209–214.

Whitley, B. E., Jr., & Frieze, I. H. (1985). Children's causal attributions for success and failure in achievement settings. A meta-analysis. *Journal of Educational Psychology*, 77, 608–616.

Whitley, B. E., Jr., & Frieze, I. H. (1986). Measuring causal attributions for success and failure: A meta-analysis of the effects of question wording style. *Basic and Applied Social Psychology*, 7, 35–51.

Whitman, R. M., Kramer, M., & Baldridge, B.

(1963). Which dream does the patient tell? *Archives of General Psychology*, 8, 277–282.

Whittaker, J. O., & Meade, R. D. (1967). Social pressure in the modification and distortion of judgment: A cross-cultural study. *International Journal of Psychology*, 2, 109–113.

Wichman, H., & Healy, V. (1979). In their own spaces: Student-built lofts in dormitory rooms. Paper presented at the American Psychological Association convention.

Wicker, A. W. (1969). Attitudes versus actions: The relationship of verbal and overt behavioral responses to attitude objects. *Journal of Social Issues*, 25, 41–78.

Wicker, A. W. (1971). An examination of the "other variables" explanation of attitude-behavior inconsistency. *Journal of Personality and Social Psychology*, 19, 18–30.

Wicker, A. W. (1979). Ecological psychology: Some recent and prospective developments. *American Psychologist*, 34, 755–765.

Wicklund, R. A. (1982). Self-focused attention and the validity of self-reports. In M. P. Zanna, E. T. Higgins, & C. P. Herman (Eds.), *Consistency in Social Behavior: The Ontario Symposium*, Vol. 2. Hillsdale, N.J.: Erlbaum.

Wiegman, O. (1985). Two politicians in a realistic experiment: Attraction, discrepancy, intensity of delivery, and attitude change. *Journal of Applied Social Psychology*, 15, 673–686.

Wiesel, E. (1985, April 6). The brave Christians who saved Jews from the Nazis. *TV Guide*, pp. 4–6.

Wilder, D. A. (1977). Perception of groups, size of opposition, and social influence. *Journal of Experimental Social Psychology*, 13, 253–268.

Wilder, D. A. (1978). Perceiving persons as a group: Effect on attributions of causality and beliefs. *Social Psychology*, 41, 13–23.

Wilder, D. A. (1981). Perceiving persons as a group: Categorization and intergroup relations. In D. L. Hamilton (Ed.). *Cognitive processes in stereotyping and intergroup behavior*. Hillsdale, N.J.: Lawrence Erlbaum.

Wilder, D. A., & Shapiro, P. N. (1984). Role of out-group cues in determining social identity. *Journal of Personality and Social Psychology*, 47, 342–348.

Wilder, D. A., & Shapiro, P. N. (1989). Role of competition-induced anxiety in limiting the beneficial impact of positive behavior by out-group members. *Journal of Personality and Social Psychology*, 56, 60–69.

Wiley, M. G., Crittenden, K. S., & Birg, L. D. (1979). Why a rejection? Causal attribution of a career achievement event. *Social Psychology Quarterly*, 42, 214–222.

Wilke, H., & Lanzetta, J. T. (1970). The obligation to help: The effects of amount of prior help on subsequent helping behavior. *Journal of Experimental Social Psychology*, 6, 488–493.

Wilkes, J. (1987, June). Murder in mind. *Psychology Today*, pp. 27–32.

Williams, J. E., & Best, D. L. (1986). Sex stereotypes and intergroup relations. In S. Worchel & W. G. Austin (Eds.), *Psychology of intergroup relations*. Chicago: Nelson-Hall.

Williams, K. D. (1981). The effects of group cohesion on social loafing. Paper presented at the Midwestern Psychological Association convention.

Williams, K. D., Harkins, S., & Latané, B. (1981). Identifiability as a deterrent to social loafing: Two cheering experiments. *Journal of Personality and Social Psychology*, 40, 303–311.

Williams, R. M., Jr. (1975). Relative deprivation. In L. Coser (Ed.), *The idea of social structure: Papers in honor of Robert K. Merton*. New York: Harcourt Brace Jovanovich.

Williams, T. M. (Ed.) (1986). *The impact of television: A natural experiment in three communities*. Orlando, Fl.: Academic Press.

Willis, F. N., & Hamm, H. K. (1980). The use of interpersonal touch in securing compliance. *Journal of Nonverbal Behavior*, 5, 49–55.

Wills, T. A. (1978). Perceptions of clients by professional helpers. *Psychological Bulletin*, 85, 968–1000.

Wilson, D. K., Kaplan, R. M., & Schneiderman, L. J. (1987). Framing of decisions and selections of alternatives in health care. *Social Behaviour*, 2, 51–59.

Wilson, D. K., Purdon, S. E., & Wallston, K. A. (1988). Compliance to health recommendations: A theoretical overview of message framing. *Health Education Research*, 3, 161–171.

Wilson, D. K., Wallston, K. A., & King, J. E. (1987). The effects of message framing and self-efficacy on smoking cessation. Paper presented at the Southeastern Psychological Association Convention.

Wilson, D. W., & Donnerstein, E. (1979). Anonymity and interracial helping. Paper presented at the Southwestern Psychological Association convention.

Wilson, E. O. (1978). *On human nature*. Cambridge, Mass.: Harvard University Press.

Wilson, J. P., & Petruska, R. (1984). Motivation, model attributes, and prosocial behavior. *Journal of Personality and Social Psychology*, 46, 458–468.

Wilson, R. C., Gaft, J. G., Dienst, E. R., Wood, L., & Bavry, J. L. (1975). *College professors and their impact on students*. New York: Wiley.

Wilson, R. S., & Matheny, Jr., A. P. (1986). Behavior-genetics research in infant temperament: The Louisville twin study. In R. Plomin & J. Dunn (Eds.), *The study of temperament: Changes, continuities, and challenges*. Hillsdale, N.J.: Erlbaum.

Wilson, T. D. (1985). Strangers to ourselves: The origins and accuracy of beliefs about one's own mental states. In J. H. Harvey & G. Weary (Eds.), *Attribution in contemporary psychology*. New York: Academic Press.

Wilson, T. D., Dunn, D. S., Kraft, D., & Lisle, D. J. (1989). Introspection, attitude change, and attitude-behavior consistency: The disruptive effects of explaining why we feel the way we do. In L. Berkowitz (Ed.), *Advances in experimental social psychology*, Vol. 22. San Diego, Ca.: Academic Press.

Wilson, T. D., Laser, P. S., & Stone, J. I. (1982). Judging the predictors of one's mood: Accuracy and the use of shared theories. *Journal of Experimental Social Psychology*, 18, 537–556.

Wilson, T. D., & Lassiter, G. D. (1982). Increasing intrinsic interest with superfluous extrinsic constraints. *Journal of Personality and Social Psychology*, 42, 811–819.

Wilson, W. R. (1979). Feeling more than we can know: Exposure effects without learning. *Journal of Personality and Social Psychology*, 37, 811–821.

Winch, R. F. (1958). *Mate selection: A study of complementary needs*. New York: Harper & Row.

Wing, R. R., & Jeffery, R. W. (1979). Outpatient treatments of obesity: A comparison of methodology and clinical results. *International Journal of Obesity*, 3, 261–279.

Winter, F. W. (1973). A laboratory experiment of individual attitude response to advertising exposure. *Journal of Marketing Research*, 10, 130–140.

Wirth, L. (1977). Cited by J. P. Wogaman in *The great economic debate*. Philadelphia: Westminster Press, p. 29.

Wicklund, R. A. (1979). The influence of self-awareness on human behavior. *American Scientist*, 67, 187–193.

Wispe, L. G., & Freshley, H. B. (1971). Race, sex, and sympathetic helping behavior: The broken bag caper. *Journal of Personality and Social Psychology*, 17, 59–65.

Wittenberg, M. T., & Reis, H. T. (1986). Loneliness, social skills, and social perception. *Personality and Social Psychology Bulletin*, 12, 121–130.

Wixon, D. R., & Laird, J. D. (1976). Awareness

and attitude change in the forced-compliance paradigm: The importance of when. *Journal of Personality and Social Psychology*, **34**, 376–384.

Wolf, S. (1987). Majority and minority influence: A social impact analysis. In M. P. Zanna, J. M. Olson, & C. P. Herman (Eds.), *Social influence: The Ontario symposium on personality and social psychology*, Vol. 5. Hillsdale, N.J.: Erlbaum.

Wolf, S., & Latane, B. (1985). Conformity, innovation and the psycho-social law. In S. Moscovici, G. Mugny, & E. Van Avermaet (Eds.), *Perspectives on minority influence*. Cambridge: Cambridge University Press.

Woll, S. (1986). So many to choose from: Decision strategies in videodating. *Journal of Social and Personal Relationships*, **3**, 43–52.

Wood, W. (1987). Meta-analytic review of sex differences in group performance. *Psychological Bulletin*, **102**, 53–71.

Worchel, S., & Brown, E. H. (1984). The role of plausibility in influencing environmental attributions. *Journal of Experimental Social Psychology*, **20**, 86–96.

Worchel, S., & Norvell, N. (1980). Effect of perceived environmental conditions during cooperation of intergroup attraction. *Journal of Personality and Social Psychology*, **38**, 764–772.

Word, C. O., Zanna, M. P., & Cooper, J. (1974). The nonverbal mediation of self-fulfilling prophecies in interracial interaction. *Journal of Experimental Social Psychology*, **10**, 109–120.

Workman, E. A., & Williams, R. L. (1980). Effects of extrinsic rewards on intrinsic motivation in the classroom. *Journal of School Psychology*, **18**, 141–147.

Worringham, C. J., & Messick, D. M. (1983). Social facilitation of running: An unobtrusive study. *Journal of Social Psychology*, **121**, 23–29.

Worth, L. T., Allison, S. T., & Messick, D. M. (1987). Impact of a group decision on perception of one's own and others' attitudes. *Journal of Personality and Social Psychology*, **53**, 673–682.

Worth, L. T., & Mackie, D. M. (1987). Cognitive mediation of positive affect in persuasion. *Social Cognition*, **5**, 76–94.

Wright, P., & Rip, P. D. (1981). Retrospective reports on the causes of decisions. *Journal of Personality and Social Psychology*, **40**, 601–614.

Wrightsman, L. (1978). The American trial jury on trial: Empirical evidence and procedural modifications. *Journal of Social Issues*, **34**, 137–164.

Wu, C., & Schaffer, D. R. (1988). Susceptibility of persuasive appeals as a function of source credibility and prior experience with the attitude object. *Journal of Personality and Social Psychology*, **52**, 677–688.

Wu, D. Y. H., & Tseng, W. S. (1985). Introduction: The characteristics of Chinese culture. In D. Y. H. Wu and W. S. Tseng (Eds.), *Chinese culture and mental health*. San Diego, Ca.: Academic Press.

Wyer, R. S., Jr., & Srull, T. K. (1986). Human cognition in its social context. *Psychological Review*, **93**, 322–359.

Wylie, R. C. (1979). *The self-concept (Vol. 2): Theory and research on selected topics*. Lincoln, Neb.: University of Nebraska Press.

Yancey, W. L. (1971). Architecture, interaction, and social control: The case of a large-scale public housing project. *Environment and Behavior*, **3**, 3–21.

Yankelovich, Skelly, & White. (1980). Surveys conducted for the American Council of Life Insurance, 1973–1978. Reported in *Public Opinion*, December–January, p. 34.

Yinon, Y., Sharon, I., Gonen, Y., & Adam, R. (1982). Escape from responsibility and help in emergencies among persons alone or within groups. *European Journal of Social Psychology*, **12**, 301–305.

Young, W. R. (1977, February). There's a girl on the tracks! *Reader's Digest*, pp. 91–95.

Younger, J. C., Walker, L., & Arrowood, J. A. (1977). Postdecision dissonance at the fair. *Personality and Social Psychology Bulletin*, **3**, 284–287.

Yuchtman (Yaar), E. (1976). Effects of social-psychological factors on subjective economic welfare. In B. Strumpel (Ed.), *Economic means for human needs*. Ann Arbor: Institute for Social Research, University of Michigan.

Yuille, J. C., & Cutshall, J. L. (1986). A case study of eyewitness memory of a crime. *Journal of Applied Psychology*, **71**, 291–301.

Yukl, G. (1974). Effects of the opponent's initial offer, concession magnitude, and concession frequency on bargaining behavior. *Journal of Personality and Social Psychology*, **30**, 323–335.

Zabelka, G. (1980, August). I was told it was necessary. *Sojourners*, pp. 12–15. (Interview by C. C. McCarthy.)

Zaccaro, S. J. (1984). Social loafing: The role of task attractiveness. *Personality and Social Psychology Bulletin*, **10**, 99–106.

Zajonc, R. B. (1965). Social facilitation. *Science*, **149**, 269–274.

Zajonc, R. B. (1968). Attitudinal effects of mere exposure. *Journal of Personality and Social Psychology*, **9**, Monograph Suppl. No. 2, part 2.

Zajonc, R. B. (1970, February). Brainwash: Familiarity breeds comfort. *Psychology Today*, pp. 32–35, 60–62.

Zajonc, R. B. (1980). Feeling and thinking: Preferences need no inferences. *American Psychologist*, **35**, 151–175.

Zajonc, R. B., Murphy, S. T., & Inglehart, M. (1988). Emotional consequences of facial muscular movement: An implication of the vascular theory of emotion. Unpublished manuscript, University of Michigan.

Zajonc, R. B., & Sales, S. M. (1966). Social facilitation of dominant and subordinate responses. *Journal of Experimental Social Psychology*, **2**, 160–168.

Zander, A. (1969). Students' criteria of satisfaction in a classroom committee project. *Human Relations*, **22**, 195–207.

Zann, M. P., Crosby, F., & Loewenstein, G. (1987). Male reference groups and discontent among female professionals. In B. A. Gutek & L. Larwood (Eds.), *Women's career development*. Newbury Park, Ca.: Sage.

Zanna, M. P., Klosson, E. C., & Darley, J. M. (1976). How television news viewers deal with facts that contradict their beliefs: A consistency and attribution analysis. *Journal of Applied Social Psychology*, **6**, 159–176.

Zanna, M. P., & Olson, J. M. (1982). Individual differences in attitudinal relations. In M. P. Zanna, E. T. Higgins, & C. P. Herman, *Consistency in social behavior: The Ontario symposium*, Vol. 2. Hillsdale, N.J.: Erlbaum.

Zanna, M. P., Olson, J. M., & Fazio, R. H. (1981). Self-perception and attitude-behavior consistency. *Personality and Social Psychology Bulletin*, **7**, 252–256.

Zanna, M. P., & Pack, S. J. (1975). On the self-fulfilling nature of apparent sex differences in behavior. *Journal of Experimental Social Psychology*, **11**, 583–591.

Zanna, M. P. & Rempel, J. K. (1988). Attitudes: A new look at an old concept. In D. Bar-Tal & A. Kruglanski (Eds.), *The social psychology of knowledge*. New York: Cambridge University Press.

Zanna, M. P., & Sande, G. N. (1987). The effects of collective actions on the attitudes of individual group members: A dissonance analysis. In M. P. Zanna, J. M. Olson, & C. P. Herman (Eds.), *Social influence: The Ontario symposium*, Vol. 5. Hillsdale, N.J.: Erlbaum.

Zebrowitz-McArthur, L. (1988). Person perception in cross-cultural perspective. In M. H. Bond (Ed.), *The cross-cultural challenge to social psychology*. Newbury Park, Ca.: Sage.

Zeisel, H., & Diamond, S. S. (1978). The jury

selection in the Mitchell-Stans conspiracy trial. *American Bar Foundation Research Journal*, 1976, **1**, 151–174 (see p. 167). Cited by L. Wrightsman, The American trial jury on trial: Empirical evidence and procedural modifications. *Journal of Social Issues*, 34, 137–164.

Zenker, S., Leslie, R. C., Port, E., & Kosloff, J. (1982). The sequence of outcomes and ESP: More evidence for a primacy effect. *Personality and Social Psychology Bulletin*, 8, 233–238.

Zillmann, D. (in press). Aggression and sex: Independent and joint operations. In H. L. Wagner & A. S. R. Manstead (Eds.), *Handbook of psychophysiology: Emotion and social behavior*. Chichester: John Wiley.

Zillmann, D. (1988). Cognition-excitation interdependencies in aggressive behavior. *Aggressive Behavior*, **11**, 51–64.

Zillmann, D., & Bryant, J. (1974). Effect of residual excitation on the emotional response to provocation and delayed aggressive behavior. *Journal of Personality and Social Psychology*, 30, 782–791.

Zillmann, D., & Bryant, J. (in press). Effects of prolonged consumption of pornography on family values. *Journal of Family Issues*.

Zillmann, D., Katcher, A. H., & Milavsky, B. (1972). Excitation transfer from physical exercise to subsequent aggressive behavior. *Journal of Experimental Social Psychology*, 8, 247–259.

Zimbardo, P. G. (1970). The human choice: Individuation, reason, and order versus deindividuation, impulse, and chaos. In W. J. Arnold & D. Levine (Eds.), *Nebraska Symposium on Motivation, 1969*. Lincoln: University of Nebraska Press.

Zimbardo, P. G. (1971). *The psychological power and pathology of imprisonment*. A statement prepared for the U.S. House of Representatives Committee on the Judiciary, Subcommittee No. 3: Hearings on Prison Reform, San Francisco, Calif., October 25.

Zimbardo, P. G. (1972, April). Pathology of imprisonment. *Transaction/Society*, pp. 4–8. (a)

Zimbardo, P. G. (1972). The Stanford prison experiment. A slide/tape presentation produced by Philip G. Zimbardo, Inc., P.O. Box 4395, Stanford, Calif. 94305. (b)

Zimbardo, P. G. (1983). Transforming experimental research into advocacy for social change. In H. H. Blumberg, A. P. Hare, V. Kent, & M. Davies (Eds.), *Small groups and social interaction*, Vol. 1. London: Wiley.

Zimbardo, P. G., Ebbesen, E. B., & Maslach, C. (1977). *Influencing attitudes and changing behavior*. Reading, Mass.: Addison-Wesley.

Zimbardo, P. G., & Hartley, C. F. (1985). Cults go to high school: A theoretical and empirical analysis of the initial stage in the recruitment process. *Cultic Studies Journal*, 2, 91–147.

Zukier, H. A. (1982). The dilution effect: The role of the correlation and the dispersion of predictor variables in the use of nondiagnostic information. *Journal of Personality and Social Psychology*, 43, 1163–1174.

Zukier, H., & Pepitone, A. (1984). Social roles and strategies in prediction: Some determinants of the use of base-rate information. *Journal of Personality and Social Psychology*, 47, 349–360.

ACKNOWLEDGMENTS

CHAPTER 1

0   Richard T. Conway © 1988/*The Plain Dealer*, Cleveland, Ohio
4   © 1978 Michael Hayman/Black Star
6   Sidney Harris
12   *Doonesbury*, © 1980 G. B. Trudeau. Reprinted with permission of Universal Press Syndicate. All rights reserved.
18   Sidney Harris
22   Ronald C. James
24   Nancy Bates/The Picture Cube

PART ONE

30–31 © Joel Gordon 1981

CHAPTER 2

32   Wide World Photos
39   © Michael Hayman/Stock, Boston
43   Drawing by Joseph Farris; © 1984 The New Yorker Magazine, Inc.
47   © Mary Ellen Mark
49   Sybil Shelton/Monkmeyer
52   Drawing by Weber; © 1987 The New Yorker Magazine, Inc.
54   Drawing by Richter; © 1977 The New Yorker Magazine, Inc.
55   © 1982 Karen Zebulon
59   Courtesy of Fritz Strack
63   Drawing by C. Barsotti; © 1988 The New Yorker Magazine, Inc.

CHAPTER 3

68   Wide World Photos
71   Drawing by Modell; © 1976 The New Yorker Magazine, Inc.
77   Wide World Photos
84   Drawing by Sempé; © 1984 The New Yorker Magazine, Inc.
85   © Mareuen Fennelli/Photo Researchers
88   Drawing by Ross; © 1988 The New Yorker Magazine, Inc.
90   © Barbara Rios 1981/Photo Researchers
92   Drawing by Dana Fradon; © 1983 The New Yorker Magazine, Inc.
96   © Abigail Heyman
97   Drawing by Koren, © 1983 The New Yorker Magazine, Inc.

CHAPTER 4

100 © Peter Miller/Photo Researchers
103 Wide World Photos
109 Myron Rothbart
111 Tom Cheek/Stock, Boston
114 Wide World Photos
119 © 1988 Robert Nichols/Black Star
122 Peter Steiner
126 © 1980 Paul Fortin/Stock, Boston

CHAPTER 5

134 © David M. Grossman/Photo Researchers
141 © Ed Lettau/Photo Researchers
143 Wide World Photos
146 © Michael Hayman/Photo Researchers
150 © Sandra Johnson 1983/The Picture Cube
153 Drawing by Frascino; © 1982 The New Yorker Magazine, Inc.
156 Wide World Photos
159 Michael Kagan/Monkmeyer

PART TWO

164–165 A. Tannenbaum/Sygma

CHAPTER 6

166 © Frank Siteman 1979/The Picture Cube
169 John Benton Harris
170 Drawing by Handelsman; © 1979 The New Yorker Magazine, Inc.
172 Drawing by P. Steiner; © 1980 The New Yorker Magazine, Inc.
173 © 1978 Bernard Pierre Wolff/Photo Researchers
175 Philip Zimbardo
179 Drawing by Dana Fradon; © 1985 The New Yorker Magazine, Inc.
181 Reuters/Bettmann Newsphotos
186 Tom Renner
192 Drawing by Whitney Darrow; © 1976 The New Yorker Magazine, Inc.
194 Drawing by Koren; © 1988 The New Yorker Magazine, Inc.

CHAPTER 7

200 Jean-Claude Lejeune/Stock, Boston
203 Drawing by W. B. Park; © 1988 The New Yorker Magazine, Inc.

206 William Vendivert
211 © 1965 by Stanley Milgram, from the film *Obedience*, distributed by the Pennsylvania State University, PCR.
215 Eric Kroll/Taurus
221 Drawing by Mankoff; © 1980 The New Yorker Magazine, Inc.
225 *The Far Side* cartoon by Gary Larson is reprinted by permission of Chronicle Features, San Francisco, California
227 © Charles Kennard 1982/Stock, Boston

CHAPTER 8

234 © Lynne J. Weinstein/Woodfin Camp & Assoc.
238 Drawing by C. Barsotti; © 1987 The New Yorker Magazine, Inc.
241 Wide World Photos
241 The Granger Collection
245 Courtesy of NW Ayer, Partnership for a Drug-Free America
257 Drawing by Chas. Addams; © 1982 The New Yorker Magazine, Inc.
259 *The Far Side*, © 1987. Reprinted with permission of Universal Press Syndicate. All rights reserved.
265 Randy Matusow/Monkmeyer

CHAPTER 9

268 © Jon Hofman
272 © 1983 Nancy J. Pierce/Photo Researchers
274 UPI/Bettmann Newsphotos
277 Courtesy of Herman Miller Inc.
278 Alan G. Ingham
281 Tom Renner
283 Philip Zimbardo
285 Bettmann Archive
293 Okamato/Lyndon B. Johnson Library, University of Texas, Austin
295 Drawing by H. Martin; © 1979 The New Yorker Magazine, Inc.
302 Wide World Photos

CHAPTER 10

306 © Jim Pickerell 1985/Stock, Boston
310 Drawing by Joe Mirachi; © 1984 The New Yorker Magazine, Inc.

313   From Loftus, Miller & Burns, 1978. Photos courtesy of Elizabeth Loftus
315   *The Far Side,* © 1985. Reprinted with permission of Universal Press Syndicate. All rights reserved.
317   *The Far Side* cartoon by Gary Larson is reprinted by permission of Chronicle Features, San Francisco, California.
319   Drawing by Lorenz; © 1977 The New Yorker Magazine, Inc.

PART THREE

328–329   © Barbara Rios/Photo Researchers

CHAPTER 11

330   © Spenner C. Grant III/Photo Researchers
336   UPI/Bettmann Newsphotos
338   Porter & Geis, 1981
340   Drawing by Vietor; © 1981 The New Yorker Magazine, Inc.
342, left   Library of Congress
342, right   Kashahara/Wide World Photos
346   Drawing by Ed Fisher; © 1987 The New Yorker Magazine, Inc.
348   Jack Edwards
350   Drawing by Maslin; © 1985 The New Yorker Magazine, Inc.
354   Ellis Herwig/The Picture Cube
356   UPI/Bettmann Newsphotos
361   Drawing by Mankoff; © 1981 The New Yorker Magazine, Inc.

CHAPTER 12

368   Bob Mayer, *News/Sun-Sentinel,* Ft. Lauderdale, Fla.
373   John Ruge
375   © Jeff Share/Black Star
376   © Photo News/Gamma-Liaison
378   Christian Simonpietri/Sygma
380   Margaret Bourke-White, *Life* Magazine 1937, 1965 Time Inc.
383   *Peanuts,* United Media
387   Dr. Nathan Azrin
392   Charles Gatewood/Stock, Boston
396   John Garrett/Woodfin Camp & Assoc.

CHAPTER 13

408   Nancy Durrell McKenna © 1985/Photo Researchers
412   *Miss Peach* by Mell Lazarus. Courtesy of Mell Lazarus and Field Newspaper Syndicate
414   © Susan Lapides 1988/Design Conceptions
416   William Mayer
419   © Bill Bachman 1986/Photo Researchers
420   Reuters/Bettmann Newsphotos

422   *Doonesbury,* © 1981 G. B. Trudeau. Reprinted with permission of Universal Press Syndicate. All rights reserved.
424, left   Michael Childers/Sygma
424, right   UPI/Bettmann Newsphotos
426   Drawing by Ziegler; © 1988 The New Yorker Magazine, Inc.
432   Charles Campbell/Taurus
438   © Ellis Herwig/The Picture Cube

CHAPTER 14

444   © Jill Freedman
449   © 1983 Bernard Pierre Wolff/Photo Researchers
450   Drawing by B. Tobey; © 1972 The New Yorker Magazine, Inc.
453   Scott Shaw, *The Odessa* (Texas) *American*
459   George Malave/Stock, Boston
464   Tom Cheek/Stock, Boston
467   Mimi Forsyth/Monkmeyer
473   American Red Cross

CHAPTER 15

480   Wide World Photos
485   Reprinted by permission of Tribune Media Services
491   Muzafer Sherif
499   David Strickler/Picture Cube
505   H. Armstrong Roberts
510   Rex F. May

COLOR ESSAYS

Ideas to Remember

1, left   David C. Fritts, Animals, Animals
1, top right   Rio Branco/Magnum Photos
1, bottom right   Wide World Photos
2, top left   American Cancer Society
2, bottom left   © 1988 Peter Turnley/Black Star
2, top right   © 1988 Christopher Morris/Black Star
2, bottom right   © Paolo Koch/Photo Researchers
3, left   Wally McNamee Woodfin Camp & Assoc.
3, right   Eric Kroll/Taurus Photos
4, top left   Ellis Herwig/The Picture Cube
4, top right   Dave Schaefer/The Picture Cube
4, bottom   Bill Stanton/Magnum Photos
5, top left   David S. Strickler/The Picture Cube
5, top right   Mimi Forsyth/Monkmeyer Press

5, bottom left   Michal Heron/Woodfin Camp & Assoc.
5, bottom right   Wide World Photos
6, left   Wide World Photos
6, right   Dave Schaefer/The Picture Cube
7, left   Adam Woolfitt/Woodfin Camp & Assoc.
7, top right   Stock, Boston
7, bottom right   Freda Leinwand/Monkmeyer Press
8, top   Wide World Photos
8, bottom left   Wide World Photos
8, bottom right   Wide World Photos

Social Behavior around the World

1, top left   © Carol Lee/The Picture Cube
1, bottom left   © 1980 Rick Smolan/Stock, Boston
1, top right   © Chad Ehlers/International Stock Photography
1, bottom right   © Patrick Montagne 1981/Photo Researchers, Inc.
2, top left   © 1986 Peter Turnley/Black Star
2, center left   © Brent Winebrenner/International Stock Photography
2, bottom left   Frank Siteman/Stock, Boston
2, top right   © Peter Menzel/Stock, Boston
2, bottom right   © Chad Ehlers/International Stock Photography
3, top left   © Jim Weiner 1982/Photo Researchers
3, bottom   © Bob Daemmrich/Stock, Boston
3, top right   © Marcel Minnée/International Stock Photography
4, top left   © C. S. Perkins/Magnum Photos
4, bottom left   © 1986 David Turnley/Black Star
4, right   Chip Hires/Gamma-Liaison
5, top right   © Rick Strange/International Stock Photography
5, center left   Focus on Sports
5, bottom left   © Dennis Stock/Magnum
5, bottom right   Focus on Sports
6, top left   © Norris Clark 1983/International Stock Photography
6, bottom left   © 1983 Stanley Rowin/The Picture Cube
6, center right   © Julian Calder/International Stock Photography

6, bottom right	© Sally Cassidy/The Picture Cube
7, top left	© John Roshelly 1980/Photo Researchers, Inc.
7, bottom left	© M. Courtney-Clarke/Photo Researchers, Inc.
7, right	© Helene Tremblay/Peter Arnold, Inc.
8, top	© Djukanovic/Daily Telegraph/International Stock Photography
8, bottom	David Austen/Stock, Boston